FROM FARM TO FACTORY...AND BEYOND

ECONOMIC HISTORY

of the Northern

SHENANDOAH VALLEY

1720 – 2020

Peter D. Heerwagen

Quad-State Publishing Company
Winchester, Virginia

Copyright 2023 by Quad-State Publishing Company

All rights reserved. No part of this publication can be reproduced, stored in a retrieval system, or transmitted in any form or by any means, electronic, mechanical, photocopying, recording or otherwise, without the prior permission of Peter D. Heerwagen.

ISBN 978-0-9678447-1-8

Cover Design: Lynn Mocarski Maurer
Interior Design: Creative Publishing Book Design

CONTENTS

Preface 1

Chapter 1: Colonial Period 3
    Settlement of the Northern Valley: Disputes Over Land Ownership . . 3
    Northern Valley Economy: Trade Opens with Eastern Seaboard 8
    French and Indian War: Spending Boosts Economy 13
    Agriculture: Wheat Becomes Primary Commercial Crop 14
    Manufacturing: Adding Value to Farm Products and
        Natural Resources 16

Chapter 2: American Revolution to 1830 23
    Revolutionary War: Supplying Continental Army
        with Guns and Butter 23
    National Economy: New Nation's Growing Pains 24
    Internal Improvements: Need for Turnpikes and Bridges 26
    Northern Valley Economy: No Longer a Backcountry Frontier . . . 32
    Agriculture: Farmers and Planters Feast on Wheat 37
    Manufacturing: Flour and Iron Production Lead the Sector. 39
    Banking: Financial Institutions Open 51
    Newspapers: Owners Advocate Their Political Agendas 53
    Tourism: Springs Resorts Promote Healing 53

Chapter 3: 1830 to Civil War 57
    National Economy: Industrial and Transportation
        Revolutions Arrive. 57
    Internal Improvements: Railroads and Canal Boost
        Trade with East Coast 58
    Northern Valley Economy: Grows at Slower Pace Than the Nation's. . 67
    Agriculture: Farmers Face Competition from the Midwest 70
    Manufacturing: Pig Iron Rides the Nation's Rails 73
    Extractive Industries: Prospecting for Copper and Manganese 82

    Newspapers: Politics Dominate the News 83
    Tourism: Railroads Bring More Patrons to Springs Resorts. 84

Chapter 4: Civil War and Reconstruction. 89
    Conflict Devastates Region's Economy 89
    Postwar: Economic Doldrums in the South, Prosperity in North . . . 94
    Recovery Strategy: Rebuild Farms and Start New Businesses 94

Chapter 5: Post-Reconstruction to World War I 113
    National Economy: Prospers from Inventions and New Industries . .113
    Internal Improvements: More Trains and Arrival of Electricity. . . .114
    Northern Valley Economy: Cities and Towns Look to
        Recruit Industry 123
    Agriculture: Farmers Switch to Orcharding and Dairying. 131
    Warehousing: Apples Go into Cold Storage 137
    Manufacturing: Industry Arrives in Urban Centers 138
    Extractive Industries: Digging Up Limestone and Sand. 163
    Banking: Every Town Has At least One 172
    Newspapers: Daily Papers Roll Off Presses 174
    Higher Education: Not All Colleges Are Normal 176
    Tourism: Visitors Drawn to Springs, Mountains and Caverns 176
    Health Care: Patients Leave Homes for Hospitals. 181
    Federal Government: Sites Open in Blue Ridge Mountains. 183

Chapter 6: World War I to World War II. 185
    National Economy: Roaring Twenties End with Great Depression . .185
    Infrastructure: Adapting to New Modes of Travel. 185
    Northern Valley Economy: More Jobs Move from Farm to Factory . .193
    Agriculture: Dieting on Apples and Milk 196
    Warehousing: Keeping More Apples Longer 199
    Manufacturing: Producing Various Finished Goods. 201
    Extractive Industries: Mining More Limestone and Sand. 215
    Federal Government: It Becomes More Active in the Region. 219
    Banking: Fewer Formations 220
    Great Depression: Will it Ever End?. 220
    New Deal Winds Down, But Big Government Remains 229
    Media: Radio Stations Compete with Newspapers for Ad Dollars . .229

Health Care: Community Hospitals Open 230
Tourism: Venues Profit from More Leisure Time 231
World War II: Conflict Jump Starts Nation's Economy 237
Some Federal Proposals Get Mixed Reviews 240

Chapter 7: Post-World War II to 2020 243
    National Economy: More Ups than Downs 243
    Northern Virginia: Westward Expansion Accelerates 244
    Northern Valley Economy: Population Growth Outpaces
        the Nation's 244
    Economic Development Strategy: Fill New Parks with Industry . . .245
    Recruitment Incentives: An Era of Corporate Welfare 247
    Local Development Agencies: Making the Recruitment Sale. 248
    Infrastructure: Upgrades Accommodate Growth 253
    Education: Improving Workforce Skills. 261
    Agriculture: Farmers and Orchardists Face Challenges 264
    Extractive Industries: Participants Change Hands 269
    Manufacturing: Factories and Jobs on the Move 272
    Warehouses: Interstate 81 Becomes the Logistics Corridor 299
    Call Centers: Employees and Companies Turn Over 303
    Fulfillment Centers: E-Commerce Arrives in Region 304
    Residential Real Estate: Northern Virginia's Market
        Affects Region's. 305
    Commercial Real Estate: Construction Follows Rooftops 309
    Banking: Mergers Leave Few Community Banks 312
    Retailing: Customers Leave Main Street for Shopping Centers. . . .317
    Health Care: Modern Hospitals Are Prescription for Survival 320
    Tourism: History and Nature Bring Visitors 325
    Recreation: Hitting Links and Circling Tracks 327
    Media: All News is Not Printed 331
    Federal Government: More Installations Arrive in Region 336

Chapter 8: Postscript 341
    Endnotes 343
    Bibliography 425
    Index 433

Map of Northern Valley
North Valley Business Journal

PREFACE

Few economic history books have focused on a small geographical area within the United States. This one covers eight counties and one independent city in the Northern Shenandoah Valley, referred to as the "Northern Valley." The region is defined by the Potomac River on the north, the Blue Ridge Mountains to the east, the Allegheny mountains to the west and Page and Shenandoah counties to the south. It includes the Eastern Panhandle of West Virginia, which was part of Virginia until 1863.

The book's title, *From Farm to Factory and Beyond,* describes the Northern Valley's economic transition from agriculture to manufacturing, and its more recent movement beyond the Blue Ridge into the orbits of Northern Virginia and Washington, D.C. Arranged into seven chronological periods from 1720 to 2020, each chapter begins with an overview of the nation's and Northern Valley's economies. The narrative continues with more detailed discussions in each period of the region's agriculture and manufacturing sectors, along with its various industry and business groupings. Economic history is a study of change. Through the years, Northern Valley farmers adjusted their crops and livestock to the evolving marketplace, and entrepreneurs started up new industries that replaced older ones. This book attempts to answer why those changes occurred.

A handful of writers have compiled survey histories either of the Shenandoah Valley or individual counties, with limited references to their economies. More recently, history professors Warren Hofstra at Shenandoah University in Winchester and Kenneth Koons from Virginia Military Institute in Lexington have done seminal work on the region's settler life and the emergence of its wheat economy. University of Maryland professor Robert Mitchell examined how the agriculture and manufacturing sectors evolved during the Shenandoah Valley's early years. Two authors wrote books on specific industries in the region. Winchester resident Wilbur Johnston traced its woolen mills, while Norman Scott from Verona, Virginia, chronicled the iron industry.

From Farm to Factory and Beyond not only incorporates the research of those five authors, but also includes other important aspects of the region's economy, as it evolved from colonial times to the early twenty-first century. The book looks at the development of economic relationships within the region and the roles key business persons and companies played in its growth. Unlike authors who conducted their research prior to the arrival of the internet, I had the good fortune to access information from digitized copies of newspapers, trade journals, court records, government proceedings and other primary sources.

Life is serendipitous, in a way. Internal improvements, later called infrastructure, were key drivers of economic development. I first learned about their importance when I took a course in American economic history in college. Little did I know that years later, I would be writing about turnpikes, bridges, canals and railroads in the Northern Shenandoah Valley. The textbook used in that course was Harold Underwood Faulkner's *American Economic History*. Many footnotes in this book reference it.

Some footnotes in Chapter 7 of *From Farm to Factory and Beyond* come from my two monthly newspapers, North Valley Business Journal and Quad-State Business Journal, published from 1989 to 2009. I wish I had completed the book before I wrote articles for those newspapers. They would have been much more interesting if relevant material from this book had been used as background information.

I am indebted to several friends for their help in producing *From Farm to Factory and Beyond*. The aforementioned Warren Hofstra edited parts of the manuscript for historical accuracy and Maggie Wolff Peterson proofread it. Any mistakes and errors are mine alone. Lynn Mocarski Maurer designed the book's cover, while Hugh Wachter, publisher of reunion books, encouraged me to include pictures.

CHAPTER 1

COLONIAL PERIOD

Settlement of the Northern Valley: Disputes Over Land Ownership

During the early colonial period, North American settlers lived on small farms in what became the eastern United States. Their subsistence lives were based on simple techniques brought from Europe, modified with concepts learned from Native Americans.[1] With family members supplying the labor, these yeoman farmers raised food for themselves, not for the commercial market.[2] They turned hides into leather for shoes and harnesses and in winter months cut hardwoods for fuel, furniture and tools.[3] Farm wives spun and wove wool and flax for clothes, made soap and candles, ground wheat into flour and corn into meal and preserved vegetables, fruits and meats.[4]

When colonial America's population reached 1.2 million in the mid-eighteenth century, handcraft production moved from the home into small shops in villages.[5] Trained artisans turned out shoes, pottery, ironware, furniture, wagons, barrels and other goods to sell or trade with farmers and merchants. Larger industries emerged to reduce colonial reliance on expensive imports from Great Britain. They included gristmills, sawmills, woolen mills, paper mills, iron furnaces, shipyards, distilleries and tanneries.[6]

Regions Work Their Comparative Advantages

By the 1750s, the economies of colonial America's three regions—New England, Middle and Southern—had developed differently. Each one's unique soil, natural resources, climate and geography gave it a comparative advantage in producing certain goods at low cost. Regional specialization also responded to Great Britain's needs and to markets in southern Europe and the West Indies.[7] While ships moved large quantities of goods over oceans, poor roads throughout North America limited trade among regions.[8]

Rocky soil, inhospitable climate and a short growing season made large-scale farming difficult in New England.[9] With abundant forests and the North Atlantic nearby, the area focused on logging, shipbuilding, fishing and whaling. The Middle colonies benefited from a longer growing season, a mild climate and rich soil where farmers planted grains and other crops and raised cattle, hogs and sheep.[10] The region was home to colonial America's first iron furnaces, paper mills and gristmills. The Southern colonies—those below the Mason-Dixon Line—had several comparative advantages. Hemp and wheat were grown on limestone-laden fertile land in central and western Maryland and in the Shenandoah Valley, areas that also had a moderate climate. In parts of Maryland, Virginia and the Carolinas, plantation owners used slave labor to grow tobacco, rice and indigo for export to England.[11]

British Mercantilism

Beginning in the 1650s, Britain pursued a policy of mercantilism, under which its colonies existed for the economic welfare of the mother country.[12] Between 1651 and 1673, Parliament passed four Navigation Acts to monopolize shipping.[13] They required staples such as tobacco, rice, indigo, cotton and wool be shipped only to the mother country and on its boats.[14] Goods imported from the rest of Europe had to pass through England and be taxed, before they entered the colonies.[15] Because the Navigation Acts were not strictly enforced in North America, smuggling was ever-present.

To encourage colonial production of favored commodities, Britain eliminated import duties on hemp, flax, indigo and the naval stores of tar and potash, and paid bounties—monetary rewards—for some of them.[16] When incentives worked, they lessened the mother country's need to import those goods from rival European nations. The Carolinas profited from bounties on naval stores, indigo and rice, while Virginia farmers benefited from those paid on hemp sold to Britain.

Migrants Purchase Disputed Land

Although driven westward into the Appalachian Mountains and beyond, Native Americans still lived in the Shenandoah Valley when settlers first arrived in the 1720s. To deal with them, Virginia Governor William Gooch, who represented the British Royal government in Williamsburg, looked to encourage farmers from Pennsylvania to move south of the Potomac River.[17] He hoped such settlement would form a barrier against Native American attacks and French encroachments, deter runaway slaves from establishing an independent colony west of the Blue Ridge Mountains, and help settle land claims made by the Maryland colony and Englishman Lord Fairfax.[18]

Beginning in 1728, the British Royal government divided 400,000 acres of Shenandoah Valley land into large tracts, then gave several men land orders to negotiate their sale.[19] Each was tasked with recruiting at least 100 families to purchase 1,000 acres apiece.[20] Through personal and family ties, word-of-mouth and printed advertisements, the men marketed the land to European settlers in eastern Pennsylvania. The sales pitch was simple; prices in the Shenandoah Valley were six or seven pounds per 100 acres cheaper than where they lived, and the limestone-enriched soil produced crop yields twice those in the rest of Virginia.[21]

In 1730, Governor Gooch granted two Pennsylvania men large parcels in what later became Frederick County. German-native Jost Hite received 140,000 acres, on the condition he recruit 140 families, while Irishman Alexander Ross was given 40,000 acres, which he sold to 40 fellow Quaker families.[22] But some Germans had already settled in the Shenandoah Valley. In 1726, they crossed the Potomac River at Pack Horse Ford and established the village of New Mecklenburg, later known as Shepherdstown.[23] The squatters subsequently gained legal possession of the land through payments to a Gooch representative.[24]

In the early 1730s, other settlers followed Native American trails that served as highways into the Shenandoah Valley. They included Germans, Quakers and Scots-Irish from the Philadelphia area and Dutch families from New York. When wagon traffic widened those trails in the mid-1740s, they became the Great Wagon Road, which passed west of Philadelphia, through present-day Lancaster, York and Chambersburg, then headed south to Hagerstown and Williamsport, where covered wagons forded the Potomac River to reach Martinsburg and Winchester.[25] During the 1740s and 1750s, an estimated 50,000 migrants took that road into the Shenandoah Valley.[26] Many stayed, but some continued on to the Carolinas and Georgia after discovering that earlier settlers had taken the most productive farmlands.[27]

As settlement of the Shenandoah Valley continued, a problem arose with the British Royal government's land grants and sales. In 1719, Englishman

*Map of Great Wagon Road
Image from Wikipedia, Wikimedia Foundation*

Thomas Fairfax, Sixth Lord Fairfax of Cameron, inherited the 3.45 million-acre Northern Neck Proprietary, which dated to 1649.[28] Despite the Royal government's legal challenge that his land lay east of the Blue Ridge Mountains, Lord Fairfax's agent, Robert "King" Carter, the richest man in colonial Virginia, disposed of thousands of acres to its west.[29] In 1730, he granted himself 50,212 acres of choice land, situated near the Shenandoah River in present-day Clarke County, and gave it to his sons and grandsons living in the Tidewater area.[30] Within two years, he granted himself 208,000 acres of Fairfax's other productive land.[31] He gave it to his Tidewater friends, relatives and their children, some with the surnames of Byrd, Burwell, Nelson, Page, Lee and Whiting.[32]

When Fairfax discovered that Williamsburg was patenting land—assigning its ownership—in the Shenandoah Valley, he moved there in 1734 to take charge of his affairs and collect land taxes called quitrents.[33] Eleven years later, England's Privy Council finally resolved the dispute between Fairfax and the colony over the Northern Neck Proprietary's boundaries.[34] When the lines were extended from the Blue Ridge westward to the Potomac River's headwaters in present-day Tucker County, West Virginia, the original 3.45

million acres became 5.2 million acres.[35] One-third of it included what became the eight counties in the northern Shenandoah Valley, hereinafter referred to as the Northern Valley.[36]

With the boundary dispute settled, the Privy Council allowed Fairfax to control and sell his acreage, but representatives working for the British Royal government had already sold much of it.[37] Fairfax returned to Virginia in 1749 and moved to his Greenway Court hunting lodge in present-day Clarke County to claim his land and collect quitrents from settlers living on it.[38] As a result, some yeoman farmers packed their belongings and moved into Augusta County, farther up the Valley of Virginia.[39] Those who stayed were forced to purchase their land a second time, but after a series of payments, Fairfax gave them outright ownership.

Greenway Court, the seat of Lord Fairfax.

Engraving of Lord Fairfax's Greenway Court.
Henry Howe (1845) Historical Collections of Virginia,
Charleston, SC: S. Babcock & Co.

While surveying for Fairfax in the early 1750s, young George Washington became aware of the Northern Valley's agriculture potential. His family members in Tidewater acquired 6,000 acres in present-day Jefferson County.[40] In 1752, Washington took possession of 1,459 acres on Bullskin Run near Summit Point, and added 2,315 acres two years later.[41] Part of that land was payment for work he performed for Fairfax.

When the Declaration of Independence was signed in 1776, the frontier phase of the Northern Valley's settlement was mostly completed.[42] Yeoman farmers worked limestone-enriched soil and less fertile shale lands in its central and western sections.[43] One hundred planter families from the Tidewater region had moved across the Blue Ridge to raise crops on rich bottomlands near the Shenandoah River in present-day Clarke, Warren and Jefferson counties.[44] Others either leased or sold their lands to yeoman farmers or placed overseers on them with instructions on how they should be managed.[45]

Northern Valley Economy: Trade Opens with Eastern Seaboard

Prior to the French and Indian War, yeomen farmers in the Northern Valley produced basic foodstuffs and necessities for their own consumption. They exchanged any excess food, clothes and household items with neighbors, merchants and backcountry traders. As the region's population grew, artisan shops appeared in towns and villages located along north-south migration routes.

While hemp and tobacco were the region's first commercial crops, yeoman farmers shifted to wheat when its price rose in the 1750s, during the Seven Years War in Europe and the French and Indian War in North America.[46] Besides an expanding agriculture sector, a handful of industries turned natural resources and agricultural produce into semi-fabricated goods. Wheat was milled into flour, pig iron was extracted from ore, wool was carded and cloth finished, grains were distilled into whiskey and logs were sawed into lumber.

Emergence of Counties and Towns

The eight counties that comprised the northern section of the Shenandoah Valley—Berkeley, Jefferson, Morgan, Frederick, Clarke, Shenandoah, Warren and Page—were created from Orange County, whose courthouse was 85 miles southeast of the Blue Ridge. As the region's population grew, citizens petitioned the British Royal government in Williamsburg for a more convenient place to conduct business. Their request was granted in 1738, when Frederick County separated from Orange County and six years later, a courthouse was established in Winchester.[47] With its county seat and crossroads location, the town became the Northern Valley's center of commercial activity, especially when markets were held on court days and during the colonial government's required two-day fairs in June and October.[48] Winchester's census of shops grew from five in

1757 to 21 in 1787, and its population of 1,500 made it one of the largest towns in the Virginia colony.[49]

Towns and villages also grew up along large creeks that powered gristmills and sawmills. On the Great Wagon Road, later known as the Valley Turnpike and U.S. 11, they included Martinsburg on Tuscarora Creek, Bunker Hill on Mill Creek, Edinburg on Stony Creek and Mount Jackson on another Mill Creek. Settlements on the East Valley Road grew into the towns of Front Royal on Happy Creek and Luray on Hawksbill Creek. Years later, that north-south corridor between the Shenandoah River and the Blue Ridge Mountains became U.S. 340.

After Frederick County's population increased from an estimated 4,000 in 1745 to 10,000 in 1763, citizens north and south of Winchester looked to establish their own courthouses.[50] In 1772, two counties—Berkeley in the north and Dunmore (later Shenandoah) in the south—were carved out of what was known as Old Frederick County.[51] Between 1801 and 1836, the five other counties that comprised the Northern Valley were formed from those first three.

Exchange Economy

Absent a banking system, universal coinage and paper money, the region's yeoman farmers traded their produce, handicrafts and services with neighbors, and with town merchants for imported coffee, tea, sugar and salt.[52] Participants in that exchange economy kept a ledger book to record their trades. A debtor wrote out a personal note or an IOU, which the creditor used to obtain something of value from a third party.[53] Although the bearer's payment history determined an IOU's worth, the holder often had to shop it around. Currency was used to balance an account.[54]

Because few coins were minted in the colonies, foreign ones circulated widely. Sales of wheat and hemp to Great Britain brought pence, shillings and pounds to colonial America.[55] Trade with Spain, France and Portugal generated coinage from those countries, but it was difficult to determine the exact amount of precious metal in them, and therefore their value.[56] Although colonial governments sometimes issued paper money as legal tender, the British Currency Acts of 1751, 1764 and 1773 prohibited the practice.[57]

Demands Grow for Better Transportation Networks

Justices of the peace in the Old Frederick County Court were powerful forces in the local economy. Appointed by the British Royal government, they enforced laws, levied and collected taxes and disbursed revenue when and where needed. Justices also decided on the construction of roads and public buildings and they regulated commercial activities on rivers.[58] Their workloads grew as increased commercial activity drove the need for better roads and more ferries.

Wagon Roads

Virginia's leaders recognized early on that economic development in its rural areas depended on a transportation system that facilitated trade and commerce. Without year-round navigable rivers and creeks, Northern Valley travelers had to rely on dirt roads—muddy in inclement weather and dusty in dry weather—for their transportation needs. County courts required yeoman farmers and plantation owners to fill in ruts on roads bordering their property. As trade developed among settlements, their residents petitioned the court to connect them with roads. Justices of the peace tried to respond expeditiously, using local tax collections for that purpose.[59] The Virginia House of Burgesses in Williamsburg, made up of elected representatives, oversaw maintenance of regional roads.[60]

While the Great Wagon Road served as the main route from the Shenandoah Valley to Philadelphia, trails through wind gaps in the Blue Ridge had to be widened for wagons loaded with wheat and flour to reach other Eastern Seaboard markets.[61] Farmers and millers successfully petitioned the Orange County Court for a wagon road through Chester Gap, west of Front Royal.[62] Trails through Snicker's Gap and Ashby's Gap, which connected Winchester and Berryville with Alexandria, were also widened.[63] By 1755, wagons could navigate through both Keyes' Gap, east of Charles Town, and Gregory's Gap, near Harpers Ferry.[64] Ten years later, they proceeded eastward from Front Royal through Manassas Gap, and from Luray through Thornton's Woods, later known as Thornton Gap.[65]

Ferries

To increase trade east and north of the region, the county court licensed ferries that crossed the region's two rivers at former fording points. A boatman pushed a flat-bottomed ferry forward with a pole, while an overhead rope with winch and pulley guided it to the other side. In 1730, Samuel Taylor ferried passengers from what became Shepherdstown, across the Potomac River to Maryland.[66] Settlers could cross at Pack Horse Ford, one mile to the south, but most opted to stay dry and pay for the ferry ride. As traffic on the Great Wagon Road picked up, Taylor's business became very profitable.[67] Thomas Van Swearingen purchased it in 1755; after his passing five years later, youngest son Benoni operated the ferry.[68]

In 1734, Thomas Chester from Philadelphia started a ferry service on the forks of the Shenandoah River to serve the public traveling between Winchester and Front Royal.[69] At former fording points 25 miles to the south, men named Ruffner, Strickler, Bixler and Bealer ferried passengers and wagons traveling between New Market and Luray. In 1748, Keyes' Ferry, also known as Vestal's Ferry, crossed the Shenandoah River where the Route 9 bridge in Jefferson County was later built.[70] Launched in 1752 near the present-day U.S. 50 bridge in Clarke County, Ashby's Ferry became Berry's Ferry in 1767, while Snicker's Ferry, which started up in 1760 below the future Route 7 bridge, changed hands as Castleman's Ferry in 1790.[71]

Castleman's Ferry on Shenandoah River in 1901
Photo by Charles Littler in Clarke County Album, VAGenWeb Archives

For easier access into the Shenandoah Valley's central section, the Great Wagon Road shifted 15 miles northwest of Shepherdstown to Light's Ford, a Potomac River crossing between present-day Williamsport and northern Berkeley County.[72] Beginning in 1744, settlers took Evan Watkins' Ferry, whose subsequent owners gave it the names of Light, Lemen and finally Williams.[73] Twenty miles upstream, Edward Joseph Hancock Jr. ferried passengers in 1774 from what became his namesake town to a road that led to Bath, later known as Berkeley Springs.[74]

In 1747, Philadelphia native and millwright Robert Harper was persuaded to forego crossing the Potomac River at Pack House Ford and enter the region at the confluence of the Potomac and Shenandoah rivers, then known as The Hole.[75] Soon afterwards, Harper acquired Peter Stephens' ferry service that ran between the village of Shenandoah Falls and present-day Sandy Hook, Maryland.[76] His purchase of 125 acres in 1751 from Lord Fairfax later became the site of Harpers Ferry.[77]

Trading Patterns with Eastern Seaboard

Besides distance and ease of travel to various markets, Northern Valley trading patterns were determined by where its products went for export, the source of its imported goods and the availability of credit from Eastern Seaboard merchants. With roots in Pennsylvania, many farmers, millers and merchants oriented their business dealings to Philadelphia, America's largest city and its leading exporter of foodstuffs. Wheat went directly from farms on the Great Wagon Road to Philadelphia, where commission merchants with foreign buyers purchased it.[78] Drawn by a team of four horses traveling 30 miles per day, each wagon carried up to three tons of cargo. To minimize the weight, wagoners—known as teamsters—walked on its left side or rode the horse positioned in front of the left wheel.[79] Wagons returned from Philadelphia full of household supplies and foodstuffs not found locally, and imported clothing, sundries and luxury goods for the region's merchants to sell in their general stores.

By the 1760s, as wagons replaced packhorses hauling goods through Blue Ridge wind gaps, the Northern Valley's trade shifted away from Philadelphia. Flour, wheat, preserved meat, furs, poultry and other products went by wagon to Alexandria on the Potomac River and to a lesser extent, Fredericksburg and Falmouth on the Rappahannock River.[80] Teamsters returned with salt, glass, coffee and other supplies imported from Europe, and sugar from the West Indies.

French and Indian War: Spending Boosts Economy

While the French and British fought the Seven Years War in Europe from 1756 to 1763, the North American conflict started two years earlier as the French and Indian War. The French sought to prevent English settlers in the Ohio River Valley from destroying their lines of communication that stretched from Canada, south to present-day Louisiana. They also did not appreciate traders from Virginia and Pennsylvania selling merchandise to their Native American neighbors at one-fourth the prices they charged.[81]

At the same time, England needed to protect settlers living in the backcountry from French-encouraged Native American raids. To shelter them when the need arose, the House of Burgesses financed construction of a chain of forts along the western Virginia frontier.[82] In 1755, George Washington was appointed colonel of the Virginia regiment and given responsibility for oversight of the forts. Thirteen lay within 15 miles of Winchester, where he built Fort Loudoun to function as his headquarters, house troops and serve as a supply depot for the other forts.[83] When the House of Burgesses paid for its construction and the wages of 450 soldiers and civilian workers with treasury notes, their circulation generated economic activity for the region.[84] The French and Indian War also offered yeoman farmers the opportunity to furnish meats, grains and other supplies to the troops stationed in Winchester and at the other forts.[85]

Postwar Economic Activity in Region

When the Treaty of Paris ended the war in 1763, Great Britain gained much of France's possessions in North America.[86] Despite sporadic resistance from Native Americans, settlement proceeded west of the Shenandoah Valley into the area between the Appalachian Plateau and the Mississippi River. A larger market opened for Winchester's merchants when those backcountry residents came into town to conduct business. In addition, the British Royal government paid Frederick County millers and farmers to supply flour and beef to its troops remaining in the Ohio and Mississippi river valleys. It also contracted with Winchester merchants to send dry goods to those areas and hired local teamsters to haul them there.

Agriculture: Wheat Becomes Primary Commercial Crop

As the region became settled, each yeoman farmer owned between 100 and 400 acres. Lacking slaves and mechanized equipment, he cultivated only 10 to 15 acres at first, with the balance held for speculation or for the next generation to work.[87] He engaged in mixed farming: raising livestock, maintaining a small orchard, planting a vegetable garden and growing corn for animal feed, wheat for bread, rye for whiskey and flax for cloth and oil. The yeoman farmer's livestock consisted of cattle, hogs, sheep and chickens. Surplus foodstuffs were exchanged with new settlers and among town merchants and artisans on court days.[88] His move to commercial farming—raising greater quantities for sale in a larger market—began with hemp and to a lesser extent tobacco, crops that required much labor to grow and harvest. With European men fighting, not farming during the Seven Years War, prices for wheat exported to England doubled.[89] As it became the main cash crop for Northern Valley farmers and planters, their financial well-being depended on the laws of supply and demand for the commodity in international markets.[90]

Tobacco

Introduced into the region in the 1740s, tobacco was grown on one or two acres to pay both local taxes and those owed to the colonial government in Williamsburg.[91] Absentee Tidewater landlords had their tenants near the Shenandoah River devote greater amounts of acreage to tobacco.[92] Teamsters hauled it to Virginia ports for shipment to Britain, which re-exported 90 percent to continental Europe.[93]

Tobacco prices fell during the late 1750s and 1760s, due to over-production in Virginia's Tidewater and Piedmont regions.[94] By 1775, it was raised on only 350 to 400 acres in the Shenandoah Valley, mostly in Berkeley and Frederick counties, which at the time included land that later became Clarke and Jefferson counties.[95] Tobacco exports from colonial America ended during the Revolutionary War.[96]

Hemp

From 1750 to 1800, Northern Valley farmers raised long-fiber hemp as a cash crop, which unlike tobacco, could be grown in the same spot forever. Although resistant to decay, mold and the sun's ultraviolet rays, the plant required a considerable amount of labor to cultivate and harvest.[97] Not consumed as a cannabis, fibers from the hemp's outer bark were spun into yarn used in the naval stores of sailcloth and rope. When mixed with pine pitch, the fibers became caulk that kept ships waterproof. The Northern Valley's strong and durable hemp yarn was also woven into burlap cloth and canvas for covered wagons. When combined with flax as osnaburg, the rough, textured fabric was used to clothe slaves.[98]

For the nation that ruled the seas, Great Britain considered hemp a strategic naval store. To reduce its reliance on Russian imports, in 1722 the House of Burgesses placed a bounty on each unit of hemp yarn delivered to British ships.[99] Despite a 50 percent bonus offered in 1745, most hemp not used in the Shenandoah Valley went for production of naval stores at colonial ports.[100]

After the Revolutionary War, farmers in Kentucky and Tennessee raised more hemp, and prices on world markets dropped when Russia and the Baltic countries increased their output.[101] Most Shenandoah Valley production ended in the early 1800s, when wool and cotton emerged as more comfortable fibers for clothing.

Flax

Scots-Irish and German settlers brought with them the knowledge of turning flax into linen, which became a favored cloth in the region's exchange economy.[102] Because flax quickly depleted nutrients from the soil, the one- or two-acre crop was rotated with wheat or corn every three years. Making linen was a labor-intensive process. At harvest time, seeds were removed from the flax plant and saved. After the stalk was soaked in water, farm wives collected fibers from its inner bark and spun them into yarn, which they wove into linen cloth. Flax seeds went to a specialty mill that extracted linseed oil from them.[103]

Wheat

The first wave of English colonists introduced wheat to North America. Because it was easier to grow and less labor intensive to process than tobacco or hemp, wheat became a popular crop to raise in the exchange economy.[104] Harvested with a sickle, the stalk was threshed with a flail to loosen the kernels, which were either ground by hand into flour on the farm or hauled in sacks to a gristmill for processing.

At first, most Northern Valley wheat went for local consumption. When its price increased rapidly during the Seven Years and the French and Indian wars in the 1750s, wheat surpassed hemp as the region's leading crop grown for the commercial market. Because much of it was exported to Britain and the West Indies, wheat prices there drove those in the colonial market. From 1720 to 1740, the price per bushel of colonial wheat ranged between 1.5 and 2.5 British shillings, then fluctuated between 2 and 3 shillings in the 1740 to 1760 period, before it increased to 5 shillings a bushel in the next two decades.[105] Although some wheat went to local millers, most of the harvest was sent by wagon, first to Philadelphia, then to Alexandria and Fredericksburg, where higher prices offset transportation costs.[106]

Manufacturing: Adding Value to Farm Products and Natural Resources

In colonial times, the region's gristmills, sawmills and woolen mills were located on rivers, creeks and streams. A mill race was dug to channel running water to a large, vertical wheel on the building's outside. Its rotation turned gears on equipment inside the mill that converted raw materials into semi-fabricated goods. Because their dams, sluices and ponds might alter a waterway's flow through neighboring properties, the county court's permission was needed, prior to a mill's construction.[107]

Before the Revolution, the value-added process of grinding wheat into flour was the Northern Valley's largest industry. Some millers converted gristmills to sawmills during down times in spring and early summer and others operated distilleries.[108] Next in importance were charcoal-fired furnaces, whose pig iron local blacksmiths and foundries used to make farm implements and household items.

Gristmills

Using technology imported from Europe, Northern Valley gristmills mechanized the farm wife's manual task of using a mortar and pestle to grind wheat kernels into flour. At the mill, the grain's starchy endosperm was moistened prior to its placement between two four-foot in diameter stones, whose rotating action separated the bran and broke the kernels into a powdery substance.[109] The flour fell into a chute, passed through a sifter and was bagged or placed in a barrel. At first, millers dumped the bran residue into streams, but later sold it for animal feed. Some millers also ground corn into meal, and rye that they distilled into whiskey.[110]

Because most of the cost to produce flour came from wheat, their prices tracked one another. The region's earliest gristmills dated to the 1730s, and for the next two decades, almost all their flour was used locally for breadstuffs made in farm kitchens.[111] In 1734, Josiah Jones located a flour mill on what became known as Rocky Marsh Run, near the Potomac River in the northeast section of present-day Berkeley County.[112] Four years later, Western Maryland native Thomas Shepherd Sr. built a large gristmill on the Town Run in his namesake village.[113] That same year, John Hite, son of early settler Jost Hite, started up Springdale gristmill on Opequon Creek, south of Winchester.[114] Other early ones appeared on Cedar Creek, the North Fork of the Shenandoah River and on Mill Creeks that passed through present-day Mount Jackson and Bunker Hill.

Iron Furnaces

Before the Revolution, the Northern Valley's iron industry consisted of one bloomery forge and three cold-blast furnaces, built near orebanks to minimize transportation costs. The local industry benefited from abundant supplies of timber, lime and running water needed to extract or smelt iron from the ore. To encourage its export to Great Britain, Parliament passed the Iron Act of 1750.[115] In mercantilist fashion, iron bars went tax free to the mother county, but the colonies were not allowed to manufacture hollowware and castings; those value-added goods had to be imported from England.[116] Because the prohibition was difficult to enforce in rural areas, it failed to put Northern Valley blacksmiths and iron founders out of business. They continued making nails, gun parts, knives, horseshoes, tools, cooking utensils, stoves, wagon wheels and farm implements.

In the industry's early days, picks, shovels and animal power were used to mine ore that contained iron. Before being loaded into a furnace, it was washed to remove clay and other impurities. Crushed limestone served as a flux that helped extract iron from the ore. Charcoal came from logs burned in a covered pit, 30 to 40 feet in diameter.[117] Because the fuel broke up into dust when transported long distances over rough roads, pits were located near furnaces.[118]

The region's iron industry began in 1742, when German settler William Vestal Jr. hired Thomas Mayberry from Pennsylvania to build a bloomery forge on his plantation in Jefferson County, seven miles south of Harpers Ferry.[119] Vestal owned a ferry service on the Shenandoah River that travelers took before and after passing through his namesake gap in the Blue Ridge. Using a charcoal-burning open hearth furnace, Vestal Bloomery employed a simple, inexpensive method of extracting small amounts of iron from the ore.[120] Because the iron never reached a high-enough temperature to melt, the resulting spongy, malleable substance was hammered on a forge to eliminate impurities called slag.[121] After Vestal's death in 1745, son John ran the forge and ferry for a short while, before moving with his family to North Carolina.[122] Vestal Bloomery passed into the hands of the Fairfax family and other owners, who operated it until the Civil War.[123]

In the 1760s, three larger, more productive cold-blast furnaces—Keep Tryst, Marlboro and Bean-Zane—appeared in the Northern Valley. The cold blast designation referred to the air temperature that a bellows sent into the furnace's firebed. Reaching a height of 35 feet in truncated pyramid form, its outer wall was constructed of limestone, while heat-resistant brick lined the inside wall. After the furnace was in blast for nine months—fueled with charcoal made from 300 acres of woodland—it was shut down to replace the firebricks.[124] An average furnace reduced between two to four tons of ore down to one ton of iron.[125]

To facilitate loading the ore, charcoal and limestone down their chimneys, most furnaces were built on hillsides, near a stream where a small water wheel powered bellows that caused the charcoal to burn between the 2,700 and 3,000 degrees Fahrenheit needed to separate iron from the ore.[126] Molten metal flowed outside the furnace into oblong-shaped molds with configurations that resembled piglets sucking on a sow.[127] When full, each mold weighed between 50 and 60 pounds.[128]

Because pig iron was actually brittle cast iron, a blacksmith at a refinery forge reheated and pounded it into a bar form; large forges used a heavy tilt hammer to achieve the same result.[129] A rolling mill thinned the bars into a flat sheet, while a slitting mill cut them into the width needed for the iron's end use.[130] Almost all furnaces had a foundry where workers poured melted iron into molds shaped as tools, stove parts, skillets, pots and other utensils.[131] The industry's greatest profits came from producing those value-added products.[132]

Employing 100 or more workers, iron plantations were self-sufficient villages that included the furnace, a charcoal house and some or all of the following: casting house, foundry, forge, stable, wagon shed, sawmill, store, church, farm and housing for workers.[133] The ironmaster-owner supervised the miners digging the ore, colliers preparing the charcoal, fillers charging the furnace and founders who oversaw iron casting. Indentured servants who exchanged work for their ocean passage, food and shelter were sources of unskilled labor on iron plantations, as were slaves and freed blacks.

Backed by investors from his native Scotland, John Semple built the region's first cold-blast furnace in 1764, at the confluence of Elks Run and the Potomac River, several miles upstream from Harpers Ferry.[134] The brown hematite ore for his Keep Tryst Furnace came from an orebank on 10,000 acres that he purchased from Israel Friend, one of the region's first settlers.[135] Semple's business plan was to ship pig iron 60 miles downriver to Occoquan Iron Works in Prince William County.[136] There it would be converted to bar iron and sent to Great Britain, which had exhausted its supply of timber to make charcoal, and was importing the metal from Sweden and Russia.[137]

But portaging iron-laden boats around the Potomac River's numerous falls drove up Semple's shipping costs. Several times he discussed possible river improvements with nearby landowner George Washington, but nothing came of it.[138] Instead, he shipped Keep Tryst's pig iron four miles upstream to Antietam Forge in Maryland, but its poor quality caused the business to fail.[139] In 1773, Semple died in debtor's prison, and the furnace was later sold at auction.[140]

In the early 1760s, Lewis Stephens and three men from Pennsylvania fired up Marlboro Furnace and Forge on Cedar Creek, five miles west of the town he founded, later known as Shephens City.[141] After leaving Philadelphia with his ironmaster uncle, Isaac Zane Jr. purchased Stephens' one-quarter interest in the Marlboro business in 1767.[142] Although from a wealthy Quaker family, he then took on debt to buy out the interests of the other men.[143]

Three years later, Zane and Mordecai Bean built an iron furnace in Mountain Falls, 10 miles from the renamed Marlboro Iron Works.[144] As with ironmasters that later came into the region, Bean learned the trade in Pennsylvania's iron ore belt in Berks and Chester counties. Producing several tons of pig iron per day, the Bean-Zane Furnace provided Marlboro Iron Works with additional raw material to produce household items and farm implements.[145] Several years later, Zane sold his interest to Bean, with the understanding that the renamed Bean's Smelter would continue to supply him with iron.

In the 1770s, the annual output of Marlboro Iron Works' furnace included 600 tons of pig iron and 150 tons of wrought and cast iron.[146] To provide his growing enterprise with iron ore and charcoal, Zane accumulated 20,000 nearby acres, financed with mortgages.[147] With a farm, sawmill, gristmill, distillery, retail store and 150 workers, including 12 slaves, Marlboro Iron Works was the region's first iron plantation and its largest industry.[148] The foundry produced hundreds of stoves, firebacks and cooking utensils that were known throughout the Virginia colony for their quality. Pig iron not used locally went by wagon to Alexandria and Fredericksburg, then by boat into the Chesapeake Bay and the Atlantic Ocean, bound for Boston and the British Isle cities of Bristol, London and Glasgow.

A leading citizen of Frederick County, Zane was a local magistrate and served in the House of Burgesses. Disowned by the Quaker's Philadelphia Meeting for his involvement in politics, Zane represented the county at Virginia's Conventions of the Revolution, held in 1775 and 1776.[149] While sales to Great Britain ceased during the Revolutionary War, Marlboro Iron Works supplied ordinance and cooking utensils to George Washington's troops.

Distilleries

In the 1700s and early 1800s, nearly every adult in colonial America imbibed alcoholic drinks during social occasions and for medicinal purposes. The Eastern Seaboard's liquor of choice was rum, a drink tied to the triangular slave and molasses trade with Africa and the West Indies. After Scots-Irish migrants brought their distilling skills with them, less-expensive whiskey became the Northern Valley's most popular alcoholic drink. Using spring water, they boiled yeast and ground-up rye or corn until it fermented, then poured the mush into a heated copper still that slowly turned it into whiskey. If production outstripped a family's needs, the excess was traded or sold.

While most whiskey was made on farms or in wayside inns, several commercial distilleries started up in the Northern Valley, often in combination with a gristmill that supplied it with ground-up grain. The distillers included Strasburg's founder Peter Stover, who made whiskey and brandy north of the town, and Gersham Keyes' family in the Bakerton area of present-day Jefferson County.[150] In 1770, William Patterson built a gristmill and distillery on Tuscarora Creek in Martinsburg and Joseph Carter did likewise at his family's Spout Spring Mill complex along Opequon Creek in eastern Frederick County.[151] On the same creek in Berkeley County, James Forman made whiskey at his gristmill in the 1780s, while Adam Eichelberger operated a distillery near the Vestal Bloomery.[152]

Sawmills

Before sawmills arrived in the region, two men sawed a log positioned over a pit or elevated on trestles. With the top sawyer standing above the log and a pitman situated below it, they moved a long, two-handled, iron saw in a vertical direction until the cut was completed. Requiring much less manpower, a sawmill produced up to 1,500 board-feet of lumber per day.[153] Its water wheel-powered saw, reciprocating straight up and down inside guide blocks, cut a resting log into boards and planks. The one-half inch thick blade generated large volumes of sawdust that found various farm uses.

Until the early 1800s, most sawmills operated on a small scale, often set up at gristmills before the wheat harvest.[154] Logs came from farmers who timbered their woodlands in the winter months for additional income. Lacking the ability to ship large quantities of the bulky material long distances, sawmill owners met the local needs of homebuilders and craftsmen that assembled furniture, barrels, wagons and carriages.

Woolen Mills

In colonial times, wool eventually surpassed linen as the favored clothing material, because it could be worn in both warm and cold weather. At first, a farm wife sorted, picked, scoured and wire-brushed raw wool, then spun it into yarn that she wove into cloth. She thickened the fabric by pounding it with her hands. Later, several of those labor-intensive steps were outsourced to two types of water-powered woolen mills. Carding mills brushed raw wool fibers into evenly aligned strands the farm wife spun into yarn. A fulling mill shrunk and thickened cloth into a finished product, ready for cutting and sewing.

In present-day Jefferson County, Benjamin Beeler opened a carding mill and gristmill in 1761 on Evitts Run.[155] Eight years later, John Rion started up a fulling mill on Howard's Branch, later called Flowing Springs Run, near present-day Halltown.[156] On Opequon Creek in Frederick County, several men built Pine Grove Woolen Factory in 1771 to card and full wool.[157] In the late 1770s, James Kelso and James Wilson opened fulling and carding mills on Abrams Creek, east of Winchester.[158] By the 1820s, integrated woolen mills in the region produced finished cloth.

CHAPTER 2

AMERICAN REVOLUTION TO 1830

Revolutionary War: Supplying Continental Army with Guns and Butter

As the 1770s approached, the colonies entered into an increasingly hostile relationship with England, which argued that they had not provided the mother country with financial support for the French and Indian War. America's leaders pointed out that their sons had fought and died in a war that benefited British interests more than its own.[1] To pay down a huge debt left from wars in Europe and North America, England taxed goods the colonists used, actions that resulted in the colonial phrase, "No taxation without representation."[2]

When the Revolutionary War broke out on April 19, 1775, colonial leaders formed the Continental Congress and established an army and navy. While no battles took place in the Northern Valley, its citizens, farmers and nascent industry pitched in to help win the conflict. Farmers in Berkeley and Frederick counties provided wheat, cattle and pigs to feed the troops, and packhorses to carry supplies for the Virginia regiments.[3] The region's hemp was made into naval stores for the Continental Navy.

Several businesses manufactured weapons and munitions. Brothers Adam, Henry and Philip Sheetz assembled flintlock muskets in Shepherdstown.[4] The armory of Adam Stephen, one of Martinsburg's founders, produced one dozen muskets per week. Its pig iron came from Keep Tryst Furnace near Harpers Ferry, which also cast cannons.[5] West of Stephens City, Isaac Zane's Marlboro Iron Works became a munitions factory that made four- and six-pound ordnance, swivel balls and chain shot.[6]

The Revolutionary War ended with the 1783 Treaty of Paris, in which England recognized the sovereignty of the United States of America. Its territory stretched from the Atlantic Ocean to the Mississippi River, and was bounded by British Canada on the north and Spanish Florida to the south.[7] Besides managing that large expanse of land, the new nation had to create tax and monetary systems and refinance its war debt. It also needed to establish credit, because paper money issued to finance the war was "Not worth a Continental." [8]

A postwar compromise between America's northern and southern states settled questions on establishing the nation's creditworthiness and locating its capital.[9] Recommendations that Treasury Secretary Alexander Hamilton made in his First Report on the Public Credit were incorporated into the Funding Act of 1790 and the Assumption Bill of 1790.[10] They required the federal government to pay its Revolutionary War debts and those incurred by the states. However, southern legislators opposed the Assumption Bill, because their citizens might be forced to pay part of the larger debt burden of the northern states, where the most fighting took place. To appease them, the Residence Act of 1790 called for the nation's capital to be located in an agrarian state near its geographic center, rather than in a financial hub such as New York or Philadelphia.[11] Given authority to determine its location, President George Washington in 1790 toured several sites along the Potomac River before choosing Virginia's Georgetown area.[12] It was located several miles upstream from his 8,000-acre Mount Vernon estate. Two hundred years later, the Northern Valley's economy would benefit greatly from that decision.

National Economy: New Nation's Growing Pains

Despite throwing off the mother country's governing shackles, the United States remained in its mercantilist grip because England accounted for three-quarters of its imports and exports. Responding to the new nation's pent-up demand caused by wartime shortages, English merchants flooded it with manufactured goods sold on easy credit.[13] In addition, the Navigation Act of

1783 blocked American exports of foodstuffs and lumber to the British West Indies.[14] That action, along with Spain's closure of New Orleans and the Mississippi River to commerce, resulted in a huge decline in United States exports.[15] The trade deficit soared from 1 million pounds-sterling to 2.7 million.[16] That imbalance, coupled with excessive federal and state government debt, mounting inflation and a shortage of gold and silver, threw the nation into recession in 1785 and 1786.[17]

Better times lay ahead. Foreign goods bound for the United States no longer went through England to be taxed, and the commerce clause of the United States Constitution prohibited tariffs on trade among the states.[18] In 1789, the United States government implemented the first tariff system, which placed duties on foreign articles that were also made domestically.[19] Its purpose was twofold: protect an emerging industrial base and raise funds to discharge the nation's Revolutionary War debt.

In 1791, Hamilton and economist Tench Coxe wrote the "Report on Manufactures," which called on the nation to produce goods to end reliance on British imports.[20] Despite that country's efforts to keep its technology and skilled mechanics at home, advances in America's manufacturing sector began when the Industrial Revolution reached its shores.[21] In 1790, on the Pawtucket River in Rhode Island, Samuel Slater built the new nation's first water-powered cotton mill.[22] When England blockaded the American coast during the War of 1812, similar mills soon appeared in several New England towns.[23]

In the early 1820s, Henry Clay and other politicians championed the American System to boost manufacturing and further reduce the nation's economic dependence on England and Europe.[24] It called for continued high tariffs and improved transportation networks to speed economic growth in a nation whose population had more than tripled, from 3.9 million in 1790—the first year of the federal census—to 12.9 million in 1830.[25] Contributing factors were larger family sizes on farms and the arrival of 500,000 immigrants.[26]

Trade Wars Between the United States and England

After 1800, wars, embargos and high tariffs affected the fortunes of Northern Valley farmers, planters and millers. Those groups benefited when the Napoleonic Wars, waged from 1803 to 1815, damaged Europe's agricultural sector and increased its demand for imported foodstuffs.[27] At first, the United States' neutrality allowed its ships to travel the Atlantic Ocean without incident.

When France and Britain seized them, however, Congress passed the Embargo Act of 1807, which closed American ports to foreign trade.[28] That caused the nation's exports to drop from $108 million to $22 million and squeezed the finances of Northern Valley wheat and flour producers, whose livelihoods had become dependent on exports.[29]

After the Napoleonic Wars, Parliament passed Corn Laws in 1815 to protect its farmers—mostly large landholders—against competition from imports.[30] Because all seed-bearing plants and their derivatives were called corn in England, Northern Valley farmers and millers faced another export headwind.[31] Congress responded with the Tariff of 1816, which placed duties averaging 20 percent on many imported goods.[32] Whenever tariffs on manufactured goods were increased, however, the economic interests of the North and the South came into conflict. Owners of northern mills and factories increased prices, but residents of the agricultural South paid more for the products.

The Panic of 1819

Financial panics occurred when a rapid increase in business activity was magnified by speculation in a particular sector or commodity, and the good times were followed by a sudden economic collapse.[33] Despite America's population growth, westward settlement and increased manufacturing activity, the first of many panics occurred in 1819. After the Napoleonic Wars drove up agriculture prices, banks in the Midwest and Great Plains provided easy money to speculators who purchased increasingly valuable public lands. In response, the Second Bank of the United States, chartered in 1816, restricted credit that it believed was over-extended. When other banks called in loans on heavily mortgaged farms, the deflationary spiral that began in 1819 hurt the finances of America's farmers.[34] However, prosperity returned two years later.

Internal Improvements: Need for Turnpikes and Bridges

In the nation's formative years, the term internal improvements referred to the construction of turnpikes, bridges and canals and better river navigation. Political and business leaders believed investments in transportation networks drove economic growth; unresolved was who had the resources and willingness to pay for them. In 1808, Treasury Secretary Albert Gallatin's "Report on Roads, Canals, Harbors and Rivers" argued for a $20 million federal expenditure to build and upgrade them, financed from tariffs and sales of public lands.[35] When Congress failed to provide the funds, states and local governments invested in internal improvements, along with private sector interests. Between 1790 and 1860, they spent $450 million on transportation projects, while the federal government provided only $54 million of financial support.[36]

As settlement reached the trans-Appalachian region in the early 1800s, leaders in New York, Pennsylvania, Maryland and Virginia sought to develop trade with it. To achieve that goal, they engaged in an internal improvements arms race, using turnpikes and canals as weapons. In 1816, the Virginia General Assembly established the $1 million Fund for Internal Improvements, which a Board of Public Works used to finance transportation projects.[37] Its principal engineer was tasked with coordinating road construction throughout the state, rather than have each county go its separate way.[38] The board purchased between 40 and 60 percent of the shares of Virginia-chartered private companies that built toll roads and canals.[39]

East-West Internal Improvements North of Region

Despite Virginia's creation of a public works fund, several large canal and turnpike projects to the north soon left the Northern Valley outside the rapidly expanding flow of east-west commerce and migration. Using technology borrowed from England, the $7 million Erie Canal gave New York State a first mover advantage in the trade wars.[40] After the 1825 opening, it cost $6 to ship one ton of midwestern wheat by barge 363 miles from Buffalo to Albany and down the Hudson River to New York City, compared to between $90 and $125 per ton when hauled by wagon.[41] The canal made the price of midwestern wheat competitive with that grown in Pennsylvania, Maryland and Virginia.

The National Turnpike, later known as U.S. 40, also bypassed the Northern Valley. Completed in 1835, it was a combination of the Cumberland Road—laid west from its namesake Maryland town—and the Baltimore National Pike. The toll road competed for western trade with the Erie Canal, and to a lesser extent, with the Pennsylvania Portage and Canal System, completed in 1834.[42] On that system's 390-mile route between Philadelphia and Pittsburgh, it took five days to navigate cargo through a series of canals, railways and inclined ramps.[43]

By the late 1830s, new transportation routes across New York, Pennsylvania and Maryland had become problematic for the economies of the Northern Valley's two largest towns, Winchester and Martinsburg. With poor roads, the

Shenandoah Valley no longer served as the primary route for northern pioneers migrating into the Ohio River Valley. And with access to the National Road, backcountry traders to the west conducted business in the alternative markets of Hagerstown, Cumberland, Wheeling and Pittsburgh.[44]

Turnpikes

When wider and smoother roads became a priority, Virginia chartered and invested in turnpike companies. A concept borrowed from Great Britain, road construction was financed through the sale of shares in a joint stock company.[45] Attendants at toll houses—five to ten miles apart—collected a fee from persons passing through a gate. After deducting expenses from receipts, any profits went to stockholders as a return of investment and later as dividends.[46] Because their businesses stood to benefit from better roads, turnpike investors included nearby merchants, inn and tavern owners and stagecoach operators.

To attract and retain users, a turnpike company had to maintain its road in good condition. In 1820, Scotsman John Macadam introduced a major improvement in road engineering.[47] Using his method, a turnpike's surface was covered with seven to ten inches of crushed stone, with larger ones placed on the bottom and smaller stones on top. Over time, buggy, wagon and stagecoach wheels ground the stones together to create a smooth macadamed surface.[48]

Valley Turnpike being macadamed
Painting by Carl Rakeman in Federal Highway
Administration's collection, Washington, DC

Between 1785 and 1840, Virginia chartered 46 turnpike companies, but few were in its western mountainous region, where construction costs were high.[49] By the early 1800s, turnpikes from Alexandria went through Snicker's and Ashby's gaps to the east bank of the Shenandoah River. Northern Valley farmers, planters and millers petitioned the General Assembly to charter companies that built turnpikes to the river's west bank, but that did not happen until the 1850s. Because improving the Great Wagon Road was a priority, the General Assembly chartered the Valley Turnpike Company in 1817 to improve travel from Winchester to Salem.[50] Due to the Panic of 1819, an insufficient number of shares were sold, but a second attempt in 1834 was successful.[51]

Bridges

Although justices of the peace regulated ferries in colonial days, the traveling public and commercial interests still complained of high fares. Post-Revolution, counties used bridge allowances to build wooden structures over small streams too deep to ford. But when traffic became heavy on major roads leading to the Potomac and Shenandoah rivers, toll bridges went over those waterways. Resting on stone abutments, their wooden roofs and sideboards preserved timbers on the floor from the elements.

In 1824, Gerard Wager's family built an 800-foot toll bridge in Harpers Ferry that replaced the ferry business they inherited from Robert Harper.[52] Their namesake bridge carried traffic between the town and present-day Sandy Hook in Maryland.[53] In 1850, the Virginia and Maryland Bridge Company finished one that connected roads between Shepherdstown and Sharpsburg and ended Swearingen's ferry service.[54] In 1815, Williamsport Bridge Company received a charter for a Potomac River bridge to speed travel on the Great Wagon Road between Martinsburg and Hagerstown.[55] However, none was built until 1909.

Several bridges spanned the Shenandoah River, beginning with the White House Bridge in 1808, which sped traffic on the turnpike between Luray and New Market.[56] In 1892, the General Assembly authorized the issuance of $40,000 worth of bonds for bridges to be built at the Berry's Ferry and Castleman's Ferry crossings.[57] Truss bridges were built in the early 1900s.[58] In 1854, the Front Royal and Winchester Turnpike Company's bridge replaced the ferry service between Riverton and Front Royal.[59]

Potomac River Improvements

While a member of the House of Burgesses, George Washington introduced a bill in 1774 to build skirting canals at several spots on the Potomac River, with construction costs recouped through user tolls.[60] With those improvements, he felt navigable tributaries and portage roads on the Allegheny Plateau could link the Potomac and Ohio rivers and bring commerce from Virginia's vast western territory to the Eastern Seaboard. Washington also knew a navigable river would bolster the economy of Alexandria, sitting several miles upstream from his Mount Vernon estate. It would also make his land in Jefferson County and the 60,000 acres he owned farther west of the Blue Ridge more valuable. Those holdings included 33,100 acres on the Ohio and Kanawha rivers.[61]

Although the Revolutionary War interrupted Washington's proposal for skirting canals, he and other investors revived it by forming the Patowmack Company in 1785.[62] But Baltimore merchants opposed the improvements, because commerce would be diverted from their city to Georgetown and Alexandria. Washington argued that trans-Appalachian area residents might align themselves with Britain or Spain, unless the Ohio River Valley was economically tied to the Atlantic Coast.[63] A navigable Potomac River would also divert trade from the Mississippi River, controlled at the time by the Spanish in New Orleans, and the St. Lawrence River, held by the British in Canada. After Virginia and Maryland signed the Mount Vernon Compact in 1785, each purchased Patowmack Company shares, as did individual investors. Speculators quickly bought up land fronting the river.[64]

The Patowmack Company deepened channels to remove small rapids at Little Falls, just north of Georgetown; at Seneca Falls, eight miles farther upriver; and at the falls near Harpers Ferry.[65] Impressed by James Rumsey's invention of a steamboat that traveled upstream, Washington hired him as the company's chief engineer to solve the problem of skirting the Great Falls near Georgetown. The Shepherdstown resident once ran a boarding house and tavern in Bath, later known as Berkeley Springs, and also built a house there for Washington.[66] A surveyor and mechanic—the 1780s equivalent of an engineer—Rumsey designed locks that lowered boats 77 feet as they passed through a canal alongside the falls.[67] Frustrated over construction delays, he left the company after one year to resume experimenting with steam-powered boats.

The Patowmack Company finally completed its skirting canals in 1802, at a cost of $750,000, well over budget due to labor problems, dangers from blasting rock with black powder and the river's erratic flows.[68] Flatboats—75-feet long, five-feet wide and pointed at both ends—carried flour, corn, whiskey, furs, iron ore and timber from Cumberland to Georgetown. It took five days to pole a boat the 185 miles downriver, but the return trip took from 10 to 12 days.[69] The company initially made money, but the river was navigable only part of the year. That meant tolls collected were insufficient to pay interest on its debt. Unable to secure more private or state financing, in 1828 the Patowmack Company turned its charter and assets over to the Chesapeake and Ohio Canal Company.[70]

Shenandoah River Improvements

While improved roads and new bridges sped the movement of Northern Valley freight wagons headed eastward, they did not measurably lower shipping costs for flour, wheat or pig iron. To achieve that goal, the region's farmers, planters, millers, ironmasters and merchants lobbied Richmond—Virginia's capital since 1780—to turn the Shenandoah River into a commercial artery. In 1798, the General Assembly chartered the Shenandoah Company to improve navigation from Harpers Ferry to Port Republic, 12 miles southeast of Harrisonburg.[71] After it failed to raise funds from private investors, the company was absorbed into the Patowmack Company in 1802, which hoped to gain traffic from a more navigable sister river.[72] Five years later, the Shenandoah Canal was dug between Virginius Island, a short distance upstream from Harpers Ferry, and the shoreline.[73] The Patowmack Company also deepened the river's channels above and below the canal, so boats could bypass a series of dangerous river ledges known as the Staircase.[74]

When no further improvements were made, due to the Patowmack Company's financial problems, the New Shenandoah Company was chartered in 1815 to dredge its namesake river and collect tolls.[75] At points where the water level was exceptionally low, partial dams and channels were built to create sluices along one of the river's banks. After the company spent $70,000, navigation opened from Harpers Ferry to Port Republic in 1823.[76] Two years and $5,000 later, the river's North Fork was made navigable from Riverton to Strasburg.[77] Flat bottom, 75-foot-long gundalows soon carried Northern Valley cargo to Harpers Ferry. When the river ran high in the spring, one boat could haul up to 12 tons of pig iron or 110 barrels of flour. Each boatman received from $14 to $18 for the three-day trip.[78] Because gundalows could not be poled against the current on return trips, most were sold in Harpers Ferry for lumber. The crews walked back to Warren and Page counties. Some boats continued down the Potomac River to Georgetown.

Gundalow boat used on Shenandoah River
Photo of George Erdman's pine scale boat, located in Shenandoah Valley Cultural Heritage Museum, Edinburg, VA

Northern Valley Economy: No Longer a Backcountry Frontier

Between 1790 and 1830, the region's population grew by a modest 38.7 percent, from 49,904 to 69,241, but it soared by 231 percent in the United States, from 3.9 million to 12.9 million.[79] Large waves of European immigrants settling into urban areas in the East and Midwest accounted for much of the difference. In addition, some second-generation Northern Valley residents left to purchase inexpensive federal land and start new lives in Kentucky, Tennessee and Ohio.

Raising wheat and livestock were the region's main agrarian pursuits, while gristmills and iron furnaces led a more diversified manufacturing sector. Martinsburg and Winchester served as market towns for their surrounding populations and for backcountry traders. With improved transportation through the Blue Ridge, the region's trade with the outside world continued to shift from Philadelphia to Alexandria. Nevertheless, the Embargo Act of 1807, the

War of 1812 and England's Corn Laws of 1815 resulted in reduced exports of wheat and flour. Then came the Panic of 1819.

Plantations in Eastern Part of Region

After the Revolution, several hundred Tidewater families with unproductive tobacco fields moved into the eastern part of present-day Clarke, Jefferson and Warren counties. The planters settled on Lord Fairfax's former lands near the Shenandoah River that Robert Carter granted to their ancestors in the 1730s, and since then had been leased to tenants.[80] Joining a much smaller Tidewater group already in the region, they came with hundreds of slaves that labored in fields, performed domestic chores and used their artisan skills to turn plantations into self-contained economic units.[81] After experimenting with tobacco and hemp, the planters raised the more profitable wheat.

Millwood became eastern Frederick County's commercial center. By 1810, the village had between 50 and 60 residents, along with a gristmill, tannery, blacksmith, tailor, cobbler and a wagon maker.[82] Its name came from the Burwell-Morgan Mill, built in 1782 on Spout Run, a Shenandoah River tributary.[83] Its owners were local planter Nathaniel Burwell and Revolutionary War General Daniel Morgan, who used German prisoners to build it.[84] To improve access to the mill, Morgan successfully petitioned the Frederick County Court in 1785 to reroute the main road from Winchester to Berry's Ferry through Millwood.[85] Born on a James River plantation, Burwell built

Carter Hall near Millwood in Clarke County
Postcard published by Williamsport Paper Company,
Williamsport, PA

the nearby Carter Hall mansion in the 1790s on 8,000 acres his grandfather, Robert Carter, acquired through grants of Fairfax's land to himself.[86] Wanting his own gristmill, Burwell built a smaller one on his property, downstream from the other one.[87]

Western Migration Through the Valley

In colonial days, migrants to the Carolinas took the Great Wagon Road through the Shenandoah Valley. Between 1790 and 1810, a larger wave of settlers—as many as 4,000 annually—traveled the same road. Northern Valley merchants thrived by selling them provisions. Rather than head directly into the Carolinas, most turned their covered wagons westward at Big Lick, later renamed Roanoke.[88] They took the Wilderness Road through the Cumberland Gap in the Allegheny Mountains to inexpensive lands in Kentucky, Tennessee and the Northwest Territory.[89] To pay down Revolutionary War debts, the federal government offered to sell anyone settling there a minimum of one square mile—the equivalent of 640 acres—for just $1 an acre.[90] Families that took the deal included those from eastern Virginia, whose land had been ruined from over-planting of tobacco, and the offspring of indentured servants. At the time, they made up three-quarters of the white population in Pennsylvania, Maryland and Virginia. The restless group also included second-generation Northern Valley farmers, who saw advertisements for fine wheat lands and moved west for better economic opportunities.[91]

Towns and Marketplaces

After the Revolution, bartering and trading goods and services among Northern Valley neighbors, merchants and artisans declined. With the introduction of the American dollar and a decimal system of coinage in 1785, market participants used cash to complete transactions.[92] By 1800, a hierarchy of commercial centers had developed along the Great Wagon Road.[93] Martinsburg and Winchester were at the top, because their merchants and artisans offered consumers the widest variety of goods. To serve more localized markets, other towns and villages grew up along the Great Wagon and East Valley roads.[94] East-west secondary roads connected the settlements on the two north-south corridors.[95]

To survive as commercial centers, Northern Valley jurisdictions needed to develop and maintain their streets, water supplies and public buildings.

Commercial property owners paid the cost of filling holes and grading streets in front of their establishments.[96] Levies placed on tithables—residents able to work—financed other infrastructure needs.[97] To keep animal mess off the streets, hogs and unattended horses were prohibited from running through them.[98] With clean water an issue for its residents, Winchester installed a central delivery system in 1808, using the spring-fed Town Run as its water source.[99] Five years later, Martinsburg prohibited washing clothes in or near the Town Spring, which supplied its residents and businesses with water.[100]

In the 1790s, Winchester's streets were lined with a dozen taverns, artisan shops and 30 stores selling goods that came from wholesalers in Philadelphia, Alexandria and Fredericksburg.[101] High-end items were found at the Daniel Norton & Co. store, which advertised in 1787 that it received, "Fall goods from the ship Dade, which just arrived in Alexandria." [102] Included were "duffil and rose blankets, negroe cottons, bath coatings, calliniancoes, wild bores, lady's fashionable hats and ribbons of the newest taste." [103] Thomas Smith & Co. in Martinsburg advertised in 1802 that it, "Just received from Philadelphia a fresh supply of merchandise, consisting of Irish linens; dowlas; Russia sheeting; German rolls; blue, striped, clouded and plain India nankeens; Imperial hyson; skin hyson; Bohen teas; coffee; sugar; Crowley; and blistered steel." [104]

Goods not found in stores in the region's two largest towns were bought and sold at an organized venue. In 1813, the open-air City Market started up at Martinsburg's main square, on the corner of Queen and King streets; four years later, the floor was paved in bricks and its ends were enclosed in gates. The town set the duties of a market master, who opened the building by shouting, "You may buy and sell." [105] He also kept the premises clean, and if requested, weighed a vendor's produce to ensure the scale's correctness. In 1817, a Market House replaced two open spaces on the corner of Winchester's Water (later Boscawen) and Market (later Cameron) streets.[106] An ordinance required a clerk to set the prices sellers charged, and any goods not sold in a store had to be offered for sale inside the Market House.[107]

Before the Revolution, Frederick, Berkeley and Shenandoah were the Northern Valley's only counties. Because their courthouses were located in Winchester, Martinsburg and Woodstock, respectively, those towns were designated as county seats. As the region's population grew, citizens wanted to transact business at a more convenient courthouse. Between 1801 and 1836, five counties were created from the original three, and each county seat became a center of commercial activity.[108] Woodstock's profile of businesses was similar to other county seats. In 1835, its 950 residents frequented a variety of establishments that included five general stores, two taverns, three tan yards, four saddlers, two hatters, five carpenters, three wheelwrights, three chair makers, four tailors, two blacksmith shops, two saddle tree makers, two bricklayers, two plasterers, five boot and shoe factories and two potters.[109] Woodstock businesses with the local market all to themselves included a watch maker, cartwright who made wagons, tinsmith and printer.[110]

Because the Northern Valley's small villages had only one or two general stores with limited merchandise, traveling salesmen from New England, New York and Pennsylvania stepped into the void. The peddlers sold pots, pans, pails, tinware, clocks, cleaning items and utensils, either door-to-door to farm families or displayed them on village street corners. Northern manufacturers stored the salesman's merchandise in Pennsylvania warehouses.[111] During economic downturns, the region's merchants and politicians viewed peddlers as disruptive, labeling them drummers because they constantly drummed-up business.[112] Virginia issued them licenses, but most peddlers had left by the early 1840s, when railroads shipped a wider variety of less-expensive goods directly to merchants.[113]

Trading Patterns

From 1770 to 1800, the region's primary exports remained wheat and flour, and to a lesser extent, pig iron and hemp. At the same time, owners of cottage industries that produced gunpowder, nails, furniture, leather goods and textiles reduced the Northern Valley's dependence on imports. Some family-run businesses sold small amounts of linen, cast iron goods, liquor, rope and sailcloth into Eastern Seaboard markets, but they had high shipping costs and limited financial resources to expand production, establish distribution systems and extend credit to customers. As a result, no large industry developed in the region.

By the early 1800s, Northern Valley trade had shifted from Philadelphia to much closer Alexandria, a former tobacco and hemp trading post on the Potomac River. It was a more active commercial center than Falmouth and Fredericksburg, located on the narrower and shallower Rappahannock River. The town's leaders initiated several projects to boost commerce. In 1792, they formed the Bank of Alexandria, which enabled 20 mercantile firms to extend credit to retailers, including those in the Northern Valley.[114] To create a deep-water channel for ocean going ships, part of the town's shoreline was filled in and wharfs were built over it.[115] Alexandria also financed construction of the 34-mile Little River Turnpike to bring wheat and flour from Loudoun County, and eventually Frederick County, to its port.[116] In 1806, that road joined the Aldie and Ashby's Gap Turnpike, which six years later reached the Shenandoah River's east bank.[117] Although Alexandria lacked falling water to power gristmills, it became a leading center for buying, selling, inspecting, storing and exporting the powdery commodity. It was also one of the nation's 10 most active ports of entry, handling imports of rum, wine, sugar, coffee and manufactured goods.[118]

Alexandria soon faced competition from Baltimore, which had become the nation's third largest city and a leading center for flour milling and trading.[119] Originally intended to function as a tobacco port, its surrounding land was not well-suited for the crop. Planters on waterways leading to the Chesapeake Bay shipped tobacco directly from their wharfs to Great Britain.[120] However, much of the new nation's wheat was grown close to Baltimore, in southern Pennsylvania and in the middle and western parts of Maryland. Capitalizing on that proximity and an abundance of water power, its businessmen built 50 large gristmills along Jones Falls, Gwynns Falls and beside the strong currents of the Patapsco and Gunpowder rivers.[121] In the early 1820s, they erected warehouses on wharfs that extended 1,000 feet into Fells Point harbor, which led to the Chesapeake Bay.[122] Using speedy Clipper ships—top sail schooners with V-shaped hulls—the city's flour trade with Europe, the West Indies and South America flourished. By 1830, the center of nation's processing, inspection and export of flour had moved from Philadelphia to Baltimore. Later in that decade, when railroads arrived in Winchester and Harpers Ferry, the Northern Valley's wheat and flour trade followed suit.

Agriculture:
Farmers and Planters Feast on Wheat

When tobacco and hemp markets declined after the Revolution, Northern Valley farmers and recently arrived planters made wheat their cash crop. Businesses that provided them with goods and services added to the region's economic activity.[123] They included blacksmiths forging farm implements, coopers fabricating barrels, cartwrights assembling freight wagons and leather workers making harnesses for draft horses.[124]

Despite high levels of wheat production, the region's farmers continued to practice mixed farming as a hedge against the grain's frequent price movements. They raised cattle and hogs for the Eastern Seaboard market, grew rye for whiskey and flax for cloth and oil. To put food on the table, farmers planted a vegetable garden and tended to a small orchard. Some devoted a few acres to broom corn, whose tightly bound stalks were used to sweep floors and clear ashes from fireplaces.[125]

Wheat Farming

In the 1760s and 1770s, England was a net exporter of wheat.[126] Between 1750 and 1800, however, its population rose by 46 percent, compared to only 9 percent in the previous 50 years.[127] That increase occurred when the Industrial Revolution drew farmers off their lands for higher-paying work in factories and coal mines.[128] By the 1780s, the nation had become an importer of wheat, causing its price to rise. When Britain's exports to southern Europe declined, those countries were forced to buy wheat on world markets.[129] Additional demand came from the West Indies, whose planters grew sugar cane, rather than wheat, in the hot climate.[130]

When the price of wheat nearly doubled between 1775 and 1800, almost every Northern Valley farmer and planter raised it for the commercial market.[131] They cleared more acreage, invested in mechanical devices, enriched their soil with lime and gypsum, practiced crop rotation and deep plowing, and used animal manure as fertilizer.[132] To learn those farming techniques, they read "A Treatise on Practical Farming," written in 1803 by Loudoun County farmer John Alexander Binns.[133] The Shenandoah Valley became the largest wheat-producing region in Virginia, the Mid-Atlantic and in the South.[134] Advertisements for its farms and raw land highlighted their suitability for commercial production of the grain.[135]

Where Northern Valley farmers sold their wheat depended on prevailing domestic and foreign prices and transportation costs. Its export price responded to events, especially wars in the much larger European market, whose estimated population of 185 million citizens in 1820 compared to 10 million in the United States.[136] In England, the price moved from 5 shillings per bushel in 1792 up to 15 shillings when the Napoleonic Wars ended in 1815.[137] But the postwar recovery of Europe's agriculture sector depressed commodity prices on world markets, as did England's enactment of the

Corn Laws in 1815. Wheat prices in the United States dropped in half, from $1.80 a bushel in 1810 to 93 cents in the Panic of 1819.[138] They rebounded to $1.36 a bushel in 1823, when America's exports shifted from England and Europe to South America.[139] Nevertheless, those volatile prices put Northern Valley wheat growers on a financial roller coaster, one that continued into the twentieth century.

Raising Livestock

Some Northern Valley farmers engaged in the livestock trade, driving cattle and hogs on hoof to Eastern Seaboard markets. At first, their animals joined those coming from western Virginia, southern Ohio and Kentucky on the Great Wagon Road, headed to Philadelphia.[140] In the early 1800s, the region's farmers organized their own droves, during which a horseman and two footmen took herds of either 120 cattle or 520 hogs to Philadelphia, Baltimore or Alexandria.[141] Averaging 10 to 20 miles a day, they rested at commercial livestock stands, known as drover inns, which provided food and lodging for the men and pens and pasture for the animals.[142] Prior to Thanksgiving, flocks of turkeys were driven 10 to 12 miles a day to eastern markets.[143] The birds followed feed sprinkled on the ground or noise from a bell tied around the dominant turkey's neck.[144]

Rather than have livestock driven eastward, some of the region's farmers dressed their cattle and hogs and shipped the dried, smoked or salted meats by wagon to those same markets.[145] To lessen their reliance on wheat's fluctuating price, plantation owners fattened cattle.[146] During spring and summer, farmers in the Allegheny Mountain foothills raised and grazed the young animals, which the planters purchased in the fall and fed during the winter months.[147] The cattle were put out to pasture the following spring and summer, before being driven to East Coast markets.[148]

Manufacturing: Flour and Iron Production Lead the Sector

When the new nation's leaders called for more domestic manufacturing to lessen America's dependence on English and European imports, the Northern Valley responded with more gristmills, sawmills, iron furnaces, distilleries, tanneries and woolen and oil mills. Artisans and craftsmen—cartwrights, wheelwrights, blacksmiths, potters and cabinetmakers—also contributed to the region's production of goods. An 1835 inventory of manufacturers in Page County, whose population was 6,500 at the time, revealed a variety of participants: 24 gristmills, 61 sawmills, 10 tan yards, six carding machines, three linseed oil mills, six hemp-rope mills, one iron furnace and two forges.[149]

Because Northern Valley mills had to be located near a water source for their power, they were scattered throughout the countryside, making it difficult to consolidate resources and gain efficiencies of scale. Developed in England in the late 1700s, steam technology enabled industry to locate anywhere. But with iron furnaces, tanneries and sawmills denuding Northern Valley forests, large quantities of wood were not available to power steam engines. And coal was nowhere to be found.

Gristmills

In 1810, the 441 toll and merchant gristmills in Virginia produced one-quarter of the nation's flour.[150] A Northern Valley farmer who operated a toll mill ground a neighbor's wheat kernels into flour or corn into meal. He kept one-eighth of the finished product as a commission and bagged the rest for the grower's use.[151] A merchant miller, however, purchased wheat outright and assumed market risk. Working year-round, he packed the flour in barrels and sold it either locally or in East Coast markets. Some merchant millers also sawed logs, distilled whiskey, raised cattle, assembled barrels and operated general stores.[152] With their limestone mansions dotting the landscape, they were among the region's wealthiest and most influential citizens.

After the Revolution, it appeared that every Northern Valley creek with rapidly moving water had multiple gristmills alongside it. They included Tuscarora Creek near Martinsburg; Mill Creek, running from Gerrardstown through Bunker Hill in southern Berkeley County; and Bullskin Run in southeastern Jefferson County. The Milldale village in Warren County was named for the many gristmills found on its creek that emptied into the Shenandoah River. They also appeared on Frederick County streams: Opequon Creek, Red Bud Run, Green Spring Run, Cedar Creek and Abram's Creek. In Shenandoah County, multiple mills were located on Stony Creek, Mill Creek, Passage Creek and on the North Fork of the Shenandoah River. In Page County, they were found on the river's South Fork and on Hawksbill Creek.

The region's larger gristmills that produced 50 or more barrels of flour per day were the Burwell-Morgan Mill in Millwood; Lantz Mill, built in the early 1800s on Stony Creek in western Shenandoah County; and Willow Grove Mill, which ground flour on a branch of Hawksbill Creek near Luray. In 1824, James Stubblefield processed 150 to 200 barrels of flour per day at his Island Mills, located on Virginius Island in the Shenandoah River near Harpers Ferry.[153]

The gristmill industry had a multiplier effect on the Northern Valley's economy, because various tradesmen provided services and products to it. They included millwrights who built and maintained the equipment, blacksmiths that fabricated the metal workings inside the mill, sawyers who provided wood for its construction, cartwrights that built freight wagons and coopers who assembled barrels to store and ship flour. In its early years, producing the commodity was a labor-intensive enterprise, but that changed when Delaware native Oliver Evans published "The Young Mill-Wright and Miller's Guide" in 1790. It suggested ways to automate a mill's internal workings by putting specific functions on separate floors and using leather belts to move buckets along an assembly line.[154] The water wheel not only powered the grinding stones, but also ran machinery that poured in grain at the start of the process and filled barrels with flour at the other end.[155] To improve productivity, Northern Valley millers purchased Evans' patented equipment.[156]

While several of the region's gristmills had a daily capacity of 50 barrels of flour, large ones in Baltimore produced more than 500 barrels a day.[157] As a result, that city was more interested in purchasing the Northern Valley's wheat than its flour. But with few gristmills in Alexandria, its commission merchants sourced most of their flour from millers in Loudoun County and the Northern Valley. In 1785, Alexandria and Baltimore passed inspection laws.[158] Millers paid a fee to an inspector who drilled a hole in the barrel, removed a sample of flour and examined it for texture, moisture and odor. He then stamped or burned "superfine" or "fine" on the barrel, along with the gristmill's name.[159] Northern Valley and other rural millers claimed the laws disadvantaged them, because the prices they received were below those paid to urban millers with too close a relationship with the inspectors.[160]

As with wheat, flour prices responded to international events. In 1800, one barrel sold for $4.50, but when the Napoleonic Wars began three years later, it soared to an all-time high of $11.[161] The price remained at that level until England enacted the Corn Laws in 1815, then bottomed at $4.50 in 1825, a time when wheat prices also dropped in half.[162]

Oil Mills

Not all Northern Valley mills located next to running water ground wheat into flour. Several pressed flax seeds into linseed oil used as a lubricant, a drying agent in paint and was found in soap. When in solid form, it became a putty-like sealant. At harvest time, farmers separated seeds from the flax stalk and brought them to an oil mill. There they were heated, then crushed by burrstones before a wedge press extracted the yellowish oil.

In the early 1800s, Virginia led the South in linseed oil production. Much of it came from Shenandoah County's five mills, which in 1810 produced 15,000 gallons or 45 percent of the commonwealth's oil.[163] Two of the region's large oil mills were Townsend Beckham's on Virginius Island and Adam Stephen's on Tuscarora Creek in Martinsburg. Those in Frederick County included Kline's Mill on the West Run tributary of Crooked Run; Meshach Sexton's mill on Red Bud Run; and several in the Opequon settlement along its namesake creek.[164] However, when the Shenandoah Valley's clothing of choice shifted from linen to wool and cotton in the 1850s, flax harvests and linseed oil production declined.

Iron Furnaces

Prior to the Revolutionary War, the Northern Valley's iron industry consisted of one forge and three cold-blast furnaces. Built in 1742 in Jefferson County, the Vestal Bloomery shut down in 1760. Bean's Smelter, started up in 1770 in the Mountain Falls area of western Frederick County, continued in blast after Mordecai Bean's passing in 1814. His son James replaced the furnace in 1848 with a smaller one on nearby Furnace Run, which he sold seven years later to A. P. Taylor.[165] The renamed Taylor's Furnace produced 500 tons of pig iron a year, used locally in the fabrication of utensils and tools.[166]

Fired up in 1764 near the Potomac River in Jefferson County, creditors foreclosed on John Semple's Keep Tryst Furnace in 1786.[167] They operated it for six years, until Philadelphia merchants and Henry "Light-Horse Harry" Lee III, father of Robert E. Lee, purchased the furnace at auction and hired Philadelphia ironmaster Thomas Mayberry to rebuild it.[168] After a second one went into blast at the site, Keep Tryst's workforce grew to 50 men, including slaves.[169]

Founded in 1767 in Frederick County, Marlboro Iron Works became one of the largest suppliers of ordnance to the Continental Army, but owner Isaac Zane went largely unpaid.[170] In addition, the postwar brigadier general gave pensions to soldiers, widows and heirs, often without government reimbursement.[171] With his extensive land holdings heavily mortgaged, Zane soon encountered financial difficulties and tried to sell the business.[172] After his passing in 1795, creditors shuttered the furnace and forge and sold them for parts.[173] Sarah Zane from Philadelphia used some of her brother's 5,000 pounds-sterling estate for construction of a fire house, private school and Quaker meeting house in Winchester, a place she often visited.[174]

Post Revolution, several ironmasters from Pennsylvania settled in the Northern Valley after hearing reports of its rich quantities of iron ore, along with inexpensive and abundant land and labor.[175] Those with the Pennybacker, Arthur, Mayberry, Blackford and Newman surnames formed partnerships among themselves, their relatives and with other ironmasters. They built the Redwell, Columbia and Liberty furnaces and several forges.

In 1778, Dirck Pennybacker and son Benjamin moved from the Philadelphia area to Sharpsburg, Maryland, and leased a furnace near Antietam Creek, but a flood ruined the business and left them in financial straits.[176] Undaunted, Pennybacker moved his family to Shenandoah County in 1784 and purchased Pine Forge on Smith Creek, several miles northwest of New Market.[177] A former co-worker supplied the forge with pig iron from a furnace in nearby Rockingham County.[178]

Wanting his own source of iron, Pennybacker moved across Massanutten Mountain in 1786 to the western part of present-day Page County, and built Redwell Furnace near Luray.[179] With Yager Springs powering its bellows, a workforce of 160 men, including 33 slaves, smelted several tons of pig iron a day.[180] Most of Redwell's bar iron was either cast into iron stoves, sold to local blacksmiths or sent back to Pine Forge, which son Benjamin managed.[181] The furnace's remaining output was either hauled in wagons eastward to Fredericksburg or sent to Bixler's Landing, where gundalows carried it to Harpers Ferry for transfer to wagons bound for Baltimore and Philadelphia.[182] After Dirck Pennybacker built Paoli Forge in 1799 on Stony Creek, eight miles west of Edinburg, some pig iron went there to meet that area's growing demand for higher-value farm implements and household items.[183]

After Pennybacker's death in 1802, Redwell Furnace came under several ownerships; the last group included son Benjamin and two brothers-in-law, Isaac Samuels and George Mayberry, brother of Thomas, who worked at the Keep Tryst Furnace.[184] In 1803, the three partners built Columbia Furnace on Stony Creek, three miles west of Paoli Forge, later renamed Union Forge, because of its location between the Redwell and Columbia furnaces.[185] In 1807, they sold the latter furnace, which produced 800 tons of pig iron a year, to John Arthur & Co.[186] Before relocating to the Northern Valley in the early 1800s, Arthur had been a principal in Pine Grove Furnace on South Mountain, east of Chambersburg.[187] As Columbia Furnace's production increased under his ownership, a village with a store, hotel, school and houses grew up around it.[188]

Benjamin Blackford also emerged as a key figure in the Northern Valley's iron industry. Beginning his career in Cumberland County, Pennsylvania, in 1801 he leased and operated Catoctin Furnace on South Mountain in Frederick County, Maryland, before moving south.[189] Seven years later, he and John Arthur formed Blackford, Arthur & Co., which purchased Union Forge and the Redwell Furnace from Benjamin Pennybacker.[190] Following an industry practice of naming an iron furnace after a loved one, Blackford gave the furnace his wife Isabella's name.[191] In 1812, Blackford, Arthur and two other men purchased Isaac Zane's former Marlboro Iron Works to salvage its machinery.[192] To process pig iron closer to Isabella Furnace, the partners built Speedwell Forge No. 1 in 1815 on Hawksbill Creek, north of Luray, and five years later, Speedwell Forge No. 2.[193] In 1820, their furnace consumed 2,700 tons of ore, 140 tons of limestone and 216,000 bushels of charcoal to produce 250 tons of pig iron and 300 tons of castings poured into molds.[194] The two forges became Virginia's largest fabricators of plough shares, which found a ready market of wheat farmers expanding their acreage under cultivation.[195]

Five miles northwest of Columbia Furnace, Walter Newman, son-in-law of Benjamin Pennybacker, built Liberty Furnace in 1821 on Laurel Run, a branch of Stony Creek.[196] Through outright purchases and land grants from Virginia, Newman accumulated 3,845 acres that contained large quantities of iron ore, limestone and timber.[197] Rather than ship bar iron to Union Forge, which Blackford, Arthur & Co. owned, in 1828 Newman built Liberty Forge near his furnace.[198]

Tanneries

Responding to a growing population that needed shoes and boots, the number of tanneries in America increased from 1,000 in 1750 to 8,000 in 1840.[199] After the Revolution, the smelly task of turning animal hides into leather moved off Northern Valley farms and into tanneries located along waterways. The region possessed all the natural resources required for leather production: tannin-laden bark, lime and clean water. From early April through May, farmers felled chestnut oak and sumac trees, peeled the bark and seasoned it during the summer. The bark then went to a tannery, which ground it into a fine powder that was placed in large vats filled with boiling water.

Tanning was a lengthy process. Hides were soaked in a mixture of water and lime to de-hair them, then were placed in the vats for between 12 and 18 months. During that time, the chemical action of the tannin solution made the hides supple and prevented their normal decomposition. But the pungent odors gave birth to the phrase, "Smells like a tannery," and their discharges of water containing lime and tannin residue polluted rivers and creeks. [200]

While the 50 tanneries in Frederick and Shenandoah counties together employed hundreds of workers in 1810, most operated on a small scale.[201] James Verdier from Maryland opened tanneries on Shepherdstown's Town Run and on Tuscarora Creek in Martinsburg in the 1770s.[202] Solomon Van Meter tanned hides along Happy Creek in Front Royal, while the tanneries of Squire Obed Funk and Obed Chandler were located on Strasburg's Town Run.[203] Beginning in 1824, oil mill owner Townsend Beckham operated one for 11 years on Virginius Island.[204]

Forests in Little North Mountain, near the western border of Frederick and Shenandoah counties, were full of chestnut oak trees. In 1803, Samuel Sydnor opened a tan yard near the village of Gravel Springs, later known as Star Tannery. He stored, dried and ground the bark, then shipped it to tanners in the region's towns.[205] Located a few miles south of Sydnor were Zepp Tannery, also called Prospect Tannery, and Eli Peer's Tan Yard.[206]

In 1800, Joseph Tuley from New Jersey established a large tannery on Spout Run in Millwood, then built one on Front Royal's Water Street, 20 years later.[207] In 1806, Tuley used his wife's inheritance to purchase the 420-acre Rattlesnake Spring Tract, three miles west of Millwood, and renamed it Tanner's Retreat.[208] More than a century later, part of the renamed Tuleyries estate became Blandy Experimental Farm, managed by University of Virginia.

Wagon Manufacturing

As the region's roads improved, freight wagons hauled large quantities of goods longer distances. Assembling them became a big business in Newtown, later known as Stephens City, and in Front Royal. The industry began in the early 1770s when Isaac Zane called on Newtown craftsmen to make sturdy ones for his nearby Marlboro Iron Works. As the region's wheat economy grew, more demand came from farmers and millers. They hired teamsters to haul grain and flour over the Blue Ridge to Alexandria and Fredericksburg, and north on the Great Wagon Road to Philadelphia.[209] Pulled by teams of four, six or eight horses, a wagon carried between 3,000 and 4,000 pounds of goods. The costlier alternative was to burden each of 15 to 20 packhorses with 200 pounds.[210] Teamsters camped at night or stayed at taverns, referred to as wagon stands.[211]

By 1810, twenty-seven master cartwrights were based in Frederick County, which included present-day Clarke and Warren counties.[212] Local saddle and harness makers, wheelwrights and sawmill operators supplied them with needed materials.[213] The 13 cartwrights residing in Newtown patterned their land schooners after the Conestoga wagon, made in its namesake Pennsylvania town. The lighter Newtown wagon came with large diameter wheels designed for travel over rough, steep and often muddy roads.[214] A white hemp or linen canvas cover, waterproofed with linseed oil, protected cargo from the elements.

The region's wagon boom cooled during the Panic of 1837, when a sudden drop in wheat and flour prices hit the pocketbooks of local farmers and millers. Demand declined further in the 1840s, when railroads hauled bulk goods to and from the region.[215] In the early 1850s, the local industry briefly profited from sales to prospectors headed to the California gold rush, but the end came when mass-produced wagons in the North proved too great a competitive challenge.

Newtown Freight Wagon, 1800-1815, Stephens City
Photo of model displayed in Colonial Williamsburg
Foundation museum

Rifle Manufacturing

At a time when the new nation imported most of its rifles from France, President George Washington looked to source them domestically. He persisted in building an armory at Harpers Ferry, despite resistance from his cabinet and a military engineer's report that waterpower there was unreliable, due to periodic flooding.[216] But the site happened to be near Washington's and his family's Jefferson County land holdings. In 1794, Congress approved construction of armories in Harpers Ferry and in Springfield, Massachusetts, towns that were near iron furnaces and waterpower.[217]

In 1796 in Harpers Ferry, the federal government located the U.S. Armory and Arsenal along the Potomac River, on 118 acres purchased from John Wager Sr.'s family.[218] Next year, 310 acres were acquired beside the Shenandoah River, just upstream from the town.[219] To ensure a supply of pig iron, the United States purchased Keep Tryst Furnace on Elks Run and acquired mining rights at nearby Friend's Orebank.[220] In 1803, twenty-five workers at the U.S. Armory began manufacturing muskets and rifles.[221] With increased federal funding, 70 employees at seven workshops grew annual production in 1810 to 10,000 muskets, with most warehoused in the arsenal.[222] By then, the armory's iron came from Pennsylvania furnaces, because management claimed the local metal lacked the quality needed for its guns. Keep Tryst Furnace and the mining rights at Friend's Orebank were later sold.

U.S. Armory buildings along Potomac River in Harpers Ferry
Postcard published by W. E. Dittmeyer, Harpers Ferry, WV

In 1819, gunsmith John Harris Hall from Maine arrived in Harpers Ferry with a federal contract to produce 1,000 of his patented flintlock rifles.[223] Compared to conventional muzzle-loaders, the Hall Breech Loader took one-third the time to load, was lighter and gave greater accuracy with less recoil.[224] Manufacturing took place inside a former armory sawmill on a 15-acre island in the Shenandoah River, upstream from Harpers Ferry. When the weapons contract was successfully completed, Hall's Rifle Works received an order for another 1,800 rifles.[225]

By 1826, Hall had perfected the American System of manufacturing, whereby rifles were assembled with interchangeable parts, which also simplified their repair.[226] Production quickly increased when unskilled laborers on an assembly line fit and placed each part into Hall Breech Loaders. Using precise cutting and drilling tools, Hall had more success machining parts than Eli Whitney, who supplied rifles to the Springfield Armory.[227] Hall's Rifle Works eventually filled four buildings on the island, where upwards of 250 employees produced a total of 23,500 rifles and 13,700 carbines.[228] Three years after his passing in 1841, the federal government replaced the Hall's Island workshops with a brick factory that produced the U.S. Model rifle.[229]

Distilleries

The Revolutionary War disrupted the triangular trade that brought West Indies molasses to Boston and New York to be made into rum. After whiskey became America's favorite drink, some Northern Valley gristmill owners built commercial distilleries that turned rye and corn into alcohol. A typical farmer-distiller produced several hundred gallons of whiskey per year. In 1791, the federal government taxed alcohol to pay for its Revolutionary War debts. In response, some Scots-Irish farmers from western Pennsylvania moved south into the Allegheny Mountains to make untaxed moonshine.[230]

At the same time, the Shenandoah Valley became the largest producer of taxed liquor in Virginia. In 1810, the 177 licensed distilleries in Frederick County and the 44 in Shenandoah County, which included Page and Warren counties, produced 92,000 gallons of alcohol.[231] Besides households, whiskey was sold to liquor distributors east of the Blue Ridge, to the region's tavern owners and later to its springs resorts.

In the late 1700s, Belle Grove plantation near Middletown was home to one of the region's largest distilleries.[232] In Strasburg, the Hupp Homestead's still house was on the Town Run, but clean water for its whiskey and brandy was sourced from a nearby spring.²³³ In the Edinburg area, farmer Joshua Foltz was licensed in 1817 to "distill spirits from domestic materials during the term of two months," while Robert Bryarly in Darkesville made whiskey from rye ground at his nearby gristmill on Middle Creek, south of Martinsburg.²³⁴

Despite the Northern Valley's robust liquor industry, much of the nation's legal production shifted to Kentucky and Tennessee in the 1820s.²³⁵ Distillers in those states, including Scots-Irish migrants from the Shenandoah Valley, turned corn into bourbon and rye into whiskey. They benefited from the availability of soft water, a steady supply of grains and hot summers and cold winters that helped age their liquor.²³⁶

Woolen Mills

For several decades after the 1783 Treaty of Paris was signed, woolen mills along Northern Valley waterways either carded raw wool, fulled cloth to finish it or performed both functions. Jonah Hollingsworth operated a fulling mill at the confluence of Winchester's Town Run and Abrams Creek, then added a carding mill.²³⁷ Prior to leaving for Ohio in 1815, his son Samuel fabricated carding machines sold to area millers.²³⁸ On Tuscarora Creek near Martinsburg were James Mendenhall's fulling mill, Jonathan Cushwa's carding mill and Martinsburg Woolen Mill, whose owner Edward Gibbs advertised in 1814 that a customer could have, "Wool carded and spun while waiting." ²³⁹

After the English invented the spinning jenny in 1764 and the power loom in 1785, they were combined with carding and fulling equipment to turn raw wool into finished cloth.²⁴⁰ When that integrated milling technology came to the United States, Congress passed the Tariff of 1816 to restrict imports of British cloth and encourage its production in New England's factories and mills.²⁴¹ Three years later, integrated woolen mills appeared in the Northern Valley when Green Spring Woolen Factory produced cloth on its namesake waterway, northwest of Winchester.²⁴² By the 1820s, Friendly Grove Woolen Factory turned out flannels, worsteds and blankets on Abrams Creek, south of Winchester.²⁴³ Beginning in 1822, Christian G. Conradt made wool carpets in Martinsburg for several decades, before moving the business to Baltimore.²⁴⁴

Paper Mills

In the early days of making paper, rags from discarded linen and hemp clothes were mashed into pulp, which a multi-step process turned into writing paper and newsprint. After the Revolution, skilled craftsmen and sophisticated machinery at Philadelphia's mills made that city the center of paper production.[245] Virginia was home to seven paper mills, including two in the Northern Valley.[246] Joseph Carter operated the first one, along with two gristmills and an oil mill on Opequon Creek, near the village of Burnt Factory, northeast of Winchester. But after making printer's paper for several years in the early 1800s, son James repurposed the unprofitable Carter's Paper Mill as Millbrook Woolen Mill.[247] In 1808, Conrad Kownslar from Baltimore opened Phoenix Mill on Mill Creek, east of Bunker Hill. It annually produced 2,000 reams—each containing 500 sheets—of high-quality writing sheets and paper currency for the federal government, but the Phoenix Mill closed after a fire in 1852.[248]

Brickyards and Potters

In colonial times, builders made bricks from clay dug at construction sites. They molded it into oblong shapes, which portable kilns melted into bricks. As the Northern Valley's population grew, builders and masons sourced larger quantities from local brickyards.[249] Each produced a brick with a distinctive appearance that depended on the owner's preferred style and the local clay's characteristics.

Agrarian societies needed containers to hold, store and cook foods and beverages. Potters provided them with milk crocks, jars, pitchers, vases and baking pans. Although they focused on utilitarian items for the household, potters also created decorative figures for display purposes. Because shipping heavy jars and crocks was expensive and susceptible to breakage, the local industry enjoyed a cost advantage over competitors from Philadelphia, Alexandria and Baltimore.

Before the American Revolution, Hagerstown was the ceramic center of the Cumberland and Shenandoah valleys. As competition increased in the Western Maryland town, some potters migrated to Shepherdstown and Winchester, while others settled farther south in Strasburg. First- and second-generation German tradesmen influenced the Northern Valley's style of pottery.[250] Among them was John George Weis, who arrived in Hagerstown in the 1750s, then moved to Shepherdstown four decades later. Due to his influence on the local trade, other potters called him the father of Shenandoah Valley pottery.[251]

In 1805, Adam Keister Sr., who learned the craft in Germany's Palatinate region, was the first potter to locate in Strasburg, situated near an abundance of high-quality clay found near the North Fork of the Shenandoah River.[252] After producing pottery in Hagerstown for almost two decades, Peter Bell Jr. moved to Winchester in 1824 and went into business with John Miller.[253] Both men relocated to Strasburg in the 1830s.[254] In the next decade, Bell's two sons joined him in the town that became home to six potters, known for the quality of their products.[255]

Cabinetmakers

Northern Valley cabinetmakers turned locally sourced chestnut, walnut and cherry lumber into hand-crafted furniture sold to the region's middle and upper classes. By 1800, their patterns had been influenced by high-style designs from Philadelphia and Baltimore, cities with whom they maintained mercantile and family connections. The cabinetmakers also trained numerous apprentices and journeymen, some of whom carried their furniture designs throughout the Shenandoah Valley and into the trans-Appalachian frontier.

The Frederick County area, which included Clarke County at the time, had 165 cabinetmakers, many of them Quakers with distinctive forms and styles.[256] Most prominent were the Frye-Martin shops, with Christopher Frye making furniture in Winchester, while partner James Lee Martin held forth in Berryville.[257] One of the region's best-known Quaker craftsman was Goldsmith Chandlee, who made tall case clocks in Winchester.[258] Working in Woodstock, clockmaker Jacob Fry and cabinetmaker Christian Baer co-mingled elements of German and Anglo traditions in their work.[259]

Scotsman native John Shearer led Martinsburg's cabinetmakers. From 1798 to 1818, he blended popular classic styles—baroque, rococo and neoclassical— with his own quirky ideas.[260] The "God Save the King" phrase appeared on many of the avowed loyalist's works.[261] In 1799, Shepherdstown cabinetmaker William Eaty advertised in the Berkeley Intelligencer that, "His work shall be inferior to none, at a much more reduced price than those found at seaports." [262]

Banking: Financial Institutions Open

Because the Constitution denied individual states the right to coin money, foreign currencies were widely used after the Revolution. To complete its financial independence, the new nation replaced the English pound with the American dollar in 1785. Six years later, it established the First Bank of the

United States in Philadelphia to circulate cash, regulate credit markets and develop a network of banks to expedite commercial transactions.[263] The nation's leaders hoped that private banks lending to new and expanding businesses would unleash America's entrepreneurial spirits.

Banks that opened in Philadelphia, Baltimore and Alexandria helped their businesses solidify relationships with the Northern Valley's agricultural and mercantile sectors. Farmers required working capital to plant crops, millers needed cash to purchase wheat, and merchants had to either prepay Eastern Seaboard wholesalers for goods or buy them on credit. With larger incomes and the ability to use their land holdings and slaves as collateral, plantation owners had an easier time obtaining credit.[264]

Northern Valley farmers, millers and merchants preferred to borrow from banks with a local presence, whose officers knew them and their businesses. That issue was resolved when two commercial banks in Richmond established branches in Winchester. In 1804, Bank of Virginia, chartered with capital stock not to exceed $1.5 million, was authorized to open branches in several urban areas.[265] Citizens in each locality first had to subscribe to a minimum number of shares, based on population. When Winchester's residents purchased $52,500 worth of stock, a Bank of Virginia branch opened in the town.[266] In 1812, Farmers Bank of Virginia was incorporated with $2 million of capital, to be spread among six branches in the commonwealth. After residents subscribed to $166,600 worth of stock, Farmers Bank of Winchester took deposits and made loans.[267]

In 1817, Valley Bank became the first commercial bank based in Winchester. Using the trade name Bank of the Valley of Virginia, its charter provided that branches could be added in nearby towns if citizens in each one subscribed to $100,000 worth of stock.[268] After that requirement was met, branches opened in Charles Town, Leesburg, Romney and Moorefield. The bank's directors visited them semi-annually to review operations.[269]

Unchartered banks, also known as voluntary associations, appeared in the region to make loans, receive deposits and issue paper money without interference from the commonwealth. They included Bank of Winchester; Bank of Martinsburg; Farmers, Mechanics and Merchants Bank of Jefferson County; and Farmers and Mechanics Bank of Harpers Ferry.[270] In 1816, however, Virginia passed legislation that forced unchartered banks to stop circulating notes and cease doing business.[271]

Newspapers:
Owners Advocate Their Political Agendas

After the U.S. Post Office Department reduced mailing rates for newspapers in 1792, their numbers increased to more than 150 in 1800.[272] Most Northern Valley papers were family-run weeklies with circulations in the hundreds, not thousands. Because newspapers carried no local news, advertisements announced the formation of new businesses and upcoming community events.[273] With papers selling for just pennies apiece, those ads paid the bills. Less concerned with profits, publishers and their wealthy backers courted readers who agreed with their policies for advancing the nation's interests. Fierce competition in the same town led to mergers.

Winchester's first post-Revolution newspaper was the Virginia Gazette and Winchester Advertiser, which rolled off the press in 1787. Henry Wilcox, owner of weeklies in Pennsylvania and Maryland, was the publisher.[274] One year later, Richard Bowen launched the Virginia Centinel as a competitor, but the two papers soon combined as the Winchester Gazette.[275] In New Market, brothers Ambrose and Solomon Henkel started the Henkel Press in 1806 as one of the South's first German language publishing companies.[276] Their Virginia and New Market Popular Instructor and Weekly News also became an important source for devotional material, song books and children's books.[277] The business began in the home of their father, a prominent Lutheran minister.

In 1790, Boston newspaperman Nathaniel Willis moved to Shepherdstown and founded the Potowmac Guardian.[278] After relocating the paper to Martinsburg, it became the Potowmac Guardian and Berkeley Advertiser, but its banner was changed to Potomak Guardian in 1798. Next year, Willis's apprentice, John Alburtis, started the Berkeley Intelligencer in Martinsburg as a Federalist rival to his former boss's Jeffersonian leaning newspaper.[279] Costing subscribers $2 a year, it merged several times with other papers, before becoming the Martinsburg Gazette.[280] In 1808, the Charles Town Farmers' Repository became the first agricultural journal to circulate west of the Blue Ridge.[281]

Tourism:
Springs Resorts Promote Healing

Native Americans were the first group to visit the Northern Valley's mineral springs. In the 1600s, Shawnees used water from Warm Springs Run in rituals

Winchester Gazette issue of May 9, 1822
Photo in Library of Congress collection, Washington, DC

and ceremonies held in what became the village of Bath, 20 miles northwest of Martinsburg.[282] While surveying for Lord Fairfax, George Washington first visited the so-called medicinal springs in 1748; on later visits, he wrote, "We found of both sexes about 250 people at this place, full of all manner of diseases and complaints." [283] With Virginia planters and merchants taking in the waters, Bath became the Northern Valley's first tourist attraction. In 1784, the village contracted with resident James Rumsey to replace its stone pools with five formal bathhouses—separate ones for ladies and gentlemen—managed by a bathkeeper.[284] Ten years later, the Fairfax Inn was built on its namesake street, facing the public bathing area. To avoid confusion with another Virginia springs to the south, the village was renamed Berkeley Springs in 1802.[285]

Post-Revolution, people seeking a cure frequented Orkney Springs at the foot of Great North Mountain, 13 miles west of Mount Jackson. They stayed in tents and log huts owned by local residents.[286] Six miles north of Winchester, the Catawba tribe frequented a spring at the foot of Devil's Backbone Ridge.[287] In the early 1800s, Rezin Duvall built several cabins on the property and marketed the medicinal qualities of his White Sulphur Springs water to invalids.[288]

In 1820, two Jefferson County businessmen purchased 60 acres on the east side of the Shenandoah River's Horseshoe Bend, seven miles east of Charles Town.[289] At Shannondale Springs, they erected a two-story, 25-room hotel and bathhouse and 12 cottages.[290] Iron in water that came from three nearby springs was thought to be a cure for cholera, dyspepsia and all afflictions of the stomach, liver and kidneys.[291] Several decades later, Shannondale and the region's other resorts would benefit when passenger trains brought patrons to depots located near their hotels.

CHAPTER 3

1830 TO CIVIL WAR

National Economy: Industrial and Transportation Revolutions Arrive

The United States census soared from 12.9 million in 1830 to 31.5 million in 1860, due to immigration, a population shift westward and larger family sizes.[1] During those three decades, 5 million immigrants—mostly from northern Europe—came to America seeking economic opportunities and relief from famines and political revolutions.[2] Opting not to compete for work with slave labor, most moved into large cities in the North and Midwest and took jobs in mills and factories.

Prior to the 1830s, high shipping costs had kept American commerce local and regional, but private capital and state government investments in turnpikes, canals and railroads made for a more mobile populace and increased the geographical reach of many businesses. The nation's 4,000 miles of turnpikes in 1820 had nearly quadrupled to 15,000 miles in 1845, while its world-leading 8,571 miles of railroad tracks in 1850 more than tripled to 28,920 miles in 1860.[3]

After the Industrial Revolution reached American shores in the first half of the nineteenth century, steam engine technology, assembly line production and numerous inventions powered the manufacturing sector. The workload of the U.S. Patent Office reflected that creativity; its 173 utility patents issued in 1815 increased to 544 in 1845 and soared to 4,363 in 1860.[4] That same year, the United States counted 140,000 large and small factories and mills, mostly based north of the Mason-Dixon line.[5] Within them, skilled managers organized and supervised workers who used machines to produce standardized products that replaced those previously made by hand in the home or in small shops.[6] Increased productivity on the factory floor raised the standard of living for millions of Americans; despite two economic downturns, per capita income grew by 50 percent in the 1830 to 1860 period.[7]

The agriculture sector also participated in the prosperity.[8] During the 1850s, America's farmers increased their land under cultivation by more than one-third to 100 million acres, with almost half cleared in seven midwestern and north-central states.[9] The nation's wheat production doubled, from 85 million bushels in 1840 to 170 million in 1860, while the number of bushels of corn harvested went from 378 million to 839 million.[10]

Two depressions interrupted the good times. Bank failures in New York City triggered the Panic of 1837, the worst economic crisis since the nation's founding.[11] The Mexican War helped bring the nation out of its economic malaise.[12] The boom times that followed ended with the Panic of 1857, triggered by the failure of the New York City branch of the Ohio Life Insurance and Trust Company.[13] The two-year downturn ended when real estate speculation and railroad over-building worked their way through the economy.[14]

Internal Improvements: Railroads and Canal Boost Trade with East Coast

As the nation's economy expanded in the antebellum years, internal improvements helped the Northern Valley participate in that growth. The Valley and Northwestern turnpikes were completed in the late 1830s, while the Chesapeake and Ohio Canal reached Cumberland in 1850. Most impactful, however, was the 1836 arrival of the Baltimore and Ohio Railroad's main line in Harpers Ferry, where it connected with the Winchester and Potomac Railroad. And in the late 1850s, the Manassas Gap Railroad gave several other towns rail access to Alexandria. Farmers, planters and millers shipped wheat and flour on those three railroads, which also brought manufactured goods into the Northern Valley. While those less-expensive items forced many skilled artisans and master craftsmen to close shop, passenger rail service from Baltimore and Alexandria increased patronage at the region's mineral springs.

Turnpikes

Two roads from Winchester leading to the Shenandoah River needed upgrades to connect with turnpikes coming from Leesburg and Alexandria. But with the Winchester and Potomac Railroad providing access to rapidly growing Baltimore, that was not a high priority for Winchester's commercial interests. The Berryville Turnpike Company was incorporated in 1831 to improve the road from Winchester through Berryville to Castleman's Ferry, opposite the terminus of the Leesburg and Snicker's Gap Turnpike.[15] Finally completed to the Shenandoah River in 1851, the Berryville Turnpike later became part of Route 7.[16]

In 1839, organizers of the Winchester and Berry's Ferry Turnpike Company hoped to improve the road to the same river. There it would meet the Aldie and Ashby's Gap Turnpike, which connected to the Little River Turnpike coming out of Alexandria.[17] Unable to raise enough private funds, a second attempt succeeded in 1848.[18] Completed in four years, the Winchester and Berry's Ferry Turnpike later became part of U.S. 50.

To offset the negative impact of the Cumberland Road to the northwest and to increase trade with the Ohio River Valley, the Virginia legislature chartered the Northwestern Turnpike Company in 1827 to improve a wagon road between Winchester and Romney.[19] After failing to raise the capital needed to begin construction, it was re-incorporated in 1831 as the Northwestern Turnpike Road Company.[20] Financed entirely by the commonwealth and completed in 1838, its 273 miles—later part of U.S. 50—went from Winchester through Hampshire County to Parkersburg on the Ohio River.[21] Trade with the Potomac Highlands also increased when the Hardy and Winchester Turnpike, also known as the Winchester and Moorefield Turnpike, was completed in 1849. Later renamed Route 55, it went through Wardensville on its way to Moorefield, located on the South Branch of the Potomac River.[22]

Heavily used by long-distance stagecoaches and teamsters, the Great Wagon Road remained the main corridor through the Shenandoah Valley. The General Assembly chartered the Valley Turnpike Company in 1817, but fundraising was halted during the Panic of 1819. Re-incorporated in 1828 with a capitalization of $100,000, the Virginia Board of Public Works required the company to realign, smooth and toll the Great Wagon Road from Winchester to Edinburg.[23] Six years later, a revised charter extended the turnpike to Harrisonburg and increased its capital to $250,000.[24]

When Valley Turnpike Company shares were offered to the public, businessmen in Frederick, Shenandoah and Rockingham counties, hoping to benefit from an improved road, bought most of them.[25] Looking to gain trade from the resource-rich Shenandoah Valley, Baltimore businessmen also purchased shares in the 68-mile turnpike.[26] Bushrod Taylor, the company's first president, owned the McGuire's tavern and hotel in Winchester. Situated on the corner of Main Street—a section of the Great Wagon Road—and Taylor Lane, the terminus of the Northwestern Turnpike, the building's crossroads location served as a stop for stagecoaches and mail deliveries.[27] After it burned in 1848, Taylor built his namesake 70-room hotel on the site.[28]

In 1837, another revision to Valley Turnpike Company's charter provided for construction of a 25-mile extension from Harrisonburg to Staunton, but it also required that the entire road be macadamed with crushed stone.[29] Two years later, the turnpike with 18 tollgates was completed at a cost of $425,000.[30] To travel the 93 miles from Winchester to Staunton, a person on horseback paid $4.38, with the fee for a wagon based on its weight.[31]

Two more turnpikes improved travel from Winchester to the Potomac River. In 1838, Virginia chartered the $45,000 Martinsburg and Winchester Turnpike Company to upgrade the 26-mile section of the Great Wagon Road

Valley Turnpike at Hillman's Tollgate, one mile south of Winchester
Postcard published by Shenandoah Publishing House, Strasburg, VA

that separated the two towns.³² It was completed in 1849, the same year the Martinsburg and Potomac Turnpike Company was chartered to extend the road to the northern Berkeley County ferry crossing to Williamsport, Maryland.³³ Years later, those roads and the Valley Turnpike, became part of U.S. 11.

Improvements to another north-south road benefited commerce in the Page Valley, an area between the Blue Ridge and the Massanutten mountains that extended from Front Royal south through Page County. In the early 1780s, the East Valley Road went from Charles Town through Berryville, Front Royal and Luray on its way to Elkton.³⁴ The Berryville and Charles Town Turnpike Company and the Luray and Front Royal Turnpike Company, chartered in 1847 and 1852, respectively, improved travel on what years later became U.S. 340.³⁵

Chesapeake and Ohio Canal

Concerned over the negative impact the Erie Canal and the Pennsylvania Portage and Canal System would have on their economies, politicians representing jurisdictions near the nation's capital looked at revisiting George Washington's effort to open up the Potomac River Valley for western trade. In 1820, plans were drawn for a canal that would eventually link the Chesapeake Bay with Pittsburgh on the Ohio River. Eight years later, the defunct Patowmack Company's holdings were ceded to the newly formed Chesapeake and Ohio (C&O) Canal Company.³⁶ Its president was U.S. Congressman Charles Mercer from the Loudoun County village of Aldie, who happened to be chairman of the House Committee on Roads and Canals.³⁷ Cost estimates for a 185-mile canal from Georgetown to Cumberland were between $4.5 million and $5.4 million.³⁸

Although the C&O Canal would be located on the Maryland side of the Potomac River, leaders in Berkeley and Jefferson counties lobbied Richmond for financial support, because it would serve their business communities. However, the General Assembly turned the counties down, arguing that limited funds should only underwrite river improvements wholly within the commonwealth, namely construction of the James River and Kanawha Canal near Richmond.³⁹ Most of the C&O Canal's funds came from the federal government, Maryland and the District of Columbia, which at the time included Alexandria.⁴⁰

When work on the canal began in 1828 in Georgetown, it faced competition from a new transportation mode.⁴¹ One year earlier, Baltimore businessmen organized and financed the Baltimore and Ohio (B&O) Railroad Company, whose trains steamed into Cumberland in 1842, eight years ahead of canal traffic.[42] Because barges pulled by mules had to pass through 74 canal locks, the faster B&O trains were formidable competitors. Furthermore, cost overruns—the $5.4 million estimate became an $11 million project—left the C&O Canal Company with a burdensome debt load in 1850.[43] Management dropped plans to build the 180-mile section into the Ohio River Valley, an expensive endeavor that also meant portaging freight over the Eastern Continental Divide and the Allegheny Plateau.[44]

Although travel by barge was slow, the C&O Canal remained a viable transportation mode until the Civil War. For farmers and millers in Berkeley and Jefferson counties, shipping wheat and flour on it to Georgetown and Alexandria was less than half the cost of hauling those goods in wagons.[45] Canal cargo bound for Baltimore was transferred to B&O trains at Point of Rocks, eight miles downriver from Harpers Ferry. After the C&O built seven dams across the Potomac River to fill the canal with water, Shenandoah River gundalows headed to Georgetown and Alexandria entered it at Lock Number 32, east of Sandy Hook.[46] Cargo bound for Baltimore was transferred to B&O trains in Harpers Ferry.[47]

C&O Canal boat at Lock No. 33 at Sandy Hook, MD
Photo from National Park Service, Washington, DC

The C&O Canal made Shepherdstown a thriving port. Flatboats laden with wheat and flour accessed it at Lock Number 38.[48] By 1850, the 60-year old Mecklenburg Tobacco Warehouse had been repurposed to store wheat, flour and other goods, prior to shipment on the canal. The building also received imported salt, sugar and coffee, along with other dry goods and manufactured products suitable for Northern Valley consumers.[49]

River Improvements

By 1825, gundalow boatmen were paying tolls for passage through sluices the New Shenandoah Company had constructed on the river's north and south forks.⁵⁰ However, low water levels in summer and fall made much of the river south of Luray unnavigable when farmers and millers shipped wheat and flour.⁵¹ Not satisfied with New Shenandoah Company's work, Northern Valley farmers, planters, millers and merchants kept searching for better access to Eastern Seaboard markets. In 1831, the General Assembly directed the Virginia Board of Public Works to conduct a survey to determine the best way to open the Shenandoah River area to more commerce.⁵² Planters living close to it supported a canal that would join with the C&O Canal at Harpers Ferry.⁵³ The board looked at the possibility of building locks and dams on the river, digging a canal beside it or bringing a railroad into the Shenandoah Valley, but no plan was forthcoming.⁵⁴

Railroads

In the 1750s, the English discovered that horse-drawn wagons riding on iron rails, rather than over roads, could move much larger loads of coal.⁵⁵ When Middleton Wagonway in Leeds replaced those horses with steam locomotion in 1812, the renamed Middleton Railway attracted curious visitors and transportation engineers from near and far, including the United States.⁵⁶ While canals might freeze in winter, railroads operated year-round and their tracks could be laid into areas not reached by river or canal. With speeds of up to 30 miles per hour, trains were much faster than mules pulling canal boats or men poling gundalows. Although shipping cargo by rail was up to three times more expensive than moving it slowly on a canal, it was one-fifth the per-ton-mile cost of a freight wagon.⁵⁷

Leaders of rapidly growing Baltimore realized their city faced economic stagnation from the Erie and C&O canals, because they would divert its midwestern trade to New York City and Alexandria.⁵⁸ In 1822, surveys were taken of connecting Baltimore with either the Susquehanna River to the north or the Potomac River to the south.⁵⁹ A better alternative was a 275-mile rail line from the city, through Cumberland to Wheeling, where travelers and cargo could be transferred to and from Ohio River steamboats.⁶⁰ In 1827, Maryland chartered the Baltimore and Ohio Rail Road Company, an action the Virginia General Assembly confirmed, because the main line would go through the commonwealth. B&O officials originally wanted the tracks to follow the C&O Canal on the Maryland side of the Potomac River, but the canal company held the legal right-of-passage on that land.⁶¹ After considering a northern route to

Hagerstown, the B&O decided to lay tracks to Harpers Ferry for a possible connection with another railroad that would bring Shenandoah Valley produce, natural resources and semi-fabricated goods to Baltimore.

Winchester leaders argued for a southerly B&O route, one that brought its tracks through their town, before heading west to a point south of Parkersburg on the Ohio River.[62] Because rail engineering was just developing in the 1830s, laying track through a Blue Ridge wind gap to Winchester and across Great North Mountain to the west would have been a challenge.[63] Instead, the B&O line went on more level land through Harpers Ferry to Martinsburg and Hedgesville, then followed the Virginia side of the Potomac River to Paw Paw—named for a local fruit-bearing tree—and on to Cumberland. Raising $3 million from Maryland, the City of Baltimore and private investors, in 1830 the B&O laid down tracks that seven years later reached the Harpers Ferry area.[64] Baltimore and Maryland pledged another $3 million to extend the line to Cumberland and Wheeling.[65]

Well aware that the B&O Railroad would pass north of Winchester, its politicians and businessmen, along with planters to the east, lobbied for ways to link up with it. The Winchester group argued for a railroad that would join the B&O in Harpers Ferry, while planters continued their support for a canal along the Shenandoah River.[66] In 1831, the Virginia General Assembly received applications to charter two railroads: the Staunton and Potomac Railroad Company's proposed $1.5 million line from Staunton to Martinsburg and the Winchester and Potomac Railroad Company's much shorter $300,000 line from Winchester to Harpers Ferry.[67] After proponents of the less-expensive railroad prevailed in Richmond, farmers, millers and merchants in the Northern Valley subscribed to three-fifths of its shares, while the Virginia Board of Public Works took the balance.[68]

When the Winchester and Potomac Railroad's 32-mile line reached Harpers Ferry in 1836, its $575,000 cost was way over budget.[69] While Virginia agreed to lend the railroad $150,000, B&O officials declined to subscribe to a stock offering, but helped it secure several loans. The B&O's 1837 completion of a Potomac River bridge enabled it to connect to the Winchester and Potomac's tracks.[70] Both railroads quickly gave an economic boost to the town best known for the U.S. Armory and Arsenal. In 1825, Harpers Ferry counted one hotel and seven stores; one year after the B&O arrived, those numbers had increased to four hotels and 18 stores carrying a wide variety of goods received by rail.[71] In contrast, the B&O caused Shepherdstown's economy to decline, because its business and industry depended on the less-competitive C&O Canal for their shipping needs.

After the railroad lines interconnected in Harpers Ferry, most Northern Valley commerce was routed towards Baltimore, rather than Alexandria. Farmers and millers who once shipped wheat and flour in wagons through wind gaps in the Blue Ridge, sent them instead to the freight depot on Winchester's Market (Cameron) Street. And wagons filled with goods from Virginia's most western counties came on the Northwestern and the Hardy and Winchester turnpikes to the same depot, which was soon surrounded with warehouses.

With its merchants reselling goods that arrived by rail from Baltimore, Winchester kept its status as a regional market center.[72] In 1814, Jacob and George Baker, sons of German immigrants, established a retail and wholesale grocery business on Main (Loudoun) Street. In 1837, they moved it closer to the rail depot to receive larger quantities of merchandise directly from Baltimore.[73] Jacob, who started the Jacob Baker & Sons mercantile business, served as president of the Winchester and Potomac.[74] After working in the store, son William became a partner in 1841 in W. B. Baker & Sons, then opened a branch in Martinsburg in 1856, followed by one in Staunton.[75]

While two-thirds of the Winchester and Potomac's revenue originated from freight cargo, its trains hauled more outbound than inbound traffic. That imbalance, combined with the depression that followed the Panic of 1837, caused the railroad's finances to weaken. After a proposed sale to the B&O fell through in 1846, the Virginia General Assembly gave up its $120,000 equity interest in the Winchester and Potomac and forgave its $150,000 loan.[76] In return, the railroad issued $270,000 of debt with a 20-year maturity to the Virginia Board of Public Works.[77]

Winchester's days as the Northern Valley's economic leader lasted until 1842, when the B&O's main line reached Martinsburg. Seven years later, the railroad moved maintenance work from Sandy Hook to the town and the B&O soon became the largest employer in Martinsburg.[78] It built a roundhouse on Tuscarora Creek, along with machine shops, an engine house, iron foundry, warehouses and the Depot House Hotel.[79] The Winchester and Martinsburg Turnpike's arrival at same time further increased the town's status as a regional transportation hub.[80]

While Baltimore merchants had access to railroads that reached into the Northern Valley market, Alexandria businessmen did not. In 1847, several of them received a charter for the Alexandria and Harpers Ferry Railroad

B&O Roundhouse in Martinsburg, 1850s
Photo from Berkeley County Historical Society, Martinsburg, WV

Company, which would lay tracks from Alexandria to Leesburg, then through Snicker's Gap and on to Harpers Ferry for a connection with the B&O's main line.[81] Hoping for direct rail access to Alexandria, Clarke County residents voted to purchase $100,000 worth of stock in the new company and Winchester businessmen promised to invest after the line crossed the Blue Ridge.[82] Renamed the Alexandria, Loudoun and Hampshire Railroad in 1855, its 37 miles of track between Alexandria and Leesburg were damaged during the Civil War.

Also determined to win back Shenandoah Valley trade lost to Baltimore, Fauquier County resident Edward Marshall, son of former Chief Justice John Marshall, led a group of Northern Virginia farmers and merchants who organized the Manassas Gap Railroad Company in 1850.[83] The plan was to lease the Orange and Alexandria Railroad's tracks from Alexandria to Manassas Station, and from there build a new line to several Northern Valley towns. After the Virginia Board of Public Works subscribed to two-fifths of the company's $800,000 stock offering, track construction started westward, through low-elevation Manassas Gap to Front Royal.

To eliminate the $30,000 annual lease payment to the Orange and Alexandria Railroad for use of its track, Manassas Gap Railroad officials sought to build a line from Alexandria to Manassas Station. In 1853, the company received a charter for the 35-mile Independent Line to parallel the other railroad's tracks.[84] But after four years of grading a gravel bed, the debt-ridden parent company halted work during the Panic of 1857.[85]

Notwithstanding, the Manassas Gap Railroad's 87 miles of track originating in Manassas Station did reach Front Royal and Strasburg in 1854, Woodstock in 1857 and Mount Jackson in 1859.[86] The Alexandria Gazette declared, "This road is destined to be of immense advantage to Alexandria, pouring into her lap the products of the richest and most productive sections of this country."[87] Cargo that previously traveled by gundalow down the Shenandoah River to Harpers Ferry was diverted to the new rail line. And some shipments originating in Shenandoah County went to Alexandria rather than to Winchester and Baltimore. To offset the decline in traffic, Winchester's leaders hoped to extend the Winchester and Potomac Railroad's tracks southward to join the Manassas Gap Railroad in Strasburg. The General Assembly authorized the extension in 1861, but the start of the Civil War meant that scarce Confederate iron would be used for munitions, not rails.[88]

Northern Valley Economy: Grows at Slower Pace Than the Nation's

Despite the Northern Valley's expanding iron smelting, tanning and woolen industries, its population increased by 15 percent from 1830 to 1860, a much slower pace than the nation's 80 percent.[89] Several trends caused the disparity. Most significantly, the Industrial Revolution that bypassed the region brought commercial activity and jobs to cities in the North and Midwest. Unskilled European immigrants settled in those urban, industrial areas, not in places where they would have to compete with slave labor for jobs.

As demand for the Northern Valley's produce grew at home and abroad, its agriculture sector prospered, but faced several headwinds. Commodity price fluctuations, especially during the recessionary times following the panics of 1837 and 1857, were a continual problem for farmers. A greater challenge was the emergence of large wheat farms in the Midwest and livestock ranches in the Great Plains. Railroads and canals lowered the cost to deliver their foodstuffs to the same Eastern Seaboard markets the region's farmers served.

Northern Valley millers faced competition from large midwestern flour producers with rail access to eastern markets. But with the railroad industry's rapid expansion, furnace owners thrived on supplying pig iron to manufacturers of wheels for its rolling stock. The region's tanners discovered Baltimore as a wholesale market for their leather, and new woolen factories produced finished cloth for both the local and East Coast markets.

Slave Economy in the Region

The 1860 census revealed the Northern Valley was home to 14,475 slaves, who represented 18.3 percent of its population.[90] Not surprisingly, the counties with plantations had the highest percentages of slaves: Clarke 47.2, Jefferson 39.6 and Warren, 24.4.[91] Counties where small farms prevailed had lower percentages: Frederick 13.7, Berkeley 13.2, Page 10.5, Shenandoah 5.4 and Morgan with 2.5 percent slaves.[92] Beginning in the 1820s, the slave trade became a big business in the region, because plantation owners in Mississippi and Louisiana needed them to pick cotton. Itinerant agents of Baltimore and Alexandria firms advertised in Winchester for slaves that could be sold for much higher prices in New Orleans.[93] With the words "Cash for Negroes" printed on their hats, the agents met prospective sellers in downtown Winchester at Bryarly's Tavern and McGuire's, later the Taylor Hotel.[94] Many of the purchased slaves ended up in a Franklin & Armfield holding pen in Alexandria. Some went by ship to New Orleans, while others were chained together in coffles of 300 and marched to Winchester.[95] From there, they turned south onto the Valley Turnpike for a 1,000-mile, three-month journey to auctions in New Orleans and Natchez.[96]

While most slaves in the Northern Valley resided on plantations, others worked at various businesses. The iron industry used them to mine ore and limestone and to cut and haul timber burned for charcoal. Slaves also labored at gristmills, in the tanning and distilling businesses, at carding and fulling mills and later in woolen cloth factories.[97] The owners used positive incentives to motivate them, not the physical coercion found on plantations.[98] An overwork system avoided the possibility of a slave sabotaging equipment or disrupting the operation through carelessness. Those who exceeded quotas were rewarded with sundries.[99] In the long run, slave labor proved harmful to the region's economy. It reduced the need for planters and owners of semi-fabricating industries to invest in productivity-enhancing equipment, which became a problem when competitors in the North and Midwest modernized their farms and industries.

Towns and Markets

The Baltimore & Ohio, Winchester and Potomac and the Manassas Gap railroads stimulated commercial activity in the Northern Valley towns they served. Merchants, wholesalers, farmers and manufacturers stored goods in warehouses that sprung up near freight depots. Wagons from southwest Virginia and eastern Tennessee brought goods on the Valley Turnpike to Winchester for rail shipment to the Baltimore market. When the Manassas Gap Railroad reached Front Royal, Strasburg and Mount Jackson in the 1850s, increased trade with Alexandria boosted commercial development in those towns.

In 1860, almost 10 percent of the Northern Valley's citizens lived either in Winchester, whose population stood at 4,392, or in Martinsburg, which counted 3,364 residents.[100] Their public markets were expanded to meet the increase in commerce. In 1847, Martinsburg replaced the open-air City Market on its town square with a brick building called the Market House.[101] In 1840 and 1848, annexes were built at each end of Winchester's Market House, with nearby fenced-in space used for livestock sales.[102] The town's 50 stores included one owned by Charles Baltzell Rouss, whose German parents settled in Martinsburg, before moving to Winchester in 1846. After attending a private academy, the 15-year-old clerked in a local store before opening his own soft goods establishment three years later. Rouss advertised that its merchandise would, "Keep everything calculated to make a man fashionable, a lady irresistible and a family comfortable." [103] By the late 1850s, he had become one of town's wealthiest merchants.[104]

After losing everything in the Civil War, Rouss borrowed heavily and entered New York City's competitive retail market with a discount store on Broadway. Taking bankruptcy in the Panic of 1873, his Charles Broadway Rouss Wholesale Auction Dry Goods emporium recovered by offering distressed merchandise for "quick sales and small profits." [105] With his wealth restored, Rouss gave $200,000 to Winchester for a city hall and fire station and gifted funds to Mount Hebron Cemetery and Winchester Memorial Hospital.[106] He also donated $30,000 to Winchester for a system to supply the city with water.[107] In 1896, he gave $1,500 to Charles Town for the Independent Fire Hall, built close to his parents' home.[108] After a New Market retailer asked him to support a cultural venue, the town received $2,500 for what became the Rouss Center, a fire station with an opera house on the second floor.[109]

Agriculture:
Farmers Face Competition from the Midwest

While the Northern Valley's agriculture sector dealt with fluctuating commodity prices, it also met competitive threats from midwestern farmers. Before the arrival of canals and railroads, steamboats hauled their bushel sacks of grain down the Ohio and Mississippi rivers to New Orleans for export to Europe, the West Indies, South America and to cities on the Atlantic Coast.[110] After the Erie Canal opened in 1825, greater quantities of midwestern foodstuffs went directly to the Eastern Seaboard. More significant competition for Northern Valley farmers came in the 1850s, when railroads lowered the cost and time needed to ship midwestern wheat and livestock eastward. The Baltimore and Ohio Railroad reached the Ohio River in 1852, and six years later the Pennsylvania Railroad established connections with trains that went through Pittsburgh and Fort Wayne, on their way to Chicago.[111] With numerous grain elevators, the Windy City was a hub for 10 railroads, whose combined schedules listed 100 trains arriving and departing every day.[112]

Wheat Farming

During the 1830 to 1860 period, wheat prices in the United States fluctuated widely, making it difficult for Northern Valley farmers to manage annual plantings. Due to a poor grain harvest in the Midwest, the price rose to $2.15 a bushel in 1836, from a low of $1.36 in 1823.[113] During the Panic of 1837, it dropped rapidly to $1.00 a bushel for several months, causing steamboat pilots on the Mississippi and Missouri rivers to burn wheat for fuel.[114] After a failed harvest in 1845, Britain repealed its Corn Laws.[115] Having protected the landed gentry from foreign competition since 1815, the laws also produced high prices that the British working class bitterly resented.[116] Removing restrictions on imported grain caused sales of American wheat to increase dramatically in England and on the European continent.[117] Bringing $1.08 per bushel in 1845, the price soared to $2.46 in the mid-1850s, a time when Russian wheat was cut off from world markets during the Crimean War.[118]

As wheat prices rose, 96 percent of Northern Valley farmers grew it on the limestone-rich soil, which they improved with fertilizer and better farming practices.[119] Many saw the cash value of their properties increase by 35 percent.[120] Rising prices also motivated farmers in the Midwest and northern Great Plains—some of whom had migrated from the Shenandoah Valley—to plant more wheat. While only 80 bushels left Chicago in 1839, the number soared to 2 million in 1850, and 50 million in 1860.[121] Likewise, wheat shipments from Milwaukee rose from just 317 bushels in 1851 to 13 million in 1860.[122] Cyrus McCormick's mechanical reaper made those increased outputs possible, because the cost to harvest wheat had long been the limiting factor in its cultivation.[123] Invented while he farmed 20 miles south of Staunton, the reaper harvested more grain in the same time that five men could with hand scythes.[124] After moving to Chicago in 1847, his McCormick Harvesting Machine Company's annual sales quadrupled in the 1850s.[125]

McCormick Reaper and Twine Binder
Photo of ad in Abilene Reflector, Kansas,
in Library of Congress collection

In 1848, grain merchants organized the Chicago Board of Trade that set standards to measure the quality of midwestern wheat sold in the marketplace.[126] Prior to its placement in storage, an inspector graded the wheat, which gave East Coast wholesalers and millers the confidence to purchase it.[127] The board also provided a platform for trading grain futures. A farmer sold them to guarantee the price he received when he delivered the wheat on a certain date.[128] Given fluctuating commodity prices, owners of large midwestern farms sold the contracts to hedge against lower prices. However, Northern Valley farmers were 650 miles from Chicago and lacked the financial resources to benefit from wheat futures.

While the nation's farmers received robust wheat prices in the early 1850s, the good times lasted only several years. The end of the Crimean War brought more European wheat on world markets, just as the Panic of 1857 reduced consumption in America. The supply-demand imbalance caused the per bushel price to fall from $2.46 in 1855 to $1.54 in 1860.[129] That decline also occurred when disease and insects plagued the crops of Northern Valley farmers. Those losses were minor, however, compared to the devastation that war soon brought to their livelihoods.

Raising Livestock

Meat was a discretionary item on the menus of many American households. Consumption rose when prices were low and fell when they were high, because families substituted less-expensive foods to satisfy their protein needs. The price of beef also depended on the speed with which grazing lands for cattle opened in the Midwest and West, relative to the nation's population growth. For most of the antebellum period, a balance between supply and demand kept meat prices level, except during the depressions that followed the 1837 and 1857 panics. Per hundred weight cattle prices rose from $65 in 1830 to $102 in 1836, then dropped in the Panic of 1837 to $68, when consumption declined.[130] It peaked at $150 in 1855, then fell to between $70 and $90 per hundred weight in the Panic of 1857.[131] The nation's rapid economic recovery two years later took the price back to $150.[132] Those price swings made it difficult for farmers who had to decide on herd sizes.

Until the 1850s, the region's beef cattle and swine went on foot to markets in Philadelphia, Baltimore and Alexandria. With rail access, some animals were sent in ventilated stock cars to those cities. Others went to local butchers, who cured and salted the meat, then packed it in barrels for rail shipment to eastern markets. But the region's livestock farmers faced competitive threats from the Midwest. Chicago's large slaughter houses processed 21,806 cattle in 1851, a number that grew to 34,623 in 1860.[133] Their salt-packed beef was placed in airtight containers, which a network of 15 railroads shipped to eastern markets.[134] Cincinnati's meatpacking houses developed assembly line methods for butchering and processing pork products. In 1833, they handled 85,000 hogs, a number that grew to 500,000 in 1850.[135] As with cattle, their prices fluctuated with the nation's economic cycles.

Manufacturing:
Pig Iron Rides the Nation's Rails

By the early 1840s, owners of the region's leading semi-fabricating industries—gristmills and iron furnaces—profited from their ability to ship products by less-costly rail to eastern markets. While tanneries and woolen mills also used railroads to send leather and cloth eastward, cooperages, cabinetmakers, distillers, sawyers, brewers and potters continued to serve local markets. Industrial centers developed in the Harpers Ferry area, which benefited from access to shipping goods on canal boats and two railroads. Using assembly line manufacturing, the United States Armory underwent several expansions and renovations.[136] With 250 workers producing 10,000 muskets annually in 1855, it was the largest industry in the region.[137]

Upstream from Harpers Ferry, the 15-acre Virginius Island became a diversified manufacturing center, with the Shenandoah River supplying water power to various mills and shops. In 1836, the Winchester and Potomac Railroad laid tracks across the island and built a freight depot on it. By 1860, Virginius Island's industry included a large gristmill, machine shop, iron foundry, sawmill, blacksmith shop and a chopping mill that coarsely ground grain.[138]

Virginius Island in Shenandoah River, 1857
Lithograph print produced by Edward Sachse, Baltimore, MD

While Harpers Ferry and Virginius Island prospered in the antebellum period, the rest of the Northern Valley failed to participate in the nation's Industrial Revolution. Instead of assembly lines producing finished goods quickly and inexpensively, skilled craftsmen that remained in business competed with each other, making one item at a time.[139] The region remained an importer, not exporter of value-added goods for several reasons: its manufacturers had limited access to capital; the owners relied on slave labor, rather than investing in productive equipment; the facilities were located on creeks and streams, not concentrated in urban areas; and coal to power steam engines was not readily available.

Gristmills

As breadstuff became an important part of everyone's diet, the worldwide demand for flour soared during the first half of the nineteenth century. Mirroring the growth in wheat cultivation, the nation's flour production increased ten-fold between 1810 and 1860, from 4 million barrels to 39.8 million.[140] As the region's wheat harvest increased and railroads reduced shipping costs, several larger mills came on the scene. On Virginius Island, the Island Mills shipped thousands of barrels of flour to Baltimore each fall.[141] Destroyed by fire in 1839, owner Abraham Herr and his brother replaced it with a much larger gristmill. In 1860, the Herr's Mill processed 145,000 bushels of wheat into 32,000 barrels of flour, 13 times the average annual production of a typical Jefferson County mill.[142] In 1832, George Grandstaff inherited a gristmill on Stony Creek, then built the larger Edinburg Mill on the site in 1849.[143] When the Manassas Gap Railroad arrived several years later, he shipped flour to Alexandria. In 1851, Samuel Fitz, a Pennsylvania foundry owner, purchased an iron works business in Martinsburg. On Tuscarora Creek, he built the large Equality Mill and used it to test his all-metal water wheel made from locally sourced bar iron.[144] Soon Northern Valley millers switched from wooden wheels to his smoother running metal ones, because they lasted longer and kept turning during harsh winters.

By the 1850s, the future of the Northern Valley's flour industry was uncertain. As with wheat growers, millers had to deal with fluctuating flour prices in the United States and on world markets. In the 1825 to 1860 period, they ranged from $4.50 a barrel to $20.[145] And along with those in Baltimore, the millers felt competitive winds from beyond the Ohio River. Concurrent with wheat production, the nation's center of flour milling had shifted away from the Mid-Atlantic region. In 1860, a majority of the nation's flour mills were located in the Midwest, and they ran on steam, not water power.[146]

Iron Furnaces

After the Revolution, United States pig iron exports to Britain languished. When wood needed to make charcoal for the island's furnaces became scarce, bituminous coal was mined and converted to coke. Using that fuel, it cost the British $11.75 to smelt one ton of iron, compared to $15 to $20 at America's charcoal furnaces.[147] To protect the domestic iron industry from cheaper British imports, Congress enacted tariffs in 1816, 1824 and 1828.[148] And the Black Tariff of 1842 raised duties even higher on imported manufactured goods, especially those made of iron.[149]

The 1825 to 1855 period was the most profitable time for the Northern Valley's pig iron industry. During those 30 years, 11 furnaces were in blast, with seven situated in Shenandoah County and the rest spread among Frederick, Page and Jefferson counties. Much of the region's pig iron not used locally went to manufacturers of wheels for railroad cars located in Wilmington, Philadelphia and several Pennsylvania counties. Smelting ore that contained manganese, Northern Valley furnaces produced high-tensile iron. It withstood a car wheel's heavy use on metal rails better than pig iron made from ore found in Pennsylvania.[150]

Prior to the Panic of 1857, two furnaces in the Paddy Mountain area in western Shenandoah County smelted iron that was shipped to fabricators of railroad car wheels.[151] In 1833, a businessman from New York City fired up Paddy Furnace, located seven miles west of Strasburg, and shipped between 25 and 35 tons of pig iron per week by wagon to the Winchester rail depot.[152] To the southwest, in 1838 Lorenzo and George Sibert from Woodstock started

Fitz Steel Water Wheel on Shepherd's Mill, Shepherdstown, late 1800s Photo in April 30, 2018 edition of Herald Mail, Hagerstown, MD

up Van Buren Furnace, named for the sitting president.[153] Rebuilt in 1854, the brothers sold it to a local businessman, who shut it down after 500 tons of pig iron had been produced.[154]

In 1836, Daniel and Henry Forrer organized Shenandoah Iron Works in southern Page County. The sons of a Pennsylvania ironmaster partnered with Samuel Gibbons, who contributed 1,000 acres of forests and orebanks to the business. The men built Furnace No.1 on the banks of the South Fork of the Shenandoah River.[155] After the Panic of 1837, the partnership purchased Benjamin Blackford & Son's two Speedwell Forges near Luray. When Gibbons moved to Harrisonburg in 1846, the Forrers bought out his interest. On Cub Run, five miles south of Furnace No. 1, they built Catherine Furnace, named after their mother.[156] The pig iron from both furnaces not used at the forges went on gundalows to Harpers Ferry, for transfer to the B&O Railroad.

Catherine Furnace on Cub Run, southwest of Newport in Page County Photo from Cedar Creek and Belle Grove National Historic Park, Middletown, VA

The Forrers gave the Shenandoah Iron Works name to the village's post office, purchased thousands of additional acres and added a refinery forge in 1856 that annually made 300 tons of wrought iron blooms and bars.[157] The following year, the brothers built Furnace No. 2 on Naked Creek in Rockingham County, near the Page County border.[158] In 1859, they converted it from cold-blast to hot-blast; when the furnace's bellows delivered oven-made steam to the charcoal, it burned faster and hotter.[159]

In 1834, Blackford, Arthur & Co., owner of Isabella Furnace and the two Speedwell Forges near Luray since the early 1800s, expanded into Shenandoah County's Fort Valley with the construction of Caroline Furnace, named after one of Blackford daughters.[160] However, the company fell on hard times when the price of pig iron fell from $55 a ton to $22 in the Panic of 1837.[161] With debts exceeding $60,000, the business was reorganized as Benjamin Blackford & Son, with Thomas Blackford replacing John Arthur as his father's partner.[162] Keeping Caroline Furnace and Union Forge, they paid creditors with proceeds from the 1841 sale of the Speedwell forges to the Forrer brothers, and Isabella

Furnace to the company's secretary, Nicholas Yager.[163] But when molten iron inside the furnace hardened, it was never restarted.[164]

Recovering from its predecessor's financial troubles, in 1845 Benjamin Blackford & Son purchased Fort Furnace, also known as Fort Mouth's Furnace, which local businessmen had built nine years earlier.[165] Located several miles from Fort Valley's northern entrance, it was renamed Elizabeth Furnace, after Benjamin Blackford's second daughter.[166] The Caroline and Elizabeth furnaces each produced three tons of pig iron per day that went by wagon, eastward over Massanutten Mountain to Bixler's Landing on the South Fork of the Shenandoah River.[167] Gundalows carried the pig iron to B&O trains in Harpers Ferry for eventual delivery to manufacturers of rail car wheels in Wilmington and Philadelphia.[168]

Despite finding success in Fort Valley, Benjamin Blackford & Son eventually left the iron industry. They sold Elizabeth Furnace to local businessmen Hugh Galise and Cornelius Pritchard in 1849. When the new owners added an oven to provide steam for the bellows, it was renamed Fort Steam Furnace.[169] Before going out of blast in 1859, its pig iron went several miles to Harmony Forge, built in 1855 near Fort Valley's northern entrance.[170]

In 1854, the Blackfords sold Caroline Furnace and Union Forge—both purchased from Benjamin Pennybacker in 1808—to the Bush & Lobdell Company in Wilmington, the nation's largest manufacturer of cast iron wheels for railroad cars.[171] At the time, the company was buying high-tensile pig iron from Columbia and Liberty furnaces in western Shenandoah County. Not needing Union Forge, Bush & Lobdell sold it to gristmiller Samuel Lantz in nearby Lantz Mills on Stony Creek.[172]

George Hupp, owner of a 1,000-acre plantation north of Strasburg, was another iron industry participant.[173] A paymaster for the Virginia Militia during the War of 1812, he served as Strasburg's postmaster from 1829 to 1845 and operated a finance business in Winchester.[174] In the early 1840s, Hupp purchased Columbia Furnace and the Capon Iron Works, near Wardensville in Hampshire County. He also ran a mercantile business at the Columbia and Fort Steam furnaces.[175] By 1851, Walter Newman, owner of nearby Liberty Furnace for three decades, had joined Hupp as a partner in Columbia Furnace.[176]

Several years later, Hupp exited the iron business, first selling Capon Iron Works in 1856 to a Wardensville businessman. He and Newman then sold Columbia Furnace to Samuel Myers and his wife's uncle, John Wissler, both from Lancaster, Pennsylvania.[177] With 200 workers, including 20 slaves, the new owners increased its output from 800 tons of pig iron to 1,365 tons in 1860, the year Myers sold his interest to Wissler.[178] Myers had joined the industry in 1852, when he and younger brother John built Henrietta Furnace.[179] Named after Samuel's wife, it was located on Alum Run in western Shenandoah County, between the villages of Basye and Orkney Springs.

Not all the region's pig iron was smelted in Page and Shenandoah counties. In 1839, Jefferson County businessmen Thomas Perdue and William Nichols formed Perdue, Nichols and Co. and built Shannondale Furnace near the Shenandoah River, adjacent to the resort with the same name.[180] Each day, 50 men made three tons of pig iron that went by wagon through Keyes' Gap to Alexandria or were sent on gundalows to Harpers Ferry for transfer to the B&O Railroad.[181]

Despite its growth, the Northern Valley's iron industry never rivaled that of Pennsylvania, which accounted for almost 60 percent of the nation's production.[182] Several reasons accounted for the disparity; its small furnaces, scattered throughout the region, were not located near railroad tracks; the owners used slave labor, rather than invest in productive equipment; the orebanks held relatively small amounts of iron; and charcoal, not the less-costly coal, fired the furnaces. By contrast, Pittsburgh's industry benefited from access to bituminous coal found in the mid-1830s near Connellsville, 50 miles south of the city. Beehive ovens there turned it into coke, which burned at an even temperature.[183] Pittsburgh's furnaces smelted iron for $11.75 per ton, compared to the $20 cost that Northern Valley ironmasters incurred using charcoal.[184]

Tanneries

In the antebellum years, several large tanneries joined smaller ones located along Northern Valley town runs. While New England cobblers made most of the nation's shoes and boots, Baltimore developed as a wholesale market for leather, much of it shipped on steamers to northern ports. With rail access to that city, the region's tanners found a ready market for their product. In the 1830s, James Bean Wigginton operated a tannery on Cedar Creek in western Frederick County, where his tan bark came from nearby chestnut oak trees.[185] Teamsters hauled the leather from Gravel Springs, later renamed Star Tannery, to the Winchester and Potomac Railroad's depot in Winchester, for shipment to the city on the Chesapeake Bay.[186] At the same time, Townsend Beckham's tannery, which opened in 1824 on Virginius Island, turned upwards of 1,000 hides each year into leather sent to Baltimore wholesalers.[187]

When Joseph Tuley died in 1825, Joseph Jr. continued operating the tanneries his father started in the early 1800s. He produced leather in Front Royal until 1855 and in Millwood until his passing in 1860. The latter tannery was put up for sale, but there were no buyers.[188] In the late 1830s, Lewis V. Shearer started Mt. Vernon Tannery on Parish Run, several miles west of Winchester.[189] Peter Bock Borst came from New York to Luray in 1847 to practice law, then was elected Commonwealth's Attorney for Page County.[190] In the mid-1850s, he ventured into the leather business, building a three-story tannery on the town's Hawksbill Creek.[191] After the Borst Tannery was burned twice during the Civil War, another one built on its site became the nation's largest leather producer in the 1890s.

Breweries and Distilleries

Despite the many offspring of Pennsylvania Dutch and German settlers living in the Northern Valley, commercial brewing was not widespread. Beer was more complicated to make than whiskey and hops were difficult to grow in the warmer climate south of the Mason-Dixon line. Nevertheless, German native Philip Shutt opened a brewery in 1792, near the spring-fed Town Run in Shepherdstown.[192] Selling Shutt's Cream Beer to locals, the business grew in the early 1830s when Irishmen laboring on the C&O Canal crossed the Potomac River and became customers.[193] Patronage declined after Shutt's death in 1833, and when canal work near Shepherdstown ended.[194]

In the 1850s, two lager breweries opened near Tuscarora Creek in Martinsburg's Buena Vista area, home to many German and Irish employees of the B&O Railroad. In 1855, Rosana Oberdorff Lang started up Buena Vista Brewery, which changed hands several times after the Civil War, then closed in 1874.[195] In 1859, Christian Wegenast established his namesake brewery on East Burke Street, which made beer into the late 1870s.[196]

In the antebellum years, numerous licensed and unlicensed distilleries operated in the Northern Valley. German immigrant Henry L. Staub established a gristmill and distillery along Tuscarora Creek in Martinsburg. After John Quincy Adams Nadenbousch, owner of the nearby Beeson Flour Mill, purchased it in 1857, his namesake distillery became a leading producer of whiskey in the region.[197] Several years later, Union troops helped themselves to Nadenbousch

Distillery's inventory, then partially destroyed the building.[198] Postwar, the nation's largest whiskey company built a distillery complex on the site.

Woolen Factories and Cotton Mills

In the 1830s, water-powered, integrated woolen factories came on line in the Northern Valley. While some carding and fulling mills still served farm wives who made their own cloth, the newer factories turned raw wool into the finished product. Their emergence encouraged some farmers to raise sheep on rocky soil in the western part of the region.[199]

Woolen factories that produced flannels, worsteds and blankets were found along Abrams, Cedar and Opequon creeks in Frederick County. In Jefferson County, the Jenkins, Kable, Johnson Woolen Factory opened in 1841 at Kabletown, near the confluence of Bullskin Run and the Shenandoah River. To the south, Watson's Woolen Mill started up in 1850 on the same river, near Keyes' Gap.[200] In 1840, the Webb and Markell Factory carded, spun and dyed wool on Shepherdstown's Town Run. One decade later, the nearby White Henkle Cotton and Woolen Factory milled tweeds, flannel and linsey, with some of its cloth retailed at John White's store.[201]

In the 1830s, cotton replaced wool as America's favorite clothing fabric, because it was easier to care for and wash. Few cotton mills were found in the Northern Valley. It was expensive to convert woolen mills to cotton production, and unlike locally sourced wool, cotton had to be shipped into the region from the Deep South. Most importantly, New England's mills controlled the nation's market for cotton cloth. Despite those obstacles, two mills spun and wove cotton for a decade on Virginius Island near Harpers Ferry. Maryland farmer James Giddings and several local businessmen formed Harpers Ferry & Shenandoah Manufacturing Co., which built a four-story mill on the island in 1848 to produce cotton sheeting and shirting.[202] One year later, the Giddings group doubled down on its investment with construction of a second cotton mill, Valley Mills, also known as the Valley Cotton Factory.[203] It quickly reached daily production of 400 pounds of cotton yarn, 100 pounds of batting and 50 pounds of candlewick.[204]

After a fire destroyed Valley Mills in 1852, it was never rebuilt.[205] That same year, Harpers Ferry & Shenandoah Manufacturing Co., having struggled financially since its founding, took bankruptcy.[206] Its bottom line had been adversely affected by an over-supply of milling capacity in the North, coupled with the rising cost of raw cotton.[207] In 1854, the vacant building was sold for

$25,000 to Abraham Herr, who at the time owned Virginius Island. He used the mill to make brown cottons, then closed it during the Panic of 1857.[208]

Cement Mill

The region's first cement mill was situated on the Potomac River, one-half mile downstream from Shepherdstown.[209] In 1827, local physician Henry Boteler and businessman George Reynolds formed the Potomac Mills partnership, purchased a gristmill and built a dam to power it.[210] But they soon discovered a vein of limestone which could be made into hydraulic cement that hardened under water. After inspecting a sample, the Chesapeake and Ohio Canal Company told them it was suitable for building canal locks. The partners then purchased kilns to burn limestone which the gristmill ground into cement.[211] At peak production, 50 workers at Potomac Mills produced 1,000 bushels of cement per day, enough to build one lock every four days.[212]

Boteler sold his interest in the company to Reynolds in 1834, the year canal construction reached Shepherdstown. However, it lost business to the Round Top Cement Mill, which opened four years later on the Potomac River's north bank, three miles west of Hancock.[213] In 1846, Boteler's son, Alexander, purchased the financially stressed Potomac Mills for $15,000 at auction, then shipped cement down the canal to builders in Washington, D.C., until Union troops burned the Shepherdstown complex in 1862.[214]

Sawmills and Cooperages

In the first half of the nineteenth century, the region's sawmill owners prospered from the growing demand for lumber used in the construction of houses, commercial buildings, covered bridges, railroad tracks and plank roads, as well as from cabinetmakers, cartwrights and coopers. After Lewis and Joel Lupton invented a circular saw in 1835, the Frederick County brothers supplied crossties and trestles to the Winchester and Potomac Railroad.[215] They also milled wooden planks for sections of the Winchester and Front Royal Turnpike and the North Frederick Turnpike near Winchester.[216] By the 1850s, lumbermen in Page County were using portable, steam-powered sawmills in the Blue Ridge and Massanutten mountains.[217] Burning dead wood for fuel, they moved their equipment from one tree stand to another. In the Warren County village of Browntown, sawmills on Gooney Creek produced flooring, wooden handles for farm tools and staves for barrels.[218]

While gristmills were the first Northern Valley industry to use large quantities of barrels, the 42-gallon containers also stored preserved meat, hides and whiskey. Barrels were assembled from oak staves—long, narrow strips of wood—that when held together with metal or wooden hoops, formed the container's round sides. Made from staves with precisely beveled edges, tight barrels held liquids, and because they kept out moisture, flour. Slack barrels were used for goods that did not require airtight sides.

At first, few independent cooperages were found in the Northern Valley. Large gristmills—Herr's Mill on Virginius Island, Edinburg Mill on Stony Creek and Burwell-Morgan Mill in Millwood—made their own barrels. But the cooperage industry grew rapidly in the early 1900s, when orchardists and limestone companies needed large quantities of barrels to store and transport apples and burnt lime.

Potters

Prior to the Civil War, Strasburg potters produced utilitarian jars and vases, along with decorative ceramics that mimicked the urban styles of their American and European counterparts. After Adam Keister Sr. moved from Strasburg to Ohio in 1830, sons Adam Jr. and Henry operated A. Keister and Co.[219] In 1843, Samuel and Solomon Bell started up Samuel Bell Pottery in Strasburg, which utilized a glazing process learned from their father, Peter Bell Jr.[220] The local industry flourished after Samuel designed a round kiln that melted stoneware clay more evenly and saved on firewood and labor. In 1853, he built a shop and kiln close to his home and sold the older equipment to Samuel H. Sonner.[221] Not a potter by trade, Sonner hired journeymen to throw clay and apply glazes, while he delivered S. H. Sonner Pottery's finished products to retail merchants and other customers.[222]

Extractive Industries: Prospecting for Copper and Manganese

While tons of iron ore came from Northern Valley orebanks during the antebellum period, out-of-area prospectors had limited success finding copper deposits along the western slope of the Blue Ridge. Local businessmen and others had more success extracting manganese in the Great North Mountain area of western Frederick and Shenandoah counties. In the late 1850s, Pittsburgh's iron industry became a major market for the metal.

Copper Mining

Prized for its ability to transmit heat quickly and evenly, copper was used in the fabrication of kettles, frying pans, skillets and distilling equipment. The region's copper belt extended from an area northeast of Front Royal, southward into the Page Valley. In the early 1800s, shallow pits were dug in several places, but the small amounts extracted were of poor quality. Commercial interest in mining copper resumed in the mid-1840s. The participants included Shenandoah Copper Mining Company, South Shenandoah Copper Company, Front Royal Mining & Copper Company and owners of the Sealoch Copper Mine, near the Warren County village of Linden.[223] In 1858, Stony Man Mining Company paid $550,000 for 5,371 acres east of its namesake's peak in the Blue Ridge, southeast of Luray.[224] Owned by New York and Massachusetts investors, the small amounts of copper found caused the company to discontinue operations.[225] Years later, Skyland Resort opened on part of the property.

Manganese Mining

Manganese was found near iron oxide deposits in the Cedar Creek Valley in southwestern Frederick County. In 1834, local operators extracted the hard, brittle, gray-white metal at the Mineral Ridge Mine, one mile from the Paddy Furnace, then washed and ground it at a mill on Paddy Run.[226] Each year, teamsters hauled upwards of 52,000 tons of manganese to the Winchester and Potomac freight depot in Winchester for shipment to coke-fired iron furnaces in Pennsylvania. Near the village of Zepp in northwestern Shenandoah County, Joel Williams leased the Godlove mine from its namesake family in 1847 and extracted large amounts of manganese, also delivered to the Winchester depot.[227] By the 1850s, Northern Valley miners faced competition from abundant supplies of better-quality manganese found in the western United States and overseas. Mineral Ridge Mine closed, but was reopened when the nation's steel industry ramped up production in World War I.[228]

Newspapers: Politics Dominate the News

With sectional politics heating up, the number of newspapers published in the United States more than tripled, from 1,300 in 1830 to 4,051 in 1860.[229] Increased revenues from paid circulations allowed Northern Valley publishers to carry more local news, along with articles reprinted from city papers.²³⁰ The industry benefited from improved printing equipment and less-expensive newsprint made from wood pulp, rather than rags. In the 1850s, the region's publishers and editors grew circulations by focusing on partisan political issues surrounding slavery. Some also served as officials in local political parties, which in turn subsidized their newspapers.²³¹

Several papers surfaced in Winchester during the antebellum period. In 1824, Peter Printz published the Winchester Republican, while Joseph Sherrard started the Virginian, three years later.²³² James Beller launched the Democratic-leaning Spirit of Jefferson newspaper in 1844 in Charles Town, in editorial opposition to the Virginia Free Press in the same town.²³³ Published since 1821, the latter paper became known as a Federalist, then a Whig newspaper. In 1849, Henry Hardy and H. W. McAnly launched the politically neutral Shepherdstown Register.²³⁴ All newspapers ceased publishing during the Civil War.

Tourism: Railroads Bring More Patrons to Springs Resorts

The build-out of railroads and turnpikes in the region led to more and larger mineral springs resorts that provided hundreds of local citizens with seasonal jobs. Arriving by rail from Baltimore, Washington, Alexandria and points in between, patrons took stagecoaches to their final destination. And they stayed in hotels, not the tents and cabins of the pre-railroad era.

The so-called healing power of mineral waters was an alternative to patent medicines that were sold as cures for every ailment known to man. Each springs resort marketed the ability of its waters to treat one or more ailments that included neuralgia, dyspepsia, anemia, rheumatism and skin rashes. Wealthy patrons also came to socialize and escape the oppressive summer heat of eastern cities. Because of their remoteness, many guests stayed one month, or spent a week or two at several resorts. Charges that averaged $3 a day or $70 a month included all meals and a never-ending supply of water.

Beginning in the late 1830s, more tourists came to Berkeley Springs after the Baltimore and Ohio Railroad established a passenger station at Sir John's Run, near the Potomac River. Following train passage, they took a three-mile stagecoach ride over Warm Springs Ridge to the town's springs. To ease tourist travel from Winchester, the Winchester and Berkeley Springs

Turnpike Company was chartered in 1839 to build a road that later became part of U.S. 522 North.[235]

Colonel John Strother, clerk of the Berkeley County Court, leased several downtown Berkeley Springs properties in 1834 and turned them into the Pavilion Hotel.[236] Four years after an 1844 fire destroyed it and other buildings, Strother opened the 300-room Berkeley Springs Hotel, south of the town's bathhouses.[237] In the late 1840s and early 1850s, United States presidents James K. Polk and Millard Fillmore stayed at the hotel.[238] After son David took over its management in 1855, dress balls and band concerts were held during the town's Golden Decade.[239] In addition to hotelier duties, the younger Strother, using the Porte Crayon pseudonym, became a well-known magazine illustrator and travel writer.[240]

Berkeley Springs Hotel
Photo from West Virginia and Regional History Collection, WVU Libraries, Morgantown, WV

Opened in the early 1820s, near the Potomac River in eastern Jefferson County, Shannondale Springs Hotel struggled amid ownership disputes that left it in rundown condition.[241] Hoping to take advantage of new rail service to Harpers Ferry, local investors formed Shannondale Springs Corporation in 1838 and purchased the hotel.[242] After expanding the property's footprint from 60 to 200 acres, the group added cottages, a gambling casino, a bowling green and horse stables.[243] Frequented by the nation's social and political elite, the resort's popularity peaked in the late 1840s. Another owner renovated the hotel in 1856, but a fire destroyed it two years later.[244]

Branch Jordan, an early visitor to White Sulphur Springs, six miles north of Winchester, purchased the property in 1834, built a hotel and bathhouse and renamed it Jordan Springs.[245] Guests rode Winchester and Potomac trains from Harpers Ferry to the Stephenson depot, then proceeded by stagecoach to the resort. In 1855, Jordan's nephew, Edwin Clarenden Jordan Sr., added a larger 48-room hotel.[246] When his uncle died at the outset of the Civil War, Edwin took sole ownership of the business.[247]

The western part of Frederick County was home to two resorts. In the early 1850s, Dr. William Keffer built the modest Pembroke Springs Hotel on his farm near Great North Mountain, southwest of Winchester.[248] At the time, completion of the Winchester and Moorefield Turnpike, later part of Route 55, made it easier for stagecoaches to access the hotel.[249] When not attending to his hostelry duties, Keffer practiced medicine in Strasburg. Closed during the Civil War, the Pembroke Springs Hotel never reopened after his passing in 1866.[250]

Several miles northwest of Gore, William Marker purchased 942 acres in 1856 in the Capper Springs area, whose six springs were named after settler John Capper.[251] The new owner built a modest hotel and marketed the property as Rock Enon Springs and Mineral Baths.[252] Patrons arriving in Winchester took a stagecoach on the Northwestern Turnpike, followed by a six-mile ride on Back Creek Road to the hotel.

In 1845, Naason Bare acquired land in the Orkney Springs area, 13 miles west of Mount Jackson, and built a log hotel in the foothills of Great North Mountain.[253] Five years later, A. R. Seymour added a weatherboard building and opened what was advertised as a sylvan retreat at Yellow Springs. The color came from chalybeate iron salts that covered the rock beds in the 11 springs on the property.[254] In 1853, a joint stock company built the two-story Maryland House, later known as the Orkney Springs Hotel.[255] In summers the resort held jousting tournaments, after which the Queen of Love and Beauty was crowned.[256] To reach the hotel in the late 1850s, guests took the Manassas Gap Railroad to Mount Jackson, followed by a stagecoach ride on Howard's Lick Turnpike, later renamed Route 263.[257]

Two springs resorts were built in 1851 in the Fort Valley area in anticipation of Manassas Gap Railroad providing passenger service to Front Royal and Strasburg. Three years later, the railroad brought their patrons to the Waterlick Station, located halfway between the towns. Local businessman John Smith Davidson opened the 60-room Warren White Sulphur Springs Hotel on a hill overlooking Passage Creek, one mile south of the station.[258] Land speculator

Orkney Springs Maryland House
Postcard published by G. F. Norton Publishing Co., Winchester, VA

Noah Burner built the three-story Burner's White Sulphur Springs Hotel and numerous cottages in the center of Fort Valley.[259] Twenty-two springs were within a half-mile diameter of the accommodations, which held up to 600 guests who paid $6 a week or $20 a month for room and board.[260] With a brass band greeting stagecoaches, it was considered one of Virginia's premier vacation spots.[261] After Burner encountered financial problems in 1852 and again during the Panic of 1857, creditors forced him to sell the resort. The new owners renamed it Seven Fountains.[262]

CHAPTER 4

CIVIL WAR AND RECONSTRUCTION

Conflict Devastates Region's Economy

After the April 1861 attack on Fort Sumter, southern representatives left the halls of Congress. Those from the North passed two programs needed to finance its war effort: a federal income tax and a tariff that ended more than 15 years of declining duties.[1] As the fighting continued, Congress paid the North's bills with higher income taxes and tariffs, supplemented by bond sales and the Treasury Department's printing press. To fund its military, the South also printed money, and later sold cotton-backed bonds on the Amsterdam market.[2] While Virginia voted to join the Confederate States of America, 39 counties in its western section, including Berkeley, Jefferson and Morgan, voted against secession. They hoped to form the State of Kanawha, but that did not happen.[3]

War's Initial Impact on the Region

At the start of the conflict, Northern Valley manufacturers and tradesmen profited from goods sold to the Confederacy.[4] Tanneries produced leather, furnaces smelted pig iron, forges fabricated munitions and skilled craftsmen made boots, harnesses, saddles and other equipment for Confederate troops to wage war.[5] Woolen mills provided cloth for their pants, shirts, overcoats and socks.[6] While the region's farmers were cut off from export markets, that loss was initially offset by sales of crops and livestock to the South. They also hired out teams of horses and wagons to the Confederacy's Quartermaster General, which used them to move supplies and equipment.

Within a short time, however, basic foodstuffs imported into the Northern Valley were in short supply and priced beyond the means of most citizens. In September 1861, the price of coffee more than doubled, while salt soared from $8 a sack to $30, three months later.[7] A gross of matches, priced at less than 65 cents before the war, cost households $6.[8] When the Confederacy's Commissary General sent agents to confiscate the region's excess livestock in 1862, it caused a shortage of beef, bacon and pork.

Northern Valley merchants saw sales decrease when loyal customers left the region and those that stayed refrained from unnecessary spending in uncertain times.[9] And as the fighting continued, soldiers on both sides pilfered goods from their stores, while obtaining replacement inventory from northern manufacturers was problematic.[10] At the start of the war, the president of Berkeley Savings Bank in Martinsburg suspended business and buried $60,000 worth of cash on his farm.[11] The branches of Bank of Virginia and Farmers' Bank in Winchester shut down.[12] Headquartered in the same town, with branches in neighboring counties, Bank of the Valley of Virginia went into receivership and closed.[13]

War's Impact on the Region's Industry

The war was disastrous for Harpers Ferry's economy when 400 workers lost their jobs at the U.S. Armory and Arsenal.[14] The federal garrison stationed there attempted to burn buildings and destroy machinery to prevent the South from making rifles.[15] But Virginia militiamen seized 300 pieces of equipment, along with the component parts for thousands of muskets.[16] Loaded on rail cars bound for Winchester, they ended up at the Virginia Manufactory of Arms in Richmond, which the Confederacy returned to service.[17]

Despite its success at Harpers Ferry, the South needed to manufacture many more armaments from pig iron made in Virginia and Tennessee.[18] After the Union Army quickly overran the latter state, Virginia's furnaces supplied the metal to Tredegar Iron Works. Situated along the James River near Richmond, America's third largest fabricator of iron products soon became the Confederacy's major producer of weapons and ammunition.[19] Tredegar arranged to source pig iron from 10 Virginia furnaces, but the Federal Army burned a number of them.[20] Although its workforce grew from 700 to 2,500 during the war, Tredegar never obtained more than one-third of the iron needed to operate at full capacity.[21]

At the war's outset, two Northern Valley furnaces stopped smelting iron. Believing that Confederate soldiers were hiding inside Shannondale Furnace in Jefferson County, Union forces burned it.[22] When Pennsylvania natives Samuel and John Myers decided to fight for their adopted Virginia, the brothers shut down their Henrietta Furnace, west of Mount Jackson.[23]

Five furnaces did produce pig iron for Tredegar. Cornelius Pritchard rebuilt his Fort Steam Furnace in Fort Valley in 1861.[24] Wagons hauled its iron eastward over Massanutten Mountain to the Virginia Central Railroad depot in Gordonsville, where it was put on trains headed to Tredegar. Iron from Columbia Furnace in western Shenandoah County went by wagon on the Valley Turnpike to the same railroad's depot in Staunton.[25] Because Shenandoah Iron Works' furnaces in Page County were not damaged, its iron and munitions went by wagon through gaps in the Blue Ridge to Tredegar.[26] Although the Bush and Lobdell Company in Wilmington owned Caroline Furnace in Fort Valley, when war broke out, local managers Joshua Clem and Joseph Marston sent its pig iron to Tredegar.[27]

Near war's end, Union forces put the Caroline and Fort Steam furnaces out of commission and neither returned to service.[28] They burned Columbia Furnace three times, but production resumed after each incident.[29] While its wooden interior parts, bellows and water wheels caught on fire, repairing the furnace was relatively easy, because its outside stone and inside brick walls remained intact.[30] Five miles west of Columbia Furnace, Federal troops burned Liberty Furnace in 1864, but it was quickly repaired and returned to service.[31] After they destroyed nearby Union Forge, it was never rebuilt.[32]

In 1861, the Union army disabled Abraham Herr's large gristmill on Virginius Island to prevent enemy use of it.[33] But when sympathizer Herr offered those troops wheat stored in his warehouse, Confederate soldiers torched it.[34] In 1863, Union forces burned the three-story Borst Tannery on Hawksbill Creek in Luray, a major supplier of leather to the Confederacy.[35] Although owner Peter Buck Borst attempted to rebuild it, Union General Philip Sheridan's troops destroyed it again in October 1864, during their Burning of the Shenandoah Valley.[36]

After Sheridan's campaign ended, he reported to General Ulysses Grant that his troops had set 70 gristmills on fire, mostly in an area from Strasburg to Staunton.[37] Among those destroyed were Lantz Mill on Stony Creek, west of Edinburg; Willow Grove Mill, on a Hawksbill Creek tributary near Luray; and Mauck's Mill, on the South Fork of the Shenandoah River.[38] Two large gristmills were spared. After Edinburg Mill was set on fire, owner George Grandstaff's granddaughters convinced Sheridan to order his men to extinguish it.[39] And fortunately for Clarke County planters, Burwell-Morgan Mill in Millwood was not burned. Instead, soldiers from both sides camping nearby made bread from flour stored on the mill's premises.[40]

War's Impact on the Region's Transportation Network

Moving soldiers and supplies quickly to where needed was critical for a successful military outcome. When the war began, the B&O Railroad employed hundreds of local residents at its Martinsburg maintenance shops. To keep their jobs, they remained loyal to the Union.[41] At the same time, B&O trains brought grain from the Ohio River Valley to the Union Army and delivered Western Maryland coal to federal naval ships anchored in the Chesapeake Bay.[42]

Knowing the importance of the B&O's main line to the Union, in 1861 Confederate General Thomas "Stonewall" Jackson's troops destroyed 37 miles of its track between Harpers Ferry and an area west of Hedgesville.[43] In Martinsburg, they burned its engine house and stripped the roundhouse and machine shops of their contents, then shipped them southward, along with torn-up track.[44] Jackson's men also captured 17 engines and more than 100 rail cars, which they hauled to the Manassas Gap Railroad's track in Strasburg, for use within the Confederacy's rail network.[45]

Jackson was also determined to stop barge shipments of Western Maryland coal on the Chesapeake and Ohio Canal to factories in the Washington, D.C. area. He also wanted to disrupt the delivery of supplies the Union needed to rebuild the B&O's tracks.[46] To keep the Potomac River's water from refilling the canal, in 1861 Jackson's men destroyed the wood-cribbed Dam No. 5, seven miles upstream from Williamsport, but Union forces quickly rebuilt it.[47]

As the war progressed, Confederate troops destroyed B&O tracks in Berkeley and Jefferson counties nine times, but they were always returned to service.[48] When Union forces seized the Winchester and Potomac Railroad in 1862, the other side had already removed the tracks.[49] That same year, their destruction of the Manassas Gap Railroad left only traces of its roadbed between Manassas Junction and Strasburg.[50]

Burning wooden bridges was another strategy to impede the transport of enemy troops and supplies through the Northern Valley. Those set on fire included the B&O's bridge at Harpers Ferry; one over Opequon Creek, two miles east of Martinsburg; and the Back Creek bridge near Hedgesville.[51] Also destroyed were the two bridges across the forks of the Shenandoah River at Riverton and the White House Bridge, southwest of Luray.[52]

War's Impact on the Region's Agriculture

Winchester and Martinsburg changed hands many times during the war.[53] As the fighting continued into early 1862, soldiers on both sides availed themselves of the region's crops and livestock.[54] Some farmers drove their herds of horses, cattle, hogs and sheep over the Blue Ridge to the relative safety of the Piedmont area, while those who stayed planted only a few acres, fearing the crops would be lost to invading armies and marauders.[55] Desperate soldiers even resorted to stealing vegetables from gardens of families living in towns and villages.

Berkeley and Jefferson counties were also not spared, as both sides confiscated livestock, looted homes and destroyed mills. In 1862, Jedediah Hotchkiss, Stonewall Jackson's cartographer, observed from his campsite in Bunker Hill that, "This county's almost destitute of every kind of forage or subsistence, for it has been full of armies for a long time."[56] Strategically placed Harpers Ferry changed hands eight times and Shepherdstown's residents saw both armies appear twice at their doorsteps.[57] When General Philip Sheridan's raids were conducted in the fall of 1864, not many crops or livestock remained on the region's farms, either for local consumption or to feed Confederate soldiers fighting elsewhere.[58]

Slaves Emancipated and New State Formed

Planters and owners of semi-fabricating industries in the Northern Valley found that in the confusion of war, many of their slaves sought freedom, even before Lincoln's Emancipation Proclamation was delivered on January 1, 1863.[59] Released from bondage, other former slaves packed their belongings and left.[60]

For years, residents in the western and most northern counties of Virginia were unhappy with the way the commonwealth's eastern politicians had treated them, particularly their lack of support for internal improvements. In June 1863, they officially joined the Union as West Virginia, with Charleston its capital.[61] Berkeley, Jefferson and Morgan counties were included, because the strategically important B&O's tracks passed through them. Based on their geographic location and footprint, they became known as the Eastern Panhandle. After the war, disputes arose over whether Berkeley and Jefferson counties should rejoin Virginia, because they were culturally, socially and economically closer to the Valley of Virginia than to the rest of West Virginia. That never transpired.

Postwar: Economic Doldrums in the South, Prosperity in North

When the Civil War ended in April 1865, the economic and physical conditions of the two sides differed greatly. Businesses and farmers in the South who were paid for goods and services in Confederate currency, script or warrants, found they were worthless. With its banks insolvent, financing an economic recovery became problematic. In contrast, the conflict stimulated a full-fledged Industrial Revolution in the North, driven by an increased demand for goods used to prosecute the war and the imposition of high tariffs on imports. In the 1860s, the number of manufacturing firms in the United States jumped from 140,433 to 252,148, with most domiciled in the North and Midwest.[62]

The nation's Reconstruction period ended with the Compromise of 1877, which settled the disputed presidential election and resulted in the United States pulling its last troops out of the South.[63] To revitalize their economies, the former Confederate states proposed a New South strategy that emphasized economic diversification through industrialization, and restoration of business relationships with the North.[64] Southern political leaders felt the key to attracting northern investors was to offer them tax incentives and building sites, improve the region's transportation network, advance public education and minimize racial conflict.

Recovery Strategy: Rebuild Farms and Start New Businesses

With their physical assets destroyed, the war left many Northern Valley residents on the verge of bankruptcy, but farmers repaired and rebuilt their barns and fences, and millers returned to producing flour and corn meal. Northern investors purchased some businesses and started new ones. Unfortunately, manpower was in short supply. During the war, an estimated 50 percent of the region's men either enlisted or were drafted, with one-quarter never returning home.[65] Hundreds of residents had left towns and farms for Baltimore and other places east of the Blue Ridge. Craftsmen and their apprentices joined them, leaving artisan shops empty. After the B&O yard was destroyed, Martinsburg experienced a mass exodus of railroad workers and Union sympathizers.

The Thirteenth Amendment to the Constitution, which abolished slavery in 1865, added to the Northern Valley's manpower shortage. Many slaves who had not left during the war moved to Pennsylvania and New York as freedmen in search of employment. Between 1860 and 1870, the number of African Americans living in Jefferson County dropped by 22 percent, while they declined by 37 percent in Clarke County.[66] The emancipation of slaves created financial hardships for business owners and planters forced to pay wages to freedmen. Some African Americans who remained bought land at auction from financially stressed whites and established communities around schools and churches they built.[67] Others became sharecroppers, working the land for themselves and giving a portion of the harvest to their former masters.[68]

While Northern Valley men were lost to soldiering, and former slaves moved north, families that fled the conflict eventually returned home. Between 1860 and 1870, the region's population grew, but the 1.7 percent increase was much lower than the 22.6 percent the United States experienced.[69] Not surprisingly, the only counties to lose population during that decade—Clarke, Jefferson and Warren—also had the highest percentage of slaves in 1860.

During Reconstruction, Northern Valley business leaders engaged in activities designed to foster an economic recovery.[70] They served as elected officials, joined boards of civic and non-profit organizations, and became cheerleaders for their communities.[71] The Winchester Times editorialized in 1871 that the town needed to grow its manufacturing sector.[72] One year later, a mayoral-appointed committee recommended Winchester reconcile with northern investors to bring in capital, encourage immigration to increase the labor pool and improve the rail network to lower shipping costs.[73]

Despite the optimism, the Northern Valley economy experienced several setbacks. The United States decided not to re-establish rifle and musket production in Harpers Ferry and instead rely on the Springfield armory, whose output had grown exponentially during the war.[74] The area was dealt a second blow in 1870, when a Shenandoah River flood caused extensive damage and 43 deaths in Harpers Ferry and destroyed almost all manufacturing on nearby Virginius Island.[75] When the water level on its South Fork rose rapidly without warning, many residents of western Page County drowned, crops and farm animals were lost and the once fertile land was ruined.[76] The flood also washed away the town of Shenandoah Iron Works, damaged its namesake furnace and destroyed gristmills and bridges in that area.[77]

Then came the Panic of 1873. It began when prominent investment banker Jay Cooke announced his Philadelphia-based Cooke & Co. was insolvent due to unpaid real estate loans.[78] During the five-year depression that followed, half the nation's iron and steel furnaces were shuttered and coal production went into free fall.[79] Although the panic's impact was less severe on the mainly agrarian Northern Valley economy, it caused the prices of pig iron, wheat and livestock to drop, reduced occupancies at the springs resorts and delayed completion of two north-south railroads.

Notwithstanding weather-related problems and the panic, the Northern Valley's population rose 15.8 percent from 1870 to 1880. Although much greater than the 1.7 percent increase in the prior decade, it was only half the nation's 30 percent growth.[80] The populations of each county went up, with Morgan, Warren and Shenandoah leading the way. From a low base, Morgan County's census soared by 34 percent when visitor activity picked up in its resort town. Warren County's 29 percent population increase resulted from the return to service of the Manassas Gap Railroad, construction of the Shenandoah Valley Railroad, and new mining and milling activity in Riverton. With a 22 percent gain, Shenandoah County benefited from the restart of its iron and flour milling industries, and the B&O's extensions of track between Mount Jackson and Harrisonburg and from Winchester to Strasburg.[81]

Although Martinsburg suffered war damage, the West Virginia legislature designated it a city in 1868. Residents moved into new gas-lit brick homes that were connected to a modern water works, which also enhanced Martinsburg's ability to fight fires. Two modern hotels opened in 1876: The B&O's hotel was remodeled as the Berkeley Hotel, while the Continental Hotel advertised its fancy bathrooms and large windows.[82] Repairs and additions to the B&O's maintenance shops created hundreds of jobs, causing Martinsburg's population to reach 6,355 in 1880, almost double its 1860 census of 3,360 citizens.

Within those two decades, Winchester's population advanced at a more modest 12.9 percent pace, from 4,392 to 4,960, but that made it large enough for Virginia's legislature to classify it as a city in 1874, independent from Frederick

County.⁸³ With more dry goods stores and specialty shops open, its Market House closed in 1882 and seven years later, was torn down for construction of Rouss City Hall.

Baltimore's Ties to Northern Valley Increase

Maryland stayed in the Union during the Civil War, even though it was located below the Mason-Dixon Line and a large slave population lived on its plantations. Some of its men crossed the Potomac River and fought for the Confederacy. Postwar, three Baltimore groups helped Virginians get back on their feet.⁸⁴ Formed in 1865, the Baltimore Agricultural Aid Society gave $76,500 to farmers in Frederick, Clarke and Warren counties and others in the Piedmont region.⁸⁵ The society advanced each farmer between $50 and $400 to purchase wheat seed and farm implements at wholesale prices.⁸⁶ In 1866, the Union Relief Association of Baltimore sent gifts of food, farm tools, cooking utensils and dishes to the Northern Valley. At its Southern Relief Fair, the Secessionist Women of Baltimore raised $160,000 for destitute citizens living in the former Confederacy.⁸⁷

To solidify their financial ties to Winchester, Baltimore businessmen in 1866 became majority shareholders in the new Shenandoah Valley National Bank.⁸⁸ Four years later, the City of Baltimore invested $1 million in the Valley Railroad Company, which planned to build a line from Harrisonburg to Salem.⁸⁹

Region's Agriculture During Reconstruction

With thousands of acres of Northern Valley farmland overgrown with weeds, bushes and small trees, the corn harvest in its Virginia portion had fallen 52 percent, rye 35 percent and hay by 11 percent.⁹⁰ The region's wheat production grew from 1.59 million bushels in 1860 to 1.68 million in 1870, then went up by 17 percent to 1.96 million in 1880.⁹¹ Northern Valley farmers used cash raised from wheat sales to rebuild barns, repair fences, replace implements and restock their herds.⁹² To offset labor shortages, they invested in mechanical equipment that included drills for sowing seed, reapers for harvesting wheat, and threshers and fans for cleaning it.⁹³ Higher per-acre yields resulted from crop rotation and more extensive application of chemical fertilizers and guano imported from South America.⁹⁴

With more land under cultivation and improved machinery, the nation's wheat harvest soared from 170 million bushels in 1860 to 460 million in 1880.⁹⁵

Because that increase outpaced the rate of population growth by almost three times, prices fell during economic downturns.[96] While one bushel of wheat brought farmers $1.04 in 1870, the price dropped to 85 cents two years after the Panic of 1873, then fell to 72 cents a bushel during the Depression of 1882-85.[97]

In addition to lower wheat prices, Northern Valley farmers faced more competition from large farms in the Midwest and Great Plains, which benefited from improved rail access to East Coast markets and lower freight rates.[98] In the 1850s, it cost 20.8 cents to transport one bushel of wheat from Chicago to New York; by the early 1880s, it was down to 8.6 cents.[99] With the B&O hauling more midwestern wheat eastward, Baltimore's exports grew exponentially, from 2.3 million bushels in 1850 to 36.4 million in 1880.[100]

As with most of the grain crops, the livestock count in the Virginia portion of the region fell from prewar levels. The horse population in 1870 was down by 15 percent, sheep herds declined by 30 percent, and there were 24 percent fewer beef cattle.[101] By 1880, the census for each category of livestock, except hogs, was above the 1860 level.[102] But farmers who raised beef cattle faced competition from Great Plains ranchers. They filled the open ranges of Nebraska, Kansas, Wyoming and Texas with cattle that grazed on grass that buffalo once ate.[103] The herd increased from 28.6 million in 1867 to 43.3 million in 1880.[104] The low prices Chicago meatpackers paid ranchers for them, coupled with reduced shipping costs, kept prices low in East Coast markets.[105]

While Northern Valley farmers faced increased competition for wheat and livestock, another business opportunity opened up for them. Fortunately, orchards were not significantly damaged during the Civil War. Starting from a low base, the region's apple production increased nearly four-fold from 1860 to 1880, despite problems of ever-changing weather conditions and the prevalence of diseases, harmful insects and rodents.[106] By the turn of the twentieth century, orcharding had become a viable alternative to raising wheat and livestock.

Internal Improvements During Reconstruction

After many of the Northern Valley's roads were torn up during the conflict, counties in Virginia and West Virginia struggled to find the resources to rebuild them. While the B&O Railroad returned the Winchester and Potomac Railroad to service, three new railroads—the Shenandoah Valley, the Valley and the Martinsburg and Potomac—brought more freight and passenger traffic to the region.

Roads

An 1874 amendment to Virginia's constitution stated that the Board of Public Works would no longer invest in turnpike companies, because the risk of loss was too great.[107] After the board's mission shifted from financial support to regulation, Virginia's cash-strapped counties assumed responsibility for rebuilding roads. One decade later, however, their condition was far worse than before the Civil War.[108] West Virginia also required its county governments to pay for repairing roads torn up during the conflict. The Valley Turnpike Company collected tolls into the early twentieth century, despite wartime destruction of its bridges and toll houses and competition from two railroads in the 1880s.[109] Because receipts never covered operating expenses of the region's other turnpikes, county governments eventually took them over as toll free roads.

Railroads

By the early 1870s, southern railroads were returned to service and 8,000 miles of new track had come on line. Before their last advance towards Winchester in late 1864, Union troops replaced the Winchester and Potomac tracks the Confederates had seized.[110] After the war, the federal government returned that railroad to its stockholders, who leased the right–of-way to the B&O for 99 years, at an annual rent of $27,000.[111] The freight depot on Winchester's Cameron Street was put back in service, which helped neighboring businesses recover.

After securing a damage claim from the federal government, the B&O repaired its tracks in the Eastern Panhandle. In 1866, it rebuilt the roundhouse in the Martinsburg rail yard, followed four years later with new shops that fabricated replacement parts for bridges and track switches.[112] With hundreds of new railroad jobs, Martinsburg regained its role as a center of economic activity.

Looking to participate in the Age of the Railroad and anxious to stimulate economic development in its war-torn state, the Virginia General Assembly approved charters for several new railroads, even though little public or private money was available to finance them. Two groups announced plans to build lines through the Shenandoah Valley to Salem, six miles south of Big Lick, later known as Roanoke.[113] There the tracks would join with those of the Virginia and Tennessee Railroad, which connected with a railroad that served southern cities.[114] One group promoted the Shenandoah Valley Railroad, a 234-mile line that paralleled the western foothills of the Blue Ridge. The other group backed the Valley Railroad, whose 113 miles of track would run through the Valley of Virginia's central spine. To build them, the promoters had to rely on outside financing from bitter rivals, the Pennsylvania and the B&O railroads.[115] Although both carriers had north-south lines in the Piedmont area, they wanted a more direct route into the Shenandoah Valley to bring its natural resources, agricultural produce and semi-fabricated goods to their home cities of Philadelphia and Baltimore.[116]

Because the proposed routes of the railroads were close to one another—only 10 miles apart in some places—their financial viability was questionable from the start.[117] And although Virginia's political leaders granted them charters, they were not anxious for either line to succeed, for it meant more Shenandoah Valley trade would be directed to other states and away from Richmond, Norfolk and Alexandria.[118] Valley Turnpike Company directors were in the same camp. They feared competition from the two railroads would hurt traffic and reduce toll collections.

Valley Railroad

In 1866, the Virginia General Assembly indicated it would issue Valley Railroad Company organizers a charter, after they raised $3 million in capital.[119] At a convention held in Staunton, the promoters realized that for their railroad to be profitable, its trains needed to reach northern and midwestern markets.[120] They partnered with the B&O, which already leased the Winchester and Potomac Railroad and had taken ownership of the Orange and Alexandria and the Manassas Gap railroads, whose tracks reached Strasburg and Mount Jackson.[121] After making repairs to the merged Orange, Alexandria and Manassas Railroad, the B&O extended its tracks to Harrisonburg in 1867.[122] Following up on a prewar proposal, it organized the Winchester and Strasburg Railroad in 1870, which built a line that connected the Winchester and Potomac with the Orange, Alexandria and Manassas in Strasburg. As a result, the B&O's Shenandoah Valley footprint went from Harpers Ferry to Harrisonburg.[123]

Farther south, Robert E. Lee, president of Washington College in Lexington, hoped to raise funds to pay for the Valley Railroad's track built between Harrisonburg and Salem, but citizens of Big Lick and Botetourt and Rockbridge counties were hesitant to approve the issuance of bonds.[124] Their concerns centered on the location of the tracks and the extent of B&O control over the new railroad. Nevertheless, by 1871, $3.3 million of equity capital had been raised from the B&O, the City of Baltimore, central Shenandoah Valley counties and towns and private investors.[125]

Although construction from Harrisonburg to Staunton had begun, the Panic of 1873 delayed the sale of $3 million worth of mortgage bonds needed to finish the line.[126] When further attempts to raise funds failed, the Valley Railroad Company was declared insolvent. Faced with its own financial issues, the B&O suspended track construction south of Staunton, even though rights-of-way had been purchased and the roadbed started.[127] In 1883, the line was finally completed to Lexington, 50 miles short of Salem.

Shenandoah Valley Railroad

Its organizers planned to build a 234-mile line from Hagerstown to Salem, with much of its track following the iron and copper belt along the Blue Ridge's western slope. That route would provide the least expensive and fastest way to ship those natural resources to Pennsylvania steel mills and northeastern fabricators of copper products.[128] In 1867, the Virginia General Assembly approved a charter for the Shenandoah Valley Railroad Company, which proposed to spend $7.8 million to develop the line.[129] The Pennsylvania Railroad guaranteed $3.5 million of the new railroad's mortgage bonds, because it would connect in Hagerstown to a branch of the Cumberland Valley Railroad, which it controlled since 1859.[130]

In 1870, the Pennsylvania Railroad assumed majority ownership of the Shenandoah Valley Railroad Company, but suspended work on the line during the Panic of 1873.[131] Six years later, Philadelphia-based E. W. Clark and Company purchased the struggling railroad, whose tracks finally reached Big Lick in June 1882, seven miles short of Salem.[132]

Martinsburg and Potomac Railroad

After the Civil War, Martinsburg's leaders looked to recruit a second railroad to provide competition for the B&O and reduce shipping costs for its business and industry. The Martinsburg and Potomac Railroad Company was incorporated in 1868 to build a 12-mile line from the city to the Potomac River in northern Berkeley County.[133] At Powell's Bend, it would connect to a Cumberland Valley Railroad line that came south from Hagerstown. The extension would give Martinsburg's commercial interests rail access to markets in central Pennsylvania and the Philadelphia area.[134] It would also provide the Pennsylvania Railroad, through its Cumberland Valley Railroad, with access to Shenandoah Valley commerce. When completed in 1873 at a cost of $431,000, the Martinsburg and Potomac's line was leased to the Cumberland Valley Railroad.[135]

Shenandoah River Improvements and C&O Canal

The 1830s arrival of railroads in Harpers Ferry and Winchester provided too much competition for the New Shenandoah Company, which had failed to make its namesake river navigable to Port Republic. Nevertheless, business and agricultural interests in Harpers Ferry, Berryville and in Page and Rockingham counties convinced West Virginia to charter the Shenandoah River Company in 1869.[136] After purchasing its predecessor's assets, the new company planned to dig canals, construct locks and connect the system to the Chesapeake and Ohio Canal at Harpers Ferry, but the 1870 flood intervened.[137]

Two years later, another effort to improve navigation surfaced with West Virginia's charter of the Shenandoah River Navigation Company.[138] Based in Harpers Ferry, its goal was to charge tolls and make improvements from the Jefferson-Clarke County border to the Shenandoah Iron Works village in southern Page County. To accommodate boats drawing 18 inches or less of water, the company built locks, dams and chutes, but a flood destroyed them in 1877.[139] Five years later, the Shenandoah Valley Railroad finished laying down tracks that paralleled the river's course through the Page Valley. Because of that competition, the Shenandoah River Navigation Company made no further improvements.[140]

After the Civil War, barge traffic resumed on the Chesapeake and Ohio Canal. Between 1866 and 1878, the boats transported 415,000 bushels of Northern Valley and Western Maryland wheat to Georgetown, compared to 275,000 bushels shipped in the prewar decade.[141] The peak year for the coal trade was 1875, when 16 steam-powered boats hauled 905,000 tons of the fuel from Cumberland.[142] But the 1870s were the only time the C&O Canal Company turned a profit, because Western Maryland's coal mining companies shifted most of their business to the B&O Railroad.[143]

Banking During Reconstruction

The National Banking Acts of 1863 and 1864 established the Office of Comptroller of the Currency in the Treasury Department to charter, supervise and examine national banks. The goal was to assure bank customers that federal regulators were keeping a watchful eye on the safety of their deposits. With Confederate currency worthless at war's end, the Virginia General Assembly made its state-chartered banks liquidate their remaining assets in 1866. The three with a presence in Winchester had previously closed their doors.

With no financial institutions, Northern Valley leaders organized banks to provide businesses with credit needed to revive their local economies. In 1866, Shenandoah Valley National Bank opened for business in the former Bank of the Valley of Virginia building, at the corner of Winchester's North Loudoun and Piccadilly streets.[144] Anxious to have a banking presence in a town they did business with, Baltimore investors purchased 80 percent of the bank's $130,000 of capital.[145] In 1870, local businessmen raised $50,000 and opened the state-chartered Union Bank of Winchester, also on North Loudoun Street.[146] In Front Royal, local farmer Isaac Newton King organized the Bank of Warren in 1872.[147] That same year, Bank of Berryville was launched, but when customers without adequate deposits wrote worthless checks, the bank was declared insolvent in 1876.[148]

In the Eastern Panhandle, National Bank of Martinsburg, later known as Old National Bank, opened on Queen Street in 1865 with capital stock of $50,000.[149] Eight years later, People's Deposit Bank of Martinsburg, with $12,000 of capital opened nearby, but soon became People's National Bank.[150] In 1869, Jefferson Savings Bank, renamed Jefferson Security Bank in 1909, opened in a Shepherdstown residence.[151] In 1873, its president, David Billmyer, a local grain dealer, merchant, councilman and farmer, built a permanent facility at the corner of German and Church streets.[152] In 1871, thirty-eight farmers, orchardists and businessmen organized the Bank of Charlestown. Later known as Bank of Charles Town, it was located in the former West Washington Street branch of Bank of the Valley of Virginia.[153]

To serve postwar residents with limited funds, Jefferson County leaders formed two non-traditional financial institutions.[154] In 1867, the Shepherdstown Building Association and the Jefferson County Building Association in Charles Town opened as cooperatives. County residents bought small amounts of shares each week, borrowed from the association and participated in any profits.[155]

Northerners Invest in Region

After the Civil War, entrepreneurs from Maryland, Pennsylvania and elsewhere came into the Northern Valley in search of business opportunities.

Emigrating from Germany in 1859, Henry Baetjer established a wholesale business in Baltimore, then postwar moved to Winchester to open a dry goods store on the southeast corner of Loudoun and Boscawen streets.[156] Until his passing in 1912, Henry Baetjer & Company was one of the largest retail establishments in the city.[157] Joseph Hable, also from Baltimore, started up a men's store in 1870 on Winchester's Loudoun Street. Two years later, his brother Solomon opened the S.H. Hable clothing store nearby, which he and son Herman expanded into a three-story, 9,000-square-foot emporium.[158]

Several tanners with the same surname came from Carroll County, Maryland, to the Northern Valley to be closer to abundant supplies of tan bark. In 1868, Thomas Cover paid $7,500 for the dilapidated James Bean Wigginton tannery on Cedar Creek, in the western Frederick County village of Gravel Springs.[159] After repairing the renamed Star Tannery, he shipped leather to Jenkins Brothers, a Baltimore wholesaler that marketed it under the Baltimore Star brand.[160] In 1874, Franklin, William Henry and Tobias Cover moved to Warren County and opened Cover Brothers Tannery on Gooney Creek, near Browntown.[161] Distant relatives of Thomas, the brothers employed more than 100 full-time workers at the tannery, while 150 seasonal workers peeled bark from chestnut oak trees in the Blue Ridge, and hauled it to the Cover's tan yard.[162]

After the war, two Pennsylvania companies brought a new industry to Jefferson County. Their mills made strawboard from residue left over from the wheat harvest. Besides providing farmers with income, sales of straw helped them dispose of an agricultural waste that previously was plowed under or burned. To make the material, straw placed in water containing resin was beaten into a pulp, which was then compressed with heat to form the coarse yellow boards.[163] Strawboard outperformed wood-based cardboard as a packaging material, due to its higher strength, lighter weight and better machining characteristics.

In 1869, Eyster & Son from Chambersburg purchased a gristmill on Flowing Springs Run in Halltown and repurposed it to produce six tons of strawboard each day. The Winchester and Potomac Railroad hauled it from a nearby depot to Harpers Ferry for transfer to the B&O line.[164] In 1870, Ashton Whelan & Company from Philadelphia acquired the Mecklenburg Tobacco Warehouse in Shepherdstown.[165] After putting a brick addition onto the building, its New Dominion Paper Mill made strawboard sold to businesses that cut and folded it into boxes.[166]

Moving from Scranton to Warren County in 1868, Dorastus Cone and several partners formed Riverton Mills Co., which acquired land near the confluence of the forks of the Shenandoah River.[167] The group's gristmill produced 125 barrels of flour daily, marketing it as coming "From the cream of Shenandoah Valley wheat."[168] Shipped on the Orange, Alexandria and Manassas Railroad, the flour was sold in the nation's capital under the Cherry Blossom brand.

Despite competition from Pittsburgh's steel industry, entrepreneurs from Pennsylvania and New York purchased pig iron businesses. During the war, the Forrer brothers, owners of Shenandoah Iron Works in western Page County, sent large quantities of pig iron to Tredegar Iron Works, but were paid in Confederate notes that became worthless.[169] In 1866, they sold the business for $240,000 to William Milnes Sr., his son and other investors from Pennsylvania.[170] The sale included Furnace No. 1 at company headquarters, Catherine Furnace near the village of Newport, Furnace No. 2 in Rockingham County, a finery forge, several orebanks and 31,483 forested acres lying between the Blue Ridge and Massanutten mountains.[171]

One year after the purchase, William Milnes Jr. assumed management of Shenandoah Iron Works from his aging father and invested in modern tools and machinery to improve productivity at the furnaces and forge.[172] However, the 1870 Shenandoah River flood caused extensive damage to the business and the town of Shenandoah Iron Works.[173] That same year, the Milnes group formed Shenandoah Iron, Lumber, Mining and Manufacturing (SILMM) Company with a capital stock of $1 million.[174] Milnes hoped its name and broad corporate charter would make the business appear as a large customer of the newly-organized Shenandoah Valley Railroad Company. That might convince investors to buy stock in it. While waiting for the railroad to deliver coal to his company and ship pig iron from it, Milnes rebuilt the flood-damaged complex and repaired buildings in the town.

The SILMM Company barely survived the Panic of 1873, when overbuilding of railroads caused the price of pig iron to drop in half.[175] During the economic downturn, Milnes shuttered Furnace No. 1, but kept the other two furnaces in blast.[176] In 1875, he became the Shenandoah Valley Railroad Company's fifth president and invested $60,000 in its stock. When the tracks finally passed by SILMM Company's works in 1882, trains brought coal from southwest Virginia and shipped more than 600 tons of pig iron each week to fabricators of rail car wheels in Harrisburg and Wilmington.[177]

Another northerner joined the region's postwar iron industry. In 1870, Dr. Frank King moved from New York to northwestern Shenandoah County and purchased the 22-year-old, Van Buren Furnace near Paddy Run.[178] Failing to revive it, he built the larger hot-blast King Furnace nearby, which shipped high-tensile pig iron from the Woodstock depot of the Orange, Alexandria and Manassas Railroad to car wheel manufacturers in Wilmington and Philadelphia.[179] During the Depression of 1882-85, however, the furnace went out of blast and was never fired up again.

In 1868, Irishman Samuel Carson moved to Warren County and purchased limestone-laden land near the village of Riverton, along the North Fork of the Shenandoah River.[180] Carson Lime Company soon became the largest such business in the Northern Valley, annually selling 100,000 tons of crushed stone to road contractors. Heating it in kilns at temperatures above 1,515 degrees Fahrenheit, the company shipped barrels of burnt lime on the Orange, Alexandria and Manassas Railroad to manufacturers of chemical and agricultural products in Northern Virginia.[181]

Commercial activity resumed on Virginius Island near Harpers Ferry, but it never returned to the level achieved under the prewar ownership of industrialist Abraham Herr. After moving to Baltimore in 1867, he sold the island and adjacent water rights for $75,000 to Ohio industrialists Jonathan Child and John McCreight, who moved to Jefferson County.[182] Adding several partners, Child, McCreight & Co. repaired and leased many of the island's 28 buildings.[183] The four-story cotton factory was repurposed as the Child & McCreight gristmill, which annually converted 400,000 bushels of wheat kernels into 80,000 barrels of flour.[184] However, the 1870 Shenandoah River flood destroyed almost all manufacturing operations on Virginius Island, including the foundry, sawmill, carriage and machine shops.[185] The damaged gristmill survived, but after flour production dropped by two-thirds, it was sold in 1884 to Philadelphia businessmen.[186] Two more floods caused its closure five years later.[187]

During Reconstruction, some businessmen who purchased or started companies in the Northern Valley managed them from distant headquarters. In 1865, Washington, D.C. investors purchased the Potomac Mills cement factory in Shepherdstown, which the Union Army destroyed in 1862.[188] Their Potomac Mills Mining and Manufacturing Company spent $100,000 to rebuild the facility, then shipped cement down the C&O Canal for use in the Washington Monument and numerous federal buildings.[189] After the city suspended all construction in 1877 to institute building codes, Washington, D.C. businessman

H. H. Blunt acquired the Potomac Mills property.[190] Forty employees resumed daily production of 250 barrels of cement until 1889, when a flood closed shipping on the canal.[191] Increased competition from manufacturers of Portland cement—a slower drying, but more durable building material—led to the Shepherdstown factory's closure in 1901.[192]

In 1867, Philadelphia businessman Henry Hannis paid $25,000 for the war-damaged Nadenbousch Distillery in Martinsburg.[193] A few years earlier, Hannis Distilling Co. purchased Mount Vernon Distillery in Baltimore, but needed more capacity after heavily promoting its nationally known rye whiskey.[194] After Hannis rebuilt and expanded the Martinsburg facility, daily output from its copper and wood stills increased to 50 barrels.[195] Known as Hannisville, the complex included a gristmill, granary and a mill that ground Nova Scotia-sourced plaster into fertilizer applied to the company's nearby rye and corn fields.[196] With an in-house cooperage, Hannis Distilling added a warehouse that stored up to 12,000 barrels of whiskey.[197] When Hannis died in 1886, his company led the nation in the production of rye whiskey.

Hannisville Distillery in Martinsburg Advertisement by Brueker & Kessler Co., Philadelphia, PA

In the late 1860s, Joseph Hoyt noticed that the B&O shipped large volumes of chestnut oak bark from Paw Paw in western Morgan County. For his New York City-based manufacturer of leather belts, it made logistical sense to haul much lighter hides from Chicago's stockyards to a tannery located close to the tan bark's source.[198] In Paw Paw in 1869, Hoyt opened Vesuvius Tannery, named after the Italian volcano that was near numerous tanneries.[199] The facility benefited from the Potomac River's running water, nearby rail and canal shipping and a good climate for drying leather.

Copper prospectors returned to the region in 1866, when northern investors opened the Larkin Lake and Rose Hill copper mines in the Linden area of Warren County.[200] That same year, Stony Man Mining Company, organized in 1858, sold its 5,731 acres in the Blue Ridge to Miners Lode Copper Company from New York City, but copper in paying quantities was never found on the property.[201] In 1882, New York and Philadelphia businessmen formed Linden Virginia Copper Co., then promoted their nearby Ravenswood mine as, "So rich that one could walk in and pick up chunks of copper," but actual production proved much different.[202]

One out-of-area company tried to sell its Northern Valley property. In 1870, Lobdell Car Wheel Company in Wilmington, successor to the Bush & Lobdell Company, put its war-damaged Caroline Furnace in Fort Valley on the market.[203] It advertised the 6,000-acres as containing, "Iron ore of superior quality and limestone and wood in great abundance." [204] But the property had no takers; 90 years later, 400 of those acres became a Lutheran camp and retreat center.

Local Entrepreneurs Are Active in Region

Not all of the region's postwar entrepreneurs were outsiders. After serving in the Confederate Army, George W. Kurtz returned to Winchester in 1867 to work in John Kerr's cabinetmaking shop on the corner of Boscawen and Loudoun streets.[205] Three years later, he opened Kurtz Funeral and Furniture Store on Cameron Street, which became one of the largest undertaking businesses in the region.[206] Serving on Winchester City Council for 26 years, Kurtz was a member of the Handley Board of Trustees and helped establish Stonewall Cemetery as a final resting place for Confederate soldiers.

Born into slavery in 1841, Robert Orrick's master allowed him to establish Orrick's Livery Stables to board and rent out horses and wagons on Winchester's South Braddock Street.[207] In 1865, he became the first African American to receive a contract with the United States government to deliver mail twice a week to towns between Winchester and Leesburg.[208] In the 1880s, Orrick received another contract to deliver mail between Winchester and Romney.[209] He invested the profits in real estate and preached in several African American Methodist churches in the Winchester area. He donated construction material for the Orrick Chapel in Stephens City and set aside land for Orrick Cemetery on Winchester's Valley Avenue.[210]

In 1872, William Boyer, a gristmill, sawmill and general store owner from Strasburg, purchased several thousand acres that contained iron ore in the Powell Mountain area of Fort Valley. There he built Mine Run Furnace, which alternatively smelted ore extracted from two orebanks.[211] The area's manganese-rich ore improved the strength of Boyer's pig iron, which wagons hauled to the

Waterlick depot of the Orange, Alexandria and Manassas Railroad.[212] Iron from one orebank went to Pittsburgh for conversion into Bessemer steel, while iron smelted from the other one was shipped to the Lobdell Car Wheel Company in Wilmington.[213] One year after the Panic of 1873, Boyer shut down Mine Run Furnace because the railroad industry's over-building reduced demand for pig iron from both steel mills and rail car wheel manufacturers.[214] Operating the furnace intermittently, he put it and his recently opened manganese mines up for sale in 1880, and three years later, Powell's Fort Mining Company from Alexandria purchased them.[215]

Because John Wissler, resident owner of Columbia Furnace in western Shenandoah County, had lived in Lancaster for some time, he sided with the North during the Civil War. After his family relocated to Wissler's native Canada in 1862, the furnace's overseer watched Union troops burn it three times.[216] On their postwar return to Virginia, Wissler and son Franklin repaired and operated Columbia Furnace. It passed into Franklin's hands upon his father's death in 1870.[217] Two years earlier, Benjamin Pennybacker Newman inherited the nearby Liberty Furnace, which his father Walter built in 1821.[218] When his finances suffered after the Panic of 1873, the U.S. District Court ordered the furnace's sale.[219] Franklin Wissler was the buyer.

After the war, commerce resumed near the rebuilt Winchester and Potomac Railroad depot in Winchester. Because the W. B. Baker and Sons store was destroyed, William Baker's suppliers in Baltimore extended him credit to reopen the business on Cameron Street.[220] He later closed the retail store and concentrated on growing his Baker & Co. wholesale grocery business into one of the largest enterprises in Winchester. In 1872, he built a steam-powered flouring mill adjacent to the company's warehouse, along with a feed mill and a building that stored fertilizer.[221] Community leader Baker was a founder and president of both Winchester Gas Company and Shenandoah Valley National Bank.[222]

Not all Northern Valley bark ended up in tanning vats. After German Smith left war-torn Harpers Ferry in 1866, he opened a general store in Winchester, then started up German Smith Bark & Sumac Mill on the corner of Wolfe and Braddock streets.[223] He purchased sumac bark from local farmers, then ground it into a yellow powder known as quercitron.[224] Smith shipped the natural dye to textile mills north and east of Winchester.

Born into a tanning family in Germany, Fred Graichen came to Winchester from Baltimore in 1853 to start the F. A. Graichen Glove Company.[225] Located on East Boscawen Street, its 100-worker payroll grew to 300 after the Civil War.[226] Learning the business from his father, William Graichen started W. C. Graichen Glove Company on North Cameron Street, and within several decades, it was one of the nation's largest glove manufacturers.[227]

Postwar, local businessmen resumed production at several gristmills and textile mills and one opened a large distillery. Destroyed by Sheridan's troops in 1864, Willow Grove Mill near Luray was rebuilt, as was Kauffman's Mill on the South Fork of the Shenandoah River.[228] In 1870, Jacob Lantz's gristmill, along Stony Creek west of Edinburg, produced 1,600 barrels of flour, 112,000 pounds of rye chop, and 112,000 pounds of corn meal.[229] Near his family's hotel in Riverton, Thomas Kenner in 1877 constructed a wooden dam on the Shenandoah River that powered a new gristmill and sawmill.[230]

After service in the U.S. Army during the war, John W. Bishop opened a wholesale grocery business and gristmill in 1871 on Martinsburg's North Queen Street and grew the business into one of the largest in the region.[231] Bishop Flour Mill-branded flours and granular table meals were sold in neighboring states. With six buildings and a spur to the B&O line, Bishop advertised that his coal yard's capacity of 1,000 tons made it the largest in the Eastern Panhandle.[232]

In 1868, N. W. Yager built the four-story Page Woolen Mill beside his namesake springs, on the former Isabella Furnace's foundation near Luray.[233] His Page Woolen & Cotton Manufacturing Co. converted raw wool and cotton into imitation satin, blankets and yarn.[234] When it burned in 1880, the mill was one of Page County's largest employers.[235] In 1875, brothers-in law Ambrose Timberlake and Thomas Maslin purchased the 31-year old Valley Woolen Mills on Cedar Creek, near Middletown.[236] After they upgraded the equipment and replaced its water wheel with a more efficient turbine—a rotary machine with blades turned by flowing water—the mill produced hundreds of blankets and 350 yards of cassimere and kersey cloth per day, shipped by rail from Winchester.[237]

In 1870, Shenandoah County native Lycurgus Savage formed L. E. Savage's & Sons Distillery, also known as Kernstown Distillery.[238] Located several miles south of downtown Winchester, under son Joseph's ownership it became one of the region's largest producers of rye whiskey, marketed for its "purity, maturity and excellent tonic qualities." [239]

Newspapers During Reconstruction

After Federal troops destroyed the presses at the Winchester Republican and the Winchester Virginian in 1862, townspeople relied on rumors for their news.[240] Postwar newspapers were full of political commentary that included editorial support for programs to restart local economies. In 1865, several former Confederate soldiers published the Winchester Weekly News, at the same time the Winchester Times and the Shenandoah Herald in Woodstock rolled off the presses.[241] In 1867, James Clark founded the Page Valley Courier in Luray, and G. W. Murphy started the Shenandoah Valley newspaper in New Market.[242] Two years later, James Trout launched the Warren Sentinel in Front Royal.[243] In 1871, the Martinsburg Statesman and the Valley Star competed for readership in Berkeley County, but the Martinsburg Independent replaced the latter paper in 1875.[244] And the Gerrardstown Times circulated from 1870 until 1905 in the southern part of the county.[245]

Higher Education During Reconstruction

Because more students drove the need for teachers, normal schools were organized to train them in the North, then in the South. The normal name was derived from the notion that primary schools were expected to teach students norms, based on rules or standards.[246] While some young women matriculated at liberal arts colleges, many attended normal schools to become teachers.

Upon receiving a $10,000 matching grant from John Storer, a white abolitionist from Maine, Storer Normal School was founded in 1865 in Harpers Ferry to prepare African Americans to teach thousands of freedmen.[247] On a hill above the town, the federal government gave the school four mansions that executives at the U.S. Armory and Arsenal once used as residences and offices.[248] Opened in 1867 to all applicants, regardless of race or sex, Storer graduated 19 African Americans in its first class.[249]

In 1871, Shepherdstown's leaders leased Jefferson County's former government offices in the town, then obtained a charter for a classical and scientific institute.[250] The following year, the West Virginia legislature designated Shepherd College as one of the state's six normal schools.[251] In several years, the co-ed institution had 160 students, but without adequate financial support from the state for what it considered a high school, enrollments declined.[252] When its physical plant and curriculum were improved years later, Shepherd's mission as a teachers' college returned.

Mineral Springs Resorts During Reconstruction

Popular tourist destinations in the antebellum period, springs resorts were closed to the public during the Civil War. For patrons to return, it was important that the region's railroad tracks were returned to service. Several resorts expanded with larger hotels, while a new one opened in western Shenandoah County. In 1869, Baltimore investors paid $50,000 for the 300-room Berkeley Springs Hotel.[253] When refurbished for the nation's 1876 centennial celebration, it helped re-establish the town as a popular summer resort.

Northeast of Winchester, Jordan Springs Resort, which Union and Confederate armies used as a hospital during the war, reopened.[254] Soldiers from both sides rested in the Maryland House at the Orkney Springs Resort in western Shenandoah County. Afterwards, Confederate soldiers convalesced at the property, which J. M. Bradford & Co. purchased in 1867 from the Orkney Springs Company. Wilmington native Bradford and two local partners built the three-story Pennsylvania House and added the four-story, 175-room Virginia House in 1876.[255] It featured the nation's largest ballroom without pillar support.

A new resort opened not far from Orkney Springs. With the wartime deaths of Samuel and John Myers, their parents moved from Lancaster to the Alum Springs area near Henrietta Furnace, which the sons put out of blast before joining the Confederate Army.[256] Rather than operate the furnace, in 1870 Abraham and Fyanna Myers built the three-story, 100-room Shenandoah Alum Springs Hotel near it.[257] They hoped guests would be attracted to the alleged medicinal power of the water's aluminum sulfate. They advertised the resort as, "The nearest alum springs to Washington, Baltimore and the northern cities." [258]

After several ownership changes, Washington, D.C. investors in 1869 purchased Rock Enon Springs and Baths in western Frederick County.[259] They expanded the hotel to 450 rooms and added a large ballroom, a bowling alley and band pavilion. Before taking over as sole proprietor in 1874, partner A. S. Pratt marketed the resort's air-dry atmosphere and healing waters.[260] Guests paid an all-inclusive $2.50 per day, $9 to $14 per week or a monthly rate that ranged from $30 to $50.[261]

While the modest Warren White Sulphur Springs hotel in Warren County was not destroyed during the war, the Waterlick White Sulphur Springs hotel replaced it.[262] Washington and Baltimore patrons looking for a cure arrived at the Orange, Alexandria and Manassas Railroad's nearby Waterlick Station and either stayed there or took a stagecoach ride into Fort Valley for a respite at the reopened Seven Fountains Resort.[263]

CHAPTER 5

POST-RECONSTRUCTION TO WORLD WAR I

National Economy: Prospers from Inventions and New Industries

From 1880 to 1910—the Gilded Age—industrialization, immigration and creativity fueled America's unparalleled economic growth. During those three decades, the national wealth more than quadrupled, from $43.6 billion to $186.3 billion, while the population grew by 84 percent, from 50.2 million to 92.2 million.[1] Two-thirds of that growth resulted from larger families, a reflection of America's optimism about the future.[2] The balance came from 17 million immigrants looking to improve their economic well-being.[3]

High tariffs protected the nation's manufacturers, which also benefited from an abundant supply of natural resources that included iron ore, copper, coal and oil. A nationwide rail system, whose footprint expanded from 30,000 miles of track in 1860 to 254,000 miles in 1915, moved raw materials to factories and finished products to consumers.[4]

An explosion of new discoveries and inventions also powered the economy. While the U.S. Patent Office registered 12,926 utility patents in 1880, that number almost doubled to 24,656 in 1900.[5] Some caused creative destruction, a term that Austrian economist Joseph Shumpeter used years later to describe innovations in manufacturing, the development of new products and the startup of industries that made older ones obsolete.[6] Most notable was the automobile ending the horse and buggy era.[7]

Notwithstanding the Gilded Age's prosperity, all was not well in America. Its industry had become concentrated in the hands of owners of pools, trusts and holding companies that restricted competition.[8] The monopolies made those captains of industry extremely rich in the midst of abject poverty, as millions of southern and eastern European immigrants poured into United States cities.

While America moved rapidly toward industrialization and urbanization, farming remained a big business. An agricultural revolution shifted the sector's profile from small farms to large, commercial enterprises that took advantage of mechanization and economies of scale. Increased supplies of food put pressure on prices in the 1870 to 1900 period, but farm finances improved during the first decade of the twentieth century, when agricultural prices increased by almost 50 percent, and the value of rural property doubled.[9] That occurred because the United States population increased at a much faster rate than new acreage brought under cultivation.[10]

Along with the nation's economic growth came cyclical downturns. After a boom in railroad construction ended, the Depression of 1882-85 negatively affected the iron, steel and coal industries.[11] The more problematic Panic of 1893, the worst one since the nation's founding, resulted from another period of railroad over-building. During the downturn that followed, America's unemployment rate soared to an estimated 18 percent.[12] The Panic of 1907 occurred when the failure of New York City trust companies caused runs on bank deposits in other cities.[13] That led to the 1913 establishment of the Federal Reserve System to oversee monetary policy and hopefully provide economic stability for the nation.[14]

Internal Improvements: More Trains and Arrival of Electricity

To grow the economy after Reconstruction, the region needed to improve its rail and road networks and adopt the new technologies spreading across the nation. From 1860 to 1890, the railroad industry's southern footprint quadrupled, from 10,000 miles of track to more than 40,000 miles.[15] The Northern Valley participated in that expansion with the arrival of two railroads and the build-out of a third one.

In the early 1890s, privately owned electric and telephone companies strung lines on poles across the nation, including parts of the Northern Valley.

As their populations and commerce grew, municipalities paid more attention to upgrading water and sewer systems. With car ownership increasing after Henry Ford mass produced his Model T in 1913, politicians at the local, state and federal levels heard calls for better roads. Those that received government money under the Federal Highway Act of 1916 had to be made free of tolls.[16]

Railroads

By the outbreak of World War I, railroads that served the Northern Valley included the Baltimore and Ohio Railroad and its Valley Branch, the Southern Railway, the Norfolk and Western Railway and the Cumberland Valley Railroad. Commercial interests in Martinsburg, Winchester and several towns benefited when two lines competed for their business.

Shenandoah Valley Railroad

First proposed in 1867, the Shenandoah Valley Railroad changed Northern Valley commerce in several ways. When completed in 1882 between Hagerstown and Roanoke, it took some freight traffic away from the Orange, Alexandria and Manassas Railroad in Front Royal and ended gundalow traffic on the South Fork of the Shenandoah River. The railroad gave an economic boost to Page County. Big Gem Cast Iron Furnace and Deford Tannery were built there to take advantage of rail access to urban markets and to supplies of coal from southwest Virginia. The Shenandoah Valley Railroad's divisional headquarters was based in the town of Shenandoah Iron Works, located halfway between Hagerstown and Roanoke. Its Shenandoah Yard was also in the town. The large maintenance facility included machine shops, a roundhouse and coaling and watering stations for steam engines.[17]

The Shenandoah Valley Railroad also gave an economic lift to the Clarke County village of Boyceville, named after Col. Upton Boyce.[18] For the railroad to purchase land there, he sold $100,000 worth of its stock to local residents.[19] With stores and warehouses, the renamed Boyce became a commercial center with a freight depot that handled outbound shipments of wheat and flour and inbound deliveries of agricultural supplies.

Although its trains reached speeds of more than 90 miles an hour on some sections of track, the Shenandoah Valley Railroad's revenues from cargo originating in the Roanoke Valley and Lynchburg regions never met projections. Defaulting on its debt in the Depression of 1882-85, it was reorganized as the

Norfolk & Western Rail Yard, Shenandoah City
Photo from Town of Shenandoah, VA

Shenandoah Valley Railway.[20] In 1890, the Norfolk and Western Railway in Roanoke purchased it for $6 million worth of stock.[21]

Valley Railroad

When the Valley Railroad's track reached Lexington in 1883, it failed to connect with a Richmond and Alleghany Railroad branch line, which could have brought much-needed coal to the Northern Valley. In addition, the Shenandoah Valley Railroad's earlier arrival in Roanoke—55 miles south of Lexington—cut into its freight traffic, which meant the Valley Railroad never turned a profit.[22] As expected, the new line had a negative financial effect on the Valley Turnpike, which paralleled the road in many places. And its trains often blocked wagon traffic at rail crossings.

Baltimore and Ohio Railroad

After the B&O's Winchester and Strasburg Railroad passed one-half mile west of Stephens City in the 1870s, its freight depot there attracted numerous businesses.[23] Within two decades, the Stephens City Station's neighbors included M. J. Grove Lime Company, Stephens City Cooperage, Virginia Chemical Company, Stephens City Evaporating Company and Stephens City Milling Company.[24] Shenandoah Valley Cider and Vinegar Company in Winchester joined them later with an apple evaporating plant.[25]

When its freight traffic slowed in the Panic of 1893, the B&O struggled to service its heavy debt load.[26] The following year, the Southern Railway in Washington, D.C. gained control of the B&O's Orange, Alexandria and Manassas Railroad, which went from Alexandria to Front Royal and Strasburg.[27] With the B&O in receivership in 1896, the Southern Railway took over its Strasburg and Harrisonburg Railroad, which diverted some of the region's freight traffic from Baltimore to Alexandria.[28]

After a reorganization in 1898, the B&O's finances recovered.[29] However, the Winchester and Potomac Railroad, whose right-of-way the B&O leased, struggled financially due to competition from the Cumberland Valley Railroad in Winchester and the Southern Railway in Strasburg. When shareholders sold the line to the B&O in 1899, it became the new owner's Valley Branch, headquartered in Winchester.[30]

The B&O's roundhouse and maintenance buildings in Martinsburg remained in use as a locomotive service and repair facility. When its finances deteriorated in the mid-1890s, the B&O moved that work to Baltimore to save money. But after the reorganization, management found those shops were too small to serve the railroad's footprint, which had expanded to 3,000 miles of track.[31] In 1902, workers returned to the vacant Martinsburg buildings and resumed fabricating parts used to repair bridges, switches and rolling stock, east of the Ohio River.[32]

As its tracks stretched westward, the B&O needed space to break down and re-assemble freight trains traveling between the East Coast and the Midwest.[33] In 1890, it opened a rail yard in Brunswick, Maryland, a company town the B&O established near its main line, eight miles downriver from Harpers Ferry.[34] In 1913, it moved the contents of a shop that assembled coal cars from Martinsburg to Brunswick; one decade later, headquarters of the B&O's Valley Branch was relocated there from Winchester.[35]

Cumberland Valley Railroad

A victim of the Depression of 1882-85, the Martinsburg and Potomac Railroad Company ended up in foreclosure in 1887.[36] Next year, the Cumberland Valley Railroad Company, which had leased the line since its completion in 1873, purchased the railroad. From Hagerstown, its tracks connected to the Martinsburg and Potomac's line at Powell's Bend on the Potomac River. The Pennsylvania Railroad, which gained control of the Cumberland Valley

Railroad in the late 1850s, believed a 22-mile extension to Winchester would bring more Shenandoah Valley freight traffic to its main line.[37]

At the same time, business leaders in the Winchester area hoped the presence of a second railroad would keep the B&O's rates down and bring in coal from eastern Pennsylvania.[38] Most of the extension's $450,000 cost was paid for when Frederick County, along with Winchester citizens and other investors purchased Cumberland Valley's common stock.[39] After the Pennsylvania Railroad subscribed to the remaining shares, the tracks from Martinsburg reached Winchester in 1889.[40]

Cumberland Valley depots sprung up in Inwood; Clear Brook; at the corner of Welltown Road and the Valley Pike, north of Winchester; and on the city's Amherst Street, where a coal trestle was built. One of the busiest stops was the Inwood depot, where wheat, flour, tan bark and railroad ties were loaded onto Cumberland Valley trains.[41] The railroad's presence was a catalyst for construction of Inwood Park, where an annual fair was held from 1892 to 1913.[42] The depot later served an apple packing house and an apple slice canning plant.

Chesapeake and Ohio Canal

Post-Reconstruction, barges on the Chesapeake and Ohio Canal continued to haul coal from Western Maryland, as well as goods to and from the Northern Valley and Washington, D.C. But Potomac River floods that disrupted canal traffic in 1877 and 1886 severely strained the company's finances, as did competition from the B&O Railroad.[43] Another flood forced the C&O Canal Company into receivership in 1889. Its days of shipping goods ended when no repairs were made after the river flooded in 1924.[44]

Roads

The arrival of automobiles gave a new urgency to improving America's roads, including those in the Northern Valley. In 1906, a State Highway Commission replaced the Virginia Board of Public Works as overseer of the commonwealth's roads.[45] Four years later, the General Assembly sought to control motor vehicle speeds by setting them at a maximum 20 miles per hour in open country and eight miles per hour in towns, around curves and at key intersections.[46] In 1913, the West Virginia legislature created the State Road Bureau, soon renamed State Road Commission, to coordinate a road system that previously had been under the direct authority of county courts and their engineers.[47]

Electric Power Providers

After Thomas Edison invented the incandescent light bulb, he introduced the concept of generating and distributing electricity into homes, businesses and factories. With financial backers, he formed New York City-based Edison Electric Light Company in 1878, which became the prototype for similar power providers across America.[48] As the industry matured, the nation's consumption of electricity increased exponentially, from 6 billion kilowatt-hours in 1900 to 57 billion in 1920.[49] Households substituted electric bulbs for oil lamps and plugged new time-saving appliances into wall outlets. Factories switched their power source from coal-fired steam engines to electric motors.[50]

Martinsburg Power Company

In 1889, local businessmen organized the Edison Electric Illuminating Company of Martinsburg to provide power to homes and businesses.[51] It purchased the Schwartz flour mill on Tuscarora Creek and contracted with Edison Electric Light Company to convert it to a coal-burning electric generating station.[52] But the Panic of 1893 forced the new company into receivership.

Re-incorporated as Martinsburg Electric Light Company in 1896, the utility needed to increase capacity to serve Berkeley County's expanding industrial base of woolen mills, textile factories and limestone processors.[53] Management considered building a hydroelectric plant on the Potomac River, which required less labor to operate than a generating station and had no fuel cost.[54] In 1901, the renamed Martinsburg Power Company purchased the vacant Honeywood Paper Mill at Dam Number 5. Repurposed as a hydroelectric plant, its 1.2 megawatts of output were transmitted to the downtown station.[55]

When Martinsburg Power's management saw potential competition from Winchester Gas and Electric Light Co., it upgraded the Potomac River plant in 1906 and added capacity at the Martinsburg station.[56] Three years later, the utility spent $223,000 to build a 2-megawatt hydroelectric plant at Dam Number 4, eleven miles upstream from Shepherdstown.[57]

Other Eastern Panhandle Electric Companies

In 1899, Thomas Savery and several investors formed Harpers Ferry Electric Light & Power Co. to produce electricity at the Potomac Paper Mill.[58] Over-capacity in the paper industry had made it difficult for Savery & Company

*Martinsburg Power Company plant at Dam No. 4
on Potomac River, 1909
Photo from West Virginia and Regional History Collection,
WVU Libraries, Morgantown, WV*

to profit from its two pulp mills near Harpers Ferry. To make electricity, water power from the Potomac and Shenandoah rivers was diverted from the mills' wood grinding machines to new turbine-powered generators.[59] By 1913, Harpers Ferry Electric Light & Power was selling electricity to 305 customers in Harpers Ferry and in Brunswick, Maryland.[60]

In the Morgan County village of Great Cacapon, local investors organized the Hydro-Electric Developing Co. in 1909 with $100,000 of capital stock.[61] Next year, its successor, Great Cacapon Power Company, built a dam and hydroelectric plant on the Cacapon River, which generated 0.55 megawatt of electricity, transmitted to Berkeley Springs, Hancock and Martinsburg.[62] To serve the county's emerging silica sand industry, the company built a steam-powered electric plant in Berkeley Springs.[63]

Northern Virginia Power Company

By the early 1890s, Winchester businessmen were aware that the availability of electricity had drawn manufacturing enterprises to Martinsburg. In 1895, they raised $88,000, formed Winchester Gas and Electric Light Co. and acquired Winchester Gas Company, which had lit the city's street lamps since 1853.[64] The new company purchased a timber-crib dam on the Shenandoah

River that once powered a gristmill near Millville, four miles upstream from Harpers Ferry.[65] In 1906, the dam was replaced with a stone and Portland cement structure and a 0.55-megawatt hydroelectric plant was built next to it.[66]

Hoping to join the interurban railway craze sweeping the nation, the utility organized Winchester & Washington City Railway Co., with plans to build an electric rail line from Winchester over the Blue Ridge to Bluemont.[67] There it would connect with the Southern Railway-owned Washington and Old Dominion interurban line that originated in Leesburg.[68] Electric-powered trolley cars riding on tracks offered a cleaner alternative to the soot and cinders of coal-fired steam engines. In the early 1900s, several interurban companies received charters to connect towns within the Northern Valley, but the industry's prospects ended with the automobile's arrival.

After Winchester Gas and Electric Light doubled the Millville plant's capacity in 1909 to 1.1 megawatts, its transmission lines furnished power to Winchester, Hedgesville, Martinsburg, Charles Town, several villages in Jefferson County and to limestone quarries and kilns in the Eastern Panhandle.[69] To focus on electric power generation and distribution, the company abandoned its railway project. In 1913, it purchased Citizens Electric Light Company of Charles Town and Great Cacapon Power Company in Morgan County.[70] The following year, Winchester Gas and Electric Light spent $150,000 to raise the Millville dam's height from 12 feet to 21 feet. That doubled the plant's output to 2.2 megawatts of electricity.[71] The company also built a substation in Berryville and a reserve power plant in Winchester. To better reflect its expanded footprint, the name was changed to Northern Virginia Power Company.[72]

Other Electric Companies in Virginia Portion of the Region

Between 1891 and 1922, nine hydroelectric and steam-powered electric plants came on line to serve communities in Warren, Page and Shenandoah counties. After receiving a franchise from Front Royal in 1891, William Campbell organized Royal Light, Heat and Power Co., which built a small steam plant on Happy Creek that served several customers and lit the town's streetlights.[73] When the company took bankruptcy during the Panic of 1893, Front Royal operated the plant. Needing more capacity, the town purchased the wooden Kenner Dam at Riverton in 1904, reinforced it with concrete and built the Riverton Hydro Plant that served residents until 1930.[74] Between 1904 and 1906, five power companies were organized in Page County. Except for Shenandoah City's Steam Electric Power Plant, they built dams and hydroelectric plants on the South Fork of the Shenandoah River.

*Riverton Hydro Plant and Kenner Dam on Shenandoah River, 1905
Photo from Warren Heritage Society, Front Royal, VA*

In Shenandoah County, Dr. Joseph I. Triplett operated two hydroelectric plants. In 1893, he purchased the Old Rush's Mill at Burnshire Dam on the North Fork of the Shenandoah River.[75] After placing a turbine inside it in 1904, his Woodstock Electric Light & Power Co. furnished electricity to Woodstock and Edinburg.[76] When a 1917 fire destroyed a gristmill on Mill Creek near Mount Jackson, Triplett repurposed it as a hydroelectric plant to serve the town.[77]

Practicing medicine until 1881, Triplett was involved in many local businesses. His Shenandoah Farmers Milling Company built a gristmill on Mill Creek in 1872. He organized the Mount Jackson National Bank, ran a wholesale tobacco business, was an orchardist and operated a farmer's supply and hardware business.[78] In the early 1920s, he donated land and funds for the Triplett High and Vocational School in Mount Jackson.[79]

Telephone Providers

In 1877, American Bell Telephone Company brought the nation's first telephone exchange on line in New Haven, Connecticut.[80] Locally owned companies provided telephone service in parts of Frederick County, but following industry trends, in 1913 they were consolidated into Chesapeake and Potomac Telephone Company in Baltimore.[81] Two years later, that telecom provider acquired switchboards and lines in Berkeley and Jefferson counties.[82] Some Northern Valley companies had mutual in their names, which meant subscribers were also the owners. The Farmers Mutual Telephone System of Shenandoah County, which began operations in 1902 in Edinburg, was the region's only carrier that remained independent.[83] It was the forerunner of Shenandoah Telecommunications Company, later known as Shentel.

Water and Sewer Services

To recruit businesses and residents, municipalities needed a centralized water supply to replace privately owned artesian wells. In 1873, the newly formed Martinsburg Water Board built a brick plant along Tuscarora Creek to pump water from the Spring Run into the city.[84] After manufacturing surged in the 1890s, the board purchased Kilmer Springs in 1903 and built a more modern plant on Baltimore Street to move greater quantities of water through the city's pipes.[85]

In 1890, Winchester acquired and repurposed the Hollingsworth Mill to pump water from nearby Thatcher Springs into a network of pipes.[86] Former Winchester retailer Charles Rouss donated $30,000 toward the project.[87] The renamed Rouss Springs served as Winchester's main source for water until 1956, when it was piped in from the North Fork of the Shenandoah River.

Northern Valley Economy: Cities and Towns Look to Recruit Industry

By the start of World War I, the factories and mills in Martinsburg and Winchester meant the Industrial Revolution had finally arrived. The Martinsburg Board of Trade's success in recruiting manufacturers caused its population to jump by 69 percent, from 6,335 in 1880 to 10,698 in 1910.[88] During those three decades, Winchester's census grew by a more modest 18 percent, from 4,958 to 5,864.[89] Their combined populations increased from 10 percent of the region's total headcount in 1880 to 15.4 percent in 1910.[90] The region had become more urbanized.

Despite the jobs that new industries created, the Northern Valley's population rose by just 15 percent from 1880 to 1910, compared to the 84 percent increase the United States recorded.[91] With a population gain of 42 percent, Page County was the fastest growing county, due to the industrial activity that the Shenandoah Valley Railroad brought with it.[92] Not far behind was Morgan County's 36 percent increase, driven by growth in its sand mining and tourism industries.[93]

Efforts to Boost Local Economies

With production at the Northern Valley's gristmills, iron furnaces and tanneries in decline, civic leaders looked to expand the industrial base of their hometowns. Hoping to attract factories, jobs and residents, the region became engulfed in a wave of boosterism. In 1890, businessmen and real estate promoters organized improvement companies in Martinsburg and Winchester, and in 10 towns in the region. They also sprung up in cities in Virginia and other states.

The improvement company business model was raise funds by selling shares of its stock, then purchase a swath of land within a city or on the outskirts of a town. After subdividing the acreage, small lots were marketed to residential buyers and large tracts were offered to business and industry. The shares of stock were often sold to investors by subscription, which called for a small down payment, followed by monthly installments. However, a four-year depression that followed the Panic of 1893 dashed the hopes and finances of organizers and shareholders of most improvement companies. Those in Martinsburg and Charles Town attracted the most industry, but others either did not raise enough capital or failed to sell many building lots.

Improvement Companies in Eastern Panhandle

In the late 1880s, Martinsburg's leaders feared the B&O Railroad would close its maintenance shops and move work to a proposed rail yard in Brunswick, resulting in the loss of between 1,000 and 1,500 jobs.[94] In 1890, they organized the Martinsburg Mining, Manufacturing and Improvement Company to raise up to $1 million and use the funds to buy land and divide it into lots.[95] The leaders also formed the Martinsburg Board of Trade to recruit businesses and the Martinsburg Improvement, Building and Loan Association to finance them.[96] With those organizations in place, the city's infrastructure assets were promoted to industrial prospects. The B&O and Cumberland Valley railroads competed to provide businesses with shipping services to northern and mid-Atlantic urban markets. And the city's newly organized Edison Electric Illuminating Company offered factory owners the option of using electricity—less costly and more reliable than water and steam power—to run their equipment.

In 1891, Martinsburg Mining, Manufacturing and Improvement Company acquired 525 acres in the southwestern section of the city, laid out industrial lots and advertised them in the Northeast.[97] The lots were located in what became known as the Boomtown District.[98] Textile recruits included Middlesex Knitting Co. from Philadelphia, Kilbourn Knitting Machine Co. from New Jersey and Crawford Woolen Co. and Shenandoah Pants Co., whose owners were from New York.[99] With plenty of hardwood forests nearby, several companies that used wood as a raw material purchased lots in Martinsburg: Auburn Wagon Company, A. F. Kembler Picture Frames and Martinsburg Furniture Works.[100] Other recruits included Brooklyn Brass Manufacturing Co., Lock and Hardware Company and Martinsburg Cold Storage and Canning Company.[101]

Not all Martinsburg Improvement, Building and Loan Association investments and loans were profitable. The Martinsburg Street Railway Company, an interurban train that ran between the B&O and Cumberland Valley rail depots, went into receivership in 1895. After the Panic of 1893, loans totaling $80,000 made to Brooklyn Brass and the Auburn Wagon companies were not repaid; three years later, the association was declared insolvent.[102] Despite the financial challenges, activity in the Boomtown District made Martinsburg the Northern Valley's leading industrial center.

Four improvement companies were formed in Jefferson County, but only one was successful. In 1890, Roger Preston Chew and six local promoters received a charter for the Charles Town Mining, Manufacturing and Improvement Company.[103] A former Confederate officer, Chew was a state politician, real estate investor and son-in-law of John Augustine Washington II, owner of the family's Blakeley estate.[104] Just north of Charles Town, the improvement company purchased 850 acres from the Ranson family, laid out streets and lots and recruited industry. It built the four-story Hotel Powhatan, promoted as the area's premier accommodation, and a large headquarters building. A hub of industrial activity developed around a Belt Railroad that linked the Norfolk and Western, formerly the Shenandoah Valley Railroad, with the B&O's leased Winchester and Potomac line.[105]

A key recruit was A. D. Goetz Company, which made harnesses, collars and saddlery for riding horses, a sport that was gaining popularity in the region.[106] Operating as United States Harness Company during World War I, Goetz made those products for the U.S. Cavalry in Warren County.[107] Other new industry included Shenandoah Brass and Iron Works from New Jersey, which later became Powhatan Brass; A. H. Maxwell Garment Company; Elmer E. Beachley Saw and Planing Mill; and the John Farrin Boiler and Machine Shop.[108] Recruited from Pennsylvania, Vulcan Road Machine Company later manufactured steel truss bridges, several of which spanned waterways in the region.[109]

Despite its initial success, the Panic of 1893 forced the sale of the company's headquarters building to the Jefferson County Board of Education, and the Hotel Powhatan was repurposed into a girl's school in 1900.[110] Ten years later, residents voted to incorporate Ranson as a town, independent from Charles Town.

In 1890, promoters from Hagerstown and several states organized Antietam Manufacturing and Land Improvement Company, hoping to profit from increased rail traffic in Shenandoah Junction, six miles north of Charles Town.[111] Despite projections of two large steel factories, a hotel and a bustling town of 20,000, the group failed to raise enough capital to exercise options it had taken on 5,000 acres.[112] In 1891, both the Shepherdstown Mining, Manufacturing and Improvement Company and the Harpers Ferry Mining, Manufacturing and Improvement Company were formed, but neither became operational.

Improvement Companies in Virginia Portion of the Region

In 1890, the Strasburg Land and Improvement Company purchased land in its namesake town and subdivided it into five-acre lots.[113] Next year, it organized the Strasburg Stone and Earthenware Manufacturing Co. to produce pottery in a factory setting on East King Street.[114] After the business closed in 1909, the building was repurposed as a Southern Railway passenger and freight depot, which in 1970 became the Strasburg Museum.[115] Partnering with entrepreneur William H. Smith, the improvement company also built the Strasburg Steam Flouring Mills in 1891.[116] With a daily production of 160 barrels of Acme, Climax and Pilot flour, it was one of the largest gristmills in the Northern Valley. In 1894, the business was sold to W. B. Baker & Sons, the Winchester wholesale grocer that operated a steam-powered gristmill on North Cameron Street.[117]

Organized in 1890, Berryville Land and Improvement Company's signature project was the Greenway Court Hotel, located off Boom Road, near the Norfolk and Western tracks.[118] When the large Victorian structure was not built during the Panic of 1893, the improvement company shut down in the midst of stockholder lawsuits over sums still owed on their installment purchases of stock.[119] South of Winchester, Middletown Land and Improvement Company was capitalized with $1 million to develop iron properties and create New Middletown, a 292-acre industrial and commercial center, west of the village.[120] A carriage factory and cannery opened, but both businesses closed during the Panic of 1893 and local investors lost everything.[121]

The Front Royal and Riverton Improvement Company was formed in 1890 to develop land on each side of the Shenandoah River's two forks, giving prospective industry access to the Orange, Alexandria & Manassas and the Norfolk and Western railroads.[122] Fauquier County lawyer H. H. Downing served as president of the company, which hoped to sell $500,000 worth of stock, but raised only two-thirds of it.[123] The improvement company purchased 1,700 acres between the two towns, and subdivided them into manufacturing and residential building sites.[124] It secured leases on 15,000 acres near Riverton, claiming they held deposits of iron, copper, asbestos, fire clay, galena, manganese, slate and marble.[125] Options were taken on land in the Green Hill area of Front Royal, which supposedly held enough iron ore to run Pennsylvania furnaces for years.[126] The improvement company's promotional map highlighted the Twin Cities of Front Royal and Riverton. It also guaranteed that lots in the Boom areas would soon be worth 10 times their current value.[127]

The improvement company sought to recruit a variety of industries, but neglected to conduct due diligence on the only one that showed interest. It offered an incentive package to George Leicester, owner of a piano manufacturer, if he moved it from Westboro, Massachusetts, to Front Royal. The deal included donated land, $15,000 for construction of a factory and a $20,000 investment in his Leicester Piano Company.[128] The improvement company soon stopped work on the building, claiming Leicester falsely represented the profitability and financial condition of his enterprise. In fact, the Westboro factory had been dormant for 10 years. After a lawsuit, a judge agreed with the improvement company's claim of Leicester's false statements. Pianos were never made in Front Royal.[129]

Nevertheless, Front Royal and Riverton Improvement Company successfully competed with Middletown Land and Improvement Company in attracting a boys' preparatory school.[130] It offered the Baltimore Conference of the United Methodist Church five acres in Front Royal, if it spent between $20,000 and $100,000 on a campus.[131] In 1892, Randolph Macon Academy moved into a $75,000 building, situated on a hill overlooking the town.[132] Two years later, the improvement company built cast iron bridges to speed commerce between Front Royal and Riverton, but it soon went into receivership, a victim of the Panic of 1893.

In 1890, locally-owned D. F. Kagey and Company formed Valley Land and Improvement Company in Luray, which offered 1,000 villa sites for sale to the public and free building lots to industry.[133] The prospectus claimed the private bank owned the Luray Inn, Luray Caverns, 2,500 acres of choice land and 8,000 acres with large deposits of iron and manganese ores.[134] But it turned out Kagey only held options on the properties and land. During the Panic of 1893, the Kagey and improvement companies became insolvent; speculators who purchased villa sites, at prices ranging from $900 to $1,500, saw them sold at auction for between $1.50 and $17 each.[135]

Although Page County had received an economic boost from the 1882 arrival of the Shenandoah Valley Railroad, promoters of two improvement companies projected additional prosperity for several small towns south of Luray. When Stanley Furnace and Land Improvement Company offered a limited number of lots for sale in 1890, investors from Baltimore and New York showed interest, but none was a buyer.[136] Thirteen miles to the south, Shenandoah Land and Improvement Company surveyed and laid out streets, produced a map and sold lots in Shenandoah City, formerly known as Shenandoah Iron Works. Because of its large Norfolk and Western rail yard, the town was promoted as the next Roanoke.[137] The improvement company built the Hotel Shenandoah in 1890, but after a fire damaged it, the building was repurposed as an apartment house.[138] Other structures were erected, but over time, floods and fires destroyed most of them.

With assistance from a wealthy Scranton, Pennsylvania, investor, Winchester's leaders threw their hats into the improvement company ring. In 1889, John Handley and his friend, local lawyer Major Holmes Conrad, organized the Equity Improvement Company of Winchester.[139] The former judge had profited from purchases of land near Scranton that contained large amounts of anthracite coal.[140] He also had invested in the successful Equity Improvement Company of Scranton, which owned coal and iron ore deposits.[141] In 1869, he organized and served as president of John Handley & Company, which two years later became Merchants and Mechanics Bank of Scranton. Near his residence on Scranton's Lackawanna Avenue, he owned the upscale Wyoming House hotel, named after a county located several miles northwest of Scranton.[142]

In 1883, Handley formed the Wyoming Manufacturing Company to mine coal in West Virginia's Kanawha County.[143] He invested $50,000, sold shares of company stock, then purchased land in Upper Creek, located along the Kanawha River and the Chesapeake and Ohio Railway.[144] The property included houses, stores, a saw mill, planning mill and coal tipple.[145] After laying out streets, he renamed the village Handley and took out leases on several hundred acres of land that held deposits of coal.[146] But Wyoming Manufacturing Company's finances suffered during the nation's Depression of 1882-1885, which negatively affected the coal, steel and railroad industries. It was sold in 1886 for several thousand dollars.[147]

The judge came to know the Winchester area through a former law partner who owned land in western Frederick County. In the Panic of 1873, Handley paid $1.25 for each of 1,375 acres near Taylor Furnace in the iron ore region of Mountain Falls.[148] One year later, he became the largest stockholder in Union Bank of Winchester.[149] Growing fond of the city in the late 1880s, Handley hoped to build a public park for its citizens to enjoy, but Holmes Conrad convinced him that a resort hotel would be more beneficial to the local economy, for it would attract wealthy patrons who might invest in the city.[150] Borrowing from his Scranton experience, Handley proposed that Winchester organize an improvement company to recruit industry, whose factories would be located along a belt railway that linked the tracks of the B&O's leased Winchester and Potomac line and the Cumberland Valley Railroad.[151]

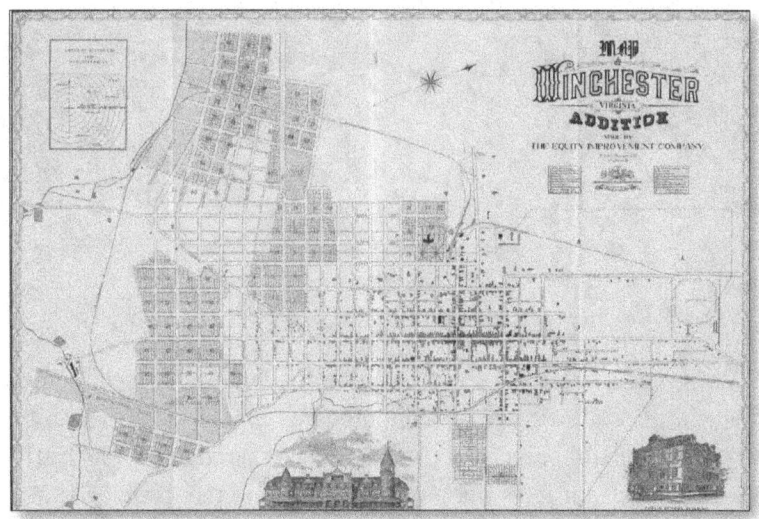

Equity Improvement Company of Winchester's proposed layout
Photo from prospectus in archives of Library of Virginia,
Richmond, VA

The Equity Improvement Company of Winchester was chartered in 1890 with an authorized capital of $1 million, which included a Handley investment of $50,000. The offering prospectus allowed investors to purchase $5,000 worth of stock, with a $250 payment made up front and the balance due in monthly installments.[152] When sales ended after subscriptions for $734,000 were taken, Handley pledged to raise the $266,000 balance by selling one of his Scranton properties.[153] The company purchased and subdivided 90 acres in Winchester's western and southern suburbs. It marked off streets and began construction of the Hotel Winchester, later known as the Winchester Inn, on a hill west of Stewart Street.[154] With an estimated cost of $100,000, it would offer 250 patrons fresh air views and medicinal water, presumably from the nearby Town Springs.[155] Completed in 1891 for $150,000, the inn's lavish appointments and furnishings surprised investors.[156]

Winchester Inn
Postcard published by A. W. Bailey & Co., Winchester, VA

When management dissention and cash shortages ensued, enthusiasm for Winchester's anticipated economic boom quickly faded. To raise more money, the Equity Improvement Company sued shareholders who had ceased making payments on their stock subscriptions, but the Panic of 1893 made collections problematic.[157] To satisfy liens against the Winchester Inn, it was sold at public auction to Holmes Conrad and a partner for $31,000.[158] Failing to attract any industry, company's directors closed the corporate books in

1899. The remaining land holdings were sold to pay debts and redeem shares of stock, and previous lawsuits against delinquent shareholders were dropped.

Two years after Handley's passing in 1895, the appraised value of his $900,000 estate in the Lackawanna County's Orphan's Court revealed that the Equity Improvement Company of Winchester had raised only $250,000 in cash from stock sales.[159] With no heirs, Handley's will left the City of Winchester $250,000 to build a library.[160] It was a time when Andrew Carnegie and other philanthropists financed construction of hundreds of them across America.[161] Handley Library opened in Winchester in 1913.

After bequests earmarked for several Scranton charities and individuals were disbursed, the remainder of his estate was set aside for two schools in Winchester. In 1923, Handley High School was built on former Equity Improvement Company land, and a school for African American children went up on the city's north end.[162] Handley's charitable interest in a city where he never resided may have been due to guilt from the failure of the Equity Improvement Company of Winchester. In addition, he had felt mistreated by Scranton officials. Despite his objections, in 1890 they paved Lackawanna Avenue near his Wyoming House and other properties, then raised their assessments to pay for the work.[163]

The ill-fated Winchester Inn stood empty until 1900, when a private school briefly occupied the building.[164] Reopened in 1911 as a summer hotel, it was auctioned four years later for $25,000. A renovated and updated Winchester Inn appeared in 1916, but the onset of World War I caused patronage to suffer. Sold the following year to Frederick Land Corp., the inn was torn down in 1918 and the surrounding acreage was subdivided into residential building lots.[165]

Agriculture: Farmers Switch to Orcharding and Dairying

Between the end of Reconstruction and 1900, the nation's over-production of foodstuffs kept prices low. In response, several Northern Valley farmers switched from wheat to orcharding, while a few that raised livestock exchanged beef cattle and hogs for cows, whose milk they delivered to dairies and creameries. Some farmers in the Page Valley and in Morgan County grew beans, tomatoes and other vegetables for canneries. To offset weak markets, fairs were held in Woodstock and Shepherdstown to promote farming. As the apple industry expanded, the Berkeley County Horticultural Society in 1909 sponsored an Apple Show and Apple Carnival in Martinsburg; 15 years later, the first Apple Blossom Festival was held in Winchester.[166]

Wheat Farming

Post-Reconstruction, Northern Valley farmers invested in expensive machinery to raise more wheat.[167] From 1.68 million bushels harvested in 1870, production increased by 37.5 percent to a decennial census record 2.31 million bushels in 1900.[168] But farmers in the Midwest and Great Plains also benefited from agriculture's mechanical revolution, using threshing machines that separated kernels from the plant and reapers that self-raked wheat into piles automatically bound with wire.[169] By the mid-1880s, the McCormick Harvesting Machine Company in Chicago was manufacturing 50,000 reapers per year.[170]

From 1870 to 1900, the nation's wheat production quadrupled, from 175 million bushels to 655 million bushels, while its population doubled, from 39 million citizens to 76 million.[171] That surplus of wheat also came at a time when Canada and Russia exported millions of bushels to Europe and South America, in competition with United States growers. The price of wheat, which averaged $1.17 a bushel from 1870 until the Panic of 1873, dropped to 71 cents during the Panic of 1893, then bottomed at just 66 cents in 1900.[172]

In the following decade, the nation's population grew at a faster rate than foodstuff production, which caused prices of agriculture commodities to increase. Wheat rebounded to $1.09 per bushel in 1909 and surged to $2.20 during World War I, when European men were fighting, not farming.[173] By then, however, decades of reduced profits from raising wheat had caused some Northern Valley farmers to engage in another agricultural pursuit: orcharding.

Orcharding

Apples were a staple food of settlers in the colonial period. Because Lord Fairfax liked the fruit, each of his land-grant recipients and tenants was required to plant 100 apple trees in the mid-1700s.[174] And George Washington made tenants plant small orchards to provide their families with apples, cider and brandy.[175] Large quantities of peaches were once grown in the Northern Valley, but spring frosts often killed blossoms that formed earlier than those on apple trees. With friendlier climates, California, South Carolina and Georgia became the nation's dominant peach growing states. Nevertheless, some of the region's orchardists did plant peach trees, whose fruit was picked at least one month earlier than apples.

Farmers have traditionally been a conservative lot when making changes to their business practices. In the early 1890s, those in the Northern Valley that experimented with orcharding first planted apple trees on their roughest and poorest fields. Discovering the blossoms needed protection from late spring frosts, they located the trees on hillsides, ridges and slopes, then waited six or seven years for the first harvest. Fruit not preserved through a drying or evaporating process was sent fresh to local merchants or pressed into liquids.

The region's first commercial orchards appeared in an area known as Apple Pie Ridge, which ran 15 miles through Berkeley and Frederick counties, west of the Valley Turnpike. The name originated when Quaker settlers made pies for their religious services held in the vicinity.[176] In 1851, William Smith Miller started a 16-acre nursery of apple, peach and plum trees on the ridge near Gerrardstown, southwest of Martinsburg.[177] When the Civil War interrupted sales, Miller turned his inventory of 4,000 apple trees and 2,500 peach trees into a 35-acre orchard.[178] In 1875, he sold it to a New York buyer for $17,000, a price that motivated some neighbors to enter the business.[179] Three years later, Miller's son John planted 50,000 apple trees in the same area. One of the largest orchards in the East, it produced 25,000 bushels in 1910.[180]

At the same time, Alexander Clohan became involved in several businesses within Berkeley County's apple industry. In 1906, he organized the Highland and Gold orchard companies, which owned 2,000 acres in the Gerrardstown area.[181] He was also a large stockholder in the Tomahawk, Cherry Run and Cherry Hill orchard companies in the northern part of the county. Clohan was president of both a farm implement dealer and a company that made wooden boxes to store and transport apples.[182] He led the West Virginia State Horticultural Society for nine years, and held numerous appointed offices in the state, including postmaster for Martinsburg.[183]

In the late 1870s, Dr. John Lupton planted 40 acres of Newtown Pippins on Apple Pie Ridge, several miles northwest of Winchester.[184] At the 1908 auction of his father's estate, S. Lucien paid $27,800 for what had become a 267-acre orchard.[185] To promote uniform grading and standard-size containers, he organized the five-state Eastern Fruit Growers Association in 1914.[186]

The unique sweet taste and rich red color of the Northern Valley's apples made them popular with consumers, both in America and abroad. The early 1880s introduction of refrigerated railcars and cargo ships, known as reefers,

Apple Picking near Martinsburg, postcard published by Ripple & Baker, Martinsburg

allowed orchardists such as John Thwaite to ship apples to the Eastern Seaboard for export. In 1876, he and his parents left Ohio and settled in the Apple Pie Ridge area of Frederick County.[187] Three years later, Thwaite planted 500 York and Baldwin apple trees and in 1888 harvested his first commercial crop.[188] After expanding the orchard, he became one of the area's largest exporters of York apples to England, which were popular, but difficult to grow there.[189]

In 1910, Thwaite organized and took a controlling interest in the Winchester-based Shenandoah Valley Apple Cider & Vinegar Co.[190] One of the founders of Winchester Cold Storage in 1917, he was also active in the cooperage industry and served as president of the Frederick County Fruit Growers Association.[191]

In the early 1900s, George Whitacre planted 40 acres of apple trees on the family farm near Cross Junction in western Frederick County.[192] Teamsters hauled barrels of York apples on the Winchester and Berkeley Springs Turnpike, present-day U.S. 522 North, to the B&O's Valley Branch depot in Winchester for eventual shipment to England.[193] With the addition of peach trees, the Whitacre orchard's footprint expanded to 350 acres.

In 1898, Henry W. Miller, another son of the Gerrardstown orchardist, formed Allegheny Orchard Co. and planted 500 acres of apple and peach trees near Paw Paw in western Morgan County.[194] When two brothers joined the company, the Miller family's footprint reached into nearby Hampshire and Allegany counties. Renamed Consolidated Orchard Co. in 1912, the B&O, whose tracks passed through Paw Paw, shipped apples from company's packing house to eastern ports for export.[195]

George and Henry Glaize cut timber in Frederick County forests and sold lumber at Glaize and Bros., founded in Winchester in 1854.[196] In 1910, George's grandsons Fred Jr. and Philip planted fruit trees on those clear-cut lands. Eleven years later, Fred L. Glaize & Co. packed apples in Winchester for the fresh market.[197] Active in the local business community, Fred Glaize had an ownership interest in Winchester Lumber Company, was a founding director of Virginia Woolen Company, an organizer of the George Washington Hotel Corporation, president of Virginia Apple Storage and a director of Shenandoah Valley National Bank. Glaize also served on the Winchester City Council for a number of years.[198]

While Winchester called itself the Apple Capital, orcharding soon expanded into nearby counties. Nineteen-year-old Harry Flood Byrd leased a Clarke County orchard in 1906, purchased another in 1912 and within 20 years owned one of the largest apple businesses in the nation.[199] The Strasburg Orchard & Produce Company began as a commercial orchard in 1907. Two-thirds of its apples went on Southern Railway reefers headed to New York and Boston for shipment to Glasgow and distribution throughout the British Isles.[200] From 1900 to the 1950s, the Blue Ridge Mountains in eastern Warren County were home to 25 orchards, whose apples left Southern Railway depots in Linden and Markham, bound for Alexandria. Taking advantage of a favorable climate on the hillside of Blue Mountain, Benjamin Lacy's family grew Freezeland Orchard's footprint from its first planting in 1906 to 20,000 apple trees on 800 acres.[201]

After selling the struggling Winchester Paper Company in 1888, Franklin Wissler sought better returns from the fruit industry. Five years later, he purchased the Strathmore estate in the Mount Jackson area near Meem's Bottom, a stretch of productive land along the North Fork of the Shenandoah River.[202] Wissler turned the property into apple and peach orchards and to access them, he built the Meem's Bottom Covered Bridge.[203] In 1911, heirs sold his 400 acres of fruit trees to a New York businessman for $150,000 or $375 per acre, a record price for Shenandoah Valley orchard property.[204]

The 1890 to World War I period was a profitable time for the region's orchardists; fresh apples were exported duty-free to Great Britain and culls and drops went to two processing plants. During that time, out-of-town con artists offered the public the opportunity to benefit from the industry's presumed riches. They purchased large tracts of land unsuitable for apples and subdivided them into 10- and 20-acre lots that were sold to would-be orchardists for $300 to $500 an acre.[205] Without proper care, the trees never bore fruit.

Raising Livestock

The region's livestock farmers continued to face competitive headwinds from Midwest farmers and Great Plains ranchers who sent their cattle to Chicago meatpackers. In the 1870s, Gustavus Swift financed development of a boxcar that was refrigerated by circulating fresh air over a combination of salt and ice.[206] By the turn of the century, 68,000 reefers had been integrated into the rolling stock of America's railroads.[207] Swift Bros. & Company used them to ship freshly processed meat to the East Coast at less expense than stuffing live animals in boxcars. In eastern cities, the company assembled networks of refrigerated warehouses and salesforces that introduced its meats to local butchers.[208] Swift also began a national advertising campaign to convince the public that meat not slaughtered locally was safe to eat.[209] By 1900, its meatpacking plants and those in other midwestern cities processed more than three-quarters of the beef and pork consumed in the United States.[210]

When the census of beef cattle rose more rapidly than the nation's population, the oversupply allowed midwestern meatpackers to pay low prices to Great Plains cattle ranchers. That pressured prices in East Coast cities, where Northern Valley farmers sent their livestock. While cattle sold for $6.47 per hundred-weight in 1870, the price fell to $3.16 in 1886, the end of a four-year national depression, during which cash-strapped consumers put less-expensive protein into their daily diets.[211]

At the turn of the twentieth century, several large woolen mills opened in Martinsburg and Winchester. To supply them with raw wool, some Shenandoah Valley farmers grazed sheep on their less productive land, and their numbers increased from 50,000 in 1870 to 120,000 in 1900.[212] As the region's woolen industry expanded, however, the mills sourced much larger quantities of wool from the western United States and Australia.

Dairying

To provide milk to the masses crowding into American cities in the 1880s, it became necessary to increase production, make the liquid safe to drink and transport it, without spoilage, from farms to distant dining room tables. In the late 1800s, pasteurization solved the safety issue by eliminating bacteria-based diseases prevalent in milk.[213] Farmers no longer sold raw milk directly to consumers, but sent it to commercial dairies to be pasteurized, bottled and shipped in reefers to urban markets.

With low prices received for beef cattle and hogs, some Northern Valley livestock farmers switched to dairying, which caused the census of cows to increase from 17,768 in 1870 to 26,060 in 1910.[214] And due to better disease control, breeding and genetic selection techniques, the average yield per cow increased by 40 percent.[215] From a few thousand pounds in 1870, milk production in the Shenandoah Valley skyrocketed to more than 13 million pounds in 1890.[216]

Warehousing: Apples Go into Cold Storage

When railroads arrived in the 1830s, the region's first warehouses were built near freight depots. They held cargo waiting for shipment and temporarily stored inbound goods destined for wholesalers, local merchants and itinerant salesmen. The next group of warehouses were cork-insulated, cold storage buildings that served the local apple industry. The air inside was kept at a high humidity level and ammonia—a chemical that absorbed heat—maintained a temperature of 32 degrees. Some cold storage companies engaged in a related business, the manufacture of ice.

By placing apples in cold storage, orchardists gained greater marketing flexibility. Rather than receive depressed prices when apples were dumped on the market at harvest time, storing them enabled growers to better match supply with demand. As a result, their apples were sold at higher prices over a longer period of time, often into late January or early February. And apple processors put the fruit in cold storage until needed on the production line.

Charles Lee Robinson, owner of a Fairmont, West Virginia, ice and coal business, saw a business opportunity in the Northern Valley's burgeoning apple industry. In 1901, he purchased W. H. Palmer's ice plant on Winchester's North Cameron Street, near the B&O's Valley Branch tracks.[217] Four years later, his C. L. Robinson Ice and Cold Storage Corporation built a warehouse nearby that stored up to 20,000 barrels of apples.[218] In 1908, the company added a 25,000-barrel facility in Charles Town, then doubled its capacity.[219] To ensure that the cold storage buildings would be filled, Robinson formed his namesake orchard company in 1910, which later owned 1,200 acres of fruit trees in Frederick and Jefferson counties.[220]

Diversifying his business interests, Robinson purchased Winchester Steam Laundry on North Kent Street in 1907. Three years later, he bought the Snapp Foundry on Winchester's North Cameron Street, near the B&O freight depot. Originally located on flood-prone Virginius Island near Harpers Ferry, the business fabricated steel items and gray iron castings that were shipped throughout the East, and repaired equipment for local industry.[221] The Snapp business soon made the electric-driven Robinson Power Ice Saw, marketed to ice plants through trade journals.[222]

In 1897, Ohio lawyer C. P. Rothwell, along with John Lovett and several other Martinsburg businessmen, organized Rothwell Lovett Company.[223] Near the B&O tracks in Martinsburg, it opened an apple storage and ice plant, then added orchards, a cider mill and a fruit packing operation to the enterprise.[224] Rothwell bought out the other investors in 1905. Five years later, the renamed Rothwell & Co.'s retail business was split off as Martinsburg Ice & Coal Co.[225] In 1913, Rothwell's son James doubled the size of the cold storage and ice plant complex in Martinsburg.[226] Within two years, Rothwell & Co. operated an apple buying and export business in New York City, and owned cold storage facilities in Charlottesville and Staunton and in Frederick, Maryland.[227]

In 1911, Mannington, West Virginia, businessman Fred Bartlett and several partners formed Morgan County Cold Storage Company to tap into that area's expanding apple industry.[228] They built a $100,000, four-story warehouse in Berkeley Springs that held 40,000 barrels of apples.[229] In 1916, the partners sold it to local merchant and hotelier George Biser, who re-sold it two years later to Pittsburgh businessmen.[230] In the 1990s, the Morgan Arts Council repurposed the cold storage building as a visual and performing arts venue.

Manufacturing: Industry Arrives in Urban Centers

In the late 1880s, most Northern Valley manufacturing was still scattered throughout the countryside and the pig iron and tanning industries were in decline. Within three decades, however, apple vinegar plants, woolen mills and textile factories had opened in Martinsburg and Winchester. Other industries in those cities and in and near the region's towns included brick, woodworking, cigar rolling and glove factories, strawboard and pulp mills and cooperages, canneries, bakeries, dairies and creameries. Growth in the region's manufacturing sector benefited from several trends in agriculture. Improvements in crop management and animal husbandry, along with more productive machinery, allowed labor to leave the farm and find employment in an urban setting. And reduced profits caused some farmers to work part time on the farm and full time in a factory.

Gristmills

Between 1870 and 1900, a 37.5 percent increase in the Northern Valley's annual wheat harvest failed to translate into more business for millers.[231] In the decade after Reconstruction, much of the region's wheat went to large gristmills in Baltimore, which paid more for the commodity than local millers could afford to offer. By the late 1880s, however, the nation's flour center had moved from Baltimore to St. Louis and Minneapolis. Flour shipments from the latter city increased from 1 million barrels in 1876 to 10 million in 1894, with much of it sent by rail to the East Coast.[232] With 20 large gristmills, Minneapolis billed itself as the Milling Capital of the World.[233]

While most Northern Valley gristmills were water-powered, newer ones in urban areas ran on steam or when it became available, electricity. To stay competitive, millers with the financial resources replaced their burr millstones with faster and more efficient roller systems.[234] Rather than crush grain between stones, rollers ground it multiple times into finer, whiter flour that brought millers one or two dollars more per barrel.[235] The cylindrical metal rollers could turn 90,000 bushels of wheat into 20,000 barrels of flour, a four and one-half-to-one ratio compared to the six-to-one ratio of millstones.[236] They also required less space and power, were easier to operate and the miller was spared from grinding down a millstone's grooves every two years.[237]

The roller system's white flour was sold to consumers as family flour for home baking.[238] Northern Valley millers packaged it in five- to 12-pound bags that were shipped by rail to food distributors in Washington and Baltimore.[239] Brand names were used to differentiate each miller's flour from the competition. Lantz Roller Mill Co., on Stony Creek west of Edinburg, marketed six-pound bags of Lilly White, Choice Family Flour.[240] Bishop Flour Mills in Martinsburg sold its flour products under the Pride of Berkeley Cream of Wheat and the Gold Dust brands.[241]

Four gristmills in Page County ground wheat from a local harvest that had increased by 41 percent, from 123,000 bushels in 1880 to 174,000 bushels in 1910.[242] Willow Grove Mill near Luray sold its Lilly White and Dutch Girl soft flour as, "Made from selected VA. Valley wheat." [243] Page Milling Co. turned out Luray Pancake and Buckwheat Flour, while Foltz Milling Co. in Stanley marketed its 12-pound bag of Skyline Flour as, "Milled near the famous Skyline Drive in Ole Virginia." [244] Nine miles to the south, Shenandoah Milling Company made self-rising flour, marketed under the Stonewall Jackson, Shenandoah and Robert E. Lee names.[245]

Foltz Milling Company Flour Sack, Town of Stanley
Image of item advertised on eBay

Following the 1914-15 recession, Winchester businessmen Lewis F. Cooper and Shirley Carter paid $40,000 at auction for W. B. Baker & Sons gristmill, elevator and warehouse on Winchester's North Cameron Street.[246] Converting the roller mill's power from steam to electricity, their Winchester Milling Corporation produced 250 barrels a day of self-rising, Supreme Quality Flour and Crystal Corn Meal.[247]

Lewis Cooper was one of several Winchester entrepreneurs involved in multiple businesses in the first part of the twentieth century. A partner in the wholesale grocery firm of Cooper Brothers, he formed Cooper Merchandise and Oil Company after his two siblings left the business.[248] He was one of the organizers of Winchester Gas and Electric Light Co., and an officer and board member of Berkeley Woolen Company, Shenandoah Valley National Bank, Colonial Brick Company and two building and loan companies.[249]

By the early 1900s, Northern Valley millers opting not to invest in roller systems used their mills to turn marl limestone into fertilizer, or to grind rye for their distilleries or corn for animal feed. Some owners of water-powered mills installed turbines to generate electricity sold to neighboring towns. They included the John Funk Mill on Tumbling Run in Fishers Hill; Whissen's Mill on Stony Creek, west of Edinburg; Zirkle's Mill and Manor's

Mill, both located on the North Fork of the Shenandoah River, west of New Market; and Old Rush's Mill on the same river, east of Woodstock.

Iron Furnaces

Before the Civil War, owners of charcoal-fired, cold-blast furnaces in the Northern Valley prospered from sales of high tensile pig iron to manufacturers of railroad car wheels. During Reconstruction, those buyers purchased stronger, more durable steel from Pittsburgh's mills.[250] By the mid-1890s, all the region's furnaces had ceased smelting pig iron.

In 1883, William Boyer sold Mine Run Furnace in Fort Valley to Powell's Fort Mining Company in Alexandria, which closed it one decade later.[251] Also in 1883, a Philadelphia businessman purchased the nearby Elizabeth Furnace, rebuilt and renamed it Locust Grove Furnace, then shut it down five years later.[252] After the National Forest Service in 1913 acquired the furnace and 1,200 surrounding acres, they became the Elizabeth Furnace Recreation Area within George Washington National Forest.[253]

Two large, coke-fired, hot-blast furnaces gave Northern Valley leaders hope for a resurgence in the local industry's fortunes. Twice the height of a charcoal-fired furnace, the Big Gem Cast Iron Furnace and a second Liberty Furnace went into blast in 1883 and 1891, respectively. They burned a mixture of coke and charcoal that produced three to five times more pig iron per day than cold-blast, charcoal-fired furnaces.[254] And by adding coke, it cost $10.25 to smelt one ton of pig iron, compared to $16 with only charcoal.[255]

In 1882, the Shenandoah Valley Railroad's tracks finally reached Shenandoah Iron, Lumber, Mining and Manufacturing (SILMM) Company, 18 miles south of Luray. With access to southwestern Virginia coke now assured, William Milnes Jr. and his partners looked to build a larger, more modern furnace than the company's two that remained in blast. To finance it, they borrowed $800,000 from Philadelphia businessmen who were familiar with the iron business.[256] Milnes closed Catherine Furnace and brought Big Gem Cast Iron Furnace on line.[257] With towering smokestacks, the 70-foot-tall structure was equipped with huge boilers and stoves that supplied its bellows with hot air to make charcoal and coke burn hotter.[258] In late 1883, Furnace No. 2 in Rockingham County, the last of the company's older furnaces, went out of blast.[259]

Big Gem Iron Furnace, Town of Shenandoah, VA
Photo from Irvin Judd Jr. collection, Shenandoah, VA

The SILMM Company's several orebanks supplied Big Gem with ore. The Norfolk and Western Railroad hauled coke from the Bluestone Flat Top-Pocahontas Coalfield to Roanoke for transfer to the Shenandoah Valley Railroad, which made final delivery to Big Gem. Four hundred workers smelted 250-pound blooms of pig iron, shipped by rail to Baltimore, Wilmington, Harrisburg and other cities for fabrication into finished products that included locomotive parts, church bells and iron hoops.[260] Big Gem's daily output of 70 to 80 tons made it the fourth most productive furnace in Virginia.[261] Sparks from its red-hot cinders that poured down the river bank lit up the area at night and created a popular tourist attraction.[262]

When pig iron prices dropped by one-third during the Depression of 1882-85, the good times ended for William Milnes and his partners.[263] He shut down Big Gem in 1884, the same year the town of Shenandoah Iron Works was renamed Milnes.[264] Meanwhile, the SILMM Company continued mining and selling iron ore to other furnaces. After defaulting on its debt in 1886, the company was placed in receivership. The U.S. District Court sold it for $100,000 to the superintendent of the Shenandoah Valley Railroad.[265] Upon Milnes' passing in 1889, the town was renamed Shenandoah City.

Big Gem Cast Iron Furnace operated intermittently until 1899, when the Empire Steel & Iron Company in New York City purchased the renamed Shenandoah Furnace Company for $85,000.[266] Two years later, Allegheny Ore and Iron Company from Clifton Forge acquired the business as part of its strategy to combine several Virginia furnaces to gain efficiencies of scale.[267]

However, the price of bar iron remained low in the early 1900s. In 1907, Lukens Iron & Steel Company in Pennsylvania purchased Allegheny Ore & Iron Company, including its Page County furnace.[268] Lukens soon discontinued operation of Big Gem due to the bursting of its smoke stack and competition from much larger steel furnaces.[269]

The charcoal-fired Liberty and Columbia furnaces in western Shenandoah County, which Franklin Wissler owned since 1873, also changed hands several times. Their 300 workers annually produced 3,000 tons of iron, shipped to manufacturers of railroad car wheels in Pittsburgh, Baltimore and Richmond.[270] When those companies substituted more durable steel for pig iron, Wissler sold Columbia and Liberty furnaces and 1,800 nearby acres in 1883 for $260,000 to Samuel Merrick in Philadelphia.[271] He then moved to Winchester to enter the more promising strawboard business.

When newly formed Columbia-Liberty Iron Company ended up in receivership in 1891, Philadelphia businessman H. H. Yard purchased it at auction.[272] He shuttered Columbia Furnace, changed the corporate name to Liberty Iron Company and replaced cold-blast Liberty Furnace with a larger, hot-blast one that burned a mixture of coke and charcoal.[273] Davis Coke and Coal Company in Tucker County, West Virginia, shipped coke by rail to the Southern Railway depot in Edinburg.[274] Rather than move coke and iron bars over an unreliable wagon road, Yard had 11 miles of narrow-gauge track built from Edinburg to Liberty Furnace.[275] However, the dinky railroad made more money hauling timber and tan bark than the furnace did smelting iron.[276] It also held a U.S. Postal Service contract to haul mail to the village of Columbia Furnace.[277]

After the Panic of 1893 and ownership changes among Philadelphia investors, Liberty Iron Company was reorganized as Shenandoah Iron & Coal Company in 1905. Faced with operational problems and low prices for pig iron, Liberty Furnace closed two years later, ending almost 150 years of pig iron production in the Northern Valley.[278] The federal government purchased most of the company's land in 1911 for eventual inclusion in the George Washington National Forest. Losing business to gasoline-powered trucks traveling over improved roads, the dinky railroad stopped running in 1917.[279]

Tanneries

Between 1880 and 1900, the number of tanneries in the United States declined by four-fifths, from 7,569 to 1,306.[280] The owners of smaller ones either left the business or sold out to larger tanneries that cut costs with labor-saving machinery.[281] In the late 1890s, a blight introduced from Asia struck chestnut oak trees that provided the Northern Valley's leather producers with much of their tan bark.[282] By 1899, three of the five tanneries had closed, and within 30 years, all chestnut oak trees had been destroyed.[283]

In 1887, Loring Cover joined his father at the Star Tannery, which had produced leather in southwestern Frederick County since 1868. Thomas Cover & Son expanded the business to include Snowflake Tannery in Giles County, Virginia, and three tanneries in the Potomac Highlands of West Virginia: Lost City Tannery near Wardensville, Potomac Tannery in Moorefield and Capon Bridge Tannery.[284] The Covers shipped leather to the Baltimore and Philadelphia tannage markets, where wholesalers sold it under the Baltimore Star, Capon and Snowflake brands.[285] After exhausting the supply of bark in the Cedar Creek Valley, they closed Star Tannery in 1895, but kept the others operating.[286]

Although the Covers faced increased competition, they rejected an offer from United States Leather Company to join the trust and fix prices. Instead, they formed the Cover, Drayton & Leonard partnership in 1899 with two leather wholesalers in Philadelphia.[287] Six years later, the partners sold the business to the Leather Trust, which folded it into the Union Tanning Company in New York City.[288]

Another Cover family continued producing leather in Warren County. By 1885, however, Franklin Cover had bought out his two brothers' interests in Cover Brothers Tannery, founded in 1874 on Gooney Creek near Browntown.[289] The renamed Mount Vernon Tannery continued shipping leather to Baltimore wholesalers, but when the blight hit the chestnut oak trees in the Blue Ridge Mountains, Franklin Cover closed the tannery in 1899.[290]

In 1823, Baltimore industrialist Benjamin Deford started Deford Leather Company, which became one of the nation's leading producers of oak-tanned leather.[291] After his passing in 1870, sons B. F. and Thomas took over the business, which included tanneries in Frederick, Maryland, and Covington, Virginia.[292] When the Shenandoah Valley Railroad came through Luray in 1882, the brothers built Virginia Oak Tannery on the Hawksbill Creek site of the former Borst Tannery.[293] Employees turned steer hides sourced from midwestern meatpackers into leather used in shoe soles, straps and gun holsters. As the business grew, the Defords purchased parcels of forested land in Page, Madison and Shenandoah counties to provide the tannery with larger quantities of chestnut oak bark.²⁹⁴ By the 1890s, Virginia Oak's 250 workers processed 1,800 hides daily, which made it the largest tannery in the United States.²⁹⁵

Deford Company's Virginia Oak Tannery, Luray
Photo provided by Dan Vaughn, author of Luray
and Page County Revisited, Luray, VA

In the early 1880s, Deford Leather Company acquired First National Tannery on Warm Springs Run in Berkeley Springs.²⁹⁶ Its chestnut oak bark came from nearby Great Cacapon Mountain and the Tonoloway Ridge. In 1888, the B&O's new Berkeley Springs and Potomac Railroad brought hides to the Deford tannery and shipped to Baltimore leather that won first place at the 1886 World Exposition in New Orleans.²⁹⁷

By the end of the decade, the Berkeley Springs complex included bark sheds and a 103-foot brick chimney. However, its pungent odors offended hotel guests during a time when the town experienced a resurgence in tourism.²⁹⁸ After the tannery encountered legal problems from polluting Warm Springs Run, the Defords closed it in 1893; five years later, the vacant buildings burned down.²⁹⁹ Fifteen miles southwest of Berkeley Springs, the vats at Vesuvius Tannery in Paw Paw were filled with hides. Opened in 1869, its 100 employees continued to make belt leather.³⁰⁰

Leather Glove Manufacturing

Although most leather produced in the Northern Valley was shipped to Baltimore wholesalers, some went to Winchester's three glove factories that utilized a putting-out system. Leather was cut into various glove sizes and styles that were then delivered to women who sewed them in their homes. The finished gloves were returned to the factory for inspection, packaging and shipping.[301] In 1853, Frederick Graichen opened Winchester's first glove factory, which he ran on Boscawen Street until 1890.[302]

After the Civil War, the city became home to two other glove manufacturers, which benefited from their access to large quantities of soft sheepskin, goat and calf leather. D. H. Anderson and Son, successor to the business his father Morgan started, made gloves on South Loudoun Street, while Frederick Graichen's son William opened W. C. Graichen Glove Company on North Cameron Street.[303] To control the quality of his gloves, Graichen opened a tannery in Winchester that finished leather to the company's specifications.[304] Successfully competing against less-expensive products, Graichen's 225 styles of gloves and mittens were sold in the East and Midwest and exported to Europe.[305]

After expanding into a multi-story building in Winchester, the company opened a factory in America's glove capital, Gloversville, New York, and a sales office in New York City.[306] By 1880, the Graichen payroll totaled 1,000 workers, and the 450 in Winchester made it one of the Northern Valley's largest employers. William Graichen and his father were leading citizens of Winchester, both having been elected as Republican mayors in a heavily Democratic city in the 1880s and 1890s.[307] William also served as a director of Farmers and Merchants National Bank and Virginia Woolen Company.[308] Upon his passing in 1915, the W. C. Graichen Glove Company was sold to local businessmen C. T. Owen and Charles Trenary.[309]

Textiles

Prior to the First World War, America's textile industry benefited from a rising population and the trend towards urban living. City dwellers required larger wardrobes to conduct their daily activities. In the 1880s, labor unrest and union activity spread from New England to New York, New Jersey and Pennsylvania. Owners of woolen and cotton mills and clothing factories looked to shift production to regions where labor was friendlier to management. Jurisdictions in the New South recruited them with financial incentives, promises of low wages and taxes and most importantly, no unions.

The availability of steam power and electricity in the early 1900s meant large textile factories could be located anywhere, including in the Northern

Valley's cities and towns. At the same time, family members in the struggling agriculture sector looked for steady paychecks. One hundred years after the Industrial Revolution arrived in America, textiles became the region's first industry to concentrate in its urban areas.

Martinsburg's Textile Industry

In 1890, the Martinsburg Board of Trade used the city's assets—available labor, electric power and rail access—to recruit owners of textile mills and factories that together employed thousands of workers. The first one to establish a presence in its Boom District was Boynton J. Hickman, owner of the Waterloo Hosiery Mill in Philadelphia.[310] In 1890, the Martinsburg Improvement, Loan and Building Association loaned him $14,000 and spent another $12,000 for construction of a men's sock factory, but he soon died.[311]

To fill the building, the Martinsburg Board of Trade turned to Charles Kilbourn, owner of Middlesex Knitting Company, a New Jersey manufacturer of men's hosiery.[312] The board raised $7,000 in equity capital and the association lent him $35,000, which he used to modify Hickman's factory and build one on the B&O line. Machines that Kilbourn's father invented wove seamless men's socks inside the nation's first textile factory to run on electricity.[313] After serving as Middlesex Knitting's treasurer for two years, lawyer John Mettler purchased the company in 1905.[314] With 660 employees, the renamed Interwoven Stocking Company billed itself as the largest manufacturer of men's socks in the world.[315] Made from cotton and worsted material, they were advertised as, "Light-weight, seamless ones that wear as well as heavy, clumsy ones." [316]

Interwoven Stocking Company mills in Martinsburg, 1920
Postcard published by Neff Novelty Co., Cumberland, MD

For 13 years, William Henry Crawford was a prominent leader in the Northern Valley's emerging textile sector. Gaining industry experience in

Rochester, New York, he started up Crawford Woolen Company in Martinsburg in 1891 to produce woolen and cashmere cloth.[317] Thirty-seven city residents donated land for his South Stephens Street factory, which by 1905 had tripled in size to 85 looms and 300 workers. Its cloth was sold to another business Crawford owned, Martinsburg Worsted and Cashmere Company, whose factories were in Martinsburg and Bunker Hill. He also held a financial interest in the local Shenandoah Pants Company and organized the Virginia Woolen Company in Winchester.[318]

Crawford Woolen Company mill in Martinsburg Postcard published by W. E. Holfheins & Co., Martinsburg, WV

Over-leveraged during the nation's 1914 financial crisis, Crawford ran into money problems and died, after which Martinsburg and Winchester businessmen paid $27,200 for Crawford Woolen Company, once valued at $250,000.[319] The reorganized Berkeley Woolen Company continued producing suiting and top coating cloth sold to apparel manufacturers.[320] After Crawford's Martinsburg Worsted and Cashmere Company went into receivership in 1914, citizens guaranteed a $35,000 loan to local industry executive Thomas Dunn, who purchased the business. Carding and spinning equipment were added at the renamed Dunn Woolen Company's mills in Martinsburg and Bunker Hill.[321] Born in Frederick County, Dunn had been general manager at the Jobe Mill in Brucetown, then held the same position for several years at Virginia Woolen in Winchester, before taking over management of Crawford Woolen in 1904.[322]

Three textile companies in Martinsburg produced trousers and skirts from locally sourced woolen cloth. In 1898, Charles Bert from Greencastle, Pennsylvania, started up Shenandoah Pants Company, whose 90 employees made 1,000 pairs of wool trousers a day.[323] Three years later, William Bert left his brother's business to launch Southern Merchant Tailoring Co., which produced Waldorf brand trousers from material that Martinsburg Worsted and Cashmere made.[324] Renamed Berkeley Manufacturing Co. in 1907, it specialized in ladies walking skirts and men's business suits, marketing them as, "Cheaper than those made by tailors." [325] With $300 borrowed on his life insurance policy, Martinsburg resident John Poland Sr. started up Perfection Garment Company in 1902 in a North Queen Street factory.[326] Traveling within a 200-mile radius of the city,

Poland took orders for women's skirts made from muslin and returned to cut material for the next day's production.[327]

Winchester's Textile Industry

Winchester's first woolen mill opened in 1891, after brothers C. A., Thomas and James Williams purchased the former Swartz Flouring Mill on Abrams Creek and moved equipment from their Stonewall Woolen Mills in eastern Jefferson County into it.[328] When the C. A. Williams & Bros. mill burned in 1896, they rebuilt it as the Winchester Woolen Mill.[329] Its capacity was doubled to 800 spindles and 16 looms in 1909. Eight years later, the brothers sold it to a Chicago company, with Winchester businessman Shirley Carter serving as treasurer of the local mill.[330] The descendant of Robert Carter and Nathaniel Burwell in Millwood, he played a key role in Winchester's industrial growth in the early 1900s.[331] He was a partner in the Hansbrough & Carter insurance and investment firm and Winchester Milling Corporation, and held directorships in Northern Virginia Power Company, National Fruit Product Company and the George Washington Hotel Corp.[332] Carter was also involved in non-profit organizations, including Winchester Memorial Hospital and Western State Hospital in Staunton.[333]

When labor-management issues heated up in the Philadelphia area, Lewis Jones relocated his women's cotton underwear and hosiery business to Winchester in 1895. With financial help from Albert Baker, son of wholesale grocer William Baker, the Lewis Jones Knitting Company opened a factory near the Winchester and Potomac Railroad's freight depot.[334] After the hosiery department was relocated to Woodstock in 1907, production on North Kent Street included men's cotton athletic underwear.[335]

In 1900, Winchester Woolen Mill faced a cross-town rival when William Crawford, the leader of Martinsburg textile industry, formed Virginia Woolen Company.[336] To build and equip a mill, he received financial help from the Shenandoah Valley National Bank and Hansbrough & Carter, which raised $25,000 from local businessmen. A city council desirous of bringing jobs to Winchester gave Virginia Woolen a five-year exemption from municipal taxes and a free supply of water.[337] With money in hand, Crawford purchased the former Shady Elm Woolen Factory in Bartonsville, several miles south of Winchester.[338] He moved its machinery into Virginia Woolen's new mill on North Kent Street, near the Lewis Jones Knitting Mill.

Thomas Dunn, at the time superintendent of Crawford Woolen Company's mill in Martinsburg, became general manager at Virginia Woolen Company, and received an equity stake in it.[339] A deal was struck to market its products through Crawford Woolen Company for six years for a 6 percent commission. With a payroll of 100 workers, Winchester's largest industrial complex burned in 1904, then was rebuilt and expanded.[340]

Five years later, Virginia Woolen's directors promoted an original investor, H. B. (Hollie) McCormac, to superintendent of the mill.[341] Born in the White Hall area of northern Frederick County, he worked in Philadelphia's woolen industry before taking the general manager job at Southern Merchant Tailoring in Martinsburg.[342] After Dunn left Virginia Woolen in 1914 to manage his Martinsburg and Bunker Hill mills, McCormac was promoted to general manager.[343] By the 1920s, he owned a controlling interest in Virginia Woolen Company.

Silk Mills

In the early part of the twentieth century, silk mills opened in Strasburg and Front Royal. In 1907, Fred Bertschinger, a member of a Swiss textile family, formed Strasburg Textile Manufacturing Company.[344] Its workers wove silk hammocks on 40 broad looms and 20 narrow looms, before producing material for parachutes during World War I.[345] When labor troubles began in 1913 at Schwarzenbach-Huber's silk mill in Union Hill, New Jersey, the Swiss company moved the machinery to Front Royal.[346] Its Royal Silk Mill made the fabric in the same building where piano manufacturing was to take place in the early 1890s.[347]

Ice Industry

For thousands of years, blocks of sawed ice used as a refrigerant came from frozen lakes, ponds and rivers. But with America's growing population and increased industrial activity, sewage pollution of waterways became a problem for natural ice companies. By 1900, manufactured ice had become the primary means of keeping food fresh. The number of plants making frozen water jumped from 200 in 1890 to 4,800 in 1920.[348] Using an ammonia compressing system, it took up to three days to produce one 300-pound block of ice. Some cold storage companies made ice as a natural extension of their primary business.

While most frozen water went into iceboxes in the home, some ended up in refrigerated boxcars. In the early 1900s, the Norfolk and Western Railroad, successor to the Shenandoah Valley Railroad, purchased ice from Front Royal

Ice and Storage Company, Luray Ice Company and Arctic Ice Company in Shenandoah City.[349] By the 1920s, however, the manufactured ice business had become a victim of creative destruction when America's households and industry substituted electric refrigerators for iceboxes. And mechanical refrigeration, combined with improved insulation, eventually replaced ice-based cooling systems in railroad cars.

Dairies and Creameries

After some Northern Valley livestock farmers switched from raising beef to milking cows, commercial dairies opened in the 1880s. They pasteurized and sold milk to the public and to creameries and ice cream factories. Creameries appeared in the Northern Valley after the Swedes invented a centrifugal cream separator that determined the exact butterfat content of milk and cream.[350] E. R. Thatcher and John V. Tavenner started a butter creamery in 1884 at the former Hollingsworth Woolen Mill in the Winchester area.[351] Five years later, Frederick County dairyman J. S. Haldeman opened Winchester Creamery on South Kent Street.[352] Using the J.S.H. brand, he processed milk into butter and cottage cheese in the city, made American cheese at a Stephens City branch and opened a retail outlet in Toms Brook.[353]

In 1909, E. C. Harnsburger made ice cream, butter and buttermilk in Luray Ice Company's former cold storage facility.[354] When his Luray Creamery's building burned in 1935, the business reopened as Blueridge Creamery.[355] In 1913, Jefferson Creamery in Kearneysville shipped milk in tank cars on the nearby B&O line. Five years later, Kearneysville Creamery took over the business, added a cheese line and sold condensed milk to ice cream factories in Hagerstown and Cumberland.[356] By World War I, however, refrigerated boxcars that brought butter and cheese from the Midwest, created competition for the region's dairy and creamery businesses.

Ice Cream Industry

Quakers brought their ice cream recipes from England to the colonies, and over the years, the homemade variety became a favorite American treat. In 1851, a Baltimore milk dealer invented a method of producing large quantities of ice cream in a factory setting.[357] In 1874, the ice cream soda was created and within several decades, soda fountains and ice cream parlors became popular gathering places.[358]

Using electric-powered freezers, several factories in the Northern Valley turned milk into ice cream, as did some bakeries. In 1903, A. W. Nicodemus & Sons made it in Woodstock, then added an artificial ice plant and cold storage building.[359] Seven years later, Chapin-Sachs Manufacturing Company in Washington, D.C., America's leading ice cream producer, purchased the business and built a larger facility in Woodstock. Each day, it turned 12,000 pounds of milk into what Chapin-Sachs advertised as the velvet kind of ice cream.[360]

In 1913, two ice cream factories opened in downtown Winchester: Jones Creamery on East Piccadilly Street and Jack Frost Ice Cream on South Braddock Street.[361] In 1919, Garber's Ice Cream, which began seven years earlier with a parlor in Moorefield, West Virginia, moved into the former location of Jones Creamery, which had relocated to Valley Avenue.[362] The Garber family's wholesale and retail ice cream business remained in downtown Winchester until 1939, when a larger factory opened near Front Royal Pike in Frederick County.[363]

Bakeries

Before 1900, only five percent of the bread consumed in America was made outside the home; by the First World War, 30 percent came from bakeries, including several in Martinsburg and Winchester.[364] Bakers had to dispel the notion that machine-made bread was less sanitary than kneading dough with clean hands. Compared to a wood-fired oven in the home, a baker's steam-tube oven improved the end product by adding moisture and employing a milder heat. Some bakers also made ice cream to complement their cake offerings.

After W. Rufus Caskey apprenticed for four years at the A. Quenzel Bakery in Martinsburg, he and his brother started up the Standard Steam Bakery in 1898.[365] Fifteen years later, the renamed Caskey Bakery & Ice Cream Co., which made bread under the Mothers, Snow Flake and Tip Top brands, opened branches in Hagerstown and Chambersburg.[366] In 1901, J. W. Lloyd began a career in several retail businesses in Martinsburg.[367] In 1912, he opened J. W. Lloyd Steam Bakery that made whole wheat bread and ice cream.[368]

Apple buyer F. A. Beck formed Winchester Steam Bakery in 1914, which seven years later became Beck's Steam Bakery.[369] Its bread, rolls, cakes and pies produced for the local market also went on the B&O's Valley Branch to urban areas. In 1925, businessman U. S. Rinaca opened Shenandoah Bakery in its namesake Page County town, and shipped quantities of baked goods on the Norfolk and Western Railroad.[370]

Distilling, Brewing and Soft Drink Industries

Moonshining on Northern Valley farms and in its forested hillsides continued as a popular way to avoid paying federal liquor taxes. But after the Civil War, licensed distilleries in the Northern Valley also made whiskey from rye and brandy from apples. Despite paying excise taxes, the distilling business was profitable, for it only took one 40-cent bushel of ground rye to make three gallons of whiskey worth $1.20.[371]

Producing whiskey in Martinsburg since 1867, the large Hannisville complex was joined by several distillers in Berkeley County: Josiah Flagg on Tuscarora Creek, east of Martinsburg, and Jacob Sencindiver and Robert Bryarly, both located on Middle Creek in the village of Darkesville, north of Inwood.[372] The latter man's distillery operated from 1810 until 1900, and was affiliated for a time with the Hannisville business.[373]

Beer sales soared in the United States after pasteurization was introduced in 1875 and mechanized methods to fill bottles were developed. In 1895, more than 1,700 breweries produced 33 million barrels of lager beer, but few were located in the Northern Valley.[374] In 1885, merchant James McGraw bottled Milwaukee Lager Beer and soft drinks in Harpers Ferry.[375] After his passing in 1893, son J. C. formed Harpers Ferry Brewing Company and built an ice plant and a brewery with a capacity of producing 10,000 barrels of beer annually.[376] When fire damage and too much debt caused financial difficulties for McGraw's company in 1898, Winchester liquor dealer Perry Haddox and partners purchased it.[377] The company changed hands and names several times until 1909, when a fire destroyed the brewery. The remaining buildings were sold to German Brewing Company in Cumberland, which used them for warehousing its Old German Beer.[378]

In 1903, Owens Bottle Machine Co. in Ohio invented equipment that made glass bottles on a large scale and spurred growth of the carbonated soft drink industry.[379] In 1915, Virginia Beverage Corp. was formed in Roanoke to market King-Cola as The Royal Drink.[380] Its Northern Valley bottlers included Charles Town Bottling Works, Martinsburg Bottling Works and Edinburg Bottling Works.[381] In 1917, Coca-Cola Company sued Virginia Beverage for infringement of its trademark. Although the Roanoke company changed the soft drink's brand name to Dixie Flip, it soon went out of business, along with the bottlers.[382]

In 1903, William Buser opened Berkeley Springs Bottling Works, which used the town's water in its Cascade Ginger Ale, French Vigo Regal Tonic and other drinks.³⁸³ Five years later, W. T. Buser, his nephew and former general manager, started up Crown Bottling Works on Martinsburg's West Race Street. He claimed the company's flavored, soda water soft drinks were, "Guaranteed under the new Food and Drug Act of 1906." ³⁸⁴

Canneries

As Americans settled into crowded cities, they lacked space to plant gardens and had less time to preserve vegetables. Those food processing chores moved from the home into canning factories that provided consumers with vegetables packed in airtight, hermetically sealed tin cans. The number of canneries in the United States increased from less than 100 in 1870 to almost 1,800 in 1900.³⁸⁵ The Northern Valley's industry participated in that growth, as thousands of wooden cases, each containing 24 cans of green beans, tomatoes and other vegetables and fruit, were sent by rail to East Coast markets. Operating in the late summer and fall in Page, Warren, Berkeley and Morgan counties, canneries also gave farm families an opportunity to earn wages after the harvest.

In 1890, Charles H. Miller, son of Berkeley County's pioneering orchardist W. S. Miller, and other investors organized Berkeley Canning Company, which built a factory on Martinsburg's Winchester Avenue to pack corn, beans, tomatoes and peaches in cans.³⁸⁶ After a fire destroyed the building in 1899, the local Rothwell-Lovett Cold Storage Company took over the business as Rothwell-Lovett Canning Company.³⁸⁷ In 1912, Charles Hart and Alexander Clohan, owners of an orchard and a vegetable farm southeast of Martinsburg, built the nearby Hart-Clohan Canning Factory.³⁸⁸ A channel was dug from Opequon Creek to supply it with water needed to process tomatoes and fruit. The partners also owned a factory that assembled wooden cases and shipping crates for their cannery and others in the region.³⁸⁹

In 1906, four partners formed Luray Canning Company to process green beans and tomatoes. Eight years later, I. N. Dovel purchased the business and renamed it Hawksbill Cannery.³⁹⁰ In 1910, Front Royal paper salesman J. B. Harnsberger dipped apples in jam and packed them in 30-pound cans.³⁹¹ When that sideline business grew, he and several partners started up Old Virginia Orchard Company several years later to turn apples into cans of jam, jelly and butter.³⁹²

Morgan County's porous sandstone soil was well-suited for raising tomatoes. The area also had above-average rainfall and temperatures that ranged from 50 to 80 degrees during the May through October growing season. In

1892, two men from Harford County, Maryland, home to numerous tomato canneries, opened Morgan County's first one in the hamlet of Sleepy Creek.[393] Many local farmers soon joined them, each raising tomatoes on 10 to 15 acres. Some owned and operated canneries on their property. By World War I, annual production from the county's 25 tomato canneries filled as many as 200 B&O rail cars. The cans were shipped to warehouses of packaged food companies.[394]

Apple Processing Industry

As orcharding expanded in the Northern Valley and bottling and canning techniques improved, two companies opened plants that processed imperfect apples—culls and drops unsuitable for the fresh market—into apple cider vinegar. It took 150,000 bushels of apples to make 10,000 barrels of vinegar.[395]

In 1910, Shenandoah Valley Apple Cider & Vinegar Company opened a plant on Winchester's Fairmont Avenue, next to the Cumberland Valley Railroad line and near the C. L. Robinson Ice and Cold Storage building.[396] Orchardist owners of the cooperative supplied the vinegar plant with between 75 and 80 percent of the apples it processed, and family members worked there after the harvest. In 1911, James Kistler, owner of Kistler Vinegar Works in Stroudsburg, Pennsylvania, and several businessmen formed Cumberland Valley Fruit Product Co.[397] It opened an apple cider vinegar plant south of downtown Martinsburg, near the Cumberland Valley Railroad's tracks.[398]

For years, dried slices of apples were used for baking. In the 1890s, the process was brought from an orchardist's kitchen or dry house into an evaporating plant, where hot air circulating from kilns dried apples not suitable for the fresh market.[399] But the kilns frequently caused fires, making it difficult for owners to obtain loans and insurance. In the 1910s, John W. Hallauer & Sons Company in Webster, New York, formed Valley Evaporating Company, which opened plants in Winchester, Stephens City and Inwood.[400] The latter facility was destroyed in 1922, when flames escaped from its kiln.[401] Shenandoah Valley Apple Cider & Vinegar Company operated apple evaporating facilities in Winchester and at Stephens City Station. In 1936, a huge fire inside the latter facility engulfed it and the nearby commercial buildings.[402]

Woodworking Industry

Dense forests in the region's surrounding mountains gave rise to industries that further processed their timber. In the early 1890s, improvement companies in the Eastern Panhandle recruited several woodworking businesses: Martinsburg Furniture Works, which made bedsteads from oak and poplar lumber; A. F. Kembler from Baltimore, who opened a picture frame business in Martinsburg; and the Elmer E. Beachley Saw and Planing Mill, which fabricated wooden sashes, doors and blinds in Ranson.[403] In Front Royal, Virginia Locust Pin Company opened a factory in 1902 that milled wooden insulator pins and brackets from locust and oak trees found in the nearby Blue Ridge Mountains.[404] They were sold to electric and telephone utilities, whose lines were spreading across the Mid-Atlantic area.[405]

In 1854, George F. Glaize left his father's farm to enter the lumber business in Winchester.[406] After serving in the Virginia Cavalry during the Civil War, he joined Henry at the Glaize and Bros. Lumber Company on North Cameron Street, near the Winchester and Potomac depot.[407] Son Frederick inherited the company and started up Glaize Bros. Saw and Planing at the same location, and by 1900, the combined enterprise was one of the largest in Winchester.[408] After a 1910 fire at the lumber business, Glaize put up a larger building supply store at the site, along with storage buildings.[409]

Wagon, Buggy and Auto Manufacturers

At the start of the twentieth century, 109,000 companies made carriages and wagons in the United States, including two in Martinsburg.[410] In 1893, Auburn Wagon Company moved from its namesake New York town to make steel-axle farm wagons in leased space in Greencastle, Pennsylvania.[411] In 1896, the Martinsburg Improvement, Loan & Building Association recruited Auburn and financed construction of its factory on West Race Street. Recovering from insolvency three years later, it became one of the Mid-Atlantic's largest manufacturers of farm wagons, marketing them as the lightest running and strongest in the world.[412] But Auburn closed in 1923, a victim of the growing use of motorized vehicles on the farm.[413]

Starting with $15,000, brothers R. N. and Claude Stewart launched Stewart Vehicle Co. in 1907 to make two-person buggies on Martinsburg's Winchester Avenue.[414] An addition to its three-story factory brought daily production up to 75 vehicles. In 1912, the Stewart's building burned in the most destructive fire in Martinsburg's history; 650 finished and unfinished buggies were lost, as well as 400 jobs.[415] Because lawsuits over its insurance claim dragged on for years, the factory was never rebuilt.

Auburn Wagon Company model of farm wagon
Photo from Berkeley County Historical Society, Martinsburg, WV

Even without the fire, Stewart Vehicle Co. would not have survived the Age of the Automobile. In 1893, brothers Charles E. and J. Frank Duryea demonstrated the first American gasoline-powered car in a short road test held in Springfield, Massachusetts.[416] With Henry Ford's introduction of the low-cost Model T in 1908, the automobile soon revolutionized transportation. Two years later, car ownership in America soared to 600,000 households.[417] As that trend continued, the number of carriage companies in America declined to just 200 in 1925, victims of creative destruction.[418] In the early 1900s, Howard Shockey switched from assembling stagecoaches and farm wagons in Winchester to building houses.[419] At the same time, Henry Heller converted his Martinsburg carriage company into an auto body and paint shop.[420]

Hoping to participate in the rapidly growing automobile industry, Martinsburg's leaders recruited the Norwalk Motor Car Company.[421] Organized in 1910 in its namesake Ohio town, it made a low-riding luxury car, but soon took bankruptcy.[422] After owner Arthur E. Skadden lined up financing from Martinsburg investors, he moved manufacturing into the former Brooklyn Brass & Foundry building in the city's industrial center. In 1912, Norwalk Motor Car began assembling the Underslung Six, which it marketed as the car of absolute exclusiveness. Priced at three times the Model T, it was sold mainly to wealthy residents of New York, Philadelphia and Toronto.[423]

Norwalk survived the nation's 1914 financial crisis, a time when many auto manufacturers failed, but after assembling 75 Underslung Six roadsters, Skadden's widow closed the company in 1922.[424] Nevertheless, the Northern Valley's ties to the industry continued into the 1920s, when several woolen mills produced fabric for automobile seat covers.

Norwalk Motor Car Company's Underslung Six roadster, Martinsburg
Photo from Berkeley County Historical Society, Martinsburg, WV

Cooperage Industry

By the turn of the twentieth century, the region's flour industry was in decline, as was its need for wooden barrels, but demand from the expanding apple and limestone industries more than made up for it. Some users found it cost-effective and more convenient to assemble their own barrels. Local mills supplied them with wooden staves and precut headers for the tops and bottoms, while blacksmiths provided the iron hoops that held staves together. Companies making their own barrels included Hannis Distillery in Martinsburg, Page Milling Co. in Luray, Powhatan Lime Co. in Strasburg. West of Stephens City, M. J. Grove Lime Company and Shenandoah Valley Apple Cider and Vinegar Company made barrels for their own use.[425] In the village of Bakerton in Jefferson County, five coopers at Standard Lime and Stone Company turned out 200 barrels a day.[426] In 1910, Fred Glaize partnered with Harry Byrd Sr. to make barrels for their orchard businesses and sell them to other fruit growers.[427]

Many Northern Valley companies outsourced their barrel requirements to independent cooperages that included the F. H. Bordon Barrel and Stave Factory in Page County, Berkeley Cooperage Co. in Martinsburg, and in Charles Town, the Jefferson Cooperage Co. and Shenandoah Valley Barrel Company.[428] In 1910, Sandusky Cooperage and Lumber Company in Ohio organized Virginia Barrel Co., which built a factory on Winchester's Wyck Street, near the C. L.

Robinson cold storage facility. Doubling its annual capacity to 80,000 barrels, Virginia Barrel later became the region's largest cooperage.[429]

Brick Manufacturing

The demand for bricks soared in the early 1900s, when America's cities and towns paved their dirt streets with them and used brick and mortar for underground water and sewer lines and the manholes that accessed them. And industrial and commercial structures, especially hotels, were built with brick, rather than fire-prone wood. To produce more bricks, the industry mined shale and clay with steam-powered shovels. Production moved from brickyards into factories with electric-powered pug mill mixers, extruding machines and improved kiln designs. The industry's best year was 1908, when 9.8 billion bricks were manufactured in the United States.[430]

After serving as a Union soldier stationed in Martinsburg, George Buxton from Bedford, Pennsylvania, returned to the city as a building contractor.[431] In 1875, he opened the G. W. Buxton Brick Yard and 20 years later, fired up kilns inside the region's first brick factory, at a site one-half mile northeast of Martinsburg.[432] With a daily capacity of 30,000 bricks, G. W. Buxton Brick Works made them from shale found in the North Mountain area, west of Hedgesville.[433] The factory provided most of the bricks used to build mills and factories during Martinsburg's booming industrial era.

North Mountain's shale-clay soil attracted several local and out-of-area investment groups looking to manufacture bricks, but only one built a factory. In 1900, Martinsburg businessmen raised $75,000 and organized Adamantine Clay Products Co., whose name meant a very hard material. Eleven years later, its North Mountain Brick Plant opened near Hedgesville with a capacity to produce 1.1 million bricks per month.[434] The B&O Railroad delivered coal from Western Maryland to Adamantine's drying furnaces and shipped its sidewalk and ornamental bricks to Baltimore and other eastern cities. The brick company advertised that customers saved on freight charges because its factory was 300 miles closer than those of its competitors.[435]

Another industry participant at first chose not to manufacture bricks in western Berkeley County. In 1911, United Clay Products Co. from Washington, D.C. purchased land in the North Mountain area and mined clay that the B&O shipped to its New York Avenue brick yard.[436] By 1926, however, the company was firing bricks at two factories in Berkeley County.

Cigar Rolling

By the early 1800s, America's taste for tobacco had shifted from pipes to cigars. In the antebellum years, independent proprietors purchased small quantities of tobacco leaves, then rolled them into cigars that were dried in wooden forms. An experienced roller made hundreds of smokes in a day; when extra help was needed, he hired one or two journeymen. In 1862, the federal government taxed cigars and other items to help pay its Civil War expenses. It also established a permitting system that forced self-employed cigar rollers to work for bonded manufacturers.[437] However, sales took off after the Tariff and Internal Revenue Act of 1883 cut the cigar tax in half, and high-quality tobacco became available in Connecticut and was imported from Sumatra, Indonesia and Cuba.[438]

Post-Reconstruction, numerous cigar companies were found in Northern Valley cities and towns. Frederick County had 10 of them in 1885, with each business employing from five to 40 workers.[439] Martinsburg, Stephens City and Front Royal were home to two cigar companies.[440] Cuba Rica Tobacco Co. in Winchester made the five-cent Charley Rouss Grand Cigar, named after the well-known retailer in his hometown and New York City.[441]

The cigar businesses eventually faced competition from a new tobacco product. In 1880, James A. Bonsack invented a machine that rolled cigarettes, and within 30 years, those less-expensive smokes eclipsed cigars in popularity.[442] The number of cigar factories in the United States declined from 23,000 in 1910 to 6,000 in 1929, a time when most Northern Valley rollers had closed shop.[443]

Potteries

After the region's potter wheels stopped turning during the Civil War, rebuilding the industry was a slow process. When competition kept earnings below normal, the "poor as a potter" phrase described their plight. Notwithstanding, the Northern Valley's golden age of pottery began in 1875, with 10 shops and 50 potters working in Strasburg, also known as Pot Town.[444] The clean quality of yellow clay found nearby was well-suited for making high-grade crocks, jugs, jars, pitchers and vases. And the ability to ship heavy pottery from Strasburg to urban markets on the Orange, Alexandria & Manassas and the B&O's Winchester and Strasburg railroads also contributed to the industry's growth.

Founded in 1843, Samuel Bell Pottery's voluminous production led Strasburg's postbellum industry. Brothers Samuel and Solomon Bell advertised the business as, "A manufacturer of stone, earthen & fancy wares and flower pots." [445] Upon Solomon's death in 1882, Samuel's sons Richard and Charles became partners with their father in the renamed Samuel Bell & Sons.[446]

Two years earlier, local farmer and businessman Jacob Jeremiah Eberly purchased A. Keister & Co., the Strasburg pottery that brothers Adam, Jr. and Henry Keister founded in 1830.[447] At J. J. Eberly & Co., the new owner hired journeymen potters to turn clay into housewares. After son Lechter took it over, the business turned out polychrome-glazed, ornamental and decorative pieces.[448] Other Strasburg stoneware potters were William H. Lehew & Co., which threw clay from 1877 to 1887, and John Henry Sonner, who took over his father's business in 1884 and ran it for eight years as J. H. Sonner & Co.[449]

In 1891, the Strasburg Land and Improvement Company and an investor group organized Strasburg Stone and Earthenware Manufacturing Co.[450] Its Strasburg Steam Pottery factory employed a number of the town's potters whose businesses had slowed.[451] Facing competition from much larger companies in Ohio and Trenton, New Jersey, it closed in 1909. Shortly thereafter, the expanded use of Mason glass jars for food storage ended Strasburg's golden age of pottery.[452]

Pulp Mills

In the mid-nineteenth century, the rising cost of cotton and linen rags used to make paper, coupled with increased demand for newsprint, triggered the search for an alternative raw material. By 1867, European and American inventors employed mechanical and chemical methods of grinding wood into pulp, whose fibers were then washed, pressed and dried into strips suitable for making paper.[453] Because they used large amounts of water, pulp mills were located along rivers, into which they also discharged tons of waste material.[454]

In 1887, Potomac Pulp Company of Pennsylvania purchased Honeywood Mills, a fire-damaged gristmill, sawmill and kiln complex that Edward Colston built in 1835 at Dam Number 5 on the Potomac River.[455] Repurposed as Honeywood Paper Mill, the water wheels were replaced with more efficient turbines to power machinery that ground pine logs into pulp shipped to paper mills in Philadelphia.[456] But after three years, Martinsburg Power Company purchased the Honeywood property and converted the mill to a hydroelectric plant.[457]

In the late 1880s, Thomas Savery, a paper company executive from Wilmington, built two pulp mills near Harpers Ferry.[458] In 1884, Savory & Company submitted the winning bid of $25,100 for the federal government's musket factory lot along the Potomac River, and another bid of $810 won the former rifle factory site on Hall's Island in the Shenandoah River.[459] After the U.S. Armory's closure in 1861 and the 1870 flood damage done to businesses on Virginius Island, the Harpers Ferry community welcomed the new industry.[460] On the banks of each river, Savery & Company built a pulp mill equipped with water-powered turbines. Shenandoah Pulp Mill began grinding up logs on Hall's Island in 1887 and three years later, Potomac Paper Mill made pulp where the armory's iron rolling mill once stood.[461] Because of their soft, long fibers, poplar and spruce logs were used at first, but as local supplies diminished, pine became the raw material of choice.[462]

Potomac Paper's pulp mill on Potomac River, 1900
Photo from National Park Service, Washington, DC

By the time Savery & Company's mills began producing pulp, the economics of the industry had changed; the nation's eight pulp mills in 1870 expanded to 80 in 1890.[463] The resulting over-capacity brought down pulp prices and caused financial problems for Savery.[464] To make money, he and several investors formed Harpers Ferry Electric Light & Power Co. in 1899, which built a hydroelectric plant inside the Potomac Paper Mill. It provided power to the mill and sold surplus electricity to several communities in the area.[465]

Strawboard Mills

With wheat production on the rise after Reconstruction, the region's third strawboard mill came on stream. Upon selling Columbia and Liberty furnaces in western Shenandoah County in 1883, Franklin Wissler and other investors formed Winchester Paper Company.[466] They purchased the Jonathan Smith woolen mill on Abrams Creek, south of the city and repurposed it as Winchester Paper Mill.[467] Every 24 hours, 50 workers used steam-powered machines to turn wheat straw into seven tons of strawboard.[468]

When over-capacity pressured strawboard prices, attempts were made to limit industry output through pooling of interests. In 1888, the Union Strawboard Co. in New York City purchased Winchester Paper Company, the New Dominion Paper Mill in Shepherdstown and others, giving it control of 90 percent of the industry's mills.[469] Eyster & Son Company in the Jefferson County village of Halltown never joined the company. One year later, American Strawboard Company in Chicago, also known as the Strawboard Trust, merged with Union Strawboard, but that transaction failed to solve the over-capacity problem.[470]

To reduce costs, Winchester Paper Company and Eyster & Son switched their raw material from straw to recycled newspapers, which the B&O Railroad shipped to their mills from Baltimore and Washington.[471] Instead of yellow strawboard, the companies produced corrugated cardboard used in large boxes and paperboard for smaller ones.[472]

In 1905, American Strawboard renamed its Winchester Paper Company subsidiary Old Dominion Paper Co.[473] After the financial Panic of 1907, it took bankruptcy and creditors idled the mill for several years.[474] Because American Strawboard had difficulty sourcing shipments of wastepaper at the start of World War I, the Winchester mill was retooled to make manila cardboard from wood chips.[475] At the same time, Eyster & Son's steam-powered mill in Halltown turned out 15 tons per day of chip cardboard.[476] After owner J. A. Eyster died in 1912, the business was incorporated as Halltown Paper Board Company.[477]

Extractive Industries: Digging Up Limestone and Sand

From 1880 to World War I, thousands of tons of manganese, limestone and silica sand were extracted from the Northern Valley, with much of it shipped to steel and glass industries in Pittsburgh and Wheeling. Renewed interest in mining began when Staunton engineer Jedediah Hotchkiss promoted the possibility that mineral riches could be found in the western foothills of the Blue Ridge Mountains. He previously served as Stonewall Jackson's chief topographical engineer for the Confederacy's Valley District.

Postbellum, Hotchkiss returned to his hometown, hung out a shingle as a consulting mining engineer and became involved in activities that promoted the Valley of Virginia's economic recovery.[478] His monthly publication, "The Virginias, A Mining, Industrial, and Scientific Journal Devoted to the Development of Virginia and West Virginia," reported on prospecting and mining that took place in the two states in the early 1880s.[479] The Father of Booms also wrote a pamphlet, "Mineral Deposits along the Line of the Shenandoah Valley Railroad," which projected that it could ship to distant markets the plentiful iron, copper and manganese found between the Blue Ridge and the Massanutten mountains.[480] Mining engineers followed his advice and searched for minerals in eastern Warren and Page counties, but their discoveries were minimal.[481]

Copper and Ochre Mining

From 1875 to 1905, Virginia and Pittsburgh Copper Company and the Gooney Manor Copper Company excavated soil in the Bentonville-Browntown-Overall area, south of Front Royal, but found limited quantities of the yellow metal.[482] In 1905, Virginia Consolidated Copper Company in Pennsylvania purchased 160 acres near the eastern Page County hamlet of Ida.[483] Investing $1 million, the company drilled a 150-foot shaft, but digging was suspended when no large vein of copper was discovered.[484]

Hotchkiss wrote of possible ochre deposits in the Page Valley, but discoveries of the natural earth pigment were limited. Used to tint paint, ochre appeared as a soft deposit intermingled with pockets of harder, crystalline iron ore. In the 1880s, Superior Ochre Company mined the mineral in Warren County and sent it to Bentonville for shipment on the Shenandoah Valley Railroad.[485] Oxford Ochre Company in Detroit opened a mine and processing mill near the Page County town of Stanley. In 1882 and 1883, more than 1,000 tons of ochre were shipped by rail to paint manufacturers in the Northeast[486] Due to the availability of higher-grade ochre found elsewhere in America, the Oxford mill closed in 1911.[487]

Manganese Mining

From Northern Valley earth, mining companies extracted much larger quantities of manganese than copper and ochre. Often found near iron ore deposits, the silvery-white metal's sulphur fixing and deoxidizing properties made it an essential alloy in steel production.[488] Small amounts of manganese—36 pounds per ton of steel—not only improved its workability at high temperatures, but also increased its strength.[489] The nation's output peaked at 34,534 tons in 1887, then declined to 2,825 tons in 1903, a time when Russia exported high-grade manganese to the United States at prices lower than the cost to mine it domestically.[490]

For several decades after 1834, manganese was extracted from the Paddy Run Mine in southwestern Frederick County, but mining stopped in the late 1850s.[491] After 1,000 feet of tunnels were dug in 1882, the mine produced 2,500 tons of ore during the next seven years.[492] In 1893, Charles Nelson from Strasburg purchased and reopened it as the Mineral Ridge Mine, which he leased to several operators, promising them it would become the largest producer of manganese in the United States.[493]

In 1876, ironmaster William Boyer secured mineral rights to the Oregon and Manganese tracts near his Mine Run Furnace, fired up four years earlier in the Powell's Fort section of Fort Valley.[494] Wagons hauled 400 barrels of manganese each month to the Waterlick Station of the Orange, Alexandria & Manassas Railroad, for eventual shipment to Pennsylvania steel mills. In 1883, Boyer sold the mines, surrounding land and his iron furnace to Powell's Fort Mining Company in Alexandria.[495] In 1885, the Manganese & Iron Company in Baltimore purchased the 531-acre property, upgraded the equipment and reopened two mine shafts.[496] New owners—Oregon Mining Company and the Woodstock Mining Company—worked the manganese mines from time to time until 1908.[497]

In the 1890s, Shenandoah Manganese Company opened the Eureka Mine, one mile south of the Page County village of Stanley, and sent the metal on a narrow-gauge spur to the tracks of the Norfolk and Western Railroad, formerly the Shenandoah Valley Railroad.[498] Dry Run Mining and Development Company in Norfolk purchased the Eureka Mine in 1908, and two years later opened the Compton Mine, 15 miles to the north, near the Page County village of Rileyville.[499] Pittsburgh-based Compton Manganese Corporation worked the latter mine intermittently, from 1916 to the 1950s.[500]

Three miles east of Front Royal, H. J. Seibel Jr. from Philadelphia opened Happy Creek Mine in 1907, near an iron ore mine he had operated for years. Steam shovels extracted the manganese, which a narrow-gauge tramway hauled to his other mine's processing mill, located near the Southern Railway station in Front Royal.[501] At peak production, water from Happy Creek washed 300 tons of manganese per month until the mine closed in 1917, just as demand increased during World War I.[502]

Limestone Quarrying

Located in a large seam running through its midsection, the region's limestone was formed during the Ordovician Period, 450 million to 500 million years ago.[503] Considered high quality, it tested 99.5 percent pure, compared to the 55 percent found in limestone in most of the United States.[504] The Northern Valley's yeoman farmers and planters discovered that it enhanced crop yields by neutralizing the soil's acidity. In the 1800s, iron furnaces and tanneries consumed small amounts of burnt lime. It was made by feeding crushed limestone into a rotary kiln, whose fire burned it into a white, powdery substance, free of impurities.[505] In the 1830s, unburned crushed limestone was used to macadamize the region's turnpikes and as ballast for railroad tracks.

By 1900, the limestone industry had become a major contributor to the Northern Valley's economy. Crushed limestone and burnt lime went to Washington and Baltimore for use as building materials. The steel industry consumed large quantities of high-quality burnt lime in its open-hearth furnaces, where it served as a flux that carried away impurities. It took between 50 and 120 pounds of lime to make one ton of steel.[506] New industrial applications increased the demand for the region's burnt lime, which was high in calcium content. Customers included chemical and glass manufacturers, sugar processing factories, paper mills and sewage treatment plants.

By the early 1900s, the region's limestone industry was mechanized. Steam-powered excavating equipment replaced the arduous tasks of drilling and shoveling limestone by hand. With one scoop, a steam shovel loaded more stone onto a wagon than a worker could in one day.[507] Large crushing machines broke up the stone for road and rail construction and for placement in rotary kilns.[508]

Unlike the region's pig iron furnaces, most limestone deposits were located near railroad tracks. By 1900, the B&O's Valley Branch was hauling 300 to 500 carloads of burnt lime per day to Cumberland, where its Pittsburgh and Connellsville Railroad subsidiary made final delivery to the Steel City.[509] The B&O also sent crushed limestone on its main line to Baltimore and on its Metropolitan Branch, initially from Point of Rocks, later from Brunswick, to Washington, D.C. Except for coal, the railroad moved more tons of limestone than any other bulk commodity.

Eastern Panhandle's Limestone

In the early 1900s, five million tons of limestone per year were extracted from quarries in Jefferson and Berkeley counties.[510] They employed 1,500 men, including many immigrants from Eastern Europe. Mining in Jefferson County took place in the Engle, Bakerton, Kearneysville and Millville areas. In 1883, brothers Charles and Otto Keller, seeking limestone deposits suitable for their Buckeystown, Maryland, tannery, purchased 240 acres in Jefferson County from William Engle. Their O. J. Keller Lime Company mined limestone at a quarry in what became known as the Engle area, situated between Harpers Ferry and Duffields, close to the B&O line.[511] In 1904, the Kellers formed Potomac Limestone Company and opened a quarry on 180 acres near their other one.[512]

In 1884, Daniel Baker Sr., a partner with the Kellers in the Buckeystown tannery, purchased 87 acres in the Engle area from them.[513] Upon their father's passing in 1888, Daniel Jr., Joseph and William formed Standard Lime & Stone Company. They purchased 47 acres from William Engle, then opened a quarry and built a spur to the B&O line.[514] The Bakers also acquired the rights to a patent Engle held on a kiln that turned high-calcium limestone into cement.[515] Fifty men worked in their newly-formed Washington Building Lime Company's quarry and at four kilns that daily burned 11,000 bushels of crushed lime shipped to builders in the nation's capital.[516] The workers' families lived in Bakerton, a company town that included employee housing, stores and a church.[517]

Growing rapidly, Standard Lime & Stone Company added a quarry near Kearneysville in 1892, from which lower-grade limestone was sold to the B&O Railroad for track ballast. That same year, the Washington Building Lime unit expanded into Berkeley County. At the southern edge of Martinsburg, it opened a limestone quarry with nine kilns.[518] The B&O built the two-mile Frog Hollow Branch from its main line to the quarry, which later supplied limestone to a Portland cement factory built near it.[519] To be closer to the railroad's headquarters, the Bakers moved their offices from Buckeystown to Baltimore.

In 1901, Standard Lime & Stone opened a quarry in Millville, near the Shenandoah River, where it mined and processed dolomite.[520] The steel industry used that magnesia-laden limestone to extend the refractory lives of its furnaces. Each day, the B&O's Valley Branch shipped 20 railcars of dolomite from its Millville depot to Pittsburgh.[521] Across the river, Pittsburgh investors purchased the Blue Ridge Lime and Stone Company in 1905.[522] Before they installed an aerial tram, 350 barrels of burnt lime were ferried daily to the Millville depot for shipment to builders and contractors in the Washington, D.C. area.[523]

In 1910, Standard Lime & Stone extended its footprint into Virginia with the opening of a quarry near Strasburg that produced 120 tons of commercial lime a day.[524] Two years later, the company acquired the O. J. Keller Lime Company in Engle, then leased one of the quarries to Blair Limestone Company, a unit of Jones & Laughlin Steel Company in Pittsburgh.[525]

A handful of corporations and investor groups from Pennsylvania entered Berkeley County's industry, looking to supply bunt lime to steel mills in their home state. In 1889, Pittsburgh businessmen formed Bessemer Limestone Co., which opened a quarry on the Cumberland Valley Railroad line, four miles west of Martinsburg.[526] In 1901, the 175-employee company was sold to United States Steel Company in Pittsburgh, which renamed it Martinsburg Limestone Co.[527] In 1909, former Frederick County tanner Loring Cover and other investors purchased and merged it into their Maryland Portland Cement Co., located in the village of Security, several miles north of Hagerstown.[528]

In 1908, the York, Pennsylvania-based J. E. Baker Lime Company, which owned limestone quarries in its home state and in Maryland, opened one in the Bunker Hill area of Berkeley County.[529] It built a spur to the tracks of the Cumberland Valley Railroad, which hauled hundreds of tons of fluxing stone daily to Steelton, four miles south of Harrisburg, where Pennsylvania Steel Company fabricated track for railroads.[530]

In 1908, Blair Limestone Company opened a quarry on 510 acres near Opequon Creek, east of Martinsburg.[531] It leased the land from three farmers, paying them an annual royalty of two cents for each ton of limestone quarried, capped at $5,000.[532] Burnt lime from the Blair quarry was shipped on the B&O's Valley Branch to its parent company in Pittsburgh, the Jones & Laughlin Steel Company. At what became the village of Blairton, the company built housing for its employees, primarily African Americans and immigrants from Italy and Eastern Europe.[533]

In 1904, a Philadelphia investor purchased 722 acres in the Nessle area of Berkeley County, which held a seam of limestone fronting the Potomac River.[534] In 1915, Pittsburgh Limestone Company, a Carnegie Steel Company unit, leased the property and opened a quarry that was served by a new Western Maryland Railroad short line.[535] Despite its name, the five-mile Williamsport, Nessle & Martinsburg Railroad never reached Martinsburg. It went from Charlton, Maryland, five miles west of Williamsport, on a bridge over the Potomac River to the quarry and kilns in Nessle.[536] Burnt lime was shipped to Pittsburgh, where Carnegie Steel used it as flux in open hearth and blast furnaces.[537] At one time employing 375 workers, the quarry closed at the beginning of the Great Depression.[538] In the 1940s, Carnegie Steel returned to the Eastern Panhandle with its purchase of the Moler Quarry in Jefferson County, located between U.S. 340 and Millville.[539]

Virginia Portion of the Region's Limestone

The volume of limestone extracted in Virginia more than doubled, from 114,000 tons in 1905 to 251,000 tons in 1920, with quarries in Shenandoah and Frederick counties producing half of that output.[540] The need for improved highways in the commonwealth increased the demand for crushed limestone for roadbeds and for burnt lime used to make concrete for road surfaces. Fifty-five percent of Virginia's limestone went to the construction industry, one-quarter of it became fertilizer and the balance was shipped to Pennsylvania steel mills.[541]

In the 1880s, limestone from quarries south of Strasburg went primarily for road building and agricultural uses. The owners included Rockdale Lime Company, renamed Toms Brook Lime & Stone Co.; the Virginia State Highway Commission's Flatrock Quarry in Quicksburg; and Woodstock Lime Co.[542] In 1886, the Limeton Lime Company produced agricultural lime in the Warren County village of Karo, 10 miles south of Front Royal.[543] After the quarry and kiln were abandoned in 1914, Virginia Rock Wool Company reopened them to make chemical lime, along with rock wool that plumbers used to insulate pipe.[544] The latter product was made by blowing a jet of steam through molten limestone to create the insulation's fine threads.

One-half century after Stephens City's wagon industry shut down, M. J. Grove Lime Company in Frederick, Maryland, became the town's largest employer. In 1900, it opened a limestone vein on 30 acres of leased land, one mile west of town.[545] After Grove purchased the property and 100 more acres, the open-pit quarry had become a 110-foot deep, tunneled mine in 1910.[546] Three miles of narrow-gauge track brought the lime to a crushing facility, where 10 kilns produced thousands of barrels of burnt lime, shipped on the B&O's Valley Branch to Pittsburgh.[547]

Between 1892 and 1910, five limestone companies worked quarries and kilns located several miles west of Strasburg. In 1894, the Southern Railway transported 20 carloads of burnt lime daily from its Strasburg depot to Eastern Seaboard cities.[548] West of town, the B&O's Valley Branch shipped burnt lime from its Oranda depot to Pennsylvania. Much of it came from local industry leader, the M. M. Orndorff company, whose one kiln in 1897 had increased to six in 1908.[549]

In 1905, William Carson assumed ownership of Carson Lime Company that his father Samuel started in 1868. To better indicate its location in Warren County, he changed the name to Riverton Lime and Stone Company.[550] One of the industry's largest companies in the region, its production included crushed lime for road building and burnt lime for chemical and agricultural uses.[551] From 1908 to 1920, Carson served as president of the National Lime Manufacturing Association.[552] After managing Harry F. Byrd Sr.'s successful bid for governor in 1925, he was appointed chairman of the newly created Virginia Conservation and Development Commission.[553] A leading advocate for Shenandoah National Park, Carson lobbied others to recognize its potential economic value to the Valley of Virginia.[554] He also started a system for placing historical markers on the commonwealth's roads.

Sand Mining

When combined with sodium carbonate and calcium oxide and heated at high temperatures, silica sand—broken down quartz crystals—became molten glass that could be shaped into a variety of objects.[555] By the early 1900s, glass was used for containers and in dinnerware, oil lamps, light bulbs, medicine bottles and other consumer items. The value of glass products made in the United States increased from $21 million in 1879 to $123 million in 1914.[556]

Glass sand containing at least 98 percent silica was found in quantity along Oriskany and Tuscarora sandstone formations that ran from New York State, through Pennsylvania and West Virginia, and into southern Virginia.[557] In the early 1870s, sand mining in Morgan County began along Warm Springs Ridge, a 12-mile strip of raised land between the Potomac River and Berkeley Springs.[558] After Hancock businessmen Robert Bridges and Charles W. Henderson heard rumors of large quantities of silica sand in Morgan County, in 1873 they acquired land near the B&O's Hancock Station, on the south side of the Potomac River.[559] Bridges' acreage was called the Berkeley Sand Works, while Henderson's was known as the Hancock White Sand Works.[560]

While managing his father's sand company in Pittsburgh, Noah Q. Speer invented a machine that steam-washed and cleaned sand, then received a patent for a simpler method of drying it.[561] When the company's sand reserves were exhausted, Speer came to Morgan County in 1873 and started Hancock White Sand Company on land leased from Henderson.[562] In the 1880s, Henry Harrison Hunter mined and processed silica sand at a small mill near Warm Springs Ridge. A sample he submitted to the 1893 Chicago World's Fair won a blue ribbon and the medal of excellence for its purity.[563] That recognition assured glass blowers of the quality of Morgan County's silica sand. When not mining, self-taught architect Hunter designed the Victorian-style bath houses in Berkeley Springs, and served as the town's bath keeper.[564]

At first, Morgan County miners used sledgehammers and wedges to break large blocks of sandstone into smaller pieces that were then crushed into particles.[565] Water from nearby springs was used to hand wash the sand free from clay, mud and iron. It was then poured through a screen and into a tube mill that ground it into a flour-like substance. As the local industry matured, machines pulverized, washed and dried the sand in separate mills within a plant. The 1888 completion of the B&O's Berkeley Springs and Potomac Railroad eased the task of shipping processed sand to glass manufacturers in Wheeling and Pittsburgh, cities with access to large quantities of natural gas needed to blow glass. Lacking that fuel, no such factories were built in Morgan County.

In 1902, Pennsylvania Glass Sand Company purchased the Hancock White Sand Company from Noah Speer for $100,000.[566] Located in Lewiston, 93 miles north of Berkeley Springs, the new owner rebuilt Speer's pulverizing plant to expand its daily throughput to 150 tons of sand.[567] In 1906, Pennsylvania Glass Sand leased the Berkeley Sand Works land from Robert Bridges, opened a quarry and built a plant whose daily processing capacity was 180 tons.[568]

After holding several jobs in Pittsburgh's sand and glass industries, Noah Speer returned to Morgan County in 1905. His Speer White Sand Company purchased five acres on the east side of Warm Springs Ridge and built a plant with a daily processing capacity of 140 tons of sand.[569] In 1908, he organized Great Cacapon Silica Sand Company in the western part of Morgan County.[570] It opened a quarry, near the confluence of the Potomac and Cacapon rivers, and along the B&O's main line. Several years later, Speer sold the company to Hazel-Atlas Glass Sand Company.[571] It acquired the business to guarantee a steady supply of sand for its parent company in Wheeling, which made glass jars for home canning. After expanding into depression glassware in 1920, Hazel-Atlas doubled the size of its Great Cacapon plant.

By the turn of the century, it was clear that the nation's demand for silica sand had increased and plentiful supplies were located in Morgan County.

Between 1900 and 1910, four companies purchased or opened quarries on Warm Springs Ridge.⁵⁷² The largest discovery of silica sand occurred in 1895, two miles north of Berkeley Springs. It was situated on land that Robert Bridges, through his Berkeley Springs Sand Works, had acquired four years earlier.⁵⁷³ Experts claimed that 500 tons per day of high-quality silica sand could be extracted from the vein for 200 to 300 years.⁵⁷⁴ Known locally as Bridges' Works, it became Morgan County's largest miner and processor of silica sand.⁵⁷⁵

In 1909, Baltimore businessmen Henry P. Bridges and Nelson E. Perin formed Berkeley Glass Sand Company and purchased Berkeley Springs Sand Works for $60,000 from the estate of Robert Bridges, Henry's father.⁵⁷⁶ The men replaced the 120-ton per day processing plant at Bridges' Works with a 200-ton facility.⁵⁷⁷ In 1911, Bridges, Perin and several local and Baltimore investors recapitalized Berkeley Glass Sand Company with $200,000 and used the funds to acquire Morgan County mines and plants with a combined daily processing capacity of 955 tons of glass sand.⁵⁷⁸ Berkeley Glass Sand was later sold to the Pennsylvania Glass Sand Company, which eventually became part of U.S. Silica.

Berkeley Glass Sand Company plant near Berkeley Springs, 1910
Postcard published by H. W. Disher & Son, Berkeley Springs, WV

Banking:
Every Town Has at Least One

Although six banks opened in the Northern Valley during Reconstruction, cashing a check in many towns remained difficult, as was borrowing money from sources other than relatives and friends. To meet the demand for financial services from a growing population, local businessmen formed 21 community banks prior to World War I. Within several decades, the region's two cities and most towns supported at least two banks, some with national in their name, indicating the federal government chartered and regulated them.

As industry brought more residents and commerce to Martinsburg, three banks opened to compete for deposits against National Bank of Martinsburg and Peoples National Bank, both organized under different names shortly after the Civil War. The new banks included Merchants and Farmers Bank of Martinsburg, formed in 1891; Citizens National Bank of Martinsburg, organized the next year; and Bank of Martinsburg, opened in 1902.[579]

Five banks entered the Jefferson County market to compete for customers with Bank of Charles Town and Jefferson Security Bank in Shepherdstown. The Bank of Harpers Ferry was launched in 1894, followed by the Farmers and Merchants Deposit Company in 1903 in Charles Town.[580] Next year, National Citizens Bank of Charles Town was formed to print what it called national currency, supposedly backed by United States bonds the bank had on deposit with the U.S. Treasury.[581] In 1906, The Farmers Bank opened its doors in Shepherdstown, while Peoples Bank of Charles Town was formed one year later.[582]

Post-Reconstruction, 13 banks opened in the Virginia portion of the Northern Valley. After Bank of Berryville closed in 1876, Clarke County's residents and businessmen had to travel to Winchester and Front Royal for their banking needs.[583] In 1881, community leaders raised $10,000 and started the state-chartered Bank of Clarke County in Berryville.[584] Nearby, Boyce State Bank opened in 1908, using what it claimed was the most modern equipment in the business.[585]

In Winchester, Farmers and Merchants National Bank was organized in 1902 with $100,000 of capital stock.[586] Later renamed F&M Bank, its building stood opposite Union Bank on Loudoun Street and was several blocks south of Shenandoah Valley National Bank, both formed soon after the Civil War. In 1906, People's Bank opened in Stephens City as the only commercial bank in Frederick County.[587]

By the early 1900s, Page County had several community banks. In 1893, Page Valley Bank of Virginia was chartered in Luray as a state bank, then moved into the building once occupied by D. F. Kagey and Company, the private bank that failed when the improvement company it promoted was dissolved.[588] In 1901, First National Bank of Luray was organized to compete with Page Valley Bank of Virginia, which quickly became Page Valley National Bank of Luray.[589] Formed in 1904, Farmers and Merchants Bank of Stanley moved into a new building on Main Street.[590]

After Reconstruction, Shenandoah County had no banks, but seven had opened their doors by 1907: Mount Jackson National Bank in 1884; Massanutten National Bank in Strasburg in 1890; Citizens National Bank of New Market in 1897; Shenandoah County Bank and Trust in Woodstock in 1899, which the following year became Shenandoah National Bank of Woodstock; People's National Bank of Mount Jackson in 1900; and Farmers Bank of Edinburg in 1905.[591] Peoples National Bank of Strasburg—years later known as First Bank—opened in 1907 to compete with Massanutten National Bank.[592]

During the latter part of the nineteenth century, Woodstock lawyer Edgar Douglas Newman, the son of Shenandoah County ironmaster Benjamin Pennybacker Newman, served on the boards of numerous banks.[593] A Shenandoah County Circuit Court judge from 1886 to 1898, his banking career began as organizer, director and president of Shenandoah County Bank and Trust Company in Woodstock.[594] He also sat on the boards of Massanutten National Bank in Strasburg, Peoples National Bank of Mount Jackson, First National Bank of Luray and Farmers and Merchants National Bank in Winchester.[595] At the time, banking laws did not prohibit multiple directorships of small banks. Besides his banking duties, Newman helped organize life insurance companies and orchard and fruit businesses.[596] He was also a director of the Valley Turnpike Company, trustee of Massanutten Academy in Woodstock and a leader in the Methodist Church.[597]

Newspapers: Daily Papers Roll Off Presses

George Eastman's 1885 invention of photographic film used to print newspapers greatly improved their looks, and pictures enhanced a paper's editorial content and made advertisements more effective sales tools.[598] While the Northern Valley's weekly papers continued to be bought, sold and merged after Reconstruction, daily newspapers appeared for the first time in its two cities.

In 1893, Richard Evelyn Byrd became editor and half-owner of the Winchester Times, which competed for readers against the Winchester Leader, a Republican paper that circulated from 1884 to 1899. The city's first daily rolled off the press when John I. Sloat published The Evening Item in 1895.⁵⁹⁹ The following year, he sold the single-sheet paper to the editor of the Winchester Weekly News, founded in 1865, who combined the papers as the Winchester-News Item.⁶⁰⁰ Sloat then started a competing daily, The Evening Star that covered the news in Winchester and Frederick and Clarke counties.

In 1897, Richard Byrd purchased The Evening Star, which had struggled in the aftermath of the Panic of 1893, and merged it into his Winchester Times.⁶⁰¹ Teenage son Harry quickly cut costs and put the daily on a firm financial footing.⁶⁰² In 1907, the younger Byrd bought the Winchester News-Item and combined it with The Evening Star as the Winchester Evening Star, the city's only newspaper.⁶⁰³ Later, as speaker of the Virginia House of Delegates and governor, Byrd used the conservative Democratic paper as a soapbox for low taxes, balanced government budgets and no public debt.

Newspaper mergers also carried the day in Martinsburg. In 1906, C. W. Boyer purchased the Martinsburg Statesman, founded in 1888, and combined it with the Berkeley Democrat, started up in 1869, as the Martinsburg Statesman-Democrat, which published until 1921.⁶⁰⁴ Shortly after Harry Byrd combined two Winchester papers in 1907, he started The Evening Journal, a daily that reported the news in Martinsburg and surrounding areas.⁶⁰⁵ Five years later, he sold the paper to associate Max von Schlegell, who renamed it The Martinsburg West Va. Evening Journal to avoid confusion with The Winchester Evening Star.⁶⁰⁶

In 1884, the West Virginia Publishing Company in Charles Town launched The Farmer's Advocate, and marketed the weekly as the West Virginia State Farmer's Alliance and Industrial Union's official organ.⁶⁰⁷ One year later, the West Virginia Democrat rolled off the press as a competitor, and after several ownerships, was merged into The Farmer's Advocate in 1890.⁶⁰⁸ Three years later, S. S. Buzzerd started the weekly Morgan Messenger in Berkeley Springs.⁶⁰⁹

Other Northern Valley towns had weekly newspapers. Berryville was home to the Clarke Courier, while Front Royal citizens read either the Warren Sentinel or the Warren Messenger. In 1895, E. L. Hisey and L. T. Stoneburner founded the Edinburg and Valley Advisor, which later became the Edinburg Sentinel.⁶¹⁰ In the years leading to World War I, Page County citizens supported eight newspapers, most of them based in Luray and Stanley.⁶¹¹ In 1912, E. E. Keister purchased his hometown's Strasburg News, then started the Middletown Weekly as the only paper based in Frederick County.⁶¹²

Higher Education: Not All Colleges Are Normal

The 1870s were lean times for the Shepherd Normal School, founded in 1871 in Shepherdstown. With meager state funding, its enrollment fell below 100 students in 1878.[613] After the co-education teacher's college improved its physical facilities, curriculum and faculty during the first two decades of the twentieth century, it continued as a state-supported institution.[614]

Founded in 1867 in Harpers Ferry to train teachers to educate African Americans, enrollment at Storer Normal School peaked in 1883 with 288 students. Renamed Storer College in 1938, it offered students several options: a four-year high school program, a two-year elementary teacher training program, a two-year junior college program, or separate courses in homemaking and agriculture.[615] Due to a dwindling student body during World War II, the West Virginia Board of Education ended its annual support of $20,000.[616] After graduating 7,000 students throughout its 88-year history, Storer College closed its doors in 1955.[617]

Two colleges found a home in the Virginia portion of the region. In 1883, Professor George Washington Hoenshel opened Shenandoah Normal College in Middletown to "allow rich and poor students to attend an institution of higher education." [618] To accommodate its growth, the college moved into larger quarters in Harrisonburg in 1887, before relocating farther south to Waynesboro.[619] Returning to the Northern Valley in 1890, the renamed Old Dominion Academy moved to the Warren County hamlet of Reliance, but closed after a fire destroyed its main building in 1914.[620] In Front Royal, Professor Samuel Rolfe Millar founded Eastern College as a liberal arts school in 1900.[621] To attract a diverse student body, it offered the following courses of study: collegiate, academic, preparatory, business, music, arts, drawing, elocution and teaching.[622] After a fire destroyed one of its main buildings in 1909, the college moved to Manassas.[623]

Tourism: Visitors Drawn to Springs, Mountains and Caverns

Post-Reconstruction, the Northern Valley's tourism industry benefited from more frequent passenger rail service and increased consumer spending during the nation's Gilded Age. While wealthy patrons from Eastern Seaboard cities returned to the region's mineral springs resorts that remained open, others discovered the Blue Ridge Mountains as a place to escape from the summer's heat and humidity. When show caves opened in the cool air beneath the Northern Valley's floor, sightseers paid to admire their unique geologic features.

In the last quarter of the nineteenth century, some railroads entered the tourism business, bringing excursion trains to popular venues they owned. The strategy was to increase passenger traffic, which was more profitable than hauling freight. Participants included the Shenandoah Valley Railroad, which brought tourists to its Luray Caverns and Hotel, and the Baltimore & Ohio Railroad, which took them to Island Park on Byrne's Island, an elongated mass of land in the Potomac River, upstream from Harpers Ferry.[624]

Opened in 1879 with pavilions, tents and amusement attractions, Island Park was originally designed as a day-trip destination for B&O employees. When made available to the public, as many as 28 excursion trains each day transported picnickers, bowling clubs, singing societies and honeymooners from Washington and Baltimore to the venue.[625] Advertisements described Island Park as having, "Mountain scenery, swings, croquet, boating and music and dancing on Byrne's Island." Until its closure in 1909, the park was also used for political conventions and meetings.[626]

Mineral Springs Resorts

Berkeley Springs tourism received a boost from more frequent passenger rail service and new bath houses, showers and a swimming pool in the town's park.[627] Beginning in 1888, the B&O brought guests from Washington, Baltimore and surrounds directly into the town, traveling the last six miles on its Berkeley Springs and Potomac Railroad.[628] The tourists included celebrities, politicians and the high-society set, who stayed at either the Berkeley Springs Hotel or the Fairfax Inn. However, the town's economy suffered when the former hotel burned to the ground in 1898 and a similar fate struck the Fairfax Inn, three years later.[629]

Recognizing that Berkeley Springs needed more hotel rooms, local businessman George Biser built the Washington Hotel in 1905 on the corner of Washington and Fairfax streets.[630] In 1912, Fred Bartlett, an oil and gas operator and hotelier from Mannington, West Virginia, purchased the hotel and renamed it after himself.[631] The prior year, Bartlett and other investors built a cold storage facility in downtown Berkeley Springs. In 1917, the Bartlett Hotel was sold to two businessmen from Altoona, Pennsylvania, who returned it to the original Washington Hotel name.[632]

Post-Reconstruction, the Northern Valley's remaining mineral springs resorts benefited from less competition and the deep pockets of the Gilded Age's high rollers. To attract patrons, the owners advertised the health benefits of their water in medical and scientific journals. But the four-year depression that followed the Panic of 1893 negatively affected occupancies and the bottom lines of all the resorts.

Washington Hotel in Berkeley Springs Postcard published by Ruppenthal's Studio and Camera Shop, Berkeley Springs, WV

West of Mount Jackson, the Orkney Springs resort hosted numerous social and political events from 1870 to 1890, with upwards of 8,000 guests spending time there each summer.[633] An 1885 brochure described its springs as, "Guaranteeing relief from dyspepsia, chronic diarrhea and female diseases." [634] The Orkney Springs Hotel and Improvement Company was chartered in 1892 with $250,000 in capital stock, but when no work was done after the Panic of 1893, the resort fell on hard times.[635] The H. C. Carter family from Baltimore purchased the property out of bankruptcy in 1908. Their Orkney Springs Hotel Co. advertised the baths as having, "Restorative waters equal to Carlsbad, Germany, for nervousness, poor blood, general debility, rheumatism, kidney and stomach troubles." [636]

Opened in 1870, three miles east of Orkney Springs, the Shenandoah Alum Springs resort experienced financial stress during the nation's Depression of 1882-85. Owners Abraham and Fyanna Myers ended up in litigation with several persons who had loaned them money to keep the business going.[637] The 1,001-acre property was sold in 1888 to a Harrisonburg attorney, who closed the hotel.[638]

After the Shannondale Springs Hotel burned in 1858, the eastern Jefferson County property was used for religious events, camping, picnicking and swimming in the nearby Shenandoah River. Some visitors stayed in several cabins that remained on the grounds.[639] In 1888, two Jefferson County businessmen purchased the property at auction, then built a 25-room hotel with a ballroom on the foundation of the original one.⁶⁴⁰ When its finances weakened during the Panic of 1893, Shannondale Springs closed. Charles Town businessman H. C. Getzendanner purchased it for $9,055 in 1902, and operated the resort for seven years until another fire did extensive damage to the hotel and it was never rebuilt.⁶⁴¹

Upon his father's passing in 1890, Edwin Clarendon Jordan Jr. inherited Jordan Springs Resort, six miles northeast of Winchester.⁶⁴² Three years later, he razed several older buildings on the property and added a four-story 60-room hotel.⁶⁴³ Patronage declined after the Panic of 1893, and the resort suffered further losses following a 1905 newspaper report of an outbreak of typhoid fever. Jordan sold the property to brother-in-law Henry H. Baker, who leased it to several operators until its closure in 1916.⁶⁴⁴

In 1903, Winchester businessman Orin C. Cullen, through his Waterlick White Sulphur Springs Corporation, remodeled the 53-year-old Warren Sulphur Springs Hotel on Passage Creek, near the northern entrance to Fort Valley.⁶⁴⁵ He advertised its location as, "Fishing and hunting are nearby, but not mosquitoes, gnats or malaria." ⁶⁴⁶ Until the hotel burned in 1939, guests took the Southern Railway to the nearby Waterlick Station.⁶⁴⁷

Not all spring resorts were situated in the countryside. In 1891, Strasburg businessman A. P. McInturff opened the Chalybeate Springs Hotel on Fort Street, one block from the town's Southern Railway depot.⁶⁴⁸ Traveling salesmen and summer tourists drank water that came from a spring behind the hotel, while other guests came for outdoor sports that included fishing in the North Fork of the Shenandoah River in spring and summer, and hunting quail and hare in the fall. ⁶⁴⁹ In 1901, McInturff sold the hotel to his son-in-law, Lewis Machir, who advertised the renamed Hotel Machir as the, "House of tranquility, located two miles from Massanutten Mountain, with the best drinking water in the world." ⁶⁵⁰

Inns and Resorts in Blue Ridge Mountains

In the 1890s, two hostelries near Snicker's Gap in eastern Clarke County catered to wealthy Washingtonians wishing to escape the city's oppressive summer heat.⁶⁵¹ Patrons took the 12-mile Washington, Ohio & Western Railway from Leesburg to Round Hill, followed by a stagecoach ride on present-day Route 7 to the hotels. Easier access came in 1900, when the rail line was extended four miles farther west to Bluemont, in the eastern foothills of the Blue Ridge.

In 1892, two businessmen from Loudoun County and Washington, D.C. built the Blue Ridge Inn, referred to as the Mountain House. Open from Memorial Day to Labor Day, the inn was not rebuilt after a fire destroyed it in 1913.[652] The nearby Elsea Springs Hotel was situated on one of the highest points in the Blue Ridge.[653] Guests stayed either in a farmhouse or in several cottages, with resident owner and farmer Thomas Elsea serving them fruits and vegetables from his garden.

Seventy miles to the south, George Freeman Pollock convinced his father that Miners Lode Copper Company's 5,400 acres in the Blue Ridge Mountains, southeast of Luray, had more value as part of a resort.[654] After building 50 cabins, a rustic restaurant and recreation hall near Stony Man Mountain, Pollock opened Skyland in 1895. He marketed it as, "The highest elevation in the South with no mosquitoes." [655] The gregarious Pollock managed Skyland with a showman's flair. His bugle woke up guests each morning, summoned them to meals and entertainments and announced the departure of the daily mail.[656] Patrons took trains from Washington, Baltimore and Philadelphia to Luray, followed by a stagecoach ride to Thornton Gap, then 10 miles south to the resort.[657] Enjoying cool breezes and views into the Shenandoah Valley, some guests stayed at Skyland for as long as three months.

George Pollock, owner of Skyland Resort in Blue Ridge Mountains. Photo from National Park Service, Washington, DC

Tourists Go Underground

Show caves became popular attractions in the 1880s, when the paying public came to view their unique underground arrangements of stalactites and stalagmites. Several miles from its namesake town, Luray Caverns was the Northern Valley's first and largest show cave. In 1878, five local men felt cold air rushing out of a limestone sinkhole atop a large hill.[658] After they widened the opening, climbed inside and discovered the cave's unique features, the public soon followed, paying 50 cents to view them.

Two years before its tracks reached Luray in 1882, the Shenandoah Valley Railroad entered the tourism industry with the purchase of Luray

Caverns for $40,000.⁶⁵⁹ Its Luray Cave and Hotel Company packaged tours that included stays at the railroad's newly built, Queen Anne-style Luray Inn.⁶⁶⁰ In 1889, more than 15,000 persons visited the caverns, many of whom took the train and stayed at the hotel, which burned two years later and was not rebuilt.⁶⁶¹ Following several bankruptcies and legal battles over Luray Caverns' ownership, Col. Theodore Northcott purchased it in 1905. He had previously channeled cool air from the cave to his nearby sanitarium, claiming it was the first air-conditioned residence in the United States.⁶⁶²

After two boys chasing rabbits in 1879 discovered a cave on Ruben Zirkle's property, south of New Market, his family conducted candlelit tours through the six-mile long cavern.⁶⁶³ Because of its never-ending tunnels and chambers, Zirkle Cave became known as Endless Caverns. The business prospered when tourists rode the Southern Railway to New Market, then visited the cave before taking a stagecoach 13 miles east over Massanutten Mountain to the more famous Luray Caverns.⁶⁶⁴ But that routine ended in 1882, when the Shenandoah Valley Railroad brought visitors directly to Luray.⁶⁶⁵ With patronage of Endless Caverns declining, Zirkle operated the business as Silver Hill Caverns. After the Panic of 1893, it remained closed until Col. E. T. Brown from Atlanta purchased the property in 1919.⁶⁶⁶ He installed electricity, reinstated the Endless Caverns name and opened an information office in Luray to lure motoring tourists over the mountain to his show cave.⁶⁶⁷

Health Care: Patients Leave Homes for Hospitals

In 1826, three local physicians opened the Medical College of the Valley of Virginia on Winchester's West Boscawen Street.⁶⁶⁸ The research facility's mission was to "investigate the nature of, and proper treatment of, various diseases of the human race, and of other subjects agitated among medical men." ⁶⁶⁹ Closed two years later, the building reopened in 1847 as Winchester Medical College to serve as a school for physicians and a hospital.⁶⁷⁰ During the Civil War, it was used to study cadavers, but Union soldiers burned the building in 1862.⁶⁷¹

In 1870, the United States had 172 hospitals that offered custodial care—warmth, shelter and food—to patients.⁶⁷² For most people who fell seriously ill, horse and buggy doctors attended to them in their homes. In rural areas, sick persons unable to afford such care received it at poor houses. As scientific knowledge, medical expertise and the use of penicillin and other antibiotics grew in the early 1900s, hospitals emerged as the health care facility of choice. By 1910, the United States had 4,300 private and public hospitals; many were either started by doctors, functioned as nursing homes or were adjuncts of nursing schools.[673]

After physicians attempted several times to reopen a hospital in downtown Winchester, plans were finalized in 1901 to build one at the corner of South Stewart and West Clifford streets. Financed with $15,000 raised from local donors, Winchester Memorial Hospital included 24 ward beds, 12 private rooms and a nursing school.[674] Twenty miles to the south, Dr. Mackall Bruin built Strasburg Hospital in 1902 as a central location to serve patients previously seen in their homes.[675] He added a nursing school and ran the hospital until leaving town in 1915.[676] Bruin's wife stayed behind and repurposed the building as the Hotel Strasburg.[677]

Winchester Memorial Hospital, 1907 Postcard published by C. E. Wheelock & Co., Williamsport, PA

Two small hospitals in Martinsburg competed for patients. In 1896, King's Daughter's Hospital, staffed by Sisters of the Holy Spirit, opened in the former city jail on East King Street.[678] In 1905, Dr. T. K. Oates from Capon Bridge opened his namesake hospital at the corner of Burke and Maple streets.[679] In Charles Town in 1904, Dr. Richard E. Venning, originally from South Carolina, turned the second floor of his West Congress Street residence into a hospital.[680] The facility included an operating room, sterilizing room, five bedrooms and one bath. Venning sold the building in 1911 to an investor group that remodeled and enlarged it as Charles Town General Hospital.[681] Six years later, it became a non-profit health care provider.

Patent medicines made from herbs gained favor in the last quarter of the nineteenth century. In 1888, Whitlock Herb Medicine Company compounded and bottled them on Winchester's Valley Avenue.[682] Dr. Joseph Whitlock and his uncle, Dr. William Whitlock, concocted a variety of nostrums sold through the mail, among them cough syrup, children's laxatives and pills for nerves, kidneys and rheumatism.[683] By 1922, they had run afoul of the U.S. Food and

Drug Administration, which alleged the therapeutic claims of their company's products were unwarranted.[684] The business closed two years later.

Federal Government: Sites Open in Blue Ridge Mountains

Uncle Sam's physical presence in the Northern Valley began in Harpers Ferry with construction of an armory and arsenal in 1789, followed by a tilt hammer shop in 1834 and a rolling mill in 1853.[685] Burned during the Civil War, the complex was not rebuilt. The federal government's next move came in 1895, when the $125,000 United States District Court building opened on Martinsburg's West King Street.[686]

Activity resumed in the first two decades of the twentieth century. In 1902, the U.S. Weather Bureau, a unit within the Department of Agriculture, purchased 85 acres in the Blue Ridge Mountains in eastern Clarke County.[687] The bureau used kites and balloons to take meteorological readings at what became known as Mount Weather.[688]

With automobiles fast replacing horses, the Cavalry Branch of the United States Army sought a way to ensure it had an ample supply of the animals for wartime deployment. Because of its proximity to horse farms and the Southern Railway line, Warren County was selected as a site to raise and train the animals.[689] In 1911, the Army acquired 5,133 acres through the purchase of 42 farms in the nearby Blue Ridge Mountains. Five years later, hundreds of local residents found work at the U.S. Army Remount Station.[690]

Over the years, lumber, iron and tanning companies had clear-cut numerous wooded areas in the Northern Valley and surrounding mountains. With few trees left to hold the soil, erosion clogged streams with silt and caused frequent floods. Under the Weeks Act of 1911, the National Forest Service purchased deforested mountain land to protect it for watershed purposes.[691] Six years later, the agency acquired three large parcels in the Northern Valley, including acreage surrounding the former Elizabeth and Liberty furnaces, and combined them into the Shenandoah National Forest, later renamed George Washington National Forest.[692]

CHAPTER 6

WORLD WAR I TO WORLD WAR II

National Economy: Roaring Twenties End with the Great Depression

After a five-year economic boom during the First World War, the United States emerged as the world power.[1] And the good times continued in the Roaring Twenties, when industrial production doubled and the gross national product rose by 42 percent.[2] However, after feeding millions of hungry Europeans, the wartime surge in farm incomes ended in 1920.[3] With transportation, supplies and equipment costs rising, they dropped by 25 percent.[4] Then came the Great Depression and the severe droughts of the early 1930s.

Infrastructure: Adapting to New Modes of Travel

After World War I, the nation's expanded use of automobiles and trucks caused rail traffic to decline, at the same time airplanes gained traction as a faster mode of long-distance travel. Northern Valley politicians and businessmen continued to believe that strong transportation networks brought economic gains to their jurisdictions. This time, they focused on providing toll-free highways for operators of gas-powered vehicles and airfields for pilots and their planes.

Roads

Motor vehicle registrations in Virginia soared from 10,000 in 1913 to 387,000 in 1930, and they jumped from 13,000 to 266,000 in West Virginia.[5] By the early1920s, toll-free highways had replaced most of the nation's turnpikes.[6] It was inconvenient for drivers of cars and trucks to stop every few miles to pay tolls, and the public had turned against private ownership of roads.

During its 1918 session, the Virginia General Assembly approved the state's first highway system, a 4,002-mile network of roads.[7] Serving as chairman of the Virginia Senate Committee on Roads in the 1920s, Harry Byrd Sr. convinced the commonwealth to buy out Valley Turnpike Company's stockholders for six cents on the dollar.[8] Tolls were abolished and the turnpike became part of U.S. 11 in 1926.[9] With Byrd lobbying for a pay-as-you-go system of financing highways, the General Assembly passed a three cents per gallon tax on gasoline in 1923.[10]

Five years later, the Virginia Department of Highways, successor to the Highway Commission, began a roads reconstruction program. It included engineering them for less-steep grades and better alignments and paving them with asphalt.[11] U.S. 11 was upgraded to a high-speed motor vehicle route.[12] In towns it passed through, the highway was widened, curbed and guttered to create Main Streets that were friendlier to vehicular and foot traffic. In the eastern part of the Shenandoah Valley, construction began in 1931 on improving former turnpikes on the East Valley Road, which became U.S. 340.[13]

The elimination of tolls on roads and bridges leading eastward brought the region's citizens and businesses closer to Northern Virginia and Washington, D.C. In 1919, the 18-mile Berryville and Winchester Turnpike that led to Snicker's Gap in the Blue Ridge, became part of Route 7.[14] Three years later, the two turnpikes from Winchester through Ashby's Gap to Aldie were also free of tolls. In 1926, those roads and the Northwestern Turnpike leading westward from Winchester became part of U.S. 50.[15]

In 1920, voters passed the Good Roads Amendment to West Virginia's constitution.[16] To help end the Mountain State's isolation, the legislation established a system of highways that connected county seats to major roads of adjoining states. In Berkeley and Jefferson counties, state and federal funds were used to upgrade roads that joined those in Morgan County, Virginia and Maryland.[17] At the same time, tolls on the three Potomac River bridges leading into Maryland were eliminated.

Railroads

With improved interstate roads, trucks replaced railroads as the preferred method of transporting finished goods on many long hauls. Unlike railroads, whose rolling stock often went through the cumbersome process of interchanges between lines, trucks delivered goods directly to their final destination. Nevertheless, railroads remained the preferred method of shipping the Northern Valley's bulky and heavy raw materials and products to wholesalers and end users. Those items included apples, vinegar, canned vegetables, crushed limestone, burnt lime, manganese and sand. But as long-distance travel shifted to automobiles, railroads serving the Northern Valley reduced or eliminated passenger service.

A 1916 fire destroyed much of Norfolk and Western Railway Company's yard in the Page County town of Shenandoah City, also the site of its divisional headquarters.[18] During the next nine years, the Roanoke-based railroad replaced the buildings with new maintenance shops and a larger roundhouse.[19] Employing 500 workers in the 1920s, the yard also included a lubricating station, a coal tipple and water tanks.[20] The Norfolk and Western ended passenger service in the region in 1962.[21]

In 1916, the tracks of the Cumberland Valley and Baltimore & Ohio railroads were physically connected at Stine's Crossing, north of downtown Winchester.[22] Cumberland Valley passenger trains approaching the city switched to the B&O's tracks and proceeded to its station on North Kent Street, where ticketing was conducted for both railroads.[23] Its unused passenger station on the corner of Boscawen and Stewart streets was closed. After the Cumberland Valley Railroad became a division of the Pennsylvania Railroad in 1919, passenger train frequency to Martinsburg and Winchester dropped to once daily in the late 1920s, then ended during the Great Depression.[24] Its vacant Winchester passenger station was torn down in 1934, but the freight depot on West Boscawen Street remained in service until the early 1970s.[25]

Because the B&O Railroad relied on coal cargo for much of its revenue, the Great Depression hit its bottom line more severely than those of other carriers. Passenger service on its Berkeley Springs and Potomac Railroad ended in 1935. Seven years later, the B&O either abandoned or sold parts of its Valley Branch track from Staunton to Harrisonburg, but continued freight service between that latter city and Harpers Ferry.[26] Scheduled passenger service within the Shenandoah Valley ended in 1949.[27]

During World War I, construction began on a short line between Winchester and Wardensville in Hardy County, West Virginia. Its promoters were Romney lawyers William and John Cornwell, who owned their hometown Hampshire Review newspaper, along with Potomac Highland companies in the lumber and sand businesses. To provide rail access for them, the Cornwell brothers and other investors organized the Hampshire Southern Railroad Company.[28] Completed in 1910, the short line's 55 miles of track went from Romney north to the B&O Railroad's tracks at Green Spring, West Virginia, then headed west, paralleling the South Branch of the Potomac River to Moorefield.[29] Next year, the investors received a charter for the Moorefield and Virginia Railroad Company, successor to the Hampshire Southern, and extended the track 12 miles farther west to Petersburg.[30] In 1913, they sold the railroad to the B&O, which used the renamed South Branch line to haul logs to its newly opened Timber Preserving Plant in Green Spring, rather than float them down the river.[31] That facility supplied the B&O with 1 million creosoted crossties each year.[32]

Soon after the Moorefield and Virginia Railroad sale, the Cornwells formed Lost River Lumber Company with $150,000 in capital stock, then purchased 60 tracts of timberland in Hardy and Hampshire counties that included 9,000 acres near the village of Wardensville.[33] The forests held an estimated 100 million feet of stumpage, three quarters of which was white oak.[34] Rather than ship heavy logs and lumber over wagon roads, the Cornwells organized the Winchester and Western Railroad Company in 1916, with plans to build a 40-mile short line between Winchester and Wardensville.[35] The B&O expressed interest in the new railroad, because its tracks might be extended 25 miles west to Moorefield.[36] At that town, Lost River Lumber's logs could be transferred to its South Branch trains for final shipment to the crosstie plant in Green Spring.[37]

To fund the Winchester and Western, the Cornwells raised $350,000 from investors in Winchester and in Hardy and Hampshire counties, while the B&O purchased most of a $600,000 issue of first mortgage bonds.[38] In 1917, William Cornwell moved from Romney to Winchester to serve as president of the Winchester and Western, whose standard-gauge tracks had already reached Gore in western Frederick County. Next year, the railroad's first shipment was Lost River Lumber Company's one-time sale of 16,000 untreated ties to the U.S. government.[39] They went to the short line's interconnection with the B&O's Valley Branch tracks in Winchester, near Old Dominion Paper Company's mill on Abrams Creek.[40] From there, the B&O hauled the ties to Sparrows Point in Baltimore for shipment to war-torn France.[41]

The Winchester and Western's track finally reached Wardensville in 1921. At its dedication, John Cornwell, then West Virginia's Governor, spoke of the railroad's potential to bring economic development to the Potomac Highlands.[42] He talked of recruiting an electric power plant and woodworking and limestone industries that would have access to the "only independent railroad built in the nation in the last four years."[43] While wood flooring was later milled in Gore, other industry failed to materialize.

In 1921, the Winchester and Western added passenger service, putting steel tires on a bus that allowed it to travel on tracks.[44] From the B&O passenger station at Piccadilly and Kent streets in Winchester, the railbus made two round trips daily to Wardensville. The 17 stops included stations located near the Rock Enon and Capon Springs resorts.[45]

Winchester & Western Railbus near Capon Lake Inn, 1923
Photo from L. P. Winnemore Collection,
posted on Wardensvlle's Facebook page, Wardensville, WV

In 1922, William Cornwell organized Winchester Lumber Company, along with three Winchester men, lawyer R. Gray Williams and lumberyard owners John Rosenberger and Fred L. Glaize, and other investors.[46] The company paid a West Virginia lumber dealer $825,000 for Cacapon Lumber Company, which owned 40,000 acres of timberland in eastern Hardy and Hampshire counties and in western Frederick County.[47] The Lost River Lumber Company's land holdings in the Potomac Highlands became part of Winchester Lumber, with William Cornwell serving as president and general manager. In possession of millions of feet of standing white oak, the company planned on putting 20 sawmills at various points along the Winchester and Western's tracks, but spent $35,000 on just one flooring mill, which opened in Gore in 1922.[48] That same year, the lumber company organized the Lost River Railroad to more easily access timber in the Lost River Valley, southwest of Wardensville.[49] Narrow-gauge tracks with three spurs were laid into hilly forests, where portable steam-powered saws cut logs into 2 million board feet of lumber.[50]

At the time Winchester Lumber started operations, the United States market for lumber softened. Not only were home sizes smaller, but residential builders also found substitutes for lumber that included plywood, cement, concrete block, brick, stucco and aluminum.[51] Facing those headwinds and competition from larger timber companies in the Northwest and the South, the volume of lumber hauled on the Winchester and Western's main line peaked in the early 1920s.

When both the railroad and lumber business went into receivership in 1925, the Gore sawmill closed.[52] Due to illness, William Cornwell resigned his railroad and lumber company presidencies.[53] In 1926, the B&O's Maryland and West Virginia Lumber Company, which had begun buying land in Hardy County, purchased Winchester Lumber at a sheriff's sale.[54] The Gore sawmill later reopened, but a 1930 fire destroyed it and thousands of feet of oak and pine flooring.

In 1929, R. Gray Williams and attorney Herbert Larrick purchased Winchester and Western Railroad Company from receivers for $200,000, then operated it as the Winchester and Wardensville Railway.[55] But the Great Depression caused the nation's lumber production to decline from 26.1 million board feet in 1930, to 10.1 million in 1933.[56] The Lost River Railroad stopped running in 1931.[57] When the Capon Springs and Rock Enon springs resorts closed during the economic downturn, the track between the latter resort and Wardensville was abandoned and all passenger service ended.[58] However, the Winchester and Wardensville began hauling sand from a mine that opened near Gore in 1931.

Besides his involvement in the railroad, R. Gray Williams led Winchester's four-year effort to implement the educational provisions of Judge John Handley's will.[59] He also served as counsel for both Northern Virginia Power Company and Virginia Woolen Company, was division counsel for the B&O Railroad and local counsel for the Pennsylvania Railroad.[60] Williams was president of and counsel for both the Shenandoah Valley National Bank and the

George Washington Hotel Corporation, and was a director of the Chesapeake and Potomac Telephone Company of Virginia.[61]

The struggling Winchester and Wardensville Railway returned to receivership status in 1938, and was sold two years later at auction for $48,300.[62] Under ownership of David Sencindiver, the railroad's former treasurer and general manager, the Winchester and Western name returned in 1941.[63] Three years later, the line was again shortened several miles eastward, from Rock Enon Springs to Gore, close to Virginia Glass Sand Co.'s mine.[64]

Airports

The nation's aviation era began in 1903 with the Wright Brothers' successful test flight at Kitty Hawk, North Carolina.[65] Airplanes came into their own during World War I, when fighter pilots gunned down enemy planes with much success.[66] Postwar, some airmen supported themselves by visiting small towns to show off their flying skills and take paying passengers on short rides. Charles Lindbergh's non-stop flight across the Atlantic in 1927 stirred new interest in the transportation mode.[67] At decade's end, 145 municipally owned airports dotted the nation's landscape.[68]

In the early 1920s, pilots took off and landed at two airstrips on Berkeley County farms: Van Meter Field, east of Martinsburg, and Kunkle Field to the north, later known as the North End Airport and then Ruppenthal Field.[69] In 1923, the Army Air Service mapped out the nation's first designated airway, which went from the nation's capital through Cumberland to Dayton, Ohio.[70] When the Army encouraged communities along the way to provide emergency landing fields, the Shepherd family gave newly organized Berkeley Aviation Committee enough land for an airfield that was close to the Army's proposed route.[71] After a crushed gravel runway south of Martinsburg was built with a white-washed large "M" on it, the city joined the Army Air Service's program. In 1927, the Berkeley Aviation Committee added an operations building near the runway.[72] Six years later, the renamed Berkeley Aviation Club managed Shepherd Field, sold fuel, promoted aviation and encouraged related businesses to locate near it.[73] In 1934, the club purchased the airfield and deeded it to the City of Martinsburg, and later to Berkeley County.[74]

Frederick County's introduction to aviation came in 1912 when a barnstormer landed a Curtiss Model 12 plane at the fairgrounds.[75] In 1927, Bowles Field opened east of Winchester, on part of its namesake family's farm, with

Shenandoah Flying Service, Inc. providing flights.[76] The grass runway, a small hangar and 35 acres were optioned to the Winchester Aero Club. In 1931, it leased 129 acres and built a much larger runway.[77] Located near the intersection of U.S. 522 South and U.S. 50 East, the property was renamed Admiral Byrd Field, in honor of the polar explorer and Winchester native.[78]

Shepherd Field near Martinsburg Postcard published by Neff Novelty Co., Cumberland, MD

Six years later, the City of Winchester exercised an option to buy the airfield.[79] After Virginia licensed the renamed Winchester Municipal Airport, local businessmen formed Valley Airways, Inc., which became the airport's fixed-base operator, selling fuel and providing maintenance service for planes.[80]

Electric Power Providers

When the Potomac River's low flow in 1914 reduced outputs at Martinsburg Power Company's two hydroelectric plants, the utility placed greater reliance on its costlier, coal-fired generator in the city. Northern Virginia Power Company in Winchester, which provided electricity to Jefferson and Morgan counties, had been denied a franchise to sell electricity in Martinsburg. It sought to buy the financially stressed utility, but met competition from Emory Coblentz, a Middletown, Maryland, businessman who owned several interurban electric rail lines.[81] After advertising rate reductions for Martinsburg Power's customers, his Hagerstown and Frederick Railway Company purchased the utility in 1916 for $575,000.[82] The two businesses were combined as Potomac Light and Power Company.[83]

Coblentz failed in his first attempt to acquire a majority interest in Northern Virginia Power Company. However, the Winchester utility suffered a perfect storm of operating and financial problems during World War I: labor turnover, high coal prices, severe shortages of electrical equipment and difficulties in obtaining rate increases from state regulators.[84] In 1919, Northern Virginia Power accepted a buyout offer from Coblentz and a group of Frederick City, Hagerstown and Baltimore investors.[85] They combined it with Potomac Light and Power Company as Potomac Public Service Company, based in Hagerstown.[86]

Between 1922 and 1928, Potomac Public Service was involved in various acquisitions and divestitures that resulted in the formation of West Penn Electric, a public company based in New York City.[87] Its three operating units included Potomac Edison, serving Winchester and Frederick, Clarke and Warren counties; Monongahela Power in the Eastern Panhandle; and West Penn Power, which supplied electricity to parts of western Pennsylvania. Residential and commercial customers of West Penn Electric benefited from inexpensive electricity, because its steam-generating facilities were located in the midst of one of the richest coal regions in the United States.[88] And long-term contracts with large coal companies guaranteed the utility a steady supply of the fuel at known prices.[89]

A 1925 fire destroyed Savery and Company's Potomac Paper Mill and damaged the equipment at its Harpers Ferry Electric Light and Power Company. After a smaller, more modern hydroelectric plant was built, the utility's output more than doubled to 830,000 kilowatt hours, transmitted to customers in Harpers Ferry, nearby Bolivar and several Maryland towns.[90] In 1928, Thomas Savery sold the renamed Potomac Power Plant and two pulp mills for $1.1 million to National Electric Power Company.[91] It was a subsidiary of Virginia Public Service Company, owned by utility industry consolidator Samuel Insull.

Between the two world wars, electricity providers in Shenandoah and Page counties were consolidated into large systems headquartered outside the region. By 1921, Valley Light and Power's turbines alongside Burnshire Dam, on the North Fork of the Shenandoah River, were supplying electricity to Woodstock. In 1924, floods destroyed that dam and power plant, as well as others on the river that former gristmill owners operated. Those that were rebuilt became part of Virginia Power Company in Richmond. In 1922, local businessman M. E. Roudabush organized Page Power Company in the village of Newport, which produced electricity from a plant and dam it built on the Shenandoah River, west of Luray.[92] By 1927, the five electric plants in Page County had been merged into Roudabush's company, which the Allegheny Power System, successor to West Penn Electric, later purchased.[93]

Northern Valley Economy: More Jobs Move from Farm to Factory

The Northern Valley's agriculture and manufacturing sectors benefited from a burst of export activity during World War I. As both volumes and prices of wheat and apples rose, so did the incomes of farmers and orchardists. The region's woolen mills were kept busy supplying Allied armies with blankets, overcoats and uniforms. Its quarries and mines fed lime, dolomite and manganese to the nation's steel mills, whose output went to manufacturers of armaments, warships, military vehicles and airplanes. Several canneries in the Page Valley provided the troops with food.

Between 1910 and 1930, the Northern Valley's population grew by 10.4 percent, but still lagged the 33.1 percent increase the United States posted.[94] During those two decades, headcounts in each county barely increased, ranging from Morgan County's 7.1 percent, down to Jefferson County's near zero growth.[95] However, with manufacturing jobs bringing new residents into Winchester, its population grew by 85.1 percent, while Martinsburg's 38.9 percent increase also outpaced the nation. Those cities together accounted for 21.6 percent of the region's population in 1930, compared to just 10 percent in 1860.[96]

Winchester's growth occurred after woolen and cotton mills, apple processing plants and related businesses opened.[97] In 1935, Virginia Woolen Company was the largest employer with 450 workers, followed by National Fruit Product Company's 400-person payroll.[98] Woolen and clothing industries powered Martinsburg's growth. Its largest employers in 1925 were Interwoven Stocking with 1,470 workers, followed by Berkeley Woolen with 300, the B&O Railroad's 200, and Dunn Woolen's 170 workers.[99]

Organizations Formed to Promote Business

For most United States cities and towns, boards of trade and chambers of commerce served as hometown boosters. Made up of local businessmen, the organizations sought to attract commerce and industry, which in turn would lead to increased sales and profits for their members. The Winchester Chamber of Commerce was organized in 1917 with a mission to "Promote the general welfare and prosperity of Winchester and Frederick County, and to encourage the commercial growth of the area." [100] Between 1922 and 1940, chambers were organized in Luray, Martinsburg and Front Royal.

In 1925, local businessmen formed the Edinburg Board of Trade to recruit manufacturers. Four years later, its brochure read, "Grow with us in the heart of the famous Shenandoah Valley." [101] It went on to state that Edinburg offered low taxes, good factory sites and plenty of "cooperative workers that are unorganized, and free from strife and unrest prevalent in many industrial centers." [102]

Downtown Development

The motorcar ended the farmer's isolation and gave Northern Valley families more shopping options than those found at their nearest general store. After World War I, they piled into cars and drove on U.S. 11 to Martinsburg and Winchester for a wider selection of goods at better prices. A more mobile public also traveled to county seats to conduct business at courthouses, government offices and to utilize medical and education facilities. Their Main Streets filled up with restaurants, hotels, banks and locally owned department, dry goods and general merchandise stores, with others specializing in groceries, shoes, stationary, furniture, pharmaceuticals, hardware and apparel.

But those retailers faced new competitors in the twentieth century. With rural-free delivery available nationwide in 1902, and parcel post introduced in 1913, mail order companies—Sears Roebuck & Co. and Montgomery Ward—took business away from the region's Main Street retailers.[103] In 1927, JC Penney became the first department store chain to locate on Winchester's Loudoun Street, and a Montgomery Ward store followed, three years later.

Independent retailers faced additional competition from five and dime chain stores that offered low prices. On Winchester's Main Street, McCrory's arrived in 1916 at the former Taylor Hotel and a J. J. Newberry store opened in 1929. The two stores appeared on Martinsburg's North Queen Street in 1923 and 1925, respectively.[104] Capitalizing on their popularity, local entrepreneurs opened independent five and dime stores in several of the larger towns.

The region's two cities offered the public more than a shopping experience. Their downtowns boomed with family-owned restaurants and motion picture theaters that featured silent films. In Winchester, movies were first shown in 1909 at the Empire Theater on North Cameron Street, but Warner Brothers purchased and renamed it the Capitol Theater in 1927.[105] The 305-seat Grand Moving Picture Theater appeared in 1913, then operated under various names until 1931, when it opened on South Loudoun Street as the Palace Theater.[106] In Martinsburg, the Apollo Theater on East Martin Street, later called the Apollo Civic Theater, replaced the deteriorating Central Opera House in 1914. It joined the Strand movie theater as one of the city's popular entertainment venues.[107]

Two large hotels with restaurants and meeting rooms became civic and social centers. In 1924, Winchester businessmen spent $600,000 on the 102-room George Washington Hotel, which American Hotels Corporation managed as part of its Colonial chain.[108] With a brick exterior and concrete

*Capitol Theater in Winchester, view from stage, 1929
Photo from cinematreasures.org website*

floors and walls, the GW was marketed as fire proof, contrasting itself to numerous wood-framed hotels that had burned.[109] In 1926, Martinsburg investors raised $600,000 to build the five-story Shenandoah Hotel on the corner of Queen and Martin streets.[110] Featuring the Crystal Dining and Gold Ball rooms, it advertised that travelers should, "Stop at the gateway to the Shenandoah Valley." [111]

As more local shoppers and tourists drove automobiles to the region's downtowns, entrepreneurs opened businesses along highways. Gas pumps placed in front of country stores served the driving public, but car mechanics later opened full-service stations with fueling pumps outside and repair bays inside.[112] Tourist courts and motor lodges—later known as motels—sprang up on heavily traveled routes and offered less-expensive accommodations than downtown hotels.[113] During the busy summer months, some enterprising families turned their residences into tourist homes.[114]

Agriculture: Dieting on Apples and Milk

While Europe's agricultural sector returned to normalcy after World War I, America's wheat harvest continued apace, despite a reduced market for exports. As its price dropped and apple prices rose in the 1920s, more Northern Valley farmers pursued orcharding. When an oversupply of cattle and pigs in the Midwest and Great Plains forced prices down, some livestock farmers milked cows.

The region's farmers organized to obtain technical assistance and procure less-expensive services and goods. In 1913, the Frederick County Farmers' Bureau secured federal and state funds to hire a farm demonstrator.[115] In 1921, the Page Cooperative Farm Bureau used the buying power of its members to negotiate lower prices from suppliers.[116]

County fairs promoted the region's agriculture. In the fall of 1916, fifteen exhibitors participated in a one-day show at a Berkeley County school.[117] Within five years, the non-profit Berkeley County Fair had expanded its annual event to two days with 80 exhibitors.[118] The Shenandoah County Agricultural Society ran fairs in Woodstock from 1886 into the early 1900s.[119] In 1916, the newly-formed Shenandoah County Fair Association purchased the society's grounds and buildings, then held its first event the following summer.[120] An agricultural fair took place at Luray's Massanutten Heights in 1930, followed by Frank Rosser's Page County Fair, held from 1934 to 1966 on the town's North Hawksbill Street.[121] Other Northern Valley counties followed with their own fairs, with help from local Ruritan Clubs.

Wheat Farming

The nation's wheat farmers, including those in the Northern Valley, rode an economic roller coaster from World War I through the Great Depression. With European farmers fighting, not tending to their crops, America's wheat exports jumped from 18 million bushels in 1914 to 98 million the following year.[122] When the price soared from 97 cents a bushel in 1914 to $2.16 in 1919, Northern Valley farmers harvested a decennial record 2.3 million bushels in 1920, up from 2.1 million in 1910.[123]

When Europe's wheat production recovered, the price quickly dropped to $1.03 a bushel in 1921, barely above its prewar level.[124] As some farmers switched to orcharding during the 1920s, the Northern Valley wheat harvest declined for the first time in an agriculture census. From 2.3 million bushels in 1920, it dropped by almost 40 percent to 1.4 million in 1930.[125] Wheat farmers suffered more pain during the Great Depression, when the price fell to 60 cents a bushel in 1930, and bottomed three years later at 38 cents, before recovering to 87 cents in 1940.[126] Additional hardship came when a severe drought, which began in the summer of 1930, lasted into 1932.[127] By then, a number of Northern Valley farmers had either switched to other agricultural pursuits or left the business altogether.[128]

Raising Livestock and Dairying

After World War I, an oversupply of cattle caused the hundredweight price of beef to drop from a high of $15.50 in 1919 to $10.95 in 1930.[129] And with America's economy at its most depressed level, it slid to $5.42 in 1933 when consumers switched to less expensive proteins. By the end of World War II, the price had recovered to $16.18 per hundredweight, too late for those farmers who had already traded steers for cows.[130] Although milking them was a labor- and capital-intensive endeavor, compared to raising beef cattle, the number of dairy farms in Virginia soared, from 4,300 in 1910 to 13,700 in 1920.[131]

The price farmers received for wholesale milk jumped from $1.58 per hundred pounds in 1915 to $3.29 by the end of World War I.[132] But when the fighting stopped, increased production caused milk prices to fluctuate around the $2.25 level.[133] To boost demand, specialists from the Dairy Division of the U.S. Department of Agriculture ran advertising campaigns in the 1920s to promote milk's nutritional value.[134] The ads generated increased consumption, especially in the Washington, D.C. area, the main market for Northern Valley dairy farmers. However, the campaign could not prevent the price from sinking by 43 percent to $1.28 per hundred pounds during the Great Depression.[135]

To gain more control over end markets, some dairy farmers joined the Maryland & Virginia Milk Producers Cooperative Association, Inc. to process their milk into value-added products.[136] Organized in 1920 in Reston, Virginia, its members shared in the profits in proportion to the volume of milk each one shipped to it. Two years later, other dairymen joined the Valley of Virginia Milk Producers Cooperative Association. It marketed the Shenandoah's Pride brand of milk, processed at a plant near Harrisonburg.[137]

Orcharding

Prior to World War I, Northern Valley orchardists realized high prices from apples sold duty-free to Great Britain, but that market shut down during the conflict. And with local men off fighting in Europe in 1918, harvesting apples from thousands of trees in Frederick County was problematic. In their place, hundreds of women from all classes of society volunteered to pick them. Local companies hired out their employees to orchardists and soldiers from Camp Lee in Prince Georges County provided additional help.[138]

When the export market returned to prewar levels, apple prices more than tripled, from 57 cents per bushel in 1914 to $1.78 in 1919.[139] Not surprisingly, Northern Valley orchards were sold at higher prices. In 1911, Franklin Wissler's 400-acre orchard in the Meem's Bottom area of Shenandoah County went for what was then a record $375 an acre.[140] Eight years later, S. Lucien Lupton sold his 267-acre Stonewall Orchard in Frederick County for twice that price, $750 per acre.[141] The buyers were the three sons of Charles Robinson, owner of C. L. Robinson Ice and Cold Storage Corporation in Winchester.[142]

Northern Valley's apple production grew rapidly. In the Virginia portion of the region, the harvest more than quintupled, from 658,000 bushels in 1910 to 3,560,000 in 1930, and the Eastern Panhandle's output increased by almost eight-fold, from 444,000 bushels to 3,354,000.[143] Orchards in Berkeley and Frederick counties, many located near Apple Pie Ridge, accounted for 61 percent of the region's production in 1930.[144]

Between one-quarter and one-half of the fruit rode on refrigerated apple trains to the Eastern Seaboard for export. Most ended up in England, with the balance shipped to the European continent, the Caribbean and South America.[145] In the 1920s, H. F. Byrd, Inc. in Berryville was a major exporter of apples. The company's 150,000 trees yielded one-half million bushels each year, 75 percent of which was shipped on the Norfolk and Western Railroad for eventual export to England, Germany, Argentina and Cuba.[146]

As the region's apple business matured, orchardists organized the Winchester Research Laboratory in 1921. Its mission was to consolidate studies done on fertilizer uses, cultivation techniques and chemical spraying that had previously been conducted at five experimental orchards.[147] A laboratory and insectary were built west of Stephens City, on land Shenandoah Valley Apple Cider and Vinegar Corporation owned.[148]

Warehousing: Keeping More Apples Longer

After World War I, the region's fruit storage industry mirrored the growth of the apple harvest. Founded in 1905, Winchester-based C. L. Robinson Ice and Cold Storage Corporation became one of the largest operators of those warehouses in the eastern United States. In 1917, it converted a former horseshoe factory in Strasburg into a cold storage facility that also made ice, then acquired Berryville Ice and Refrigerating Co.[149] Four years later, the C. L. Robinson company built a fireproof cold storage building next to its flagship facility in Winchester, which brought their combined capacity up to 180,000 bushels of apples. By 1929, the company's four locations could hold 500,000 bushels, but it faced competition from two orchardist-owned businesses.

Not wanting to rely on C. L. Robinson for their storage needs, Harry Byrd Sr. and other apple growers organized Winchester Cold Storage Co., Inc. in 1917. They built a warehouse near Robinson's that stored up to 550,000 bushels of apples.[150] After additions in 1920 and 1929 increased the capacity to 1.5 million bushels, the company advertised it as the world's largest cold storage facility.[151]

In 1929, Frederick County orchardists formed Virginia Apple Storage, Inc., which erected a building with a 325,000-bushel capacity on 28 acres near Winchester's Valley Pike.[152] Glaize Apple Packing House occupied the rear wing, near a rail spur from the B&O line. After Glaize moved into its own building at Pennsylvania Avenue and Commerce Street, the Winchester Apple Growers Association packed and shipped fruit from the vacated space.[153]

Winchester Cold Storage Co. warehouse
Postcard published by Shenandoah Publishing House,
Strasburg, VA

Using ammonia and similar equipment, the cold storage and artificial ice businesses were extensions of each another. Six years after Luray Ice Co. opened in 1911, it built a cold storage warehouse that held 70,000 bushels of apples.[154] In competition with the C. L. Robinson company, Winchester Cold Storage made ice at its facility. In 1921, general manager Jacob W. Gatrell purchased Rothwell & Co., a cold storage business founded in Martinsburg in 1897. The renamed Rothwell-Gatrell Corp. purchased equipment capable of producing 35 tons of ice daily.[155]

Manufacturing: Producing Various Finished Goods

Between World War I and 1930, several industries that increased their presence in the Northern Valley processed fruit, milled wool cloth, sewed clothing, machine-knitted hosiery, fabricated barrels and canned vegetables. During the same period, industries relatively new to the region packed fruit and made bricks and cement. By the early 1900s, however, producers of leather, pottery and cigars had been the victims of creative destruction. New technologies and discoveries caused their industries to either disappear or suffer reductions in size and scope.

Textile and Clothing Industry

Before America's late entrance into World War I, most of Virginia Woolen's production in Winchester was sold to the Allies as uniform cloth.[156] Berkeley Woolen in Martinsburg sent 25,000 yards to the French and was awarded a large contract from the United States Army for Khaki cloth.[157] When America joined the fight in 1917, the Clothing and Equipage Division of the U.S. War Department ensured that Northern Valley woolen mills had enough raw wool to produce blankets and cloth for military uniforms and overcoats.[158]

Postwar, Berkeley Woolen, Virginia Woolen, and Dunn Woolen companies supplied Ford, General Motors and Chrysler with seat cover material for their automobiles. Under the presidency of Martinsburg attorney Howard H. Emmert, Berkeley Woolen Company raised capital in 1919 to expand into other buildings, moves that three years later resulted in a payroll of 250 workers.[159] Emmert was also president of Old National Bank, counsel and director of Interwoven Hosiery Company and head of the Berkeley Bar Association.[160]

In Winchester, Hollie McCormac Sr. increased Virginia Woolen's loom count from 80 in 1914 to 124 in 1930.[161] Until his passing in 1937, he held important positions in the region's business and non-profit communities.[162] McCormac succeeded Emmert as president of Berkeley Woolen Company, and was a board member of Winchester Milling Corp., Colonial Brick Corporation, Winchester Credit Co., Union Bank of Winchester and Mount Clifton Orchard Corp. in Shenandoah County.[163] He also helped organize the local chamber of commerce and Rotary club, and at one time was executive committee chair of Winchester Memorial Hospital and leader of Virginia's Republican Party.[164]

One woolen company's fortune soared, then collapsed. After purchasing Winchester Woolen Mill in 1917, the Chicago Wool Company sold it in 1926 to Arthur G. Jones of Fairmont, West Virginia.[165] When an addition was put on the Abrams Creek structure, the renamed Arthur Jones Woolen Mill's product line expanded into cloth for knickers and caps. With 200 workers producing 10,000 yards weekly, output tripled.[166] But in 1929, it was discovered that Jones and the treasurer had embezzled funds, actions that resulted in prison sentences for both men and bankruptcy for the company.[167] Next year, 25 Winchester businessmen organized the Winchester Woolen Company and purchased the Jones company's mill at auction for $28,000.[168]

After World War I, the assembly lines ran continuously at Interwoven Stocking Company's facilities in Martinsburg. Artist Norman Rockwell designed ads that emphasized the durability of its high-end men's socks.[169] With 40 salesmen calling on 10,000 retail accounts in the 1920s, Interwoven opened factories in Hagerstown, Chambersburg and Berkeley Springs.[170] In 1930, its 1,800 employees in Martinsburg were the largest workforce in the region.[171]

Interwoven Stocking Company workers in Martinsburg factory
Photo from West Virginia and Regional History Collection, WVU Libraries, Morgantown, WV

When the women's skirt market declined after the war, John Poland turned to producing muslin underwear at his Perfection Garment Company in Martinsburg.[172] He added capacity at the Keyser, West Virginia, facility and at the former A. H. Maxwell Garment factory in Ranson, which Poland purchased in 1918.[173] When Perfection's postwar production shifted back to skirts, its sales rose to $1.5 million in 1930.[174]

Not all postwar textile manufacturing was based in Martinsburg and Winchester. Founded on Maryland's Eastern Shore in 1904, Casey Jones Work-Clothes Company opened an overall factory on Luray's West Main Street in 1923.[175] An employee recruitment sign read, "Wanted, learners-operators, steady work for industrious girls." [176] Several years later, Casey Jones added factories in rail-served towns of Shenandoah, Woodstock, Mount Jackson and Elkton. Sixty women in Luray cut raw cloth into various men's and boy's jean sizes.[177] The pieces were sent to the other factories, where 80 to 100 women at each one sewed them into jeans that were returned to Luray for quality control inspection, packing and shipping.[178] After Blue Bell Overall Company from Greensboro, North Carolina, purchased Casey Jones in 1943, the jeans were marketed under the Wrangler brand.[179]

Apple Processing Industry

During and after World War I, five apple processors joined the region's two vinegar plants. To be closer to orchards, National Fruit Product Company, Inc. built a facility in 1918 on Winchester's Fairmont Avenue, next to Shenandoah Valley Apple Cider & Vinegar.[180] Its origins began 10 years earlier, when B. Fleet Board and Frank Armstrong Sr. purchased an Alexandria business that repackaged New York sourced vinegar.[181] After one year, Board, Armstrong and Company, Inc. brought manufacturing in house.[182] Upon his partner's death in 1912, Armstrong formed National Fruit Product Company, Inc., with White House as the brand name.[183] The famous building could be seen from the company's Alexandria plant.

After its Winchester facility opened, National Fruit purchased the former Hannis Distillery in Martinsburg in 1919, repurposed it into a vinegar plant and added a cold storage warehouse for upwards of 100,000 bushels of apples.[184] Expanding beyond the Northern Valley, in 1921 the company built an apple processing facility in Waynesboro, Virginia.[185] An addition to the Winchester plant in 1923 tripled its capacity to press cider and vinegar.[186] After fire destroyed the Alexandria plant two years later, Armstrong moved its production to Winchester.[187] Producing 2.5 million gallons of vinegar each year, the plant was the largest of its kind in the world.[188] In 1929, National Fruit purchased companies with apple juice and vinegar factories in Atlanta; Glassboro, New Jersey; and the Pennsylvania towns of Peach Glen and Chambersburg.[189]

National Fruit Product Co. plant in Martinsburg
Postcard published by Naturecraft, Davis, WV

Besides National Fruit, other cider and vinegar plants opened in the Virginia part of the region. In Front Royal in 1920, Orchards Products Co. opened a plant to process cider and vinegar near Virginia Ice and Cold Storage Co.'s building.[190] It was led by J. B. Harnsberger, the founder of Old Virginia Orchard Co., which opened in 1912 to can apple products in the same town. In 1923, Orchards Products was sold to Richmond Vinegar Works, Inc., which expanded cider production the next year.[191] In Strasburg in 1927, Shenandoah Apple Products Co., Inc. was organized to purchase Strasburg Fruit Products Co. Inc., which had started up seven years earlier to produce cider and vinegar.[192] The new owner kept the existing plant and built another to pack apples and process apple sauce and butter.[193]

After West Virginia State Senator Gray Silver and fellow Berkeley County orchardists organized an apple packing house in Inwood in 1917, they looked for an outlet for their imperfect fruit. Three years later, Silver convinced C. H. Musselman Company in Biglerville, Pennsylvania, to build a $150,000 apple slice plant near the Inwood depot of the Cumberland Valley Railroad.[194] By the late 1920s, its 250 employees produced apple juice, cider and vinegar in what later became the nation's first plant to can applesauce.[195] Besides orcharding,

Gray Silver was the region's largest livestock dealer, breeding short-horn cattle and raising western ranch sheep that provided wool to local mills.[196] He was president of the West Virginia State Senate from 1911 to 1913, and served as director of Peoples National Bank of Martinsburg.[197]

In 1916, U.S. Department of Agriculture inspectors discovered that instead of selling pure fermented apple vinegar, the Cumberland Valley Fruit Products plant in Martinsburg added waste vinegar to its product.[198] The following year, its Pennsylvania owners consented to a judgment of $300 plus court costs.[199] Several years later, the company had to compete with the new Berkeley County plants of National Fruit and Musselman when purchasing apples, which drove up its raw material costs. Despite processing 5 million pounds of the fruit into vinegar each year, Cumberland Valley Fruit Products closed the plant in 1920.[200]

In December 1919, the third fire in 31 months destroyed Shenandoah Valley Apple Cider & Vinegar's complex on Winchester's Fairmont Avenue. The estimated loss of $75,000 included 18 of its 24 vinegar tanks and 12 tons of inventoried apples.[201] But the producer of Apple Pie Ridge Vinegar was soon back in business, after it purchased Cumberland Valley Fruit's recently shuttered Martinsburg plant for $150,000.[202] The cooperative then built a 60,000-square-foot concrete and brick replacement plant in Winchester, and conveyed the other one back to Cumberland Valley Fruit for the original purchase price.[203] No more vinegar production took place there.

In 1920, the Carl Massey family, through its Ridgewood Fruit Growers, Inc. in Winchester, made the Apple Jack Jr. brand of soda, a mixture of apple cider and ginger ale. In 1927, the Masseys formed Ridgewood Orchards Candy Company, later renamed Shenandoah Candy Company, to make apple-flavored sweets.[204] They were marketed throughout the eastern United States as, "Made from the juice of the rich red apples, cane sugar, cornstarch and walnuts." In the early 1930s, the factory on Winchester's Amherst Street produced more than 880,000 pounds of candy annually, packed in wooden containers shaped like the fruit.[205]

Fruit Packing Industry

The availability of manufactured ice and refrigerated boxcars meant fruits and vegetables could travel greater distances between grower and retailer, a separation that sometimes led to abuses in packing fresh produce.[206] After Congress passed the Apple Grading Law in 1912, the U.S. Department of

Agriculture and its state counterparts set standards for packing apples shipped to the fresh market.[207] Ten years later, another federal law required inspections at the point of shipment to certify the apples were accurately graded.[208]

For the Northern Valley's industry to comply with new consumer protection laws, orchardists no longer packed fresh apples on their premises. Instead, they went to packing houses near railroad depots for washing, sorting and grading. Imperfects were removed and sold to further processors. In 1912, several hundred persons attended a week-long Frederick County Packing School to learn how to comply with the new standards. That same year, Woodstock entrepreneurs launched Grabill Manufacturing Company, later known as Agri-Tech, Inc., to fabricate machines that automatically sorted, waxed and packed apples.[209]

In 1917, State Senator Gray Silver secured $100,000 from the West Virginia legislature for construction of the State Demonstration School for Grading and Packing Fruit, located next to the Cumberland Valley Railroad depot in Inwood.[210] Orchardists in Berkeley and Frederick counties sent apples to the renamed West Virginia Community Packing House. Its employees sorted, graded and packed them in baskets with Johnny Appleseed labels on them.[211] The Inwood operation later became part of Federated Fruit and Vegetable Growers, a New York City-based marketing cooperative.[212]

West Virginia Community Packing Plant, Inwood
Photo from West Virginia and Regional History Collection,
WVU Libraries, Morgantown, WV

To share costs, several Jefferson County orchardists in 1921 formed the Apple Products Company that turned a brick building in Shepherdstown into a packing house.[213] Its fruit was later sold through Federated Fruit and Vegetable Growers in Inwood. Fifteen other orchardists formed the Shepherdstown Fruit Growers Club, which contracted with the Apple Products Company to pack apples sold under the Rumsey brand.[214] In Martinsburg, Rothwell-Gatrell Fruit Company, Inc. packed Rothwell Farm and Orchard Company's apples, using the Gold Medal brand.[215]

Shepherdstown Fruit Growers Club display of apples
Photo from West Virginia and Regional History Collection,
WVU Libraries, Morgantown, WV

Some Frederick County orchardists built their own packing houses near Winchester's rail lines and cold storage facilities. In 1917, S. Lucien Lupton moved the task of grading and packing apples from his orchard into a building near Cumberland Valley Railroad's yard. On Wyck Street, H. W. Butler & Brothers Packing Company sorted and packed apples harvested from the family's 1,000 acres of orchards.[216] The Cather family of orchardists packed apples at its Old Mill Cold Storage facility on Valley Avenue, which Virginia Pride Fruit Packers occupied in 1985.[217] In Berryville in 1937, H. F. Byrd, Inc. built a cold storage facility and apple grading and packing house along the Norfolk and Western Railway's tracks, and added a cannery in 1948.[218] Near their Jefferson Orchards to the north, the Byrds opened a packing house in 1946.[219]

Shipping apples from the B&O's depot in Paw Paw since 1912, Consolidated Orchard Co. added a packing operation in 1920. Nine years later, owner Henry W. Miller Sr. and his brothers formed Consolidated Distributors, Inc. to market their locally grown fruit under the Mountaineer label.[220] An industry leader, Miller headed both the National Apple Institute and the International Apple Association. In 1965, Progressive Farmer magazine named him Man of the Year in West Virginia agriculture.[221] When Consolidated Orchard Co. was sold in 1977 to New York and California investors, its Paw Paw packing house was the nation's tenth largest distributor of apples.[222]

Canneries

The demand for canned vegetables expanded rapidly in the first two decades of the twentieth century. The number of cases—each with 24 cans—produced in the United States rose from 29 million in 1904 to 66 million in 1919.[223] To feed their soldiers during World War I, American military commanders sought large quantities of inexpensive canned meats and vegetables that did not spoil in transport and could survive trench warfare conditions. After I. N. Dovel purchased Luray Canning Company in 1914, the renamed Hawksbill Cannery's annual production increased to 30,000 cases of green beans and tomatoes in 1917.[224] Many of them were shipped to American troops fighting in Europe.[225] In 1915, Massanutten Canning Company opened a factory southeast of Front Royal to can tomatoes, green beans and soups marketed under the Massanutten brand.[226] Two years later, its cans were sold to the War Industries Board to feed American soldiers on the battlefields of France.[227]

Postwar, several canneries opened near Norfolk and Western depots in Page County, from which their cans were shipped to East Coast warehouses. In 1918, C. V. Shaffer enlarged and repurposed the spring house on his Leakesville farm into a cannery that produced the Willow Brook brand of tomatoes until 1955.[228] In 1925, Shaffer and neighbor Charles D. Price Jr. purchased a vacant cannery in Stanley that I. N. Dovel built five years earlier, but never operated.[229] They moved its machinery into one in nearby Ingham.[230] From the 1930s to the 1950s, Price also processed vegetables at his Riverdale Canning Company in Alma.[231] Some of its 100 seasonal workers were relocated there from the Blue Ridge Mountains when Shenandoah National Park opened in 1936.

Near the village of Stony Man, Hubert Lucas and Vincent P. Stirewalt opened Lucas & Stirewalt Cannery in 1921 to produce canned tomatoes and green beans sold under the Skyland brand.[232] In 1940, peach orchard owner W. T. Moyer & Sons purchased and renamed it Moyer Brothers Cannery.[233] Until its closure in 1974, the 500 to 600 cases of peaches produced daily were marketed under the Page Valley, Stony Man and Luray Caverns brands.[234]

Experiencing financial problems from high sugar prices, Old Virginia Orchard Company, founded in 1906 in Front Royal, was reorganized in 1924 as Old Virginia Packing Company.[235] Owner Julian Neville Major relocated the business into a new building on 24 acres, near the North Fork of the Shenandoah River.[236] With 200 workers canning apple, grape and tomato juices; apple sauce and butter; marmalade and mincemeat, Old Virginia Packing was one of the town's largest employers.[237]

By the end of World War II, most canneries in the Page Valley had closed. Amendments to the 1906 Pure Food and Drug Act in 1912 and 1913 made it more difficult for those with limited financial resources to meet much stricter sanitary standards.[238] And large farms in California and Florida grew vegetables year-round that were sold to packaged food companies, which canned them for nationwide distribution.

First grown in Morgan County in the early 1890s, tomato plants covered 1,550 acres by World War II.[239] During the two-month harvest, between 2,000 and 3,000 workers processed and packed 2.5 million quarts of tomatoes at 30 canneries.[240] While some cans ended up on shelves of the region's grocery stores, the labels on others bore the Campbell, Hunt, Heinz and Dole names. The local industry suffered during World War II, when farmers left their fields and joined the military. A tomato blight in the late 1940s presented a more serious problem for the Morgan County industry.[241]

Tomato canning also took place nine miles south of the Morgan County border, in the Frederick County village of Cross Junction. Brothers Max and Paul Braithwaite opened Shawnee Springs Foods Canning there in 1928 to pack their own brand of tomatoes.[242] Within four years, the Braithwaite Bros. business also turned small-sized apples from nearby orchards into canned products.

Cooperage Industry

By the early 1900s, a number of Northern Valley fruit processing, limestone and cold storage companies made barrels for their own use. But as their main lines of business expanded, they outsourced production to independently owned cooperages, which formed the Shenandoah Valley Barrel Group in 1919.[243] As the industry grew, Frederick County orchardist and barrel maker John Thwaite inspected and graded locally made barrels for the National Slack Cooperage Manufacturers Association.[244]

By the early 1920s, Virginia Barrel Co., which built a factory in Winchester in 1910, had become the local industry's largest producer. In 1915, the unit of Ohio-based Sandusky Cooperage and Lumber Company made 10,000 staves a day in the Frederick County village of Hayfield, west of Winchester.[245] Three years later, Virginia Barrel purchased Shenandoah Valley Barrel Company in Charles Town, then opened a factory in Shepherdstown.[246] In the early 1920s in Winchester, the company added a mill that made staves, along with headers for barrel tops and bottoms. Virginia Barrel's factory added a line of barrelettes, which were one-half the size of a regular 42-gallon barrel.[247] In 1922, it opened a factory in Paw Paw to supply Consolidated Orchard Co. with barrels.[248]

The region's other barrel fabricators included Winchester Cooperage Company, Inwood Cooperage Company and Cumberland Valley Cooperage Company in Martinsburg. In 1917, the Glaize & Bros. lumber business in Winchester made barrels in Stephens City to serve customers in southern Frederick County. Two years later, Jefferson Cooperage Co. in Charles Town purchased Shenandoah Valley Barrel Co. in Ranson from Virginia Barrel and combined the two businesses.[249] In 1921, orchardist Henry Warden and several local businessmen formed Berryville Basket Co. Inc. to assemble fruit containers at a facility on the Norfolk and Western Railway line.[250] In 1938, Herbert Smalley purchased the company, which made barrels and baskets for the apple industry, and renamed it Smalley Packaging.[251]

As the 1920s ended, the region's cooperage industry faced several headwinds. Competition came from lightweight veneer barrels that were less costly to fabricate and cheaper to ship. When gas-powered forklift trucks became available, the apple industry replaced barrels with large wooden boxes that were easier to assemble and move.[252] Forklift operators raised the heavy boxes on and off trucks and railroad cars, and stacked them inside cold storage facilities. And one-bushel baskets with nailed-down tops were sometimes used to limit bruises on fruit in transit.

Gristmills

Prior to the World War I, Northern Valley gristmill owners sold bags of white flour used in home baking. Afterwards, they faced competition from large midwestern milling companies that marketed their branded flours nationwide. With less wheat grown in the region, some Northern Valley millers ground other items. In 1919, T. H. Locke retrofitted Price's gristmill, situated along the Shenandoah River in Clarke County, to turn locally mined marl limestone into fertilizer.[253] Near the Page County village of Newport, Foltz's Mill switched from wheat to processing feed sold to the region's expanding poultry industry.[254]

Front Royal Milling Co. produced flour, feed and meal from 1901 until 1921, when a basement fire destroyed the building and 18 other downtown structures.[255] Afterwards, the concrete Proctor-Biggs Feed Mill was built on the site to grind corn and other grains into meal for livestock.[256] In 1920, Front Royal and Baltimore investors organized the Front Royal–Riverton Milling Co., which purchased the burned remains of Riverton Mills on the Shenandoah River.[257] There the company built a dam, hydroelectric plant and a gristmill with a daily output of 300 barrels of flour.[258] Facing financial problems two years later, the complex was sold at auction to several local businessmen for $20,000.[259] Rather than process flour, their Riverton Mills Corporation made commercial fertilizer from nearby limestone, until the mill burned in 1957.[260]

At the end of the Second World War, only a few Northern Valley gristmills produced flour. They included Page Mill in Luray; Stoner-Keller Mill in Fishers Hill, west of Strasburg; Bunker Hill Mill, in southern Berkeley County; Bartonsville Mill, the former Springdale Flour Mill, south of Winchester; Edinburg Mill and Lantz Mill, both on Stony Creek in Shenandoah County; Mount Jackson Mill; and the Burwell-Morgan Mill in Millwood.[261]

Tanning and Glove Industries

Several headwinds hurt the bottom lines of Northern Valley tanneries that used locally sourced tan bark to turn animal skins into leather. By the end of the nineteenth century, the industry put hides into a chromium solution that was cheaper and faster acting than tannin, even though tan bark produced a better-quality product. In addition, the availability of synthetic rubber reduced the amount of sole leather used in shoes and boots. Finally, as automobiles, trucks and tractors replaced horsepower, the demand for harness and saddle leather declined.

After World War I, Deford Tanning Company in Baltimore, which never joined the Leather Trust, was slow to recover from the rising cost of hides used at its Luray Tannery, once the largest in the nation.[262] When sales declined during the Great Depression, the company took bankruptcy in 1938. Five years later, the Federal Reserve Bank of Richmond sold the company to Arthur and Stephen Blaut, members of a German tanning family.[263] Running the Luray facility from New York City, they reopened it under the former Virginia Oak Tannery name.[264] The 250 workers used chemical solutions to process 600 hides per day for shoe leather.[265] For several years after tanning ceased in 1980, cut sole leather was finished for the western boot industry.[266]

Four companies owned Vesuvius Tannery during its 83 years in Paw Paw. In the 1930s, upwards of 450 workers processed more than 500 hides a day at the world's largest belt leather tannery.[267] In 1942, Keystone Tanning and Glue Company from Pennsylvania, part of the Leather Trust, became Vesuvius's last owner. When Paw Paw workers voted for a union in 1951, Keystone closed the tannery.[268]

After William Graichen's passing in 1915, W. C. Graichen Glove Company in Winchester was sold to local businessmen C. T. Owen and Charles W. Trenary. The renamed Owen and Trenary Glove Company became known for both extended cuffs on its railroad gauntlet gloves and the dress and automobile gloves displayed in its factory's windows.[269] It remained in business until Trenary's death in 1930, a time when large quantities of synthetic gloves made in low-wage countries came to America.[270]

Brick Manufacturing

By the early 1900s, brick factories serving regional markets had replaced most brickyards found in small towns. In the Northern Valley, the Berkeley County factories of Buxton Brick Works and Adamantine Clay Products Co. were started in 1895 and 1911, respectively. The Buxton factory closed after its namesake owner died in 1918. Two years earlier, sparks from a nearby B&O locomotive set fire to the Adamantine facility in the North Mountain area near Hedgesville, but the building and its contents were insured for much less than the $100,000 worth of damage.[271] Rebuilt with a daily capacity of 50,000 bricks, Adamantine went through bankruptcy in 1917, an outcome it repeated in 1925.[272] The following year, E. Taylor Chewning, owner of United Clay Products Co. in Washington, D.C., purchased Adamantine and gave it his company's name. Since 1911, United Clay Products had mined clay in the North Mountain area, which the B&O shipped to its brick factory in the nation's capital.

In 1916, Baltimore and New York investors organized Municipal Shale Brick & Block Company to manufacture paving bricks in Martinsburg.[273] A factory costing $250,000 was built along Charles Town Road, as was a rail spur to the B&O's tracks.[274] The company planned to put an addition on the factory and build a $500,000 facility nearby, but instead took bankruptcy in 1919.[275] Next year, Hudson Cement & Supply Co. in Baltimore acquired Municipal Shale Brick & Block for $75,000 and planned to make brick and tile at the factory, but Chewning purchased it at auction.[276] At the renamed Continental Clay Products factory, he replaced the beehive kilns with a continuous production line that made 60,000 face bricks daily.[277]

In 1922, Winchester investors organized Colonial Brick Company to meet the demand from local architects and builders for colonial style bricks and eliminate the high cost of shipping the building material to the city.[278] On the site of a former brick kiln just north of Winchester, Colonial built a factory that made bricks patterned after those found at Mount Vernon.[279] A dinky hauled shale from an open-pit mine, one-half mile to the factory.[280] Besides their local use, Colonial's bricks went into the construction of several federal buildings in the metro D.C. area.

Cement Manufacturing

By 1900, concrete, mortar and stucco had become popular substitutes for brick and stone. Portland cement, which consisted of at least 80 percent high-quality lime, was an important component of those newer building materials, because it was more durable than regular cement. From less than 1 million barrels in 1895, Portland cement production in the United States soared to 176 million barrels in 1928.[281]

With plenty of 99.5 percent pure limestone quarried in Berkeley County, two groups showed interest in building a cement plant in Martinsburg, but neither made the necessary large capital investment. Loring Cover, who with his father once owned the Star Tannery in western Frederick County and several others in the Potomac Highlands, did build a plant. Two years after the latter tanneries were sold to United States Leather in 1905, Cover and other Baltimore businessmen founded Security Cement & Lime Co. and raised $3 million.[282] In the village of Security, just north of Hagerstown, they built a Portland cement plant with a daily capacity of 1,000 barrels.[283]

Soon after World War I, Security Cement & Lime started up a similar plant south of downtown Martinsburg, near a Standard Lime and Stone Company quarry. It was also situated on the B&O's Frog Hollow Branch, a two-mile rail spur from the railroad's main line. To meet increased demand for its Portland cement, the plant's capacity was doubled in 1920.[284] Seven years later, the Baker family in Baltimore, owners of Standard Lime and Stone—the Northern Valley's largest limestone business—purchased the plant.[285] Because its product went mainly into the Washington, D.C. market, the business was renamed Capitol Cement Corp.[286]

Pulp and Cardboard Industries

The 1920s were not good times for the nation's pulp, paper and cardboard industries. To improve productivity, participants invested in more sophisticated and larger machines, and the resulting over-capacity caused pulp and paper prices to drop.[287] Operating with outdated equipment, Savery and Company's Potomac Pulp Mill, which began grinding logs in 1890 near Harpers Ferry, had difficulty in achieving profitability.[288] After a 1924 flood damaged the company's nearby Shenandoah Pulp Mill, it operated at only one-third capacity.[289] The following year, a fire destroyed the Potomac Pulp Mill, but owner Thomas Savery was able to rebuild the profitable Harpers Ferry Power and Light Company's plant, located inside the mill. In 1928, he sold the mills and power company to utility industry consolidator Samuel Insull, who seven years later closed the money-losing Shenandoah Pulp Mill.[290]

Remaining independent from the Strawboard Trust, Halltown Paper Board Company's mill in Jefferson County turned recycled wastepaper into corrugated cardboard. Demand increased after World War I, when the nation packed and shipped more items in boxes, but industry over-capacity forced the company into receivership in 1922.[291] After management invested in new machinery and renovated the mill, the business recovered and survived the Great Depression.[292] Despite three ownership changes after World War II, the renamed Halltown Paperboard mill, which first made strawboard in 1867, remained the oldest manufacturing facility in West Virginia.[293]

When war-related embargos on recycled paper subsided in 1916, American Strawboard Company reopened its Old Dominion Paper Company's cardboard mill on Winchester's Papermill Road. Experiencing financial problems from industry over-capacity, it took bankruptcy in 1923.[294] Six years later, Indianapolis industrialist Nathan Carpenter purchased it and formed Shenandoah Paper Boxboard Corporation.[295] In 1933, his son Nate reorganized it as Eastern Board and Paper Company, but after the mill lost money during the Great

Depression, he shuttered it in 1935.[296] Four years later, Kieckhefer Container Company in New Jersey, which pioneered the use of fiber-based shipping containers, purchased the property.[297] Each day, 80 employees of its Eddy Paper unit converted waste pulp from its other mills into 44 tons of linerboard used to make milk cartons.[298]

Extractive Industries: Mining More Limestone and Sand

Although owners of the region's manganese mines benefited briefly from increased sales to American steel mills during World War I, they met with mixed success in the years that followed. Lime shipments from the Shenandoah Valley declined by almost one-half during the Great Depression, then bounced back during World War II with increased sales to the steel industry. Between the two wars, Morgan County's silica sand industry came under ownership of a single company and a new mine opened near the village of Gore in western Frederick County.

Manganese Mining

During the First World War, a Turkey-German blockade of the Dardanelles Straits prevented Russia from shipping its inexpensive manganese ore to United States steel mills.[299] In response, several Northern Valley mines helped supply the industry with the metal it needed to support the Allied war effort. In 1915, H. P. Binswanger Company from New York City acquired Powell's Fort mine in Fort Valley and shipped 135 tons of manganese to Pittsburgh.[300] For the next three years, National Carbon Company in Cleveland leased the mine and extracted more than 1,000 tons of manganese used for wartime production of steel, hydrochloric acid and dry cell batteries.[301] When Powell's Fort mine closed at war's end, 275 men lost their jobs.[302] A Richmond company purchased it in 1925, but faced with strong foreign competition and high costs of extracting the remaining manganese, it shuttered the mine two years later.[303]

In 1917, several Pittsburgh investors formed Shenandoah Valley Manganese Corporation to reopen the 1890s Eureka Mine, near Stanley in Page County, and build a half-mile rail spur to the Norfolk and Western line.[304] During the First World War, 1,600 tons of manganese went to Pennsylvania steel mills.[305] The Eureka Mine was closed when Paul Tyler from Washington,

D.C. purchased it in 1928.[306] From the renamed Stanley Mine, he shipped a total of 4,000 tons of manganese until 1936, when all mineral had been extracted.[307]

The Godlove manganese mine, near the village of Zepp in southwestern Shenandoah County, was worked in the late 1840s and again in the 1890s, but limited amounts of metal were shipped from it.[308] During World War I, the locally owned U.S. Manganese & Mineral Company reopened the mine and hauled the mineral to Winchester for rail shipment to Pittsburgh steel mills.[309] In 1920, Kaylor-Fleming Manganese Company leased the Zepp property, but delivered only 25 tons of manganese to chemical companies, before closing the mine.[310]

From 1832 until 1889, several operators extracted manganese intermittently from the Paddy Run Mine, near Star Tannery in western Frederick County.[311] Four years later, Charles Nelson in Strasburg purchased the renamed Mineral Ridge Mine. At the start of World War I, he sold it along with mineral rights on 300 acres to W. B. Shaffer, owner of an engineering company in Pennsylvania.[312] After spending $50,000 to update the mine's processing plant, Shaffer and Nelson formed Mineral Ridge Manganese Corp., secured mineral rights on 400 more acres and installed equipment on Paddy Run to clean the ore.[313] From 6,000 feet of tunnels, the company extracted 1,500 tons of the metal that went to the B&O's Valley Branch depot at Oranda, west of Strasburg, for shipment to steel and chemical companies.[314]

In 1920, Nelson took full ownership of the Mineral Ridge Mine and leased it to Hy-Grade Manganese Company, which extracted a total of 10,000 tons until 1932.[315] Idled during the balance of the Great Depression, Nelson sold the mine in 1940 to American Alloy Corp. in Cleveland.[316] During World War II, it shipped manganese to the steel industry and to manufacturers of bricks and dry cell batteries.[317] Mining ended in the 1960s, when Mineral Ridge's last owner declared bankruptcy.

Limestone Quarrying

During and after the First World War, two companies made value added products from dolomite limestone found in the region. At the war's outset, magnesite imports from Austria-Hungary, which America's steel industry used in furnace linings, were halted. As a substitute, J. E. Baker Lime Company in York, Pennsylvania, produced Magdolite by twice burning dolomite at very high temperatures at its quarry in the Bunker Hill area of Berkeley County.[318]

From 1930 to 1950, Standard Lime and Stone Company in Baltimore manufactured rock wool from its dolomite quarry in Millville, near the Shenandoah River.[319] Its Capitol Rock Wool brand of pipe insulation was marketed to plumbers in the Washington, D.C. area.

During the First World War, 100 employees mined 2,000 tons of limestone daily at M. J. Grove Lime Company's quarry, opened one mile west of Stephens City in 1900. While burnt lime went to steel mills, the Frederick, Maryland-based company also shipped hydrated or quicklime to businesses that produced plaster, mortar, cement, fertilizers and water softeners.[320] In 1938, Grove opened a quarry and processing plant on a 175-acre farm it purchased near Cedar Creek, southwest of Middletown.

M. J. Grove Lime Company plant near Stephens City, 1930
Postcard published by Shenandoah Publishing House, Strasburg, VA

By 1917, the Oranda area west of Strasburg had become another Northern Valley lime center. Two-hundred fifty workers at a handful of companies quarried and processed 4,000 barrels of limestone daily, much of it shipped on the B&O's Valley Branch.[321] But as the ability to extract limestone suitable for steel furnaces diminished and competition from midwestern producers increased, the M. M. Orndorff business became the sole survivor in the Oranda limestone belt. In 1921, Palmer Lime and Cement Company in New York City acquired its quarry and five kilns.[322] They later became part of National Gypsum Company, whose customers used lime as a finish coat on lath and plaster.[323]

Rich in carbonate minerals and clay, marl limestone was quarried for fertilizer at several Northern Valley locations. Started up in 1921, Cornwell Lime Marl Co. in Romney set a goal of mining 125 tons of marl daily in western Frederick County, near the Winchester and Western Railroad's tracks.[324] Its president was former West Virginia governor John Cornwell, who with brother William had organized the railroad, five years earlier. In 1923, the Cornwell company extracted 1,942 tons of the agricultural lime from its Frederick County quarry.[325]

In the 1920s near Charles Town, the Alba Marl Lime Co. quarried marl lime that it marketed to drive-in customers as, "Nature's remedy for acid, unproductive soils." [326] To the south, Clarke County's marl producers included the Old Chapel Lime Marl Plant and J. C. Digges & Sons, Inc., both in White Post, and the E. G. Kenney Jr. business in Berryville.[327] Locke's Mill on the Shenandoah River ground the marl into fertilizer.

When Congress passed the National Labor Relations Act in 1935, union activity increased in the Eastern Panhandle lime and cement industries.[328] The Quarry Workers International Union of North America organized workers at Capitol Cement Company in Martinsburg, while the United Cement, Lime and Gypsum Workers International Union was active at the Blair Limestone quarry near Martinsburg and at Pittsburgh Limestone's Moler plant in Jefferson County.[329] The Allied Product Workers of America sought to organize M. J. Grove's workforce in Stephens City in 1941 and in 1942, but failed each time.[330]

Sand Mining

After Baltimore businessmen Henry Bridges and Nelson Perin consolidated most of Morgan County's silica sand industry in 1911 into Berkeley Glass Sand Company, Bridges bought out his partner's interest in 1924.[331] Three years later, he sold the company to Lewistown-based Pennsylvania Glass Sand Corporation, which had joined the local industry in 1902 with its purchase of Hancock White Sand Company.[332] Several miles northeast of Berkeley Springs, the new owner built the most advanced and largest sand processing plant in the United States.[333] Its location was close to where an employee of Bridges' father discovered a large vein of sand in 1895. When the plant opened in 1929, Pennsylvania Glass Sand demolished its other processing facilities, and after purchasing it in 1935, the Hazel-Atlas Glass Sand plant in Great Cacapon.[334] Each year the B&O Railroad shipped thousands of tons of Pennsylvania Glass Sand's product to flat and specialty glass, ceramics and paint factories in Wheeling and Pittsburgh.

The Oriskany sand vein found in Morgan County extended into western Frederick County. When Judge Walter R. Talbot found it on his property near Gore, he raised $150,000 from local investors and formed Virginia Glass Sand Corp. in 1930. George Hohannes, a former manager at Berkeley Glass Sand Company, was hired to run the new business.[335] After the Winchester and Western Railway built a spur from its Gore depot to Virginia Glass Sand's mine, it hauled the sand to Winchester for transfer to the B&O and Cumberland Valley railroads.[336] The short line also served Eastern Silicate & Chemical

Corp., which opened a plant in 1931 on Cold Run Ridge near Gore to further process its neighbor's sand into a fine grit known as cristobalite. After a fire, Shenandoah Silica Co., Inc., built a new facility on the site in 1932.[337]

Federal Government: It Becomes More Active in Region

In 1915, consideration was given to using the U.S. Department of Agriculture's Mount Weather site in eastern Clarke County as either a sanitarium for sick merchant marine seamen or for a summer hotel.[338] However, its remote location in the Blue Ridge Mountains was deemed both difficult to reach with food and supplies and too cold in winter to house people. Upon America's entry into World War I, the 85 acres were converted to an artillery practice range.[339]

Postwar, the 30 cottages and other buildings at Mount Weather housed 200 returning soldiers suffering from nervous disorders.[340] There was also talk of repurposing the property, two hours from Washington, D.C., as the summer capital for the president and his family.[341] In 1921, however, a federal commission recommended selling Mount Weather, because remodeling and maintaining it would be expensive.[342] No sale took place.

By 1916, the 4,133-acre U.S. Army Remount Station near Front Royal had become a breeding and training center for the U.S. Cavalry's horses and

U.S. Army Remount Station's Green Hill Stable in Warren County
Photo from Special Collections, U.S. Department of Agriculture's
National Agricultural Library, Washington, DC

mules.³⁴³ With 11 barns and stables and a race track, the complex employed 400 military and civilian personnel.³⁴⁴ Between 15,000 and 20,000 horses—some purchased from local breeders—came through the facility, prior to their deployment overseas in World War I.³⁴⁵

Established in 1905, the National Forest Service was also active in the region. By 1925, the agency had built roads, trails and lookout towers within Shenandoah National Forest, part of which was located in Warren, Page and Shenandoah counties. Available for public use, the recreation area attracted thousands of campers, fisherman, hunters and hikers who generated economic activity for the surrounding towns and villages. Several years later, those public lands took the George Washington National Forest name to avoid confusion with the new national park in the Blue Ridge Mountains to the east.³⁴⁶ In 1932, the National Forest Service combined its Massanutten and Lost River districts as the Lee Ranger District, based in Edinburg.³⁴⁷

Banking: Fewer Formations

Because Northern Valley communities were well-served with financial institutions, only three commercial banks opened between World War I and the Great Depression. They included Western Frederick Bank in 1919 in the village of Gore; Shenandoah Valley Bank and Trust in 1920 in Martinsburg; and Citizens National Bank in 1922 in New Market. Two of the region's banks changed their names. Organized in 1903 in Page County, Bank of Shenandoah became First National Bank of Shenandoah in 1918.³⁴⁸ Ten years later, Peoples National Bank of Strasburg, formed in 1907, was renamed First National Bank of Strasburg.³⁴⁹

Great Depression: Will it Ever End?

During the Roaring Twenties, the good times flowed from rising wages, salaries and corporate profits, and soaring stock prices at the end of the decade. But bad times followed the October 1929 stock market crash. Putting only 10 percent cash down on purchases of common stock, investors made highly leveraged bets on ever-rising share prices.³⁵⁰ When they fell, brokers called in those margin loans, forcing customers to sell more stocks, which drove share prices even lower.

As the economy slowed during what became the Great Depression, Americans consumed less and businesses withheld investments in plants and equipment. Between 1929 and 1933, the nation's gross domestic product declined by almost 50 percent. The number of unemployed Americans soared from 4.6 million in October 1931 to an estimated 13 million two years later.[351] The protectionist Smoot-Hawley Tariff Act of 1930 added to the economic malaise. Designed to help farmers suffering from low crop prices, it caused other nations to retaliate; between 1929 and 1933, United States exports declined by two-thirds.[352]

Northern Valley's Economy During the Depression

While not calculated at the local level, the Northern Valley's unemployment rate was undoubtedly lower than in much of the nation. Its jobs were not in heavy industry, the group hit hardest in the Great Depression. While 8.6 percent of all Virginians were given emergency relief from Washington, 4.4 percent of households in the Virginia portion of the Northern Valley were recipients.[353] The relief rolls ranged from less than one percent of Clarke County households to percentage highs of 10 and 10.5 in Page and Warren counties, respectively.[354] Meanwhile, Jefferson and Berkeley counties had the lowest percentage of West Virginian families classified as poor.[355]

In the 1930s, the populations of the Northern Valley and the nation increased at almost the same rate: 6.1 percent, compared to 7.3 percent.[356] With a 35.1 percent increase in residents in the decade, Warren County was the region's fastest growing jurisdiction, due to the opening of Shenandoah National Park and construction of the large American Viscose rayon complex in Front Royal.[357] With the exception of Clarke County's slight loss of residents, the region's other counties reported modest population gains during the 1930s. Winchester's 11.4 percent increase resulted from the presence of new fruit processing factories and related industries.[358] But labor problems at Martinsburg's clothing factories, woolen mills and nearby limestone quarries caused its population to rise by only 1.3 percent.[359]

New Deal Programs in the Region

The Franklin Roosevelt administration's New Deal adopted economist John Maynard Keynes' theory that increased government spending to boost aggregate demand would restart a depressed economy. Between 1933 and 1935, three programs were implemented to provide jobs that paid wages to previously unemployed workers: the Civil Works Administration (CWA), the Works Progress Administration (WPA) and the Civilian Conservation Corps (CCC).[360] In late 1933, several CWA projects created manual labor jobs in the Northern Valley.[361] One involved street cleaning in Luray, while another made improvements to the National Cemetery in Winchester. The United States Treasury provided funds for construction of post offices in Berryville, Luray, Woodstock and Strasburg and commissioned local artists to paint murals inside them.[362]

Following on the nationwide success of the CWA program, the Works Progress Administration employed thousands of Northern Valley men in its urban areas. They built a water system for Stephens City, a town hall for Front Royal and a courthouse and high school for Warren County.[363] In Winchester, WPA funds went for a new water works, Handley High School landscaping and a National Guard armory.[364] The program also supported Bird Haven, an artisan center near the former Alum Springs Hotel in western Shenandoah County. The only WPA projects implemented in the Eastern Panhandle were in Morgan County: construction of the Ridge State Fish Hatchery, south of Berkeley Springs, and rehabilitation of Berkeley Springs Sanitarium, damaged by the 1936 flood of Warm Springs Run.[365]

The Northern Valley benefited from other New Deal spending. In 1930, the Division of Fish Culture within the U.S. Department of Commerce built a $75,000 fish hatchery in the Jefferson County village of Leetown.[366] It restocked streams and conducted research on raising fish commercially. In eastern Clarke County, Mount Weather served as a work farm for unemployed men not participating in the CCC program.[367]

In 1933, the New Deal's Emergency Conservation Act created the Civilian Conservation Corps to provide jobs in rural areas for unemployed young men. They earned $30 a month, $25 of which went home to their families.[368] With regional headquarters in Edinburg, the CCC housed hundreds of 17- to 25-years-old "boys" at Camp Roosevelt in Fort Valley—the program's first living quarters—and at Cacapon Camp in southern Morgan County.[369] In 1933, Camp Edinburg opened west of Columbia Furnace, near the Virginia-West Virginia border.[370] Next year, several hundred African American participants made the renamed Camp Wolf Gap their temporary home.[371] Other CCC participants lived at camps at Skyland and Big Meadows in Shenandoah National Park, where they landscaped Skyline Drive and built visitor centers, campgrounds and lodges.[372]

In the George Washington National Forest, the boys cleared camping areas, blazed hiking trails and built Woodstock Tower on Massanutten Mountain. They constructed a state fish hatchery on Passage Creek, just outside Fort Valley, and built a nine-hole golf course and clubhouse along the Shenandoah River in Warren County. On Morgan County land that had previously been clear cut for timber, CCC participants developed Cacapon Park, which later became a state park.[373] The boys also planted thousands of tree saplings on hills and mountains surrounding the Shenandoah Valley, especially where logging had denuded forests.[374]

When the program closed in 1942, more than 3 million CCC young men had worked from 4,000 camp sites across the nation.[375] It had near- and long-term economic effects on the Northern Valley and surrounds. During the Great Depression, federal funds were spent locally on purchases of supplies and equipment, and on food and clothing for the participants. Afterwards, the CCC's recreational area improvements attracted hikers, fishermen, hunters, campers and tourists that spent money in the region.

Northern Valley Banks During the Depression

In 1933, President Roosevelt declared a bank holiday to prevent customer runs on deposits, but more than 5,100 banks still failed during the economic downturn.[376] In the Northern Valley, they included Bank of Harpers Ferry, founded in 1894; National Citizens Bank of Charles Town, organized in 1903; and Peoples Bank of Stephens City, formed in 1906. The Bank of Morgan County in Berkeley Springs closed in 1931, followed two years later by the Bank of Berkeley Springs. In their wake, Citizens National Bank of Berkeley Springs opened in 1934 to provide needed financial services to county residents.[377]

While regulators gave certificates of soundness in 1933 to the four commercial banks headquartered in Winchester, each eliminated its dividend to conserve cash. Several banks found new owners: Peoples Bank of Mount Jackson took over Mount Jackson National Bank, organized in 1900, and Bank of Clarke County acquired Boyce State Bank, founded in 1907.[378] In Martinsburg, the People's Trust Company assumed ownership of Shenandoah Valley Bank and Trust Company, formed in 1920.[379] In 1943, Farmers and Merchants Bank in Winchester acquired Union Bank, its Loudoun Street neighbor that opened in 1878.[380]

Northern Valley's Agriculture During the Depression

Already suffering from low crop prices in the 1920s, the finances of the region's farmers worsened during the downturn. In the summer of 1930, the nation experienced an unusually harsh drought, during which Virginia's rainfall fell to 60 percent of its normal weather patterns.[381] After the apple harvest failed, the Drought Relief Administration paid orchardists and apple pickers to survey land in the Blue Ridge, prior to construction of Skyline Drive.[382]

While depressed prices and drought caused farmers to cultivate fewer acres, the Northern Valley's wheat harvest dropped only slightly, from 1.441 million bushels in 1929 to 1.404 million in 1939.[383] Still a major cash crop for some farmers, its price declined to 66 cents a bushel in 1930, then bottomed at 38 cents, its lowest point in 130 years.[384] The hundredweight price of beef steers followed suit, falling from an already depressed price of $10.95 in 1930 to $5.42 in 1933.[385] To assist struggling farmers, Congress passed the Agricultural Adjustment Act of 1933, which maintained crop prices at levels similar to those the agriculture sector received in its more prosperous 1909 to 1914 period.[386] Despite that financial assistance, farm incomes did not increase until World War II.

Apple prices also declined during the Great Depression. While the per-bushel price had already slipped from a high of $1.78 in 1919 into a range of 99 cents to $1.39 during the Roaring Twenties, it bottomed at 61 cents a bushel in 1932.[387] In response to the Smoot-Hawley tariffs of 1930, England placed import duties on American apples and sourced them from its Commonwealth countries.[388] But the domestic market for apples picked up slightly when Americans took advantage of the low price to feed their families. The acquisitive H. F. Byrd, Inc. in Berryville purchased five apple orchards totaling 1,000 acres in Jefferson County.[389] After 200 acres were added in 1942, the company's Jefferson Orchards employed 300 full time and 1,500 seasonal workers.[390]

The economic downturn caused Michigan and Washington state orchardists to look for new sales outlets. When they began shipping apples in refrigerated rail cars to East Coast markets, Northern Valley growers took notice. In the mid-1930s, Harry Byrd Sr., president of the Virginia State Horticultural Society, initiated a voluntary effort among members to raise funds and advertise their apples in the domestic market.[391] In response, orchardists from a four-state region formed the Appalachian Apple Service that jointly promoted their fruit.[392]

Northern Valley's Textile Industry During the Depression

The Smoot-Hawley Tariff Act of 1930 protected America's woolen mills and clothing manufacturers from imports coming from countries with low labor costs, but that did not offset reduced domestic demand for their products. With sales dropping by more than 25 percent, labor-management relations became strained at Martinsburg's textile industry.[393] Berkeley Woolen's 375 workers struck in August and September of 1933 over management's failure to recognize the Textile Workers Union of America, but the National Labor Relations Board intervened and allowed them to join.[394] Along with employees at the Dunn Woolen mills in Martinsburg and Bunker Hill, they struck again in 1934 and 1935, and the mill closed temporarily in 1938.[395] Workers at Interwoven Mills, the largest employer in Martinsburg, took part in the Textile Workers Union of America's nationwide strike in 1934.[396] When 80 percent of its 1,500 employees walked out, the men's hosiery company operated with a skeleton crew. Unresolved issues contributed to another strike in 1941, just as Interwoven prepared to produce socks for the military.[397]

Winchester's textile industry also suffered sluggish sales during the Great Depression, but its workers were more amenable to negotiating grievances directly with management, rather than join a union.[398] The mills and factories operated without a work stoppage because employees were offered a choice: lose their job or work fewer hours, either through a reduced workweek or on a shortened shift.[399]

In 1935, local owners sold the Lewis Jones Knitting Mill in Winchester to a company headquartered in New York City's garment district.[400] The renamed Winchester Knitting Mills, Inc. continued to manufacture men's cotton knit underwear and athletic wear. Virginia Woolen's 530 workers produced 110,000 yards of cloth per month that went into CCC overcoats and Hart, Schaffner & Marx men's suits.[401] Cross-town rival Winchester Woolen kept its 175 employees busy processing 100,000 yards of flannel and suiting cloth each month.[402] Two years of union strikes at its

Virginia Woolen Company mill in Winchester, 1930s
Postcard published by Shenandoah Publishing House, Strasburg, VA

Hatboro, Pennsylvania, mill, caused Philadelphia-based Oscar Nebel Company to move its women's silk stocking machinery to Winchester in 1938 and open mills in Staunton and Verona.[403] After several ownership changes, the local factory closed in 1950.[404]

In 1905, British company Courtaulds plc developed a synthetic fiber called viscose that was designed to mimic silk.[405] Chemically treated wood cellulose made into a thick liquid was extruded through small holes into an acid bath, which solidified the strands into a fiber.[406] Labeled rayon in 1924, annual production in the United States soared from 13.4 million pounds in 1930 to 31.8 million in 1940.[407] Between 1910 and 1929, a Courtaulds subsidiary, American Viscose Company, built six factories along rivers in the eastern United States. A seventh went into production in 1940 in Front Royal, on the South Fork of the Shenandoah River.

Several Northern Valley textile companies worked with rayon, whose average price per pound was 53 cents, compared to wool's $1.34 and silk's $2.79.[408] After New Jersey businessman Charles Platt purchased Strasburg Textile Manufacturing Company out of bankruptcy in 1932, the renamed Strasburg Silk Mills, Inc. used rayon to produce linings for caskets.[409] The following year, M. E. Bing Company from New Jersey opened Edinburg Silk Mill in a vacant store to weave rayon fabric, but it closed in 1938.[410]

That same year, 100 employees at Shenandoah Knitting Mills, based in its namesake Page County town, made high-end women's hosiery from rayon and nylon.[411] After Chadbourne Hosiery Mills, Inc. in Charlotte, North Carolina, acquired the business in 1943, the local payroll grew to 275 workers.[412] Four years later, Winchester Knitting Mill put an addition on its North Kent Street facility to produce men's underwear from rayon cloth.[413]

Northern Valley's Apple Processors During the Depression

Despite the severe economic downturn, the region's apple processing industry expanded with three new participants. After it closed a plant in 1930 in western New York, H. J. Heinz Company in Pittsburgh produced vinegar at a new one on Winchester's Valley Avenue.[414] Specially designed rail cars transported the liquid to company headquarters for use as an ingredient in its ketchup.[415] Apples also went there to be made into mincemeat and butter. The same year Heinz arrived in Winchester, ZeroPack Company moved from Cincinnati to be closer to a source of apples. Inside the C. L. Robinson Ice and

Cold Storage facility on North Cameron Street, its employees vacuum-packed frozen apple slices that were sold to bakeries and institutional food service companies.[416] In 1939 in Mount Jackson, the Charles Bowman family organized Bowman Apple Products to make applesauce from fruit grown in its orchards.[417] The company paid $3,000 for an 80,000-square-foot factory that Gilbert Apple Products Company in New York State previously owned.[418]

In 1930, National Fruit Product Company, Inc. in Alexandria acquired Strasburg Fruit Product Co., which had made cider and vinegar for a decade.[419] Eight years later, the company's Alexandria headquarters was moved to Winchester to be closer to its largest plant. Production there was expanded from vinegar to apple butter and jelly, with apple juice and fruit pectin lines shifted to the Martinsburg plant.[420]

New Businesses Open in Region During the Depression

Undaunted by the downturn, local entrepreneurs opened businesses in the Northern Valley. In 1932, Raymond J. Funkhouser purchased the struggling O'Sullivan Rubber Co. in Massachusetts from J. P. Morgan & Co., and moved it to Winchester.[421] The company made rubber heels that eased a worker's leg fatigue from long hours of standing on the job. Because his Victor Products Co. in Hagerstown made roofing granules from reclaimed rubber scrap, Funkhouser was familiar with the business.[422] Under his leadership, O'Sullivan's sales rose from $687,000 in 1932 to $3.9 million in 1949, when he retired.[423]

Born in 1895 in Cherry Run in northwestern Berkeley County, Funkhouser grew up in the rear of his father's country store, and began his business career as owner of a sawmill and crosstie business in Morgan County.[424] In 1928, he and brother Elmer formed Victor Products Co. Besides selling roofing granules, the company ran a commercial refrigeration business that fabricated doors for cold storage facilities, then added a line of counter coolers and Quickfreezers.[425] In 1947, Victor Products opened a factory in Ranson that assembled soft drink vending machines; its successor, Dixie-Narco Inc., became one of the largest employers in Jefferson County.[426]

Through his holding company, Funkhouser owned 18 companies, including the Baltimore Trust Company, headquartered in that city's tallest building.[427] Residing in Jefferson County, he maintained penthouses in Baltimore and New York and organized Blakeley Bank and Trust Company in Ranson.[428] Beginning in 1943, he purchased and restored several George Washington family estates in Jefferson County and lived in one of them, Claymont Court. Prior to retiring in the 1950s to raise Thoroughbred horses on his 7,000-acre O'Sullivan Farms, Funkhouser lost bids for West Virginia governor and United States senator.[429]

The economic downturn failed to deter several Winchester entrepreneurs from starting fuel dealerships when Americans began to heat their homes with oil, rather than coal. John D. Glover & Son opened an oil and gas distributorship in 1931, followed by Hugh Funkhouser, who started H. N. Funkhouser & Co. to sell heating oil and kerosene.[430] In 1942, W. H. Emmart launched Emmart Oil Company, which supplied homes and businesses with heating oils, motor fuels and lubricants.[431]

In the late 1920s, Sam Shendow sold men's suits in Winchester for The Bell Clothes Shop, based in the nation's capital. Using a temporary office at the Hotel Jack, he showed samples and took measurements for his regular customers.[432] Despite the falling economy, Shendow moved to Winchester in 1931 and opened Bell's Fine Clothing on Loudoun Street to serve a loyal following that included many hard-to-fit men.[433]

After Prohibition ended in 1933, several beer distributorships were launched in the region. The Eugene Dearing family started Dearing Beverage Company in Winchester to wholesale Miller beer, followed by B. J. Sager, Inc., which warehoused and distributed Budweiser beer in the same city.[434] Martin Distributing Company in Martinsburg wholesaled Tru-Blu beer, made by Northampton Brewing Corp. in the Lehigh Valley of Pennsylvania.[435] Howard Martin later added Pabst Blue Ribbon and Schlitz to his company's offerings, along with Cumberland-brewed Old German Beer.[436]

In Winchester, two new food companies survived the Great Depression. In 1929, Douglas Brown and the Cochran family opened B&C Baking Corporation on Indian Alley. Producing Valley Pride bread, the partners also ran a retail store that sold B&C's baked goods and locally sourced food products.[437] In 1928, Bob Schenck and Howard Cahill launched Valley Foods Company to make potato chips and pretzels marketed under the Blossom brand.[438] In 1933, they opened a macaroni factory on South Kent Street. When Valley Foods carried Kraft Foods cheeses in the 1940s, it became Schenck Cheese Company.[439] After distributing a variety of foods to restaurants and institutional customers in 1952, the renamed Schenck Foods Company built a 45,000-square-foot warehouse in Kernstown, south of Winchester.[440]

Despite reduced levels of residential construction during the Great Depression, Paul Plumly saw a need for wood flooring when the mill in Gore burned in 1930. Four years later, on Winchester's North Kent Street he started P.W. Plumly Lumber Corporation to make oak flooring and other milled products, sold under the Plum Line trademark.[441] In the early 1930s, Stuart Perry used lime sourced from his quarry—the former Shawnee lime kilns—in the southeast section of Winchester to make concrete for construction projects.[442] Faced with restrictions on blasting rock close to several housing developments, Perry sold the quarry to the City of Winchester in 1936. He then purchased and reopened the Virginia Highway Department's rock quarry on U.S. 50, several miles west of Winchester.[443] Stuart M. Perry, Inc. proceeded to sell crushed and sized limestone to contractors working on state roads.

New Deal Winds Down, But Big Government Remains

Buoyed by huge federal outlays in the early 1930s, the nation's economy appeared to have improved. But the recovery faltered when government spending slowed in 1937, at the same time the Federal Reserve tightened the money supply.[444] A 10 percent drop in America's gross domestic product caused the unemployment rate to increase to 20 percent.[445] It took the nation's industrial buildup during World War II to put the economy back on a growth path.[446] Four decades later, the expanding workforce needed to manage federal programs started in the New Deal, followed by others in the Truman Fair Deal, had a significant impact on the Northern Valley's economy.

Media: Radio Stations Compete with Newspapers for Ad Dollars

Between the wars, newspapers in the region were bought and sold, although at a slower pace than in the previous century. In 1923, Harry Byrd Sr., owner of The Winchester Evening Star, bought the Daily News-Record in Harrisonburg.[447] That same year, H. C. Ogden, head of Ogden Newspapers, Inc. in Wheeling, entered the Northern Valley market. He purchased The Martinsburg West Va. Evening Journal from former Byrd associate, Max von Schlegell and renamed it The Martinsburg Journal.[448]

Six years after acquiring the Strasburg News and starting the Middletown Weekly in 1912, E. E. Keister added the Edinburg Sentinel to his portfolio of weeklies.⁴⁴⁹ In 1920, he rolled the Front Royal Record and Woodstock Times newspapers off the presses. The latter paper was eventually merged with the Edinburg Sentinel as the Woodstock Times and Edinburg Sentinel.⁴⁵⁰ In the midst of the Great Depression, Keister folded the four weeklies into the Northern Virginia Daily, based in Strasburg.⁴⁵¹ He believed readers of a regional paper would be interested in news from their neighboring towns. Keister opened a Winchester bureau to cover the city and Frederick and Clarke counties, in competition with the Winchester Evening Star.⁴⁵² His Shenandoah Publishing House also printed books on local history and postcards that showcased well-known buildings and scenes found in the region.

In 1948, the Spirit of Jefferson, started up in Charles Town in 1844, merged with the Farmer's Advocate, first published in 1884. They became the Spirit of Jefferson and Farmer's Advocate.⁴⁵³ Founded in 1849, the Shepherdstown Register closed in 1955, while in Berkeley Springs, Simeon Strother Buzzerd and his sons Jim and Lewis continued publishing the Morgan Messenger, which rolled of the press in 1893.⁴⁵⁴

In the 1940s, Northern Valley newspaper publishers faced competition from a new medium. The nation's first radio station went on the air in 1920, and within two years, 600 stations were broadcasting music and news.⁴⁵⁵ In 1939, the Fredericksburg Chamber of Commerce advertised in Broadcasting Magazine for someone to start a station in its community. California resident Richard F. Lewis Jr. answered the ad and put WFVA on the air.⁴⁵⁶ In 1941, Lewis crossed over the Blue Ridge and launched WINC-AM in Winchester as an NBC affiliate.⁴⁵⁷ In 1946, he expanded into frequency modulation with WINC-FM, which was one of the nation's first radio stations with a high-fidelity sound for music.⁴⁵⁸ That same year, WINC's production manager, C. Leslie Golliday, put WEPM-AM on the air in Martinsburg as the Eastern Panhandle's first radio station.⁴⁵⁹

Health Care:
Community Hospitals Open

At the start of World War I, there were four hospitals in the Northern Valley: Winchester Memorial, Charles Town General and in Martinsburg, King's Daughter's and Dr. Oates' hospitals. By 1950, non-profit community hospitals were also found in Luray, Front Royal, Woodstock and Berkeley Springs, whose local boards of trustees hired professional administrators to manage them.

Funded with a gift from James Ambrose Beahm's estate and other donors, Beahm Memorial Hospital opened in 1928 in a former residence on Luray's South Court Street.⁴⁶⁰ That same year, Mrs. Sidney Johnson started a nursing home in Front Royal, which she operated as a maternity ward with four attending physicians.⁴⁶¹ In 1937, two doctors opened Front Royal Community Hospital on North Royal Avenue, but along with Johnson's facility, it closed when Warren Memorial Hospital was built on North Shenandoah Avenue in 1951.⁴⁶²

For a handful of years, two physician-owned hospitals competed for patients in Woodstock. In 1937, Dr. Harold Miller founded the Cora Miller Memorial Hospital, named in honor of his mother. Closed when Shenandoah County Memorial Hospital was built in 1951, Miller's facility was repurposed as the Susan B. Miller Nursing Home, named after his wife.⁴⁶³ Returning to his hometown after the war, Dr. Roy Fravel opened his namesake hospital in Muhlenburg Hall in 1946.⁴⁶⁴ Five years later, he closed it due to health issues and the opening of the county hospital, where he served as staff medical advisor.⁴⁶⁵

In 1933, the Pines Crippled Children's Clinic became the first health-care facility in Berkeley Springs. It was thought that bathing in water from the town's mineral springs would help heal young polio victims.⁴⁶⁶ Two years later, President Franklin Roosevelt, a victim of the disease at age 39, visited the clinic.⁴⁶⁷ In 1950, the Morgan County Commission took ownership of the Pines and repurposed it as War Memorial Hospital.⁴⁶⁸

Tourism: Venues Profit from More Leisure Time

The automobile gave vacationers more travel options after World War I. To capture business from families seeking to enjoy the great outdoors, Northern Valley entrepreneurs opened campgrounds and recreation facilities at water venues. In addition to vacationing at the region's remaining mineral springs resorts, tourists cooled off in the mountains and explored underground show caves. And as farm families took factory and office jobs, they found more leisure time to play golf and patronize race tracks.

With motorists visiting the Valley of Virginia in increasing numbers, businesses that catered to them organized the Staunton-based Shenandoah Valley, Inc. in 1924 to jointly market themselves.⁴⁶⁹ The members included restaurants, hotels, motels and tourist attractions located in an area from Charles Town south to Lexington and west to Clifton Forge. Later known as Shen-Valley Inc., then Shenandoah Valley Travel Association, Inc., the non-profit published the Shenandoah Valley Travel Guide.

In 1925, the Shenandoah Valley Hotel and Inn Association jointly marketed its members' accommodations, scattered along U.S. 11.[470] When most of Skyline Drive in Shenandoah National Park opened in 1936, owners of campgrounds, motels and restaurants in Page County formed the Skyline Scenic-Route Association to jointly advertise their businesses.[471]

Tourism in the Blue Ridge Mountains

Until Shenandoah National Park opened in 1936, private firms operated two resorts in the section of the Blue Ridge Mountains west of Luray. In 1924, local businessman J. Allen Williams and partners opened the 350-acre rustic Panorama Resort, close to where U.S. 211 passed through Thornton Gap.[472] It included a tea room, a 14-room hotel, five cottages, a dining room, bathhouse, miniature golf course and tennis court.[473]

Panorama Resort in Shenandoah National Park
Postcard published by Graycraft Card Co., Danville, VA

Opened in 1895 as Stony Man Camp/Skyland, the renamed Skyland Resort was located 10 miles south of Panorama Resort. When a national park was first proposed in the late 1920s, owner George Pollock lobbied for its footprint to include the one-half million acres that surrounded his property.[474] But with liens outstanding on Skyland Resort during the Great Depression, the National Park Service took it over in 1936, along with the Panorama Resort.[475] To run them, the agency awarded contracts to Virginia Sky-Line Company, Inc. in Richmond.[476] While the Panorama's hotel and cottages were torn down in

1958, the Tea Room was renamed Panorama Restaurant, a visitor center was added and a rest stop later replaced the eatery.[477]

Mineral Springs Resorts

After the First World War, the region's remaining springs resorts faced several headwinds in addition to the Great Depression and another world war. Improvements in public health and sanitation, coupled with important drug discoveries in the 1920s and 1930s, reduced the public's interest in using mineral water as a cure for various ailments.[478] In addition, the American Medical Association joined the Federal Trade Commission in a campaign to stop what they deemed to be the industry's misleading advertisements.[479]

Several years after World War I, the Orkney Springs Company made numerous improvements to its namesake resort, west of Mount Jackson, including installation of electric lights and elevators in its main building, the Virginia House.[480] In the mid-1920s, the Episcopal Diocese of Virginia established Shrine Mont as an open-air sanctuary in the same area, and later assumed ownership of the resort.[481]

In 1919, Winchester businessmen Fred Glaize Sr. and Lee Herrellin purchased Rock Enon Springs Resort, near the village of Gore in western Frederick County.[482] They kept the hotel, but tore down most of the outlying buildings. When the Winchester and Wardensville Railroad ended passenger service to Gore in 1944, the Glaize family sold Rock Enon five years later. The Shenandoah Area Council of the Boy Scouts of America paid $5,000 for the hotel and 840 acres and used it as a summer campground.[483] Near the entrance to Fort Valley, the Waterlick Sulphur Springs Hotel burned in 1939 and never reopened.[484]

The area around Warm Springs Run in downtown Berkeley Springs became West Virginia's smallest state park in 1925. Four years later, the main bathhouse opened at its south end and gender-segregated baths, steams and massages were offered to the paying public.[485] In 1933, the Walter Harmison family built the 40-room Park View Inn on the site of the Berkeley Springs Hotel, which had burned in 1898.[486] When tourism declined during the Great Depression, the B&O Railroad ended passenger service on its short line leading to the town.[487] Notwithstanding, in 1937 the Harmisons added two wings to the Park View Inn, which they operated until 1972, when a new owner renamed it The Country Inn.[488]

Caverns

Between the two world wars, several commercial show caves joined the Luray and the Endless caverns in drawing tourists to the region's underground curiosities. In the mid-1800s, George Hupp, paymaster and iron furnace owner, used a cave on his 1,000-acre property north of Strasburg for cold storage of foods and hosted illuminations with candles and lanterns.[489] Virginia's first documented cavern, Hupp's Cave was used as a military hospital during the Civil War.[490] Years later, grandson Bruce Hupp acquired the property and cave, then built paths, installed electric lights inside it and opened Crystal Caverns to the paying public in 1922.[491] That same year, two local businessmen developed Shenandoah Caverns as a tourist attraction near the Shenandoah County village of Quicksburg, 13 miles north of Endless Caverns.[492] Automobile, bus and Southern Railway travelers stayed at a nearby hotel, air-conditioned by the caverns.[493]

In 1937, private investors hired Walter Amos, a retired geologist and mineralogist living in Winchester, to search for potential show caves in the Page Valley that might profit from tourists headed to the newly built Skyline Drive in Shenandoah National Park.[494] After more than one foot of mud and clay was cleared out, Skyline Caverns opened in 1939, near the park's Front Royal entrance, then promoted itself as, "The closest natural wonder to the nation's capital." [495]

In 1906, a cave with an underground lake was discovered in the center of Charles Town, but rather than walk on lighted paths, visitors toured Crystal Lake Cave in boats.[496] In 1929, local machinist Charles Weller purchased the site and operated Lakeland Caverns as a commercial show cave, accompanied by a dance hall and restaurant.[497] But the tourist attraction closed within three years, a victim of the Great Depression.

Golf Courses

The public's interest in golf grew in the 1920s when a trio of top professionals—Bobby Jones, Walter Hagen and Gene Sarazen—competed for trophies and tournament purses.[498] As the number of weekend golfers doubled, hundreds of private and public courses appeared on former farmland. Each was built near a stream that provided water for the greens and fairways, and hazards for players. With Northern Valley citizens prospering from the expanding apple, textile and extractive industries, several private country clubs opened for play during the Roaring Twenties. For community leaders, they added to the area's quality of life, which might also attract business and industry.

Berkeley County businessmen formed Opequon Country Club in 1922, then built a nine-hole course near its namesake creek, east of Martinsburg.[499] Next year, Winchester Golf Club, later called Winchester Country Club, built an 18-hole course along Abrams Creek, on a 250-acre former dairy farm east of the city.[500] Participants in the Blue Ridge Hunt in Clarke County founded Millwood Country Club in 1924 and built a nine-hole course along Roseville Run.[501] In the late 1920s, a golf course was added to Hawksbill Retreat, a Page County playground for Washington's rich and famous.[502] Located near the town of Stanley, the nine-hole, private course closed during World War II and never reopened.

In 1927, Roland Hill built Shenvalee Golf Resort on farmland south of New Market.[503] The region's first public course came with a hotel that catered to players from the Washington-Baltimore area. On opening day, Bobby Jones made a guest appearance at the nine-hole course, whose name was derived from the words Shenandoah, Virginia and Lee.[504] In 1938, the Civilian Conservation Corps built Front Royal Golf Course on the north bank of the Shenandoah River.[505] Riverton Lime and Stone Company owner William Carson donated the land to Warren County and helped design the nine-hole public course.[506]

Bobby Jones at Shenvalee Golf Course opening in New Market, 1927 Postcard published by Shenandoah Publishing House, Strasburg, VA

Horse Racing and Motorsports

For years, Thoroughbred horses were raised and trained on plantations and estates in Clarke and Jefferson counties. In 1808, the Charles Town Jockey

Club sponsored races that were held several days a month.[507] In the 1880s, riding, harness and steeplechase races became part of the annual Berryville Horse Show, while trotters ran at nearby Shenandoah Driving Park.[508] Formed in 1913, the Charles Town Horse and Colt Show Association held its first event at a Jefferson County farm. The 4,000 attendees made it a social and financial success.[509] While no racing took place, the association held a similar show in each of the next 20 years.

Looking for a new revenue source during the Great Depression, West Virginia's legislature legalized pari-mutuel betting on horses in 1933.[510] That year, Baltimore businessman Albert Boyle and other investors formed Shenandoah Valley Jockey Club, Inc. They purchased land in the northeast section of Charles Town from the renamed Charles Town Horse Show Association.[511] The group spent $160,000 to build Charles Town Race Track, a complex that included a three-quarter mile oval, 12 stables, a clubhouse with 44 betting windows and a 3,000-seat grandstand.[512]

Charles Town Race Track, 1940
Postcard published by Marken & Bielfeld, Inc., Frederick, MD

In December 1933, horse racing began at America's only Thoroughbred track to operate in winter, because the Charles Town Race Track's grandstand area was heated by fires inside oil drums. Gamblers from the Baltimore-Washington area took special trains and buses to the track. But when the Great Depression persisted, the Shenandoah Valley Jockey Club, Inc. was forced into receivership.⁵¹³ Creditors reorganized the company in 1934 and marketed the race track to bettors across a wider geographic area, from New York to southern Virginia.⁵¹⁴

Almost three decades after the Indianapolis Motor Speedway opened, Kermit Batt in 1936 built the Airport Speedway near Winchester Municipal Airport.⁵¹⁵ The L-shaped track held races for Model T and Model A cars and motorcycles that reached top speeds of 45 miles per hour.⁵¹⁶ In 1940, jalopy racing was added, along with bleachers capable of seating 4,000 spectators who were protected by a strong fence.

World War II: Conflict Jump Starts Nation's Economy

When Germany invaded Europe's lowland countries in May 1940, the United States began the most rapid industrial buildup in its history. Within five years, its gross national product soared from $100 billion to $212 billion.⁵¹⁷ For the first time in more than a decade, the nation's unemployment rate fell below 10 percent, and by 1945, it was negligible.⁵¹⁸ While many Northern Valley men and women went off to war, others stayed back to produce much needed goods for the military.

American Viscose Makes Synthetic Rubber in Front Royal

In 1940, American Viscose Corporation, the subsidiary of British-based Courtaulds plc, opened a rayon factory in Front Royal, on 440 acres along the South Fork of the Shenandoah River.⁵¹⁹ Company officials assured the public that water used would pass through an elaborate series of treatments before it was returned to the river, making it harmless to fish and vegetation.⁵²⁰ In 1941, the British government took ownership of American Viscose, sold it to an American banking syndicate and used the proceeds to buy much needed war supplies.⁵²¹

When Japan occupied the Malay Peninsula right after Pearl Harbor, the United States lost 90 percent of its supply of natural rubber.⁵²² To fill the gap, the War Production Board—the federal agency supervising industry during wartime—required American Viscose and its competitors to produce high-tenacity, rayon cord for heavy-duty truck and aircraft tires.⁵²³ During the conversion, the federal Defense Plant Corporation leased the Front Royal factory and effectively managed it. To satisfy American Viscose's need for

American Viscose Corporation plant in Front Royal, 1940s
Postcard published by Tichnor Brothers Inc., Boston, MA

specialty chemicals in Front Royal, in 1944 the corporation commissioned two companies to build factories near it. Stauffer Chemical Company produced carbon bisulfide just outside Bentonville in Warren County, while General Chemical Company opened a sulfuric acid factory next to American Viscose.[524]

Synthetic rubber production in the United States jumped from 28 million tons in 1942 to 922 million in 1945.[525] The Front Royal factory's output increased to 82 million tons, which the Norfolk and Western shipped to manufacturers of heavy-duty military tires.[526] Buses traveling throughout the Shenandoah Valley and Potomac Highlands transported 4,000 workers to and from their American Viscose shifts.[527]

Wartime Demand for the Region's Other Products

Parachutes were widely used in wars, not only as life-saving devices for pilots, but also for troop deployment. Strasburg Silk Mills, Inc., which made them from silk during World War I, switched its production from casket linings back to parachutes in the Second World War. But when Japan's invasion of Southeast Asia ended silk imports, the company used rayon as its raw material.[528]

The War Production Board generated a huge demand for military clothing and footwear, and companies with a presence in the Northern Valley responded in kind. In 1941, Swiss-owned Schwarzenbach-Huber Company built a yarn throwing mill on North Hawksbill Street in Luray.[529] Its Luray Textile

Corporation transferred skeins of yarn to spools that doubled, tripled or quadrupled the thread's thickness.[530] While most was sold to producers of military clothing, the 125-employee mill also received a large order in 1942 for nylon thread used to make parachutes.[531] After Blue Bell Company in North Carolina purchased Casey Jones Company in 1943, its five factories in the region produced denim, bell-bottom pants for the U.S. Navy.[532] And Virginia Oak Tannery in Luray benefited briefly from the War Production Board's increased demand for finished leather for military footwear.

The region's woolen mills also helped clothe the nation's 5 million soldiers. Military leaders insisted that they wear specially designed uniforms, many made entirely of wool. The War Production Board undertook the critical task of securing additional raw wool for the mills. The Berkeley and Winchester woolen mills sold half their cloth production to companies that made overcoats and uniforms.[533] The Dunn Woolen mills in Martinsburg and Bunker Hill worked entirely on government contracts. During the war, their 400 employees produced between 800,000 and 1 million Army blankets.[534]

The 600 employees at Virginia Woolen made as many as 1,800 blankets a day in Winchester, while Berkeley Woolen's payroll expanded to 500 workers in Martinsburg producing cloth for the war effort.[535] In that latter city, Interwoven Hosiery's 1,500 workers turned out hundreds of thousands of socks for Army and Navy personnel.[536] Also in Martinsburg, Perfection Garment's 440-person payroll produced 300,000 seersucker slips sent to Europe under the Lend-Lease Program, and made 25,000 cotton shirts for the United States Navy.[537]

One woolen entrepreneur's timing was fortuitous. William Lawrence Jr., president of Blue Ridge Woolen Company in Chambersburg, wanted a mill of his own. In 1939, he purchased the assets of bankrupt Brucetown Woolen Company in northern Frederick County.[538] Renaming the business Clearbrook Woolen Co., Inc., he replaced its aging machinery with modern dying, spinning and finishing equipment, put an addition on the original building and produced cloth for the civilian market. After military contractors called on Lawrence to turn out 1,000 olive-drab blankets per day, Clearbrook Woolen's payroll grew to more than 100 workers in 1942.[539]

Northern Valley Agriculture

Because the war eliminated the nation's crop surpluses, farmers were able to recover from the agriculture depression they experienced in the 1930s. While those who planted wheat, corn and rye benefited from higher prices, World War II shut down Northern Valley apple exports to Great Britain and Europe.[540] With many men away fighting, prisoners of war living in six work camps provided much-needed manpower for the region's apple processors and orchardists.

Some Federal Proposals Get Mixed Reviews

Before the United States entered the European conflict in December 1942, it was clear that horses were no match for motorized tanks, because in September 1939, German panzers quickly dismembered the Polish cavalry. In 1943, the U.S. Army Remount Depot in Warren County trained pack mules and muleskinners needed for deployment in the rugged terrain of the Italian Alps.[541] The depot's remaining horses and ponies and their riders patrolled the southeastern United States coastline for enemy planes and submarines.[542]

The Army Remount Depot was also tasked with training dogs for the service's Quartermaster K-9 Corps, which used them for scouting missions and sentry duties in combat zones.[543] After the war, the depot's oversight was transferred to the U.S. Department of Agriculture, which opened a Beef Cattle Research Station. Several federal agencies used the canine training center to teach dogs to detect drugs and explosives.

In 1944, the U.S. Army built the Newton D. Baker General Hospital in Berkeley County to care for thousands of wounded soldiers.[544] Two years later, the 1,727-bed hospital, named after the Martinsburg native who served as Woodrow Wilson's Secretary of War, became part of the Veterans Administration.[545] In a related development, the runway at Eastern West Virginia Regional Airport was expanded so larger aircraft could transport wounded soldiers to the hospital.[546] And during the war, the federal government's Mount Weather facility in eastern Clarke County was used as a Civilian Public Service site to provide conscientious objectors with an alternative to military service.[547]

In 1941, Jefferson County citizens turned down the opportunity to have a major military installation as a neighbor. Looking to boost their county's economy after the Great Depression, local businessmen lobbied the War Department to build a proposed ammunition depot on 15,000 acres near Opequon Creek.[548] When the county was selected for the $17 million facility, projected to bring with it 2,000 wartime and 300 peacetime jobs, citizen protests stopped the project.[549] Months later, the Letterkenny Ordinance Depot opened at a site 10 miles north of Chambersburg.[550]

In 1920, the Army Corps of Engineers considered building a large dam on the Shenandoah River to create a reserve water supply for a power station at Great Falls near Washington.[551] While no dam was erected, in 1945 the Corps looked to build a 193-foot high dam at Millville, upstream from an existing one.[552] It was part of a Potomac River flood control plan, deemed necessary after seven floods in the prior 72 years had caused extensive damage in the nation's capital. Besides generating electricity, the dam would create a huge lake, from Millville south to Front Royal.[553] Enlisting help from their congressmen, Northern Valley citizens successfully opposed the dam. Nevertheless, another Potomac River flood control plan surfaced in 1961, but construction of an 80-foot-high dam on Opequon Creek, six miles northeast of Winchester, also never gained traction.[554]

CHAPTER 7[i]

POST-WORLD WAR II TO 2020

National Economy: More Ups than Downs

When the Second World War ended in August 1945, Americans were ready to, "Let the good times roll." Responding to 15 years of pent-up demand from depression and war, the nation's factories again made consumer products. And despite 12 postwar recessions, the gross domestic product, adjusted for inflation, grew almost ten-fold, from $2.2 trillion in 1945 to $20.9 trillion in 2020.[1] During that same period, America's population more than doubled, from 151.3 million to an estimated 331 million.[2] The makeup of its labor force changed; the service sector accounted for 79 percent of all jobs in 2019, up from 52 percent in 1950, while the percentage of factory workers shrunk from 36 to 20.[3] Farm employment dropped from 11 percent to just over 1 percent.[4]

The nation's post-World War II economy had its challenges. The 1970s were marked by oil embargos and inflation, followed by abnormally high interest rates in the early 1980s. The New Millennium began with the bursting of the dot-com stock market bubble, followed by an economic shock from the September 11, 2001 terrorist attacks. Then came the collapse of residential real estate prices during the Great Recession that began in 2008. That downturn was followed by tax cuts and a soaring stock market, which fueled another era of good times. But in early 2020, the Covid-19 pandemic again put the nation's economy in jeopardy.

Northern Virginia: Westward Expansion Accelerates

Washington, D.C. boomed during World War II, when 280,000 workers moved into the district and filled 27 temporary office buildings.[5] The Cold War brought an even larger federal bureaucracy to the nation's capital, along with a growing cohort of government contractors to Northern Virginia. Fairfax County's population soared from 275,000 in 1960 to 1,150,000 in 2020, while Loudoun County's jumped from 21,000 to 376,000, fueled by an information technology industry that developed in the Dulles Corridor.[6] Both counties made the list of the nation's 10 jurisdictions with the highest average household incomes.[7] By the New Millennium, that growth and purchasing power had spilled over the Blue Ridge and into the Northern Valley's economy.

Northern Valley Economy: Population Growth Outpaces the Nation's

For decades, the region's population growth lagged that of the United States. The 1950 to 1970 period was no exception, for its headcount grew 20 percent compared to the nation's 35 percent.[8] However, a dramatic reversal occurred between 1970 and 1990, when the Northern Valley's 55 percent increase far outpaced the United States 22 percent.[9] And that differential was almost duplicated in the 1990 to 2010 period, when the region's population jumped by 49 percent, twice the nation's 24 percent increase.[10] The 2010 to 2020 period showed similar results, when the Northern Valley's headcount grew by 15.8 percent, compared to the nation's 7.4 percent.[11]

The Northern Valley's accelerated population growth resulted from expanded employment opportunities, lifestyle choices and immigration. Its first group of new residents came in the 1970s to take manufacturing jobs that Interstate 81 brought to the region. Beginning in the late 1980s, families living and working in Northern Virginia moved west of the Blue Ridge, trading less-expensive housing for longer commutes. The federal Office of Management and Budget recognized that trend in 2000 when it included most of the region's jurisdictions in the Washington-Baltimore-Arlington Combined Statistical Area.[12]

In the early 1990s, federal government and private sector retirees came from Northern Virginia in search of lower-cost housing and a slower-paced lifestyle.[13] And when federal agencies opened offices and installations in the Eastern Panhandle, their employees and contractors followed. The final cohort to arrive were Mexican and Central American immigrants, who took unskilled jobs in the agriculture, landscaping, construction, food services and hospitality sectors.

While the Northern Valley's population expanded, its agriculture sector struggled with low commodity prices, rising costs, environmental regulations and changing weather patterns. But farmers and orchardists discovered they owned an increasingly valuable commodity: land. And they sold it for the highest and best use: residential and commercial development needed to accommodate the region's growing population.

Economic Development Strategy: Fill New Parks with Industry

As the use of wool in clothing lost out to cotton, half the nation's woolen mills closed between 1900 and 1930.[14] The Northern Valley's industry survived the Great Depression, then received a boost from wartime sales of woolen cloth and blankets for military use. But when American consumers wrapped themselves in rayon, nylon and polyester, five of the region's six woolen mills had closed by 1958. The region's leaders sought to recruit new industry to replace hundreds of lost jobs. The sales pitch included a reliable labor force that worked for reasonable wages, low land acquisition costs, excellent rail and highway networks and a good quality of life for business owners and managers.

Recruiters found a receptive audience, because corporate America needed to add manufacturing capacity to meet the postwar pent-up demand for consumer and industrial goods. Their checklist included a low cost of doing business, a labor force with either factory experience or mechanical skills gained from farm work, and the ability to ship finished products quickly to populous Mid-Atlantic and Northeast markets.

To help its industrial recruitment effort, Virginia became a right-to-work state in 1947, which meant workers need not join a union as a condition of employment.[15] Because those laws suppressed union activity, Frederick County billed itself as the most northern jurisdiction in the nation's most northern right-to-work state.[16] Organized labor was more prevalent in the Eastern Panhandle, because coal mines and steel mills had a long history of union activity in West Virginia.

First Industrial Parks in Virginia Portion of Region

Winchester's leaders needed an industrial park with utilities in place to recruit industry in a timely manner. In 1959, William Battaile, local car dealer and president of the Winchester-Frederick County Chamber of Commerce, led a group of businessmen that formed the non-profit Winchester Industrial Development Corporation.[17] With financial backing from several sources, it purchased 98 acres in Kernstown, several miles south of the city's downtown.[18] It was also near the B&O Railroad's tracks and U.S. 11, which led to newly-opened Interstate 81. The acreage was subdivided into five-acre lots and water and sewer lines were installed in Winchester Industrial Park.

Chamber members took recruitment trips to fill the park. In 1965, Inter-type Corporation, a manufacturer of typesetting equipment, became its first occupant.[19] Next year, J. Schoeneman, Inc. in Owens Mills, Maryland, opened a sewing factory that made private-label, tailored men's suits for the Saks Fifth Avenue department store chain.[20] But in a precursor of manufacturing trends, 700 employees lost their jobs in 1983, after Schoeneman consolidated its production into a factory in Chambersburg.[21]

Privately-owned industrial parks in Frederick County included two rail-served ones to the north of Winchester. In 1970, local general contractor Howard Shockey & Sons, Inc. and a partner in Falls Church opened 335-acre Fort Collier Industrial Park, near U.S. 11.[22] Four years later, the Gilpin family in Clarke County, through its Lenoir City Corporation, developed 500-acre Stonewall Industrial Park, near Route 37 and the U.S. 11 interchange with I-81.[23]

As the Northern Valley's population increased, not all proposed industrial parks became a reality. In 1999, the Shockey Companies sought to develop 447-acre, rail-served Mid-Atlantic Industrial and Tech Park near Stephenson, north of Winchester.[24] Neighbors objected to the increased truck traffic it would bring, while preservationists took issue with the park's compromising a Civil War battlefield site known as Stephenson's Depot. Rather than fight them, Shockey had the land rezoned into a planned residential development known as Snowden Bridge.[25] Almost 20 years later, the company returned to that area with a less controversial rezoning request. The Frederick County Board of

Supervisors approved its 271-acre Graystone Commerce Center, just south of the housing development.[26]

Warren County's first park was the 24-acre Old Virginia Industrial Park, owned and occupied by Old Virginia Packing Company.[27] Opened in the mid-1950s, it was located in Front Royal, on Norfolk Southern's line and near American Viscose's plant.[28] The county's 1975 comprehensive plan identified farmland in the U.S. 522/340 corridor, north of Front Royal, as well-suited for industrial development.[29] Although E. I. DuPont Co. built an automotive paint factory there in 1981, fifteen years passed before other industry became its neighbor.

The Shenandoah County Industrial Development Authority purchased 200 acres in 1973 for its Mount Jackson Industrial Park, then recruited cabinetmaker Merillat Industries and satellite company Echo-Star International.[30] Without the ability to provide industry with direct access to Interstates 81 or 66, business parks appeared in Clarke and Page counties much later, in 2000 and 2008, respectively.

First Industrial Parks in Eastern Panhandle

In the late 1950s, the Martinsburg-Berkeley County Chamber of Commerce, led by radio station owner Leslie Golliday, opened rail-served, 174-acre Berkeley County Industrial Park.[31] It was located near U.S. 11, several miles south of Martinsburg. The first recruit was Corning Glass Works in New York State, which built a ceramic cookware factory in 1960. It sourced the raw material needed for its products from Pennsylvania Glass Sand Company in Morgan County.[32]

In 1979, the Jefferson County Chamber of Commerce organized the Jefferson County Development Authority, which borrowed $600,000 to acquire 80 acres on Route 9, north of Ranson. After they were subdivided into lots with roads and utilities, Bardane Industrial Park opened for business.[33] In 1981, the West Virginia Economic Development Authority loaned $172,500 to Omni Direct Mail Services Ltd. The Vienna, Virginia-based company built a plant in the park and hired 80 workers to print and mail solicitation letters for its clients.[34]

Recruitment Incentives: An Era of Corporate Welfare

In each year of the New Millennium, state and local governments recruited businesses with an estimated $80 billion in tax breaks, grants, training funds and infrastructure improvements.[35] Those arguing against incentives labeled them corporate welfare that went mostly to undeserving, large companies. Nonetheless, economic developers stressed they were used only to close a deal. The most important recruitment factors were building sites with utilities in place, a quality workforce and a robust transportation network.

When Virginia found itself losing business to North Carolina and other southern states in the mid-1970s, it established an enterprise zone program that offered tax incentives to encourage commercial development in economically depressed parts of the commonwealth.[36] In 1992, the monetary stakes were raised with the Governor's Opportunity Fund, followed by Investment Partnership Grants and finally, Major Employee Eligible Grants given to companies that invested at least $100 million and created 1,000 or more jobs.[37]

Losing jobs in its mining and heavy industry sectors, the West Virginia legislature enacted an aggressive array of incentives. In 1985, it passed the Business Investment and Job Expansion Act that offered tax credits to new and expanding businesses and for relocations of corporate headquarters.[38] That was followed by the PILOT program, which stood for Payments in Lieu of Taxes that a recipient would make to local governments.[39] Under it, West Virginia financed and took ownership of a factory or warehouse. Because the state was exempt from local property taxes, the lessor made equivalent payments directly to the school system.[40]

Local Development Agencies: Making the Recruitment Sale

Until the 1980s, economic development activities at the local level were left to chambers of commerce or boards of trade. But as competition to attract business and industry increased, state agencies took the lead. To refer relocation specialists and their corporate clients to a locality, states insisted it be capable of closing deals. That meant creation of an economic development agency that could market build-ready sites.

EDAs in Virginia Portion of Northern Valley

Formed in 1976, the Front Royal-Warren County Economic Development Authority (EDA) opened the 55-acre Happy Creek Industrial Park on Shenandoah Shores Road, east of downtown Front Royal.[41] After Avtex closed its rayon factory in 1989 and 470 high-paying union jobs were lost, the EDA purchased several farms located along the U.S. 522/340 corridor, north of Interstate 66. The EDA's newly established Stephens and Kelley industrial parks soon filled up with factories and warehouses. The number of jobs in Warren County increased by 41.5 percent, from 7,116 in 1990 to 10,072 in 2002.[42]

The Front Royal-Warren County EDA was also charged with redeveloping the 450-acre Avtex complex. The $137 million remediation on the federally designated Superfund site was finally completed in 2014.[43] The following year, U.S. Congressman Bob Goodlatte, who represented Warren County at the time, introduced government contractor IT Federal to the EDA.[44] Based on the company's claim that it had a $140 million contract with the Nuclear Regulatory Agency, the EDA loaned it $10 million to build a 600-employee facility on the Avtex site, but it was never completed.[45] A 2018 forensic accounting of the Front Royal-Warren County EDA found that the IT Federal loan was one of many suspicious transactions, including the executive director's alleged self-dealings over an eight-year period.[46] In 2020, the Virginia General Assembly granted Front Royal permission to create its own EDA.[47]

In 1982, the Shenandoah County Industrial Development Authority (IDA) became the Shenandoah County Office of Economic Development. It looked to fill several vacant clothing factories and sell lots in the 200-acre North Shenandoah Industrial Park, located west of Strasburg along I-81.[48] In 2012, economic development responsibilities reverted back to an IDA, staffed by a director of community development, who received marketing assistance from the Harrisonburg-based Shenandoah Valley Partnership.[49]

The Winchester-Frederick County Economic Development Commission (EDC) was formed in 1984.[50] After Winchester Industrial Park near Kernstown was filled, it decided not to use public funds to develop other parks, but would help recruit businesses to privately-owned Fort Collier and Stonewall industrial parks in Frederick County. In 1991, the EDC formed a call team of retired executives who periodically interviewed company managers and owners to gauge their satisfaction with the local business climate and to report on their needs and wants.[51] In 1997, the commission looked to recruit companies in the printing, food processing, metalworking and plastics industries, because they already had a strong presence in the region. It believed their skilled workforces and well-developed supply lines might attract similar companies.

As the region became more densely populated, concerns arose over new industrial projects, especially when they might negatively affect the environment. In 1997, the Winchester-Frederick County EDC threw its support behind Cardinal IG, after the Minneapolis company sought to make insulated window glass at a $76 million, 300-employee factory, south of Kernstown.[52] When a Save the Valley citizens group opposed its 200-foot tall smokestack, projected to release 1,700 tons of emissions annually, Cardinal's owner built the factory in North Carolina.[53]

Lacking land for industrial parks, the City of Winchester formed the Office of Economic Redevelopment in 2001 to repurpose vacant properties. To accomplish those goals, its director used the financial resources of the city's Industrial Development Authority, which generated fees from administering locally issued tax-exempt bonds, many from Valley Health.[54] Partnering with a Lynchburg firm, the office rehabilitated the vacant Taylor Hotel on the Loudoun Street pedestrian mall into restaurants and apartments. The director also turned land on Valley Avenue, where a fruit research facility once stood, into building lots sold to retailers, banks, fast food restaurants and for office use.

After the 9/11 terrorist attacks, the Winchester-Frederick County EDC shifted its business attraction efforts away from existing industries towards Northern Virginia companies working in information technology, life sciences, advanced manufacturing, business services and security and defense.[55] In 2003, the EDC established a Technology Zone in downtown Winchester that offered high-tech companies several tax breaks, but the main recruit stayed only two years.[56] In 2014, the city and county went their separate business recruitment ways when the EDC split into two economic development authorities.

For years, Clarke County's political leaders were committed to controlling growth and preserving as much agricultural land as possible. But in 1999, they opened a business park near Berryville and hired a coordinator for the newly created Office of Economic Development.[57] One year later, building lots in the 76-acre Clarke County Industrial Park were sold to six small construction firms, not the high-tech companies local officials had envisioned. In 2020, a tourism function was added to the renamed economic development director's job.[58]

In the twenty-first century, the Page County Economic Development Authority's business recruitment efforts were hindered by the county's distance from I-81 and I-66. To provide building sites for industry, the 60-acre, rail-served Page County Industrial and Technology Park opened in 2008 near Luray.[59] The EDA's development and tourism director later marketed its building sites, along with those in the 45-acre Shenandoah Industrial Park, near its namesake town.[60]

EDAs in Eastern Panhandle

The West Virginia Economic Development Authority was organized in 1962 in Charleston to provide loans, direct financing and operating leases to county agencies that recruited industry.[61] Formed in 1979, the Jefferson County Development Authority (JCDA) marketed Bardane and Burr industrial parks, located on Route 9, to potential occupants.[62] At the start of the New Millennium, the authority's business attraction efforts focused on light manufacturing and high-tech, business services and research and development companies. The JCDA hoped they would hire county residents that were commuting to jobs in Northern Virginia.

One industrial project the authority supported met with community opposition. In 2018, Rockwool, the North American unit of Danish company Roxul, Inc., proposed building a $150 million plant near Ranson, on land that once was part of the Byrd family's Jefferson Orchard. Rockwool used natural gas to burn stone at extremely high temperatures to produce strands of wool insulation.[63] Citing potential air pollution, a social media group known as Citizens Concerned About Rockwool-Ranson, WV was formed, but the plant's construction proceeded anyways.[64] It was not the first time that insulation was made from stone in Jefferson County. In the early 1930s and the 1940s, Baltimore-based Standard Lime and Stone Company made rock wool from dolomite limestone at its quarry in Millville, a much less populated area near the Shenandoah River.[65]

Organized in 1982, the Berkeley County Development Authority (BCDA) took over management of the chamber of commerce's Berkeley County Industrial Park, south of Martinsburg. It later opened parks opposite each other on I-81, just north of the Route 9 exits: 80-acre Mid-Atlantic Industrial Park on the east side, and 620-acre Cumbo Yard Industrial Park on the west side. In 2004, the BCDA purchased the 324-acre Criswell farm, near the intersection of U.S. 11 and Tabler Station Road, south of Martinsburg.[66] In 2012, it borrowed $2 million from the West Virginia Infrastructure and Job Development Fund to expand Tabler Station Business Park to 580 acres.[67] Three years later, Proctor & Gamble in Cincinnati decided to build a 1 million-square-foot, $800 million factory on 458 of those acres.[68] It became the largest economic development project in the region.

The Morgan County Economic Development Corporation was established in 1962 to finance a golf course at Cacapon State Park. It later recruited Vanguard Industries, which made golf and bowling bags and gun cases in

Interwoven Company's former hosiery factory in Berkeley Springs. In 1989, the renamed Morgan County Economic Development Authority opened the 102-acre U.S. 522 South Business Park, 12 miles south of Berkeley Springs.[69] In 1998, Lippert Components, a Michigan maker of recreational vehicle parts, became the first company to locate a factory in it.[70]

In western Morgan County, Paw Paw's economy suffered when the devastating 1985 Potomac River flood ruined the buildings of the town's two main employers: Vesuvius Crucible Company, which made steel nose cones on the former tannery property, and Consolidated Orchard Company, a packer and distributor of apples.[71] To offset those losses, in the early 1990s the Robert C. Byrd Industrial Park, funded with state and federal grants, opened on higher ground.[72] However, the several businesses that moved into the park soon shut down.

Region Hopes to Participate in Dot-Com Boom

By the 1990s, the internet explosion in the Dulles Corridor had caught the attention of Northern Valley economic developers. They looked to bring some of those information technology companies and their high-paying jobs over the Blue Ridge. In 1995, the Winchester-Frederick County Economic Development Commission announced that the Winchester pedestrian mall would become a CyberStreet.[73] High-tech businesses that located in the downtown Technology Zone would be eligible for incentives that included rebates on local telephone and utility taxes and on business licenses.[74] The federally-funded Shenandoah Valley Telecommuting Center on the pedestrian mall and an electronic bulletin board at Handley Library were to anchor CyberStreet.[75]

In 1998, Judd's OnLine became the first high-tech company to locate in the zone.[76] The 20-person unit of the Strasburg-based printer developed and maintained Web sites for companies.[77] As its payroll grew, however, it left downtown for larger office space in a Frederick County industrial park. After returning to the city, it eventually was sold and moved to Pennsylvania.[78]

Warren County's effort to develop an information technology cluster in the New Millennium benefited from its proximity to the Dulles Corridor. A dozen companies took Interstate 66 to Front Royal and joined the 60-member Warren County Technology Consortium, which lobbied for affordable, high-speed internet service.[79] In 2003, Happy Creek Industrial Park in Front Royal became Happy Creek Technology Park to serve those companies that needed larger quarters.[80] In 2009, the town established three technology zones—Front

Royal, Happy Creek and Avtex Area—with tax incentives offered to qualifying businesses.[81] By 2018, however, the Warren County Technology Consortium was no longer active.

Attempts to Incubate High-Tech Businesses

In the New Millennium, several business incubators were formed in the region. For a monthly fee, they provided startups with desk space, internet access, shared equipment and business counseling services. After a favorable study from the Virginia Tech Economic Assistance Development Center, the Winchester Incubation Regional Enterprise (WIRE) opened in 2000 at the federally supported NetTech Center, formerly the Shenandoah Valley Telecommuting Center.[82] Through its Small Business Incubator Program, the Virginia Department of Business Assistance granted $50,000 to the WIRE, which organized other incubators in Front Royal and Luray.[83] As high-speed internet became more widely available, however, many entrepreneurs opted to work from a home office. With low occupancies, the NetTech Center and the incubator moved in 2005 from the pedestrian mall to space on Valley Avenue and offered clients individual offices.[84] But when government funding ended the next year, the WIRE program ended.[85]

In 2001, the federally supported Jefferson County TeleCenter in Ranson started BizTech, a business accelerator for high-tech firms, but it never gained traction. In 1998, the Appalachian Regional Commission granted Morgan County $20,000 to examine the feasibility of starting an incubator in Berkeley Springs.[86] Two decades later, Blue Ridge Community and Technical College made desk space available for the town's entrepreneurs at its SpringTech Innovation Lab.[87] It was located at the Pines Opportunity Center in the former War Memorial Hospital building.

Despite efforts to incubate and grow clusters of high-tech companies, no Silicon Alley developed in the Northern Valley. The headwinds included the dot-com bust of 2000, the lack of large office spaces in its cities and towns, and a perception that few information technology workers lived in the region.

Infrastructure: Upgrades Accommodate Growth

When turnpikes, canals and railroads were built in nineteenth-century America, those transportation networks were called internal improvements.

After World War II, interstates, airports, telecommunications, high-speed internet and advanced education institutions were labeled infrastructure. As in earlier years, community leaders viewed them as essential elements for a growing economy.

The Northern Valley benefited from completion of interstates 81 and 66 and the Virginia Inland Port, all of which brought factories and warehouses with them. And improved east-west highways drew the region closer to one of the nation's fastest growing and wealthiest metropolitan areas, located 50 to 70 miles to the east. But as the twenty-first century approached, several infrastructure enhancements became a priority for the Northern Valley to stay competitive in the economic development arena. They included widespread broadband service, more vocational and higher education opportunities, improvements to Interstate 81 and upgrades to airports.

Roads

With nuclear attacks a possibility during the Cold War's early days, President Eisenhower proposed building a 41,000-mile nationwide network of four-lane interstate highways to expedite evacuation of citizens from cities to rural areas and move military equipment and supplies quickly over long distances.[88] Begun in 1957 at a cost of $1 billion, construction of the 855-mile Interstate 81 from New York to Tennessee was completed in 1971.[89] The 85 miles within the Northern Valley opened to traffic in 1966 and 1967.[90] Economic developers later promoted the fact that I-81 made the region less than a one-day's drive from one-third of the nation's population and one-half of its retail trade.

As the New Millennium approached, the number of trucks on I-81 became problematic. Originally projected to account for 15 percent of total traffic, they represented 40 percent by 2010, making passenger car travel difficult at times.[91] Calls went out for additional lanes, paid for with tolls on trucks, and shifting cargo to the nearby Shenandoah Line of the Norfolk Southern Railway. Yet the region's only significant I-81 enhancements were an expansion to six lanes through part of Berkeley County and a widened Potomac River bridge into Maryland.[92] In mid-2019, Virginia raised the gas tax by 2.1 percent in its counties located along or near I-81, and earmarked the revenue for construction projects designed to increase safety.[93]

Improvements to east-west highways in the 1960s and 1970s made it easier for Northern Valley residents, especially those living east of I-81, to commute to jobs in Leesburg, Dulles, Tyson's Corner and points farther east. The roads included four-lane highways U.S. 50 and Route 7 in Frederick and Clarke counties and U.S. 340 and Route 9 in Jefferson County. Residents in Warren and Shenandoah counties commuting to Northern Virginia jobs took Interstate 66, which joined I-81 at a point south of Middletown in 1982.

Airports

Revenue that supported the region's publicly owned airports came from fuel sales, hangar rentals and leased buildings. Winchester Regional Airport in Frederick County and Eastern West Virginia Regional Airport near Martinsburg served small jet, turboprop and general aviation planes used for business and pleasure. The Front Royal-Warren County Airport, the Luray-Page County Airport and privately-owned Sky Bryce and New Market airports in Shenandoah County catered to general aviation aircraft. As a business recruitment tool, economic developers lobbied for airport upgrades, mostly paid for with federal and state funds, to accommodate corporate jets.

The Eastern West Virginia Regional Airport benefited from the West Virginia Air National Guard's presence, which occurred when the 167th Fighter Bomber Squadron relocated there from Charleston in 1955.[94] Six years later, its mission changed to servicing and flying prop-driven cargo planes.[95] In 2006, U.S. Senator Robert Byrd from West Virginia secured $280 million from Congress to upgrade the airport's infrastructure to accommodate the renamed 167th Airlift Wing's fleet of C-5A Galaxy cargo jets.[96] When smaller Boeing C-17 Globemaster planes replaced the C-5As in 2014, the wing's $97 million budget supported 1,100 full- and part-time military and civilian jobs at the airport.[97]

The runway at the 235-acre Winchester Municipal Airport was paved in 1961.[98] By 1987, Winchester Regional Airport Authority's members came from the city and Frederick, Clarke, Warren and Shenandoah counties.[99] One year later, an instrument landing system was installed, followed by construction of several hangars, a longer runway and a 9,245-square foot terminal in 1989.[100]

After the 9/11 terrorist attacks on the nation's capital, Northern Valley airports were viewed as more favorably located than those in Leesburg and Manassas, which were inside restricted airspace created to protect Washington from another airborne disaster. As a result, some corporate and general aviation aircraft were repositioned to Winchester and Martinsburg.[101] Despite new passenger terminals and longer runways at the two airports, neither attracted a commuter service to the three large ones in the Washington-Baltimore area, because they were too close to the Northern Valley.

Railroads

Post-World War II, the Baltimore and Ohio and the Norfolk and Western railroads and the Pennsylvania Railroad's Cumberland Valley Division each continued freight service within the Northern Valley, but scheduled passenger service had ended by 1962. After Penn Central took bankruptcy in 1970, the federal government reorganized it as Consolidated Rail Corporation (Conrail), which closed the freight stations on Martinsburg's Raleigh Street and on Winchester's West Boscawen Street.[102] The latter building became home to the non-profit Winchester Little Theater in 1974.[103]

Roanoke-based Norfolk and Western Railway converted its engines from steam to diesel power in 1957.[104] In the Page County town of Shenandoah, it closed the large maintenance facility that had serviced coal-burning engines since 1883.[105] After Norfolk and Western merged with Southern Railway in 1982 as Norfolk Southern Corporation, the Shenandoah Line continued hauling freight in the eastern part of the Northern Valley.[106]

By 1980, the B&O and several railroads had been combined as CSX Corporation, based in Jacksonville.[107] Its maintenance shops remained in Martinsburg until 1988, when the work was transferred to other locations. The Berkeley County Roundhouse Authority was organized 12 years later to preserve and redevelop the site as a tourist attraction.[108] Since 1974, commuters from Berkeley and Jefferson counties rode Maryland Area Regional Commuter (MARC) trains each weekday to jobs in the metro D.C. area. Using 74 miles of the CSX—former B&O Metropolitan Branch—track for its Brunswick Line, MARC scheduled two passenger trains in each direction between Martinsburg and Union Station in Washington, D.C., with stops at Duffields and Harpers Ferry.[109]

In 1931, the Winchester and Western Railroad switched from lumber to hauling sand products from a mine and a processing plant near the western Frederick County village of Gore. Four years after Belgium-based SCR-Sibelco NV purchased both sand businesses in 1973 from Unimin Corporation, it acquired the railroad, which included a short line in Connecticut,.[110] The Winchester and Western's footprint reached into Maryland in 1986, after its purchase of 35 miles of Pennsylvania Railroad—former Cumberland Valley Railroad—track that Conrail abandoned between Hagerstown and Winchester.[111]

The railroad changed hands several times before OmniTRAX Inc. in Denver purchased it in 2019 for $105 million.[112] Eastern Panhandle leaders were hopeful that with its larger financial resources, the new owner would use the Winchester and Western Railroad to attract more industry to the area.[113]

Virginia Inland Port

In the late 1980s, the Virginia Port Authority in Norfolk proposed that containers arriving in Hampton Roads, then delivered by truck to companies in the Mid-Atlantic region, be sent 220 miles by rail to an intermodal terminal in Warren County.[114] The goals were to reduce tractor-trailer congestion at Virginia's ports and divert container traffic from the Port of Baltimore to Norfolk.[115] In 1988, Virginia International Terminals Inc., a privately owned operator of marine terminals, purchased 161 acres in northern Warren County, near four-lane U.S. 522/340.[116] Norfolk Southern's tracks passed through the property, whose location also gave container trucks access to Interstates 81 and 66. After the $15 million Virginia Inland Port (VIP) opened in 1990, containers traveled 12 hours by rail, from Hampton Roads through Lynchburg to Front Royal.[117]

From a slow start, VIP traffic picked up when warehouses that stored a variety of imported goods were built near it. Considered the nation's first successful inland port, volumes grew from 5,000 containers in 1990 to 31,000 in 2020.[118] The Virginia Port Authority claimed the VIP was responsible for adding 24 industrial buildings and 7,000 jobs in the Northern Valley.[119] A $27

Virginia Inland Port in Warren County, 2020
Photo from Virginia Port Authority, Norfolk, VA

million investment in 2020 in tracks and equipment at Front Royal expanded container handling capacity by 30 percent.[120]

Electric Utility Providers

Formed in the early 1920s, West Penn Electric Company in New York City became Allegheny Power System, Inc. in 1960, with three operating subsidiaries: West Penn Power, Monongahela Power and Potomac Edison, which served Northern Valley customers.[121] In 1995, the renamed Allegheny Energy, Inc. moved its headquarters from New York City to Hagerstown.[122] In 2010, the utility sold Potomac Edison's 102,000 customers in Virginia for $305 million to the Shenandoah Valley Electric Cooperative in Mount Crawford and the Rappahannock Electric Cooperative in Fredericksburg.[123] The following year, First Energy Corp. in Ohio paid $8.5 billion for Allegheny Energy, which included the Potomac Edison unit that served the Eastern Panhandle.[124]

To produce electricity for the wholesale, deregulated market, Competitive Power Ventures (CPV) in Silver Spring, Maryland, planned to build a 520-megawatt, gas-fired electric plant in Warren County, but high natural gas prices in 2001 made the $280 million project not feasible.[125] When fracking caused gas prices to fall, Dominion Energy in Richmond purchased CPV's land and construction permits in 2008 and completed the plant five years later.[126]

Renewable Energy

In 1991, Potomac Edison Co. of West Virginia shuttered its 102-year-old hydroelectric plant near Harpers Ferry, which produced 0.84 megawatt of power.[127] But with the New Millennium's increased interest in renewable energy, other century-old plants on the Northern Valley's two rivers remained in service. On the Potomac, the plant at Dam No. 5 near Falling Waters generated 1.2 megawatts of power, while the one at Dam No.4 near Shepherdstown continued to produce 2 megawatts.[128] The five installations on the Shenandoah River included the 2.84-megawatts plant at Millville in Jefferson County, the 0.75-megawatt plant in Warren County and three on the South Fork of the river in Page County, which together accounted for almost 4 megawatts of power.[129]

In 2014, FirstEnergy Corp. sold the region's seven hydroelectric plants, along with four others in Pennsylvania, to a New York City private equity firm.[130] Four years later, Eagle Creek Renewable Energy, a subsidiary of Canadian utility Ontario Power Generation, purchased them.[131] In 2011, locally-owned Burnshire Hydroelectric LLC restarted a plant that Dr. J. I. Tripplett built in 1892 on the North Fork of the Shenandoah River.[132] It produced 100 kilowatts, enough to power 70 homes in Woodstock.[133]

When generating renewable energy from the sun gained traction, some Northern Valley farmland found a higher and better use: fields of solar panels, which produced many more megawatts of power than the region's hydroelectric plants. Local governments benefited financially from solar farms. Property tax collections increased from the recapture of the low agriculture taxes previous owners paid, and from higher assessments and tax rates paid on commercial property. But a lingering issue was disposal of the glass and metal panels, after their 25- to 35-year lifespan.

In 2017, Chicago-based Hecate Energy LLC built a 10-megawatt solar farm in the northwest corner of Clarke County, which Dominion Energy soon purchased for $16 million.[134] In 2019, the Page County Board of Supervisors voted on two proposals from affiliates of Glen Allen, Virginia-based Urban Grid Solar Projects, which later became a unit of Canadian-based Brookfield Renewable Partners.[135] A 20-megawatt project on 340 acres in the Stanley area was approved, but the 100-megawatt solar farm on 559 acres, just north of Luray, was denied.[136] The issues were lack of consistency with Page County's comprehensive plan, large amounts of agriculture land that would be turned into industrial use and the farm's impairment of tourist view sheds from Skyline Drive.[137]

Those approved in Frederick County included Urban Grid Solar Projects' 140-megawatt Foxglove Solar farm, west of Stephens City, and Colorado-based Torch Clean Energy's 180-megawatt farm along Opequon Creek.[138] Shenandoah County approved two projects near Mt. Jackson: California-based Cyprus Creek Renewables 50-megawatt facility and a 7-megawatt farm from Randolf Solar Partners LLC, owned by EDF Renewables, a subsidiary of French national utility EDF Group.[139]

West Virginia had no solar farms until 2020, when EDF Renewables started construction on the 92.5-megawatt Wind Hill Project, three miles south of Charles Town.[140] That was followed by Torch Clean Energy's proposed 100-megawatt Bedington Energy Facility in Berkeley County.[141] It was to be located on 750 brownfield acres within the former DuPont Potomac Works, which Shockey Properties in Frederick County purchased in 2018.[142] West Virginia entered into a 15-year PILOT arrangement with the solar company, with the final lease amount based on the actual number of megawatts produced at the site.[143]

Telecom Providers

After the telephone industry consolidated in the 1920s, American Telephone & Telegraph Company in New York City owned most of the nation's exchanges, including Chesapeake & Potomac Telephone's systems in the Northern Valley. When AT&T was split into seven regional holding companies in 1984, Bell Atlantic Corporation and its successor, Verizon Communications, Inc. in New Jersey, served customers in Winchester and Frederick and Clarke counties.[144] Frontier Communications from Connecticut handled calls in the Eastern Panhandle, while Sprint, then Embarq and finally CenturyLink provided telephone service in Warren and Page counties.[145]

Founded in 1902, the Farmer's Mutual Telephone Company of Shenandoah County in Edinburg was the Northern Valley's only independent telecom provider.[146] With customers as shareholders, it was demutualized in 1981 as Shenandoah Telecommunications Company, Inc. Three years later, Warren French Jr. returned from his job with AT&T in New York to assume the general manager's role at the struggling company.[147] Upon securing a $2 million loan from the federal Rural Electrification Administration, he upgraded the service and added customers.[148] Community leader French served on the boards of Shenandoah Memorial Hospital and the Shenandoah County Economic Development Agency and raised funds for a county library.[149]

Serving as Shentel's CEO, French's son Christopher brought analog cellular service to the Northern Valley in 1990.[150] Customers used large, cordless car phones to place and receive calls that went through Shentel's base stations and cell towers, located between Edinburg and Winchester.[151] United States Cellular and Southwestern Bell's Cellular One soon became competitors. In 1995, Shentel again led the local industry when it joined forces with American Personal Communications, Inc. in Bethesda to provide personal communications service (PCS) in the region.[152] Under a license with Sprint Corporation, wireless calls were delivered through small, digital flip phones. Shentel built cell towers as far north as southern Pennsylvania, but then faced PCS competition.[153]

In 1998, CFW Communications Services, Inc., the Waynesboro, Virginia, telecom provider, obtained wireless spectrum in an area from Winchester south to Roanoke.[154] CFW changed its corporate name to nTelos in 2000, the same year AT&T and Verizon offered wireless service in the region.[155] Borrowing heavily to acquire spectrum and build towers, nTelos declared bankruptcy in

2003 and was reorganized as a private company, with bondholders owning most of the stock.[156] In 2016, Shentel purchased nTelos Holdings Corporation for $640 million and folded its customers into the Sprint wireless system.[157]

In 2020, T-Mobile in Kansas purchased Sprint for $26.5 billion.[158] Under Shentel's affiliate agreement with Sprint, the merger triggered T-Mobile's option to purchase the Edinburg company's wireless business.[159] Shentel was paid $1.95 billion for its 1.1 million subscribers. The proceeds were used to pay down debt, issue a special dividend and build out the company's Glo Fiber broadband service in the four-state region.[160]

Internet Service Providers

The nation's first internet providers used land lines of incumbent telecoms to offer dial-up access. In the early 1990s, Verizon marketed higher-speed digital subscriber line (DSL) service, but businesses and residences had to be located within a short distance of the telecom's central office to access it. By the late 1990s, cable TV companies offered internet and satellite television providers sold the service to homes that dial-up and cable did not reach. In 2020, the Northern Valley's urban areas had access to broadband service, but residents in many rural areas remained off the high-speed, information super-highway.

Education: Improving Workforce Skills

Workforce skills and education levels have long been an issue for economic developers and employers in rural areas like the Northern Valley. After World War II, good-paying factory jobs were available to persons with a high school education. But between 2000 and 2020, more than 5 million manufacturing jobs in the United States disappeared, due to automation on the factory floor and unskilled jobs going to low-cost countries.[161] While the region's labor force had a reputation for a good work ethic, human resource administrators looked for employees with greater proficiencies in math, reading, communication and critical thinking. Persons wishing to receive a career-focused education could attend one of the region's vocational-technical schools or community colleges. Its four-year colleges offered advanced education opportunities, held cultural events that enhanced the area's quality of life and sourced products and services from local businesses. In 2016, consulting firm TischlerBise concluded that Shenandoah University supported 1,570 jobs and had a $145.7 million economic impact on Winchester and Frederick County.[162] The Bureau of Business and Economic Research at West Virginia University found in 2014 that Shepherd University accounted for 1,012 jobs and added $96.1 million to the Eastern Panhandle's economy.[163]

Vo-Tech Centers

Using funds from the federal Vocational Education Act of 1963, a handful of vo-tech schools opened in the Northern Valley to meet the career interests of young adults and the workforce needs of local businesses.[164] High school students not college bound were taught skills for careers in the building and mechanical trades, health care, cosmetology and food service industries. Triplett Business and Technical Institute opened in Mount Jackson in 1966, followed four years later by the James Rumsey Vo-Tech Center near Hedgesville.[165] In 1971, the City of Winchester joined with Frederick and Clarke counties to build the Dowell J. Howard Vocational-Technical Center, east of Winchester.[166] The Warren County Vocational-Technical Center in Front Royal, later called Blue Ridge Technical Center, began taking students in 1977.[167] The Page County Technical Center opened in 1993 in the village of Marksville, between Luray and Stanley.[168]

To bring vo-tech students physically closer to their general education classes, school administrators in Winchester and Clarke County moved Dowell J. Howard's courses back into their respective high schools. In 2017, the Winchester School Board repurposed the former John Kerr Elementary School near Handley High School into the Emil and Grace Shihadeh Innovation Center. Its curriculum focused on the health professions and skills development in advanced technologies such as robotics, network engineering and 3-D printing.[169] Students were linked to work-based learning programs held at local businesses.[170]

Community and Private Colleges

Four years after Virginia created a community college system in 1966, the doors at Lord Fairfax Community College, later known as Laurel Ridge Community College, opened on a 120-acre campus near Middletown.[171] Between 1988 and 2014, the college added two Fauquier County campuses near Warrenton and repurposed the former Wrangler jeans annex building as its Luray-Page County Center.[172] Along with an expanded footprint, the number of part-time and full-time students at the college increased from 2,633 in 1990 to 6,710 in 2019.

Blue Ridge Community and Technical College had its beginnings in 1974, when Shepherd College's nursing department offered a two-year program.[173] As its curriculum expanded, the school became Shepherd Community and Technical College (CTC) in 1989, then moved into part of the former Blue Ridge Outlet Center in Martinsburg in 2001.[174] When accredited as an independent institution four years later, the CTC was renamed Blue Ridge Community and Technical College. In 2012, it moved to a campus on Route 45, west of Martinsburg, and opened two more facilities: the Morgan County Center, at the Pines Opportunity Center in Berkeley Springs, and Blue Ridge Technology Center in Berkeley Business Park, in the former Corning factory.[175] The college's enrollment reached 6,273 students in 2018, up from 2,466 in 2009.[176]

Two private colleges found a home in Martinsburg. In 1987, Valley College opened a campus in the Aikens Center in the northern part of the city.[177] The for-profit career training school offered medical, trade and business programs to high school graduates.[178] In 2000, non-profit Mountain State University in Beckley brought its degree completion program for working adults to several vacant stores in the Tanger Factory Outlet Center.[179] It purchased the center in 2003, then acquired the Martinsburg Mall to hold classes there.[180] But faced with too much debt and the loss of accreditation, Mountain State University closed and its presence in Martinsburg ended in 2012.[181]

Four-Year Colleges

Along with its community colleges, the region's three universities and one college grew their student bodies and physical plants. In the late 1940s, Shenandoah College and the Shenandoah Conservatory of Music, both founded in 1875 in Dayton, Virginia, began to experience financial issues.[182] Looking to recruit a four-year college to their city, Winchester businessmen, led by James R. Wilkins Sr., convinced the schools in 1960 to move 70 miles north onto 45 acres of donated land, southeast of the city's downtown. The community's interest in higher education was confirmed when the Winchester-Frederick County Chamber of Commerce raised $350,000 for classrooms.[183]

After both schools were combined as Shenandoah College, a satellite campus opened in Leesburg in 1990, and university status came the following year.[184] Through donations and purchases, several former school, bank and office buildings in downtown Winchester became part of Shenandoah University's expanding footprint. As its student body increased, nearby hotels were purchased for housing, and a football stadium and an athletic and event center were built on the east side of Interstate 81. Enrollment reached 3,271 in 2019.[185]

After Shepherd State Teachers College, originally Shepherd Normal School, implemented a liberal arts program in 1943, it was renamed Shepherd College.[186] As its degree offerings increased, the Shepherdstown school achieved university status in 2004. Total enrollment at Shepherd University stood at 3,554 students in 2019.[187] In Warren County, Christendom College was founded in 1977 as a Catholic liberal arts school.[188] When enrollment reached 400 students, it added buildings on the 120-acre campus near the Shenandoah River.[189] Christendom also ran a graduate theology program in Alexandria, and offered students study abroad options in Donegal, Ireland and in Rome.

In 2003, for-profit American Public University System, Inc. (APUS) moved from Manassas to Charles Town.[190] Offering online courses and degrees, mostly to military and public service personnel, it sold shares of stock on the public market in 2007.[191] Two years later, APUS built an academic center in Ranson, located on the brownfield of a metal salvage yard. By 2020, its enrollment had grown to 81,000 online students, with 980 faculty and staff located in the Jefferson County area.[192]

Agriculture: Farmers and Orchardists Face Challenges

After World War II, the Northern Valley's manufacturing and service sectors were growing, but agriculture was in decline. The contributing factors were lower profits, increased environmental regulations, an aging cohort of farmers and better opportunities for their children. Census statistics revealed a changed landscape. Frederick County had 1,850 farms on 215,000 acres in 1925, but those numbers had shrunk in half by 2017, to 762 farms on 110,000 acres.[193] The county's farm employment, not counting family and seasonal labor, dropped from 3,700 workers in 1925 to 1,016 in 2017.[194] Those trends were similar for Berkeley County, where 1,436 farms with 154,473 acres in 1925 had declined to 946 and 73,134, respectively, in 2017.[195]

In 2012, almost 50 percent of families residing on farms in Jefferson County listed non-farming pursuits as their principal occupation.[196] Some farmers supplemented their incomes with agritourism. They offered city folks activities that included picking fruit and vegetables, wandering through pumpkin patches and corn mazes, taking hay rides and cutting their own Christmas trees.

Raising Wheat and Livestock

From 1945 to 1980, the nation's wheat harvest more than doubled, from 1.1 billion bushels to 2.4 billion.[197] Much of its wheat production had moved westward, with large farms in the Great Plains—from Texas to Montana—accounting for two-thirds of the harvest.[198] Peaking at 4 million bushels per year during World War I, the Northern Valley's annual wheat output declined steadily to 2.5 million bushels in the 1940s, before dropping to 300,000 bushels in 1980.[199]

Following historical trends, wheat prices fluctuated wildly, rising from $1.09 a bushel to $1.49 during World War II, then soaring to $4.09 in 1974, when a Middle East oil embargo caused severe inflation in the United States.[200] Its price retreated to $2.42 per bushel in 1986, then rose to $4.55 in 1995, a time when most farmers in the region no longer raised the crop.[201]

After World War II, some farmers shifted from milking cows to the less labor-intensive pursuit of raising beef cattle. In 2017, Frederick County farmers owned 16,884 beef cattle, but milked only 392 cows.[202] Raising Angus beef cattle became a popular part-time farming pursuit, especially after the per hundredweight price soared from $28 in 1957 to a record $119 in 2017.[203]

Orcharding

With increased use of automation and better growing techniques, Northern Valley apple harvests offset the economic slack from the rapid decline in wheat. Production at orchards in Frederick County rose from 2.5 million bushels in 1960 to a record 4.7 million in 1979, while Berkeley County's harvest topped out at 2.16 million bushels in 1978.[204] With more apples on more trees, the region's orchardists turned to migrant workers to pick the fruit, but hiring them was a complicated process. Before requesting such seasonal help through the U.S. Department of Labor, they were required to advertise locally for workers. With few takers, Jamaicans and Puerto Ricans were hired and housed in two labor camps, one near the National Fruit Product Company's factory in Winchester and the other on Grapevine Road, west of Martinsburg.

By the early 1950s, H. F. Byrd, Inc. in Berryville owned 5,000 acres of orchards spread from Charles Town to New Market. With annual harvests of 1.5

million bushels, five packing houses and 1,500 seasonal workers, it continued to be the most expansive fruit business in the region. Industry participants called U.S. Senator Harry Byrd Sr. the Apple King of America.[205] However, a declining export market caused the Byrds to sell their 1,500-acre Jefferson Orchard near Kearneysville in 1966.[206] One of the world's largest orchards, its 60,000 trees produced 750,000 bushels of apples annually.[207] Closed down in 2015, the acreage was developed for mixed uses.

After World War II, the Orr family's orchards and farm southwest of Martinsburg became a diversified fruit business. George Orr Jr., who grew up on his grandfather's fruit farm in the Apple Pie Ridge area near Arden, purchased an adjacent 60-acre farm in 1954.[208] By the New Millennium, the George S. Orr & Sons, Inc. business annually produced one-half million bushels of fruit—apples, peaches, berries, cherries and grapes—on 1,100 acres.[209] The company marketed its apples and peaches under the Mountaineer brand, and sold its fruit and locally sourced products at Orr's Farm Market.[210]

By the 1990s, C. Robert Solenberger in Frederick County owned 3,000 acres of apple and peach trees in orchards that stretched from Gerrardstown to Strasburg.[211] The great nephew of pioneer orchardist J. Fred Thwaite, Solenberger started with just 100 acres in 1959.[212] His Fruit Hill Orchards, Inc. sold 95 percent of its annual 2 million-bushel apple harvest to processors, mainly National Fruit Product Company in Winchester.[213] Also in the fruit warehousing business, Solenberger became majority owner of Virginia Apple Storage, Inc. and held joint ownership with National Fruit in Winchester Warehousing, Inc.[214]

Several other orchardists had a large presence in the region. Started in Frederick County in 1921, Glaize Apples owned 700 acres in Frederick and Shenandoah counties.[215] The Winchester company packed its fruit for the fresh market, mostly grocery stores. At one time, the Bowman family in Shenandoah County worked 3,000 acres of orchards, with most of the harvest sent to its processing plant in Mount Jackson. National Fruit Product Company also was vertically integrated, through its ownership of several thousand acres of orchards.

After World War II, the region's industry faced various headwinds. In 1960, the 25 percent of apples not processed or sold locally went to the Eastern Seaboard for export to England, the European continent, Canada and Cuba. However, those sales declined when some countries imposed tariffs and China exported low-priced apple juice concentrates into the same markets. In 2010, that country harvested 33.3 million metric tons of apples—half the world's supply—compared to America's 4.2 million tons.[216]

Seventy percent of Northern Valley apples once went to local processing plants, but six closed between 1982 and 2008. That made it more difficult for growers to negotiate prices with the remaining processors—National Fruit and Bowman—both of which had their own orchards. To make matters worse, America's per capita consumption of fresh apples declined in the three decades after 1980.[217] In addition, consolidation in the supermarket industry gave large chains, which purchased three quarters of the nation's fresh apples, more power to negotiate prices with growers and wholesalers.[218]

Squeezed by low apple prices and increased production costs, some Northern Valley orchardists left the business in the 1990s. As a result, land devoted to apples in the Virginia portion of the region decreased by 60 percent between 1982 and 2007, from 26,800 acres to 11,000 acres.[219] The Frederick County harvest declined by two-thirds, from its peak of 4.7 million bushels in 1979 to 1.6 million in 2016.[220] Between 1987 and 2000, land devoted to orchards in the Eastern Panhandle dropped almost in half, from 15,000 acres to 7,800.[221] Berkeley County produced 600,000 bushels in 2015, a 73 percent drop from the 2.2 million bushels harvested in 1930.[222]

Orchardists that left the apple business included Alfred Snapp in Frederick County and Moore and Dorsey, Inc. in Clarke County, which switched to raising nursery stock, grain and sod. Responding to the changing market, Agri-Tech, Inc., a Woodstock fabricator of apple sorting machinery since 1912, moved production in 2001 to the larger fruit market in Olympia, Washington.[223]

Several years later, Harry Byrd III, citing a squeeze on profit margins, reduced the size of his family's orchard. Prices that remained flat for more than a decade had not offset his increased costs for labor, fuel and pesticides.[224] The last straw for Byrd occurred in 2003, when Hurricane Isabel damaged 40 percent of his 100,000 trees.[225] His brother Beverly called it quits in 2019, after excess rain the prior year left him with only 20 percent of the normal harvest from his 140-acre Clarke County orchard.[226]

Fruit stands and pick-your-own offerings kept some Northern Valley orchardists in business. By retailing directly to local customers and tourists, they obtained higher prices and incurred less labor and transportation costs. And to better compete with Pacific Northwest fruit shipped to the East Coast, they switched from the traditional Golden and Red Delicious, Granny Smith and Stayman varieties to premium-priced, specialty apples named Gala, Fuji, Pink Lady, Ida Red, Ginger Gold and Nittany.[227]

Raising Poultry

Until the 1930s, chickens were kept on family farms for egg production. When refrigeration and improved sanitary practices gave Americans more confidence to eat processed chickens, farmers raised them for the ready-to-cook market. During World War II, households consumed greater quantities of poultry when much of the nation's beef and pork went to feed the troops. Bred to be larger and juicier, sales of broilers increased from 43 million in 1935 to 1.8 billion in 1960.[228] During those same 25 years, the number of turkeys raised for the domestic market jumped from 17 million to 83 million.[229] Poultry consumption continued to grow after an American Heart Association report in 1961 warned citizens about eating too much beef.[230]

The Shenandoah Valley's agriculture sector responded to those trends. In the 1930s, Charles Wampler Sr. in Dayton, six miles south of Harrisonburg, ended the practice of free-range turkey farming, because birds ate less when confined.[231] He also pioneered a business arrangement whereby a farmer purchased baby turkeys and feed from Wampler Feed and Seed Company, then raised them inside a one-story grow-out house.[232] When the turkeys were ready for market, Wampler purchased them for processing on its assembly lines. Known as a poultry integrator, the company later expanded into the broiler market.

Transportation costs required turkey and broiler grow-out houses to be located near the feed mills, hatcheries and processing plants of the Rockingham County integrators. That made it feasible for 200 to 300 farmers in southern Page and Shenandoah counties to raise the birds. As the grower numbers increased, processing plants were built closer to them, in New Market, Stanley and Columbia Furnace. To fill their feed mills, integrators purchased locally grown corn and soybeans.

Vineyards and Wineries

In the 1770s, Thomas Jefferson planted European wine grapes at his Monticello plantation near Charlottesville, but the vines fared poorly in the Virginia Piedmont's soil and climate.[233] Two hundred years later, it was discovered that French-American hybrid grapes were well-suited to the Northern Valley's relatively dry climate, warm days and cool nights. Shenandoah Vineyard opened in 1976 on a former cattle farm, west of Edinburg. Other early movers were North Mountain Vineyard and Winery, west of Maurertown, and Deer Meadow Vineyard, near Mountain Falls in western Frederick County.[234] In 1988, Linden

Vineyard bottled Cabernet Sauvignon, Cabernet Franc, Chardonnay, Vidal and Seyval wines from grapes it grew in eastern Warren County.[235]

By the 1990s, the census of wineries in the Virginia portion of the Northern Valley had tripled. Their tastings and special events on weekends attracted visitors from the metro D.C. area. The Shenandoah Valley Wine Growers Association was formed in 2003 to promote the cultivation of varietals and to market the vineyards of its members.[236]

Extractive Industries: Participants Change Hands

While manganese mining ceased in the Northern Valley after World War II, new uses for sandstone and limestone increased the demand for those minerals. In the New Millennium, the renewable energy industry used sand to make solar panels, while the fossil fuel industry fracked natural gas with it. For years, the region's limestone was shipped to Pennsylvania's steel mills and was used in cement, plaster and fertilizer and for road building. Newer applications included remediation of soil and sludge, compliance with wastewater treatment and other environmental regulations, flue gas desulfurization in power plants, fiberglass manufacturing and metal ore refining.[237]

Hoping to profit from the nation's growing use of lime and silica sand, private equity firms and conglomerates purchased several Northern Valley companies that extracted and processed limestone and sandstone. The former group acquired them in leveraged buyouts, using assets in the ground as collateral for the loans, and cash flows to pay down the debt.

Limestone Quarrying in the Eastern Panhandle

When the Baker family in Baltimore sold its Standard Lime and Stone Company in 1954, it was the largest limestone business in the Eastern Panhandle. American-Marietta Corporation from Chicago paid $10 million for its Washington Building Lime subsidiary in Bakerton, nine quarries and processing plants in seven states, and the Capitol Cement plant in Martinsburg.[238] Three years later, American-Marietta shuttered the 68-year-old Bakerton quarry, stating it had run out of high-quality limestone needed to make cement, and laid off 115 workers.[239]

The former Standard Lime and Stone quarry and kilns in Millville, south of Harpers Ferry, continued to produce burnt lime for cement and dolomite for rock wool insulation and steel furnace linings and flux.[240] Under subsequent owners, crushed stone was also shipped by rail to the metro D.C. area for construction projects.[241] When British firm Bardon Plc purchased the Millville complex in 1999, it was West Virginia's largest limestone operation. Six million tons were extracted from the quarry in 2018.[242]

Limestone Quarrying in the Virginia Portion of the Region

Riverton Lime & Stone Company, started up in 1868 in Warren County, had several owners before Riverton Investment Corporation in Winchester acquired it in 1980.[243] Three years later, it paid Martin-Marietta Corporation, successor to American-Marietta Co., $20 million for the Blairton property in eastern Berkeley County and the Capitol Cement plant, which produced 900,000 tons per year of Portland and masonry cement.[244] In 2002, Riverton Investment was sold for $107 million to Pennsylvania-based ESSROC, a unit of Italian cement company Italcimenti Group.[245]

Other limestone properties in the Virginia portion of the region changed hands multiple times. In the late 1940s, National Gypsum Company sold its Oranda lime operation—the former M. M. Orndorff business that started up west of Strasburg in the early 1900s—to Central Chemical Corp., a Hagerstown-based blender of agricultural pesticides and fertilizers.[246] In 1967, Engelhard Minerals & Chemicals Corporation from New Jersey purchased the limestone business.[247] In 1998, Cleveland-based Oglebay Norton Company acquired the renamed Chemstone Corporation, then purchased W.S. Frey Company, Inc. in Frederick, Maryland.[248] Frey had mined limestone near Martinsburg from 1956 to 1961, before moving the business to Clear Brook.

Saddled with $560 million in debt, Oglebay Norton filed for bankruptcy in 2004.[249] Three years later, Carmeuse Lime & Stone, Inc. in Pittsburgh, a subsidiary of Belgium-based Carmeuse Group, paid $700 million for the renamed O-N Minerals, including its Northern Valley quarries and kilns.[250]

In 1975, Flintkote Corp. from Massachusetts purchased M. J. Grove Lime Company's 75-year-old quarry and kilns west of Stephens City and its quarry in nearby Middletown.[251] Five years later, it sold them to Genstar Stone Products Company in Hunt Valley, Maryland.[252] In 1983, James Bowman, whose Frederick County trucking company hauled the Stephens City lime to Northern Virginia markets, purchased the complex and leased it back to

Genstar, and finally to British company Redland Plc.²⁵³ In 1988, Bowman formed Shen-Valley Lime Corporation, which operated the business until its closure in 2003.²⁵⁴

Sand Mining

Post-World War II, Pennsylvania Glass Sand Corporation, the only such company still active in Morgan County, changed ownership several times. In 1968, New York City-based conglomerate ITT Corporation acquired it for $112 million and moved headquarters from Lewiston, Pennsylvania, to Berkeley Springs.²⁵⁵ In 1985, ITT sold the subsidiary for $80 million to U.S. Borax, Inc., the world's largest producer of borates used in the manufacture of glass and fiberglass.²⁵⁶ Next year, Borax paid $46 million for Ottawa Silica Co. of Illinois and combined it with Pennsylvania Glass Sand as U.S. Silica Company, based in Berkeley Springs. It then purchased other sand businesses that served the glass, fiberglass, plastics, metallurgical and chemical industries.²⁵⁷

In 1995, Borax sold U.S. Silica in a leveraged buyout to D. George Harris & Associates, a New York City private equity firm.²⁵⁸ The following year, the renamed Better Minerals & Aggregate Company entered the crushed rock and asphalt markets, hoping to benefit from increased federal funding of highways.²⁵⁹ Sales doubled after Better Minerals purchased five stone companies, but profits failed to materialize. The aggregates business was sold in 2003 to British-owned Hanson Building Materials, and the U.S. Silica name returned to Berkeley Springs.²⁶⁰

In the New Millennium, increased demand for sand used to make solar panels and to frack natural gas attracted more investors to the industry. In 2007 and 2008, U.S. Silica Holdings Inc., by then the nation's second largest sand company, passed through the hands of four private equity firms. Its last owner, San Francisco-based Golden Gate Capital, paid $337 million for it in 2008.²⁶¹ Two years later, its headquarters was moved to Frederick, Maryland. After revenues and profits grew for several years, Golden Gate Capital took U.S. Silica public in 2012 with a market valuation of $900 million.²⁶² To be closer to the company's fossil fuel customers, headquarters was relocated to a suburb of Houston in 2018.²⁶³

The sand mining and processing businesses near the village of Gore in western Frederick County also changed ownership. William J. Woods Jr. in New Canaan, Connecticut, formed Unimin Corporation in 1970, two years after he left his executive job with Pennsylvania Glass Sand Corporation.[264] The new company acquired several sand mines and processing plants, including Virginia Glass Sand Corporation and its neighbor, Shenandoah Silica Company. After high-grade silica sand at the Gore mine was depleted, Woods sold Unimin in 1973 to SCR-Sibelco.[265] The Belgian company spent $5 million to open a new mine, then acquired the Winchester and Western Railroad to ensure it would continue hauling sand from Gore.[266] In 2018, SCR-Sibelco sold Unimin and the railroad to Ohio-based Covia Holdings Corporation.[267] In the Gore area, 750,000 tons of sand were mined each year from 1,100 acres of owned and leased land.[268]

Manufacturing: Factories and Jobs on the Move

Just as fertile land brought settlers into the Northern Valley in the 1700s, two and one-half centuries later its industrial parks, reliable labor force and interstate highways attracted manufacturers. By the late 1990s, however, those companies grew sales not by adding capacity, but through mergers and acquisitions. They cut costs by consolidating factory space, investing in automation and moving unskilled work to low-wage countries. From 2000 to 2019, manufacturing jobs in the Virginia portion of the region dropped by 41.7 percent, from 21,428 to 12,500, while those in the Eastern Panhandle declined by 40.6 percent, from 6,230 to 3,700.[269] Despite those losses, Northern Valley's economic developers and factory owners were able to recruit businesses to fill many of the vacated facilities.

Food and Beverage Industry

Before the Second World War, the region's food industry included dairies, creameries, gristmills, bakeries, canneries and fruit processors, whose raw materials came from plants and animals raised in the Northern Valley. By the 1990s, however, some packaged food and beverage companies sourced their raw materials from outside the region.

With less wheat grown in the Northern Valley, most of the remaining gristmills were shuttered after World War II. They included Stoner-Keller Mill in Fishers Hill in 1958 and the Bunker Hill Mill in 1964.[270] On Opequon Creek south of Winchester, the Springdale Flour Mills, once known as Bartonsville Mill, closed in 1970, while Edinburg Mill on Stony Creek stopped producing flour eight years later.[271] When needed, two restored gristmills in Clarke County still ground grains: Locke's Mill on the Shenandoah River and Burwell-Morgan Mill on Spout Run in Millwood.

Fruit Processing

As Northern Valley orchardists adapted to changing market conditions in the postwar period, so did its apple processing companies. In an increasingly competitive market, some plants were sold, while outdated and inefficient ones were closed. They could not compete with newer plants in Asia, Australia, New Zealand and Europe, whose products were exported duty-free to the United States.[272]

After the Bowmans opened a factory in Mount Jackson in 1939 to process their own apples, Gordon Bowman Sr. bought out his siblings' interests in 1946 and formed Bowman Apple Products Co., Inc., which packaged private label products, including juices sold to grocery chains.[273] Worried about imports of Chinese apple concentrates, the company bottled 20 varieties of Gatorade for PepsiCo. in 2006 [274] Five years later, French fruit processor Andros et Cie acquired a majority interest in Bowman to gain a foothold in the United States food market.[275] Bowman Andros Foods was based in Mount Jackson.

In 1949, National Fruit Product Company, Inc. in Winchester sold its Pennsylvania apple processing plants in Chambersburg and Peach Glen to the newly organized Knouse Foods Cooperative, based in the latter town.[276] In 1985, National Fruit acquired its neighbor on Fairmont Avenue, the Shenandoah Valley Apple Cooperative, formerly known as Shenandoah Valley Apple Cider and Vinegar Corporation.[277] Because the purchase greatly increased National Fruit's production and warehousing capacity, it closed plants in Atlanta and Martinsburg.[278] Faced with an increasingly competitive market, the company sold its Michigan and North Carolina facilities in 1998.[279] Some of that production was brought into the 600-employee Winchester plant, and more resources were devoted to marketing its White House Foods products.[280]

In 2006, Paige and husband David Gum, National Fruit's vice president of manufacturing, and other investors purchased the company from the Armstrong family in a management-led buyout.[281] The Gums sold the office building on Fairmont Avenue and put 1,100 acres of the company's 3,000 acres of orchards in southern Berkeley County on the auction block.[282] But it retained ownership when the proposed mixed-use development failed to gain traction during the Great Recession.[283]

Two other apple processors changed hands within the Northern Valley. In 1994, the Massey family closed Shenandoah Candy Company's factory, which opened in 1927 on Winchester's Amherst Street.[284] In 1997, Millcroft Farms Company, in the Stanley area of Page County, purchased their equipment and the apple candy's Shenandoah brand name.[285] In 1966, Paul and Max Braithwaite sold what had become an apple cannery in Cross Junction to the William Whitacre family, which owned 350 nearby acres of apple and peach orchards.[286] Their Shawnee Canning Company, Inc. packaged the fruit in private label cans and jars for local grocers, while its own brands were sold at Shawnee Springs Market on U.S. 522, northwest of Winchester.

Several fruit processors closed their Northern Valley operations, either to consolidate production in other locations or due to financial issues. In 1961, PET, Inc., the St. Louis milk company, purchased C. H. Musselman Company in Biglerville, Pennsylvania, including its orchard and applesauce factory in Inwood.[287] Musselman changed hands several times before Knouse Foods Cooperative acquired the company in 1984 from an investor group.[288] It closed the 90-employee Inwood factory in 2008 and moved production to Chambersburg.[289] Knouse's management stated that more housing and fewer orchards in Berkeley County meant less apples for processing.[290]

In the decade following the 1966 death of Rudolph Rasche, owner of Zeropack Company, trustees of the Cincinnati-based fruit processor continued leasing a former cold storage building on Winchester's North Cameron Street.[291] When C. L. Robinson Corporation refused to negotiate lease extensions, Rasche's estate sold Zeropack to the landlord for $2.8 million in 1976.[292] At peak production, 30 million pounds of sliced and frozen apples were sold each year to small bakeries and cafeterias. Failing to pay orchardists in 1997, Zeropack's doors closed, 400 workers lost their jobs and its assets were liquidated while in receivership.[293]

In 1988, H. J. Heinz Company in Pittsburgh closed its apple cider vinegar plant on Winchester's Valley Avenue and consolidated production into a similar one in Michigan. Opened in 1930 to supply vinegar to its hometown ketchup factory, Heinz sold the vacant building to neighbor O'Sullivan Corporation.[294]

Undaunted by the closure of three of the region's apple processing plants, David and Philip Glaize III saw a business opportunity related to the soaring popularity of hard cider drinks. In 2018, they opened Glaize and Bro. Juice Company next to the family's apple packing house on Winchester's Pennsylvania Avenue.[295] The Fred L. Glaize orchards supplied the brothers with cider-specific apples, which were pressed into juice. At first, they sold it to hard cider producers, then made the finished product themselves.[296]

Soft Drink Bottlers

Moving from Blackstone, Virginia, to Winchester, William E. Bridgeforth Sr. signed on as a route driver for a Nehi soft drink distributor in Culpeper.[297] In 1928, he and wife Margaret founded Nehi Bottling Company of Winchester and opened a plant on North Cameron Street.[298] When Royal Crown Cola became Nehi's flagship soft drink in the 1930s, the Bridgeforths changed their company's name to Royal Crown Bottling Company of Winchester.[299] Between 1964 and 1969, son Ed Jr. acquired regional bottling franchises for Mountain Dew, Canada Dry and Dr. Pepper, and added a plant in Hagerstown.[300] In 1967, he moved Royal Crown Bottling to larger quarters in Winchester Industrial Park, where production increased to more than 2 million canned and bottled soft drinks each year.[301]

While Romney native Reynolds Hill worked for a Coca-Cola bottler in Florida, he saw a potential market for sales of pure spring water. In 1974, he formed West Virginia Spring Water Company in Berkeley Springs and sold water from the town's Warm Springs Run. With bottling outsourced to the local Berkeley Club Beverages, Inc., Hill annually shipped 1.5 million gallons of filtered and sterilized water to southern Florida.[302] He later moved production into his own plant.

In the early 2000s, a Winchester soft drink bottler consolidated the century-old Berkeley Springs water industry. Founded in 1987, family-owned DeHaven Seven Up Corporation purchased Berkeley Club Beverages in 2004, which at one time bottled ginger ale.[303] Two years later, the DeHavens acquired West Virginia Spring Water Company and moved Berkeley Club's equipment into the more modern facility.[304]

Poultry Processing

While Rockingham County became known for turkeys, several poultry integrators built broiler plants in and near the Northern Valley. They provided farmers in Page and Shenandoah counties with broiler chicks and feed, then purchased and dressed mature birds for sale to grocers and restaurants. Concerned about low prices received for their chickens, 233 farmers formed Rockingham Poultry Marketing Cooperative, Inc. in 1940 and opened a processing plant at its Broadway headquarters, 13 miles north of Harrisonburg.³⁰⁵ The co-op added facilities in New Market, Staunton and Moorefield, and one on Winchester's North Kent Street, which operated from 1947 to 1961.

Wampler Feed and Seed Company, which began in the 1930s in Dayton as a turkey integrator, added broilers to its product line. To be closer to growers in Page and Shenandoah counties, Wampler opened a plant in 1953 near Stanley, where 300 members of the United Food and Commercial Workers Union dressed 650,000 chickens per week.³⁰⁶ After Wampler purchased a turkey processor in Hinton, Virginia, it took the Wampler Foods, Inc. name.³⁰⁷

During the balance of the twentieth century, Virginia's poultry industry consolidated, first among itself, then with companies from outside the commonwealth. In 1984, Wampler Foods merged with Pennsylvania chicken processor Horace W. Longacre, Inc. and became Wampler-Longacre, Inc.³⁰⁸ When the Rockingham Poultry Marketing Cooperative joined it two years later, the new company became WLR Foods Inc., headquartered in Broadway.³⁰⁹

In 1944, Grover Holler Jr. and two brothers started up Blue Ridge Poultry & Egg Co., Inc. in Edinburg, which built a broiler plant near the village of Columbia Furnace, west of the town.³¹⁰ In 1967, its 250 employees processed 56 million pounds of poultry.³¹¹ When the company experienced financial problems four years later, Rocco, Inc. in Harrisonburg and Marval Poultry Company, Inc. in Dayton, purchased its plant.³¹² Started up in 1939, Robert and Charles Strickler transformed Rocco Feeds, Inc. two decades later into poultry integrator Rocco, Inc.³¹³ After its acquisition of Marval Poultry in 1981, the combined company operated as Rocco Farm Foods.³¹⁴

In the late 1990s, the poultry industry suffered from high feed costs and low chicken prices, a condition that forced several Shenandoah Valley companies to seek out-of-state partners. In 2001, Minneapolis grain dealer Cargill Inc. purchased Rocco Farm Foods.³¹⁵ Keeping Rocco's turkey business in Harrisonburg, Cargill sold its broiler plants in that city and in Columbia Furnace to George's Inc. in Arkansas.³¹⁶ In 2001, Pilgrim's Pride Corporation from Texas purchased WLR Foods, Inc., whose annual sales had grown to $800 million.³¹⁷ The 300 employees at the former Wampler plant in Page County soon lost their jobs when work was moved to the Broadway and Moorefield facilities.

As the Shenandoah Valley's broiler production increased, it needed to dispose of aging breeder hens and roosters. To solve the problem, the Whitt Carr family launched New Market Poultry Products, Inc. in 1989, which dressed the mature birds at Rockingham Poultry Marketing's former plant in New

Market.³¹⁸ In 2011, the 150-employee company was sold to Georgia-based Tip Top Poultry, Inc., the nation's largest processor of baking and stewing hens.³¹⁹

Rendering By-Products

After World War II, Valley Proteins, Inc. in Frederick County became one of the nation's largest renderers. The industry collected oil and animal by-products—grease, fat, meat and bones—from livestock and poultry plants, restaurants and grocery stores. The inedible matter was recycled into pet food, animal feed and biofuels. In 1949, Clyde Smith, who gathered by-products for a rendering business in Pennsylvania, purchased Winchester Rendering Company, located near Rockingham Poultry Marketing's plant on North Kent Street.³²⁰

After his father's death in 1968, Gerald Smith Sr. bought out six siblings to secure sole ownership of what had become Valley Proteins, Inc.³²¹ By 1986, the company operated 12 rendering plants in eight states, including one near its headquarters.³²² At Gerald's passing in 2003, Valley Proteins' footprint had expanded to 21 plants and 1,300 employees. Under the leadership of Clyde's grandson J.J. Smith, 2,000 employees generated $550 million in revenue for the company in 2019.³²³ Several years later, Valley Proteins was sold for $1.1 billion to Darling Ingredients Inc. in Irving, Texas.³²⁴

In 1986, Rocco Farm Foods, Inc. opened Mountain View Rendering facility next to its broiler plant in Columbia Furnace.³²⁵ When George's Inc. purchased Rocco's broiler business from Cargill in 2001, the plant annually recycled 150,000 tons of chicken entrails, from the processing plants in Columbia Furnace and Harrisonburg, into animal feed.³²⁶

Other Food Processors

In 1951, Melvin Pierce founded Pierce Pre-Cooked Foods, Inc. in Michigan to market frozen chicken to restaurants, then moved the company to Moorefield to be near poultry processors.³²⁷ One decade after salesman Wendell Hester purchased the company in 1954, he cooked chicken wings in spices and delivered them to a food wholesaler in Buffalo, where the concept of flavored wings originated.³²⁸ Finding success, he purchased them for pennies per pound and produced frozen Wing Dings at the Moorefield plant.

In 1967, Hester Industries, Inc. moved headquarters to Winchester and opened Marketeam, Inc. to sell wings to restaurants and fast food outlets. Several times Hester's son Jeff was forced to defend the company's Wing

Dings trademark against competitive threats, including Tyson Foods' launch of a similar product called Wing Flings.[329] In 1997, Hester Industries was sold to Omaha-based ConAgra, Inc., which closed the Winchester office.[330]

In 1962, Art Plummer started Shenandoah Bee Company in Gerrardstown.[331] Orchardists paid him to place hives among their fruit trees to ensure the blossoms would be pollinated. Deciding to package and sell the honey, Plummer formed Virginia Honey Co., Inc. and opened a plant on Route 7, west of Berryville.[332] In 1998, Martinsburg banker Terry Hess purchased the company from his uncle and opened a factory in Berkeley County Industrial Park to package Virginia Brand onion salad dressing and sauces, made from Plummer's recipes.[333]

In 2001, Hess sold Virginia Honey to Vita Food Products, Inc., a Chicago marketer of kosher fish, but retained ownership of both local plants.[334] After leaving Vita, he started up SVB Food & Beverage at the Berkeley County facility.[335] It produced condiments under the Shenandoah Valley Brand and bottled products for other food companies. In 2012, Hess purchased Linden Beverage Company, the Warren County bottler of Alpenglow Sparkling Cider since 1980, and moved production to Berkeley County.[336]

Between food business jobs, Hess started JayDee's Family Fun Center in 2007 in Inwood as a private recreational park.[337] He also sold Virginia Honey's original building and equipment to Greg Gunter. Started in 1965 in Clarke County, Gunter's Honey packaged and shipped buckwheat and wildflower honey to markets in Northern Virginia, New York City and for export.[338]

Several companies made frozen food products in the former Rockingham Poultry Marketing plant on Winchester's North Kent Street, because it was equipped with coolers that once kept processed chicken fresh. In 1964, Schrafft's Frozen Foods, Inc. in New York City used it to prepare pre-portioned dinners for the company's 55 restaurants and for sale to institutional cafeterias.[339] Radar ovens heated the frozen meals in 30 seconds. In 1968, PET, Inc. from St. Louis purchased Schrafft's and placed the meal business into its Food Service Division.[340]

After PET closed the Winchester plant in 1972, Rich Products Corporation from Buffalo acquired it two years later to bake and freeze breads, rolls, sweets and muffins.[341] When Rich shifted production in 2005 to Tennessee, 220 members of the Bakery, Confectionery, Tobacco Workers and Grain Millers Union lost their jobs.[342] Next year, Winchester Cold Storage Company purchased the North Kent Street plant and used it for dry, freezer and cooler storage.[343]

In 2009, Quesos La Ricura Ltd. from Long Island used $7.5 million from an industrial revenue bond to purchase and renovate the building and install machinery to process cheese.[344] When demand for its products failed to meet projections, Quesos La Ricura closed the 125-employee plant two years later.[345]

In 1995, the Cohen family, owners of the Tabard Inn in Washington, D.C., moved their potato chip business from Waldorf, Maryland, to a former feed store on Middletown's Main Street, part of U.S. 11.[346] Since 1982, their Tabard Farm in nearby Reliance had raised organic vegetables for the restaurant.[347] Made from a variety of root vegetables, Route 11 Potato Chips' kettle-cooked snacks soon gained a regional following.[348] In 2008, Sarah Cohen moved production to a larger, more modern facility in Mount Jackson Industrial Park.[349]

Several of the nation's packaged foods companies opened factories in the Northern Valley. Because General Foods, later part of Kraft Heinz, needed more capacity to produce its Capri-Sun drinks, it started up a production line in 1992 in Fort Collier Industrial Park in Frederick County.[350] That same year, newly-formed Hershey Pasta Group moved into a factory in the same park, along with Miller Milling Co. from Minneapolis, which supplied its neighbor with semolina flour.[351] Deciding that candy and pasta were not a good fit, Hershey sold the latter business in 1999 to a private equity firm that formed New World Pasta Company, based in Harrisburg.[352] When Spanish food company Ebro Puleva S.A. purchased it in 2006, the Frederick County plant, which made the Ronzoni brand of pasta, became part of its Riviana Foods unit in Houston.[353]

In 2000, HP Hood, LLC from Massachusetts opened what became the region's largest food processing plant on the same Valley Pike site where three years earlier, local opposition convinced Cardinal Glass not to build a factory.[354] HP Hood turned milk purchased from Mid-Atlantic dairy farmers into extended shelf-life, fluid milk and non-dairy products.[355] After $300 million was spent on several expansions, the plant's annual capacity increased from 45 million gallons of processed milk to 150 million in 2015, and its workforce grew to 500 employees.[356]

In 2006, Interbake Foods moved cookie production from its unionized plant in Richmond into a former truck factory in Stephens Industrial Park in northern Warren County.[357] Headquartered in Richmond, Interbake was a unit of Toronto-based George Weston, Ltd., one of North America's largest cookie and cracker companies.[358] In the same park in 2015, Montreal-based Nature's Touch Frozen Foods opened a facility in which 25 employees packed fruits, imported through the Virginia Inland Port, for the private label market.[359]

Household Products Industry

Because they manufactured consumer staples, household products companies were in a non-cyclical industry. Nevertheless, between 2002 and 2010, three of them closed factories in the Northern Valley. Two took on too much debt in leveraged buyouts and the third was a victim of creative destruction. By 2012, however, each factory had been repurposed and occupied.

In 1960, Corning Glass Works built what grew into a 460,000-square-foot housewares factory in Berkeley County Industrial Park, south of Martinsburg.[360] As the internet gained traction in the 1990s, the renamed Corning Inc. focused on its more profitable and faster growing optical fiber and telecom equipment businesses.[361] In 1998 in a leveraged buyout, the Consumer Products unit was sold to private equity firm KKR & Co., Inc., which combined it with two similar companies as World Kitchen.[362] Unable to meet its financial obligations, the new company took bankruptcy in 2002, and the Martinsburg factory, which once employed as many as 1,000 union workers, was shuttered.[363]

In 1975, General Electric hired 500 employees at the world's largest incandescent lamp factory, located south of Winchester in Kernstown.[364] GE consolidated production from several smaller, less-efficient ones into the 450,000-square-foot building.[365] In 1983, a $90 million investment expanded annual production to 400 million light bulbs.[366] In the New Millennium, the federal government forced consumers to purchase energy-saving, compact florescent and LED lights, which made GE's local factory obsolete.[367] Due to the investment needed to produce the lights, GE Consumer Products closed the Kernstown factory in 2010, and sourced them from China.[368]

As with World Kitchen, Pen-Tab Industries, Inc. suffered from too much debt. In 1995, the company's headquarters and manufacturing were relocated from New York City into a 272,500-square-foot factory in Kelley Industrial Park in Warren County.[369] Three hundred employees turned large rolls of paper, imported through the Virginia Inland Port, into school and office supplies and stationery.[370] In 1997, Pen-Tab's two founders sold the company in a leveraged buyout to Citicorp Venture Capital.[371] The new owner soon doubled revenues with the debt-financed, $140 million purchase of competitor Stuart Hall, but mounting losses forced Pen-Tab into the hands of Mead Corporation in 2001.[372] Two years later, the Warren County plant closed, costing 160 employees their jobs.[373]

Despite the Corning, General Electric and Pen-Tab plant closures, three more household product companies established a presence in the region.

In 2008, Indonesian-owned Mercury Paper Inc. in California leased a 406,000-square-foot building in North Shenandoah Industrial Park, near Strasburg.³⁷⁴ One hundred thirty workers made disposable household products—napkins, paper towels and toilet paper—from large rolls of paper imported through the Virginia Inland Port.³⁷⁵

In 2015, Proctor & Gamble Company in Cincinnati announced it would build and equip a huge factory in Tabler Station Business Park, several miles south of Martinsburg.³⁷⁶ It was part of the company's goal to slash $10 billion in manufacturing and logistics costs by consolidating production from smaller and less efficient, one-product factories into automated large ones.³⁷⁷ After the 2.5 million-square-foot facility opened in 2018 in Berkeley County, 1,400 P&G employees produced 45 different personal and household products.³⁷⁸ West Virginia's incentives for the project included $8.5 million for site preparation, an Economic Opportunity Tax Credit and a PILOT agreement.³⁷⁹

In 2019, Clorox Company in California needed more capacity to meet the growing consumer demand for cat litter. Because it neutralized the acid smell of urine, limestone was an important ingredient in the product. Clorox proposed building a 100,000-square-foot cat litter factory near Carmeuse Lime & Stone's quarry in Clear Brook, but neighbors objected to the increased truck traffic and noise that it would bring.³⁸⁰ The Frederick County Board of Supervisors turned the project down, despite its potential to bring $500,000 in annual tax revenue into county coffers.³⁸¹ Seven months later, Clorox found a willing partner in Berkeley County when it announced construction of a $190 million factory, located near the Proctor & Gamble complex.³⁸² In 2020, one hundred Clorox workers made Scoop Away and Fresh Stop cat litter, using limestone the Winchester and Western Railroad hauled from the Clear Brook quarry.³⁸³

Textile and Apparel Industry

After World War II, clothing factory jobs replaced those lost at the Northern Valley's woolen mills. Apparel sales were driven by the nation's postwar pent-up demand for consumer goods, higher disposable incomes of a growing middle class and an expanding service sector, whose workers needed larger wardrobes than those laboring on farms and in factories. To meet that demand, clothing companies in Pennsylvania and New York sought to add manufacturing capacity in the less expensive and non-unionized Northern Valley. They also found that Interstate 81 eased the task of trucking finished goods to Northeast and Mid-Atlantic markets. Paid piece work rates for each garment finished, many women left struggling family farms for clothing factory jobs.

By 1990, however, the nation's membership in the General Agreement on Trade and Tariffs and the North American Free Trade Agreement had decimated the domestic apparel industry.[384] Clothing manufacturers continued to design and market the goods, but outsourced production to low-wage factories in Asia, Mexico, Central America and the Caribbean. Global supply chains moved the finished clothing tariff free into the United States. Because of that offshoring, apparel items made in America declined from 95 percent of total units sold in 1960 to just 3 percent in 2013.[385]

Woolen Mills

As synthetic fabrics replaced wool after World War II, the six woolen mills in the Northern Valley shuttered their doors; it was too costly to invest in equipment needed to make the new cloth.[386] In 1946, Berkeley Woolen Company in Martinsburg and Virginia Woolen Company in Winchester formed Varel Mills, Inc., which built a finishing plant alongside Turkey Run Spring in the Jefferson County village of Middleway.[387] The facility solved the owners' water supply and waste disposal issues that had developed in the downtowns of the two cities. When the Berkeley Woolen Company went out of business in 1949, Virginia Woolen became sole owner of Varel Mills.[388] Operating at only half capacity, the plant lost money. In the early 1950s, Virginia Woolen also experienced losses at its antiquated complex on Winchester's North Kent Street.[389] United Merchants and Manufacturers, Inc. in New York City purchased the company in 1956.[390] Failing to make the operation profitable, it closed the Winchester mill two years later, and then shuttered the Varel finishing plant.[391]

After the war, Winchester Woolen Company switched production from flannel and suiting cloth to women's wear, but local stockholders liquidated the unprofitable company in 1948.[392] Its mill on Abrams Creek was sold to O'Sullivan Rubber Company, which warehoused rubber heels in it.[393] Due to competition from synthetics, the Dunn Woolen Company mills in Martinsburg and Bunker Hill, which produced fabric for automobile upholstery, were shuttered in 1953.[394] Facing a flood of low-cost imports of women's garments and tweeds, William Lawrence Jr. closed his Clearbrook Woolen Mill in 1971.[395] That decision ended a Northern Valley industry that 80 years earlier brought large-scale manufacturing to its two cities.

Silk and Rayon Mills

By 1989, the region's four silk and rayon mills had closed. The Strasburg Silk Mill, which substituted rayon for more expensive silk, remained in operation making casket linings until owner Nathan Platt's passing in 1977.[396] In Front Royal, Schwarzenbach-Huber Company shut down its Royal Silk Mill in 1966, where 300 workers annually wove 2 million yards of silk cloth.[397] It transferred work to its typewriter and computer ribbon factory in Pennsylvania that had excess capacity.[398] Cheap imports forced closure of the Swiss company's yarn throwing factory in Luray in 1985, and production was transferred to Honduras.[399]

Shutting down American Viscose's rayon factory in Front Royal was more problematic. After opening in 1940, it dumped chemicals into 23 waste disposal basins that emptied into the South Fork of the Shenandoah River.[400] In 1948, the Virginia Water Control Board ordered the company to install wastewater treatment equipment and submit monthly reports to it.[401] Between 1963 and 1976, the rayon factory was sold several times, while the Amalgamated Clothing and Textile Workers Union's membership declined from 2,000 persons to 470.[402] In 1976, newly formed Avtex Fibers, Inc. in Valley Forge purchased the Front Royal and four other American Viscose factories in a $200 million leveraged buyout.[403] Public outcry over its pollution of the Shenandoah River continued. After Virginia revoked Avtex's water discharge permit in 1989, the company declared bankruptcy and closed the Front Royal complex.[404]

Apparel Industry in Virginia Portion of the Region

During the 1960s, out-of-state companies opened numerous clothing factories in the Northern Valley. Deciding not to compete for labor in Winchester and Martinsburg, most were built in more rural Shenandoah and Page counties.[405] Aileen, Inc. and the Wrangler unit of VF Corporation became the Northern Valley's largest apparel employers. By the 1980s, clothing factory payrolls in Page County totaled 1,500 persons, while 1,700 apparel workers in Shenandoah County accounted for 30 percent of its manufacturing jobs.[406] But as the work shifted to low-cost countries, all clothing factories had closed by 2002.

In 1960, New York City-based Aileen, Inc. needed more manufacturing capacity for its women's knit suits. In response, the newly-formed Shenandoah County Industrial Development Corporation sold bonds that financed construction of factories in Woodstock and Edinburg.[407] After Aileen went public in 1961, it added facilities in Strasburg and New Market, and for a short time, leased the former Wanner Textile factory in Winchester.[408] When the company ran into financial problems in the early 1980s, it closed the New Market and Strasburg operations. In 1988, contract apparel maker Strasburg Manufacturing Co. purchased the latter factory to make blouses.[409] With sales of Aileen's knit suits losing market share to trendier women's wear, it took bankruptcy in 1994.[410] Five hundred women lost their jobs when the Woodstock and Edinburg factories were shuttered and production was moved to the Dominican Republic.[411]

During World War II, Blue Bell Overall Company in North Carolina purchased Casey Jones Work-Clothes Company, which opened a factory in Luray in 1923. For decades, blue jeans were considered reliable work clothes, but they gained popularity as leisure clothing after appearing in Western movies. Blue Bell rode the jeans craze into the Northern Valley, and by the 1970s, employed 1,200 workers spread among its regional headquarters and factory in Luray and others in Shenandoah, Woodstock and Mount Jackson.[412] With its purchase of Blue Bell in 1986, VF Corporation became one of world's largest jeans manufacturers. By 2002, however, it had shuttered all Northern Valley factories and outsourced production to Asian and Caribbean countries.[413] A warehouse remained in Luray to process jeans imported through the Virginia Inland Port in Front Royal.

From the 1950s into the New Millennium, other clothing factories opened and closed in the Virginia portion of the region. In 1952, John Wanner left the employ of Lewis Jones Knitting Mill in Winchester to start up Wanner Textile Company on North Cameron Street. Before its closing a decade later, the factory produced ladies' cotton knitted blouses and cardigans, in competition with those of Wanner's previous employer.

Seven months after World War II ended, the International Ladies' Garment Union struck Lewis Jones Knitting Mill, demanding an increase in wages from 45 cents to 60 cents an hour.[414] After William H. West from Clarke County purchased the property in 1954, the renamed Winchester Knitting Mill assembled women's and children's cotton sweaters that his Locksley Corporation shipped to New York City's garment district.[415] In 1963, West converted the building to an outlet store, then sold it one decade later.[416]

A labor dispute also occurred at Shenandoah Knitting Mills' women's hosiery factory, which opened in 1943 in its namesake Page County town. After North Carolina-based owner Chadbourne Hosiery Mills, Inc. laid off workers in 1957, the others struck several times in efforts to join the American

Federation of Hosiery Workers.[417] Chadbourne refused to recognize the union, but when the National Labor Relations Board ratified its formation, the factory was shuttered in 1960.[418] After World War II, three other clothing companies moved in and out of Shenandoah County. They included Windsor Knitting Mills, Inc., with two sewing factories in Edinburg, and underwear companies J. E. Morgan Knitting Mills, Inc. and Dawson International Plc., which operated facilities in other towns.[419] After their closure, Gentile Brothers Folder Factory, Coleman Microwave Company and Shenandoah Telecommunications Company purchased the empty buildings.[420]

Apparel Industry in the Eastern Panhandle

Post-World War II, Interwoven Stocking Company in Martinsburg was reorganized as Interwoven Company. At peak production in the early 1950s, more than 3,000 workers filled 450,000 square feet of space in 14 buildings in Martinsburg, making Interwoven the largest employer in the Eastern Panhandle.[421] But as cheaper imports hurt sales, its workforce had shrunk to 900 in 1960.[422] When John W. Mettler Jr. assumed ownership upon his father's passing two years later, he sold Interwoven to Chester H. Roth Company, a New York City maker of unbranded men's hosiery.[423] The new owner immediately reduced the Martinsburg headcount to 250 and moved most production to North Carolina. Local manufacturing was halted completely in 1970, leaving less than 100 employees engaged in warehousing and shipping socks to retailers. In 1976, Roth Company's successor, Kayser-Roth Corporation, closed the Martinsburg operation.[424]

With Interwoven's mills vacant and a cadre of Martinsburg workers trained in making men's socks, Benjamin Sirota sensed a business opportunity. Since 1949, his Royce Hosiery Mills, Inc. produced a high-end product in Philadelphia for specialty clothing shops.[425] In 1965, Sirota moved sock production into one of Interwoven's vacant mills, before building a factory on Baltimore Street, eight years later.[426] Royce Hosiery was sold three times before Royce Too LLC from New York City closed the 75-employee factory in 2004 and transferred production to Winston-Salem.[427] Warehousing was consolidated into the Shockey Commerce Center, the former General Motors parts facility on I-81, north of Martinsburg. Looking to secure a distribution foothold in the American market for its products, Okamoto Corporation, Japan's largest hosiery maker, purchased Royce Too in 2008.[428]

Women's apparel factories closed in the Eastern Panhandle. After a 20-year effort, in 1953 the International Ladies Garment Workers Union organized Perfection Garment Company's employees in Martinsburg. They soon struck that factory, along with those in the West Virginia towns of Ranson and Keyser.[429] In 1956, Samuel Stein from Pennsylvania purchased the company and closed its Ranson unit, putting 90 workers on the street.[430] Those in Martinsburg and Keyser continued to sew women's clothes until 1991, when new owners shifted production to a South Carolina factory to better compete against foreign imports.[431]

In 1965, the Zacharia family in New York City formed Granada Sales Corporation to sew ladies' sleepwear and loungewear at a factory in Berkeley County Industrial Park. Production was moved to Puerto Rico in 1993, the same year that Potomac Sportswear, Inc. closed its 60-year-old factory in Martinsburg and 75 union workers lost their jobs.[432]

Aircraft Industry

After World War II, three airplane manufacturers opened factories at the Eastern West Virginia Regional Airport, but each closed within a decade. In 1952, Armond Thieblot, a former chief engineer at Fairchild Aircraft in Hagerstown, started up Thieblot Aircraft to assemble cargo airplanes in Martinsburg.[433] Four years later, Vitro Corporation of America purchased the business, but its operations at the airport ceased in 1960.[434]

In the region's most chronicled business development effort, U.S. Senator John D. Rockefeller IV from West Virginia spent 12 years helping Swearingen Aircraft Corporation secure funds to manufacture SJ30 business jets in Martinsburg. In 1992, he announced the San Antonio company, which Edward Swearingen founded in 1973, would build an 800-worker factory at the Martinsburg airport.[435] While it had orders for hundreds of the $2 million SJ30s, Swearingen Aircraft needed $100 million to gain FAA certification and begin manufacturing what it billed as, "The world's fastest- and longest-range light business jet." [436]

After failing to secure funds from venture capital firms, Rockefeller convinced the Taiwanese in 2004 to invest $400 million in the renamed Sino Swearingen Aircraft Company. When the FAA finally certified the jet in 2007, a factory opened in the Martinsburg airport's new 225-acre John D. Rockefeller IV Science & Technology Center.[437] Rather than build planes, 125 employees

Chapter 7: Post-World War II to 2020   287

Sino Swearingen SJ30 airplane, 2005
Photo in advertisement from SyberJet Aircraft, Cedar City, UT

fabricated fuselages, wings and tail parts that were shipped to San Antonio for final assembly into SJ30s, whose price had risen to $5.5 million.[438] As Sino Swearingen burned through cash, the Taiwanese poured another $300 million into the company, but its leaders opposed further investments.[439] In 2008, Emirates Investment and Development Company in Dubai put up $150 million for an 80 percent stake in the renamed Emivest Aerospace Corporation.[440] After it took Chapter 11 bankruptcy two years later, the Martinsburg and San Antonio factories went on the auction block.

A second aircraft company Senator Rockefeller recruited to the Eastern West Virginia Regional Airport also encountered financial headwinds. In 1997, Taiwanese-based Tung Long Metal formed TLM Aerospace, Inc. to manufacture the Tiger AG-5B general aviation airplane, which Grumman Aerospace Corporation once made.[441] Investing $15 million in a factory at the airport in 2000, TLM projected assembling upwards of 600 of them each year.[442] But with only 51 Tiger aircraft delivered between 2001 and 2006, the company declared bankruptcy, shut down operations and the building was put up for sale.[443]

Building Materials Industry

After World War II, numerous companies opened factories in the Northern Valley to make windows, doors, kitchen cabinets and trusses from wood timbered in nearby forests. The region's economy also benefited when two Fortune 500 companies—Boise Cascade and Mobil Oil—spun off units in Clarke and Frederick counties that did not fit into their long-range plans. Sold in management led buyouts, the American Woodmark and the Trex companies expanded rapidly after going public. While most building materials companies in the region survived the nation's housing recession that began in 2007, several factories either closed or were sold.

Windows and Doors

At one time, Page County's manufacturing sector included three door and parts plants, whose parent companies went through numerous corporate mergers. They included Crown Door Company, Inc. in Stanley that Masonite International in Ontario purchased in 2014, and Genie Company, with a factory that made garage door openers north of the town of Shenandoah. The latter company was purchased by Overhead Door Company in 1994, then sold two years later to China-based Sanwa Shutter Corporation. In 2001, EMCO Enterprises, Inc.'s door factory in Luray became part of Andersen Corporation, the nation's largest manufacturer of windows and doors.[444]

In 1985, Stanley Works in Connecticut, which Masonite later purchased, made residential entry doors at a factory in Fort Collier Industrial Park in Frederick County.[445] In 2003, Barber & Ross Company received state and county incentives to move its headquarters and window and door assembly lines from Leesburg into a new building in the same park.[446] But as the Great Recession started, the company declared bankruptcy, closed the business and laid off 400 employees.[447]

Kitchen Cabinets

In 1971, Boise Cascade Corp. in Idaho purchased Raygold Corp., a Long Island cabinet maker that owned a factory in Moorefield, West Virginia.[448] To be closer to that facility, in 1974 the Boise Cabinet Division moved into the former H. F. Byrd, Inc. apple packing building in Berryville. In addition to serving as the unit's headquarters, kitchen and bath cabinets were assembled there from components made in Moorefield. In a 1980 leveraged buyout, Boise sold the cabinet unit to four executives.[449] Headquarters of the renamed American Woodmark Company were moved to Winchester Industrial Park in 1986, the same year the company went public.[450]

First marketed through dealers, after less-expensive cabinet lines were developed for home improvement retailers, Woodmark's sales grew to $241 million in 1998. As the housing market heated up in the New Millennium, the company added manufacturing capacity, but closed three of its 12 factories in the Great Recession, including the 260-employee unit in Berryville and the oldest of its three Moorefield facilities.[451] As sales rebounded to $1.25 billion in 2018, American Woodmark moved 425 employees into a new $30 million headquarters building on Shady Lane Road, south of Winchester.[452]

In 1985, Masco Corporation in Detroit acquired Merillat Industries Inc., a southwestern Michigan cabinet maker, then opened a door frame and veneering factory in Mount Jackson Industrial Park.[453] After a 2006 expansion—the third in less than two years— Merillat's employment rose to 500 workers.[454] But in the midst of the housing downturn, only 125 remained at the factory.[455]

Trusses, Decking and Modular Housing

After the Second World War, several manufacturers of trusses—triangular wood structures used to support roofs—opened in the region. Willard Fansler pioneered the local industry when he started Blue Ridge Truss and Supply Company in 1962. Until it closed in 2015, trusses were fabricated near the western Shenandoah County village of Basye.[456] In 1975, the Fred Glaize Jr. family, owners of a hardware and lumber store in Winchester, opened Glaize Components to fabricate trusses, panels and joists in a factory near U.S. 50 East in Frederick County. In 2010, ProBuilt Holdings, a Denver-based supplier of building materials, purchased Glaize's truss business, which included a North Carolina factory.[457]

Two Northern Virginia companies relocated their truss operations in the region. In 1989, the William Frogale family moved its Allied Systems, which made wall panels and roof and floor trusses, from Haymarket to a factory near Glaize Components.[458] When the housing boom began in 2003, the company added 98,000 square feet of manufacturing space.[459] Six years later, the Frogale's Annandale Lumber and Millwork joined Allied Systems at the Frederick County site and both companies became Annandale Millwork and Allied Systems Corporation.[460] In 2005, Fairfax County homebuilder Van Metre Company built a truss and wall panel factory in newly established Capon Bridge Technology and Industrial Park, located in southern Hampshire County, several miles off U.S. 50.[461] Five years later, Van Metre moved its Total Structural Solutions' production into a former recreation vehicle factory in Winchester Industrial Park.

Trusses were also made in northern Berkeley County. In 1999, three local businessmen started Code Plus Components, then moved the company into a larger factory along I-81.[462] In 2017, it was sold to BMC Stock Holdings, Inc., an Atlanta-based millwork, door and truss company.[463] In 2002, Allensville Planing Mill from Pennsylvania purchased a vacant truss factory in the Mid-Atlantic Industrial Park, but operations ended during the Great Recession.[464]

In 1992, Mobil Chemical Corporation paid $10 million for Florida-based Rivenite Corporation, which made maintenance-free outdoor decking by fusing plastic bags with wood chips and sawdust.[465] To be closer to those latter materials, Mobil moved its Timbrex unit into a former Capitol Records factory in Kernstown, south of Winchester.[466] Upon deciding that decking did not fit into its long-range plans, the oil company sold Timbrex in 1996 to its management in a $30 million leveraged buyout.[467]

After the renamed Trex Company, Inc.'s sales grew to $47 million in 1999, it went public, moved headquarters into an office building in Frederick County and opened a factory in Nevada.[468] Initially marketing its decking through independent installers, Trex made the product available at home improvement retailers in 2004.[469] As sales passed the $300 million mark two years later, the Winchester area headcount reached 450 workers.[470] Trex built a factory in Mississippi, but in 2007 mothballed it due to the slowdown in the housing market.[471] The following year, new management streamlined Trex's operations and returned it to profitability.[472] With 1,200 employees and $817 million in revenue, the company invested $200 million in 2020 to expand production by 70 percent at its Winchester and Nevada facilities.[473]

In 1982, North American Housing Corp. in Frederick, Maryland, opened a modular home factory on Route 55 in western Warren County. Industry leader Champion Enterprises, Inc. in Michigan acquired the 200-worker facility in 2006, but closed it four years later and moved production to another factory.[474] The Front Royal-Warren County Economic Development Authority later purchased and resold the building to a manufacturer of stone products.

Brick and Cement Manufacturers

After World War II, the region's three brick factories fell on hard times when other building products and steel were used on houses and large buildings.[475] Just north of Winchester, Colonial Brick Company, which started up in 1922, struggled through the Great Depression and a United Brick and Clay Workers of America strike in 1941. Seven years later, the renamed Shenandoah Brick and Tile Corporation made white-colored, sand-lime brick, block and tile.⁴⁷⁶ Until the factory's closure in 1978, they were marketed under the Shenado Chief of Construction trademark.

In 1954, the Chewning family in Washington, D.C. switched production from bricks to tile at its United Clay Products Co. factory near Hedgesville, which opened in 1911 as Adamantine Clay Products Co. Falling victim to the high cost of coal and diminished amounts of clay and shale found in the North Mountain area, the factory was shuttered in 1972.⁴⁷⁷ Locally owned LCS Services, Inc. purchased the property in 1989 for use as a landfill, which it later sold to Houston-based Waste Management, Inc., the nation's largest refuse handler.⁴⁷⁸ In 1974, the Chewnings sold Continental Clay Products Company in Martinsburg, which it owned since 1921, to General Industries, a building supply and construction company in Springfield, Virginia.⁴⁷⁹ After the subsidiary entered Chapter 11 bankruptcy in 1984, Imperial Corporation in Lynchburg and four other companies purchased and renamed it Continental Brick Company.⁴⁸⁰

For several decades, ESSROC Corporation in Nazareth, Pennsylvania, was a major factor in the region's cement and concrete industry. In 2002, the American subsidiary of the Italcementi Group in Italy paid $107 million for Riverton Investment Company in Winchester.⁴⁸¹ The acquisition included the Riverton quarry along the Shenandoah River in Warren County, the 150-employee Capitol Cement factory and quarry in Martinsburg and the Blairton quarry, west of the city.⁴⁸² In 2009, ESSROC spent $500 million to increase annual cement production from 650,000 tons to 1.6 million tons.⁴⁸³ Through its PILOT program, the West Virginia Economic Development Authority provided financial support for the expansion.⁴⁸⁴ As a condition for allowing Germany-based Heidelberg Cement AG to purchase Italcementi in 2016, antitrust authorities made ESSROC sell the factory.⁴⁸⁵ Cementos Argos in Columbia purchased the renamed Martinsburg Cement Plant for $660 million.⁴⁸⁶ Italcementi's quarry in Riverton became part of Hanson Aggregates, a unit of Heidelberg Cement.

Eight years earlier, ESSROC purchased Crider & Shockey, the ready-mix concrete division of the Shockey Companies in Frederick County.⁴⁸⁷ James Crider and James Shockey Sr. started the business in 1947, which had grown to include 100 employees at five ready-mix plants in the Northern Valley and five others in neighboring Virginia counties.⁴⁸⁸ Shockey kept the ready-mix plant at its headquarters to supply the company's Precast Group with concrete for walls that were formed, then tilted-up at construction sites.⁴⁸⁹ But in 2018, that 500-employee business was sold to Metromont Corp. in South Carolina.⁴⁹⁰

Plastics Industry

During World War II, plastics were used as substitutes for wood, glass and iron, which freed the nation from exhausting those materials needed for the war effort. Production in the United States soared from 1.1 million tons in 1939 to 4.1 million tons in 1945.[491] One decade later, resin pellets came by railroad to Northern Valley companies that heated and molded them into a variety of products. In 1953, O'Sullivan Rubber Company, which R. J. Funkhouser purchased and relocated to Winchester in 1930, realized its future was in plastics. Near its headquarters and rubber heel factory on Valley Avenue, the company built a facility that made vinyl sheeting used in flooring, wall coverings, notebook covers, pool liners and seat backs and padded dashboards for automobiles.[492]

In 1962, O'Sullivan Rubber acquired Gulfstream Corporation, a Michigan injection molding company that made plastic interior trim products for the automobile industry.[493] Because shoe manufacturing had moved offshore, the company sold the rubber heel division in 1970 and was renamed O'Sullivan Corporation.[494] Between 1982 and 1986, it opened a Gulfstream factory in Luray and acquired several calendared vinyl film companies.[495] In 1992, the company diversified into consumer products with the purchase of New Jersey-based Melnor Industries. It moved the fabricator of plastic lawn and garden equipment and snow shovels into a vacant factory in Winchester Industrial Park.[496]

Then O'Sullivan downsized. In the early 1990s, the Gulfstream Division experienced quality problems with interior trim products it supplied to Ford Motor Company. In 1994, the unit was sold for $70 million to competitor Automotive Industries, Inc. in Strasburg.[497] Realizing Melnor's weather dependent consumer products business was not a good fit, O'Sullivan sold it in 1997 to Germany-based Gardena Holding A.G.[498] Between 1999 and 2017, the renamed O'Sullivan Films, Inc. was sold three times, first to Geon Company in Ohio for $191 million.[499] Its last owner was Continental AG, a German manufacturer of rubber tires.[500]

In 1955, Larson Boat Works from Little Falls, Minnesota, opened a factory in Strasburg to make plastic components for watercraft assembled at its headquarters.[501] Three years later, the renamed Crestliner, Inc. facility made fiberglass boats that were shipped on Southern Railway flatcars to East Coast dealers.[502] After several ownership changes, Crestliner was sold in 1970 to North American Rockwell Corporation in Iowa, which soon closed the Strasburg factory.[503]

In 1967, Rubbermaid, Inc. in Wooster, Ohio, formed a division to mold and extrude plastic products for the food service, sanitary maintenance and waste handling markets.[504] The following year, the headquarters and factory of Rubbermaid Commercial Products opened in Winchester Industrial Park.[505] In 1999, Newell Company in Atlanta acquired Rubbermaid, Inc., and after several expansions, the Winchester factory's payroll reached 1,100 employees in 2010.[506] Next year, Virginia and Winchester gave Rubbermaid Commercial Products $1 million in incentives for its $65 million investment in plant and equipment.[507] But two years later, the company moved headquarters and 65 of its highest-paid staff to North Carolina.[508]

In 1969, Los Angeles-based Capitol Records hired 250 workers and opened a vinyl record factory in Kernstown, just south of Rubbermaid.[509] Several years later, work at its unionized Scranton facility was moved to Winchester, where 1,000 workers pressed Beatles albums, among others.[510] But increased competition from Far Eastern and European manufacturers forced Capitol Records in 1988 to close what had become a cassette tape duplication operation, and 535 jobs were lost.[511] Eight years later, Trex Company moved decking production into the unoccupied buildings.

In 1975, Helmut Rader relocated Monoflo International, Inc. from Northern Virginia into the vacant Virginia Woolen mill in Winchester.[512] He wanted to be closer to O'Sullivan's factory, which supplied plastic parts for Monoflo's automatic water feeders. They were sold to poultry growers, including some in Page and Shenandoah counties and the Potomac Highlands.[513] Moving into its own factory on Baker Street, just north of downtown Winchester, Monoflo added plastic folding boxes and pallets to its product line.[514]

In the early 1980s, Coca-Cola bottlers formed Southeastern Container, Inc. to make their own plastic bottles. In 1992, the North Carolina cooperative molded them at a factory in Fort Collier Industrial Park in Frederick County.[515] In the same park, M&H Plastics Ltd., a unit of British-based RPC Group, Plc, opened a factory in 2004 that produced plastic bottles and jars for the personal care market.[516] Fifteen years later, Berry Plastics in Indiana acquired the facility.[517] Just outside Fort Collier, Pactiv Corporation opened a factory in 1980 that made polystyrene containers for McDonald's restaurants, then 30 years later, switched to producing plastic wraps and rigid insulation for the construction industry.[518] After several ownership changes, Kingspan Group Plc in Ireland acquired the renamed Pactiv Building Products for $82 million in 2014.[519]

In Warren County in 1997, Toray Plastics (America), Inc., a unit of its namesake Japanese parent company, built a plastics factory in Virginia Inland Port Industrial Park.[520] Its 120 employees made polyolefin foams and film for the automotive and flooring markets and for various packaging applications.[521] A $25 million, 50,000-square-foot addition in 2016 increased the factory's capacity by 160 percent.[522]

Three companies made plastic products in the Eastern Panhandle. In 1987, the West Virginia Economic Development Authority built a factory in eastern Berkeley County for Variform, Inc. The Missouri-based extruder of residential vinyl siding leased it under the state's PILOT program.[523] In 1995, Brentwood Industries, Inc. moved into a former Crestmanor Homes factory in Berkeley County Industrial Park, south of Martinsburg.[524] The Reading, Pennsylvania, company made plastic filters for cooling and water treatment equipment. In 2018, TeMa North America, a unit of TeMa Technologies and Materials Industrial Company in Italy, opened a factory in Burr Business Park in Jefferson County to produce membrane insulation systems for residential and commercial construction.[525] Billing itself as a green company, TeMa's 30 workers made the insulation from recycled plastic bottles.[526]

Automotive Parts Industry

After World War II, several auto parts suppliers opened factories in the Northern Valley, but two closed in the New Millennium when production shifted overseas. In 1947, the American Brake Shoe and Foundry Co. in New Jersey built a factory on Winchester's Paper Mill Road that made automotive brake liners and pads.[527] Later headquartered there, the renamed Abex Friction Products Corp. changed hands a number of times among conglomerates and private equity firms.[528]

Until 1988, Abex's 900 United Auto Workers members put lead and asbestos fibers into the brake pads to prevent them from sparking under friction and causing fires. When many workers stricken with mesothelioma filed a class-action lawsuit, its last owner, Michigan-based Federal-Mogul Corporation, took bankruptcy in 2001.[529] After production had shifted to China and Mexico, the Winchester factory closed in 2013, putting the 125 remaining workers on the street.[530] Three years later, the Virginia Department of Environmental Quality found that hazardous waste landfills were left on Abex's 40-acre property.[531]

In 1977, Germany-based VDO-Argo Instruments, Inc. built two manufacturing facilities in Fort Collier Industrial Park in Frederick County.⁵³² VDO supplied instrument panels to a Volkswagen factory in Pennsylvania, while sister company Argo Instruments made them for truck manufacturers.⁵³³ Once employing 700 workers, the VDO factory changed hands among Japanese and German owners until 2002, when Siemens Automotive Systems Group closed it and moved production to Mexico.⁵³⁴

In 1975, Automotive Industries, Inc., whose CEO was a former O'Sullivan executive, made interior trim systems and blow-molded plastic parts for the auto industry at the former Crestliner boat factory in Strasburg.⁵³⁵ In 1994, the company acquired O'Sullivan Corporation's Gulfstream Division, whose 725 workers in Winchester and another 200 in Luray made similar automotive products. Next year, Lear Seating Corp. in Michigan paid $626 million for Automotive Industries.⁵³⁶ As part of a global restructuring, it closed the Winchester and Luray factories in 2005 and consolidated the work into Strasburg. One year later, the struggling auto supplier became part of IAC North America, a subsidiary of the International Automotive Components Group in Luxembourg.⁵³⁷ The United Auto Workers headcount in Strasburg fluctuated between 500 and 700 members, depending on sales volumes for Ford, Volvo and Mack vehicles.⁵³⁸

In 1981, E. I. Dupont Corporation in Wilmington built a $20 million factory in the Cedarville area, north of Front Royal.⁵³⁹ Its 400 non-union workers produced paints for the automotive aftermarket. In 2013, DuPont sold its Performance Coatings unit, including the Warren County factory, for $4.9 billion to the Carlyle Group, a private equity firm in Washington, D.C.⁵⁴⁰

Printing Industry

After World War II, several publishing and printing companies located presses in the Northern Valley, where unions found in urban areas were not present. In 1957, America's largest book publisher, Doubleday & Company, Inc., moved printing from Long Island into a new plant on a former apple orchard near downtown Berryville.⁵⁴¹ Bertelsmann AG in Germany purchased Doubleday in 1986 and renamed the 440-employee local press Berryville Graphics.⁵⁴² The new owner invested $14 million in equipment that more efficiently printed trade books sold to a general audience of readers.⁵⁴³

In 1968, Chicago-based Wallace Business Forms, Inc. opened a printing plant in Luray that employed upwards of 1,000 workers.⁵⁴⁴ In 1981, its name changed to Wallace Computer Services, Inc. to better reflect increased sales of its forms and labels to owners of desktop printers. After Moore Corporation from Canada acquired the company in 2003, it closed the Luray plant, whose payroll had dropped to 125 employees, and consolidated production into a Fredericksburg facility.[545]

Judd & Detwiler was organized in 1868 in Washington, D.C. to print legal documents for the Supreme Court.[546] To save costs, successor Judd's, Inc. moved into the former Frye Furniture building in Strasburg in 1975. Seven hundred employees at its Shenandoah Valley Press printed magazines for publishers and catalogs for retailers.[547] In 1997, Perry Graphics in Iowa acquired Judd's, and 12 years later, Chicago-based RR Donnelley & Sons Company purchased Perry.[548]

Between 1989 and 1995, three printing companies built plants in the Northern Valley, but by 2010, their presses ran under the same corporate umbrella. In 1989, Century Graphics Corporation in Louisiana printed advertising inserts in Stonewall Industrial Park in Frederick County.[549] Next year, Arcata Graphics in Baltimore built a $70 million, 360,000-square-foot book printing plant, southeast of Martinsburg, which Quebecor Printing in Canada acquired in 1994.[550] Next year, Wisconsin-based Quad/Graphics, Inc. opened a press in Cumbo Yard Industrial Park, northwest of Martinsburg.[551] Through its PILOT program, West Virginia owned the 335,000-square-foot plant, where 800 employees printed magazines and catalogs.[552]

Then came more industry consolidation. World Color Press acquired Century Graphics in 1998 and the following year, Quebecor Printing purchased World Color Press for $1.4 billion, and formed Quebecor World.[553] But a combination of too much debt, lower sales during the Great Recession and the migration to digital publishing forced Quebecor World into bankruptcy in 2008.[554] Two years later, Quad/Graphics acquired it for $1.3 billion, creating a business with 30,000 employees, including hundreds of workers at three Northern Valley presses.[555]

In 2016, R.R. Donnelley spun off its printing presses, including the one in Strasburg, into LSC Communications, Inc.[556] With sales and profits declining, LSC hoped Quad/Graphics would acquire it, but a U.S. Department of Justice antitrust lawsuit stopped the deal.[557] In 2020, LSC closed its Strasburg press and two others, causing 400 local workers to lose their jobs.[558] That same year, Quad/Graphics sold its book printing business to the Bertelsmann Printing

Group in Hicksville, NY.[559] The former Arcata Graphics' plants in Martinsburg and Fairfield, Pennsylvania, became part of the German company's Berryville Graphics division, headquartered in its namesake town.

Vending Machine Industry

During World War II, major soft drink bottlers looked for ways to provide the public with low-priced refrigerated drinks for consumption outside homes and restaurants. At the time, Victor Products Co. in Hagerstown assembled roll-top counter coolers that held bottled drinks.[560] In 1947, owners Raymond and Clyde Funkhouser moved the company into a related line of business, fabricating refrigeration equipment for soft drink vending machines.[561] A Victor Products factory in Ranson soon produced the machines themselves, which the brothers marketed to soft drink bottlers throughout the United States.

In 1957, the Funkhouser brothers sold the vending business to Dixie Foundry, a Tennessee maker of cooking equipment and stoves.[562] The new owners appointed Roy Steeley, former president of Victor Products, as vice president and general manager of the renamed Dixie-Narco, which Magic Chef acquired in 1958. Within two decades, Steeley grew sales from $2 million to $152 million, and Dixie-Narco accounted for two-thirds of the nation's vending machine market.[563]

Soon after Maytag Corporation acquired Magic Chef, including its vending machine unit, Steeley started Royal Vendors, Inc. in 1986 in Bardane Industrial Park.[564] With Dixie-Narco controlling most of the industry and smaller competitors experiencing financial problems, soft drink bottlers welcomed Royal Vendors into the market. But Steeley's former employer put up a fight, claiming he had not only taken its intellectual property with him, but also worked on the new venture while still at Dixie-Narco.[565] Steeley successfully fought off the charges in court.[566]

Royal Vendor's workforce in Jefferson County grew to 1,000 employees, while Dixie-Narco's headcount declined from 1,300 to 300.[567] In 1991, Maytag moved vending machine production from Ranson to its Admiral freezer factory in South Carolina.[568] Five years later, Steeley sold Royal Vendors to its minority shareholder, St. Louis-based Coin Acceptors, Inc.[569] Not ready to retire, the 67-year old started Automated Merchandising Systems, Inc. in Burr Business Park to fabricate vending machines that dispensed snacks.[570]

Furniture Industry

After the Second World War, two Northern Valley companies made reproduction antique furniture that did not compete directly with mass-produced furniture made in North Carolina and Michigan. Nor were cheap Chinese imports a headwind for the region's better-quality, handcrafted furniture.

Henkel Harris was born in 1946, when Carroll Henkel and friend John Harris assembled a corner cabinet in the basement of Henkel's home.[571] When Harris sold his interest to Henkel and wife Mary in 1954, the company was located in a small factory on North Loudoun Street, where 22 craftsmen made eighteenth century reproduction furniture from cherry, mahogany and walnut lumber.[572] In 1964, Henkel Harris moved into a much larger facility off South Pleasant Valley Road.[573]

After Carroll Henkel died in 1969, Mary ran the 300-employee company until 1982.[574] The first woman to serve as a director of the Southern Furniture Manufacturers Association, she was inducted into the Furniture Hall of Fame in 1996.[575] Until her passing in 2001, she served as chairman of Henkel Harris. In 2013, the company was sold to the Gum family, owners of National Fruit Product Company in Winchester.[576] To improve its finances, they switched the Henkel Harris business model from producing furniture for inventory to filling individual customer orders.

While Tom Seely ran an antique shop in Berkeley Springs in the early 1950s, he reproduced his favorite furniture pieces.[577] As sales grew, the Tom Seely Furniture factory opened in 1970 on U.S. 522, south of town. Its 140 employees assembled and finished pine furniture from component pieces outsourced to local woodworkers.[578] In 1996, Seely sold the company to former West Virginia Governor Gaston Caperton and son Gat, who added a modern, cherry furniture line, and renamed the business Gat Creek Furniture.[579]

Between 1955 and 1980, a variety of other furniture companies found a home in the region. They included Shipman Brothers Mattress and Box Spring Company in Ranson; Forecast Furniture, Inc. in Henkel Harris's original Winchester factory; Jackson Furniture Company in Front Royal, maker of Catnapper recliners; and McDole Library Furniture, Inc. in Frederick County, which former Washington pro football player Ron McDole owned.[580]

Northern Valley Factories Find New Uses

The Northern Valley was not spared from the nation's factory closures that began in the late 1990s. With a reduced demand for manufacturing space, vacant buildings were repurposed into warehouses, offices, retail space and classrooms. The region's expanding economy made those changes possible. The most active purchaser of factories was Winchester Cold Storage Company. Between 2002 and 2006, it acquired the VDO-Yazaki factory in Frederick County, which FEMA rented for use as a call center; the Pen-Tab Industries factory in Warren County, leased to a company that repaired Postal Service equipment; and the Rich Products frozen food plant in Winchester, which it used as a warehouse.[581]

In 1997, direct mail company AB&C Group in Reston moved its offices into the former Dixie Narco vending machine factory in Ranson. Six years later, Shockey Company executives purchased the shuttered Corning housewares factory in Berkeley County and repurposed it into warehouse and office space.[582] In 2006, a real estate investment trust acquired O'Sullivan Corporation's vacant Gulfstream factory in Winchester Industrial Park and leased it to Trex Company for the storage of plastic bags.[583] P. W. Plumly Lumber Company's factory in Winchester became a distribution center for flooring products of Connecticut-based Rossi American Hardwoods, Inc.[584]

The local OakCrest Companies repurposed Lewis Jones Knitting Mill in Winchester into office space for its real estate business.[585] The Jouan, S.A. centrifuge factory in Frederick County was leased to the FBI in 2008 for use as a records storage and management center.[586] In 2017, Lord Fairfax Community College repurposed a Wrangler jeans factory in Luray for satellite classrooms.[587] Rubbermaid Commercial Products purchased the vacant General Electric light bulb factory in Kernstown for use as a warehouse.[588] In 2018, Midwesco Filter Resources Inc.'s former factory in Winchester Industrial Park became retail and office space for Blue Ridge Habitat for Humanity.[589]

Warehouses:
Interstate 81 Becomes the Logistics Corridor

The Northern Valley's first significant warehouse activity coincided with the 1830s arrival of railroads, when inbound and outbound cargo was stored in buildings near freight depots. Next to appear were cold storage facilities, built in the early 1900s to serve the emerging apple industry. The final group to make its way into the region were dry storage warehouses, built after Interstate 81's completion in the 1960s, and the Virginia Inland Port's arrival in the 1990s. Later called distribution centers, they became part of corporate America's supply chains. Inside thousands of square footage, warehouses featured level floors, high ceilings and storage racks that workers accessed with motorized forklifts. Smart technologies—computers, bar codes, scanners, sensors and robotics—allowed workers to store and select goods for shipment in a timely and cost-efficient way.

Warehouses that were located in what became known as the I-81 Logistics Corridor benefited from lower real estate and labor costs, more reliable employees and less traffic congestion than sites near New York City, Philadelphia, Baltimore and Washington. When land in the Harrisburg and Carlisle areas became filled with warehouses, developers looked southward on I-81 for less-expensive acreage. Nevertheless, the flood of warehouses into the Northern Valley had its downsides: the pay was less than for factory work and on a square-footage basis, warehouses generated less machinery and tools taxes than did factories. In addition, increased truck traffic on roads and highways became a concern for local officials and their constituents.

Warehouses in the Eastern Panhandle

The first two dry storage warehouses in the Northern Valley were located along I-81 in Berkeley County. For three decades, they were the largest ones in the region. In 1968, General Motors Company opened a 1 million-square-foot facility north of Martinsburg, where upwards of 1,100 employees packed and shipped auto parts to GM dealers in the East.[590] Six years later, Western Electric Company opened a 735,000-square-foot warehouse south of the city, at the Tabler Station Road exit on I-81.[591] The AT&T subsidiary stored cable, switching gear and other telephone related items in it.

Most warehouses that followed were built in industrial parks located close to Interstate 81. In 1987, Bell Atlantic Company occupied a 191,000-square-foot warehouse in Mid-Atlantic Industrial Park, on the east side of I-81, opposite GM's building.[592] It stored thousands of telephone directories, delivered to customers in an eight-state region. After several phonebook businesses took up space in the building, Ecolab, Inc. in 2017 kept cleaning fluids in it that were produced at its nearby plant.[593]

In 1999, S. Schwab Company in Cumberland built a 187,000-square-foot warehouse in the John D. Rockefeller IV Science & Technology Center at Eastern West Virginia Regional Airport.[594] Because the park was in a Foreign Trade Zone, Schwab benefited from reduced and delayed import duties paid on children's clothes it received through the Virginia Inland Port.⁵⁹⁵ In 2004, Polo Ralph Lauren Corporation in New York City purchased Schwab; six years later, its 100 warehouse jobs in Berkeley County were moved to North Carolina.⁵⁹⁶

In 2000, Memphis-based Orgill, Inc. built a 500,000-square-foot, $20 million distribution center on Tabler Station Road, at the I-81 exit.⁵⁹⁷ The company used it to ship wholesale merchandise to independent hardware retailers in the Mid-Atlantic area. In 2005, Orgill put a 263,000-square-foot addition on the building. New York City-based real estate investment trust W. P. Carey Inc. paid $38 million in 2019 for the warehouse in a sale-leaseback transaction.⁵⁹⁸

Using West Virginia's PILOT program, General Motors built a 352,000-square-foot, $26 million Parts Distribution Center in 2001 in Cumbo Yard Industrial Park.⁵⁹⁹ Located behind the company's original parts warehouse, GM planned to gain efficiencies from a reconfigured workspace. It negotiated new work rules with the United Auto Workers union, whose members earned $60,000, more than twice that of the region's other warehouse workers.⁶⁰⁰ After GM moved the parts packing function to three Michigan facilities in 2004, the workforce at the three-year old warehouse dropped from 1,000 employees to 135.⁶⁰¹

Shockey Realty Company in Frederick County, later known as Shockey Properties, purchased GM's original parts warehouse and 226 acres in 2005.⁶⁰² Renamed Shockey Commerce Center, 500,000 square feet were leased back to GM for a collision parts distribution center.⁶⁰³ Other lessors included Rubbermaid Commercial Products, BlueSky Brands, Inc.'s fulfillment center and Rust-Oleum Corporation.⁶⁰⁴

Equus Capital Partners in Newtown Square, Pennsylvania was a major participant in the region's warehouse market. It raised funds from private investors, then purchased, developed and managed commercial real estate for them. In 2010, Equus opened Mid-Atlantic 81 Logistics Park on 150 acres south of Martinsburg, and nine years later, built a 356,700-square-foot warehouse in it.⁶⁰⁵ Half the space was leased to Proctor & Gamble for temporary storage of goods made at its nearby factory.⁶⁰⁶ Equus indicated land in the park was available for 1.4 million more square feet of warehousing.⁶⁰⁷

Warehouses in the Virginia Portion of the Region

After World War II, Winchester Cold Storage Company emerged as the region's largest operator in its industry. In the early 1960s, it installed a controlled-atmosphere system in its Winchester facility, which lengthened the time apples could be stored.[608] In an airtight, refrigerated room, a high humidity level was maintained while almost all oxygen was pumped out of it. Under those conditions, apples stayed fresh for up to two years, much longer than four months when sitting inside other cold storage buildings.

In 1979, Winchester Cold Storage expanded its footprint with the purchase of Jefferson Storage on Summit Point Road. With a 735,000-bushel capacity, it once served as an H. F. Byrd, Inc. apple packing shed and cold storage building.[609] In 1998, the company acquired the vacant Moore and Dorsey cold storage building, near Norfolk Southern's tracks in Berryville. In 2015, the renamed WCS Logistics built a 63,000-square-foot freezer storage facility in Fort Collier Industrial Park in Frederick County, which quadrupled its capacity to store goods in temperatures 20 degrees below zero.[610]

At the beginning of the New Millennium, out-of-area real estate development companies built and leased numerous warehouses in the Virginia portion of the region. In 2001, ProLogis, Inc., the nation's largest warehouse owner, built one in Fort Collier Industrial Park in Frederick County to store juice drinks that Kraft Foods produced at its nearby Capri Sun plant.[611] The San Francisco-based real estate investment trust later outsourced the supply chain function to German-owned DB Schenker Logistics, Inc.[612] In the same park in 2008, Johnson Development Associates, Inc. in South Carolina built a warehouse leased to Home Depot for a 400-employee Rapid Deployment Center.[613] It returned one decade later with construction of a warehouse that Mercury Paper, a manufacturer of household products in the Strasburg area, leased.[614]

From 2013 to 2019, Pennsylvania-based Equus Capital Partners, Ltd. and its BPG Development Company built pre-leased warehouses in Frederick County industrial parks that totaled 1.5 million square feet of space. The tenants included McKesson Corp., a distributor of medical and surgical supplies; Home Depot, which stored overflow merchandise from its Rapid Deployment Center; and additional storage space for Rubbermaid Commercial Products.[615] In 2017, Equus built a 400,000-square-foot Mopar Parts Distribution Center in Stonewall Industrial Park, from which parts were shipped to Fiat Chrysler dealers.[616] Equus later entered into a sale-leaseback transaction with Ford Motor Company for its 250,000-square-foot, 95-employee High Velocity Parts Distribution Center.[617] It was built in 2004 in Kernstown, south of Winchester.

Shockey Properties in Frederick County used its sister company, Howard Shockey & Sons, Inc. to build distribution centers. In 2016, its Graystone

Corporation of Virginia put up two warehouses in the 65-acre Blackburn Commerce Center, south of Winchester near Route 37, and leased them to Trex Company, the Frederick County producer of decking.[618] North of the city in its Graystone Commerce Center, Shockey Properties leased a 63,000-square-foot warehouse in 2020 to Kirkland's Home Furnishings and built a 175,000-square-foot one on speculation.[619]

Opened in 1990, the Virginia Inland Port (VIP) attracted numerous warehouses to the Northern Valley. The intermodal facility received containers full of imported goods that came by rail from Newport News to Warren County. From there, they were loaded onto flatbed trailers and hauled short distances to local warehouses. In 1997, Kohl's Department Stores built one in the Airport Business Center in Frederick County to receive clothing that came through the VIP.[620] Closer to the intermodal port, Family Dollar Stores, Inc., plumbing supply retailer Ferguson Enterprises, Inc. and food distributor Sysco Corporation opened warehouses in the U.S. 522/340 corridor.[621]

With few parcels of land along that Warren County highway left for development, several companies received VIP-generated containers at warehouses in Frederick County. They included a Home Depot Stocking and Distribution Center in the Eastgate Commerce Center and warehouses in the Graystone and Stonewall industrial parks that stored imported Red Bull GmbH energy drinks.[622] In the latter park, Fortessa, Inc. in Sterling, Virginia, packed and shipped imported tableware from a warehouse with a Foreign Trade Zone designation.[623]

Not all VIP container traffic in the Northern Valley was inbound. In 2000, AmeriCold Logistics, an Atlanta-based real estate investment trust, built a 245,000-square-foot, temperature-controlled warehouse in North Shenandoah Industrial Park, which bordered I-81 in the Strasburg area.[624] It froze chicken parts received from a Moorefield processing plant, then packed them in containers sent to the VIP for shipment to Asian countries.[625]

Call Centers:
Employees and Companies Turn Over

Beginning in the 1980s, corporate America used call centers to centralize either customer service or their sales and marketing functions. While some operated in-house, others were outsourced to businesses that specialized in inbound and outbound calling. Many were located in rural areas with reliable communications systems and workforces without recognizable accents. The centers were stressful environments, because employees were constantly on phones and under the watchful eyes and ears of supervisors. Annual turnover rates ranged from 35 to 40 percent, more than double the average for all United States occupations.[626]

Three call centers in the Northern Valley employed hundreds of personnel, before closing in the early years of the New Millennium. ICT Group, Inc. marketed insurance and credit cards at an outbound call center in Bardane Industrial Park in Jefferson County, while Aerotek Staffing Services handled inbound calls for Verizon on Martinsburg's Foxcroft Avenue. CFW Communications, Inc., then Telegate AG, ran an AT&T telephone directory assistance center in the former Taylor Hotel in Winchester.[627]

Another call center more than made up for the job losses at ICT, Aerotek and Telegate. After its purchase of F&M National Corporation in 2001, BB&T Corp. built a check processing and customer service center in Westview Business Centre in eastern Frederick County.[628] In 2004, Navy Federal Credit Union in Vienna, Virginia, purchased the building for use as a data recovery center in case of another terrorist attack on Washington, D.C.[629] When its plans changed, Navy Federal opened a customer-support center, at which 500 operators took calls from 4 million members. As volumes increased, the nation's largest credit union added office space and personnel that brought its Frederick County workforce up to 1,900 persons in 2020.[630]

Fulfillment Centers: E-Commerce Arrives in Region

Before the internet, fulfillment centers used mailing lists, printed catalogs, telephones, fax machines and the U.S. Postal Service to run their business. During that era, those that opened in the Northern Valley met with mixed success. Founded in 1972 in Reston, the AB&C Group's clients included catalog retailers, fundraising companies and member-based organizations.[631] In 1992, the direct marketing and response company moved its printing and fulfillment center into the former Dixie-Narco vending machine factory in Ranson.[632]

The following year, National Wildlife Federation in Reston purchased American Woodmark Company's 150,000-square-foot warehouse in Stonewall Industrial Park in Frederick County and moved its fulfillment unit into it.[633] In 2006, however, the non-profit supporter of conservation efforts outsourced the catalog operation to the AB&C Group in Ranson.[634] In 2015, Interchange

Company in Harrisonburg purchased the vacant National Wildlife building and leased 78,000 square feet to California-based Threshold Enterprises Ltd.[635] The distributor of nutritional supplements and other natural products used the space to fill wholesale orders from 6,000 retailers in the eastern United States.[636]

In 1994, Oregon-based Norm Thompson Outfitters opened a 173,330-square-foot fulfillment center in Burr Business Park in Jefferson County, where 150 workers processed orders from East Coast customers for clothing, footwear, gifts and gourmet food.[637] In 2006, private equity firm Golden Gate Capital in San Francisco purchased Norm Thompson, then consolidated the local operation into one it owned in Pennsylvania.[638]

That same year, Reliant Equity Investors LLC in Chicago purchased several fulfillment companies and combined them as BlueSky Brands, Inc., based in Rhode Island.[639] Included was the AB&C Group, whose catalog operation was moved from Ranson into leased space in the former General Motors parts warehouse in Berkeley County. Overburdened with debt in the Great Recession, BlueSky Brands shut operations down in 2008 and 400 local jobs were lost.[640]

When e-commerce gained traction in the New Millennium, sales were made on the internet and orders were filled in large automated warehouses. FedEx, UPS and the U.S. Postal Service delivered the packages. In 2012, New York City-based Macy's, Inc. built a 1.3 million-square-foot fulfillment center in Cumbo Yard Business Park in Berkeley County.[641] Financing for the retailer's $150 million project was arranged through West Virginia's PILOT program.[642] Macy's staffed the facility with 1,200 full-time employees, referred to as pickers and stowers, and 700 others hired during the peak holiday season.[643]

In 2018, the world's largest e-commerce company arrived in northern Frederick County. A 1.06 million-square-foot Amazon Fulfillment Center went up near Clear Brook, on the same 101-acre site the FBI once considered for a Central Records complex.[644] As many as 1,500 workers packed and shipped furniture and other bulky items from the $56.6 million center, for which Amazon received incentive payments from Virginia.[645]

Residential Real Estate: Northern Virginia's Market Affects Region's

As the Northern Valley's postwar economy was drawn into metro D.C.'s orbit, so was its residential real estate market. When home prices east of the Blue Ridge rose, less-expensive housing to the west became attractive to workers willing to lengthen their commutes.[646] Conversely, as Northern Virginia's prices weakened, its homeowners tended to stay put. The bottom line: when the housing market in Fairfax and Loudoun counties caught a cold, the Northern Valley's got the sniffles.

After World War II, national and regional homebuilders focused on the fast-growing Washington, D.C. suburbs, not the rural Northern Valley. Local builders had the market to themselves. Near Interstate 81 exits, 1970s subdivisions of $100,000 single-family homes and $75,000 townhouses became bedroom communities for the region's two cities. By the late 1980s, however, builders were marketing $250,000 to $500,000 custom-built homes to a growing legion of professionals and to commuters and retirees from Northern Virginia searching for more affordable housing.[647]

Faced with tighter zoning restrictions in Northern Virginia in the early 1990s, out-of-area builders Trammel Crow, Ryland Homes and Washington Homes entered the Northern Valley market. They skipped Clarke County, which had enacted restrictive residential zoning, and landed in Frederick, Warren, Jefferson and Berkeley counties. As struggling farmers and orchardists watched the values of their neighbor's land skyrocket, they were happy to sell their primary asset to developers and homebuilders. With pockets filled with cash, they echoed the refrain, "We live poor and die rich." [648] The most sought-after farms and orchards were located east of I-81, close to highways leading to Northern Virginia.

The September 11, 2001 terrorist attack on Washington renewed Northern Virginia homeowner interest in moving west of the Blue Ridge.[649] With reasonably priced, developable land in Loudoun County nearly exhausted, more national and regional builders flooded Northern Valley zoning departments with housing permits.[650] The well-publicized rapid rise in home values in the New Millennium's early years, coupled with creative mortgage arrangements, encouraged buyers to purchase homes they could not afford. The median sale price for homes in the Winchester-Frederick County market jumped from $150,000 in 2002 to $280,000 in 2006.[651]

But Northern Virginia's housing market peaked in the fall of 2005, as sales slowed and the number of listings increased.[652] When prices there dropped, the Northern Valley's market followed suit. The median sale price for homes in the Winchester-Frederick County area slid 27 percent, from $280,000 in 2006 to $205,000 in 2008.[653] Berkeley County's 16 percent decline to $180,000 was less severe, because its prices had not risen as fast.[654]

In the foreclosure epidemic that caused the Great Recession, the hundreds of houses that went on the auction block kept prices depressed. National and regional builders closed their Northern Valley offices, while local builders kept busy with remodeling and commercial work. Land developers and their banks were stuck with numerous unsold building lots. Planning and zoning departments in Berkeley and Frederick counties estimated the number of approved, but empty lots in their jurisdictions in 2009 were 5,700 and 10,000, respectively.[655]

The nation's housing market had recovered by the time the Covid-19 pandemic struck the nation in March 2020. Families fled the Washington metro area for less populated locales, including the Northern Valley. A lack of supply and unusually low mortgage rates caused homes to sell quickly at or above a homeowner's asking price. Within one year, the median sale price of homes in Frederick County had jumped by 20 percent to $245,520, while it rose in Berkeley County at a slower 4 percent to $208,500.[656]

Vacation Home Developments

One hundred years after the region's springs resorts drew the infirmed, along with wealthy patrons, to their waters, real estate developers marketed vacation lots on wooded hillsides to families east of the Blue Ridge. Several 1950s trends drove demand for the lots. An expanding federal government created a prosperous middle class in the metro D.C. area. Crowded families living in suburban housing developments looked to commune with nature. Improved roads eased the task of reaching their vacation properties. But a perfect storm of gas shortages in the 1970s, and high interest rates in the early 1980s, slowed sales and forced several vacation home companies into bankruptcy. In the 1990s, many of those second homes became primary residences, especially the ones located near commuter roads leading eastward.

In 1952, Dr. E. M. Freeman from Northern Virginia purchased 1,120 acres in the Blue Ridge Mountains of eastern Clarke County.[657] At Shenandoah Retreat Country Club, he subdivided the acreage into 1,900 lots, built a nine-hole golf course and clubhouse, a swimming pool and tennis courts, and carved out a small beach on the Shenandoah River's east bank. In 1965, Freeman sold the development to property owners, whose Shenandoah Retreat Land Corporation hoped to market the remaining lots.[658] But in the midst of high gas prices and rising mortgage rates, the company filed for bankruptcy in 1979, and unsold lots were auctioned.[659]

In 1954, local real estate broker Charles M. Johnson and partner Guy Holley formed Shannondale, Inc. to sell lots in a 2,500-acre development in the Blue Ridge Mountains in eastern Jefferson County.[660] They built an Adirondack-styled lodge, a bathhouse and large pool. After a 65-acre lake and 5,000 acres were added to Shannondale, it was the largest subdivision in West Virginia.[661] Eight miles to the north, two second-home communities—Blue Ridge Acres and Keyes Ferry Acres—opened on Loudoun Heights. After 500 homes were built in Shannondale, Johnson sold it to a consortium of property owners in 1978.[662]

Three vacation home destinations appeared in the mountains of western Frederick County. When 1,400-acre Wilde Acres, later called Mountain Falls Park, opened in the mid-1950s, it included 2,200 lots, a small lake, recreation center and playground.[663] Several miles away, Marjec, Inc. in 1955 developed Shawneeland on 7,000 acres that included 3,000 lots, Cherokee Lake, a ski slope with rope tow and a lodge and restaurant.[664] When sales at the second home community fell victim to gas shortages, the Maryland company took bankruptcy in 1978.[665] To the north near Cross Junction, Donald Bayliss and several other Winchester Realtors in the 1970s assembled 1,600 acres for vacation homes at The Summit.[666] They dammed Isaac Creek to create a 250-acre lake and laid out an 18-hole golf course at the gated, weekend retreat, but a proposed ski area never opened.[667] By the late 1980s, most homes in the renamed Lake Holiday subdivision were primary residences.

In 1909, William Bryce from Philadelphia opened Bryce Hillside Cottages and Mineral Baths near the western Shenandoah County hamlet of Basye, several miles from Orkney Springs.[668] In 1965, grandson Peter from Chicago formed Bryce Mountain Resort Corporation, added a ski area, a landing strip for general aviation planes and put 2,700 building lots on the market.[669] In 1969, Joseph Luter in Smithfield, Virginia, took a majority financial interest in Bryce Resort, then turned it over to a group of Bryce property owners, many from the metro D.C. area.[670]

During the 1950s and 1960s, developers laid out three recreational subdivisions in the Blue Ridge Mountains in eastern Warren and western Fauquier counties. High Knob, Apple Mountain Lake and Blue Mountain were located east of Linden, on the north side of Interstate 66. Developed in 1970 in an area between the Shenandoah River and the Blue Ridge's western foothills, the 2,650 lots in 7,000-acre Shenandoah Farms included some that fronted the river.[671]

In 1961, Sam Ashelman and Al Capen from the Washington, D.C. area developed Coolfont Resort on 1,300 acres near Berkeley Springs.[672] They built a lodge and restaurant, dammed a stream for Lake Siri and sold building lots; later amenities included a spa, wellness and conference centers and snow tubing.[673] In 2005, Coolfont Resort was sold to the Carl M. Freeman Companies in Rockville, Maryland, but after failing to redevelop the property, the facilities and remaining lots were auctioned in 2016.[674] Three years later, the Larry Omps family of Berkeley Springs, owners of the local Best Western motel and the Country Inn, renovated and reopened Coolfont's lodge and restaurant.[675]

In the early 1970s, two vacation home developments appeared in western Berkeley County: Glenwood Forest, where 545 acres were divided into 380 lots, several miles west of Gerrardstown, and The Woods Resort, situated farther north near Hedgesville. The latter project began in 1972, when Ray Johnston from Minneapolis and Bob Bernstein from Baltimore formed Potomac Valley Properties, Inc. The partners acquired several large parcels of land, including the 800-acre Sleepy Hollow subdivision with a lake and 500 lots.[676] After adding a swimming pool, restaurant and lodge, they sold building sites in The Woods Resort, which later included two golf courses.[677]

Commercial Real Estate: Construction Follows Rooftops

After World War II, general contractors with a national footprint built many of the Northern Valley's factories, warehouses and shopping centers. Those with a local presence worked on strip malls, hotels, restaurants, medical facilities, office buildings, schools and churches. Some contractors started out as homebuilders, but switched to the commercial side when that market gained traction, as the region's population grew. A few took on risk, building rental properties for their own account.

General Contractors

Started in Baltimore in 1860, Minghini's General Contractors, Inc. relocated to Martinsburg in the early 1920s as S. L. Minghini & Son, Inc.[678] In 1988, Craig and Berniece Collis purchased the commercial builder and kept the Minghini name.[679] After graduating from Martinsburg High School in 1934, Harley Miller learned the construction trade while in the Civilian Conservation

Corps.⁶⁸⁰ Recognizing the region's postwar need for more commercial buildings, he formed W. Harley Miller, Inc. in 1945 in his hometown.⁶⁸¹

With one truck and two employees, Charles Ricketts began building homes in 1957 in Winchester. Upon completion of a dormitory for Shenandoah College in 1966, Ricketts Construction Company, Inc. became a general contractor, specializing in office and retail space, some of which it owned. After Ricketts' passing, the company ran into financial difficulty when the new president developed hundreds of residential building lots, just before the Great Recession hit the housing market.⁶⁸² Post-bankruptcy, the business was sold to a general contractor in southern Pennsylvania.⁶⁸³

In the early 1900s, Howard Shockey switched from fabricating wagons and carriages to building houses in the Winchester area. By the time sons James R. and Ralph joined him in the 1940s, Howard Shockey & Sons, Inc. was engaged in commercial construction.⁶⁸⁴ Led by grandson Donald in the 1980s, the Frederick County-based design-build and construction management firm became one of the largest general contractors in Virginia. It specialized in schools, hospitals and senior-living facilities, and made tilt-up, reinforced concrete wall panels used in parking garage and warehouse construction. In the New Millennium, Shockey Properties repurposed several vacant industrial properties and built and leased warehouses in business parks it owned.

Several other general contractors were based in the Winchester area. In 1976, Charles Toan and son Doug founded Construction Management, Inc. in Frederick County.⁶⁸⁵ By 1983, the firm specialized in assembling prefab metal buildings for restaurants, car dealerships, warehouses and professional offices. Lantz Construction of Winchester, Inc. started in 1984 as a division of a Broadway, Virginia, general contractor.⁶⁸⁶ One year later, manager Allen Ervin purchased the local business, which built churches, schools, restaurants, apartments and medical offices, and renovated commercial buildings.⁶⁸⁷ In 2005, brothers Danny, Kenny and Tim McKee opened Kee Construction Services, Inc. in Winchester to engage in commercial construction and renovations.⁶⁸⁸

Before houses could be built, raw land needed site work that included moving dirt, blasting rock, grading land, installing utilities and building roads. In 1951, Ferman Perry launched Perry Engineering Company in Frederick County to provide land development services to the region's residential and commercial builders.⁶⁸⁹ In the early 1970s, Perry found business opportunities in related areas, so he formed Winchester Asphalt Company, Greenway

Engineering and Survey Company and Winchester Building Supply Company. After his passing in 1987, wife Kathryn and general manager Rupert Werner ran Perry Engineering.[690]

Commercial Real Estate Developers

While several local companies developed land, Washington banker and real estate investor Leo Bernstein took a different approach, one that brought tourists to the region. In the 1960s, he restored historic properties: Wayside Inn and the Wayside Theatre in Middletown, the Burwell-Morgan Mill in Millwood and the Battletown Inn in Berryville.[691] In the late 1970s, he repurposed the former Strasburg Silk Mill into the Strasburg Antique Emporium and restored the 85-year old Hotel Strasburg on Holliday Street.[692] Bernstein's Wayside Foundation of American History and Arts, Inc. opened the Museum of American Presidents and the Jeanne Dixon Museum in Strasburg. North of the town, the foundation managed the Stonewall Jackson Museum and the Crystal Caverns at Hupp's Hill.[693]

In the midst of the Great Depression, Gerrardstown native Harry Aikens worked in Winchester woolen mills by day and built houses at night.[694] In 1949, he operated a drive-in theater in Martinsburg, then owned several Tastee-Freez franchises.[695] To attract tenants to a new shopping center in Martinsburg, he opened an Aikens Sizzling Steaks restaurant in 1975.[696] In the late 1980s, he closed what became a small restaurant chain to concentrate on H&W Construction, the more profitable real estate business that he and son Walter had formed.[697] Their Aikens Group expanded into commercial and residential construction and leasing, and hotel development and management.

In Martinsburg in 1979, local developer Bruce Van Wyk purchased 70 acres on the east side of I-81, just south of the King Street exit. After bisecting the land with north-south Foxcroft Avenue, he built apartments, offices and hotels along the road.[698] In 1984, Van Wyk purchased 40 acres that joined Route 45, at the next I-81 exit south of King Street. When he extended Foxcroft Avenue through the second parcel, more commercial development came after the Martinsburg Mall opened in the 1990s.[699]

Shepherdstown developer Ken Lowe helped Senator Robert Byrd relocate federal installations to Jefferson County. With other investors, he built 343-acre Liberty Business Park near the Berkeley County border, into which the Internal Revenue Service and the U.S. Coast Guard moved their offices.[700] After Byrd convinced the U.S. Office of Personnel Management to relocate its Eastern Management Development Center from Maryland to Shepherdstown, Lowe led another investor group that built a Clarion hotel to accommodate the students.[701]

Fred L. Glaize III, through his Glaize Developments, Inc., continued his father's Winchester real estate business. Anticipating where future growth might occur, he assembled tracts of land that were later sold to homebuilders and commercial developers. Glaize also partnered with James Bowman, owner of a Stephens City trucking business, in a number of large land purchases. One deal involved the 1989 sale and donation of 158 acres south of Middletown, originally earmarked for industrial tracts, to the Cedar Creek Battlefield Foundation.[702] Another Bowman-Glaize project was the purchase of 1,000 acres around a 132-acre, man-made lake, southeast of Winchester.[703] After the partners donated what became Lake Frederick to Virginia in 1981, it was improved with $700,000 of state funds. The partnership then sold its nearby Wheatlands tract to Loudoun County homebuilders.[704]

In the early years of the twenty-first century, two historic Winchester hotels, the George Washington and the Taylor, underwent extensive restorations. The developers received federal and state historic tax credits and other incentives to complete the work. In 2003, local real estate investors Glen and Kimberly Burke paid $600,000 for the 75,000-square-foot George Washington Hotel, built in 1924 on Piccadilly Street.[705] Five years and millions of dollars later, the 90-room hotel opened as a licensee of Wyndham Worldwide Corp., which specialized in marketing historic hotels.[706]

In 2013, Roanoke-based Brian Whisneff & Associates and the Winchester Economic Development Authority formed a public-private partnership that repurposed the 1848 Taylor Hotel on Winchester's pedestrian mall into apartments and restaurants.[707] In 2019, the Whisneff group moved farther north and purchased the 104-room Shenandoah Hotel, built in 1926 on Martinsburg's North Queen Street.[708] The company looked to redevelop the upper floors of the building, which had changed ownership several times, into 40 apartments and turn the ground floor into retail, office and restaurant space.[709]

Banking:
Mergers Leave Few Community Banks

After federal legislation changed bank ownership rules, industry consolidation was inevitable. The Bank Holding Company Act of 1956 gave the green light for intrastate banks to combine.[710] In the early 1980s, Virginia, West Virginia, North Carolina and other states permitted interstate banking on a reciprocal basis.[711] In 1994, the Interstate Banking and Branching Efficiency Act gave a bank holding company permission to acquire financial institutions in any state.[712] Mergers and acquisitions enabled banks to increase profits by combining deposits and loans and closing branches, which reduced personnel, real estate and marketing expenses. Not surprisingly, the nation's census of commercial banks declined from 14,300 in 1955 to 4,600 in 2019.[713] During that period, the industry consisted of large national and super-regional banks and smaller, independent community banks. That financial landscape was also found in the Northern Valley.

Regardless of size, the Great Recession had a negative impact on the balance sheets of all Northern Valley banks, because they were forced to take large write-downs of commercial loans made to developers and homebuilders. In 2010, the federal Dodd-Frank Wall Street Reform and Consumer Protection Act doubled banking regulations and increased the capital needed to open a bank.[714] While none was formed in the region, its bank deposits increased from $4.7 billion in 2005 to almost $7 billion in 2019.[715]

Banks in the Virginia Portion of the Region

Postwar merger and acquisition activity began in 1963, when Farmers & Merchants Bank in Winchester acquired First National Bank of Berryville, founded in 1904.[716] After its board formed F&M National Corporation in 1969, Wilbur Feltner led the holding company's purchase of community banks in Virginia, the Eastern Panhandle and in Maryland. Starting his career as a cashier, the Clarke County native was named president in 1963 and served as chairman from 1970 to 2001.[717] Under Feltner, F&M National's assets grew to $1 billion in 1992 and topped $4 billion in 2000, when it also held the largest share of deposits in the region.[718]

The following year, North Carolina-based BB&T Corporation, later renamed Truist Financial Corp., purchased F&M for $1.17 billion.[719] Its shareholders and management received a lucrative deal. In addition to paying a 50 percent premium on the Winchester bank's share price, BB&T gave F&M executives the industry's usual golden parachute of three times their most recent salary, then offered them consulting contracts.[720] It also donated to a Feltner foundation F&M's art collection and one of the bank's restored downtown buildings, which he gifted to Shenandoah University in 2011.[721]

Prior to BB&T's purchase of F&M, two Virginia-based banks had acquired several of the region's older community banks. In 1967, First Virginia Bank in Reston purchased People's Bank, formed in 1900 in Mount Jackson. Two years later it bought Massanutten National Bank, founded in 1890 in Strasburg.[722] In 1980, Dominion Bankshares in Roanoke acquired the 75-year old Farmers Bank of Edinburg. Four years later, it purchased the Harrisonburg bank holding company that owned Commercial and Savings Bank, opened in Winchester in 1916.[723] Its building on Loudoun Street became headquarters for Dominion Bank of the Shenandoah Valley.

Betting on more industry consolidation, Northern Valley businessmen started three community banks in the early 1970s, and within 20 years sold each one at a profit. In 1980, First Virginia Bank bought Bank of Frederick County, organized seven years earlier in Stephens City. In 1985, F&M National purchased 11-year old Stonewall Jackson Bank & Trust in Mount Jackson. In 1992, Jefferson Bankshares, Inc. in Charlottesville purchased Peoples Bank of Front Royal, founded in 1973.[724]

Not all new community banks were success stories. Local businessmen opened Marathon Bank in 1988 on Valley Pike, several miles south of Winchester.[725] Its unusual business model consisted of a headquarters, fax machine and no branches. Suffering from bad loans made in the 1989-90 recession, shareholders recapitalized the bank with more equity and hired local banker Donald Unger to turn it around.[726] After adding branches, Marathon and Rockingham Heritage Bank in Harrisonburg merged in 2000 as Premier Community Bankshares, Inc.[727] The regional bank holding company was headquartered on Valley Pike. In 2007, United Bankshares, Inc. in Charleston, West Virginia, acquired Premier.[728]

In 2020, community banks that remained independent in the Virginia portion of the Northern Valley included First Bank and its holding company, First National Corporation in Strasburg; Bank of Clarke County, a unit of Eagle Financial Services, Inc. in Berryville; Pioneer Bank, formerly Farmers & Merchants National Bank of Stanley; and Blue Ridge Bank in Luray.

Banks in the Eastern Panhandle

Founded in 1871, Bank of Charles Town organized Bank of Harpers Ferry in 1975, named after one that failed in the Great Depression.[729] It later became a branch of the parent bank whose holding company, Potomac Bancshares,

Inc., was incorporated in 1984.[730] When Bank of Charles Town expanded into neighboring Berkeley, Loudoun and Washington counties in the 1990s, it used the BCT acronym.

In 1984, Mountaineer Bankshares of West Virginia, Inc. became the holding company for Old National Bank of Martinsburg, organized in 1865.[731] During Martinsburg attorney Lacy I. Rice Jr.'s tenure as chairman and chief executive officer, it purchased a number of community banks in West Virginia. Included was Morgan County State Bank, Inc. which opened in 1979 in Berkeley Springs.[732] With the largest deposit base in the Eastern Panhandle, Mountaineer's total assets had grown to $738 million in 1994. That year, Charleston-based One Valley Bancorp of West Virginia, Inc. purchased it for $155 million and named Rice chairman of One Valley Bank–East, N.A.[733]

In the early 1990s, two community banks with long histories in the Eastern Panhandle were acquired. In 1992, Key Centurion Bancshares in Charleston purchased Peoples Bank of Charles Town, which opened in 1906. The local branch later became part of United Bankshares, Inc.[734] In 1994, Huntington National Bank, based in its namesake Ohio city, acquired Peoples National Bank of Martinsburg.[735] Founded in 1873 as Peoples Trust Company, it had taken advantage of intrastate banking in 1983 with the acquisition of South Berkeley National Bank, opened nine years earlier in Inwood.[736]

Despite the merger activity, several community banks remained headquartered in the Eastern Panhandle in 2020: Jefferson Security Bank in Shepherdstown; Bank of Charles Town and its holding company, Potomac Bancshares, Inc.; and CNB Bank, formerly Citizens National Bank of Berkeley Springs.[737]

Savings Banks and Credit Unions

In the late 1970s and early 1980s, the savings and loan (S&L) industry suffered from disintermediation, which occurred when federal regulators capped the interest rates S&Ls paid on deposits. That caused customers to move them into higher-yielding money market mutual funds. To help the industry, S&Ls were allowed to make commercial real estate loans, in addition to their traditional home mortgages.[738] Amid a series of bad loans and scandals, the deregulation effort backfired; by 1989, one-third of the nation's 3,200 S&Ls had failed, costing the federal government $160 billion.[739]

After World War II, thrift institutions organized in the Northern Valley met with mixed success. During the industry crisis, three changed their names from savings and loan associations to savings banks, while federal regulators forced the sale of two of them. In 1951, local businessmen formed Winchester Building and Loan Association, which eight years later became Winchester Savings and Loan Association.[740] Taking the Old Dominion Savings and Loan Association name in 1971, branches were added in seven Virginia jurisdictions.[741] Assets grew to $212 million in 1983, when the renamed Old Dominion Savings Bank was sold to Jefferson National Bank in Charlottesville.[742]

Chartered in 1964 in Front Royal, First Federal Savings and Loan Association became First Federal Savings Bank of the Shenandoah Valley in 1990, then Dominion Savings Bank, F.S.B., seven years later.[743] Greater Atlantic Financial Corp. in Reston purchased the struggling thrift in 2000, but the new owner came under increased scrutiny from the Office of Thrift Supervision during the Great Recession.[744] In 2009, the McLean-based holding company for Sonabank purchased Greater Atlantic, including its Front Royal branch.[745]

Organized in Martinsburg in 1973, Shenandoah Federal Savings and Loan Association was a principal lender to two West Virginia ski areas—Snowshoe Ski Resort and Winter Place—both of which took bankruptcy in 1984.[746] Unable to recover from the bad loans, the federal Resolution Trust Corporation sold Shenandoah Federal in 1991 to Blue Ridge Bank in Martinsburg, a newly organized unit of City Holding Company in Charleston.[747] Headquartered in the former Berkeley County jail, the bank took its parent company's name in 1999.

One S&L survived the industry's crisis, changed its name and added branches in the region. Front Royal Savings and Loan Association opened for business in 1980, then became Virginia Savings Bank, three years later.[748] In 1984, branches were added in Winchester and Woodstock. President Michael Funk expanded the bank's footprint to Strasburg in 2000 and Stephens City in 2008. Four years later, City Holding Company purchased its $130 million in assets parent company, Virginia Savings Bancorp, Inc., for $13.4 million.[749]

After World War II, federal credit unions—non-profit, member-owned cooperatives—were organized to provide financial services to Northern Valley citizens. They included Front Royal Credit Union, Winchester Industrial Credit Union, UAW-Abex Employees Credit Union in Winchester, along with several smaller ones in the Eastern Panhandle.[750] Other credit unions opened to serve teachers, government employees and the community in general.

Retailing: Customers Leave Main Street for Shopping Centers

The nation's retail sales soared from $147 billion in 1950 to $1.84 trillion in 1990, then more than tripled to $5.86 trillion in 2020.[751] During those last three decades, Americans no longer shopped on Main Street, but at strip and enclosed malls, neighborhood convenience centers and power centers filled with big-box retailers. The 30,000 shopping centers that dotted the nation's landscape in 1970 almost quadrupled to 116,000 in 2017.[752]

Until the 1960s, no thought was given to redevelopment of the Northern Valley's Main Streets, but that changed when several retail chains left the downtowns of its two cities. In 1965, JC Penney and J. G. McCrory's exited Martinsburg's Queen Street for the newly built Berkeley Plaza, several miles north of the downtown.[753] In 1964, Montgomery Ward moved from Winchester's Loudoun Street to anchor Ward's Plaza Shopping Center on Valley Avenue.[754] And four years later, discounter S. E. Nichols Company in New York City built 100,000-square-foot stores in new shopping centers that were located close to the Winchester and Martinsburg downtowns.[755]

To imitate the popularity of shopping in enclosed malls, in 1974 Winchester's leaders established a pedestrian mall on Loudoun Street, between Cork and Piccadilly streets.[756] But eight years later, its retail anchors—Leggett's (later Belk's), JC Penney and Sears—moved into the 442,000-square-foot, enclosed Apple Blossom Mall, which New England Development Company built at a site near U.S. 50 and Interstate 81.[757] Loudoun Street merchants soon found it difficult to compete with the new mall's free parking and long hours.

Responding to increased competition from shopping centers and strip malls, merchants in some Northern Valley jurisdictions organized downtown associations in the 1970s and 1980s. Their missions were to jointly market member businesses and lobby politicians to physically improve Main Street and its surroundings. The groups were formed in Winchester, Martinsburg, Harpers Ferry, Shepherdstown, Charles Town, Front Royal and Strasburg. Nevertheless, their downtown merchants soon faced new competition.

In 1990, Walmart Inc. entered the market with a 110,000-square-foot store in the new Apple Blossom Corners shopping center on Winchester's South Pleasant Valley Road.[758] Three years later, the low-price retailer from Arkansas announced plans to add a Sam's Club nearby, but competitor Price Club—later renamed Costco—opened the region's first membership warehouse, on Front Royal Pike in Frederick County.[759] In 1996, Walmart relocated its Winchester store one-half mile south, into a larger 180,000-square-foot supercenter that included a grocery section.[760] Within 15 years, it had grown its Northern Valley presence to eight stores.

Besides Walmart, national retailers in the 1990s sought to reach what they considered under-served, rural markets. As the Northern Valley's population grew, developers followed the rooftops, clustering big box stores in power centers with a variety of up-market names. They included Winchester Commons and Winchester Station; Stonewall Plaza, Winchester Gateway and Rutherford Crossing in Frederick County; Crooked Run Town Center and Riverton Commons in Warren County; Potomac Marketplace in Jefferson County; and The Commons in Berkeley County.

In 1991, Crown American Realty Trust from Pennsylvania opened the Martinsburg Mall to serve Eastern Panhandle shoppers who traveled to enclosed malls in Hagerstown and Winchester.[761] Anchored by Sears, JC Penney and Bon Ton, the mall struggled for years. Shoppers frequented a Walmart, built on its own land at the mall's north end, but spent less time inside the other stores. In receivership in 2010 with its anchors leaving, the Martinsburg Mall was sold several times. Paramount Development Corporation from South Carolina purchased the property in 2013 and transformed it into the 600,000-square-foot Foxcroft Towne Center with outdoor entrances to its tenants.[762]

At the start of the New Millennium, Apple Blossom Mall experienced turnover among its in-line retailers when shoppers migrated to nearby big-box stores. In 1999, Simon Property Group in Indianapolis purchased the 30-year old mall and gave the property its first ever facelift in 2012.[763] That included a larger Carmike Cinema theater, along with new ceilings, floors, lighting, doors and signs, a renovated food court and a larger play zone for small children.[764] While financially struggling JC Penney kept its doors open, Sears left the mall in 2020.[765]

In an over-retailed nation, many stores in the region's shopping centers failed to compete with Amazon's strong online presence, first in books, later in other categories. Its growth in the New Millennium, along with the emergence of other e-commerce companies, caused the demand for brick and mortar retail space to decline. Retail chains that once had a presence in the Northern Valley included Gander Mountain, Toys R Us, Circuit City, H.H. Gregg, Payless Shoe Source, Blockbusters and Borders. The retailers who survived adopted a hybrid model of in-store and online sales.

Retail development in the Northern Valley also included local entrepreneurs. In 1990, retired American Woodmark executive Richard Graber opened Creekside Village on Valley Pike in Kernstown, several miles south of downtown Winchester.[766] The architecture of its 20 retail and office buildings was patterned after Colonial Williamsburg. In 2007, Graber built the much larger Creekside Station nearby, which attracted national clothing chains Talbot's, Jos. A. Banks and Chico's, along with other retailers and several restaurants.[767]

In 2005, the Nerangis family, owner of McDonald's restaurants in the region, announced the development of Kernstown Commons, situated south of the Route 37 overpass between U.S. 11 and Interstate 81. Within five years, it was home to an Aldi grocery store, Outback Steakhouse and Carraba's Italian Grill, plus several Nerangis-owned franchises: Country Inn & Suites, Alamo Drafthouse theater, Green Turtle Sports Bar and Grill and, not surprisingly, a McDonald's.[768]

In the 1980s, Martinsburg's economy benefited from bargain hunters shopping at factory outlet stores.[769] In 1984, Loudoun County resident Moncure Chatfield-Taylor repurposed the Dunn and Crawford woolen mills into the 265,000-square-foot Blue Ridge Outlet Center. Although met with local skepticism, when 50 manufacturers of name-brand consumer goods put off-price stores in the complex, Martinsburg became a regional shopping mecca.[770] In 1987, the 44,000-square-foot Tanger Factory Outlet Center opened on Foxcroft Drive. Located closer to I-81, the North Carolina real estate investment trust hoped to benefit from traffic the Blue Ridge Outlet Center generated.

In 1999, however, Chatfield-Taylor lost his tenants to a larger Prime Retail Outlet Center, located on Interstate 70 in neighboring Washington County.[771] That made it easier for metro D.C. area shoppers to reach bargain priced goods. Three years after the Blue Ridge Outlet Center's closure in 2000, Berkeley County repurposed the buildings into its judicial center and government offices.[772] At the same time, Tanger sold its outlet center to Mountain State University, which held classes in it.[773] In 2015, Paramount Development, which two years earlier had acquired the Martinsburg Mall, purchased the former Tanger property for $2 million, and leased the renamed Viking Way Center for retail and office use.[774]

Health Care:
Modern Hospitals Are Prescription for Survival

The public's increased usage of health care in the late 1940s started a hospital building boom in both the nation and the Northern Valley. With wage controls in place during World War II, unions negotiated health insurance benefits for their members.[775] Federal programs enacted in 1965—Medicare for the elderly and Medicaid for the indigent—resulted in millions more insured patients. In 1940, only 9 percent of Americans had health insurance, but 76 percent were enrolled in plans in 1985.[776] Not surprisingly, the insured made more trips to hospitals.

In response to the growing need for health care facilities, the federal Hill-Burton Act of 1946 provided grants and loans for their construction.[777] To be eligible for the funds, a hospital had to provide free care to citizens unable to pay for it. Using some Hill-Burton money, the non-profit Winchester Memorial Hospital increased its bed count from 36 to 300 in 1953 with a five-story, $3.45 million addition put on its Stewart Street property.[778] Unable to expand downtown, in 1984 the renamed Winchester Medical Center purchased a 94-acre orchard near Amherst Street's interchange with Route 37, the western beltway around the city.[779] Its board of trustees formed Valley Health Services—the Services was later dropped from the name—to function as an umbrella organization for the hospital and other health care entities.

After surgeons lobbied for an outpatient clinic suitable for minor operations, they partnered with Valley Health in the 1985 opening of the Surgi-Center of Winchester on the hospital's future campus. Five years later, Winchester Medical Center moved into a nearby 480,000-square-foot, $86.5 million building with 356 private rooms for patients.[780] By 2020, the campus had grown to include parking garages, medical office buildings, a wellness and fitness center, a systems office building and diagnostic, cancer and heart centers.[781]

The former Stewart Street hospital housed Valley Health's Rehabilitation Center, Blue Ridge Hospice and Shenandoah University's physical therapy program. In 2014, HealthCare Development Partners in Chicago purchased the building. Six years later, the City of Winchester approved the new owner's proposal to repurpose it into apartments for seniors, assisted living rooms and a memory care unit.[782]

In other Northern Valley jurisdictions, older hospitals were replaced with larger, more modern ones that met the needs of their growing populations. In

Chapter 7: Post-World War II to 2020　　　　　　　　　　　321

1951, Hill-Burton funds were used to build 48-bed Warren Memorial Hospital on the former Front Royal Community Hospital site.[783] That same year, the Fravel and Cora Miller Memorial hospitals in Woodstock closed when Shenandoah County Memorial Hospital opened on South Main Street.[784] In 1958, Page Memorial Hospital in Luray replaced 30-year old Beahm Memorial Hospital, then underwent expansions 20 years later.[785] In Ranson, the 35-bed Charles Town General Hospital was built in 1948 for $425,000 on the former Hotel Powhatan site that industrialist R. J. Funkhouser donated.[786] The original hospital at Dr. Richard Venning's residence became a nursing home. In 1975, the $4.5 million, 79-bed Jefferson Memorial Hospital was built beside Charles Town General, which was converted to an extended care facility.[787]

For years, Dr. Oates and King's Daughter's hospitals competed for patients in Martinsburg, but that scenario changed in the early 1970s when City Hospital replaced the Oates' facility on Tavern Road, near Interstate 81.[788] It was financed with $2.5 million worth of Hill-Burton funds, Appalachian Regional Commission grants, and $1.5 million raised locally.[789] The more modern and larger City Hospital put financial pressure on King's Daughter's, which nuns had operated since the mid-1890s on East King Street. In 1976, for-profit Hospital Corporation of America (HCA) in Nashville was recruited to find a solution for the two hospital problem.[790] It offered to purchase City Hospital for $9 million, but the board of trustees rejected the deal.[791] Instead,

City Hospital in Martinsburg, 1970s
Postcard published by Louis Kaufmann & Sons, Baltimore, MD

HCA Management Company was hired to operate it, at which point King's Daughter's closed.[792] Faced with cuts in Medicare reimbursements in 1999, City Hospital's board hired its own management team instead of renewing the HCA contract.[793]

Employers Organize Health Care Task Force

Rising health care costs became a concern for employers in the Virginia portion of the region. To service the debt on its new hospital, Winchester Medical Center raised prices at double-digit percentages for several years. In 1993, the Winchester Society for Human Resource Management formed the Northern Shenandoah Valley Health Care Task Force to search for ways to control the health care costs of its members.[794] The group sought to form a preferred provider organization (PPO) to negotiate prices with Winchester Medical Center.[795] Although the hospital rejected the idea—a PPO would only shift costs to patients not in the network—its rates did not increase in 1993 and 1994.[796] The task force did persuade Valley Health to open an urgent care center in Winchester to provide an alternative to expensive emergency room visits. [797]

The Eastern Panhandle Health and Human Service Council was formed in 1993 to coordinate health care in that delivery area, but no employer-led coalition materialized to negotiate with its health care providers.[798] Hospital charges never escalated as rapidly as in Winchester, because none was built, and unlike the Virginia Department of Health, the West Virginia Health Care Authority regulated rate increases.

Hospital Mergers and Acquisitions

Many patients at tertiary care Winchester Medical Center underwent complicated surgeries and treatments, which required long stays that filled its beds. In the 1990s, other Northern Valley hospitals found it difficult to keep their facilities occupied when insurers forced them to shorten patient stays after routine procedures. Unable to generate sufficient cash flows to modernize their equipment, the hospitals struggled to recruit physicians to fill beds with patients.

While Winchester Medical Center operated at 63 percent capacity in 1997, occupancy rates at the region's other hospitals ranged from 20 percent to 47 percent.[799] Its revenues less expenses increased five-fold, from $11.8 million in 2001 to $53.1 million in 2010, the year its cash flows totaled $84.6 million.[800] With the region's most profitable health care provider, Valley Health had the financial resources to acquire and modernize five struggling community hospitals. Between 1993 and 2010, Warren Memorial in Front Royal, Shenandoah Memorial in Woodstock, Hampshire Memorial in Romney, Page Memorial in Luray and War Memorial in Berkeley Springs joined Valley Health. Their new owner built hospitals for four of them, and between 2007 and 2016, provided Shenandoah Memorial Hospital with funds to build a new surgical center, diagnostic center and a 45,000-square-foot emergency room and medical office building.[801] Valley Health's investments in those facilities totaled $500 million, and by 2020, the system's payroll had grown to 6,000 employees, including a medical staff of 600 physicians and advanced practice clinicians [802]

Besides its non-profit hospitals, Valley Health owned businesses that competed with the private sector. They included physician practices, medical office buildings, urgent care centers, pharmacies, fitness centers and ambulance, laboratory and imaging services.[803] Those businesses operated under the corporate umbrella of Valley Regional Enterprises, Inc., a for-profit subsidiary that paid real estate, income and other taxes, when required.[804]

City Hospital in Martinsburg and Jefferson Memorial Hospital in Ranson had to upgrade and expand their services to be competitive with hospitals in Winchester and Hagerstown.[805] With rates regulated at the state level, their cash flows were weak and inconsistent, which made it difficult for them to raise funds in capital markets. In 2005, City and Jefferson Memorial hospitals joined the larger, non-profit West Virginia University Health System in Morgantown as West Virginia University Medicine East.[806] With financial backing from their new owner, they borrowed more than $100 million to upgrade equipment and facilities.[807] In 2006, a certificate of need application was filed with the West Virginia Health Care Authority for several projects at the hospitals.[808] They included medical office buildings, emergency room expansions and a diagnostic cardiac cathertization lab at City Hospital. Because the lab duplicated a service Winchester Medical Center provided, Valley Health objected to it, but the appeal failed.[809]

In 2013, West Virginia University Health System rebranded the Eastern Panhandle hospitals as Berkeley Medical Center and Jefferson Medical Center, to identify them more closely with the communities they served.[810] Despite the WVU Health System's presence in the Eastern Panhandle, Valley Health extended its reach northward. In 2012, it opened an urgent care center near Berkeley Plaza, north of downtown Martinsburg, followed five years later with one outside Ranson, near the Potomac Marketplace mall on Route 9.[811] In 2020, the $17 million Valley Health I Spring Mills office building opened to provide a variety of medical services in northern Berkeley County.[812]

Senior Living Facilities

The Northern Valley's growing senior population, which included thousands of retirees from the metro D.C. area, drove demand for living quarters outside the home. In the mid-1990s, assisted living accommodations emerged as a less-expensive alternative to nursing homes. The owners hoped seniors still performing some activities of daily living would move into their facilities.[813] Flush with bank and Wall Street financing, assisted living accommodations soon sprung up in the Northern Valley and elsewhere. The frenetic building activity ceased when over-capacity hit the industry in the New Millennium. Assisted living construction resumed in the region in 2010 when HH Hunt Corporation from Blacksburg, Virginia, built Spring Arbor on U.S. 50, close to Winchester Medical Center.[814]

Several non-profit, continuing-care retirement communities (CCRCs) provided Northern Valley seniors with life care. As a resident's health status changed, he or she moved from independent living to assisted living quarters and finally into a nursing unit. In return, CCRCs required an entrance fee, usually financed with proceeds received from the sale of a home. Because residents also paid monthly fees, certain levels of income and net worth were needed to qualify for admission.

In 1987, Westminster-Canterbury of Winchester, Inc. was the first CCRC to open in the Northern Valley. Sponsored by the Presbyterian and Episcopal churches, it was located on 65 acres, three miles from Winchester Medical Center. Residents paid high up-front costs for contracts that gave them unlimited use of Westminster-Canterbury's health care services. Saddled with too much debt and low occupancy, the CCRC soon took Chapter 11 bankruptcy.[815] The 1989-90 housing recession had made it difficult for prospects to sell their homes to pay the entrance fees. On firmer financial footing in the late 1990s, the renamed Shenandoah Valley Westminster-Canterbury expanded several times.[816] By 2017, its accommodations included 162 independent living apartments, 101 health care related apartments and 48 cottages.[817] Two years later, it purchased 21 acres near Fox Drive to develop one- and two-bedroom villas.[818]

Sensing a need for a less expensive CCRC, two other church groups entered the Northern Valley market with offerings that required lower up-front costs, but instead of providing free health care for life, residents paid for it on a fee-for-service basis. In 2008, Homewood Retirement Centers in Williamsport, Maryland, affiliated with United Church of Christ, opened a CCRC on 60 acres in the Strasburg area.[819] After spending $15 million and building 12 cottages, Homewood at the Shenandoah Valley was put up for sale in the midst of the Great Recession's housing crisis.[820] In 2007, National Lutheran Home in Potomac, Maryland, announced it would build The Village at Orchard Ridge on U.S. 50, two miles west of Winchester Medical Center.[821] But the Great Recession made it difficult for prospects to sell their homes. The Lutherans finally opened Orchard Ridge in 2013, and seven years later, the CCRC included 324 cottages and apartments.[822]

Tourism: History and Nature Bring Visitors

After World War II, Americans found themselves with increased leisure time, resulting from shorter workweeks, more national holidays and vacation days. In the late 1980s, local governments formed tourism agencies to lure day trippers and vacationers into the Northern Valley, along with tour buses, conferences and conventions. Agency officials pointed out that those visitors spent money at hotels, restaurants, gas stations and tourist attractions, but required little in the way of government services. Convention and visitor bureaus were later considered part of a jurisdiction's economic development effort; Shenandoah, Clarke and Page counties combined the functions in one position.

Tourists visited museums run by local historical societies, as well as a foundation's $20 million, 50,000-square-foot regional museum. In 2005, the Museum of the Shenandoah Valley opened on the 254-acre Glen Burnie estate that faced Winchester's Amherst Street.[823] The $50 million Glass-Glen Burnie Foundation, which Julian Wood Glass Jr. funded in 1986 with his family's Oklahoma oil interests, financed much of the building's cost and its operating budget.[824] A descendent of Winchester's founder James Wood, Glass preserved and lived part-time in the estate's 1794 Glen Burnie House, until his passing in 1992.[825]

Parks, Trails and Battlefields

After World War II, the National Park Service opened three parks that attracted heritage and recreational tourists to the region. They included some of the Harpers Ferry and Bolivar Heights area in 1963, the Chesapeake & Ohio Canal National Historical Park in 1971, and Cedar Creek and Belle Grove National Historical Park, established in 2002 in Frederick County.[826] The Northern Valley also featured three state parks: Berkeley Springs State Park, Cacapon Resort State Park in Morgan County and Shenandoah River State Park in Warren County. The latter one opened in 1999 near Bentonville, on property once earmarked for a landfill.[827]

Several government agencies and organizations mapped out themed drives for tourists traveling in automobiles. They included the Civil War Trails in Virginia and West Virginia, Washington Heritage Trail in the Eastern Panhandle, Follow the Apple Trail in Frederick County, Shenandoah Valley Wine Trail, Shenandoah Spirits Trail and the Virginia Cave and Karst Trail.

For more than one century, the Northern Valley sat on an untapped tourist attraction: Civil War battlefields. In 1967, Virginia Military Institute (VMI) in Lexington opened the 300-acre New Market Battlefield State Historical Park, on the region's first preserved battlefield.[828] Made possible by VMI graduate George Collins, the park was dedicated to the school's cadets, who on May 15, 1864 fought against Union forces. [829]

In 1990, forty million Americans watched Ken Burns' Civil War documentary on public television. With renewed interest in the conflict, Northern Valley leaders believed if former battlefields were preserved, they would attract tourists. In 1996, U.S. Representative Frank Wolf secured Congressional approval for an eight-county Shenandoah Valley National Historic Battlefields District Commission.[830] Based in New Market, it put together five geographical groupings of battlefields, along with Civil War visitor centers, between Frederick and Augusta counties.[831]

Mineral Springs Resorts

Only one of the region's six springs resorts that reopened after the Civil War still operated in the New Millennium. In the 1940s, Miles Portlock from the Newport News area purchased Orkney Springs resort in western Shenandoah County.[832] The Episcopal Diocese of Virginia, which used adjacent land for retreats, bought the property from him in 1979 and renamed it Shrine Mont.[833] After refurbishing the buildings in 1987, the Diocese opened them to the public, held church conferences and hosted the Shenandoah Valley Music Festival in summer months.

With Warm Springs Run, historic baths and contemporary spas, Berkeley Springs remained a popular tourist destination. In 2010, USA Today named it one of the 10 Best Historical Small Towns.[834] In addition, Travel Berkeley Springs advertised its town as not only the nation's first spa, but also home to three times as many massage therapists as lawyers.[835]

Recreation: Hitting Links and Circling Tracks

Golf course openings in the United States increased from 102 in 1985 to a peak of 399 in 2000.[836] With 13 new courses and others adding holes, the Northern Valley participated in that growth. As the housing market heated up, golf course developers adopted a new business model. They borrowed funds to build a course and clubhouse, sold lots for upscale homes and used the proceeds to pay down the loan. But the Great Recession and the public's declining interest in the sport hurt the bottom lines of several courses in the region. Its horse racing and motorsports tracks fared better: Attendance at Charles Town Race Track increased when a new owner added slots and table games, and two tracks opened to entertain car racing enthusiasts.

Golf Courses

With Arnold Palmer, Jack Nicklaus and Gary Player competing for ever larger purses in televised tournaments in the 1960s, more golfers hit the links. While most Northern Valley players were local, those from the D.C. metro area looked to lower their handicaps on the region's less crowded and less expensive public courses. Their owners generated extra income from charity tournaments and pro shop and food bar sales, while those with a large clubhouse hosted banquets and weddings.

In 1955, member-only, nine-hole Opequon Country Club, founded in 1922 near its namesake creek, was sold to Martinsburg investors, who turned it into Stonebridge Golf Club, an 18-hole public course.[837] Between 1962 and 1965, three golf courses opened in the region: Sleepy Hollow Golf and Country Club near Charles Town, Carpers Valley Golf Club in eastern Frederick County and Woodbrier Golf Course near Martinsburg.[838] The first residential golf community appeared in 1966, when Lynwood Morrison repurposed his Warren County hog farm into the 18-hole Shenandoah Valley Golf Club, then marketed home sites along the course.[839] Selling the property in 1979, he doubled down on the golf business with the development of two 18-hole courses on 400 nearby acres.[840] After the North and South courses opened at Bowling Green Country Club in 1984 and 1992, respectively, lots were sold for upscale housing.[841]

More golf communities appeared in the region. In 1988, the Drennen family from Northern Virginia sold lots at its member-only Cress Creek Country Club near Shepherdstown.[842] Ray Johnston offered them at two 18-hole courses he designed at The Woods Resort, near Hedgesville: the Mountain View Golf Course in 1989, followed in 2002 by the mid-length, 3,600-yard long Stony Creek Golf Course, designed for shorter hitting golfers.[843] Although Warren County had five courses, two Virginia businessmen built 18-hole Blue Ridge Shadows Golf Course in 2006 on U.S. 340/522, then sold building lots.[844]

When Tiger Woods' winning ways in the early 1990s created new interest in golf, more holes appeared in the Northern Valley. Courses that opened between 1991 and 1999 included Locust Hills Golf Course, several miles west of Charles Town; Jackson's Chase Golf Club in Warren County; and Virginia National Golf Course, on the site of the former Shenandoah Retreat course in eastern Clarke County.[845] In 2003, Denny Perry, president of Stuart M. Perry, Inc., designed and built 18-hole Rock Harbor Golf Course.[846] Located adjacent to the company's crushed stone quarry near Round Hill, several miles west of Winchester, 18 holes were added in 2015.

Golf participation in America peaked in 2005 with 30 million players.[847] While millennials found better use of their time and money, the industry's expected participation from Baby Boomer retirees never materialized. Between 2005 and 2010, more than 600 courses closed, including several in the Northern Valley.[848] After 43 years, play at Carper's Valley Golf Course ended in 2006, and two years later, Blue Ridge Shadows LLC filed for bankruptcy, but remained open.[849] The owners of Virginia National met the same fate in 2010, and three years later, it was turned into Shenandoah University's Cool Spring River Campus.[850] Locust Hills and Jackson's Chase became financially stressed before new operators purchased them. In 2013, Stonebridge Golf Club was sold at auction for $650,000 to a Florida real estate company.[851]

Horse Racing

Postwar, the horse racing industry lost popularity as a spectator sport, as did many others that featured individual competitors.[852] Nevertheless, New York investors formed Shenandoah Corporation in 1959, with hopes of building a $13 million race track and 15,000-seat grandstand, near the Charles Town Race Track.[853] After a legal battle and local opposition to more wagering in Jefferson County, the West Virginia Racing Commission granted the company permission to hold races.[854] Shenandoah Downs, the nation's first track to schedule night races, opened in 1959 and soon took business from its neighbor, which first held races in 1933.[855] In 1968, Herman and Ben Cohen, owners of Pimlico Race Course in Baltimore, bought the struggling Charles Town Race Track from the Charles Town Jockey Club.[856] The brothers made extensive renovations that included installing lighting to hold night races in competition with Shenandoah Downs.[857]

Despite the excitement Triple Crown winners Secretariat, Seattle Slew and Affirmed brought to horse racing in the 1970s, the industry faced a headwind.[858] Its near monopoly on legal gambling ended when state governments held lotteries to raise revenue for a variety of public purposes. In 1972, Shenandoah Corporation purchased Charles Town Race Track from the Cohen brothers and four years later, used Shenandoah Downs for training.[859] As the track's daily attendance declined towards the end of the 1970s, Kenton Corporation, which New York City financier Meshulum Riklis controlled, purchased Shenandoah Corporation for $16 million in 1978.[860]

Charles Town Race Track was then hit by a perfect storm of gas shortages, an IRS requirement that tracks withhold taxes from winning bets and a West Virginia tax on pari-mutuel betting.[861] Kenton closed the track soon after its purchase, citing a loss of $250,000 and projections of a larger one for 1979.[862] Four years later, Rapid American Corporation, another Riklis holding company, and 15 businessmen, including 11 from the Northern Valley, purchased the complex.[863]

Despite the ownership changes, Charles Town Race Track again fell on hard times. Low purses—money paid to owners of winning horses—did not attract best-of-breed Thoroughbreds on which gamblers preferred to place bets. As its physical condition deteriorated and attendance dropped, the owners hoped to install video slot machines that would generate revenue to support larger purses.[864] The West Virginia legislature approved slots in 1994, but Jefferson County voters turned them down by a slim margin, even though the race track played an important part in the local economy.[865]

After citizens changed their minds in 1996, casino operator Penn National Gaming, Inc. purchased the Charles Town Race Track and its 250 acres for $18 million.[866] The Wyomissing, Pennsylvania, company spent $27 million on clubhouse and grandstand renovations, new jockey quarters and paddock, two restaurants and a casino with 400 video slot machines.[867] By the New Millennium, the slot count was 2,000 and the track's payroll included 750 full-time and 250 part-time workers.[868] The total value of its annual racing purses soared from $3 million in 1998 to $33 million in 2010.[869]

Concerned with potential competition from new casinos in Maryland, Penn National looked to add table games. After Jefferson County voters and West Virginia regulators approved them in 2010, the renamed Hollywood Casino at Charles Town Races opened with roulette wheels, craps and blackjack tables.[870] Nevertheless, the Maryland casinos did force Penn National Gaming to lay off some poker dealers in 2013.[871] By the end of 2019, however, Hollywood Casino included 2,200 slot machines, 74 table games and a 1,300-person payroll.[872]

For years, harness racing was held each fall at the Shenandoah County Fairgrounds in Woodstock, but no betting took place. In 2014, the non-profit Virginia Equine Alliance saw an opportunity to fulfill its mission of promoting horse breeding and racing in the commonwealth. Taking the Shenandoah Downs name from the former track in Charles Town, the alliance spent $800,000 renovating the half-mile oval track at the fairgrounds.[873] It held harness races each September and October and managed the track's on-site betting.[874]

Motorsports

Airport Speedway, the auto racing track located east of Winchester Municipal Airport, closed during World War II. Kermit Batt and new partner Lawrence Lichliter reopened it in 1947 as Winchester Speedway.[875] They reconfigured its straight-away layout to a three-eighths mile oval and added wooden grandstands, replaced in 1974 with concrete ones.[876] After Winchester Speedway changed hands several times, Greg Gunter, owner of a honey business in Berryville, paid $1.25 million for it in 2010.[877] Open on Saturday nights from March to October, Gunter's Honey Motorsports was one of the featured racing teams.[878]

In the late 1960s, several Northern Virginia businessmen purchased a 375-acre farm near the village of Summit Point in Jefferson County, then built a 2.5-mile oval asphalt track.[879] The $3.5 million Summit Point Motorsports Park opened as a professional racing venue in 1970, but closed several years later, a victim of the nation's oil crisis.[880] In 1979, Formula Vee world champion Bill Scott purchased the track and added a 4,000 foot straight-away.[881] Besides auto racing, the U.S.

State Department used it to conduct the Foreign Affairs Security Training Center, attended by 7,000 federal law enforcement personnel each year.[882] Following Scott's passing in 1999, his widow Barbara ran the park until its sale in 2018 to Xator Corporation, a safety and security consulting firm in Reston.[883]

In 2005, Jeff Vaughan, owner of machining company KVK Precision Specialties in the Page County town of Shenandoah, ventured into the motorsports business. He built the three-eighths mile, asphalt Shenandoah Speedway for automobiles, while motocross—off-road motorcycle—races were held on a nearby dirt track.[884] Vaughn also rented the speedway to persons wishing to experience driving their cars on a banked, oval course.[885]

Media: All News Is Not Printed

Within half a century, four categories of media joined traditional newsprint to compete for audiences and advertising dollars: radio in the 1940s, television in the 1950s, cable TV in the 1980s and the internet in the 1990s. Northern Valley's media companies adapted to the competitive landscape by changing their formats, coverage areas and through mergers and acquisitions.

The internet was a major headwind for newspaper publishers. Its electronic delivery of instant news—anywhere and anytime—adversely affected subscriptions, especially from younger readers. And advertising, including the most profitable classified ads, was lost to social media and search engines. Challenged to operate profitably, newspaper publishers rolled out paid digital subscriptions. They generated less revenue, but eliminated paper, printing and delivery costs. In the New Millennium, radio found itself competing for listeners against digital upstarts Pandora, Spotify, Apple Music, Amazon Music and others. Legacy television networks and cable channels watched viewers migrate to the streaming services of Netflix, Disney Plus and NBC Universal's Peacock.[886]

Newspapers and Periodicals

Two newspaper publishers competed for readers and advertisers in the Virginia portion of the region. After E. E. Keister folded four newspapers into the Strasburg-based Northern Virginia Daily in the 1930s, the Byrd family purchased weeklies in towns located between its Winchester and Harrisonburg dailies. They included The Page News & Courier in Luray, Warren Sentinel in Front Royal and the Shenandoah Herald and Shenandoah Valley Weekly in

Woodstock, which were later combined as the Shenandoah Valley-Herald. In 2008, the Byrds purchased the weekly Clarke Times-Courier from Arundel Newspapers in Leesburg, then stopped publishing it because their Winchester Star also covered news in Berryville and Clarke County.[887]

In 1985, veteran newspaperman Keith Stickley started The Free Press in Woodstock to report Shenandoah County news each week in competition with papers owned by the Byrd and Keister families.[888] For additional revenue, his Narrow Passage Press printed weekly and monthly newspapers for publishers in the region and in Northern Virginia. Mike McCool, owner of National Media Services, Inc. in Front Royal, joined a new publishing trend. In 2016, he launched the advertising-supported Royal Examiner as an online publication covering Warren County news.[889]

In 1990, Ogden Newspapers in Wheeling changed The Evening Journal in Martinsburg, owned since 1923, into a morning newspaper and renamed it The Journal.[890] Increasing its Northern Valley footprint, the Ogden group purchased the weekly Shepherdstown Chronicle in 1999, the Northern Virginia Daily in 2013 and five years later, the Byrd family's Winchester Star, Daily News Record and its weekly papers.[891] That gave Ogden Newspapers coverage from Martinsburg to Harrisonburg.

In 1989, the advertising-supported North Valley Business Journal began covering business news in Winchester and Frederick, Clarke, Warren and Shenandoah counties. At the time, similar papers started up in other rural areas to provide more in-depth coverage of business news than local papers did. The monthly newspaper soon reached into the Eastern Panhandle, and in 1995 was renamed the Quad-State Business Journal when news coverage and circulation was expanded northward, along the I-81 corridor to Hagerstown and Chambersburg. In 2001, the Byrds published the Shenandoah Valley Business Journal, which covered the area from Harrisonburg north to Winchester. Four years later, B2B magazine started in Martinsburg to report on business in the Eastern Panhandle. In the midst of the Great Recession, the three monthly publications closed shop.

Radio Stations

After World War II, Northern Valley airwaves carried 14 radio stations, including the three oldest: WINC-AM and FM, started up in Winchester in 1941 and 1946, and WEPM-AM, which went on the air in Martinsburg in 1946.

*Last Issue of Quad-State Business Journal, June 2009
Scanned from Peter Heerwagen's collection of past issues, Winchester, VA*

Since then, many stations were bought and sold, while other owners changed formats to increase listenership. In 1948, the Front Royal-Warren County Chamber of Commerce formed Sky-Park Broadcasting Corporation, which put WFTR-AM on the air.[892] After changing hands several times, Andrew Shearer from Philadelphia purchased it in 2000 for $950,000.[893]

In 1982, the Holt Limited Partnership of Pennsylvania acquired ShenVal Communications in Winchester, owner of WEFG-FM since 1965, then switched the station's call letters to WUSQ and branded it Shenandoah Country Q102.[894] It was sold to Baltimore-based Benchmark Communications in 1991, which three years later purchased FM classic rock station WFQX in Strasburg.[895] In 1985, Art and Virginia Stamler formed Ruarch Associates in Woodstock and launched Christian station WAZR-FM to play big band music.[896]

In 1958 in Berkeley Springs, Charles S. Trump, through his Trump Broadcasting, Inc., started up WCST-AM, using his initials for its call letters.[897] In the same town, Emmitt Capper put country, bluegrass and Americana-formatted WDHC-FM on the air in 1965. Thirty years later, Capper Broadcasting Company purchased the Trump station.[898] Also in the Eastern Panhandle, brothers Rick and Gregg Wachtel, through their Shenandoah Communications, Inc., started Talk Radio WRNR in 1976 in Martinsburg.[899] In the same city, the Golliday family sold its two WEPM stations in 1987 to Prettyman Broadcasting Company in Salisbury, Maryland.[900]

The federal Telecommunications Act of 1996 allowed one company to own multiple radio stations in the same market. Not surprisingly, that legislation resulted in the sale of numerous stations, accompanied by a surge in prices. In 1999, Prettyman Broadcasting purchased a Williamsport, Maryland, station and combined it with the company's WEPM-FM station in Martinsburg as WLTF-FM or Lite 95.9.[901] In 2014, Prettyman sold it and WEPM-AM and a station in Hagerstown for $3 million to West Virginia Radio Corporation in Morgantown.[902] Next year, the Wachtel brothers sold Talk Radio WRNR for $650,000 to Michael Hornby, publisher of the Around the Panhandle Magazine.[903] In 2017, Emmitt Capper sold his two Berkeley Springs stations to Metro Radio, Inc. in Fairfax, Virginia, for $365,000.[904]

Radio station transactions also picked up in the Virginia portion of the region. In 1997, the Lewis family in Winchester added several properties to its Mid Atlantic Network, Inc., which owned WINC-AM and FM, along with stations in Fredericksburg and Harrisonburg. Mid-Atlantic paid $850,000 to locally owned Signal Knob Radio Partners for both WAPP-FM, started in Berryville in 1979, and WBPP-FM, aired from Strasburg since 1986.[905] To compete directly with Shenandoah Country Q102, which Benchmark Communications owned, Mid Atlantic converted the Berryville and Strasburg stations to country formats. It then purchased Stonewall Broadcasting Company in Harrisonburg for $1.75 million.[906]

To take advantage of more liberal ownership rules, CapStar Broadcasting, Inc. was organized in 1996 in Austin, Texas, to purchase small-market radio stations. One year later, it acquired Shenandoah Country Q102 in Winchester from Benchmark Communications.[907] In 2001, Mid Atlantic Network sold its three Harrisonburg stations for $7.2 million to CapStar, by then a subsidiary of San Antonio-based Clear Channel Communications, Inc., another serial acquirer of radio stations. Later renamed iHeartMedia, Clear Channel purchased WXVA in 1997, first aired 30 years earlier in Charles Town.[908] It moved the station's tower and studio to Winchester in 2004, then folded it into the company's WKSI-FM station in Stephens City. In 2001, Clear Channel purchased big band format WAZR-FM in Woodstock from Ruarch Associates for $1.3 million and repositioned WAZR's tower to the

Harrisonburg area.⁹⁰⁹

In 2007, Mid Atlantic Network sold its six stations in Winchester and Fredericksburg for $36 million to Centennial Broadcasting in North Carolina, a transaction that ended the Lewis family's 55 years of radio station ownership in the Northern Valley.⁹¹⁰ In 2020, the new owner closed the WINC office in Winchester and sold Mid Atlantic's 92.5 FM frequency for $1.75 million to non-profit Educational Media Foundation in California.⁹¹¹ WINC-FM's adult contemporary music format moved to Centennial's stations that remained in Strasburg and Berryville.⁹¹²

Television Stations

NBC affiliate WHAG-TV went on the air in 1970 in Hagerstown to report on news, sports and weather from Chambersburg to Winchester and from Frederick west to Cumberland. After losing its affiliation with NBC in 2017, the call letters changed to WDVM—short for District of Columbia, Virginia and Maryland—and coverage was expanded into the metro Washington market.⁹¹³

Three TV stations launched in the Northern Valley met with mixed results. In 1985, Ruarch Associates started WAZT-TV, a Christian, family-oriented station in Woodstock, the same year its radio station went on the air.⁹¹⁴ In 2006, the group sold the TV station for $3.9 million to JLA Media and Publishing, LLC in Ashburn, Virginia.⁹¹⁵ It remained in Woodstock until the owner took bankruptcy in 2010, then changed hands several times among broadcasting companies serving the metro D.C. area.⁹¹⁶

In 1991, WYVN-TV, the acronym for We're Your Valley News, began broadcasting from Martinsburg as an affiliate of Fox Broadcasting Company.⁹¹⁷ General partner and majority station owner Ralph Albertazzie received financial support from Martinsburg and Winchester investors.⁹¹⁸ WYVN competed with WHAG-TV for viewers in the Eastern Panhandle, but after three years, the former Air Force One pilot took the unprofitable WYVN off the air.

In 2007, WHSV-TV in Harrisonburg, owned by Gray Television Inc. in Atlanta, launched a station in the Winchester and Front Royal markets.⁹¹⁹ The ABC affiliate broadcast TV3 Winchester from Shenandoah University's studio, which produced public service programming over WCT Channel 20.⁹²⁰ With limited coverage of local news, TV3's paid advertising never gained traction during the Great Recession. After six years, the station went off the air.⁹²¹

Cable TV

Beginning in the late 1990s, the nation's cable TV industry spent billions of dollars upgrading its systems with high-capacity fiber optic and coaxial networks.[922] New broadband offerings included a triple-play bundle of high-speed internet, high-definition television and land-line telephone service. As the industry matured, cable TV companies purchased systems near each other to gain operating efficiencies and to reduce overhead.

In 1965, the Lewis family in Winchester, through its Mid Atlantic Network of radio stations, entered the nascent cable TV industry. When the cable business was sold in 1989 to Adelphia Communications Corporation in Pennsylvania, its 11 systems in Virginia included those in Winchester and Front Royal.[923] Through a series of acquisitions and trades, GS Communications in Frederick, Maryland, ended up with a cluster of cable TV systems in the Eastern Panhandle.[924] When Adelphia acquired GS in 2001, it became the largest participant in the Northern Valley's cable TV industry, a position that did not last for long. The company took bankruptcy in 2006, after it was discovered that the Rigas family, Adelphia's controlling shareholders, had used it as their own piggy bank. Four years later, Comcast Corporation in Philadelphia purchased its systems, including those in the Northern Valley.[925]

First offering cable TV service in Shenandoah County in 1980, Shenandoah Telecommunications Company (Shentel) in Edinburg grew its local subscriber base to 8,300 households and businesses in 2007.[926] The following year, Shentel began acquiring rural cable systems in Virginia, West Virginia and Kentucky, using its financial resources to upgrade their service with high-definition reception and faster internet speeds. By 2019, its cable TV footprint had grown to 194,000 subscribers.[927] After Shentel sold its wireless business to T-Mobile in 2020, it offered Glo Fiber service in the Winchester and Harrisonburg markets. The company claimed its fiber optic cable brought the internet to customers at faster, more reliable speeds than Comcast's Xfinity product.[928]

Federal Government: More Installations Arrive in Region

After World War II, the U.S. Government's presence in the Northern Valley expanded at an accelerated pace, most notably in the Eastern Panhandle. Federal installations diversified the region's economic base and brought with them high-paying jobs with excellent benefits. In 2019, the average salary of federal workers was $81,900 in Berkeley County and $110,865 in Jefferson County, twice that paid to the region's private-sector workers.[929]

The region's largest federal employer was the Newton D. Baker Army General Hospital in Martinsburg, which served veterans throughout the four-state region. Built to care for wounded soldiers during the Second World War, in 1946 it became part of the Veterans Administration.[930] In 1984, the original hospital was replaced with a six-story facility, in which 1,500 employees ran a 69-bed medical center, a 1,178-bed nursing home and a 312-bed domiciliary.[931] In 1960, the federal government purchased the vacant Storer College campus, located on a hill above Harpers Ferry and transferred the property to the National Park Service.[932] After the school's classrooms were repurposed into offices, the Harpers Ferry Center opened in 1970 to provide the parks with interpretive services for their exhibits.[933]

Because the United States Cavalry no longer needed horses in combat situations after World War II, ownership of the 3,100-acre Remount Depot in eastern Warren County changed several times. In 1948, Congress transferred it to the U.S. Department of Agriculture, which redeveloped it as the Front Royal Beef Cattle Research Center.[934] After the Smithsonian Institute purchased the site in 1973, its scientists studied endangered species at what became the Conservation Biology Institute.[935] The following year, the U.S. Customs Service relocated its narcotic detection dog training operation from San Antonio to the nearby 300-acre site that the Army's Quartermaster K-9 Corps once used to train dogs.[936]

In 1959 in eastern Clarke County, the U.S. Bureau of Mines excavated a network of tunnels and underground rooms at Mount Weather to shelter high-ranking federal officials in the event of a nuclear attack on Washington.[937] In 1979, the Federal Emergency Management Agency (FEMA) established training facilities at the complex, which later became an emergency response operations center during disasters.[938] After the 9/11 terrorist attacks in 2001, FEMA became part of the U.S. Department of Homeland Security. Three years later, its 300-employee information technology division moved off Mount Weather to leased space in the former VDO-Yazaki factory in Fort Collier Industrial Park in Frederick County.[939] In 2007, the unit relocated several miles north to a $28 million, 125,000-square-foot office building on U.S. 11.[940] By 2019, FEMA's 600-person staff at its renamed Disaster Operations Center directed the agency's responses to floods, hurricanes and tornadoes.[941]

In 1976, the Middle East Division of the Army Corps of Engineers moved its rear echelon unit from Washington, D.C. into the vacant J. Schoeneman men's clothing factory in Winchester Industrial Park.[942] Working on behalf of its Saudi Arabian headquarters, the local unit awarded design contracts for construction projects in that part of the world. In 2009, the renamed Transatlantic Division moved its 400 civilian and 50 military personnel into a new office building on Prince Frederick Drive in eastern Frederick County.[943]

From 1995 to 2010, the number of federal government jobs in the Eastern Panhandle grew by 45 percent, from 3,413 to 4,960, and accounted for 10 percent of all jobs in Berkeley and Jefferson counties.[944] Those figures did not include numerous private sector employees of firms that provided contractual services to the federal agencies. U.S. Senator Robert C. Byrd from West Virginia brought many of those jobs to the Eastern Panhandle. Serving either as chairman or minority leader of the Senate Appropriations Committee for 20 years, he secured funds to locate eight federal installations in the Eastern Panhandle. Responding to critics who labeled him a pork barrel politician, Byrd argued that moving them saved taxpayers money, because they were in a less-expensive area, yet remained close to Washington, D.C. And decentralizing federal operations away from the nation's capital took on greater importance after the 9/11 terrorist attacks.

As a junior senator, it took Byrd 15 years to locate the Appalachian Fruit Station Center in Jefferson County, because opponents argued the research should be conducted at an existing Virginia Tech site.[945] But in 1975, Byrd finally secured a $7.5 million Congressional appropriation for the center's construction near Kearneysville.[946] As he gained committee seniority, Byrd 's projects moved more rapidly through Congress. In 1982, he helped the Internal Revenue Service consolidate 700 employees at four Berkeley County offices into a new building in Liberty Business Park, located off Route 9 at the Jefferson County border.[947] In the early 1990s, Byrd brought the National Tracing Center of the Bureau of Alcohol, Tobacco, Firearms and Explosives to Spring Mills Business Park in northern Berkeley County.[948] As work transferred from other branches, the ATF's local payroll grew to 620 federal and contractor employees in 2016.[949]

In 1990, Byrd convinced the U.S. Coast Guard that it could save money by relocating a 400-person computer center from Governor's Island in costly New York City to the Spring Mills Business Park. In 2008, he sponsored a $12 million Congressional appropriation that centralized the Coast Guard's 17 regional centers managing its Mariner Licensing and Documentation System. As a result, 400 workers moved into a new office building on Route 9, north of downtown Martinsburg.[950]

Byrd also brought federal jobs to the Shepherdstown area. In 1997, he secured a $143 million appropriation for construction of the U.S. Fish and Wildlife Service's National Conservation Training Center. One hundred fifty employees from several agencies and private contracting firms worked in a building high above the Potomac River.[951] At Byrd's urging, the U.S. Office of Personnel Management in 1998 relocated its Eastern Management Development Center from Lancaster, Pennsylvania, to a newly built Clarion hotel in Shepherdstown. Owned by several area businessmen, it served as an off-site training center for mid-level federal employees.[952] In 2005, Byrd secured a $122 million appropriation for a U.S. Customs and Border Protection shooting range in eastern Jefferson County.[953] Three years later, he convinced the Department of Veterans Affairs to build a 150-employee, $32 million regional data center at the Martinsburg VA Medical Center.[954]

In 2015, the Eastern Management Development Center was moved from Shepherdstown to Washington, D.C., to be closer to where most federal employees worked.[955] Two years later, in a call center at the Clarion hotel site, Veteran Affairs Administration employees answered questions and took complaints from veterans.[956] Initiated by President Donald Trump, the program was labeled a White House Veterans Hotline, although calls never reached Pennsylvania Avenue.[957]

The Virginia portion of the Northern Valley benefited from Congressman Frank Wolf's seat on the House Committee on Appropriations. A proponent of telecommuting to reduce traffic congestion, he secured a $5 million appropriation for the General Services Administration (GSA) to manage an Interagency Telecommuting Pilot Program. As a result, the Shenandoah Valley Telecommuting Center opened in 1993 on Winchester's pedestrian mall, but after six months, its workstations were only 10 percent occupied.[958] Nevertheless, another center opened in Ranson in 1997, but as high-speed internet service became available at their residences, many federal employees opted to telework from home, rather than at a center. GSA ended the telecommuting program in 2011.[959]

In 2004, Wolf announced that an FBI Central Records Complex would come to Frederick County, along with 500 to 700 federal jobs.[960] It would serve as a repository for paper documents kept at 200 separate FBI locations throughout the United States. An interim center opened in the former Jouan SA centrifuge plant, south of Winchester.[961] In 2007, Wolf raised the FBI's potential local job count to 1,350, but due to the Great Recession, GSA failed to issue a contract for a permanent building.[962] The records center became more certain in 2016, when GSA paid $4.75 million for 60 acres on U.S. 50, east of Winchester. Four years later, a 265,000-square-foot, $135 million building housed 450 FBI workers who answered freedom of information inquiries from the media and the public.[963] Another 500 workers remained at the Jouan site.

CHAPTER 8

POSTSCRIPT

What about the "and Beyond" in the book's title? It references the growing economic relationship between the Northern Valley and the metro Washington, D.C. area. Interstates and improved east-west state roads have brought the two regions closer together. As private-sector jobs—many at federal contracting firms—move into Loudoun and Fauquier counties, expect more commuters to relocate into the lower cost-of-living Northern Valley. When they retire, numerous federal government workers will move west of the Blue Ridge for the same reason, and to enjoy a less stressful and better quality of life. Both groups will drive the Northern Valley's need for additional retail, restaurant, entertainment, recreational and health care offerings.

As population pressures increase, more of the region's agricultural land will be developed into housing, a trend that started in the late 1980s. To keep taxes low and make necessary infrastructure investments, local governments will be challenged to balance residential growth with commercial development that adds to the tax base, but requires fewer public services.

The sign of a vibrant region is its ability to adapt to economic change. At the beginning of the twentieth century, when wheat prices softened and Midwest and Great Plains harvests increased, Northern Valley farmers turned to orcharding. With the livestock market experiencing a similar fate, farmers switched from raising beef to dairying.

When the woolen mills closed after World War II, the region's leaders opened industrial parks to attract new businesses. Economic developers used

Interstate 81's arrival to bring corporate America's factories and warehouses to the Northern Valley. When the agriculture sector declined toward the end of the twentieth century, farmers and orchardists sold their land for residential and commercial development needed to accommodate a rapidly expanding population.

In recent years, the Northern Valley has benefited from a diverse economy that includes manufacturing, warehousing, agriculture, mining, tourism and the presence of federal installations. But as technological change disrupts many sectors of the American economy, the region's workforce must be skilled in reading, math, interpersonal communications and critical thinking to meet those challenges.

Besides a skilled workforce, the Northern Valley's current and future needs include making broadband access universal, investing in transportation networks, addressing environmental and climate change issues, maintaining a diversified economy, developing affordable housing and attracting high-paying jobs. And as population pressures increase, the demand for housing must be balanced against smart growth strategies to limit congestion and protect the region's rural heritage. For 300 years, the Northern Valley has adapted to changing economic conditions. Its leaders look to continue that legacy in the twenty-first century.

Endnotes

Chapter 1

1. Harold Underwood Faulkner, *American Economic History*, 7th *Edition* (New York, NY: Harper & Brothers Publishers, 1954), 59.
2. Joyce Hakim, *A History of US: Making Thirteen Colonies, 1600-1840, Book Two* (New York, NY: Oxford University Press, 1993), 119.
3. Samuel Kercheval, A History of the Valley of Virginia, Fourth Edition, originally published in 1833 (Strasburg, VA: Shenandoah Publishing House, reprinted 1925), 269.
4. Faulkner, *American Economic History*, 87.
5. census.gov, U.S. Census Bureau, "Population in the Colonial and Continental Periods," 9.
6. Faulkner, *American Economic History*, 83.
7. Ibid., 79.
8. Ibid., 59.
9. Ibid., 65.
10. Ibid., 66.
11. Ibid., 67.
12. Ibid., 69.
13. Ibid., 108.
14. Ibid., 109.
15. Ibid.
16. Ibid., 69.
17. Warren R. Hofstra, *The Planting of New Virginia* (Baltimore, MD: Johns Hopkins University Press, 2004), 5.
18. Ibid., 7.
19. Warren R. Hofstra, "The Colonial Road," in Hofstra and Karl Raitz, *The Great Valley Road of Virginia* (Charlottesville, VA: University of Virginia Press, 2010), 88.
20. Ibid.
21. Chester Raymond Young, "The Effects of the French and Indian War on Civilian Life in the Frontier Counties of Virginia" (PhD thesis, Nashville, TN: Vanderbilt University, 1969), 2, and Robert D. Mitchell, *Commercialism and Frontier: Perspectives on the Early Shenandoah Valley* (Charlottesville, VA: University of Virginia Press, 1977), 21.
22. Hofstra, "The Colonial Road," 79, and Thomas Kemp Cartmell, *Shenandoah Valley Pioneers and Their Descendants* (Winchester, VA: The Eddy Press Corporation, 1909), 269.
23. J. E. Norris, *History of the Lower Shenandoah Valley: Counties of Frederick, Berkeley, Jefferson and Clarke, Volume 1* (Baltimore, MD: Genealogical Publishing Company, 1923), 370.
24. Ibid.
25. Mitchell, *Commercialism and Frontier*, 35 and 149.
26. Warren R. Hofstra, *A Separate Place: The Formation of Clarke County, Virginia* (Madison WI: Madison House Publishers, 1986), 32.
27. legendsofamerica.com, Legends of America, Kathy Weiser-Alexa;nder, "The Great Wagon Road to the East," 2018.

[28] lva.virginia.gov, Library of Virginia, Dictionary of Virginia Biography, "Thomas Fairfax, Sixth Baron Fairfax of Cameron."

[29] Hofstra, *A Separate Place*, 3.

[30] Ibid. and xiv.

[31] Stuart E. Brown Jr., *Virginia Baron: The Story of Thomas, 6th Lord Fairfax* (Berryville, VA: Chesapeake Book Co., 1965), 56.

[32] Hofstra, *A Separate Place*, 4 and 6.

[33] Ibid., 5.

[34] Brown Jr., *Virginia Baron*, 95.

[35] Ibid.

[36] Ibid.

[37] Norris, *History of the Lower Shenandoah Valley*, 61.

[38] Brown Jr., *Virginia Baron*, 101 and 119.

[39] Ibid., 60.

[40] wvencyclopedia.org, e-WV, The West Virginia Encyclopedia, William B. Maxwell, "Washington's Western Lands," 11-13-2013.

[41] loc.gov, Library of Congress, Edward Redmond, "Washington as Land Speculator."

[42] Mitchell, *Commercialism and Frontier*, 37.

[43] Hofstra, *The Planting of New Virginia*, 32 and 33.

[44] Hofstra, *A Separate Place*, 6.

[45] Mitchell, *Commercialism and Frontier*, 56.

[46] Kenneth E. Koons and Warren R. Hofstra, "Introduction: The World Wheat Made," in Koons and Hofstra, editors, *After the Backcountry, Rural Life in the Great Valley of Virginia 1800-1900* (Knoxville, TN: University of Tennessee Press, 2000), xviii.

[47] Norris, *History of the Lower Shenandoah Valley*, 70.

[48] Hofstra, *A Separate Place*, 7, and vagenweb.org, VAGenWeb Project, Hening's Statutes at Large, "Laws of Virginia, February 1752 – 25th George II, Chapter XVII," 236.

[49] Frederic Morton, *The Story of Winchester in Virginia* (Strasburg, VA: Shenandoah Publishing House, 1925), 97, and Warren R. Hofstra and Robert D. Mitchell, "Town and Country in Backcountry Virginia: Winchester and the Shenandoah Valley, 1730-1800," published in The Journal of Southern History (Athens, GA: Southern Historical Association, November 1993), 632.

[50] Hofstra, *A Separate Place*, 7.

[51] John W. Wayland, *The Shenandoah Valley in History and Literature* (Harrisonburg, VA: State Normal School, 1894), 8.

[52] Hofstra, *The Planting of New Virginia*, 224.

[53] Ibid., 225.

[54] Ibid., 247.

[55] Morton, *The Story of Winchester in Virginia*, 54.

[56] Faulkner, *American Economic History*, 76.

[57] Ibid., 77.

[58] Hofstra, *The Planting of New Virginia*, 26.

[59] Cartmell, *Shenandoah Valley Pioneers*, 50.

[60] Hofstra, "The Colonial Road," 93.

[61] Karl Raitz, "The Lay of the Land," in Hofstra and Raitz, *The Great Valley Road of Virginia*, 33.

[62] Mitchell, *Commercialism and Frontier*, 151 and 153.

[63] Ibid.

[64] Ibid.

[65] Ibid., 152.

[66] perrinhistory.net, Corrine Hanna Diller, "A New Look at an Old Map, The First Whites on the Upper Potomac" (A Perrin History, Richard Perrin Day, 2018), and familysearch.org, "Samuel Taylor."

[67] training.fws.gov, National Conservation Training Center, NCTC Cultural History, "The Swearingens Become Prominent Under Lord Fairfax Rule," 2-21-2014.

[68] Road sign near Shepherdstown, "Thomas Swearingen's Ferry and Pack Horse Ford," and Norris, *History of the Lower Shenandoah Valley*, 371, and jeffersoncountyhlc.org, Paula S. Reed & Associates, August 2009, "Bellevue."

[69] local.townsquarepublications.com, Town Square Publications, Front Royal-Warren County Chamber of Commerce, "Heritage."

[70] founders.archives.gov, National Archives, Founders Online, "September 1784."

[71] Cartmell, *Shenandoah Valley Pioneers*, 66 and 67.

[72] Hofstra, "The Colonial Road," 80, and stonesentinels.com, "Light's Ford and Lemen's Ferry."

[73] Wood, *Documented History of Martinsburg and Berkeley County, Volume II*, 6 and 11.

[74] townofhancock.org, Town of Hancock, Maryland. "History."

[75] David T. Gilbert, *Waterpower: Mills, Factories, Machines & Floods at Harpers Ferry, West Virginia, 1762-1991* (Harpers Ferry, WV: Harpers Ferry Historical Association, 1999), 18.

[76] Ibid.

[77] nps.gov, National Park Service, Allison A. Crosbie and Andrew S. Lee, "Cultural Landscape Report for the United States Armory and Potomac Riverfront" (Boston, MA: Olmstead Center for Landscape Preservation, 2009).

[78] Robert D. Mitchell, "From the Ground Up: Space, Place and Diversity in Frontier Studies," in Michael J. Puglisi, editor, *Diversity and Accommodation* (Knoxville, TN: University of Tennessee Press, 1997), 40.

[79] nedhector.com, Ben Rohrbeck, "Teamsters, Wagon Drivers, The Conestoga Wagon" (NT Lewis, 2004).

[80] Mitchell, *Commercialism and Frontier*, 158.

[81] Young, "The Effects of the French and Indian War on Civilian Life," 22.

[82] frenchandindianwarfoundation.org, Norman L. Baker, "Fort Loudoun as Virginia's French and Indian War Command Center" (Winchester, VA: French and Indian War Foundation).

[83] Ibid., and Morton, *The Story of Winchester in Virginia*, 73.

[84] Hofstra, *The Planting of New Virginia*, 248.

[85] Mitchell, *Commercialism and Frontier*, 145.

[86] Faulkner, *American Economic History*, 103.

[87] Mitchell, *Commercialism and Frontier*, 135, 136 and 59.

[88] Ibid., 139 and 144.

[89] Ibid.

[90] Koons and Hofstra, "Introduction: The World Wheat Made" in *After the Backcountry*, xviii.

[91] Ibid., 139.

[92] Hofstra, *A Separate Place, Virginia*, 9.

[93] Mitchell, *Commercialism and Frontier*, 179.

[94] Ibid., 162.

[95] Ibid., 179.

[96] Ibid.

[97] Ibid., 164.

[98] projects.cah.ucf.edu, Jason Bernstein, "Osnaburg: A Sign of Wealth?" (Orlando, FL: University of Central Florida History Department).

[99] Mitchell, *Commercialism and Frontier*, 163.

[100] Ibid., 163 and 164.

[101] Ibid.

[102] Ibid.

[103] Ibid.

[104] Faulkner, *American Economic History*, 63.

[105] core.ac.uk, CORE, The Open University, Paul Sharp, "The Long American Grain Invasion of Britain: Market Integration and the Wheat Trade Between North America and Britain From the Eighteenth Century" (University of Copenhagen, Denmark, 9-26-2008), 13.

[106] Warren Hofstra and Clarence R. Grier, "Farm to Mill to Market: Historical Archeology of an Emerging Grain Economy in the Shenandoah Valley," in *After the Backcountry*, 51.

[107] Don C. Wood, *Documented History of Martinsburg and Berkeley County, Volume I* (Martinsburg, WV: Berkeley County Historical Society, 2004), 179.

[108] Ibid., 208.

[109] mountvernon.org, George Washington's Mount Vernon, "Gristmill Glossary of Terms."

[110] Wood, *Documented History of Martinsburg and Berkeley County, Volume I*, 208.

[111] Mitchell, *Commercialism and Frontier*, 144.

[112] Wood, *Documented History of Martinsburg and Berkeley County, Volume I*, 222.

[113] wvculture.org, West Virginia Department of Arts, Culture and History, National Register of Historic Places Nomination Form, Clifford M. Lewis, "Thomas Shepherd's Gristmill," 10-9-1970.

[114] U.S. Department of Interior, National Register of Historic Places Inventory, "Springdale Mill Complex," National Historic Landmarks Commission staff, 5-10-1982.

[115] Kathleen Bruce, *Virginia Iron Manufacturers in the Slave Era* (New York, NY: Century Co., 1931), 21.

[116] Ibid.

[117] Norman H. Scott, *Shenandoah Iron* (Verona, VA: self-published, 2017), 45 and 47.

[118] steelmuseum.org, "The American Iron Industry: 1800-1860" (Coatesville, PA: The National Iron & Steel Heritage Museum), 15.

[119] vestals.us, Minnie Speer Boone, "Our Family Heritage: William Vestal Jr." (New York, NY: The American Historical Company, Inc., 1936).

[120] wvencyclopedia.org, e-WV, The West Virginia Encyclopedia, Lee R. Maddex, "Shenandoah Bloomery," 10-20-2010.

[121] Scott, *Shenandoah Iron*, 7.

[122] ancestry.com, Message Boards, "John Vestal."

[123] Ibid., and Joint Committee of Hopewell Friends and John Wayland, *Hopewell Friends History, 1734 to 1934, Frederick County, Virginia* (Strasburg, VA: Shenandoah Publishing House, 1936), 167, and georgewashingtoncave.org, George Washington Masonic Cave, Jason Williams, "Business is Blooming and Blooming is Business," 11-26-2018.

[124] Scott, *Shenandoah Iron*, 43 and 63

[125] Susan Dieffanbach, *Coldwell Iron Furnace: Pennsylvania Trail of History Guide* (Mechanicsville, PA: Stackpole Books, 2003).

[126] Ibid.

[127] Ibid.

[128] Scott, *Shenandoah Iron*, 67.

[129] Ibid., 69.

[130] Ibid.

[131] Ibid.

[132] Ibid., 62

[133] angelfire.com, Hal Sharpe, The Civil War in the Shenandoah Valley, "The Early Iron Industry in the Shenandoah Valley."

[134] David Curtis Skaggs, "John Semple and the Development of the Potomac Valley, 1750-1773," in The Virginia Magazine's History and Bibliography (Richmond, VA: Virginia Historical Society, July 1984), 282.

[135] Ibid.

[136] Ibid.

[137] Ibid., 283.

[138] Ibid., 295.

[139] William D. Theriault, *History of Eastern Jefferson County of West Virginia* (Hagerstown, MD: self-published, 2009), 39.

[140] Skaggs, "John Semple," 295.

[141] newtownhistorycenter.org, Newtown History Center, "Beginnings, 1732-1783."

[142] dhr.virginia.org, Virginia Department of Historic Resources, National Register of Historic Places Nomination Form, Helen Lee Fletcher, "Old Forge Farm," 9-11-03, and The Virginia Magazine of History and Biography, Roger W. Moss Jr., "Isaac Zane Jr., a Quaker for the Times" (Richmond, VA: Virginia Historical Society, July 1969), 292.

[143] Whitfield Jenks Bell Jr., *Patriot-Improvers, 1743-1768* (Philadelphia, PA: American Philosophical Society, 1997), 287.

[144] Cartmell, *Shenandoah Valley Pioneers*, 437.

[145] Ibid.

[146] Rebecca A. Ebert and Teresa Lazazzera, *Frederick County, Virginia: From the Frontier to the Future* (Norfolk, VA: Donning Company, 1988), 35, and Garland R. Quarles, *Some Worthy Lives*, "Isaac Zane Jr." (Winchester, VA: Winchester-Frederick County Historical Society, 1988), 256.

[147] Moss Jr., "Isaac Zane Jr.," 295.

[148] Joint Committee and Wayland, *Hopewell Friends History*, 167, and Scott, *Shenandoah Iron*, 86.

[149] Ibid.

[150] John W. Wayland, *A History of Shenandoah County, Virginia* (Strasburg, VA: Shenandoah Publishing House, Inc., 1969, originally published in 1927), and jeffersoncountyhlc.org, William D, Theriault, "History of Eastern Jefferson County, The Second Wave of Settlement, 1760-1775" (Charles Town, WV: Jefferson County Historic Landmarks Commission, 2009).

[151] Wood, *Documented History of Martinsburg and Berkeley County, Volume II*, 52, and dhr.virginia.org, Virginia Department of Historic Resources, National Register of Historic Places Registration Form, Jennifer Hugman, "Millbank," 2014.

[152] bloomerysweetshine.com, "History of Bloomery SweetShine."

[153] farmanddairy.com, Sam Moore, "The Evolution of the Sawmill Industry" (Salem, OH: Farm and Dairy magazine, 9-7-2017).

[154] Mitchell, *Commercialism and Frontier*, 147.

[155] jeffersoncountyhlc.org, Nomination Form, "Beeler's Mill Water Mill" (Charles Town, WV: Jefferson County Historic Landmarks Commission, May 2015).

[156] Conrad C. Hammann, *History of Halltown Paperboard Company* (Shepherdstown, WV: self-published, 1984), 5.

[157] Wilbur S. Johnston, *Weaving a Common Thread* (Winchester, VA: Winchester-Frederick County Historical Society, 1980), 40.

[158] Ibid., 20.

Chapter 2

[1] Harold Underwood Faulkner, *American Economic History*, 7th Ed. (New York, NY: Harper and Brothers Publishers, 1954), 115.

[2] John Steele Gordon, *An Empire of Wealth: The Epic History of American Economic Power* (New York, NY: Harper Collins Publishers, 2004), 54, and history.com, History Channel, "Townsend Acts."

[3] Robert D. Mitchell, *Commercialism and Frontier: Perspectives on the Early Shenandoah Valley* (Charlottesville, VA: University of Virginia Press, 1977), 174 and 184.

[4] A. D. Kenamond, *Prominent Men of Shepherdstown During its First 100 Years* (Charles Town, WV: Jefferson County Historical Society, 1963).

[5] Bruce A. Ragsdale, *A Planters' Republic: The Search for Economic Independence in Revolutionary Virginia* (Madison, WI: Madison House Publishers), 138.

[6] Joint Committee of Hopewell Friends and John W. Wayland, *Hopewell Friends History, 1734 to 1934* (Strasburg, VA: Shenandoah Publishing House, 1936), 167.

[7] Faulkner, *American Economic History*, 169.

[8] Gordon, *An Empire of Wealth*, 68.

[9] Faulkner, *American Economic History*, 138.

[10] Ibid., 153.

[11] loc.gov, Library of Congress, Primary Documents in American History, "Residence Act."

[12] Faulkner, *American Economic History*, 154.

[13] Warren R. Hofstra, *The Planting of New Virginia* (Baltimore and London: Johns Hopkins University Press, 2004), 283.

[14] Faulkner, *American Economic History*, 144.

[15] Gordon, *An Empire of Wealth*, 6.

[16] Hofstra, *The Planting of New Virginia*, 283.

[17] Faulkner, *American Economic History*, 144 and 145.

[18] Gordon, *An Empire of Wealth*, 62, and britannica.com, "Commerce Clause, United States Constitution."

[19] Faulkner, *American Economic History*, 153.

[20] Jacob E. Cooke, "Tench Coxe and Alexander Hamilton and Encouragement of American Manufacturing" (Williamsburg, VA: William and Mary College Quarterly, 1975).

[21] Faulkner, *American Economic History*, 246.

[22] Gordon, *An Empire of Wealth*, 95, and Faulkner, *American Economic History*, 224 and 248.

[23] Ibid.

[24] Ibid., 164.

[25] Ibid., and census.gov, U.S. Census Bureau, First Census and Fifth Census.

[26] Faulkner, *American Economic History*, 179.

[27] Ibid., 221.

[28] Ibid., 222

[29] Ibid., and Kenneth W. Keller, "The Wheat Trade on the Upper Potomac, 1800-1860," in Kenneth E. Koons and Warren R. Hofstra, editors, *After the Backcountry, Rural Life in the Great Valley of Virginia, 1800-1900* (Knoxville, TN: University of Tennessee Press, 2000), 25.

[30] britainexpress.com, Britain Express, David Ross, "The Corn Laws."

[31] Ibid.

[32] Faulkner, *American Economic History*, 164.

[33] Alan Greenspan and Adrian Wooldridge, *Capitalism in America, A History* (New York, NY: Penguin Press, 2018), 41.

[34] Ibid.

[35] econ-server.umd.edu, John Joseph Wallis, "American Government and Promotion of

Economic Development in the National Era, 1790 to 1860" (College Park, MD: Department of Economics, University of Maryland, January 2004).

36 Ibid.

37 lva.virginia.gov, Library of Virginia, "The Internal Improvement Movement in Virginia."

38 Ibid.

39 Ibid.

40 Faulkner, *American Economic History*, 268.

41 eriecanalimpacts.weebly.com, Impact of the Erie Canal, "Erie Canal, How Much Did It Cost."

42 Faulkner, *American Economic History*, 270.

43 Kirk Reynolds and Dave Oroszi, *Baltimore and Ohio Railroad* (Minneapolis, MN: Voyageur Press, 2008), 15.

44 Warren R. Hofstra, *A Separate Place: The Formation of Clarke County, Virginia* (Madison WI: Madison House Publishers, 1986), 67.

45 explorepahistory.com, Stories from PA History, "Crossing the Alleghenies: Early Turnpikes."

46 Faulkner, American Economic History, 263.

47 interestingengineering.com, Interesting Engineering, Christopher McFadden, "John Loudon McAdam: The Father of the Modern Road," 10-26-2017.

48 britannica.com, Encyclopedia Britannica, "Macadam Road Construction."

49 eh.net, Economic History Association, Daniel B. Klein and John Majewski, "Turnpikes and Toll Roads in Nineteenth Century America" (Santa Barbara, CA: University of California, 2-10-2008).

50 John W. Wayland, *A History of Shenandoah County, Virginia* (Strasburg, VA: Shenandoah Publishing House, Inc., 1969), 262.

51 Kenneth W. Keller, "The Best Thoroughfare in the South," in Hofstra and Raitz, editors, *The Great Valley Road of Virginia* (Charlottesville, VA and London: University of Virginia Press, 2010), 159, and Wayland, *A History of Shenandoah County, Virginia*, 262.

52 mdcoveredbridges.com, Maryland Covered Bridges, "Harpers Ferry Covered Bridge."

53 Ibid.

54 Ibid., "Covered Bridge at Shepherdstown."

55 Mike High, *The C&O Canal Companion: A Journal through Potomac History* (Baltimore, MD: Johns Hopkins University Press, 2015), 265, and Atlantic Reporter, Vol. 77 (St. Paul, MN: West Publishing Co.), 1124, and *Laws of Maryland Made and Passed at a Session of Assembly* (Annapolis, MD: Jehu Chandler, Printer, 1816), 30.

56 luray.net, "Area Attractions, White House Bridge."

57 Acts of General Assembly of Virginia, 1892 (Richmond, VA: Richard Samuel Shepherd, printer).

58 Thomas D. Gold, *History of Clarke County, Virginia* (Berryville, VA: self-published, 1914), 24.

59 dhr.virginia.gov, Virginia Department of Historic Resources, National Register of Historic Places Registration Form, Maral S. Kalbian, "Riverton Historic District," 8-14-2000.

60 nps.gov, National Park Service, "George Washington's Influence on the C&O Canal."

61 history.org, Andrew G. Gardner, "How Did Washington Make His Millions?" (Williamsburg, VA: Colonial Williamsburg Journal, Winter 2013).

62 nps.gov, National Park Service, Great Falls Park Virginia, "The Patowmack Canal."

63 mountvernon.org, George Washington's Mount Vernon, "Mount Vernon Conference."

64 Ibid, and Douglas R. Littlefield, "The Patowmack Company: A Misadventure in Financing an Early American Internal Improvement Project" (Cambridge MA: Harvard University, The Business History Review, Winter 1984), 571.

65 nps.gov, National Park Service, Great Falls Park Virginia, "The Patowmack Canal."

66 cecildaily.com, Cecil Whig, Erika Quesenbery Sturgill, "Robert Fulton You Know, But Cecil's James Rumsey? (Greeneville, TN: Adams Publishing Company, 12-29-2018).

67 mountvernon.org, George Washington's Mount Vernon, "The Potomac Company."

68 nps.gov, National Park Service, Great Falls Park Virginia, "The Patowmack Canal."

69 Ibid.

70 gfhs.org, Great Falls Historical Society, Great Falls, VA, "NPS History of the Great Falls Park."

71 Wayland, *A History of Shenandoah County, Virginia*, 267.

72 *Acts of Various States in Relation to the Chesapeake and Ohio Canal Company* (Washington, D.C.: Gales and Seaton, 1828), 108.

73 washingtonheritagetrail.com, Washington Heritage Trail, "Shenandoah Canal."

74 nps.gov, National Park Service, "Virginius Island Trail Guide."

75 *Twenty-Fourth Annual Report of the Board of Public Works to the General Assembly of Virginia*, November 1, 1839, 19.

76 Ibid.

77 Ibid.

78 John W. Wayland, *A History of Rockingham County, Virginia* (Dayton, VA: Ruebush-Elkins Company, 1912), 419.

79 census.gov, U.S. Census Bureau, First Census and Fifth Census.

80 Hofstra, *A Separate Place*, 10.

81 J. E. Norris, *History of the Lower Shenandoah Valley: Counties of Frederick, Berkeley, Jefferson and Clarke, Volume 1* (Baltimore, MD: Genealogical Publishing Company, 1923), 483.

82 Maral S. Kalbian, *Clarke County, Images of America* (Charleston, SC: Arcadia Publishing, 2011), 57.

83 dhr.virginia.gov, Virginia Department of Historic Resources, National Register of Historic Places Nomination Form, Maral S. Kalbian, "Millwood Historic District," 7-22-05.

84 Ibid.

85 dhr.virginia.gov, Virginia Department of Historic Resources, Maral S. Kalbian, "Clarke County Reconnaissance Survey, 1989," 61.

86 encyclopediavirginia.org, Burwell, Nathaniel (1750-1814).

87 Lorraine Rehbock, "Printing a New Future for Lower Clarke Mill" (Winchester Star, 6-30-1998), B1.

88 E. R. R. Green, editor, *Essays in Scotch-Irish History* (Belfast, IRL: Ulster Historical Foundation, 1969), 75, and Warren R. Hofstra, "The Colonial Road," in Hofstra and Raitz, editors, *The Great Valley Road of Virginia*, 99.

89 u-s-history.com, United States History, "The Wilderness Road."

90 Ibid.

91 Don Worthington, "Westward Bound: Exhibit Depicts Virginian's Exit from Eden" (Winchester Star, 1-13-1995), C6.

92 Hofstra, *The Planting of New Virginia*, 330, and monticello.org, The Jefferson Monticello, "Currency."

93 Mitchell, *Commercialism and Frontier*, 189.

94 Kalbian, "Clarke County Reconnaissance Survey, 1989," 59.

95 Mitchell, *Commercialism and Frontier*, 189 and 190.

96 Norris, *History of the Lower Shenandoah Valley*, 283.

97 lva.virginia.gov, Library of Virginia, "Tithables."

98 Norris, *History of the Lower Shenandoah Valley*, 171.

99 Ibid.

100 Don C. Wood, *Documented History of Martinsburg and Berkeley County, Volume I* (Martinsburg, WV: Berkeley County Historical Society, 2004), 73.

101 Norris, *History of the Lower Shenandoah Valley*, 148.

102 Ibid., 158-159.

103 Ibid.

104 Ibid., 264.

105 Wood, *Documented History of Martinsburg and Berkeley County, Volume 1*, 51.

106 Frederic Morton, *The Story of Winchester in Virginia* (Strasburg, VA: Shenandoah Publishing House, 1925), 137.

107 Norris, *History of the Lower Shenandoah Valley*, 171.

108 Thomas Kemp Cartmell, *Shenandoah Valley Pioneers and Their Descendants* (Winchester, VA: The Eddy Press Corporation, 1909), 30.

109 Wayland, *A History of Shenandoah County, Virginia*, 133.

[110] Ibid.

[111] Mitchell, *Commercialism and Frontier*, 154.

[112] Walter A. Friedman, *Birth of a Salesman: The Transformation of Selling in America* (Cambridge MA: Harvard University Press, 2005).

[113] Joseph T. Rainer, "Commercial Scythians in the Great Valley of Virginia: Yankee Peddlers' Trade Connections to Antebellum Virginia," in Koons and Hofstra, *After the Backcountry*, 62 and 72.

[114] connectionnewspapers.com, The Connection to Your Community, Michael K. Bohn, "Old Town History: Bank of Alexandria."

[115] alexandriava.gov, City of Alexandria, Virginia, "A Brief History of Alexandria," 8-25-2017, and Office of Historic Alexandria, "Alexandria Waterfront History," 2010.

[116] ravensworthstory.org, "The Story of Ravensworth: Little River Turnpike."

[117] route50.org, Route 50 Coalition, "Geographical and Historical Background: The Piedmont."

[118] alexandriava.gov, "A Brief History of Alexandria," 8-25-2017.

[119] jeffersonpatterson.wordpress.com, Maryland History by the Object, Patricia Samford, "The Port of Baltimore."

[120] Ibid.

[121] baltimoreindustrytours.com, Baltimore Industry Tours, "Cotton Mills of Jones Falls."

[122] mht.maryland.gov, Maryland Historical Trust, National Register of Historic Places Nomination Form, Priscilla M. Thompson, "Fells Point Historic District," 11-1985.

[123] Hofstra, *The Planting of New Virginia*, 14.

[124] Koons and Hofstra, "Introduction: The World Wheat Made" in Koons and Hofstra, *After the Backcountry*, xix.

[125] broomshop.com, Warren Olney, "History of Early American Brooms."

[126] core.ac.uk, Paul Sharp, "The Long American Grain Invasion of Britain: Market Integration and the Wheat Trade Between North America and Britain From the Eighteenth Century" (University of Copenhagen, DK, 9-26,2008), 7.

[127] Brinley Thomas, "Feeding England During the Industrial Revolution: A View from the Celtic Fringe (Winter Park, FL: Agriculture History Society, January, 1982).

[128] D. B. Grigg, *Population Growth and Agrarian Change* (Cambridge, GB: Cambridge University Press, 1980), 168.

[129] Sharp, "The Long American Grain Invasion of Britain," 19.

[130] Ibid.

[131] Mitchell, *Commercialism and Frontier*, 174.

[132] Ibid.

[133] loudounhistory.org, History of Loudoun County, Virginia, "John Binns – Pioneer in Crop Improvement."

[134] Koons and Hofstra, "Introduction: The World Wheat Made" in Koons and Hofstra, *After the Backcountry*, xviii.

[135] Mitchell, *Commercialism and Frontier*, 175.

[136] census.gov, U.S. Census Bureau, Fourth Census, and William S. Rossiter, "The Adventure of Population Growth" (Journal of the American Statistical Association, March 1923).

[137] Thomas, "Feeding England During the Industrial Revolution," 357.

[138] U.S. Department of Agriculture, National Agriculture Statistics Service.

[139] Ibid.

[140] Mitchell, *Commercialism and Frontier*, 148.

[141] Ibid.

[142] Ibid.

[143] vtdigger.org, Mark Bushnell, "Then Again: Turkey Drives Were the 1800s Version of 'Farm to Table'" (Montpelier, VT: Vermont Journalism Trust, 12-20-2016).

[144] Ibid.

[145] Karl Raitz, "The Lay of the Land," in Hofstra and Raitz, editors, *The Great Valley Road of Virginia*, 42.

[146] Hofstra, *A Separate Place*, 28.

[147] Ibid.

[148] Ibid.

[149] Wayland, *A History of Shenandoah County, Virginia*, 274.

150 spoommiodatlantic.org, Robert Lundegard, "County and City Mills in Early American Flour Manufacture and Export," 4.

151 mountvernon.org, George Washington's Mount Vernon, "Ten Facts About the Gristmill."

152 Hofstra, *The Planting of New Virginia*, 307.

153 wvculture.org, West Virginia Department of Arts, Culture and History, Mary Johnson, "A Nineteenth-Century Mill Village: Virginius Island, 1800-1860."

154 Oliver Evans, *The Young Mill-Wright and Miller's Guide* (Philadelphia, PA: Lea & Blanchard, 1848), preface.

155 Gordon, *An Empire of Wealth*, 94.

156 dhr.virginia.gov, Virginia Department of Historic Resources, National Register of Historic Places Nomination Form, James C. Massey, "Stoner-Keller House and Mill," Fishers Hill, 9-25-2012.

157 Lundegard, "County and City Mills," 5.

158 Ibid., 9.

159 Ibid., 7.

160 Ibid., 6.

161 stlouisfed.org, St. Louis Federal Reserve Bank, Economic Data Series.

162 Ibid.

163 Mitchell, *Commercialism and Frontier*, 182.

164 millpictures.com, "Kline's Mill Frederick County," and Kenneth W. Keller, "From the Rhineland to the Virginia Frontier: Flax production as a Commercial Enterprise" (The Virginia Magazine of History and Biography, Vol. 95, No. 3, July 1990, Richmond, VA: Virginia Historical Society,), 506.

165 Cartmell, *Shenandoah Valley Pioneers*, 437.

166 Ibid.

167 David Curtis Skaggs, "John Semple and the Development of the Potomac Valley, 1750-1773" (Richmond, VA: The Virginia Magazine of History and Bibliography, Virginia Historical Society, July 1984), 285.

168 Ibid.

169 Ibid.

170 Roger W. Moss Jr., "Isaac Zane Jr., A Quaker for the Times" (Richmond, VA: The Virginia Magazine of History and Biography, Virginia Historical Society, July 1969), 300.

171 Ibid.

172 Linda McCarty, "It's Like Living History Here" (Winchester Star, 6-23-1999), 1.

173 dhr.virginia.gov, Virginia Department of Historic Resources, National Register of Historic Places Nomination Form, Helen Lee Fletcher, "Old Forge Farm, Zane's Furnace," 9-11-2003.

174 Brian Brehm, "Sarah Zane: The Name is Well Known, the Woman is Not" (Winchester Star, 9-11-2019).

175 H. E. Comstock, "The Redwell Ironworks" (Winston-Salem, NC: Journal of Early Southern Decorative Arts, Vol. 7, Issue 1, May 1981), 42.

176 dhr.virginia.gov, Virginia Department of Historic Resources, National Register of Historic Places Registration Form, J. Daniel Pezzoni and James R. Graves, "Redwell-Isabella Furnace Historic District," 3-4-2005.

177 Scott, *Shenandoah Iron*, 11.

178 Ibid.

179 Ibid.

180 Pezzoni and Graves, "Redwell-Isabella Furnace Historic District."

181 Comstock, "The Redwell Ironworks," 47.

182 Ibid., 48.

183 Wayland, *A History of Shenandoah County, Virginia*, 241.

184 sites.rootsweb.com, RootsWeb, "A Mayberry Family Timeline."

185 Scott, *Shenandoah Iron*, 129, and Wayland, *A History of Shenandoah County, Virginia*, 242.

186 mtnlaurel.com, Mason Cooper and Bob Zimmerman, "The Shenandoah Iron and Coal Company" (Basye, VA: The Mountain Laurel, April 1987).

187 patc.us, Potomac Appalachian Trail Club, Horace Andrew Keefer, "Recollections, Historical and Otherwise, Relating to Old Pine Grove Furnace."

188 Scott, *Shenandoah Iron*, 131.

189 vagenweb.org, Shenandoah County VAGenWeb Project, Tom Pierce, "The Blackford Iron Workers, 4-10-2008."

[190] Comstock, "The Redwell Ironworks," 39.

[191] theincline.com, MJ Slaby, "Pittsburgh's Iconic Blast Furnaces Were Named After Local Women. Here's Why" (Pittsburgh, PA: The Incline, 9-25-2018).

[192] shenandoahcountyhistoricalsociety.org, Shenandoah County Historical Society, Nancy B. Stewart, "The Presence of African Americans in the Shenandoah County Iron Industry," 2.

[193] J. P. Lesley, *Iron Manufacturers Guide to the Furnaces, Forges and Rolling Mills* (London, GB: John Wiley Publishers, 1859).

[194] Pezzoni and Graves, "Redwell-Isabella Furnace Historic District."

[195] Kathleen Bruce, *Virginia Iron Manufacturers in the Slave Era* (New York, NY: Century Co., 1931), 133.

[196] Scott, *Shenandoah Iron*, 137.

[197] Ibid.

[198] Wayland, *A History of Shenandoah County, Virginia*, 242, and Scott, *Shenandoah Iron*, 140 and 141.

[199] encyclopedia.com, "Leather and Leather Products Industry."

[200] Richard MacMaster, *The History of Hardy County, 1786-1986* (Salem, WV: Wadsworth Press, Inc., 1986), 288.

[201] Mitchell, *Commercialism and Frontier*, 206.

[202] Jefferson County Historical Society Magazine, "Rockland" (Charles Town, WV: December 1994), 142.

[203] Wayland, *A History of Shenandoah County, Virginia*, 129.

[204] Merritt Roe Smith, *Harpers Ferry Armory and the New Technology: The Challenge of Change* (Ithaca, NY: Cornell University Press, 2015).

[205] Linda McCarty, "Down in the Valley, Exploring the Foothills of Little North Mountain" (Winchester Star, 5-23-2001), A7.

[206] Cartmell, *Shenandoah Valley Pioneers*, 587.

[207] Kalbian, "Millwood Historic District," 7-22-05, and livingplaces.com, Edna Johnson and Kathryn Gettings Smith, "Front Royal Historic District," 2002.

[208] Kalbian, *Clarke County, Images of America*, 80, and Stuart E. Brown Jr., *Annals of Clarke County, Virginia, Vol. 1* (Berryville, VA: Virginia Book Company, 1983), 148.

[209] "It Is, In Its Situation, Very Delightful, Stephens City, Newtown" (Winchester Star, 10-4-2008), A7.

[210] Ibid.

[211] Wayland, *A History of Shenandoah County, Virginia*, 268.

[212] newtownhistorycenter.org, Newtown History Center, "Growth, 1789-1860."

[213] Ibid.

[214] Annette Jones, "The Foundation of Stephens City's Future: Recapturing its Heritage," (Winchester Star, 5-16-1998), B2.

[215] newtownhistorycenter.org, Newtown History Center, "Growth 1784-1860."

[216] nps.gov, National Park Service, Allison A. Crosbie and Andrew S. Lee, "Cultural Landscape Report for the United States Armory and Potomac Riverfront" (Boston, MA: Olmstead Center for Landscape Preservation, 2009), 16.

[217] Ibid.

[218] David T. Gilbert, *Waterpower: Mills, Factories, Machines & Floods at Harpers Ferry, West Virginia, 1762-1991* (Harpers Ferry, WV: Harpers Ferry Historical Association, 1999), 26.

[219] Ibid.

[220] Scott, *Shenandoah Iron*, 288.

[221] Crosbie and Lee, "Cultural Landscape Report for the United States Armory and Potomac Riverfront," 19.

[222] Ibid.

[223] nps.gov, National Park Service, Harpers Ferry National Historic Park, "John H. Hall."

[224] Gilbert, *Waterpower*, 40.

[225] Johnson, "A Nineteenth Century Mill Village."

[226] nps.gov, "John H. Hall."

[227] Ibid.

[228] Ibid.

[229] nps.gov, National Park Service, "Virginius Island Trail Guide."

[230] Faulkner, *American Economic History*, 155.

[231] archives.countylib.org, Shenandoah County Library, "Spirits, Stills and Temperance:

Tracing the History of Alcohol in Shenandoah County."

[232] savingplaces.org, National Trust for Historic Preservation, "Belle Grove."

[233] vagenweb.org, Shenandoah County GenWeb Project, Daniel W. Bly, "Identification of the Earliest Owners and Residents of the Site Now Called 'The Frontier Fort,' Strasburg, Virginia, 1835-1900," February, 2011.

[234] themsv.org, The Museum of the Shenandoah Valley, A. Nicholas Powers, "Still Kicking: The Foltz Family's Spirited History," 1-10-2018, and wvculture.org, West Virginia Department of Arts, Culture and History, National Register of Historic Places Inventory Nomination Form, Don C. Wood, "Union Bryarly's Mill," 12-10-1980.

[235] history.com, Christopher Klein, "How Kentucky Became the World's Bourbon Capital," 9-1-2018.

[236] Ibid.

[237] Wilbur S. Johnston, *Weaving a Common Thread, A History of the Woolen Industry in the Top of the Shenandoah Valley* (Winchester, VA: Winchester-Frederick County Historical Society, 1990), 30.

[238] Ibid., 31.

[239] mesda.org, Museum of Early Southern Decorative Arts, "Gibbs, Edward A."

[240] paradisefibers.com, "The Industrial Revolution's Textile Industry" (Spokane, WA: Paradise Fibers).

[241] Faulkner, *American Economic History*, 164.

[242] Johnston, *Weaving a Common Thread*, 19 and 24.

[243] Ibid., 18.

[244] maierassociates.com, Maier Associates, Christian Gottllieb Conradt, "The Story as I Know It."

[245] philadelphiaencyclopedia.org, The Encyclopedia of Greater Philadelphia, "Workshop of the World."

[246] John Bidwell, *American Paper Mills, 1690-1832: A Directory of the Paper Trade* (Hanover, NH: Dartmouth College Press, 2013), 161-163.

[247] Joint Committee and Wayland, *Hopewell Friends History, 1734-1934*, 169.

[248] Bidwell, *American Paper Mills*, 399 and 400.

[249] wvculture.org, West Virginia Department of Arts, Culture and History, National Register of Historic Places Nomination Form, Paula Reed, "New Mecklenburg/Shepherdstown Historic District," 5-26-87.

[250] Ibid.

[251] historicshepherdstown.com, Historic Shepherdstown and Museum, "John George Weiss Family."

[252] Reed, "New Mecklenburg/Shepherdstown Historic District," 5-26-87, and A. H. Rice and John Baer Stoudt, *The Shenandoah Pottery* (Strasburg, VA: Shenandoah Publishing House, 1929).

[253] Ibid.

[254] washingtoncountyhistoricaltrust.org, Washington County Historical Trust, "The Miller House Museum, and antiquesandthearts.com, "Bell Family Pottery," at the Washington County Museum of Fine Arts (Hagerstown, MD: Antiques and the Arts, 10-7-2008).

[255] Wayland, *History of Shenandoah County, Virginia*, 129.

[256] mesdajournal.org, A. Nicholas Powers, "Friends in High Places: Quaker Furniture Makers in Virginia's Northern Shenandoah Valley" (Winston-Salem, NC: Journal of Museum of Early Southern Decorative Arts, Vol. 38, 2017).

[257] Wallace Gusler, *The Furniture of Winchester, Virginia* (Lanham, MD: Altamira Press, 2011).

[258] Powers, "Friends in High Places."

[259] christopherhjones.com, "Corner Cupboard from Shenandoah County, Virginia" (Alexandria, VA: Christopher H. Jones Antiques).

[260] Elizabeth A. Davidson, *The Furniture of John Shearer, 1790-1820: A True North Britain in the Southern Backcountry* (Lanham, MD: Altamira Press, 2011).

[261] Ibid.

[262] Johanna Metzgar Brown, "A Southern Backcountry Perspective at the Winter Antiques Show" (Winston-Salem, NC: Journal of the Museum of Southern Decorative Arts).

[263] Ibid., 153 and 154.

[264] Hofstra, *A Separate Place*, 49.

[265] Cartmell, *Shenandoah Valley Pioneers*, 112.

[266] Ibid.

[267] Ibid.

[268] Ibid.

[269] Ibid.

[270] *The Revised Code of the Laws of Virginia, Being a Collection of All Such Acts of the General Assembly, March 12, 1819* (Richmond, VA: Thomas Ritchie, Printer to the Commonwealth), 116.

[271] Daniel Colt Gilman, Harry Thurston Peck, Frank Moore Colby, *The New Encyclopedia, Volume 20* (New York, NY: Dodd, Mead and Company, 1906), 161.

[272] usps.com, United States Postal Service, "Universal Service and the Postal Monopoly: A Brief History," October, 2008, and ushistory.org, James Breig, "Early American Newspapers" (Williamsburg, VA: Colonial Williamsburg Journal, Spring 2003).

[273] Norris, *History of the Lower Shenandoah Valley*, 265.

[274] loc.gov, Library of Congress, Eighteenth-Century American Newspapers in the Library of Congress.

[275] Rebecca A. Ebert and Teresa Lazazzera, *Frederick County, Virginia: From the Frontier to the Future* (Norfolk, VA: Donning Company, 1988), 36.

[276] vagenweb.org, Shenandoah County VAGenWeb Project, "Henkel Printers New Market, Virginia," The Virginia Conservation Commission and Virginia Works Progress Administration Historical Inventory Project of 1936-37.

[277] Ibid.

[278] wvpublic.org, Bob Powell, "February 1, 1798: Oldest Newspaper Takes New Name, Potowmak Guardian" (West Virginia Public Broadcasting, 2-1-2017).

[279] Ibid.

[280] Norris, *History of the Lower Shenandoah Valley*, 388.

[281] loc.gov, Library of Congress, "Farmers' Repository" (Charles Town, Va. (W. Va.) 1808-1827)."

[282] nps.gov, National Park Service, National Register of Historic Places Registration Form, Jacqueline Hovermale, "Berkeley Springs Train Depot," 2-20-2000.

[283] washingtonheritagetrail.com, Washington Heritage Trail, "George Washington's Bathtub."

[284] wvcommerce.org, West Virginia Department of Commerce, Berkeley Springs State Park, "Area History."

[285] berkeleysprings.com, Walking Tour, "Fairfax Street."

[286] dhr.virginia.gov, Virginia Department of Historic Resources, James C. Massie, Shirley Maxwell, J. Daniel Pezzoni and Judy B. Reynolds, "Shenandoah County Historic Resources Survey Report," May 1995.

[287] historicjordansprings.com, Historic Jordan Springs Event & Cultural Centre, "History."

[288] Cartmell, *Shenandoah Valley Pioneers*, 297.

[289] wvculture.org, West Virginia Department of Arts, Culture and History, National Register of Historic Places Nomination Form, William D. Theriault, "Shannondale Springs," September 1997.

[290] Ibid.

[291] Ibid.

Chapter 3

[1] census.gov, U.S. Census Bureau, Fifth Census and Eighth Census.

[2] Harold Underwood Faulkner, *American Economic History* (New York, NY; Harper & Brothers Publishers, 1954), 291.

[3] Jonathan Hughes and Louis P. Cain, *American Economic History* (Reading, MA: Addison Wesley Longman, Inc., 1998), 151, and census.gov, U.S. Census Bureau, "Railroad Active Mileage by Region, 1890."

[4] uspto.gov, U.S. Patent and Trademark Office, "U.S. Patent Activity, 1790 to the Present."

[5] Faulkner, *American Economic History*, 257.

[6] Ibid.

[7] census.gov, U.S. Census Bureau, Fifth Census and Eighth Census.

[8] Richard F. Selcer, *Civil War America, 1850 to 1875* (New York, NY: Infobase Publishing, 2006), 90.

[9] jtlu.org, Jeremy Atak and Robert A. Margo, "The Impact of Access to Rail Transportation on Agriculture Improvement" (Minneapolis, MN: University of Minnesota, Journal of Transport and Land Use, Vol. 4, Number 2, Summer 2011).

[10] census.gov, Historical Statistics of the United States, "Chapter E. Agriculture – Corn and Wheat," 106, and John Steele Gordon, *An Empire of Wealth; The Epic History of American Economic Power* (New York, NY: Harper Collins Publishers, 2004), 173.

[11] Ibid., 179

[12] Ibid.

[13] americaslibrary.gov, America's Story from America's Library, "The Panic of 1857 Began August 29, 1857."

[14] Faulkner, *American Economic History*, 166.

[15] *Journal of the House of Delegates of the Commonwealth of Virginia* (Richmond, VA: Thomas Ritchie, Printer for the Commonwealth, 12-6-1830), 252, and *Thirty-Sixth Annual Report of the Board of Public Works to the General Assembly of Virginia, 1851*, 95.

[16] Ibid.

[17] *Acts and Joint Resolutions of the General Assembly of the Commonwealth* (Richmond, VA: Davis Bottom, Superintendent of Public Printing, 1916), 211 and 212.

[18] dhr.virginia.gov, Virginia Department of Historic Resources, Maral S. Kalbian, "Clarke County Reconnaissance Survey, 1989," 63.

[19] H. L. Swisher and Hu Maxwell, *History of Hampshire County, West Virginia* (Morgantown, WV: S. Brown Boughner Printer, 1897), 57.

[20] James Lilliefors, "Go West, Old Highway" (Washington Post, 9-1-1989), and Gilbert Gude, *Where the Potomac Begins, A History of the North Branch Valley* (Cabin John, MD: Seven Locks Press, 1984), 23 and 24.

[21] Ibid.

[22] Thomas Kemp Cartmell, *Shenandoah Valley Pioneers and Their Descendants* (Winchester, VA: The Eddy Press Corporation, 1909), 57, and en.m.wikipedia.org, "List of Turnpikes in Virginia and West Virginia."

[23] Gabrielle M. Lanier, "An Early Road to the New West, 1780-1837," in Warren R. Hofstra and Karl Raitz, editors, *The Great Valley Road of Virginia* (Charlottesville, VA and London: University of Virginia Press, 2010), 119.

[24] nps.gov, National Park Service, Cedar Creek and Belle Grove, "The Valley Turnpike Company."

[25] Kenneth W. Keller, "The Best Thoroughfare in the South," in Hofstra and Raitz, *The Great Valley Road of Virginia*, 158.

[26] Ibid.

[27] Ibid.

[28] Garland R. Quarles, *Some Worthy Lives* (Winchester, VA: Winchester-Frederick County Historical Society, 1988), 223, and phwi.org, Karen Clay, "The Taylor Hotel: At the Crossroads of Prosperity" (Preservation of Historic Winchester, Inc., Taylor Hotel Edition, Spring 2011.

[29] Keller, "The Best Thoroughfare in the South," 160.

[30] nps.gov, National Park Service, Cedar Creek and Belle Grove, "The Valley Turnpike Company."

[31] Ibid.

[32] Cartmell, *Shenandoah Valley Pioneers*, 56.

[33] Willis F. Evans, *History of Berkeley County, West Virginia* (Westminster, MD: Heritage Books, Inc., originally published 1927, reprinted in 2001), 88.

[34] Robert D. Mitchell, *Commercialism and Frontier: Perspectives on the Early Shenandoah Valley* (Charlottesville, VA: University of Virginia Press, 1977), 190, and Kalbian, "Clarke County Reconnaissance Survey," 59.

[35] en.m.wikipedia.org, "List of Turnpikes in Virginia and West Virginia."

[36] nps.gov, National Park Service, The Building of the Chesapeake and Ohio Canal, "George Washington's Influence on the C&O Canal."

[37] canaltrust.org, C&O Canal Trust, "Charles F. Mercer."

[38] Harlan D. Unrau, *Historic Resource Study: Chesapeake & Ohio Canal* (historian, C&O Canal Restoration Team, Denver Service Center, 1976), 105.

[39] Warren R. Hofstra, *A Separate Place: The Formation of Clarke County, Virginia* (Madison WI: Madison House Publishers, 1986), 57.

[40] nps.gov, National Park Service, The Building of the Chesapeake and Ohio Canal, "History of the Canal."

[41] Ibid.

[42] csx.history.railfan.net, Jay Phillips, A History of the Railroads of CSX, "The Baltimore and Ohio Railroad," 1999.

[43] nps.gov, "History of the Canal."

[44] Ibid.

[45] Ibid.

[46] Ibid.

[47] Mike High, *The C&O Canal Companion: A Journal through Potomac History* (Baltimore, MD: Johns Hopkins University Press, 2015), 129.

[48] shepherdstownriverfront.org, Friends of the Shepherdstown Riverfront, "The Warehouse."

[49] Ibid.

[50] *Twenty-Fourth Annual Report of the Board of Public Works to the General Assembly of Virginia, November 1, 1839*, 19.

[51] Hofstra, *A Separate Place*, 69 and 70.

[52] Lanier, "An Early Road to the Old West," 129.

[53] Hofstra, *A Separate Place*, 70.

[54] Ibid.

[55] Kirk Reynolds and Dave Oroszi, *Baltimore and Ohio Railroad* (Minneapolis, MN: Voyageur Press, 2008), 16.

[56] middletonrailway.org.uk, "Welcome to the Middleton Railway."

[57] Reynolds and Oroszi, *Baltimore and Ohio Railroad*, 15.

[58] Phillips, A History of the Railroads of CSX.

[59] nps.gov, National Park Service, Andrew S. Lee, "Historical Background Report, Baltimore and Ohio Railroad, Harpers Ferry Station," 2003, 2.

[60] Reynolds and Oroszi, *Baltimore and Ohio Railroad*, 15.

[61] nps.gov, National Park Service, "History of the Canal."

[62] Frederic Morton, *The Story of Winchester in Virginia* (Westminster, MD: Heritage Books, Inc., 2007, originally published in 1925 in Strasburg by Shenandoah Publishing House), 128.

[63] Ibid.

[64] Reynolds and Oroszi, *Baltimore and Ohio Railroad*, 20.

[65] Ibid., 23.

[66] Hofstra, *A Separate Place*, 69.

[67] J. Randolph Kean, "The Development of the Valley Line of the Baltimore and Ohio Railroad" (Richmond, VA: Virginia Magazine of History and Biography, Virginia Historical Society, October, 1952), 538.

[68] Morton, *The Story of Winchester in Virginia*, 129.

[69] Linda McCarty, "All Aboard! Tracks Across Frederick" (Winchester Star, 7-3-1996), E6.

[70] Reynolds and Oroszi, *Baltimore and Ohio Railroad*, 23.

[71] Jill Y. Halchin, editor, *Archeological Views of the Upper Wager Block, A Domestic and Commercial Neighborhood in Harpers Ferry* (Washington, DC: National Park Service, 1994), 2.7.

[72] Morton, *The Story of Winchester in Virginia*, 113.

[73] Quarles, *Some Worthy Lives*, 14.

[74] Norris, *History of the Lower Shenandoah Valley*, 623.

[75] Quarles, *Some Worthy Lives*, 18.

[76] McCarty, "All Aboard!" E6.

[77] Ibid.

[78] historic-structures.com, Historic Structures, "B&O Railroad Repair Shops, Martinsburg, WV."

[79] Ibid.

[80] snaccooperative.org, SNAC Cooperative, Virginia Board of Public Works, Social Network and Archival Content (Charlottesville, VA: University of Virginia Library and Washington, DC: National Archives and Records Administration).

[81] alextimes.com, "Out of the Attic: Alexandria, Loudoun and Hampshire Railroad" (Alexandria, VA: Alexandria Times, 9-9-2010).

[82] Morton, *The Story of Winchester in Virginia*, 132.

[83] Kean, "The Development of the Valley Line of the Baltimore and Ohio Railroad," 545.

[84] William Page Johnson, II, "The Unfinished Manassas Gap Railroad" (Fairfax, VA: The Fare Fax Gazette, Spring 2004).

[85] Ibid.

[86] Ibid.

[87] Harold W. Hurst, *Alexandria on the Potomac: The Portrait of an Antebellum Community* (Lanham, MD: University Press of America, 1991), 7.

[88] Morton, *The Story of Winchester in Virginia*, 130.

[89] census.gov, U.S. Census Bureau, Fourth Census and Eighth Census.

[90] virginiaplaces.org, Population of Virginia – 1860 (total and slave).

[91] census.gov, U.S. Census Bureau, Eighth Census.

[92] Ibid.

[93] Wilma A. Dunaway, *The African American Family in Slavery and Reconstruction* (Cambridge, UK: Cambridge University Press, 2003), 26.

[94] Ibid.

[95] Edward Ball, "Retracing Slavery's Trail of Tears" (Washington, DC: Smithsonian Magazine, November 2015).

[96] Ibid.

[97] shenandoahcountyhistoricalsociety.org, Nancy B. Stewart, "Who Got into the Slavery Business in Shenandoah County?" (Woodstock, VA: Shenandoah County Historical Society).

[98] Norman H. Scott, *Shenandoah Iron* (Verona, VA: self-published, 2017), 52.

[99] Ibid.

[100] census.gov, U.S. Census Bureau, Eighth Census.

[101] Don C. Wood, *Documented History of Martinsburg and Berkeley County, Volume I* (Martinsburg, WV: Berkeley County Historical Society, 2004), 53.

[102] Morton, *The Story of Winchester in Virginia*, 137.

[103] Ibid., 141.

[104] Christopher Gray, "Broadway, His Middle Name" (New York Times, 8-11-1996).

[105] Morton, *The Story of Winchester in Virginia*, 141.

[106] Ibid.

[107] Ibid.

[108] Dave McMillion, "Historic Rouss Building Getting Renewed Attention" (Hagerstown, MD: Herald-Mail, 3-18-02).

[109] rousscenter.org, Rouss Center for the Arts, "History of the Building."

[110] Theodore M. Porter, *Trust in Numbers: Objectivity in Science and Public Life* (Princeton, NJ: Princeton University Press, 1995), 47.

[111] Reynolds and Oroszi, *Baltimore and Ohio Railroad*, 34.

[112] referenceforbusiness.com, Reference for Business, Chicago Board of Trade, "Company Profile – History."

[113] Robert Sullivan, *Cross Country* (New York, NY: Bloomsbury USA, 2006), 98.

[114] Ibid.

[115] historytoday.com, David Eastwood, "The Corn Laws and Their Repeal, 1815-1846" (Maidenhead, UK: History Today, 9-25-96).

[116] Ibid.

[117] John M. Murrin, etc., *Liberty, Equality, Power: A History of the American People* (Boston, MA: Cengage Company, 2014), 386.

[118] Douglass C. North, *The Economic Growth of the United States, 1790 to 1860* (New York, NY: W. W. Norton & Company, Ltd., 1966), chart of wheat and corn prices, 210.

[119] Kenneth E. Koons, "The Staple of Our Country: Wheat in the Regional Farm Economy of the Nineteenth Century Valley of Virginia," in Kenneth E. Koons and Warren R. Hofstra, *After the Backcountry, Rural Life in the Great Valley of Virginia 1800-1900* (Knoxville, TN: University of Tennessee Press, 2000), 6.

[120] Michael G. Mahon, *The Shenandoah Valley, 1861-1865: The Destruction of the Granary* (Mechanicsville, PA: Stackpole Books, 1999), 5.

[121] North, *The Economic Growth of the United States, 1790 to 1860*, 152.

[122] Ibid.

[123] Gordon, *An Empire of Wealth*, 174.

[124] Alan Greenspan and Adrian Wooldridge, *Capitalism in America, A History* (New York, NY: Penguin Press, 2018), 46.

[125] Jeremy Atak and Robert A. Margo, "The Impact of Rail Transportation on Agriculture Improvement" (Plymouth, MA: American Journal of Transportation, Vol. 4, No 2, summer 2011).

[126] britannica.com, Encyclopedia Britannica, "Chicago Board of Trade," and Porter, *Trust in Numbers*, 47.

[127] Ibid.

[128] referenceforbusiness.com, Reference for Business, Chicago Board of Trade, "Company Profile – History."

[129] North, *The Economic Growth of the United States, 1790 to 1860*, 210.

[130] Carroll D. Wright, "Wages, Prices and Cost of Living, 1752-1860" (Boston, MA: Massachusetts Bureau of Statistics of Labor), 130.

[131] Paul C. Henlein, *Cattle Kingdom in the Ohio Valley, 1783-1860* (Lexington, KY: University of Kentucky Press, 1959), 145-148.

[132] Ibid.

[133] Bessie Louise Pierce, *A History of Chicago, Vol. 2* (Chicago, IL: University of Chicago Press, 1940), 97.

[134] Faulkner, *American Economic History*, 255.

[135] Gordon, *An Empire of Wealth*, 172.

[136] nps.gov, National Park Service, "Virginius Island Trail Guide."

[137] nps.gov, Allison A. Crosbie and Andrew S. Lee, "Cultural Landscape Report for the Unites States Armory and Potomac Riverfront" (Boston, MA: Olmstead Center for Landscape Preservation, 2009), 49.

[138] David T. Gilbert, *Waterpower: Mills, Factories, Machines & Floods at Harpers Ferry, West Virginia, 1762-1991* (Harpers Ferry, WV: Harpers Ferry Historical Association, 1999), 117-112.

[139] North, *The Economic Growth of the United States, 1790 to 1860*, 168 and 169.

[140] spoommidatlantic.org, Robert Lundegard, "County and City Mills in Early American Flour Manufacture and Export" (Great Falls, VA: Society for the Preservation of Old Mills, Mid-Atlantic Chapter, Colvin Run Historic Site, 9-18-2007), 16.

[141] Johnson, "A Nineteenth-Century Mill Village."

[142] Ibid.

[143] dhr.virginia.gov, Virginia Department of Historic Resources, National Register of Historic Places Nomination Form, Virginia Historic Landmarks Commission staff, "Edinburg Mill," June 1979.

[144] waterwheelfactory.com, Robert Vitale, "History of the Fitz Water Wheel Company," and Matthew Umstead, "Owners Want to Bring Pre-Civil War Foundry Back to Life in Martinsburg" (Hagerstown, MD: Herald-Mail, 4-28-2018).

[145] newyorker.com, The New Yorker, 11-14-1931.

[146] Lundegard, "County and City Mills," 14.

[147] fsusda.gov, Forest Service, U.S. Department of Agriculture, George Washington & Jefferson National Forests, "Cultural History."

[148] Faulkner, *American Economic History*, 164, and taxhistory.org, "The Second American Party System and the Tariff."

[149] Ibid., 167.

[150] Robert B. Gordon, *American Iron, 1607-1900* (Baltimore, MD: Johns Hopkins University Press, 1996), 114.

[151] dhr.virginia.gov, Virginia Department of Historic Resources, National Register of Historic Places Nomination Form, "Van Buren Furnace," 3-17-1999.

[152] J. Peter Lesley, *The Iron Manufacturer's Guide to the Furnaces, Forges and Roller Mills of the United States* (London: John Wiley Publisher, 1859), 67.

[153] Scott, *Shenandoah Iron*, 152.

[154] Jed. Hotchkiss, "The Virginias, A Mining, Industrial and Scientific Journal, Devoted to the Development of Virginia and West

Virginia," Vol. III, No. 1 (Staunton, VA: S. M. Yost & Son, January 1882), 12, and dhr.virginia.gov, Virginia Department of Historic Resources, "Van Buren Furnace," 3-17-1999.

[155] Scott, *Shenandoah Iron*, 94 and 95.

[156] vagenweb.org, VaGenWeb Project, "Catherine Furnace," WPA Historical Inventory Project, 1937.

[157] Scott, *Shenandoah Iron*, 97.

[158] Ibid.

[159] Ibid.

[160] Ibid., 126.

[161] fs.usda.gov, Forest Service, U.S. Department of Agriculture, George Washington & Jefferson National Forests, "Cultural History."

[162] vagenweb.org, VaGenWeb Project, Tom Pierce, "The Blackford Iron Workers," 4-1-2008.

[163] Darwin Lambert, *The Undying Past of Shenandoah National Park* (Lanham, MD: Roberts Rinehart Inc., Publishers, 1989), 77.

[164] Scott, *Shenandoah Iron*, 112.

[165] Ibid., 126 and 145.

[166] Pierce, "The Blackford Iron Workers," 4-1-2008.

[167] Wayland, *A History of Shenandoah County, Virginia*, 178.

[168] "Philadelphia, Wilmington and Baltimore Railroad" (New York Times, 7-20-1864), 5.

[169] Scott, *Shenandoah Iron*, 146.

[170] Lesley, *The Iron Manufacturer's Guide*, 179.

[171] John H. White, Jr., *The American Railroad Passenger Car* (Baltimore, MD: Johns Hopkins University Press, 1978), 532.

[172] Peachy R. Grattan, *Reports of Cases in the Supreme Court of Appeals of Virginia, Volume 73* (Richmond, VA: R. F. Walker, Superintendent Public Printing, 1890), 196.

[173] ead.lib.virginia.edu, Virginia Historical Society, "A Guide to the Lupton Family Papers, 1745 to 1895," which reference letters to George Hupp, Columbia Furnace in 1842.

[174] wikitree.com, "George Franklin Hupp (1792-1885)."

[175] historichampshire.org "Iron Industry in Hampshire County," and *Thomson's Mercantile and Professional Directory, Virginia, 1851* (Baltimore, MD: William Thomson, 1851).

[176] Ibid.

[177] Wayland, *A History of Shenandoah County, Virginia*, 240.

[178] Scott, *Shenandoah Iron*, 129, and countylib.org, Shenandoah County Library System, "A Guide to the Wissler Letters Collection."

[179] vagenweb.org, VaGenWeb Project, Virginia W.P.A. Historical Inventory Project, 1937, "Henrietta Furnace."

[180] Stanley K. Dickinson, "Extracting Iron in Jefferson County" (Charles Town, WV: Jefferson County Historical Society Magazine, 2004), 101.

[181] Ibid.

[182] *Manufactures of the United States in 1860*, compiled from the Original Returns of the Eighth Census, Under the Direction of the Secretary of the Interior (Washington, DC: Government Printing Office, 1865), clxxx.

[183] North, *The Economic Growth of the United States, 1790 to 1860*, 164.

[184] Gordon, *An Empire of Wealth*, 245, and fs.usda.gov, Forest Service, U.S. Department of Agriculture, George Washington & Jefferson National Forests, "Cultural History."

[185] Cartmell, *Shenandoah Valley Pioneers*, 439.

[186] Ibid.

[187] Johnson, "A Nineteenth-Century Mill Village."

[188] "Tuleyries for Sale" (Staunton, VA: Staunton Spectator and General Advertiser, 10-23-1860).

[189] Cartmell, *Shenandoah Valley Pioneers*, 498.

[190] revolvy.com, Revolvy, "Peter Bouck Borst."

[191] Ibid.

[192] historicshepherdstown.com, Marc Briod, "Historic Shepherdstown & Museum, Family Histories," presented at Shepherdstown's 250th Anniversary Coming Home Parade, 11-11-2012, and Briod, "The Colorful History of Stone House Row on New Street."

[193] Ibid.

[194] Ibid.

[195] Wood, *Documented History of Martinsburg and Berkeley County, Volume I*, 98.

[196] Ibid.

[197] F. Vernon Aler, *Aler's History of Martinsburg and Berkeley County, W. VA.* (Hagerstown, MD: The Mail Publishing Company, 1888), 283.

[198] civilwarintheeast.com, The Civil War in the East, "John Q. A. Nadenbousch."

[199] Koons, "The Staple of Our Country," 4.

[200] civilwarscholars.com, Jim Surkamp, "The Civil War in Jefferson County: Homes in 1860," and "West Virginia Route 9, Charles Town to Virginia Line, Jefferson County, WV" (Final Environmental Impact Statement, WVDOT, 10-6-2000).

[201] Jefferson County Historical Society Magazine, 2006, reprint from Shepherdstown Register, 33, and Historic Shepherdstown Commission, *Shepherd's Town, Vol. III*, 1996.

[202] Gilbert, *Waterpower*, 100 and 102.

[203] nps.gov, National Park Service, Virginius Island, "The Landscape of Industrial Development," and riverexplorer.com, Potomac River Guide, "Shenandoah Falls Canal."

[204] Johnson, "A Nineteenth-Century Mill Village."

[205] Ibid.

[206] Kate Coleman, "Walk the Path of Industrial History" (Hagerstown, MD: Herald-Mail, 9-20-2002).

[207] Ibid.

[208] Johnson, "A Nineteenth-Century Mill Village."

[209] Bill Theriault, "A Site Worth Saving" (Charles Town, WV: Spirit of Jefferson Farmers Advocate, 5-30-2002), 4.

[210] jeffersoncountyhlc.org, Jefferson County Historic Landmarks Commission, "The Shepherdstown Cement Mill," 2016, and canaltrust.org, C&O Canal Trust, Landmark Nomination Report, "Potomac Mills/Boteler's Cement Mill," 9-19-2012.

[211] Ibid.

[212] Ibid.

[213] Ibid.

[214] Ibid.

[215] Joint Committee of Hopewell Friends and John W. Wayland, *Hopewell Friends History, 1734 to 1934* (Strasburg, VA: Shenandoah Publishing House, 1936), 173.

[216] Ibid.

[217] Lambert, *The Undying Past of Shenandoah National Park*, 164.

[218] browntowncommnity.com, Rebecca Poe, "History of the Village of Browntown VA" (Browntown Community Center Association, 2013).

[219] A. H. Rice and John Baer Stoudt, *The Shenandoah Pottery* (Strasburg, VA: Shenandoah Publishing House, 1929).

[220] shenandoahpottery.com, "Historic Shenandoah Pottery, 2017."

[221] Josette Keelor, "Pot Town Earned its Title in the Early Years" (Strasburg, VA: Northern Virginia Daily, 4-11-2011).

[222] Ibid.

[223] Wayland, *A History of Shenandoah County, Virginia*, 29, and Wilma A. Dunaway, *The First American Frontier: Transition to Capitalism in Southern Appalachia, 1700-1860* (Chapel Hill, NC: University of North Carolina Press, 1990), and si.edu, Smithsonian Institute, Historic Preservation Reports, "National Zoological Park Comprehensive Facilities Master Plan, Front Royal Campus," 9-20-2007.

[224] nps.gov, National Park Service, "Skyland Resort History."

[225] patc.us, G. Freeman Pollock, "Why Skyland?" (reprint from Potomac Appalachian Trial Club Bulletin, October 1935).

[226] Eric Force, "Manganese Contents of Some Lower Paleozoic Carbonic Rocks of Virginia" (U.S. Geological Survey Bulletin, 1916), B-2.

[227] Chester Keeler Wentworth and George Willis Stose, "Manganese Deposits of Western Virginia" (Charlottesville, VA: Virginia Division of Mineral Resources, Issues 22-23, 1922), 81.

[228] Ibid., 58.

[229] William A. Dill, "Growth of Newspapers in the United States" (master's thesis, Lawrence, KS: University of Kansas, 3-15-1928), 11 and 12.

[230] Norris, *History of the Lower Shenandoah Valley*, 274.

231 encyclopedia.com, Encyclopedia of the New American Nation, Thomas Gale," Political Parties and the Press," 2006.

232 Cartmell, *Shenandoah Valley Pioneers*, 156.

233 chroniclingamerica.loc.gov, Library of Congress, "About the Spirit of Jefferson."

234 William D. Theriault, *Jefferson County's (Virginia) Fourth Estate* (Berwyn Heights, MD: Heritage Books, Inc., 2017).

235 Journal of the House of Delegates of Virginia, Session 1845-1846, 19.

236 museumoftheberkeleysprings.com, Museum of the Berkeley Springs, "1834–1860: The Golden Age Returns."

237 Ibid.

238 Ibid., "Fires of Berkeley Springs Exhibit."

239 Candice Boxley, "Berkeley Springs Has a Fiery History" (Hagerstown, MD: Herald-Mail, 8-13-2006).

240 Editor, "Strother Exhibit Added to the Museum of the Berkeley Springs in Time for Reopening" (Berkeley Springs, WV: Morgan Messenger, 5-13-2020).

241 wvculture.org, West Virginia Department of Arts, Culture and History, National Register of Historic Places Nomination Form, William D. Theriault, "Shannondale Springs," September 1997.

242 Ibid.

243 Ibid.

244 Ibid.

245 historicjordansprings.com, Historic Jordan Springs Event & Cultural Centre, "History."

246 Ibid.

247 Ibid.

248 Cartmell, *Shenandoah Valley Pioneers*, 57.

249 Ibid.

250 findagrave.com, Find A Grave, "Dr. William H Keffer."

251 Handley Library, Winchester, VA, Stewart Bell Jr. Archives, "Rock Enon Springs Records, 1887-1920."

252 Rebecca A. Ebert and Teresa Lazazzera, *The Frederick County, Virginia: From the Frontier to the Future* (Norfolk, VA: Donning Company, 1988), 106.

253 Ibid.

254 dhr.virginia.gov, Virginia Department of Historic Resources, National Register of Historic Places Nomination Form, Virginia Historic Landmarks Commission staff, "Orkney Springs Hotel," 4-22-1976, and shenandaohstories.com, Shenandoah County Library, "Orkney Springs Resort."

255 Ibid.

256 John W. Wayland, *A History of Shenandoah County, Virginia* (Strasburg, VA: Shenandoah Publishing House, Inc., 1969, originally published in 1927), 151.

257 Ibid., 273.

258 dhr.virginia.gov, Maral S. Kalbian, *Rural Historic Resource Survey Report of Warren County, Virginia, 1991,* 59.

259 archives.countylib.org, Shenandoah County Library, Shenandoah Stories, "Burner's Resort," 2-2-2018.

260 Ibid.

261 "Fort Valley Rich in History, Minerals, Beauty" (Woodstock, VA: Shenandoah Herald and Shenandoah Valley, 7-1-1976), 42.

262 Shenandoah Stories, "Burner's Resort," 2-2-2018, and Wayland, *A History of Shenandoah County, Virginia*, 181.

Chapter 4

1 John Steele Gordon, *An Empire of Wealth; The Epic History of American Economic Power* (New York, NY: Harper Collins Publishers, 2004), 195.

2 Alan Greenspan and Adrian Wooldridge, *Capitalism in America, A History* (New York, NY: Penguin Press, 2018), 82.

3 virginiaplaces.org, "Why Virginia Split Into "East" and "West" Virginia (But with Only Three Shenandoah Valley Counties, and Without Southwest Virginia)," and history.com, "8 Things You May Not Know About West Virginia."

4 Michael G. Mahon, *The Shenandoah Valley, 1861-1865* (Mechanicsburg, PA: Stackpole Books, 1999), 29.

5 Ibid., 28

6 Ibid.

7 Ibid., 45
8 Ibid.
9 Ibid., 29.
10 Ibid., 58.
11 Don C. Wood, *Documented History of Martinsburg and Berkeley County, Volume II*, (Martinsburg, WV: Berkeley County Historical Society, 2007), 86.
12 Thomas Kent Cartmell, *Shenandoah Valley Pioneers and Their Descendants* (Winchester, VA: The Eddy Press Corporation, 1909), 112.
13 Ibid.
14 Mahon, *The Shenandoah Valley, 1861-1865*, 21.
15 David T. Gilbert, *Waterpower: Mills, Factories, Machines & Floods at Harpers Ferry, West Virginia, 1762-1991* (Harpers Ferry, WV: Harpers Ferry Historical Association, 1999), 122.
16 Ibid.
17 Ibid., and ead.lib.virginia.edu, Library of Virginia, Virginia Heritage, "A Guide to the Virginia Manufactory of Arms Records, 1798-1864."
18 Norman H. Scott, *Shenandoah Iron* (Verona, VA: self-published, 2017), 161.
19 Dennis Maher Hellerman, "The Tredegar Iron Works, 1865-1876" (master's thesis, Richmond, VA: University of Richmond, 5-14-1978).
20 Ibid.
21 Gordon, *An Empire of Wealth*, 201.
22 Scott, *Shenandoah Iron*, 89.
23 vagenweb.org, VaGenWeb Project, Virginia W.P.A. Historical Inventory Project, 1937, "Henrietta Furnace."
24 Scott, *Shenandoah Iron*, 146.
25 Ibid., 95.
26 Ibid., 98.
27 Staff writers, *History of Virginia, Volume VI, Virginia Biography* (Chicago and New York: The American Historical Society, 1924), 73, and Scott, *Shenandoah Iron*, 126.
28 dmme.virginia.gov, Virginia Department of Mines, Minerals and Energy, "Virginia's Mineral Resources and the American Civil War," 2015.
29 Scott, *Shenandoah Iron*, 135.

30 Ibid., 158.
31 Ibid., 141.
32 John W. Wayland, *A History of Shenandoah County, Virginia* (Strasburg, VA: Shenandoah Publishing House, Inc.,1969), 242.
33 nps.gov, National Park Service, "Virginius Island Trail Guide."
34 Ibid.
35 revolvy.com, Revolvy, "Peter Bouck Borst."
36 Ibid.
37 nps.gov, National Park Service, Cedar Creek and Belle Grove National Historic Park, "The Burning: The Shenandoah Valley in Flames."
38 Dan Vaughn, *Luray and Page County, Images of America* (Charleston, SC: Arcadia Publishing, 2005), 38.
39 edinburgmill.com, Shenandoah Valley Cultural Heritage Museum at the Edinburg Mill, "History of the Mill."
40 colonialghosts.com, "Phantom Coach at Carter Hall."
41 Mahon, *The Shenandoah Valley, 1861-1865*, 37.
42 Joel Danoy, "Great Train Raid" (Winchester Star, 4-16-2011), A6.
43 John F. Stover, *History of the Baltimore and Ohio Railroad* (Lafayette, IN: Purdue University Press, 1987), 105.
44 Ibid.
45 David Bright and Andrew H. Hall, *Locomotives Up the Turnpike* (Shelby, NC: Westmoreland Printers, Inc., 2016).
46 Wood, *Documented History of Martinsburg and Berkeley County, Volume II*, 85, and blueandgraytrail.com, "America's Civil War, Attack on Dam Number 5."
47 Ibid.
48 Su Clauson-Wicker, *Scenic Routes & Byways, West Virginia* (Guilford, CT: Morris Book Publishing, LLC, 2013), 50.
49 Handley Library, Winchester, VA, Stewart Bell Jr. Archives, "Winchester and Potomac Railroad Records."
50 historynet.com, Earl McElfresh, "Unfinished Railroad Cut at Second Manassas," 10-5-2011.
51 nps.gov, National Park Service, Harpers Ferry National Historic Park, "Harpers Ferry – Baltimore & Ohio Bridge in Ruins."

Endnotes: Chapter 4

52 virginia.org, Virginia Is for Lovers, Historical Sites, "White House Bridge, Critical Crossing, 1862 Valley Campaign," 7-20-2011.

53 Don C. Wood, *Documented History of Martinsburg and Berkeley County, Volume I*, (Martinsburg, WV: Berkeley County Historical Society, 2004), 30.

54 Mahon, *The Shenandoah Valley, 1861-1865*, 28.

55 Ibid., 30 and 60.

56 Wood, *Documented History of Martinsburg and Berkeley County, Volume II*, 90.

57 Mahon, *The Shenandoah Valley, 1861-1865*, 21, and stationatshepherdstown.com, The Station at Shepherdstown, "History."

58 nps.gov, "The Burning," and Mahon, *The Shenandoah Valley, 1861-1865*, 137.

59 Ibid., 59.

60 Ibid., 77.

61 National Public Radio staff, "West Virginia Birthday Recalls a State Born of the Civil War," 2-3-2013.

62 Gordon, *An Empire of Wealth*, 200.

63 Eric Foner, *Reconstruction, America's Unfinished Revolution, 1863-1877* (New York, NY: Harper & Row Publishers, 1988), 582.

64 Mary Sullivan Linhart, "Up to Date and Progressive: Winchester and Frederick County, Virginia, 1870-1980" (PhD dissertation, Fairfax, VA: George Mason University, 2014), 10.

65 battlefields.org, American Battlefield Trust, "Civil War Casualties."

66 visitlongbranch.org, Long Branch Historic House and Farm, "Enslaved Workers," and wvvulture.org, West Virginia Archives and History, "West Virginia Population by Race."

67 Maral S. Kalbian, *Clarke County, Images of America* (Charleston, SC: Arcadia Publishing, 2011), 8.

68 visitlongbranch.org, "Enslaved Workers."

69 census.gov, U.S. Census Bureau, Eighth Census and Ninth Census.

70 Linhart, "Up to Date and Progressive," 44.

71 Ibid.

72 Frederic Morton, *The Story of Winchester in Virginia*, (Strasburg, VA: Shenandoah Publishing House, 1925), 253.

73 Linhart, "Up to Date and Progressive," 49.

74 nps.gov, National Park Service, "Harpers Ferry Armory and Arsenal," and nps.gov, "Springfield Armory."

75 nps.gov, "Memorable Floods at Harpers Ferry."

76 vagenweb.org, VaGenWeb Project, Virginia W.P.A. Historical Inventory Project, 1937, Don Silvus, "The Flood of 1870."

77 Ibid.

78 Gordon, *An Empire of Wealth*, 227.

79 Ibid.

80 census.gov, U.S. Census Bureau, Ninth Census and Tenth Census.

81 Ibid.

82 wvencyclopedia.org, e-WV, The West Virginia Encyclopedia, Don C. Wood, "Martinsburg," 4-11-2016.

83 winchesterva.gov, Winchester, Virginia, "Chronological History," and census.gov, U.S. Census Bureau, Eighth Census and Tenth Census.

84 Linhart, "Up to Date and Progressive," 55.

85 *The Farmer: Dedicated to Agriculture, Horticulture and Mechanical Arts, Vol. 1, No. 1* (Richmond, VA: Elliot & Shields, January 1866), 85.

86 Ibid.

87 shenandoahatwar.org, Kenneth E. Koons, "Our Once Beautiful, but Desolated Valley" (New Market, VA: Shenandoah Valley Battlefields Foundation, 6-11-2015), and "Southern Relief Fair" (New York Times, 3-18-1866), 5.

88 Linhart, "Up to Date and Progressive," 65.

89 J. Randolph Kean, "The Development of the Valley Line of the Baltimore and Ohio Railroad" (Richmond, VA: The Virginia Magazine of History and Biography, October 1952), 547.

90 Kenneth E. Koons, "The Staple of Our Country: Wheat in the Regional Farm Economy of the Nineteenth Century Valley of Virginia," in Kenneth E. Koons and Warren R. Hofstra, editors, *After the Backcountry, Rural Life in the Great Valley of Virginia 1800-1900*

(Knoxville, TN: University of Tennessee Press, 2000), 8.

91 usda.gov, U.S. Department of Agriculture, "Census of Agriculture Historical Archives, Agriculture in United States in 1860, 1870 and 1880."

92 Koons, "The Staple of Our Country," 8.

93 Ibid., 12.

94 Ibid., 11.

95 census.gov, U.S. Census Bureau, Agricultural Statistical Atlas.

96 census.gov, U.S. Census Bureau, Eighth Census and Tenth Census

97 usda.gov, U.S. Department of Agriculture, "Census of Agriculture Historical Archives, Agriculture in United States in 1870, 1880 and 1890."

98 Richard MacMaster, *The History of Hardy County, 1786-1986* (Salem, WV: Wadsworth Press, Inc., 1986), 261.

99 Greenspan and Wooldridge, *Capitalism in America, A History*, 121.

100 baltimoreindustrytours.com, Deane Nettles, "Early Mill History of Baltimore: Cotton Mills of the Jones Falls," 2013.

101 Koons, "The Staple of Our Country," 9.

102 Ibid.

103 okhistory.org, "Removal of Tribes to Oklahoma" (Oklahoma, OK: Oklahoma Historical Society).

104 census.gov, U.S. Census Bureau, Chapter E. Agriculture (Series E1-269), "Historical Statistics of the United States, 1789-1945," 290.

105 Koons, "The Staple of Our Country," 8.

106 Ibid., 14.

107 vdot.org, Virginia Department of Transportation, History of Roads in Virginia, "The Most Convenient Wayes," 6-20-2012.

108 Ibid.

109 Ibid.

110 Chas. E. Fisher, "The U.S. Military Railroads" (Railway and Locomotive Historical Society Bulletin, No. 59, October 1942), 59.

111 *Sixty-Eighth Annual Report of the Baltimore and Ohio Railroad Company*, "Leases of the Company," 21.

112 historic-structures.com, Historic Structures, "B&O Railroad Repair Shops, Martinsburg, West Virginia," 10-4-2017.

113 John R. Hildebrand, *Iron Horses in the Valley: The Valley and Shenandoah Valley Railroads 1866–1882* (Shippensburg, PA: Burd Street Press, 2001), 31.

114 Ibid., 7.

115 Ibid., 6.

116 Ibid.

117 Ibid., 3.

118 Ibid., 10.

119 Ibid., 47

120 Ibid., 49.

121 Ibid., 47 and 48.

122 Ibid., 49.

123 Ibid.

124 Ibid., 13.

125 Kean, "The Development of the Valley Line of the Baltimore and Ohio Railroad," 547.

126 Hildebrand, *Iron Horses in the Valley*, 55.

127 Ibid., 84.

128 Ibid., 51.

129 Ibid., 20.

130 Ibid.

131 Ibid., 25.

132 Ibid., 36 and 45

133 Fourth Annual Report of the State Corporation Commission of Virginia, Part II, Year Ending December 31, 1906 (Richmond, VA: Davis Bottom, Public Printer).

134 "Cumberland Valley and Martinsburg Railroad Company, History" (Eighth Annual Report of the State Corporation Commission of Virginia, Year Ending December 31, 1910), 417.

135 "Martinsburg and Potomac Railroad" (New York, NY: Poor's Manual of Railroads, 1874), 183.

136 Acts of the Legislature of West Virginia at its Session Commencing January 19, 1869, "Act to Incorporate the Shenandoah River Company," 52.

137 Ibid., 55.

138 usgpo.gov, United States Congressional Serial Set, Volume 2371, "Improvement of Shenandoah River, West Virginia"

(Washington, DC: Government Printing Office, 1886), 957.

[139] Ibid.

[140] Ibid.

[141] nps.gov, National Park Service, *Chesapeake and Ohio Canal, A Guide to the National Historic Park* (Washington DC: Division of Publications, 1991), 60.

[142] Ibid., 64.

[143] Ibid.

[144] Linhart, "Up to Date and Progressive," 65.

[145] Ibid.

[146] Norris, *History of the Lower Shenandoah Valley*, 215.

[147] frontroyalva.com, "Walking Tour of Front Royal, Virginia."

[148] John Hudson, *History of Bank of Clarke County* (Berryville, VA: Bank of Clarke County, 2006), 7.

[149] Norris, *History of the Lower Shenandoah Valley*, 311.

[150] Ibid.

[151] jsb.bank.com, Jefferson Security Bank, "Bank History & Mission."

[152] A. D. Kenamond, *Prominent Men of Shepherdstown During its First 200 Years* (Charles Town, WV: Jefferson County Historical Society, 1963), 40.

[153] mybct.com, Bank of Charles Town, "About Us, Our History," and Doug Perks, "History Matters: A Banking Future Across Charles Town" (Charles Town: Spirit of Jefferson, ^-8-2022)

[154] Bill Theriault, "Rebuilding Jefferson County" (Charles Town, WV: Spirit of Jefferson Farmer's Advocate, 1-15-2004).

[155] Ibid.

[156] Handley Library, Winchester, VA, Stewart Bell Jr. Archives, "Henry Baetjer Records Collection."

[157] Ibid.

[158] isjl.org, Institute of Southern Jewish Life, "Encyclopedia of Southern Jewish Communities - Winchester, Virginia."

[159] Norris, *History of the Lower Shenandoah Valley*, 715.

[160] Shoe and Leather Reporter, Vol. 20 (New York, NY: Joseph R. Lorenz, 1-8-1880), advertisement on page 862.

[161] hpo.ncdcr.gov, North Carolina State Historic Preservation Office, National Register of Historic Places Nomination Form, Jim Sumner, "Franklin Pierce Cover House," May 1982.

[162] Darwin Lambert, *The Undying Past of Shenandoah National Park* (Lanham, MD: Roberts Rinehart, Inc. Publishers, 1989), 164.

[163] shepherdstownriverfront.org, Friends of the Shepherdstown Riverfront, Charles Belfoure, "Historic Structures Report for the Mecklenburg Tobacco Warehouse," 8.

[164] Conrad C. Hammann, *A History of Halltown Paperboard Company*, (Shepherdstown, WV: self-published, 1984).

[165] Belfoure, "Historic Structures Report for the Mecklenburg Tobacco Warehouse," 8, and Kenamond, *Prominent Citizens of Shepherdstown*, 41.

[166] Ibid.

[167] livingplaces.com, The Gomback Group, "Riverton Historic District."

[168] Northwestern Miller, Volume 51 (Minneapolis, MN: Miller Publishing Co., 6-19-1901), advertisement on page 1200.

[169] Scott, *Shenandoah Iron*, 99.

[170] Ibid.

[171] Lambert, *The Undying Past of Shenandoah National Park*, 79, and townofshenandoah.com, "Town of Shenandoah History."

[172] Ibid.

[173] Scott, *Shenandoah Iron*, 99.

[174] *Acts of the General Assembly of the State of Virginia Passed at the Session of 1869-70* (Richmond, VA: James A. Goode, Printer, 1870), 216.

[175] David Glaser, editor, *Business Cycles and Depressions: An Encyclopedia* (New York, NY: Garland Publishing, Inc., 1997), 150.

[176] Scott, *Shenandoah Iron,* 102.

[177] Ibid., 101.

[178] Jed. Hotchkiss, "The Virginias, A Mining, Industrial and Scientific Journal, Devoted to the Development of Virginia and West Virginia" (Staunton, VA: S. M. Yost and Son, printer January 1882), 12.

[179] Scott, *Shenandoah Iron*, 153, and Allister Baker, "Furnaces in Area May Get Historic Status" (Strasburg, VA: Northern Virginia Daily, 3-15-1999), 9, and Hotchkiss, "The Virginias," January 1882, 12.

[180] dhr.virginia.gov, Virginia Department of Historic Resources, National Register of Historic Places Nomination Form, Maral S. Kalbian, "Riverton Historic District, Town of Front Royal, Warren County, Virginia," 8-14-2000.

[181] lime.org, National Lime Association, "How Lime is Made."

[182] Gilbert, *Waterpower*, 128.

[183] Ibid., 132 and 129.

[184] Ibid., 129.

[185] nps.gov, National Park Service, "Virginius Island Historic Overview."

[186] Gilbert, *Waterpower*, 138.

[187] Ibid.

[188] Elmer Epenetus Barton, *Historical and Commercial Sketches of Washington and Environs, Our Capital City* (Washington, DC: E. E. Barton, Publisher, 1884), 157.

[189] Ibid.

[190] Ibid.

[191] Ibid.

[192] jeffersoncountyhlc.org, Jefferson County Historic Landmarks Commission, "The Shepherdstown Cement Mill."

[193] preprowhiskeymen.blogspot.com, Jack Sullivan, "Henry S. Hannis: The Millionaire Goes Mad," 5-2-2012.

[194] Ibid.

[195] newspapers.com, "Newspapers by Ancestry" (Hagerstown, MD: The Mail, 6-9-1899), 6.

[196] Sullivan, "Henry S. Hannis."

[197] Ibid.

[198] berkeleysprings.com, "The Washington Heritage Trail in Morgan County, Paw Paw."

[199] Ibid.

[200] skylandestates.com, "Skyland Estates, Linden, Virginia History."

[201] nps.gov, National Park Service, "Skyland Resort History."

[202] skylandestates.com, "Skyland Estates, Linden, Virginia History."

[203] The Bulletin of the American Iron and Steel Association, Volume 4 (Philadelphia, PA, 9-22-1870), advertisement on page 397.

[204] Ibid.

[205] Norris, *History of the Lower Shenandoah Valley*, 665, and Handley Library, Winchester, VA, Stewart Bell Jr. Archives, "Kurtz Funeral Home Records."

[206] Ibid., and Garland R. Quarles, *The Story of One Hundred Old Homes in Winchester, Virginia* (Winchester-Frederick County Historical Society, 1967), 179.

[207] places.afrovirginia.org, Virginia Humanities, "Robert Orrick Home."

[208] Alexandria Gazette, 9-9-1865.

[209] "Wealthiest Colored Man's Death Regretted" (Winchester Evening Star, 7-9-1902).

[210] Virginia Humanities, "Robert Orrick Home."

[211] Wayland, *A History of Shenandoah County, Virginia*, 178.

[212] Ibid.

[213] Ibid.

[214] William Needham and Jack Thorsen, "Massanutten Mountain: Geology and Iron" (Washington, DC: Potomac Appalachian Trail Club newsletter, April 2003), 7.

[215] The Bulletin of the American Iron and Steel Association, Vol. 14 (Philadelphia, PA, 1-7-1880), advertisement on page 23, and Scott, *Shenandoah Iron*, 149.

[216] Henry Wissler, "The Wissler Family Record, Being a Brief Account of Andrew Wissler's Branch," 40.

[217] Ibid., 53.

[218] Scott, *Shenandoah Iron*, 141.

[219] archives.countylib.org, Shenandoah County Library, Shenandoah Stories, "Liberty Furnace."

[220] Garland R. Quarles, *Some Worthy Lives* (Winchester, VA: Winchester-Frederick County Historical Society, 1988), 18.

[221] Ibid.

[222] Ibid.

[223] Norris, *History of the Lower Shenandoah Valley*, 788.

[224] Hotchkiss, "The Virginias," July 1884, 187.

225 Norris, *History of the Lower Shenandoah Valley*, 664.

226 Quarles, *Some Worthy Lives*, 109.

227 Norris, *History of the Lower Shenandoah Valley*, 664.

228 Vaughn, *Luray and Page County*, 44.

229 archives.countylib.org, Shenandoah Public Library, Shenandoah Stories, "Lantz Mill."

230 Roger Bianchini, "Riverton Dam: A Political and Historical Perspective" (Front Royal, VA: Warren County Report, November 2010), 2.

231 Berkeley County Historical Society, John W. Bishop, 12-1-2018.

232 Ibid.

233 dhrvirginia.gov, Virginia Department of Historic Resources, Historic District Nomination Form, David Pezzoni and James R. Graves, "Redwell-Isabella Furnace," 3-4-2005.

234 Ibid.

235 Ibid.

236 Norris, *History of the Lower Shenandoah Valley*, 694.

237 Ibid.

238 Ibid., 793.

239 phwi.org, Preservation of Historic Winchester, Inc., "Friday Photos: The Kernstown Distillery and Other Commercial Enterprises, 1904," 7-26-2013.

240 Darcy Spencer, "A Pleasant Place to Stay," in *Standing Ground, The Civil War in the Shenandoah Valley* (Strasburg, VA: Northern Virginia Daily, 1996), 87.

241 lva.virginia.gov, Library of Virginia, "Frederick County and Shenandoah County Newspapers."

242 Ibid.

243 Ibid.

244 Willis F. Evans, *History of Berkeley County, West Virginia* (originally published 1927, and reprinted by Heritage Books, Inc., Westminster, MD, 2001), 315.

245 loc.gov, Library of Congress, Search Newspapers, "Gerrardstown Times."

246 jmu.edu, "JMU Centennial Celebration – What's a Normal School" (Harrisonburg, VA: James Madison University).

247 nps.gov, National Park Service, "Storer College."

248 Vivian Verdell Gordon, "A History of Storer College, Harpers Ferry, West Virginia" (Washington, DC: Journal of Negro Education, autumn 1961), 445.

249 Ibid.

250 shepherd.edu, Shepherd University, "History."

251 Ibid.

252 wvencyclopedia.org, e-WV, The West Virginia Encyclopedia, "Shepherd University."

253 wvculture.org, West Virginia Department of Arts, Culture and History, National Register of Historic Places Nomination Form, David L. Taylor, "Town of Bath Historic District," December, 2008.

254 Rebecca A. Ebert and Teresa Lazazzera, *The Frederick County, Virginia: From the Frontier to the Future* (Norfolk, VA: Donning Company, 1988), 128.

255 archives.countylib.org, Shenandoah County Library, Shenandoah Stories, "Orkney Springs Resort."

256 vagenweb.org, VaGenWeb, Virginia W.P.A. Historical Inventory Project, 1937, "Henrietta Furnace."

257 Ibid.

258 archives.org, Library of Congress, advertisement printed at the Valley Farmer Book and Job Office, Mount Jackson, 1878.

259 Norris, *History of the Lower Shenandoah Valley*, 793.

260 archives.org, Rock Enon Springs & Baths, Frederick County, VA, 1880 promotional material (Washington, DC: Judd & Detweiler, Inc.), and Norris, *History of the Lower Shenandoah Valley*, 794.

261 archives.org, Library of Congress, "Full Text of Rock Enon Springs and Baths in Frederick County, Virginia."

262 vachronicle.com, Richmond Times Dispatch, 7-14-1907.

263 Ibid.

Chapter 5

[1] census.gov, U.S. Census Bureau, "National Wealth – Historical Statistics of the United States, 1789-1945," 10, and U.S. Census Bureau, Tenth Census and Thirteenth Census, and U.S. Bureau of Economic Analysis.

[2] Alan Greenspan and Adrian Wooldridge, *Capitalism in America* (New York, NY: Penguin Press, 2018), 95.

[3] Jonathan Hughes & Louis P. Cain, *American Economic History, Fifth Edition* (Reading, MA: Addison Wesley Longman, Inc., 1998), statistics on inside back cover, and Harold Underwood Faulkner, *American Economic History* (New York, NY: Harper and Brothers, 1924), 474 and 475.

[4] american-rails.com, "Railroad History, An Overview of the Past."

[5] uspto.gov, U.S. Patent and Trademark Office, "U.S. Patent Activity, 1790 to the Present."

[6] investopdia.com, Carol M. Kopp, "Creative Destruction," 11-20-2019.

[7] Greenspan and Wooldridge, *Capitalism in America*, 14.

[8] businessinsider.com, Business Insider, Gus Lubin, Michael Kelley and Rob Wile, "Meet the 24 Robber Barons Who Once Ruled America," 3-20-2012.

[9] Eric Goldman, *Rendezvous with Destiny*, (New York, NY: Vintage Books, 1952), 55.

[10] J. L. Coulter, "Agricultural Development in the United States, 1900-1910" (Oxford, GB: Oxford University Press, Quarterly Journal of Economics, November 1912), 3 and 9.

[11] thehistorybox.com, The History Box, Miriam Medina, "The Financial Crisis of 1884," 4-22-2012.

[12] u-s-history.com, United States History, "1893."

[13] federalreservehistory.org, Federal Reserve History, Jon R. Moen and Ellis W. Tallman, "The Panic of 1907."

[14] Ibid.

[15] Faulkner, *American Economic History*, 477.

[16] ibtta.org, International Bridge, Tunnel and Turnpike Association, "Legislative History of Federal Tolling Policies."

[17] Dan Vaughn, *Luray and Page County, Images of America* (Charleston, SC: Arcadia Publishing, 2005), 99.

[18] boyceva.net, Town of Boyce, "Town."

[19] railwaymailservice.org, Maral S. Kalbian, "Norfolk & Western Railway Station at Boyce," 12-22-2004.

[20] John R. Hildebrand, *Iron Horses in the Valley: The Valley and Shenandoah Valley Railroads 1866–1882* (Shippensburg, PA: Burd Street Press, 2001), 46.

[21] Ibid.

[22] Ibid., 67.

[23] Linda McCarty, "Welcome to Mudville" (Winchester Star, 6-18-2002), A7.

[24] Linden A. Fravel and Byron C. Smith, *Stephens City, Images of America* (Charleston, SC: Arcadia Publishing, 2008), 92.

[25] newtownhistorycenter.org, Newtown History Center, "The Twentieth Century and Today."

[26] Kirk Reynolds and Dave Oroszi, *Baltimore & Ohio Railroad* (Minneapolis, MN: Voyageur Press, 2008), 49.

[27] wvencyclopedia.org, e-WV, The West Virginia Encyclopedia, Robert L. Frey, "Baltimore and Ohio Railroad," 11-14-2010.

[28] Reynolds and Oroszi, *Baltimore & Ohio Railroad*, 49, and Linda McCarty, "All Aboard! Tracks Across Frederick" (Winchester Star, 7-3-1996), E6.

[29] Reynolds and Oroszi, *Baltimore & Ohio Railroad*, 49.

[30] McCarty, "All Aboard! Tracks Across Frederick," E7.

[31] Don C. Wood, *Documented History of Martinsburg and Berkeley County, Volume I* (Martinsburg, WV: Berkeley County Historical Society, 2004), 79.

[32] Ibid., 80.

[33] msa.maryland.gov, Maryland State Archives, Richard Love, "Brunswick's Blessed Curse: Surviving an Industrial Legacy" (Baltimore, MD: Maryland Historical Magazine, summer 1993), 135.

[34] Ibid.

35 Frederic Morton, *The Story of Winchester in Virginia* (Strasburg, VA: Shenandoah Publishing House, 1925), 130.

36 William Bender Wilson, *History of the Pennsylvania Railroad Company, Volume 1* (Philadelphia, PA: Henry T. Coates & Company, 1895), 397.

37 Paul J. Westhaeffer, "A Brief History of That Part of the Cumberland Valley Railroad Between Hagerstown and Winchester, 1867-1919" (Martinsburg, WV: Berkeley County Historical Society, BCHS Journal, Issue 12, 1983).

38 Thomas Kemp Cartmell, *Shenandoah Valley Pioneers and Their Descendants* (Winchester, VA: The Eddy Press Corporation, 1909), 63 and 64.

39 "Fifty-Fifth Annual Report of the Cumberland Valley R.R. Co. to Stockholders for Year Ending 2-20-1890" (Chambersburg, PA), 10.

40 Morton, *The Story of Winchester in Virginia*, 131.

41 Willis F. Evans, *History of Berkeley County, West Virginia*, published in 1927 (Westminster, MD: Heritage Books, Inc., reprinted in 2001), 332.

42 Ibid.

43 nps.gov, National Park Service, "Chesapeake and Ohio Canal National Historic Park."

44 *A Guide to Chesapeake and Ohio Canal National Historic Park* (Washington, D.C: Division of Publications, National Park Service, 1991), 67.

45 virginiadot.org, *A History of Roads in Virginia*, "The Most Convenient Wayes," Special Centennial Edition (Richmond, VA: Virginia Department of Transportation, 2006), 23 and 24.

46 Ibid.

47 James Norton Callahan, *History of West Virginia, Old and New, Vol. II* (Chicago and New York: American Historical Society, Inc., 1923), 548.

48 edn.com, EDN Network, Suzanne Duffree, "Edison Electric Light Co. Begins Operation, October 15, 1878," 10-15-2017.

49 census.gov, "Power, Net Production of Electric Energy," 506.

50 Gordon, *An Empire of Wealth*, 307.

51 *Acts of the Legislature of West Virginia at its Twentieth Regular Session, Commencing January 14, 1891* (Charleston, WV: Moses W. Donnally, Public Printer), 807.

52 loc.gov, Library of Congress, "Dam Number 4 Hydroelectric Plant, Potomac River" (Martinsburg, WV: Historic American Emergency Record, 1868), 37.

53 Ibid., 42.

54 Ibid., 46.

55 Ibid., 55.

56 Ibid.

57 Ibid., 74.

58 David T. Gilbert, *Waterpower: Mills, Factories, Machines & Floods at Harpers Ferry, West Virginia, 1762-1991* (Harpers Ferry, WV: Harpers Ferry Historical Association, 1999), 156.

59 Ibid.

60 Ibid., 158.

61 Municipal Journal and Engineer, Vol. 27 (New York, NY: Swetland Publishing Co., July-December 1909), 732.

62 Ibid.

63 Electrical Review and Western Electrician, Volume 56 (Chicago, IL: Electrical Review Publishing Co., 1-1-1919), 56.

64 The Electrical World and Engineer, Volume 46 (New York, NY: McGraw Publishing Company, 7-8-1905), 81.

65 ferc.gov, "Draft Environmental Assessment for Hydropower License" (Washington, DC: Federal Energy Regulatory Commission, August 2017), 65.

66 Ibid.

67 Ibid.

68 Ibid.

69 Ibid.

70 "Dam Number 4 Hydroelectric Plant, Potomac River," 83 and 84, and Kate Shunney, "The Birth of Local Power" (Hancock, MD: The Hancock News, 4-24-2013), 6.

71 "Draft Environmental Assessment for Hydropower License," 65.

72 John Moody, *Moody's Analyses of Investments, Part II* (New York, NY: Moody's

Investment Service, Public Utilities, Fifth Section, 1917), 1951.

[73] Electrical Industries, Vol. III, 1892 (Chicago, IL: Electrical Industries Publishing Co.), 213.

[74] Ibid.

[75] Ibid.

[76] burnshirehydro.com, "Burnshire Hydroelectric LLC, Historical Pictures."

[77] dhrvirginia.gov, Virginia Department of Historic Resources, National Register of Historic Places Nomination Form, David A. Edwards, "Mount Jackson Historic District," 2-23-1993.

[78] Ibid.

[79] Ibid.

[80] telcomhistory.org, "Telecommunications History Group."

[81] Rebecca A. Ebert and Teresa Lazazzera, *Frederick County, Virginia: From the Frontier to the Future* (Norfolk, VA: Donning Company, 1988), 150.

[82] Session Laws, Acts of the Legislature of West Virginia (Wheeling, WV, 1886), 325.

[83] shentel.com, "Shentel History."

[84] Wood, *Documented History of Martinsburg and Berkeley County, Volume I*, 74.

[85] Ibid., 75.

[86] Ibid.

[87] winchesterhistory.org, Winchester-Frederick County Historical Society, "Hollingsworth Mill History."

[88] Wood, *Documented History of Martinsburg and Berkeley County, Volume I*, 45, and census.gov, U.S. Census Bureau, Tenth Census and Thirteenth Census.

[89] Ibid.

[90] Ibid.

[91] Ibid.

[92] Ibid.

[93] Ibid.

[94] Wood, *Documented History of Martinsburg and Berkeley County, Volume I*, 65.

[95] *Acts of the Legislature of the State of West Virginia at its Twentieth Regular Session, 1-24-1891* (Charleston, WV: Moses W. Donnally, Public Printer, 1891), 1558.

[96] Wood, *Documented History of Martinsburg and Berkeley County, Volume I*, 44.

[97] Ibid., 45.

[98] Ibid.

[99] Wilbur S. Johnston, *Weaving a Common Thread* (Winchester, VA: Winchester-Frederick County Historical Society, 1980), 7.

[100] Wood, *Documented History of Martinsburg and Berkeley County, Volume I*, 46 and 47.

[101] Ibid.

[102] The Southeastern Reporter, Volume 38 (St. Paul, MN: West Publishing Co. (March 26 to June 18, 1901), 670.

[103] revolvy.com, Revolvy, "Roger Preston Chew."

[104] Sue Schell, "Biography of Roger Preston Chew," in Callahan, *History of West Virginia, Old and New*, 321 and 322.

[105] scripophily.net, Historic Stock and Bond Certificates, "Charles Town Mining, Manufacturing and Improvement Company Stock Certificate," 1891.

[106] ransonrenewed.com, "City of Ranson/City of Charles Town Brownfields Area-Wide Plan," December 2012.

[107] United States Congressional Serial Set, Issue 7777 (Washington, DC: U.S. Government Printing Office, 12-6-1920), 18.

[108] wvculture.org, West Virginia Department of Arts, Culture and History, National Register of Historic Places Registration Form, Geoffrey Henry, "Charles Town Mining, Manufacturing and Improvement Company," 4-10-2001.

[109] "Our Bridge Company" (Charles Town, WV; Spirit of Jefferson, 7-26-1892), 3.

[110] Ibid.

[111] Financial and Mining Record, Volume 29 (New York, NY: The Unit Company Publishers, 1-24-1891), 58.

[112] Ibid.

[113] strasburgmuseum.org, "A Brief History of the Museum."

[114] shenandoahstories.org, Shenandoah County Library, "Strasburg Steam Pottery-Depot-Museum."

[115] Ibid.

[116] csonner.net, "Strasburg Steam Flouring Mills" (Strasburg, VA: Strasburg News, 5-10-1917).

[117] Ibid.

[118] Maral S. Kalbian, *Clarke County, Images of America* (Charleston, SC: Arcadia Publishing, 2011), 43.

[119] Southeastern Reporter, Vol. 37 (St Paul, MN: West Publishing Co. (10-16-1900 to 3-19-1901), 814.

[120] cambridge.dlconsulting.com, Cambridge (MA) Public Library, Edward J. Stack, "Middletown, Virginia, One of the Great Coming Cities" (Cambridge Tribune, Volume XIII, Volume 25, August 1890).

[121] William Hanlon, "Aside from the Civil War Period, Middletown's History Remains Little Known," (Winchester Star, July 2, 1994).

[122] Thomas Bruce, *Southwest Virginia and the Shenandoah Valley* (Richmond, VA: J. L. Hill Publishing Company, 1891), 241.

[123] Ibid.

[124] Ibid.

[125] Ibid.

[126] Ibid.

[127] warrencountyva.net, Warren County, Virginia, "Regional Setting/History."

[128] United States Court of Appeals Reports: Cases Adjudged in the United States Circuit Court of Appeals for the Fourth Circuit, 1895, 378.

[129] Ibid., 379.

[130] rma.edu, Randolph-Macon Academy, "An Academy is Born," 5-17-2017.

[131] Ibid.

[132] Ibid.

[133] Dan Vaughn, *Luray and Page County, Images of America Revisited* (Charleston, SC: Arcadia Publishing, 2008), 16.

[134] Stephen Harnsberger, "Luray: A Splendid Town" (New York, NY: The Christian Union, 9-4-1890), 1 and advertisement.

[135] Norman H. Scott, *Shenandoah Iron* (Verona, VA: self-published, 2017), 179, and Shenandoah Herald (Woodstock, VA, 4-27-1893), 4.

[136] "Stanley Lots for Sale" (Page News and Courier, 10-30-1890).

[137] townofshenandoah.com, "Town of Shenandoah."

[138] Ibid., "Town of Shenandoah Comprehensive Plan, 2015."

[139] "Prospectus, Equity Improvement Company of Winchester, Virginia," 1890.

[140] Garland R. Quarles, *John Handley and the Handley Bequests* (Winchester VA: Winchester-Frederick County Historical Society, 1969), 31.

[141] Ibid., and 32.

[142] Ibid., 30.

[143] Jed Hotchkiss, "The Virginias: A Mining, Industrial and Scientific Journal, Vol. IV" (Staunton, VA: S. M. Yost & Son, October, 1883), 164.

[144] Mary Ann Rosenagle, Appellant, v. H. W. Palmer, John T. Richards and Lemeul Ammerman, Executors of John Handley, deceased, in *State Reports, Volume 186, Containing Cases Decided by the Supreme Court of Pennsylvania at May and July Terms, 1898*, reported by Wilson C. Kress, state reporter (New York and Albany, NY: Banks and Brothers, Law Publishers, 1898), 32-42.

[145] Ibid.

[146] Ibid.

[147] Ibid.

[148] Quarles, *John Handley and the Handley Bequests*, 39.

[149] Ibid.

[150] Ibid., 40.

[151] Ibid.

[152] Ibid.

[153] Ibid., 41.

[154] Ibid., 44.

[155] Prospectus, Equity Improvement Company of Winchester.

[156] Quarles, *John Handley and the Handley Bequests*, 50.

[157] Atlantic Reporter, Vol. 50, October 16, 1901 to February 5, 1902 (St. Paul, MN: West Publishing Co., 1902), 524.

[158] Quarles, *John Handley and the Handley Bequests*, 51.

[159] Weekly Notes of Cases Argued and Determined in the Supreme Court of

Pennsylvania, etc., March 1897 to September 1897, "Handley's Estate," 2-26-1897, 305.

[160] Quarles, *John Handley and the Handley Bequests*, 66.

[161] carnegie.org, Carnegie Corporation of New York, "Andrew Carnegie's Story."

[162] Quarles, *John Handley and the Handley Bequests*, 66.

[163] Ibid., 54.

[164] Ibid., 49.

[165] Priscilla Lehman, "Out of the Past . . . from the Archives of the Winchester Star, 100 Years Ago" (Winchester Star, 6-25-2018).

[166] wvculture.org, West Virginia Department of Arts, Culture and History, Cynthia Molle Oates, "Honoring the Apple, Mountain State Apple Harvest Festival," 2019.

[167] Kenneth E. Koons, "The Staple of Our Country: Wheat in the Regional Farm Economy of the Nineteenth Century Valley of Virginia," in Kenneth E. Koons and Warren R. Hofstra, editors, *After the Backcountry, Rural Life in the Great Valley of Virginia 1800-1900* (Knoxville, TN: University of Tennessee Press, 2000), 8.

[168] usda.gov, Census of Agriculture Historical Archives, Agriculture in United States in 1870, 1890, 1900 and 1910 (U.S. Department of Agriculture).

[169] Walter Licht, *Industrializing America, The Nineteenth Century* (Baltimore, MD: Johns Hopkins University Press, 1995), 116.

[170] Ibid.

[171] encyclopedia.com, Encyclopedia of Food and Culture, "The Natural History of Wheat" (Farmington Hills: MI: The Gale Group, Inc., 2003), and census.gov, U.S. Census Bureau, Ninth Census and Twelfth Census.

[172] usda.gov, U.S. Department of Agriculture, Census of Agriculture Historical Archives.

[173] U.S. Department of Commerce, Statistical Abstract of the United States, "Grains—Prices and Supply" (Washington DC: Government Printing Office, 1923), 221.

[174] Helen Lee Fletcher, *Shenandoah Apple Blossom Festival, Images of America* (Charleston, SC: Arcadia Publishing, 1999), 38.

[175] Susan Futrell, *Good Apples: Behind Every Bite* (Iowa City, IO: University of Iowa Press, 2017), 23.

[176] Evans, *History of Berkeley County, West Virginia*, 23.

[177] wvencyclopedia.org, e-WV, The West Virginia Encyclopedia, Richard Zimmerman and Henry Hogmire, "Orchards," 10-22-2010.

[178] Ibid.

[179] Report of the West Virginia Agricultural Experimental Station (Morgantown, WV: West Virginia University, 1911-1912), 73.

[180] Ibid.

[181] Thomas Condit Miller and Hu Maxwell, *West Virginia and Its People, Volume II* (New York, NY: Lewis Historical Publishing Company, 1913), 543.

[182] Ibid.

[183] wvgenweb.org, The WVGenWeb Project, Berkeley County, West Virginia, Marilyn Gouge, "Biography of Alexander Clohan."

[184] "Dr. Lupton's Orchards Sold," Fruit Trade Journal and Produce Record, Volume 40 (New York, NY: Fruit Trade Journal Company, 1-2-1909).

[185] Ibid.

[186] Ibid.

[187] Staff writers, *History of Virginia, Vol. IV*, "Virginia Biographies" (Chicago and New York: American Historical Society, Inc., 1924), 399-400.

[188] Ibid.

[189] Ibid.

[190] Ibid.

[191] Ibid.

[192] shawneesprings.com, "About Shawnee Springs Market."

[193] Ibid.

[194] "Henry W. Miller Obituary" (Cumberland, MD: Cumberland Evening Times, 10-26-1960), 20.

[195] Ibid., and Kate Shunney, "When Paw Paw Smelled Like Apples in the Fall" (Berkeley Springs, WV: Morgan Messenger, 10-3-2018).

[196] Johnston, *Weaving a Common Thread*, 158.

[197] U.S. Apple Association, Congressional Testimony of Phil Glaize, Glaize Orchards,

Winchester, Virginia, "Protecting America's Harvest," 9-24-2010.

[198] Johnston, *Weaving a Common Thread*, 159.

[199] Ronald L. Heinemann, *Harry Byrd of Virginia* (Charlottesville, VA: University of Virginia Press, 1996), 125.

[200] csonner.net, "Trees Must Be Cultivated" (Strasburg, VA: Strasburg News, 5-10-1917).

[201] wceda.com, EDA News, "The Apple House Celebrating 50 Years'" (Front Royal-Warren County Economic Development Authority newsletter, June 2013).

[202] Henry Wissler, *The Wissler Family Record* (Toronto, Canada: The Bryant Press, 1904), 59-61, and "400 Acres Brings $150,000" (Harrisonburg, VA: Daily News-Record, 3-29-1911), 1.

[203] waymarking.com, Waymarking, "Meem's Bottom Covered Bridge."

[204] "400 Acres Brings $150,000," 1.

[205] Terry Sharrer, *A Kind of Fate: Agricultural Changes in Virginia 1861-1920* (Ames, IO: Iowa State University Press, 2000), 161.

[206] britannia.com, Encyclopedia Britannica, "Gustavus Swift, American Businessman."

[207] Standard & Poor's Manual of Railroads, and the Interstate Commerce Commission, 1900.

[208] Ibid.

[209] encyclopedia.chicagohistory.org, Encyclopedia of Chicago, Susan E. Hirsch, "Economic Geography."

[210] Faulkner, *American Economic History*, 353.

[211] fred.stlouisfed.org, Federal Reserve Economic Data, Federal Reserve Bank of St. Louis, "Wholesale Price of Cattle for Chicago, IL, 1860 to 1940" (Washington, DC: National Bureau of Economic Statistics).

[212] Koons, "The Staple of Our Country," 11.

[213] idfa.org, International Dairy Foods Association, "Pasteurization."

[214] U.S. Department of Agriculture, Census of Agriculture, Historical Archive, Agriculture in United States in 1870 and 1910.

[215] Greenspan and Woodridge, *Capitalism in America*, 118.

[216] Koons, "The Staple of Our Country," 11.

[217] Handley Library, Winchester, VA, Stewart Bell Jr. Archives, "C. L. Robinson Ice and Cold Storage Co. Records," 1470THL.

[218] Ibid.

[219] Ibid., and Ice and Refrigeration (Chicago and New York: Nickerson & Collins Co., September, 1912), 111.

[220] *Annual Report of the Secretary of the Commonwealth to the Governor and General Assembly of Virginia, for Year Ending September 30, 1911* (Richmond, VA: Davis Bottom, Superintendent of Public Printing).

[221] wvculture.org, West Virginia Department of Arts, Culture and History, Mary Johnson, "A Nineteenth Century Mill Village: Virginius Island 1800-1860" (Charleston, WV: West Virginia Archives and History, 1995).

[222] Ice and Refrigeration, Volume 62 (January 1922), 75.

[223] Legislature of West Virginia at its Twenty-Third Regular Session Beginning January 13, 1987, "Corporations," 129.

[224] Ibid.

[225] The Butcher's Advocate and Market Journal, Volume 35 (New York and Chicago, 5-10-1905), 24, and Ice and Refrigeration, Volume 36 (January 1909), 83, and Volume 39 (December 1910), 113.

[226] Ibid., Volume 44, June 1913, 375.

[227] American Fruit-Grower, Vol. 2-5 (Charlottesville, VA: Virginia Horticulture Society August 1916), 2.

[228] The Glass Worker (Pittsburgh, PA: Consumer Publishing Co., 6-24-1922), 12.

[229] Ibid.

[230] Ice and Refrigeration, Volume 50 (May 1916), 341; and Volume 54 (June 1918), 350.

[231] usda.gov, Census of Agriculture Historical Archives, Agriculture in United States in 1870 and 1900 (U.S. Department of Agriculture).

[232] Theodore R. Hazen, *Flour Milling in America, A General Overview* (Washington, DC.: National Park Service, 2003).

[233] mnhs.org, Minnesota Historical Society, "Minneapolis Flour Milling Boom," and Hazen, *Flour Milling in America*.

[234] G. Meissner, "Roller Milling," The Northwestern Miller, Volume 14 (Minneapolis,

MN: Miller Publishing Company, 10-8-1882), 192.

[235] Ibid.

[236] alimentarium.org, Alimentarium, Vevey, Switzerland, "Milling."

[237] Hazen, *Flour Milling in America*.

[238] angelfire.com, Theodore R. Hazen, "How the Roller Mill Changed the Milling Industry," 1996.

[239] Ibid.

[240] shenandoahstories.org, Shenandoah County Library, "Lantz Mill," photograph.

[241] Wood, *Documented History of Martinsburg and Berkeley County, Volume I*, 61.

[242] usda.gov, Census of Agriculture Historical Archives, Agriculture in United States in 1870 and 1900 (U.S. Department of Agriculture).

[243] millpictures.com, "Willow Grove Mill."

[244] Vaughn, *Luray and Page County, Images of America*, 40, and ebay.com, advertisement for Skyline Flour Bag.

[245] Ibid.

[246] The Operative Miller, Volume 21 (Chicago, IL: The Operative Miller Co., January 1916), 254.

[247] Handley Library, Winchester, VA, Stuart Bell Jr. Archives, Photo Record, "Winchester Milling Corporation Flour Product Prints."

[248] Johnston, *Weaving a Common Thread*, 151.

[249] Ibid.

[250] Robert B. Gordon, *American Iron, 1607-1900* (Baltimore, MD: Johns Hopkin University Press, 1996), 114.

[251] Scott, *Shenandoah Iron*, 149, and Acts and Joint Resolutions of the General Assembly of the Commonwealth of Virginia, Session of 1877-78, 124.

[252] dhrvirginia.gov, Virginia Department of Historic Resources, National Register of Historic Places Nomination Form, Heather Crowl and Steven H. Mofson, "Elizabeth Furnace," 3-17-1999.

[253] Allister Baker, "Furnaces in Area May Get Historic Status" (Strasburg, VA: Northern Virginia Daily, 3-15-1999), 8.

[254] Scott, *Shenandoah Iron*, 179.

[255] Ibid., 173.

[256] Virginia Department of Historic Resources, National Register of Historic Places Nomination Form, Maral S. Kalbian, "Shenandoah Historic District," 12-12-2003.

[257] Jed. Hotchkiss, "The Virginias, A Mining, Industrial and Scientific Journal, Devoted to the Development of Virginia and West Virginia" (Staunton, VA: S. M. Yost & Son, 1881), 152.

[258] Scott, *Shenandoah Iron*, 184.

[259] Ibid., 103.

[260] Ibid.

[261] Ibid.

[262] townofshenandoah.com, Town of Shenandoah, "History."

[263] Scott, *Shenandoah Iron*, 202.

[264] Ibid.

[265] Ibid., 205 and 206.

[266] Ibid., 210.

[267] Darwin Lambert, *The Undying Past of Shenandoah National Park* (Lanham, MD: Roberts Rinehart Inc., 1989), 79, and Scott, *Shenandoah Iron*, 210, and David T. Fay, *Mineral Resources of the United States, Calendar Year 1904* (U.S. Geological Survey, Department of Interior), 75.

[268] Scott, *Shenandoah Iron*, 211.

[269] Vaughn, *Luray and Page County, Images of America*, 30.

[270] U.S. Treasury Department, Wm. F. Switzler, *Report of the Internal Commerce of the United States* (Washington, DC: Government Printing Office, 12-20-1886), 157.

[271] "The Wissler Family Record, Being a Brief Account of Andrew Wissler's Branch," 40.

[272] Scott, *Shenandoah Iron*, 136.

[273] Ibid.

[274] Ibid., 243.

[275] Ibid.

[276] Ibid., 237.

[277] Ibid., 225 and 266.

[278] Ibid., 233.

[279] Ibid., 274.

[280] census.gov, U.S. Census Bureau, "Twelfth Census of the United States, Bulletins Published Between April 29 and June 21, 1902," 6.

[281] Ibid.

[282] nps.gov, National Park Service, Reed Engle, "Shenandoah: An Abused Landscape?" 6-29-2017.

[283] Ibid.

[284] Cartmell, *Shenandoah Valley Pioneers*, 506 and 242, and Richard MacMaster, *The History of Hardy County, 1786-1986* (Salem, WV: Wadsworth Press, Inc., 1986), 288, and landuse.law.wvu.edu, West Virginia University Law, "Moorefield Comprehensive Plan, Adopted July 2016," 2-2.

[285] Shoe and Leather Reporter, Vol. 57 (New York, NY: Joseph R. Lorenz, January – July 1894), 999.

[286] Ebert and Lazazzera, *The Frederick County, Virginia*, 109.

[287] Hide & Leather (Chicago, IL: The Jacobson Publishing Co., 10-2-1920), 55.

[288] Cartmell, *Shenandoah Valley Pioneers*, 242.

[289] Ibid.

[290] Shoe and Leather Reporter, Vol. 20 (1-8-1880), advertisement on page 862, and Lambert, *The Undying Past of Shenandoah National Park*, advertisement on page 164.

[291] John Thomas Scharf, *History of Baltimore City and County, From the Earliest Period to the Present Day* (Philadelphia, PA: Louis H. Everts, 1881), 403.

[292] Ibid.

[293] Lambert, *The Undying Past of Shenandoah National Park*, 163.

[294] Ibid.

[295] Ibid., and Vaughn, *Luray and Page County, Images of America*, 34.

[296] Shoe and Leather Reporter, Vol. 27, 1-2-1889, 903.

[297] bguthriephotos.com, Bruce Guthrie Photos, "Washington Heritage Trail: Tannery vs. Hotels in Berkeley Springs."

[298] Jeanne Mozier and Betty Lou Harmison, *Berkeley Springs, Images of America* (Charleston, SC: Arcadia Publishing, 2011), 10.

[299] Ibid., 39.

[300] Editor, "Bicentennial Lecture on County Tanneries Live-Streamed This Saturday" (Berkeley Springs, WV: Morgan Messenger, 4-24-2020).

[301] encyclopedia.com, Oxford University Press, "Domestic System."

[302] J. E. Norris, *History of the Lower Shenandoah Valley: Counties of Frederick, Berkeley, Jefferson and Clarke, Volume 1* (Baltimore MD: Genealogical Publishing Company, 1923), 664.

[303] Ibid., 791, and Lyon Gardiner Tyler, ed., *Men of Mark in Virginia: Ideals of American Life; A Collection of Biographies of Leading Men in the State* (Washington, DC: Men of Mark Publishing Company, 1906), 293.

[304] Ibid.

[305] Ibid.

[306] Ibid.

[307] Johnston, *Weaving a Common Thread*, 162.

[308] Ibid.

[309] *Annual Report of the Secretary of the Commonwealth to the Governor and Virginia General Assembly, for Year Ending September 30, 1916* (Richmond, VA: Davis Bottom, Superintendent of Public Printing), 335.

[310] Wood, *Documented History of Martinsburg and Berkeley County, Volume I*, 66.

[311] Ibid., 67.

[312] Ibid.

[313] uspo.gov, U.S. Patent Office, *Commissioner of Patents Annual Report for the Year 1912* (Washington, DC: Government Printing Office, 1913), 296.

[314] Kristina Marie McIntyre, *Adaptive Reuse in Martinsburg: The Interwoven School of Crafts* (master's degree in architecture, College Park, MD: University of Maryland, 2008), 38.

[315] Bureau of Labor, *Eighth Biennial Report for the State of West Virginia* (Charleston, WV: The Tribune Printing Co., 1904, and advertisement for Interwoven Socks.

[316] Journal of Marketing Communications, Volume 85 (New York, NY: Printers Ink, 1913), 6.

[317] Johnston, *Weaving a Common Thread*, 54 and 55.

[318] Ibid., 58.

[319] Ibid., 59 and 68.

[320] Ibid.

[321] Callahan, *History of West Virginia, Old and New, Vol. II*, 354.

[322] Johnston, *Weaving a Common Thread*, 41.

[323] Callahan, *History of West Virginia*, 397.

[324] Ibid.

[325] Ibid.

[326] wvculture.org, West Virginia Archives and History, Jerra Jenrette, "Labor-Management Conflict in the Eastern Panhandle: Perfection Garment Company Battles the ILGWU."

[327] Ibid.

[328] Johnston, *Weaving a Common Thread*, 50.

[329] Ibid.

[330] Ibid.

[331] Ibid., 149.

[332] Ibid.

[333] Ibid.

[334] dhr.virginia.com, Virginia Department of Historic Resources, National Register of Historic Places Nomination Form, Maral S. Kalbian, "Winchester Historic District (Boundary Increase 2008)," 9-12-2008.

[335] Fibre and Fabric (2-10-1906), 15.

[336] Johnston, *Weaving a Common Thread*, 77.

[337] Ibid., and 82.

[338] Ibid., 34 and 14.

[339] Ibid., 83 and 84.

[340] Ibid., 86.

[341] Ibid., 87.

[342] Ibid., 175 and 176.

[343] Ibid., 90.

[344] Virginia Hinkins Cadden, The Story of Strasburg (Strasburg, VA: Northern Virginia Daily, 1961, reprinted by Strasburg Heritage Association in 2011, with credit to Kathy C. Kehoe).

[345] Ibid.

[346] Textile World and Industrial Record (April 1913-September 1913), 153.

[347] Thomas Blumer and Charles W. Pomeroy, *Front Royal and Warren County* (Charleston, SC: Images of America, 2004), 56.

[348] history-magazine.com, History Magazine, Barbara Krasner-Khait, "The Impact of Refrigeration," January, 2016.

[349] *Norfolk and Western Railway Industrial and Shippers Guide* (Roanoke, VA: N&W Agricultural and Industrial Department, 1916), 273.

[350] dairyprocessinghandbook.com, Dairy Processing Handbook, "Centrifugal Separators and Milk Standardization."

[351] Ebert and Lazazzera, *The Frederick County, Virginia*, 45.

[352] Norris, *History of the Lower Shenandoah Valley*, 795.

[353] "History of Toms Brook, VA" (Strasburg, VA: Strasburg News, 1905).

[354] Vaughn, *Luray and Page County, Images of America*, 57.

[355] Ibid.

[356] Elsie Hamstead, *One Small Village: Kearneysville, 1842-1942* (Hagerstown, MD: Hagerstown Printing and Binding Co., 2000).

[357] idfa.org, International Dairy Foods Association, "History of Ice Cream."

[358] Ibid.

[359] The National Provisioner, Volume 38 (Chicago and New York: BNP Media, January 4, 1908), 22.

[360] "Chapin-Sachs Manufacturing Company" (Strasburg, VA: Strasburg News, 5-10-1917), and thehillishome.com, The Hill Is Home, Robert Pohl, "Lost Capitol Hill: Chapin-Sachs Manufacturing Company," 9-30-2013.

[361] Handley Library, Winchester, VA, Stuart Bell Jr. Archives, "Businesses of the Area Collection."

[362] garbersicecream.com, Garber's Ice Cream, "About Us."

[363] Ibid.

[364] mnhs.org, Minnesota Historical Society, "Minneapolis Flour Milling Boom."

[365] "W. Rufus Caskey" (Martinsburg, WV: Berkeley County Historical Society, 5-23-2018).

[366] Ibid.

[367] files.usgwarchives.net, USGenWeb Archives, Jefferson County, West Virginia, "Biography of John W. Lloyd" (Chicago and New York: The American Historical Society Inc., 1922), 433.

[368] Ibid.

Endnotes: Chapter 5

[369] The Weekly Northwestern Miller (Minneapolis, MN: Miller Publishing Company, 5-17-1914), 543.

[370] townofshenandoah.com, Town of Shenandoah, "History."

[371] The Congressional Globe: The Debate and Proceedings, Second Session, Fortieth Congress (Washington, DC: Office of the Congressional Globe, 1868).

[372] Evans, *History of Berkeley County, West Virginia*, 62.

[373] wvculture.org, West Virginia Department of Arts, Culture and History, National Register of Historic Places Inventory, Don Wood, "Union Bryarly's Mill," 12-1-1979.

[374] Paul A. Shakel, *Culture Change and New Technology: An Archeology of the Early American Industrial Era* (New York and London: Plenum Press, 1996), 50.

[375] Deborah A. Hull-Walski and Frank L. Walski, *There's Trouble a-Brewin: The Brewing and Bottling Industries at Harpers Ferry, West Virginia* (Society for Historical Archeology, New York, NY: Springer International Publishing, 1995), 106.

[376] Ibid., 107.

[377] potomacbottlecollectors.org, The Potomac Pontil, Jack Sullivan, "The Singing Frog Was No Help to J. P. Haddox," September 2015.

[378] Walski, *There's Trouble a-Brewin*, 117.

[379] centralohiohistory.org, Central Ohio History, "Owens Bottle Machine Co."

[380] tazewell-orange.com, The History of Soda Bottlers of Southwest Virginia, Joseph T. Lee, "King Cola, The Royal Drink," June 2008.

[381] Ibid.

[382] Ibid.

[383] "The Purity of the Spring Water," pamphlet, Museum of the Berkeley Springs.

[384] American Bottler, Volume 28, (New York, NY: American Bottler Publishing Company, 1-15-1908), 54.

[385] Ibid.

[386] Evans, *History of Berkeley County, West Virginia*, 214.

[387] Ibid., 215.

[388] wvgenweb, WVGenWeb Project, Marilyn Gouge, "Alexander Clohan Biography," 1928.

[389] Ibid.

[390] Vaughn, *Luray and Page County, Images of America*, 40.

[391] National Dairy Products Corporation v. Federal Trade Commission, United States Court of Appeals for the Seventh District, No. 16455 (4-1-1964), 325.

[392] Ibid.

[393] "When Tomato Was King," pamphlet, Museum of the Berkeley Springs.

[394] James Morton Callahan, *Semi-Centennial History of West Virginia* (published by Semi-Centennial Commission of West Virginia, 1913), 346.

[395] "Berkeley County Orchard Survey" (Morgantown, WV: West Virginia University Agriculture Experiment Station, June 1915), 62.

[396] The Packages, Volume 13 (Milwaukee, WI: Packages Publishing Co., January 1910), 78.

[397] The Barrel and Box, (Chicago, IL: E. F. Defebaugh, March 1911), 60.

[398] Ibid.

[399] appleparermuseum.com, Mike Viney, "The Commercial Evaporator, an American Innovation in Drying Apples: The First Fifty Years—1864-1914" (International Society of Apple Parer Enthusiasts newsletter, December 2017).

[400] Ibid.

[401] "Fruit Drying Plant at Inwood Burned" (Washington Times, 11-11-1922), 6.

[402] newtownhistorycenter.org, "The Twentieth Century and Today."

[403] wvgenweb.org, WVGenWeb Project, Berkeley County, West Virginia, "Early Newspaper Extracts," and scripophily.net, Historic Stock and Bond Certificates, Charles Town Mining, Manufacturing and Improvement Company Stock Certificate, 1891.

[404] dhrvirginia.gov, Virginia Department of Historic Resources, National Register of Historic Places Nomination Form, Edna Johnston and Kathryn Gettings Smith, "Front Royal Historic District," 4-11-2003.

[405] Ibid.

[406] Garland R. Quarles, *Some Worthy Lives* (Winchester, VA: Winchester-Frederick County Historical Society, 1988), 99.

[407] Ibid., 95.

[408] Kalbian, "Winchester Historic District (Boundary Increase)," 9-12-2008.

[409] Quarles, *Some Worthy Lives*, 95.

[410] Greenspan and Woodridge, *Capitalism in America*, 421.

[411] Matthew Umstead, "Museum Gets a Rare Auburn Wagon Built in Martinsburg" (Hagerstown, MD: Herald-Mail, 5-27-2014).

[412] Ibid.

[413] Ibid.

[414] Wood, *Documented History of Martinsburg and Berkeley County, Volume II*, 284.

[415] wvgenweb.org, WVGenWeb Project, Berkeley County, West Virginia, "Early Newspaper Extracts," 9-16-1912.

[416] amhistory.si.edu, Smithsonian Institution, "America on the Move, Duryea Automobile History."

[417] history.com, "1908, Ford Motor Company Unveils the Model T."

[418] ARK Investment Management, Sam Korus, "The Automotive Industry is on the Threshold of Massive Consolidation," 8-26-2016.

[419] Kristen Green, "Shockey's Solid Foundation" (Winchester Star, 7-4-1996), F1, and winchesterva.gov, City of Winchester, What Can You Do in Winchester, "Snapp Foundry, Completed Project.

[420] "John Heller" (Martinsburg, WV: Berkeley County Historical Society, 9-29-1918).

[421] Wood, *Documented History of Martinsburg and Berkeley County, Volume II*, 286.

[422] wvencyclopedia.org, e-WV, The West Virginia Encyclopedia, "Norwalk Motor Car," 3-4-2013.

[423] Ibid.

[424] Wood, *Documented History of Martinsburg and Berkeley County, Volume II*, 286.

[425] Vaughn, *Luray and Page County, Images of America*, 40, and Rock Products and Building Materials, Volumes 14 -15 (Chicago, IL: Tradepress Publishing Corporation, 5-7-1914), 40, and newtownhistorycenter.org, Newtown History Center, "The Twentieth Century and Today."

[426] William D. Theriault, "History of Eastern Jefferson County of West Virginia: Establishment of Bakerton (1883-1921), Part 1" (Charles Town, WV: Spirit of Jefferson Farmer's Advocate, 3-14-1996), 17.

[427] National Lumberman, Volume 45 (St. Louis, MO: Commercial Journal Co., 4-1-1910), 87.

[428] Vaughn, *Luray and Page County, Images of America*, 65, and Industrial Development and Manufacturers Record, Volume 51 (Baltimore, MD: Conway Publishers, 1-17-1907), 291, and Corporation Report of Secretary of State of West Virginia, Volume 2, (Charleston, WV: Crossman Printers Company, March 4, 1905 to March 1, 1906), 730, and The Tradesman, Volume 66 (Chattanooga, TN: Tradesman Publishing Company, 10-19-1911), 58.

[429] National Coopers Journal, Volume 26 (Philadelphia, PA: John A. McCann, December 1910), 12.

[430] Historical Statistics of the United States, 1789-1945, "Physical Output of Manufactured Commodities, 1899-1939."

[431] *History of West Virginia, Old and New, Vol. III* (New York and Chicago: The American Historical Society, Inc., 1913), 371.

[432] "The Clay Worker," Volumes 25-26 (Indianapolis, IN: National Brick Manufacturers Association, 1896), 170.

[433] George P. Grimsley and I. C. White, *West Virginia Geological Survey, Jefferson, Berkeley and Morgan Counties* (Wheeling, WV: Wheeling News Litho. Co., 1916), 533.

[434] Washington Herald (Washington, DC, 2-22-1912), 9, and Martinsburg Statesman-Democrat, 9-20-1912.

[435] Ibid.

[436] Kathy Orton, "Tacaro Farm in Maryland's Horse County is an Ode to Brick" (Washington Post, 3-3-2017).

[437] Cigar Makers International Union, "Organizational History."

[438] Frank L. Olmsted, "The Tobacco Tax" (Oxford University Press, The Quarterly Journal of Economics, January 1891), 209, and Cigar Makers International Union, "Organizational History."

[439] *Lake's Atlas of Frederick County, Virginia, 1885* (Philadelphia, PA: D. J. Lake & Co.).

[440] stephenscity.org, "Walking Tour of Stephens City, Va., formerly Newtown and Stephensburg," Map Key, and *Annual Report of the Secretary of the Commonwealth to the Governor, Year Ending September 30, 1903* (Richmond, VA: Superintendent of Printing), 158.

[441] uspo.gov, Official Gazette of the U.S. Patent Office, Volume 97 (12-15-1901), 2527.

[442] Tracy Campbell, *The Politics of Despair: Power & Resistance in the Tobacco Wars* (Lexington, KY: Kentucky University Press, 1993), 22-23.

[443] madehow.com, How Products Are Made, "Cigar History."

[444] shenandoahpottery.com, "Historic Shenandoah Pottery," 2018.

[445] vagenweb.org, VAGenWeb Project, "Samuel Bell Home, Also Known as Bell Pottery."

[446] Ibid.

[447] A. H. Rice and John Baer Stoudt, *The Shenandoah Pottery* (Strasburg, VA: Shenandoah Publishing House, 1929).

[448] Jane Etter, "Strasburg Pottery is Very Collectible" (Valley Overlook, Byrd Newspapers, 9-19-2002), 8.

[449] Ibid.

[450] strasburgmuseum.org, Strasburg Museum, "A Brief History of the Museum."

[451] Ibid.

[452] archives.countylib.org, Shenandoah County Library, Truban Archives, "Strasburg Steam Pottery-Depot-Museum."

[453] David C. Smith, "Wood Pulp and Newspapers" (Cambridge, MA: The Business History Review, Autumn 1964), 334.

[454] Gilbert, *Waterpower*, 140.

[455] Wood, *Documented History of Martinsburg and Berkeley County, Volume II*, 199.

[456] Ibid.

[457] wvculture.org, West Virginia Department of Arts, Culture and History, National Register of Historic Places Inventory, Don C. Wood, "Power Plant and Dam No. 5 (Honeywood Dam)," 1980.

[458] nps.gov, National Park Service, Andrew S. Lee, "The U.S. Armory at Harpers Ferry, Historic Resource Study," 2006, 86.

[459] Gilbert, *Waterpower*, 139.

[460] wvculture.org, West Virginia Department of Arts, Culture and History, National Register of Historic Places Registration Form, Paula S. Reed, "Hydroelectric Power Plant, Harpers Ferry," June 1999.

[461] Teresa S. Moyer and Paul A. Shackel, *The Making of Harpers Ferry National Historical Park: A Devil, Two Rivers and a Dream* (Lanham, MD: Altamira Press, 2008), 22.

[462] Gilbert, *Waterpower*, 149.

[463] Ibid., 154.

[464] Ibid.

[465] Ibid., and Moyer and Shackel, *The Making of Harpers Ferry National Historical Park*, 22.

[466] "John L. (Franklin) Wissler, 70, Dies Suddenly" (Harrisonburg, VA: Daily News-Record, 1-14-1931), 1.

[467] *The Paper Mill Directory of the World* (Holyoke, MA and New York, NY: Clark W. Bryan & Co., 1884), 124.

[468] Ibid.

[469] Lyman H. Weeks, *A History of Paper-Manufacturing in the United States, 1890-1916* (New York, NY: Ayer Co. Publisher, 1969), 306.

[470] Ibid.

[471] Conrad C. Hammann, *A History of Halltown Paperboard Company* (Shepherdstown, WV: self-published, 1984), 32.

[472] Ibid., 80.

[473] *Lockwood's Directory of the Paper and Allied Trades* (New York, NY: Lockwood Trade Journal Co., September, 1909), 162.

[474] The Paper Box Maker and American Bookbinder, Volume 23-24 (New York, NY: L. D. Post, publisher, May 1916), 14.

[475] Ibid.

[476] *Lockwood's Directory of the Paper and Allied Trades*, 162.

[477] Hammann, *A History of Halltown Paperboard Company*, 11.

478 revolvy.com, Revolvy, "Jedediah Hotchkiss."

479 wvencyclopedia.org, e-WV, The West Virginia Encyclopedia, "Jedediah Hotchkiss."

480 *Travelers' Official Railway Guide for the United States and Canada* (Philadelphia and New York: National Railway Publication Company, April 1881), 42.

481 Crystal Cook Marshall, "Making and Breaking Big Rural: Science and Technology Construct the Coalfield" (PhD thesis, Blacksburg, VA: Virginia Polytech Institute, 12-20-2017), 100-102.

482 mindat.org, Hudson Institute of Mineralogy, "Epidote from Virginia and Pittsburgh Copper Company Prospect, Northern Section-Blue Ridge Province, Warren County, Virginia."

483 Thomas Leonard Watson, *Mineral Resources of Virginia* (Lynchburg, VA: J. P. Bell Company, 1907), 509.

484 Ibid.

485 revolvy.com, Revolvy, "Shenandoah Valley Railroad."

486 Hotchkiss, "The Virginias, A Mining, Industrial and Scientific Journal" (November 1880), 173.

487 americantowns.com, "Town of Stanley."

488 pubs.usgs.gov, U.S. Geological Survey, William F. Cannon, "Manganese—It Turns Iron into Steel (and Does So Much More)."

489 William Ascarza, "Manganese Mine in Arizona Fed US Need in World War II" (Tucson, AZ: Arizona Daily Star, 4-8-2018).

490 Thomas Leonard Watson, "Granites of the Southeastern Atlantic States, U.S. Geological Survey," U.S. Department of Interior (Washington, DC: Government Printing Office, 1910), 269.

491 G. W. Stose and H. D. Miser, "Manganese Deposits in Western Virginia, Issues 22-23" (Charlottesville, VA: Virginia Division of Mineral Resources, 1922), 58.

492 Ibid.

493 Ibid.

494 Ibid.

495 *Acts and Joint Resolutions of the General Assembly of the State of Virginia During the Session of 1877-78* (Richmond, VA: R. F. Walker, Superintendent of Public Printing, 1878), 324.

496 Scott, *Shenandoah Iron*, 149, and Stose and Miser, "Manganese Deposits in Western Virginia," Issues 22-23, 94.

497 Ibid.

498 Vaughn, *Luray and Page County, Images of America*, 31.

499 thediggings.com, Diggings, "Compton Manganese Mine, Rileyville, Virginia."

500 pubs.usgs.gov, U.S. Geological Survey, D. F. Hewett, "Some Manganese Mines in Virginia and Maryland," 1916, 30.

501 Ibid.

502 Ibid., 69.

503 Randal C. Orndorff and Jack B. Epstein, "A Structural and Stratigraphic Excursion Through the Shenandoah Valley, Virginia" (U.S. Department of the Interior, U.S. Geological Survey, 5-7-1994).

504 Linda McCarty, "Into the Tunnels of the M. J. Grove Lime Co." (Winchester Star, 10-3-2001), A6.

505 lime.org, National Lime Association, "How Lime is Made."

506 Ibid., "Iron and Steel."

507 geo.msu.edu, Department of Geology, Michigan State University, "Limestone Mining."

508 John Ashurst and Francis G. Dimes, editors, *Conservation of Building & Decorative Stone* (New York, NY: Taylor and Francis Group, 1990), 78.

509 greatamericanstations.com, The Great American Stations, "Connellsville, PA."

510 Grimsley and White, *West Virginia Geological Survey, Jefferson, Berkeley and Morgan Counties*, 404.

511 Ibid.

512 Ibid.

513 Ibid.

514 Ibid.

515 Ibid., 399.

516 Theriault, "History of Eastern Jefferson County," 17.

517 Ibid.

518 Grimsley and White, *West Virginia Geological Survey*, 399.

[519] Matthew Umstead, "Martinsburg Eyes Use of a Rail Spur for Trail" (Hagerstown, MD: Herald-Mail, 9-20-2020).

[520] Grimsley and White, *West Virginia Geological Survey*, 402.

[521] Ibid.

[522] Ibid.

[523] Ibid.

[524] Ibid.

[525] Theriault, "History of Eastern Jefferson County," 17.

[526] "Biennial Report, State of West Virginia," Department of Labor, Volume 7, 1901-1902 (Charleston, WV: The Tribune Company, 1902), 49.

[527] Stone, Vol. XXII (New York, NY: Frank W. Hoyt, January 1901 – June, 1901), 562.

[528] Grimsley and White, *West Virginia Geological Survey*, 408.

[529] Ibid., 406.

[530] Ibid.

[531] Caryle Murphy, "Town Fights Threat to Turn off Their Spigot" (Washington Post, 7-25-1999).

[532] Ibid.

[533] Grimsley and White, *West Virginia Geological Survey*, 408.

[534] Ibid.

[535] Ibid.

[536] Southeastern Reporter, Vol. 84 (St. Paul, MN: West Publishing Co., February 13-May 8, 1915), 910.

[537] Grimsley and White, *West Virginia Geological Survey*, 407.

[538] Mike High, *The C&O Canal Companion: A Journal through Potomac History* (Baltimore, MD: Johns Hopkins University Press, 2015), 276, and Southeastern Reporter, Vol. 84 (St. Paul, MN: West Publishing Co., February 13-May 8, 1915), 910.

[539] caselaw.findlaw.com, Court of Special Appeals of Maryland, "Lyon v. Campbell," 4-1-1998.

[540] dmme.virginia.gov, Palmer C. Sweet, "Virginia's Lime Industry" (Richmond, VA: Virginia Division of Mines, Minerals and Energy, November 1986), 34.

[541] Ibid.

[542] archives.countylib.org, Shenandoah County Library, Truban Archives, "Rockdale Lime Quarry," and Preston Knight, "Mundy Quarries Sells Two Locations" (Strasburg, VA: Northern Virginia Daily, 7-12-2011), and Thomas Leonard Watson, *Annual Report on the Mineral Production of Virginia During 1908* (Charlottesville, VA: University of Virginia, 1909), 84.

[543] Raymond S. Edmunston, "Industrial Limestone and Dolomites in Virginia: Northern and Central Parts of Shenandoah Valley," Virginia Geological Survey, Bulletin 65 (Charlottesville, VA: University of Virginia, 1945), 24.

[544] Ibid.

[545] Fravel and Smith, *Stephens City, Images of America*, 93.

[546] Ibid.

[547] Ibid.

[548] Wayland, *History of Shenandoah County, Virginia*, 130.

[549] Ibid.

[550] dhr.virginia.gov, Virginia Department of Historic Resources, National Register of Historic Places Nomination Form, Shirley Maxwell, "Killahevlen," 4-23-1993.

[551] Blumer and Pomeroy, *Front Royal and Warren County*, 61.

[552] encyclopediavirginia.org, A Publication of Virginia Humanities, "William E. Carson (1870-1942)."

[553] Ibid.

[554] Ibid., and Maxwell, "Killahevlen."

[555] Grimsley and White, *West Virginia Geological Survey*, 321.

[556] census.gov, U.S. Census of Manufacturers, General Statistics, "Glass Industry in the United States, 1869 to 1924."

[557] wvencyclopedia.org, e-WV, The West Virginia Encyclopedia, John Douglas, "Glass Sand Mining," 8-7-2012.

[558] Grimsley and White, *West Virginia Geological Survey*, 326.

[559] woodmontwritersenclave.com, "Woodmont of Maryland and Woodmont of Virginia."

[560] William Bauman, "Benjamin Mitchell Family History," October, 2017, 14 and 15.

561 files.usgwarchives.net, US GenWeb Archives, Valerie Crook, "Biography of Noah Q. Speer."

562 Ibid.

563 Ibid.

564 Mozier and Harmison, *Berkeley Springs, Images of America*, 17 and 122.

565 Ibid., 41.

566 Cook, "Biography of Noah Q. Speer."

567 Grimsley and White, *West Virginia Geological Survey*, 333.

568 Ibid., 332.

569 Ibid., 337.

570 Crook, "Biography of Noah Q. Speer."

571 Ibid.

572 Talk given by George Didawick on the "History of Silica Sand Mining in Morgan County," 10-17-2020, at Church of Christ, Berkeley Springs, commemorating Morgan County's Bi-Centennial, and Grimsley and White, *West Virginia Geological Survey*, 336 and 338.

573 "An Immense Vein of Sand Discovered at Berkeley Springs After Four Years of Prospecting" (Hagerstown, MD: The Herald and Torch Light, 8-29-1895), 5.

574 Ibid.

575 Didawick, "History of Silica Sand Mining in Morgan County."

576 Rock Products and Building Materials, Volume 9 (Chicago, IL: The Francis Publishing Company, 12-22-1909), 32.

577 Paint, Oil and Drug Review (Van Ness Publishing Company, 7-5-1911), 3.

578 Industrial World, Volume 28 (Pittsburgh, PA: Wentworth Press, 7-10-1911), 4, and Callahan, *Semi-Centennial History of West Virginia*, 364.

579 Evans, *History of Berkeley County, West Virginia*, 326, and Federal Deposit Insurance Corporation records; and antiquemoney.com, "Old Money from the Citizens National Bank of Martinsburg."

580 Evans, *History of Berkeley County, West Virginia*, 326.

581 Ibid.

582 West Virginia Blue Book, Jefferson County Register (Charleston, WV: The Tribune Printing Co.), 64.

583 John Hudson, *History of Bank of Clarke County* (Berryville, VA: Bank of Clarke County, publisher, 2006), 15.

584 Ibid.

585 dhr.virginia.gov, Virginia Department of Historic Resources, National Register of Historic Places Registration Form, Maral S. Kalbian, "Boyce Historic District," 8-1-2003, 50.

586 ffiec.gov, Federal Financial Institutions Examination Council, Federal Reserve System National Information Center, "Institution History for Winchester VA Main Branch (990325)."

587 Fravel and Smith, *Stephens City, Images of America*, 51.

588 Vaughn, *Luray and Page County, Images of America*, 54.

589 Ibid.

590 Ibid., 55.

591 ffiec.gov, Federal Financial Institutions Examination Council, Federal Reserve System National Information Center.

592 Ibid.

593 John William Leonard, editor, *Who's Who in Finance and Banking, A Biographical Dictionary of Contemporaries, 1920-1922* (New York, NY: Joseph & Sefton, 1922), 497.

594 Ibid.

595 Ibid.

596 Ibid.

597 Ibid.

598 pbs.org, Public Broadcasting System, Who Made America, "George Eastman."

599 winchesterstar.com, Winchester Star, "About Us."

600 Ibid.

601 Ibid.

602 Ibid.

603 Ibid.

604 loc.gov, Library of Congress, "Martinsburg Statesman."

605 wvencyclopedia.org, e-WV, The West Virginia Encyclopedia, "Martinsburg Journal," 10-8-2010.

[606] Ibid.

[607] chroniclingamerica.loc.gov, Library of Congress, "About the Farmers' Advocate" (Charles Town, W.Va.) 1890-1948."

[608] Ibid.

[609] Mozier and Harmison, *Berkeley Springs, Images of America*, 44.

[610] townofedinburg.org, Town of Edinburg Comprehensive Plan, (Front Royal, VA: Northern Shenandoah Valley Regional Commission), 12.

[611] Vaughn, *Luray and Page County, Images of America*, 71, and lva.virginia.gov, Library of Virginia, Searching Virginia County Newspapers: "Page."

[612] virginiachronicle.com, Library of Virginia, Middletown Weekly, Volume 1, Number I, 7-12-1912 and 9-30-1910.

[613] wvencyclopedia.org, e-WV, The West Virginia Encyclopedia, Jerry Bruce Thomas, "Shepherd University," 7-18-2016.

[614] Ibid.

[615] nps.gov, National Park Service, "Storer College."

[616] Ibid.

[617] Ibid.

[618] visitwaynesboro.net, "The Founding of Basic City, Virginia to its Merger with Waynesboro, Virginia, 1890-1923" (Waynesboro, VA: Waynesboro Historical Commission, 2005), 15 and 16.

[619] Ibid.

[620] Ibid.

[621] Tyler, *Men of Mark in Virginia: Ideals of American Life*, 259.

[622] lost.colleges.com, "Eastern College, Front Royal and Manassas, 1902-1920."

[623] Ibid.

[624] lcweb2.loc.gov, Library of Congress, "Baltimore and Ohio Railroad, Harpers Ferry Station" (Historic American Engineering Record, 1894).

[625] Ibid.

[626] harpersferrywv.us, Harpers Ferry Community Newsletter, "History of Harpers Ferry Bandstand/Gazebo," May 2017.

[627] wvculture.org, West Virginia Department of Arts, Culture and History, National Register of Historic Places Nomination Form, Jacqueline Hovermale, "Berkeley Springs Train Depot."

[628] Ibid.

[629] berkeleysprings.com, "Berkeley Springs Town History."

[630] Mozier and Harmison, *Berkeley Springs, Images of America*, 84.

[631] usgwarchives.net, US GenWeb Archives Project, *The History of West Virginia, Old and New* (Chicago, IL: The American Historical Society, Inc., 1923), 70.

[632] Engineering News (New York, NY: Hill Publishing Company, 8-8-1912), 95, and the Hotel/Motor Hotel Monthly, January, 1916 (Chicago, IL: John Willy), 76.

[633] Federal Writers' Project, *WPA Guide to Virginia: The Old Dominion State* (San Antonio, TX: Trinity University Press, reprint 2014).

[634] dhr.virginia.gov, Virginia Department of Historic Resources, National Register of Historic Places Nomination Form, Virginia Historic Landmarks Commission staff, "Orkney Springs Hotel," March 1975.

[635] *Annual Report of the Secretary of the Commonwealth to the Governor, Year Ending September 1903*, (Richmond, VA: Davis Bottom, Superintendent of Public Printing), 221.

[636] Richmond-Times Dispatch, 6-10-1916, advertisement, page 6.

[637] "Myers et al vs Rollins et al" (St. Paul, MN: West Publishing Co., Southwestern Reporter, January 1 to March 26, 1889), 488.

[638] Ibid.

[639] wvculture.org, West Virginia Department of Arts, Culture and History, National Register of Historic Places Nomination Form, William D. Theriault, "Shannondale Springs," September 1997.

[640] Ibid.

[641] Ibid.

[642] historicjordansprings.com, "Historic Jordan Springs Event & Cultural Center, Post-Civil War History."

[643] Ebert and Lazazzera, *Frederick County, Virginia: From the Frontier to the Future*, 128.

[644] Ibid.

645 "Orin C. Cullen Under Arrest" (Roanoke, VA: The Evening News, 9-14-1903), 1.

646 The Virginia Magazine of History and Biography, Volume 11, (Richmond, VA: Wm. Ellis Jones, Printer, July 1903), advertisement.

647 Maral S. Kalbian, "Rural Historic Resources Survey Report of Warren County, Virginia, 1991," 59.

648 csonner.net, Strasburg, Virginia (Strasburg, VA: Strasburg News, 5- 10-1917).

649 Ibid.

650 Ibid.

651 abandonedrails.com, Abandoned Rails, "Alexandria to Bluemont."

652 Handley Library, Winchester, VA, Stewart Bell Jr. Archives, Photo Record, "Blue Ridge Inn, Bluemont, VA."

653 dhr.virginia.gov, Virginia Department of Historic Resources, National Register of Historic Places Nomination Form, Maral S. Kalbian, "Bear's Den Rural Historic District," 6-13-2008.

654 patc.us, G. Freeman Pollock, "Why Skyland?" (Reprint from October 1935 edition of Potomac Appalachian Trial Club Bulletin).

655 John Kelly, "An Investment Fueled by a Reckless Affair" (Washington Post, 10-29-2012).

656 nps.gov, National Park Service, Shenandoah National Park, "Skyland Resort History."

657 Ibid.

658 Bill Baskervill, "A Tale of a Fortune Found and Lost" (Washington Post, 8-6-1987).

659 Ibid.

660 Ibid.

661 Vaughn, Luray and Page County, Images of America, 49.

662 showcaves.com, "Luray Caverns History."

663 caves.org, The Journal of Spelean History, "Endless Caverns" (Virginia and the Explorers Club, American Spelean History Association, Volume 22, Number 4, October-December, 1988).

664 Ibid.

665 Ibid.

666 Ibid.

667 Ibid.

668 Handley Library, Winchester, VA, Stewart Bell Jr. Archives, "Winchester Medical College Collection," 190 THL/WFCHS.

669 Ibid.

670 Ibid.

671 Jerry W. Holsworth, Civil War, Winchester (Charleston, SC: The History Press, 2011).

672 Milton I. Romer, National Health Systems of the World (Oxford, GB and New York, NY: Oxford University Press, 1993), 49.

673 Ibid.

674 Handley Library, Winchester, VA, Stewart Bell Jr. Archives, "Winchester Medical Center," 1926 THL/WFCHS.

675 shenandoahstories.com, Shenandoah County Library, "Hotel Strasburg."

676 Charles Paullin, "Hotel Strasburg Owner Aims to Sell Complex o the Right Buyer" (Strasburg, VA: Northern Virginia Daily, 12-25-2020).

677 Ibid.

678 wvhistoryonview.org, West Virginia History on View, "Kings Daughters Hospital, East King Street; Martinsburg, WV."

679 ewvcf.org, Eastern West Virginia Community Foundation, "2014 Report to the Community, Dr. T.K. Oates Nursing Scholarship Established to Honor City Hospital Founder."

680 shannondale.org, Shannondale and Beyond, Inc., "Jefferson County's First Hospital," 9-15-2016 (reprint from the Jefferson Republican, 9-20-1951).

681 Ibid.

682 Quarles, Some Worthy Lives, 242.

683 Ibid.

684 Ibid.

685 nps.gov, National Park Service, "Harpers Ferry Armory and Arsenal."

686 Wood, Documented History of Martinsburg and Berkeley County, Volume II, 288.

687 Wayde Byard, "War, Disaster Gave it a Place in History" (Winchester Star, 10-24-1994).

688 Ibid.

689 si.edu, Smithsonian Institution, Historic Preservation Reports, "Front Royal Site Cultural Resource Assessment," 9-20-2007.

690 fs.usda.gov, Gerald W. Williams, "The USDA Forest Service – The Firsts Century," April 2005, 8

691 Ibid., 37.

692 fs.usda.gov, George Washington and Jefferson National Forests, "History and Culture, Background."

Chapter 6

1 Harold Underwood Faulkner, *American Economic History* (New York, NY: Harper & Brothers Publishers, 1954), 583.

2 Ibid.

3 Ibid., 625.

4 Ibid., 627.

5 virginiadot.org, *A History of Roads in Virginia, The Most Convenient Wayes, Special Centennial Edition* (Richmond, VA: Virginia Department of Transportation, 2006), 31.

6 eh.net, Daniel B. Klein and John Majewski, "Turnpikes and Toll Roads in Nineteenth Century America" (La Crosse, WI: Economic History Association, 2-10-2008).

7 virginiadot.org, *A History of Roads in Virginia*, 27.

8 vagenweb.org, Shenandoah County GenWeb Project, Don Silvius, "The Valley Turnpike," 6-20-1997.

9 Ibid.

10 fhwa.dot.gov, U.S. Department of Transportation, Federal Highway Administration, Richard F. Weingroff, "Harry Flood Byrd of Virginia – The Pay-As-You-Go Man," 6-27-2017, and virginiadot.org, *A History of Roads in Virginia*, 29.

11 Ibid., 30.

12 Karl Raitz, "U.S. 11 and a Modern Geography of Culture and Connection," in Warren R. Hofstra and Karl Raitz, editors, *The Great Valley Road of Virginia* (Charlottesville, VA and London, GB: University of Virginia Press, 2010), 248.

13 Dan Vaughn, *Luray and Page County Revisited, Images of America* (Charleston, SC: Arcadia Publishing, 2008), 17.

14 Priscilla Lehman, "Out of the Past . . . from the Archives of the Winchester Star, 100 Years Ago" (Winchester Star, 8-19-2019), B5.

15 Raitz, "U.S. 11 and a Modern Geography," 248.

16 Klein and Majewski, "Turnpikes and Toll Roads in Nineteenth Century America."

17 wvculture.org, West Virginia Division of Arts, Culture and History, "The Road Ahead for West Virginia, Passage of the Good Roads Amendment" (West Virginia State Roads Federation, 1920).

18 townofshenandoah.com, Town of Shenandoah, Virginia, "History."

19 Ibid.

20 Vaughn, *Luray and Page County Revisited, Images of America*, 94.

21 F. C. Lowe, "When Trains Ruled the World" (Winchester Star, 10-7-2010), A2.

22 Priscilla Lehman, "Out of the Past . . . from the Archives of the Winchester Star, 100 Years Ago" (Winchester Star, 8-6-2018), B6.

23 Ibid.

24 Paul J. Westhaeffer, *History of the Cumberland Valley Railroad, 1835-1919* (Washington, D.C. Chapter: National Railway Historical Society, 1979), 45.

25 Ibid.

26 John R. Hildebrand, *Iron Horses in the Valley: The Valley and Shenandoah Valley Railroads, 1866–1882* (Shippensburg, PA: Burd Street Press, 2001), 67.

27 Lowe, "When Trains Ruled the World."

28 potomaceagle.info, "Potomac Eagle History."

29 Ibid.

30 awpa.com, Wood-Preserving, "The B&O Timber Preserving Plant" (Baltimore, MD: American Wood Preservers' Association, January – March, 1915), 8.

31 Ibid.

32 Ibid.

33 Lumber World Review (Chicago, IL: Lumber Review Company, 8-25-1913), 42.

34 American Lumberman (Chicago, IL: American Lumberman Co., 2-14-1914), 76.

[35] Railroad Review (Chicago, IL: Willard A. Smith, publisher, 8-6-1916), 199.

[36] Ibid.

[37] Lawrence P. Winnemore, *Winchester and Western Railroad* (Washington, D.C. Chapter: National Railway Historical Society, 1976), 1.

[38] Ibid.

[39] Winchester Evening Star, 1-14-1918.

[40] Ibid., 10-17-1916.

[41] Ibid.

[42] Ibid., 5-25-1921.

[43] Ibid.

[44] american-rails.com, Railroads: A Long and Storied History of America By Rail, "Winchester and Western Railroad."

[45] Winnemore, *Winchester and Western Railroad*, 8.

[46] Lumber World Review, 3-10-1922, 59.

[47] Ibid., and Winnemore, *Winchester and Western Railroad*, 9.

[48] Ibid.

[49] Ibid.

[50] Ibid.

[51] Walter J. Meade, *Competition and Oligopoly in the Douglas Fir Lumber Industry* (Berkeley and Los Angeles, CA: University of California Press, 1966), 43.

[52] Winnemore, *Winchester and Western Railroad*, 9.

[53] Ibid., 22.

[54] Ibid., 9.

[55] Linda McCarty, "All Aboard! Tracks Across Frederick" (Winchester Star, 7-3-1996).

[56] U.S. Department of Commerce, *Statistical Abstract of the United States, 1946*, 70, and fraser.stlouis.org, Joseph L. Muller and Charles W. Slifko, "Lumber Industry Under Wartime Conditions" (St. Louis Federal Reserve Bank Survey of Current Business, August 1942), 18.

[57] Winnemore, *Winchester and Western Railroad*, 19.

[58] McCarty, "All Aboard! Tracks Across Frederick."

[59] Wilbur S. Johnston, *Weaving a Common Thread* (Winchester, VA: Winchester-Frederick County Historical Society, 1980), 191 and 192, and Kenneth W. Rose, "The Problematic Legacy of Judge John Handley" (Winchester, VA: Winchester-Frederick County Historical Society Journal, Volume 25, 2003).

[60] Ibid.

[61] Ibid.

[62] McCarty, "All Aboard! Tracks Across Frederick."

[63] Ibid.

[64] Ibid.

[65] Faulkner, *American Economic History*, 502.

[66] Ibid.

[67] charleslindbergh.com, "Charles Lindbergh Biography, An American Aviator."

[68] centennialofflight.net, U.S. Centennial of Flight Commission, Roger Mola, "The Earliest Airports."

[69] flymrb.com, Eastern West Virginia Regional Airport, "History."

[70] Ibid.

[71] Ibid.

[72] Ibid.

[73] Ibid.

[74] Ibid.

[75] Laura Arenschield, "The History of Aviation in the Winchester Area is a Chronicle of Continuing Growth and Progress" (Winchester Star, March 13, 2007).

[76] Ibid.

[77] virginiaaviationhistory.org, "A Brief History of Winchester's Three Airports" (Fredericksburg, VA: Virginia Eagles, Official Newsletter of the Virginia Aeronautical Historical Society, Oct.-Dec. 1999), 14.

[78] Arenschield, "The History of Aviation in the Winchester Area."

[79] "A Brief History of Winchester's Three Airports," 14 and 15.

[80] Ibid.

[81] loc.gov, Library of Congress, "Dam Number 4 Hydroelectric Plant, Potomac River" (Martinsburg, WV: Historic American Emergency Record, 1968), 100.

[82] Ibid., 99, and Frederick Post (Frederick, MD, 8-19-1916).

[83] Ibid.

84 "Dam Number 4 Hydroelectric Plant, Potomac River," 128.

85 Ibid., 129.

86 Ibid.

87 Ibid.

88 Ibid.

89 Ibid.

90 wvculture.org, West Virginia Department of Arts, Culture and History, National Register of Historic Places Nomination Form, Edith Wallace, "Hydroelectric Power Plant," December 2000, and David T. Gilbert, *Waterpower: Mills, Factories, Machines & Floods at Harpers Ferry, West Virginia, 1762-1991* (Harpers Ferry, WV: Harpers Ferry Historical Association, 1999), 166.

91 Ibid., 167.

92 Industrial Development and Manufacturers Record, Volume 81 (Baltimore, MD: Conway Publishers, 6-29-1922), 68.

93 *Federal Register* (Washington, D.C.: National Archives of the United States, 4-3-1945), 4284.

94 census.gov, U.S. Census Bureau, Thirteenth Census and Fifteenth Census.

95 Ibid.

96 Ibid.

97 Ibid, and Eighth Census.

98 Mary Sullivan Linhart, "Up to Date and Progressive: Winchester and Frederick County, Virginia, 1870-1980" (PhD dissertation, Fairfax, VA: George Mason University, 2014), 115.

99 trace.tennessee.edu, Joseph Paul Guttmann, "Agricultural Land-Use Change and Local Context: The Shenandoah-Cumberland Valley Apple Growing District in the Eastern United States" (PhD dissertation, Knoxville, TN: University of Tennessee, August 2012), 62.

100 Handley Library, Winchester, VA, Stuart Bell Jr. Archives, "Top of Virginia Regional Chamber Records."

101 Mary Ann Lutz Williamson and Jean Allen Davis, *History of Edinburg, Virginia* (Edinburg, VA: Edinburg Heritage Foundation, 1994).

102 Ibid.

103 postalmuseum.si.edu, Smithsonian National Postal Museum, "Precious Packages – American's Parcel Post Service."

104 Don C. Wood, *Documented History of Martinsburg and Berkeley County, Volume I* (Martinsburg, WV: Berkeley County Historical Society, 2004), 55.

105 handley.pastperfectonline.com, Handley Library, Stewart Bell Jr Archives, "Empire Theater" and Capital Theater Collection, 1584 WFCHS/THL.

106 cinematreasures.org, Cinema Treasures, "Palace Theater."

107 Ibid., "Apollo Civic Theater."

108 Kathryn Parker, *Winchester, Images of America* (Charleston, SC: Arcadia Publishing, 2006), 64.

109 Ibid.

110 shenandoahwv.com, The Shenandoah, "History."

111 Ibid., and John McVey, "Unique Events Venue Available in Martinsburg's Shenandoah Hotel" (Martinsburg, WV: The Journal, 12-30-2015).

112 Raitz, "U.S. 11 and a Modern Geography," 258.

113 Ibid., 264 and 265.

114 Ibid.

115 "Notes from Frederick County" (Richmond, VA: The Southern Planter, Volume 74, May 1913), 538.

116 pagecountygrown.com, "Page County Grown, From the Heart of the Shenandoah Valley, Retailers."

117 Doug Havatter, "The History of the Berkeley County Fair, 1915-2017" (Martinsburg, WV: The Journal, 7-29-2017).

118 Ibid.

119 shenandoahstories.com, Shenandoah County Library, "Shenandoah County Fair."

120 Ibid.

121 Vaughn, *Luray and Page County Revisited, Images of America*, 20.

122 Gordon, *An Empire of Wealth*, 288.

123 nass.usda.gov, "All Wheat Area Planted and Harvested, Yield, Production, Price and Value in the United States: 1866-2017" (National Agricultural Statistics Service,

U.S. Department of Agriculture), 206, and agcensus.mannlib.cornell.edu, Census of Agriculture Historical Archives, "Agriculture in United States in 1920" (U.S. Department of Agriculture).

[124] nass.usda.gov, "All Wheat Area Planted and Harvested," 206.

[125] usda.gov, Census of Agriculture Historical Archives, "Agriculture in the United States in 1910, 1920, 1930 and 1940."

[126] Ibid.

[127] virginiaplaces.org, Virginia Places, "Rain and Drought in Virginia."

[128] Ibid.

[129] usda.gov, Census of Agriculture Historical Archives, "Agriculture in the United States in 1910, 1920, 1930 and 1940."

[130] Ibid.

[131] census.gov, Fourteenth Census of the United States, State Compendium: Virginia (U.S. Government Printing Office, 1925).

[132] fsa.usda.gov, Cornell Program on Dairy Markets & Policy, "Price Volatility in US Dairy Markets" (Farm Service Agency, U.S. Department of Agriculture).

[133] Ibid.

[134] nal.usda.gov, National Agriculture Library, U.S. Department of Agriculture, Bureau of Dairy Industry.

[135] fsa.usda.gov, Cornell Program on Dairy Markets & Policy, "Price Volatility in US Dairy Markets" (Farm Service Agency, U.S. Department of Agriculture).

[136] mdvamilk.com, Maryland & Virginia Milk Producers Cooperative Association, "Our Roots."

[137] Hutzel Metzger, "Cooperative Marketing of Fluid Milk" (U.S. Department of Agriculture, May 1930), 87.

[138] Priscilla Lehman, "Out of the Past . . . from the Archives of the Winchester Star, 100 Years Ago" (Winchester Star, 10-1-2018), E7.

[139] census.gov, U.S. Census Bureau, "Historical Statistics of the United States, 1789-1945: Agriculture" (Series E1-219).

[140] "400 Acres Brings $150,000" (Harrisonburg, VA: Daily News-Record, 3-29-1911), 1.

[141] Priscilla Lehman, "Out of the Past . . . from the Archives of the Winchester Star, 100 Years Ago" (Winchester Star, 10-28-2019), B5.

[142] Ibid., and ancestors.familysearch.org, Family Search, "Fred Albert Robinson."

[143] census.gov, U.S. Department of Agriculture Census, 1910 and 1930.

[144] Ibid.

[145] Winnemore, *Winchester and Western Railroad*, 10.

[146] Ronald L. Heinemann, *Harry Byrd of Virginia* (Charlottesville, VA: University of Virginia Press, 1996), 138.

[147] arec.vaes.vt.edu, Virginia Agricultural Research and Extension Centers, "History of the Alson H. Smith Jr. Center" (Blacksburg, VA: Virginia Tech).

[148] Ibid.

[149] Ice and Refrigeration, Volume 52 (Chicago and New York: Nickerson & Collins Co., March 1917), 171.

[150] Heinemann, *Harry Byrd of Virginia*, 136, and Priscilla Lehman, "Out of the Past . . . from the Archives of the Winchester Star, 100 Years Ago (Winchester Star, 3-23-2020), B5.

[151] Ibid.

[152] dhr.virginia.gov, Virginia Department of Historic Resources, National Register of Historic Places Registration Form, William T. Frazier, "Virginia Apple Storage Warehouse," 2-9-2018.

[153] Ibid.

[154] Ice and Refrigeration, Volume 52 (March 1917), 171.

[155] American Fruit-Grower, Vol. 2-5 (Charlottesville, VA: Virginia Horticulture Society, August 1916), 2.

[156] Johnston, *Weaving a Common Thread*, 88.

[157] Ibid., 68.

[158] wwiusarmyservicecoats.wordpress.com, "U.S. Army Service Coats of World War I."

[159] Johnston, *Weaving a Common Thread*, 70.

[160] Ibid., 156.

[161] Ibid., 88.

[162] Ibid., 174.

[163] Ibid., and 175.

[164] Ibid.

[165] Ibid., 50.

[166] Ibid., 51.

[167] Ibid., 52.

[168] Ibid.

[169] collections.nrm.org, Norman Rockwell Museum, "Browse the Digital Collection of Interwoven Socks Advertisements."

[170] wvencyclopedia.org, e-WV, The West Virginia Encyclopedia, Jerra Jenrette, "Interwoven Mills," 2-3-2012.

[171] Kristina Marie McIntyre, *Adaptive Reuse in Martinsburg: The Interwoven School of Crafts* (master's thesis, College Park, MD: University of Maryland, 2008), 46.

[172] wvculture.org, Jerra Jenrette, "Labor-Management Conflict in the Eastern Panhandle: Perfection Garment Company Battles the ILGWU" (Vol. 52, 1993), 109-126.

[173] Bob O'Connor, "The Centennial History of Ranson, W.Va. – 1910–2010" (Charles Town, WV: Spirit of Jefferson Farmers Advocate, 6-23-2010), 3C.

[174] Jenrette, "Labor-Management Conflict in the Eastern Panhandle."

[175] Dan Vaughn, *Luray and Page County, Images of America* (Charleston, SC: Arcadia Publishing, 2005), 36.

[176] Ibid.

[177] Henry M. Strickler, *A Short History of Page County, Virginia* (Richmond, VA: Dietz Press, Incorporated, 1952), 328.

[178] Ibid.

[179] menstylefashion.com, "Wrangler Jeans – The History," 12-20-2018.

[180] alextimes.com, Office of Historic Alexandria, "Out of the Attic: National Fruit Product Co. Goes Up in Flames," 11-26-2013.

[181] Ibid.

[182] whitehousefoods.com, "The Story of White House Foods."

[183] "Out of the Attic," and fohbc.org, Federation of Historical Bottle Collectors, Wade Cox, "White House Vinegar," Winter 2003, 40.

[184] whitehousefoods.com, "The Story of White House Foods."

[185] Ibid.

[186] "Out of the Past . . . from the Archives of the Winchester Star, 100 Years Ago (Winchester Star, 1-22-2023), A6.

[187] "Out of the Attic."

[188] Ibid.

[189] whitehousefoods.com, White House, "The Story of White House Foods."

[190] Warren Sentinel (Front Royal, 3-19-1920).

[191] Warren Sentinel (Front Royal, 8-17-1923).

[192] The Packages Vol. 23 (Milwaukee, WI: Packages Publishing Co., February, 1920), 48, and Canner and Dried Fruit Packer, Vol. 64, 1927 (Chicago, IL: Conner Publishing Co., 4-2-1927), 24.

[193] Ibid.

[194] Don Silvius, Berkeley Journal, Issue #33 (Martinsburg, WV: Berkeley County Historical Society, 2007).

[195] Ibid.

[196] wvgenweb.org, WVGenWeb Project, Berkeley County, West Virginia, "Biography of Gray Silver."

[197] Ibid.

[198] U.S. Department of Agriculture, Bureau of Chemistry, "Service and Regulatory Announcements," Issues 31-40 (11-7-1917), 267.

[199] *Notices of Judgment Under the Food and Drug Act, Volume 5001, PT. 5500* (Washington, DC: U.S. Food and Drug Administration, 1918).

[200] Chicago Packer, "Big By-Products Plant Sold" (Chicago, IL: Barrick Publishing Co., 1-3-1920), and West Virginia Secretary of State Mac Warner, Business Organization Detail, "Cumberland Valley Fruit Products Company."

[201] Priscilla Lehman, "Out of the Past . . . from the Archives of the Winchester Star, 100 Years Ago (Winchester Star, 12-10-2019), B5.

[202] Chicago Packer, "Big By-Products Plant Sold."

[203] realmarkets.com, RealMarkets, Real Estate-Auctions-Investments, "Sold – Foreclosure Auction, July 2, 2019 – Concrete Production Facility Located Near I-81."

[204] millcroftfarms.com, "About Millcroft Farms,"

205 Ibid., and worthpoint.com, "Antique Shenandoah Apple Candy Advertising Wood Apple."

206 Raymond Leslie Spangler, "Standardization and Inspection of Fresh Fruits and Vegetables," U.S. Department of Agriculture (Superintendent of Documents, U.S. Government Printing Office, August 1956), 4.

207 Ibid., 7.

208 Ibid., 8.

209 Peter Heerwagen, "Agri-Tech Hits 85" (Winchester, VA: Quad-State Business Journal, July 1997), 27.

210 archive.org, Internet Archive, F. J. Schneiderman, "West Virginia Community Packing House in Inwood as a State Service to Apple Growing" (Morgantown, WV: College of Agriculture, West Virginia University, November 1930), 3.

211 "As Far as We Know It . . . a Look at History" (Bunker Hill, WV: Bunker Hill Historical Committee, 1993), 243.

212 Schneiderman, "West Virginia Community Packing House," 3.

213 The Packages, Volume 24 ((Milwaukee, WI: Packages Publishing Co., January 1921), 37.

214 Archives (Hagerstown, MD: Daily Mail, 10-28-1938), 2.

215 James Norton Callahan, *History of West Virginia, Old and New, Vol. II* (Chicago and New York: American Historical Society, Inc., 1923), 111.

216 Priscilla Lehman, "Out of the Past . . . from The Archives of the Winchester Star, 100 Years Ago" (Winchester Star, 10-16-2017), B7.

217 Handley Library, Winchester, VA, Stewart Bell Jr. Archives, photo of 2424 Valley Avenue, Winchester, "Old Mill Cold Storage."

218 Heinemann, *Harry Byrd of Virginia*, 138.

219 Ibid.

220 Kate Shunney, "When Paw Paw Smelled Like Apples in the Fall" (Berkeley Springs, WV: Morgan Messenger, 10-3-2018).

221 agriculture.wv.gov, West Virginia Department of Agriculture, "Henry W. Miller Sr."

222 Cumberland (MD) Evening Times, 10-26-1990.

223 encyclopedia.com, Martin H. Stack, "Canning Industry."

224 Vaughn, *Luray and Page County Revisited, Images of America*, 40.

225 Henry M. Strickler, *A Short History of Page County, Virginia* (Richmond, VA: Dietz Press, Incorporated, 1952).

226 skylineranchresort.com, Skyline Ranch Resort, "Our History."

227 Ibid.

228 Henry H. Douglas, "The Alshire – Schaffer Farm, Page County, Virginia," Pioneer America, Vol. 2, No. 2 (International Society for Landscape, Place & Material Culture, July 1970), 45.

229 Douglas, "The Alshire – Schaffer Farm," 45.

230 Ibid.

231 Vaughn, *Luray and Page County, Images of America*, 38.

232 Ibid., 37.

233 Ibid.

234 Ibid.

235 U.S. Court of Appeals for the Seventh District, "National Dairy Products Corporation v. Federal Trade Commission, No. 16455," 4-22-1968, 325, and Blumer and Pomeroy, *Front Royal and Warren County, Images of America*, 63.

236 Ibid.

237 Ibid.

238 u-s-history.com, United States History, "Pure Food and Drug Act: A Muckraking Triumph."

239 "WV 9 Corridors, Berkeley Springs to Martinsburg, Environmental Impact Statement" (Charleston, WV: West Virginia Department of Transportation, 9-17-1996).

240 Jeanne Mozier and Betty Lou Harmison, *Berkeley Springs, Images of America* (Charleston, SC: Arcadia Publishing, 2011), 54.

241 obitcentral.com, Obituary Central, Miscellaneous Morgan County, West Virginia, Obituaries, "Paul Kesecker."

242 antiquelabel.com, photo of "Rare Historic Shawnee Brand Tomato Canning Label."

243 Barrel and Box and Packages, Volume 24 (Chicago, IL: Edward Harvey Defebaugh, Publisher, March 1919), 38.

244 The Barrel and Box (Chicago, IL: E. H. Defebaugh, March 1913), 35.

245 The Packages, Volume 21 (August 1918), 37.

246 Ibid.

247 Priscilla Lehman, "Out of the Past . . . from the Archives of the Winchester Star, 100 Years Ago" (Winchester Star, 3-2-2020), B7.

248 National Coopers Journal, Volume 36-37 (Philadelphia, PA: Associated Cooperage Industries, October 1921), 14.

249 Ibid., Volume 35-36 (May 1919), 10.

250 Priscilla Lehman, "Out of the Past . . . from the Archives of the Winchester Star, 100 Years Ago" (Winchester Star, 2-22-2020), B5, and Veneers (Indianapolis, IN: H. S. Smith Co., April, 1921), 49.

251 clarkecountypastperfectonline.com, Clarke County Historical Association, "Smalley, H. M., 1962."

252 nationalapplemuseum.com, National Apple Museum, Biglerville, PA, "Packing."

253 Priscilla Lehman, "Out of the Past . . . from the Archives of the Winchester Star, 100 Yeats Ago" (Winchester Star, 5-13-2019), B5.

254 Strickler, *A Short History of Page County, Virginia*), 327.

255 The Northwestern Miller, Volume 132 (11-22-1922), 856.

256 millpictures.com, Mills and Covered Bridges from All Over the World, "Proctor & Biggs Feed Mill" pictures.

257 American Miller and Processor, Volume 47 (Chicago, IL: Mitchell Brothers Publishing Co., 7-1-1919), 658.

258 Industrial Development and Manufacturers Record, Volume 78 (Baltimore, MD: Industrial Development Research Council, 12-23-1920), 115.

259 Manufacturers Record, Volume 82 (Baltimore, MD: Manufacturers Record Publishing Co., 7-6-1922), 100.

260 Ibid.

261 Laura Hutchinson Grant, "Milling Through the 18th Century" (Winchester Star, 9-29-1995), C2.

262 dhr.virginia.gov, Virginia Department of Historic Resources, National Register of Historic Places Nomination Form, "Ruffner House," J. Daniel Pezzoni, 3-7-2001.

263 Ibid.

264 Vaughn, *Luray and Page County, Images of America*, 35.

265 Strickler, *A Short History of Page County, Virginia*, 328.

266 hawksbillgreenway.org, "Greenway History."

267 berkeleysprings.com, Welcome to Berkeley Springs, "Washington Heritage Trail in Morgan County."

268 Cumberland (MD) Times (7-20-1951), 6.

269 Ibid.

270 The News Leader (Staunton: VA, 11-8-1930).

271 Brick and Clay Record, Volume 47 (Chicago, IL: Industrial Publications, Inc., 10-5-1915), 529.

272 *American Bankruptcy Reports* (Albany, NY: Matthew Bender Inc., 1920), 367.

273 The Clay-Worker, Volumes 71 and 72 (Indianapolis, IN: T.A. Randall & Co., January 1919), 509.

274 Ibid.

275 Standard Corporation Service (New York, NY: Standard Statistics Company, Inc., 9-1 to 12-31-1917), 256, and Brick and Clay Record, Volume 51 (9-11-1917), 481, and The Clay-Worker, Volumes 71 and 72 (January 1919), 509.

276 Brick and Clay Record, Volume 57 (11-2-1920), 323, and The Clay-Worker, Volumes 75-76 (January 1921), 590.

277 wvculture.org, West Virginia Department of Arts, Culture and History, National Register of Historic Places Nomination Form, Don Wood, "Continental Clay Brick Plant," May 1998.

278 Brick and Clay Record, Volume 59 (12-27-1921), 1031.

279 Ibid, and The Clay-Worker, Volumes 77-78 (June 1922), 60.

280 Brick and Clay Record, Volume 64 (5-13-1924), 756.

281 Joseph B. Shaw, "The Ceramic Industries of Pennsylvania" (State College, PA: School of Mineral Industries, Pennsylvania State College Bulletin, 1930), 84.

282 The Morning Herald (Hagerstown: MD, 9-14-1953), 111.

283 Ibid.

284 Cement Mill and Quarry (Chicago, IL: International Trade Press, Inc., 7-5-1920), 44.

285 Ibid.

286 Ibid.

287 eh.net, Gene Smiley, The U.S. Economy in the 1920s, "Productivity Developments" (La Crosse, WI: Economic History Association).

288 Wallace, "Hydroelectric Power Plant."

289 loc.gov, Library of Congress, "Shenandoah Pulp Mill, Shenandoah Street, Harpers Ferry, Jefferson County, WV," photos from 1968 survey, Historic American Engineering Record, WV-59.

290 Wallace, "Hydroelectric Power Plant," and loc.gov, "Shenandoah Pulp Mill, Shenandoah Street, Harpers Ferry."

291 Conrad C. Hammann, *A History of Halltown Paperboard Company* (Shepherdstown, WV: self-published, 1984), 11.

292 Ibid., 12.

293 oxindustries.com, Ox Industries, "Halltown Paper Mill - Celebrating 150 Years."

294 "Rehabilitating Paper Mill," The Paper Box Maker and Bookbinder, Volumes 23-24, (New York, NY: L. D. Post, 5-12-1916), 14.

295 findagrave.com, "Nathan Harold Carpenter Sr."

296 Ibid.

297 Winchester Star (12-12-1939), and revolvy.com, Revolvy, "John W. Kieckhefer."

298 Winchester Star (7-8-1941).

299 "Manganese Ores of Bukowina," Engineering and Mining Journal (New York, NY: Hill Publishing Company, 11-25-1916), 935.

300 G. W. Stose and H. D. Miser, "Manganese Deposits in Western Virginia," Issues 22-23 (Charlottesville, VA: Virginia Division of Mineral Resources, 1922), 94.

301 Ibid.

302 Ibid.

303 Ibid.

304 pubs.usgs.gov, U.S. Geological Survey, D. D. Hewett, "Some Manganese Mines in Virginia and Maryland," 48.

305 Philip B. King, "Geology of the Elkton Area of Virginia," Geological Survey Professional Paper 230 (Washington, DC: U.S. Government Printing Office, 1950), 66 and 67.

306 Norman H. Scott, *Shenandoah Iron* (Verona, VA: self-published, 2017), 294.

307 Ibid.

308 Watson H. Monroe, "Mineral Ridge Deposits of Cedar Creek Valley, Frederick and Shenandoah Counties" (U.S. Department of Interior, GPO, 1942), 129.

309 thediggings.com, "Godlove Mine in Shenandoah, VA, Manganese Past Producer, Discovered in 1847."

310 Ibid.

311 Stose and Miser, "Manganese Deposits in Western Virginia." 59.

312 Ibid.

313 "New Virginia Manganese Ore Property," The Iron Age, Volume 101 (New York, NY: Chilton Company, 4-4-1918), 893.

314 Ibid.

315 Stose and Miser, "Manganese Deposits in Western Virginia," 59.

316 Ibid.

317 Monroe, "Mineral Ridge Deposits of Cedar Creek Valley, 129.

318 Betty Clock Peckham, *The Story of a Dynamic Community, York, Pennsylvania* (York, PA: York Chamber of Commerce).

319 lcweb2.loc.gov, Library of Congress, "Standard Lime & Stone Quarry (Millville Quarry)" (National Park Service, Historic American Engineering Review, No. WV- 49, 9-24-1991), 6.

320 dmme.virginia.gov, Virginia Minerals (Charlottesville, VA: Virginia Division of Mineral Resources, January 1960), 4.

[321] csonner.net, "Strasburg, Virginia" (Strasburg, VA: Strasburg News, 5-10-1917).

[322] "Past, Feb. 15, 1923 – Mar 2, 1923," The Free Press (Edinburg, VA: Shenandoah Free Press, 6-28-2012).

[323] fundinguniverse.com, Funding Universe, Company Profiles, "National Gypsum Company History."

[324] Cement Mill & Quarry, Volume 19 (Chicago, IL: International Trade Press, Inc., 7-29-21), 43.

[325] dmme.virginia.gov, David A. Hubbard Jr., William Giannini and Michelle M. Lorah, "Virginia Minerals: Travertine-Marl Deposits of the Valley and Ridge Province of Virginia" (Charlottesville, VA: Virginia Division of Mines, Minerals and Energy, February 1985), 7.

[326] National Stockman and Farmer, Volume 45 (Pittsburgh, PA: Stockman-Farmer Publishing Co., 4-2-1921), advertisement on page 2.

[327] The Iron Age (New York, NY: Iron Age Publishing Company, 7-17-1924), 186.

[328] history.com, Erin Blakemore, "The 1936 Strike That Brought America's Most Powerful Automaker to its Knees."

[329] John Martin Heneghan, "A History of the United Cement Lime and Gypsum Workers International Union" (master's thesis, Chicago, IL: Loyola University).

[330] reuther.wayne.edu, Walter P. Reuther Library, "Quarry Union International of North America Papers" (Detroit, MI: Wayne State University).

[331] Henry Bridges obituary, (Hagerstown, MD: The Morning Herald, 4-27-1957), 20.

[332] David P. Bridges, *The Bridges of Washington County: Spanning Work and Nature* (Bookman Publishing and Marketing, 2003), and wvencyclopedia.org, e-WV, The West Virginia Encyclopedia, John Douglas, "Glass Sand Mining," 8-7-2012.

[333] Ibid.

[334] Douglas, "Glass Sand Mining," and George Didawick, "History of Silica Sand Mining in Morgan County," talk given on 10-17-2020 at Church of Christ, Berkeley Springs.

[335] Winchester Star (7-23-1930) and (8-30-1930).

[336] Ibid.

[337] Geological Survey Bulletin, Issue 1019 (Washington, DC: U.S. Department of Interior, 1-1-1949), 662.

[338] Letter from the Secretary of Agriculture, "Report on Present Condition and Value of Tract of Land Known as Mount Weather" (U.S. Department of Agriculture, 12-9-1914).

[339] Garrett M. Graff, *Raven Rock: The Story of the U.S. Government's Secret Plan to Save Itself, While the Rest of Us Die* (New York, NY: Simon & Schuster, 2017).

[340] Priscilla Lehman, "Out of the Past . . . from the Archives of the Winchester Star, 100 Years Ago" (Winchester Star, 8-24-2020), B4.

[341] Graff, *Raven Rock*.

[342] Priscilla Lehman, "Out of the Past . . . from the Archives of the Winchester Star, 100 Years Ago" (Winchester Star, 1-4-2021), B4.

[343] Lynn Rainville, *Virginia and the Great War: Mobilization, Supply and Combat, 1914-1919* (Jefferson, NC: McFarland & Company, Inc., 2018), 21.

[344] Ibid., 36.

[345] Ibid.

[346] fs.usda.gov, U.S. Department of Agriculture, Jean L. Satterthwaite, "A History of the George Washington National Forest," March 1993, 15.

[347] Ibid.

[348] Vaughn, *Luray and Page County Revisited, Images of America*, 54, and townofshenandoah.com, Town of Shenandoah, "History."

[349] fbvirginia.com, First Bank, "Our History."

[350] bostonfed.org, Peter Fortune, "Perspective: Is Margin Lending Marginal?" (Federal Reserve Bank of Boston, 9-1-2001).

[351] Faulkner, *American Economic History*, 645.

[352] Ibid., 646.

[353] Ronald L. Heinemann, *Depression and the New Deal in Virginia: The Enduring Dominion* (Charlottesville, VA: University of Virginia Press, 1983), 202-206.

[354] Ibid.

[355] Jerry Bruce Thomas, *An Appalachian New Deal: West Virginia in the Great Depression*

(Lexington, KY: The University Press of Kentucky, 1998), 61.

356 census.gov, U.S Census, Fifteenth Census and Sixteenth Census.

357 Ibid.

358 Ibid.

359 Ibid.

360 Faulkner, *American Economic History*, 673.

361 livingnewdeal.org, The Living New Deal, "Civil Works Administration (CWA), 1933."

362 wpamurals.com, Work Progress Administration, "New Deal WPA Art in Virginia."

363 The Living New Deal, "Projects in Front Royal, Warren County Courthouse," and Mildred Lee Grove, "History of Stephens City, Va." (Stephens City, VA: Newtown News, February-May 1993).

364 The Living New Deal, "Projects in Winchester."

365 Ibid., "Projects in Berkeley Springs and Morgan County."

366 lsc.usgs.gov, U.S. Geographical Survey, "A Brief History of the Leetown Science Center."

367 globalsecurity.org, "Mount Weather, High Point Special Security."

368 John P. Byrne, "The Civilian Conservation Corps in Virginia, 1933-1942" (PhD dissertation, Missoula, MT: University of Montana, 1982), 1.

369 Byrne, "The Civilian Conservation Corps," 4.

370 shenandoahstories.org, Shenandoah County Library, "Camp Wolf Gap."

371 Ibid.

372 guidetosnp.com, Guide to Shenandoah National Park and Skyline Drive, "Civilian Conservation Corps."

373 Byrne, "The Civilian Conservation Corps," 4.

374 Ibid.

375 Ibid.

376 Gordon, *An Empire of Wealth*, 328.

377 occ.gov, Office of the Comptroller of the Currency, Administrator of National Banks, "Citizens National Bank of Berkeley Springs," 1-5-2004.

378 archivescountylib.org, Shenandoah County Library, Shenandoah Stories, "Mt. Jackson National Bank," and John Hudson, *History of Bank of Clarke County* (Berryville, VA: Bank of Clarke County, publisher, 2006).

379 Willis F. Evans, *History of Berkeley County, West Virginia* (published 1927, reprinted 2001 (Westminster, MD: Heritage Books, Inc., 2001), 327.

380 Priscilla Lehman, "Out of the Past . . . from the Archives of the Winchester Star, 75 Years Ago" (Winchester Star, 8-20-2018), B5.

381 Heinemann, *Depression and the New Deal in Virginia*, 4.

382 nps.gov, National Park Service, Shenandoah National Park, Reed Engle, "Skyline Drive Historic District."

383 usda.gov, Census of Agriculture Historical Archive, "Agriculture in United States in 1929 and 1939" (U.S. Department of Agriculture, and Ithaca, NY: Cornell University).

384 Ibid., "Agriculture in the United States in 1930."

385 Ibid.

386 Faulkner, *American Economic History*, 662.

387 census.gov, U.S. Census Bureau, "Historical Statistics of the United States, 1789-1945: Agriculture" (Series E1-219).

388 Percy Wells Bidwell, "The New American Tariff: Europe's Answer" (New York, NY: Council on Foreign Affairs, Foreign Affairs Magazine, October 1930).

389 Frederick Kunkle, "Development Sneaks Up on W.Va. (Washington Post, 3-5-2000).

390 Ibid.

391 Linhart, "Up to Date and Progressive," 101.

392 Ibid.

393 Johnston, *Weaving a Common Thread*, 71.

394 wvencyclopedia.org, e-WV, The West Virginia Encyclopedia, Jerra Jenrette, "Berkeley Woolen Mills," 12-22-2010.

395 Johnston, *Weaving a Common Thread*, 71.

396 Jenrette, "Interwoven Mills.

397 Ibid.

398 Johnston, *Weaving a Common Thread*, 127.

399 Ibid.

400 dhr.virginia.gov, Virginia Department of Historic Resources, National Register of

Historic Places Nomination Form, Maral Kalbian, "Winchester Historic District (Boundary Increase)," 11-19-2002.

[401] Johnston, *Weaving a Common Thread*, 131 and 110.

[402] Ibid., 53.

[403] New York Times (9-15-1938), 20, and Textile World, Vol. 60, (New York, NY: Bragdon, Lord & Nagel Co., Inc., October 1, 1921), 97.

[404] Handley Library, Winchester, VA, Stuart Bell Jr. Archives, "Winchester Hosiery Co."

[405] museumtextiles.com, Museum Textile Services, Carmille Myers Breeze and Tegan Kehoe, "Rayon Through the Years, Part II," 6-3-2013.

[406] Ibid.

[407] fred.stlouisfed.org, Federal Reserve Bank of St. Louis, Economic Research, "Production of Rayon Yarn for the United States."

[408] minkyvintage.com, Minky Vintage, "Vintage Fabrics – 1940's Rayon."

[409] isjl.org, Encyclopedia of Southern Jewish Communities-Winchester, Virginia, "Jewish Businesses in Winchester" (Jackson, MS: Goldring/Woldenburg Institute of Southern Jewish Life).

[410] The Free Press, 4-29-1932.

[411] Vaughn, *Luray and Page County Revisited, Images of America*, 35.

[412] Daily Times News (Burlington, NC, 7-15-1944), 10.

[413] Priscilla Lehman, "Out of the Past . . . from the Archives of the Winchester Star, 75 Years Ago" (Winchester Star, 12-5-2022), B5.

[414] "History of the Heinz Plant" (Rochester, NY: Westside News, Inc., 2-20-2017).

[415] Pittsburgh Post-Gazette, 7-2-1930, 4.

[416] The Zeropack Company v. Commissioner, United States Tax Court, Docket No. 20515-80, 10-27-1983.

[417] Ibid.

[418] archives.countylib.org, Shenandoah County Library, Shenandoah Stories, "Bowman Apple Products Plant" (4-15-2018).

[419] whitehousefoods.com, "The Story of White House Foods," and The Packages, Vol. 23 (February 1920), 48.

[420] fohbc.org, Federation of Historical Bottle Collectors, Wade Cox, "White House Vinegar," 40.

[421] Stan Hinden, "O'Sullivan Rubber's Well-Heeled Beginnings to Diversified 1980s" (Washington Post, 8-15-1988).

[422] Hearings Before the Select Committee on National Defense Migration, House of Representatives, Seventy-Seventh Congress, June 27 and 28, 1941, "The Victor Products Co., 5924.

[423] justjefferson.com, Jim Surkamp, "R. J. Funkhouser (1885-1965), The Lord of the Manse."

[424] Ibid.

[425] Ibid.

[426] Ibid.

[427] Ibid.

[428] Ibid.

[429] Ibid.

[430] Onofrio Castiglia, "Longtime Petroleum Provider Funkhouser, a Family Run Firm," (Winchester Star, 8-30-2017).

[431] emmartoil.com, Emmart Oil Company.

[432] bellsfineclothing.com, "Our Story."

[433] Ibid.

[434] bloomberg.com, Bloomberg L.P., "Company Overview of Dearing Beverage Co., Inc. and B. J. Sager, Inc."

[435] martindist.com, Martin Distributing Company, "About Us."

[436] Ibid.

[437] Handley Library, Winchester, VA, Stewart Bell Jr. Archives, Photo Record, "19 North Indian Alley, B&C Baking Company."

[438] schenckfoods.com, Schenck Foods Co., "Our History, The Beginnings."

[439] Ibid.

[440] Ibid.

[441] trademarkia.com, Search Trademarks, "Plum Line."

[442] stuartperry.com, Stuart M. Perry, "Our History."

[443] Ibid.

[444] Faulkner, *American Economic History*, 696.

[445] federalreservehistory.org, Federal Reserve History, "Recession of 1937-38."

[446] Faulkner, *American Economic History*, 696.

[447] dnronline.com, Daily News Record, Harrisonburg, VA: "About Us."

[448] wvencyclopedia.org, e-WV, The West Virginia Encyclopedia, "Martinsburg Journal," 10-8-2010.

[449] John W. Wayland, *A History of Shenandoah County, Virginia* (Strasburg, VA: Shenandoah Publishing House, Inc., 1969), 30.

[450] Ibid.

[451] Ashley May, "E. E. Keister Founded the Northern Virginia Daily at the Height of the Depression" (Strasburg, VA: Northern Virginia Daily, 12-16-1999), 43.

[452] loc.gov, Library of Congress, Search Newspapers, "About Northern Virginia Daily."

[453] Ibid., "About Spirit of Jefferson Farmer Advocate."

[454] chroniclingamerica.lic.gov, "About the Farmers' Advocate and the Shepherdstown Register," and Mozier and Harmison, *Berkeley Springs, Images of America*, 44.

[455] xroads.virginia.edu, American Studies at the University of Virginia, "Radio in the 1920s."

[456] enacademic.com, Academic Dictionaries and Encyclopedias, "WINC-FM."

[457] Ibid.

[458] Stephanie M. Mangino, "Sold! $36M for WINC's Corporate Parent" (Winchester Star, 5-17-2007), 1.

[459] obittree.com, ObitTree, "Obituary for C. Leslie Golliday."

[460] Vaughn, *Luray and Page County Revisited, Images of America*, 124.

[461] Blumer and Pomeroy, *Front Royal and Warren County, Images of America*, 64.

[462] valleyhealthlink.com, Valley Health, Warren Memorial Hospital, "Our History."

[463] dhr.virginia.gov, Virginia Department of Historic Resources, National Register of Historic Places Registration Form, David A. Edwards, "Woodstock Historic District," 5-30-1995.

[464] Daily News-Record (Harrisonburg, VA, 2-5-1938), 4.

[465] shenandoahcountyhistoricalsociety.org, "Mable Lee Walton House" (Edinburg, VA: Shenandoah County Historical Society Newsletter, Winter 2014), 4.

[466] Mozier and Harmison, *Berkeley Springs, Images of America*, 47.

[467] Ibid.

[468] Ibid., 50.

[469] Ebert and Lazazzera, *Frederick County, Virginia: From the Frontier to the Future*, 132.

[470] Wayland, *A History of Shenandoah County, Virginia*, 38.

[471] Vaughn, *Luray and Page County Revisited, Images of America*, 22.

[472] nps.gov, National Park Service, Shenandoah National Park, Carrie Janney-Lucas, "Why Not Panorama?"

[473] Ibid.

[474] nps.gov, National Park Service, Shenandoah National Park, "Skyland Resort History."

[475] Ibid.

[476] Ibid.

[477] Ibid.

[478] 1920-30.com, The 1920s in History, "1920s Medicine."

[479] Columbia Law Review Association, "The Consumer's Protection Under the Federal Pure Food and Drugs Act" (New York, NY: Columbia Law Review, April, 1932).

[480] New York Hotel Record, Volume 18, No. 19 (New York, NY: Hotel Record Company, June 14, 1921), 9.

[481] shenandoahstories.org, Shenandoah County Library, "Orkney Springs Resort."

[482] sac-bsa.org, Boy Scouts of America, Shenandoah Area Council, "Camp Rock Enon."

[483] Priscilla Lehman, "Out of the Past . . . from the Archives of the Winchester Star, 70 Years Ago" (Winchester Star, 2-25-2019), B5.

[484] dhr.virginia.gov, Virginia Department of Historic Resources, Maral S. Kalbian, *Rural Historic Resource Survey Report of Warren County, Virginia, 1991*, 59.

[485] Mozier and Harmison, *Berkeley Springs, Images of America*, 19.

[486] Christine Snyder, "By a Country Mile: Couples Find Small-Town Charm, Elegance at the Country Inn in Historic Berkeley Springs"

(Charles Town, WV: Spirit of Jefferson and Farmer's Advocate, 6-20-2017).

[487] wvculture.org, West Virginia Department of Arts, Culture and History, National Register of Historic Places Registration Form, Jacqueline Hovermale, "Berkeley Springs Train Depot," 8-22-2000.

[488] museumoftheberkeleysprings.com, "Berkeley Springs Walking Tour: Berkeley Springs Inn & Spa."

[489] Wayland, *A History of Shenandoah County, Virginia*, 687.

[490] Ibid.

[491] Ibid.

[492] Philip Holman, "History Under Ground" (Woodstock, VA: Shenandoah Valley-Herald, July 1992), 14.

[493] Ibid.

[494] skylinecaverns.com, "History of Skyline Caverns."

[495] Ibid., "Welcome to Skyline Caverns."

[496] Missy Sheehan, "The Cave Beneath Charles Town, W.Va.," Blue Ridge Country (Roanoke, VA: LeisureMedia 360, 1-25-2016).

[497] Ibid.

[498] thepeoplehistory.com, "History of the Game of Golf."

[499] Matthew Umstead, "Future of Stonebridge Golf Course Still Up in the Air" (Hagerstown, MD: Herald-Mail, 5-6-2015).

[500] winchestercountryclub.net, Winchester Country Club, "History."

[501] millwoodcc.org, "History of Millwood Country Club."

[502] prweb.com, Cision PR Web. "Hawksbill Retreat – Virginia Cabin Rental History Dating Back to 1785," 1-30-2013.

[503] shenvalee.com, "Shenvalee History."

[504] Ibid.

[505] Roger Bianchini, "Carson Heirs Located, Will Support FR Golf Club Usage Change Request" (Front Royal, VA: Royal Examiner, 7-4-2018).

[506] Ibid.

[507] Millard Kessler Bushong, *A History of Jefferson County, West Virginia, 1719-1940* (Boyce, VA: Carr Publishing Company, Inc., 1972), 69.

[508] Maral S. Kalbian, *Clarke County, Images of America* (Charleston, SC: Arcadia Publishing, 2011), 86.

[509] Dolly Nasby, *Charles Town, Images of America* (Charleston, SC: Arcadia Publishing, 2004), 7.

[510] wvpublic.org, West Virginia Public Broadcasting, Bob Powell and Gail Thornhill, "Charles Town Race Track Opens December 2, 1933," 12-2-2016.

[511] Ibid.

[512] wvencyclopedia.org, e-WV, The West Virginia Encyclopedia, "Charles Town Races."

[513] Ibid.

[514] Bushong, *A History of Jefferson County, West Virginia*, 274.

[515] indianapolismotorspeedway.com, Indianapolis Motor Speedway, "The World When IMS Opened," and racingvirginia.com, Racing Virginia, "About Winchester Speedway."

[516] Ibid.

[517] Gordon, *An Empire of Wealth*, 358.

[518] Ibid., 357.

[519] Christina Wulf, "The River and the Factory: Momentum and Shifting Dynamics Between the Shenandoah River and Avtex Fibers, 1939-1989" (master's thesis, Harrisonburg, VA: James Madison University, 2010), 76.

[520] Ibid., vii.

[521] Ibid., 40 and 37.

[522] Ibid., 38.

[523] Ibid., 39.

[524] Ibid., 46.

[525] Ibid., 45.

[526] Ibid., 48.

[527] Ibid.

[528] isjl.org, Institute of Southern Jewish Life, Encyclopedia of Southern Jewish Communities-Winchester, Virginia, "Jewish Businesses in Winchester."

[529] Strickler, *A Short History of Page County, Virginia*, 330.

[530] Ibid.

[531] Vaughn, *Luray and Page County Revisited, Images of America*, 41.

[532] Vaughn, *Luray and Page County, Images of America*, 36 and 37.

[533] Johnston, *Weaving a Common Thread*, 160 and 114.

[534] Alger, "Berkeley County in World War II," 62.

[535] Johnston, *Weaving a Common Thread*, 116, and Jenrette, "Berkeley Woolen Mills," 12-22-2012.

[536] Jenrette, "Labor-Management Conflict in the Eastern Panhandle," 109-126.

[537] Ibid.

[538] Ebert and Lazazzera, *The Frederick County, Virginia: From the Frontier to the Future*, 126.

[539] Ibid.

[540] Ruth G. Tucker and Marguerite F. Golden, "FRUIT, United States Foreign Trade Related to Production, 1910-1949" (U.S. Department of Agriculture, Foreign Agriculture Report No. 60, June 1951), 6.

[541] Patrick Farris, U.S. Army Remount Depot Supported Two World Wars (Byrd Newspapers, Shenandoah Summer, 2008)," 42.

[542] Ibid.

[543] Ibid., 41, and u-s-history.com, United States History, "K-9 Corps."

[544] hmdb.org, Historical Marker Database, "Veterans Administration Center, Martinsburg, West Virginia."

[545] Ibid.

[546] flymrb.com, Eastern West Virginia Regional Airport, "History."

[547] swarthmore.edu, "List of CPS (Civilian Public Service) Camps" (Swarthmore, PA: Swarthmore College).

[548] Daily Mail, Hagerstown, MD, 9-20-1941, and John Edmund Stealey III, "Stages of Development of West Virginia's Shenandoah Valley Counties" (Charles Town, WV: Jefferson County Historical Society Magazine, Vol. XLIII, December, 1977), 18.

[549] Ibid.

[550] letterkenny.army.mil, "1940s History of Letterkenny Army Depot."

[551] Priscilla Lehman, "Out of the Past . . . from the Archives of the Winchester Star, 100 Years," 10-12-2020, B4.

[552] Chris J. Magoc, *Chronology of Americans and the Environment* (Santa Barbara, CA: ABC-CLIO, LLC, 2011), 89.

[553] *Federal Power Commission Reports, July 1, 1964-December 31, 1964* (Washington, DC: U.S. Government Printing Office), 585.

[554] Potomac River Basin Report: Letter from the Secretary of the Army, Vol. 4 (Washington, DC: U.S. Government Printing Office, 1970), 66.

Chapter 7

Key – NVBJ = North Valley Business Journal
QSBJ = Quad State Business Journal

[1] bea.gov, U.S. Bureau of Economic Analysis, "U.S. Economy by Year."

[2] census.gov, U.S. Census Bureau, Seventeenth Census, and Eric Jensen, "Census Bureau Provides Estimates for Independent Evaluation of Census Results," 12-15-2020.

[3] bls.gov, U.S. Bureau of Labor Statistics, "Employment by Major Industry Sector."

[4] Ibid.

[5] A. J. Baime, *The Accidental President, Harry S. Truman* (Boston, MA: Houghton Mifflin Harcourt, 2017), 9.

[6] fairfaxcounty.gov, Fairfax County Profile (Fairfax County Office of Research and Statistics, Research Branch, November 1973), 9, and Thomas Grubisich, "Fairfax 2nd in Area Population" (Washington Post, 8-9-1980), and U.S. Census Bureau, Twenty-Fourth Census.

[7] Carol Morello and Ted Mellnik, "Seven of the Nation's 10 Most Affluent Counties Are in Washington Region" (Washington Post, 9-20-2012).

[8] census.gov, U.S. Census Bureau, Sixteenth Census and Nineteenth Census.

[9] Ibid., Nineteenth Census and Twenty-First Census.

[10] Ibid., Twenty-First Census and Twenty-Third Census.

[11] Ibid., and Twenty-Fourth Census, and Tara Bahrampour, et al, "2020 Census Shows U.S. Population Grew at Slowest Pace Since the 1930s" (Washington Post, 4-26-2021).

[12] Ibid., Twenty-Second Census, and Metropolitan Statistical Areas and Components, November 2004.

[13] Onofrio Castiglia, "Retirees Making up Bulk of Region's Population Growth" (Winchester Star, 2-5-2019).

[14] L. D. Howell, "Changes in the American Textile Industry" (Marketing Research Division, U.S. Department of Agriculture, November 1959), 4.

[15] nrtw.org, National Right to Work Legal Defense Foundation, "Right to Work States: Virginia."

[16] yesfrederickva.com, Frederick County Economic Development Authority, Why Frederick County, "Workforce."

[17] Mark Krikorian, "Local History of Industrial Development Corporation Recounted" (Winchester Star, 10-8-1992), C1.

[18] Ibid., C2.

[19] Handley Library, Winchester, VA, Stewart Bell Jr. Archives, "Battaile Drive," Photo Record, 1598-16 wfchs, and harris.com, "Harris Corporation Marks its 100th Anniversary," 12-19-2005.

[20] Handley Library, "Battaile Drive," Photo Record, 1598-20a wfchs.

[21] Peter Heerwagen, "Apparel Industry May Be Out of Fashion" (Winchester, VA: NVBJ, August 1993), 1.

[22] "Industrial/Business Parks," *The Book of Lists, 2009 Edition* (Winchester, VA: QSBJ), 14.

[23] Ibid.

[24] "Shockey's Back" (Strasburg, VA: Northern Virginia Daily, 11-13-2018), editorial.

[25] "Winchester Fights to Save Battlefield" (Washington Times, 6-25-2001).

[26] "Shockey's Back."

[27] Thomas Blumer and Charles W. Pomeroy, *Front Royal and Warren County, Images of America* (Charleston, SC: Arcadia Publishing, 2004), 63.

[28] Ibid.

[29] warrencountyva.net, "Warren County 2004 Comprehensive Plan."

[30] "Industrial/Business Parks," *The Book of Lists, 2009 Edition,* 14.

[31] "Work Begins for Lockheed Plant at Martinsburg Park" (Hagerstown, MD: Morning Herald, 7-14-1966).

[32] etradingpost.com, "The CorningWare Story."

[33] jcda.net, Jefferson County Development Authority, "About JCDA."

[34] "New Omni Direct Mail Plant at Bardane Park Dedicated: To Employ About 80 People" (Charles Town, WV: Spirit of Jefferson Farmer's Advocate, 10-23-1981), 1.

[35] citylab.com, CITY LAB, Richard Florida, "The Uselessness of Economic Development Incentives" (Washington, DC: The Atlantic Monthly, 12-7-2012).

[36] yesvirginia.org, "Business Incentives, Investing in Each Other" (Richmond, VA: Virginia Economic Development Partnership).

[37] Ibid.

[38] tax.wv.gov, "Business Investment and Jobs Expansion Credit and Corporate Headquarters Relocation Credit" (Charleston, WV: West Virginia Tax Department).

[39] wvcommerce.org, "West Virginia State Tax Department Program: Payment in Lieu of Taxes" (Charleston, WV: West Virginia Department of Commerce).

[40] wvjit.org, West Virginia Jobs Investment Trust Board, "Our History."

[41] "Economic Development Agencies," *The Book of Lists, 2009 Edition,* 60.

[42] Peter Heerwagen, "The Heavener Legacy in Warren County" (Winchester, VA: QSBJ, August 2003), 5 to 7.

[43] Joan Tuppance, "Front Royal Celebrates Return of Avtex Property" (Richmond, VA: Virginia Business, August 2014).

[44] Norma Jean Shaw, "Documents Indicate Goodlatte Pushed for $10-Million Loan to Tran and IT Federal" (Front Royal, VA: Warren Examiner, 4-5-2019).

[45] Ibid., and Josh Gully, "The $10 Million IT Federal Loan" (Strasburg, VA: Northern Virginia Daily, 3-26-2019).

46 Gary Robertson, "New EDA Chief Tries to Do Business Amid Scandal" (Richmond, VA: Virginia Business, December 2019), 10.

47 Josh Gully, "Town Nears Creation of its Own EDA" (Strasburg, VA: Northern Virginia Daily, 6-23-2020).

48 "Economic Development Agencies," *The Book of Lists, 2009 Edition,* 60.

49 shenandoahcountyva.us, "Minutes of Industrial Development Authority of Shenandoah County," 5-31-2017.

50 "Economic Development Agencies," *The Book of Lists, 2009 Edition,* 60.

51 Peter Heerwagen, "Three Cheers for Area's Existing Industry" (Winchester, VA: QSBJ, July 1997), 6.

52 siteselection.com, Project Watch, Jack Lyne, "Rejected in '98, Cardinal Glass Returns to Virginia with Plant That May Employ 300" (Peachtree Corners, GA: Site Selection Magazine, 10-27-2003).

53 Ibid.

54 Peter Heerwagen, "Jim Deskins Sees Many Opportunities for Development in Winchester" (Winchester, VA: QSBJ, October 2006), 1.

55 yesfrederickva.com, "Targeted Growth Sectors" (Winchester, VA: Frederick County Economic Development Authority).

56 Peter Heerwagen, "Economic Developers Talk Up the Start of the New Millennium" (Winchester, VA: QSBJ, January 2000), 5.

57 Ibid.

58 Mickey Powell, "Hart Named Clarke County's Economic Development Director" (Winchester Star, 6-23-2020).

59 shenandoah-valley.biz, "2015-16 Annual Report, Page County" (Harrisonburg, VA: Shenandoah Valley Partnership).

60 pagecountyvirginia.gov, "Page County Commercial and Industrial Properties."

61 wveda.org, "Welcome to the West Virginia Economic Development Authority Website."

62 "Economic Development Agencies," *The Book of Lists, 2009 Edition,* 60.

63 Matthew Umstead, "Mountaineer Gas: First Segment of Distribution Line Project Nearly Complete" (Hagerstown, MD: Herald-Mail, 1-3-2019).

64 Onofrio Castiglia, "Pollution Issues Spur Stone Wool Plant Opposition" (Winchester Star, 8-14-2018), 1.

65 icweb2.loc.gov, Library of Congress, "Standard Lime & Stone Millville Quarry" (National Park Service, Historic American Engineering Review, No. WV- 49, 1968), 6.

66 Peter Heerwagen, "Developers Assess Prospects for 2004" (Winchester, VA: QSBJ, January 2004), 6.

67 Matthew Umstead, "Land Deal Expands Business Park in Berkeley County" (Hagerstown, MD: Herald-Mail, 1-2-2013).

68 Umstead, "Proctor & Gamble to Open Facility in Berkeley County" (Hagerstown, MD: Herald-Mail, 2-10-2015), and "Berkeley Co. Approves Proctor & Gamble PILOT Agreement," 8-24-2017.

69 Peter Heerwagen, "Sun Begins to Rise on Morgan County Park" (Winchester, VA: NVBJ, November 1997), 16.

70 Ibid.

71 Peter Heerwagen, "Talon Manufacturing First to Land in Paw Paw Park" (Winchester, VA: NVBJ, February 1993), 8.

72 Ibid.

73 "CyberStreet aka Downtown Mall" (Winchester, VA: NVBJ, April 1995), 15.

74 Ibid.

75 Ibid.

76 Peter Heerwagen, "Online Firm to Winchester Tech Zone" (Winchester, VA: QSBJ, February, 1998), 7.

77 Ibid.

78 Peter Heerwagen, "Judd's Online Sold for $6.6 Million to York Media Company" (Winchester, VA: QSBJ, December 2000), 20.

79 Peter Heerwagen, "Warren County Builds Its Roster of High-Tech Firms" (Winchester, VA: QSBJ, August 2003), 1.

80 Ibid.

81 Town of Front Royal Municipal Code, "Tech Zone Ordinance."

82 Peter Heerwagen, "Business Incubators Venture Forth" (Winchester, VA: QSBJ, December 2000), 1.

83 Quad-State Bits and Bytes, "Getting WIREd" (Winchester, VA: QSBJ, January

2001), 17, and Thru the Valleys, "Incubator Hatched" (Winchester, VA: QSBJ, March 2002), 8.

[84] Peter Heerwagen, "Business Incubator Goes Cold" (Winchester, VA: QSBJ, September 2006), 11.

[85] Ibid.

[86] arc.gov, Appalachian Regional Commission, "Grants Made in 1998."

[87] Michael Neary, "SpringTech Offers Incubator Space, Resources in Berkeley Springs" (Martinsburg, WV: The Journal, 2-27-2019).

[88] fhwa.dot.gov, U.S. Department of Transportation, Federal Highway Administration, "History of the Interstate Highway System."

[89] interstate-guide.com, "Interstate 81."

[90] roadstothefuture.com, Scott Kozel, "Roads to the Future, Interstate Highway System in Virginia," 3-6-2004.

[91] Christian Davenport, "Our Accident Plagued Interstate 81 in Va.; Fear Becomes a Traveling Companion" (Washington Post, 8-1-2009).

[92] Peter Heerwagen, "An Update on Interstate 81 Widening and 511" (Winchester, VA: QSBJ, September 2004), 5, and Coleen McGrath, "I-81 Potomac River Bridge Project Approaching Completion" (Hagerstown, MD: Herald-Mail, 12-2-2020).

[93] Onofrio Castiglia, "Gas Tax Going Up Along I-81 to Pay for Road Improvements" (Winchester Star, 4-19-2019).

[94] 167aw.ang.af.mil, "History of the 167the Airlift Wing," 12-18-2012.

[95] Ibid.

[96] Matthew Umstead, "Air Force: Eight C-17s Would Replace C-5A Fleet at W.Va. 167th Airlift Wing" (Hagerstown, MD: Herald-Mail, 2-3-2012).

[97] Richard Belisle, "167th Airlift Wing Ushers in New Era of Flight in Martinsburg" (Hagerstown, MD: Herald-Mail, 12-6-2014).

[98] virginiaaviationhistory.org, "A Brief History of Winchester's Three Airports" (Virginia Eagles, Official Newsletter of the Virginia Aeronautical Historical Society, Oct.-Dec. 1999), 16.

[99] Ibid.

[100] Ibid., 17, and doav.virginia.gov, Virginia Department of Aviation, "Site Work Begins for New Winchester Regional Airport Terminal."

[101] aopa.org, Aircraft Owners and Pilots Association, Federal Aviation Administration, Washington, D.C., "Special Flight Rules Area," Public Meeting, Washington Dulles Airport, 1-18-2006.

[102] library.hbs.edu, Lehman Brothers Collection, "Penn Central Transportation Company" (Cambridge, MA: Baker Library, Harvard Business School).

[103] wltonline.org, Winchester Little Theatre, Shirley Echelman, "Tragedy Tomorrow, Comedy Tonight: Eighty-Five Years of Community Theatre in Winchester."

[104] Dan Vaughn, *Luray and Page County Revisited, Images of America* (Charleston, SC: Arcadia Publishing, 2008), 102.

[105] Ibid.

[106] trainvideos.com, Big "E" Productions, "NS Valley Line North of Front Royal, VA."

[107] american-rails.com, Rail History, "The Chessie System."

[108] historic-structures.com, Historic Structures, "B&O Railroad Repair Shops, Martinsburg, West Virginia," and Matthew Umstead, "Berkeley County Roundhouse Authority Still Waiting for Review of Plans to Build Restrooms" (Hagerstown, MD: Herald-Mail, 9-12-2013).

[109] ggwash.org, Alex Holt, "MARC's Commuter Train Connecting West Virginia to DC May Drop to Only One Round Trip Per Day" (Greater Greater Washington, 10-22-2019).

[110] Linda McCarty, "Hard Times, Tragedy Didn't Derail the W&W" (Winchester Star, 6-1-2000), B1.

[111] virginiaplaces.org, "Winchester and Western Railroad in Virginia."

[112] Josh Janney, "Winchester and Western Railroad Sold for $105M" (Winchester Star, 10-15-2019).

[113] Liz McCormick, "Proponents Say Railroad Deal Could Boost W.Va.'s Economy, Attract Jobs to Eastern Panhandle" (Charleston, WV: West Virginia Public Broadcasting, 1-16-2019).

114 Stuart Auerbach, "Port of Call Front Royal, VA. Inland Facility Tries to Steer Cargo Shippers Toward Norfolk" (Washington Post, 5-15-1989).

115 Ibid.

116 Ibid.

117 Ibid.

118 Robert McCabe, "Front Royal Sees Port-Driven Progress" (Richmond, VA: Virginia Business, 4-28-2022).

119 joc.com, John D. Boyd, "Virginia's Intermodal Crossroads" (New York, NY: Journal of Commerce, 6-24-2011).

120 joc.com, Ari Asche, "Virginia Terminal Expansion to Speed Rail Flow" (New York, NY: Journal of Commerce, 6-10-2019).

121 Ibid.

122 Peter Heerwagen, "Allegheny Power Streamlines" (Winchester, VA: QSBJ, June 1995),1.

123 businesswire.com, "Key Parties Reach Agreement on Sale of Potomac Edison's Virginia Assets" (Shenandoah Valley Electric and Rappahannock Electric cooperatives joint press release, 4-28-2010).

124 crainscleveland.com, Scott Suttell, "FirstEnergy Corp. Agrees to Buy Allegheny Energy in $8.5 billion Deal" (Crain's Cleveland Business, 2-11-2010).

125 Peter Heerwagen, "Power Plant to Warren County" (Winchester, VA: QSBJ, September 2001), 1.

126 cpv.com, "Dominion, Competitive Power Ventures Announce Dominion's Purchase of CPV Power Station Development in Warren County, VA" (Competitive Power Ventures press release, 3-4-2008).

127 David T. Gilbert, *Waterpower: Mills, Factories, Machines & Floods at Harpers Ferry, West Virginia, 1762-1991* (Harpers Ferry, WV: Harpers Ferry Historical Association, 1999), 169.

128 Staff reports, "W.Va., Va., Pa Hydro Plants Being Put Up for Sale" (Hagerstown, MD: Herald-Mail, 11-3-2013), and power-eng.com, Power Engineering, "First Energy Sells 11 Hydropower Plants for $395 M."

129 Ibid.

130 Ibid.

131 prnewswire.com, Press release, Ontario Power Generation, Inc., 11-28-2018.

132 burnshirehydro.com, Burnshire Hydroelectric LLC, "History and Our Environmental Goals."

133 Ibid.

134 Cathy Kuehner, "Solar Farm Planning to Break Ground in Weeks" (Winchester Star, 1-26-2017), and "Dominion Energy Acquires Virginia Solar Facility; Plans to Purchase Another" (Richmond, VA: Dominion Energy press release, 6-30-2017), and sec.gov, Dominion Energy Inc. 10-K Annual Report for 2017, filed with U. S. Securities and Exchange Commission, 2-27-2018), 102.

135 Rebecca Armstrong, "Solar Farms: Cape Killed 3-3; Dogwood Approved 4-2 (Luray, VA: Page News and Courier, 4-5-2019).

136 Ibid.

137 Ibid.

138 Josh Janney, "Supervisors OK Permit for $101M Solar Plant" (Winchester Star, 7-10-2020), A1, and Janney, "Second Solar Facility Eyeing Southern Frederick" (Winchester Star, 9-16-2020), A1.

139 Brad Fauber, "Shenandoah Supervisors Approve Permit for Solar Facility" (Strasburg, VA: Northern Virginia Daily, 10-12-2020), and edf.re.com, EDF Renewables, "Who We Are."

140 wvmetronews.com, Jeff Jenkins, "PSC Considers Evidence Concerning Large Solar Energy Project in Jefferson County" (Charleston, WV: Metro News, 1-29-2021).

141 Breanna Francis, "Colorado-Based Company to Bring $100 Million Solar Production Facility to Berkeley County" (Martinsburg, WV: The Journal, 1-7-2021).

142 Ibid.

143 Ibid.

144 businessinsider.com, Matthew Stuart, "How AT&T Conquered All Forms of Communication After the Government Forced it to Break Up," 3-5-2018.

145 David Twiddy, "Embarq Begins Journey into Uncertain Future" (Associated Press article in Washington Post, 5-17-2006).

146 shentel.com, Shentel, "Timeline of History."

147 Carolyn Keister Baker, "A Vision for the Future, Warren B. French Leaves Mark on County Politics, Business" (Strasburg, VA: Northern Virginia Daily, 3-1-2006), 51.

148 shentel.com, Shentel, "Timeline of History."

149 Baker, "A Vision for the Future, Warren B. French."

150 Peter Heerwagen, "Cutting the Cord: Cellular Telephones Arrive in the Area" (Winchester, VA: NVBJ, December 1990), 1.

151 Ibid.

152 Heerwagen, "Competition Heats Up for Wireless Service" (Winchester, VA: QSBJ, March 1996), 1.

153 Heerwagen, "Telecoms Grow Wireless Business" (Winchester, VA: QSBJ, January 2002), 21.

154 Heerwagen, "CFW Marches Up I-81" (Winchester, VA: QSBJ, March 1998), 12.

155 Heerwagen, "Competition Heats Up for Wireless Service," 1.

156 Yuki Noguchi, "Va. Telecom Firm nTelos files for Bankruptcy Protection" (Washington Post, 3-5-2003).

157 Kevin Green, "Shentel Reaches Agreement to Acquire nTelos" (Strasburg, VA: Northern Virginia Daily, 8-12-2015).

158 Matt Welch, "Shentel, T-Mobile Progressing in Wireless Assets and Operations Acquisitions Deal" (Strasburg, VA: Northern Virginia Daily, 11-23-2020).

159 Ibid.

160 Matt Welch, "Shentel to Sell Wireless Assets to T-Mobile for $1.95 B" (Strasburg, VA: Northern Virginia Daily, 2-3-2021).

161 Charisse Jones, "Where Have the Manufacturing Jobs Gone as U.S. Factories Closed? (McLean, VA: USA Today, 1-1 2022).

162 Karin Kapsidelis, College Profile: Shenandoah University, "A Different Animal" (Richmond, VA: Virginia Business, November 2018), 77.

163 shepherd.edu, "Shepherd Ranks 3rd in Regional Economic Impact," 8-11-2016.

164 education.stateuniversity.com, State Departments of Education, "Vocational Education."

165 "Quad-State Vocational-Technical Schools," *The Book of Lists, 1995 Edition*, (Winchester, VA: QSBJ, August 1995), 13.

166 Ibid.

167 Ibid.

168 publicschoolreview.com, Public School Review, "Page County Technical Center."

169 Julia Kazar, "Winchester Career and Technical Center Gets New Name After $1M Gift" (Winchester Star, 10-10-2017).

170 Ibid.

171 lfcc.edu, Lord Fairfax Community College, History of the College, "Where We've Been."

172 Staff report, "Vint Hill Closes Deal with Lord Fairfax Community College Center" (Charlottesville, VA: The Daily Progress, 7-7-2014).

173 blueridgectc.edu, "About Blue Ridge Community and Technical College."

174 Ibid.

175 blueridgectc.edu, "Locations – Blue Ridge Community and Technical College."

176 lfcc.edu, Lord Fairfax Community College, "LFCC Overall Enrollment Trends by Demographic," and blueridgectc.edu, Blue Ridge Community and Technical College, "Demographics – Fall 2018," and *The Book of Lists, 2009 Edition* (Winchester, VA: QSBJ), 22.

177 Peter Heerwagen, "Valley Training Centers Targets Office Technology" (Winchester, VA: NVBJ, August 1994), 18.

178 valley.edu, About Us, "Locations."

179 Peter Heerwagen, "Graduating from College to University" (Winchester, VA: QSBJ, August 2001), 18.

180 sec.gov, "Tanger Factory Outlet Centers, Inc. Form 10-K for Year Ending December 31, 2003," filed with the U.S. Securities and Exchange Commission, 23.

181 wvmetronews.com, "Mountain State Loses Accreditation," 7-11-2012.

182 su.edu, Shenandoah University, "History."

183 Susan Burke, "It All Started in a 2-Story Stucco Building in Dayton" (Winchester Star, 11-29-1977).

184 Ibid.

185 su.edu, Shenandoah University, "Quick Statistics."

186 shepherd.edu, "History of Shepherd University."

187 Ibid., "Chronology," and "Quick Facts Fall 2018."

188 christendom.edu, "About Us. Welcome to Christendom College and A History of Christendom College."

189 Ibid.

190 Peter Heerwagen, "Online College Enrolls in Charles Town" (Winchester, VA: QSBJ, February 2004), 3.

191 nasdaq.com, "American Public Education Inc. (APEI) Initial Public Offering," 11-9-2007.

192 apus.edu, American Public University System, "APUS Breaks Ground on New Academic Center in Charles Town, WV" (company press release, 10-15-2019), and "APUS Fast Facts."

193 usda.gov, U.S. Department of Agriculture Historical Archives, 1925 Census and 2017 Census.

194 Ibid.

195 Ibid.

196 census.gov, U.S. Census Bureau, 2012 Census of Agriculture.

197 Ibid., Crop Production Historical Track Records, April 2019, "All Wheat Area Planted and Harvested, Yield, Production, Prices and Value – United States: 1866-2018."

198 Economic Research Service, U.S. Department of Agriculture, "Overview of Wheat Farming."

199 nass.usda.gov, "2017 Census of Agriculture" (Washington, DC: National Agricultural Statistics Service, U.S. Department of Agriculture).

200 Ibid.

201 Ibid.

202 ext.vt.edu, Virginia Cooperative Extension, Virginia Tech, "Beef Cattle."

203 Ibid.

204 nass.usda.gov, "2017 Census of Agriculture, Frederick County, 1960 and 1979, and Berkeley County, 1978" (Washington, DC: National Agricultural Statistics Service, U.S. Department of Agriculture).

205 John D. Morris, "3,000,000 Apples a Day Keep the Senator Away, In Season" (New York Times, 11-6-1955).

206 wvnews.com, Christine Snyder, "Jefferson Apple Orchard Set to Close Up Shop" (Charleston, WV: The State Journal, 10-29-2015).

207 Ibid.

208 orrsfarmmarket.com, Orr's Farm Market, "About Our Farm & Family."

209 Ibid.

210 Ibid.

211 Karen Bogan, "Area's Top Orchardist Always on the Go" (Special Section, The Core of the Community, Winchester Star, 10-28-1997), 5.

212 Scott Jost, *Shenandoah Valley Apples* (Chicago, IL: Columbia College Chicago Press, 2013), 18.

213 Bogan, "Area's Top Orchardist Always on the Go," 5.

214 Ibid.

215 glaizeapples.com, Glaize Apples, "History."

216 goodfruit.com, Richard Lehnert, "Chinese Apple Production Still Rising" (Yakima, WA: Good Fruit Grower, 1-1-2011).

217 fruitgrowersnews.com, Matt Milkovich, "Supermarkets Reshape the Global Apple Industry," 1-29-2015.

218 Ibid.

219 U.S. Department of Agriculture Census statistics.

220 Onofrio Castiglia, "Growers Expect 400 Migrant Workers for Beautiful Apple Crop" (Winchester Star, 7-31-2019), A1.

221 Ibid.

222 Matthew Umstead, "Apple Production Up Across Mid-Atlantic Region" (Hagerstown, MD: Herald-Mail, 10-12-2015).

223 washingtoncompany.net, "Agri-Tech, Inc."

224 "Man's Story Shows Va. Apple Industry Going Sour" (Winchester Star, 1-4-2004).

225 Ibid.

226 Castiglia, "Growers Expect About 400 Migrant Workers," A1.

[227] Milkovich, "Supermarkets Reshape the Global Apple Industry."

[228] nal.usda.gov, Floyd A. Lasley et al, "The U.S. Broiler Industry" (National Agricultural Library, U.S. Department of Agriculture, November 1988), 8.

[229] usda.gov, U.S. Department of Agriculture Census, 1935 and 1960.

[230] circ.ahajournals.org, "Dietary Fat and its Relation to Heart Attacks and Strokes" (Dallas, TX: American Heart Association, 1961).

[231] Vic Bradshaw, "Valley Poultry Icon Charles Wampler, 101, Dies" (Harrisonburg, VA: Daily-News Record, 11-17-2017).

[232] Ibid.

[233] Suzanne Hamlin, "Jefferson's Vision Finally Bears Fruit" (New York Times, 9-15-1996), 8.

[234] virginiawine.org, Virginia Wine, Shenandoah Valley Region, "Shenandoah Vineyards."

[235] lindenvineyards.com, "About Linden Vineyards."

[236] shenandoahvalleywinetrail.com, Shenandoah Valley Wine Trail Association Magazine, "Who We Are."

[237] lime.org, National Lime Association, "Lime's Myriad Uses."

[238] lcweb2.loc.gov, Jill A. Chappel, "Standard Lime & Stone Quarry (Millville Quarry)," (Historical American Engineering Record, Mid-Atlantic Region, National Park Service, 1993), and manisteenews.com, Mark Fedder, "Standard Lime and Stone" (Manistee, CA: Manistee News Advocate, 8-23-2007).

[239] jeffersoncountyhlc.org, Jefferson County Historic Landmarks Commission, Bill Theriault, "Bakerton Now."

[240] Chappel, "Standard Lime & Stone Quarry (Millville Quarry)."

[241] Clyde Ford, "Bank Stops Quarry Sale" (Hagerstown, MD: Herald-Mail, 12-12-1997).

[242] Jenni Vincent, "W.Va. Permit Hearings Draw Fewer Than Expected (Hagerstown, MD: Herald-Mail, 10-4-2018).

[243] Hon. Emanuel Celler, "Industrial Concentration Accelerated by Mergers" (Congressional Record: Proceedings and Debates of Congress, 7-16-1956), and Robert W. Wood, "Stock Acquisitions Given Unattractive Redemption Treatment, Riverton Investment Decision" (New York, NY: Panel Publisher, M&A Tax Report, January 2001).

[244] Minerals and Materials (U.S. Department of Interior, U.S. Bureau of Mines, Feb.-March, 1983), 8.

[245] Peter Heerwagen, "Foreign Grip on Local Cement Industry Hardens" (Winchester, VA: QSBJ, May 2002).

[246] fundinguniverse.com, Funding Universe, Company Profiles, "National Gypsum Company History."

[247] David J. Kusler, James L. Calver and Harold F. Heffernan, *The Mineral Industry of Virginia*, Bureau of Mines, Minerals Yearbook.

[248] Minerals Yearbook, "Markets and Minerals, Vol. I" (Bureau of Mines, U.S. Department of Interior, 1996), 830, and dmme.virginia.gov, Palmer C. Sweet, "Virginia's Lime Industry" (Richmond, VA: Virginia Department of Mines, Minerals and Energy, November 1986), 39.

[249] Thru the Valleys, "Digging Out of a Hole" (Winchester, VA: QSBJ, March 2004), 12.

[250] Peter Heerwagen, "Limestone Company Extracts Sales Price" (QSBJ, Winchester, November 2007), 12.

[251] Linda McCarty, "Into the Tunnels of the M. J. Grove Lime Co." (Winchester Star, 10-3-2001), A7.

[252] Ibid.

[253] Ibid.

[254] newtownhistorycenter.org, Newtown History Center, "The Twentieth Century and Today."

[255] wvencyclopedia.org, e-WV, The West Virginia Encyclopedia, John Douglas, "Glass Sand Mining," 8-7-2012, and "ITT Set to Buy Silica Supplier" (New York Times, 1-30-1968).

[256] Ibid.

[257] ussilica.com, U.S. Silica, "History and Vision."

[258] Peter Heerwagen, "U.S. Silica Digs into Aggregates Business" (Winchester, VA: QSBJ, July 2000), 1.

259 Ibid.

260 Peter Heerwagen, "Better Minerals to Unload Aggregates Business" (Winchester, VA: QSBJ, July 2003), 17.

261 "Golden Gate Capital Completes $337M Acquisition of U.S. Silica" (San Francisco Business Times, 1-26-2008).

262 marketwatch.com, MarketWatch, "U.S. Silica Goes Public After 111 Years," 2-1-2012.

263 Kate Shunney, "Handful of Silica Corporate Staff to Return to Local Office" (Berkeley Springs, WV: Morgan Messenger, 3-6-2019).

264 "Obituary: William J. Woods, 90, Former New Canaan Resident Who Founded Unimin Company" (New Canaan, CT: New Canaan Advertiser, 10-2-2012).

265 cisa.org, "Unimin Corporation Company History" (Rockford, IL: Casting Industry Suppliers Association).

266 Ibid.

267 sibelco.com, Media Releases and Case Studies, "Unimin Merges with Fairmount Santrol," 12-12-2017.

268 sec.gov, Covia Holdings Corporation, 10-K, Fiscal Year End 12-31-2018, 46.

269 ES-202 Reports, Labor Market Information, Virginia Employment Commission and West Virginia Department of Labor.

270 burwellmorganmill.org, "History of the Burwell-Morgan Mill;" and dhr.virginia.gov, Virginia Department of Historic Resources, National Register of Historic Places Nomination Form, "Stoner-Keller House and Mill," James C. Massey, 9-25-2012, and lcweb2.loc.gov, "Bunker Hill Mill," Historic American Engineering Review No. WV-29.

271 dhr.virginia.gov, Virginia Department of Historic Resources, National Register of Historic Places Nomination Form, Virginia Historic Landmarks Commission staff, "Springdale Mill Complex," March 1981, and dhr.virginia.gov, Virginia Department of Historic Resources, National Register of Historic Places Nomination Form, Virginia Historic Landmarks Commission staff, "Edinburg Mill," June 1979.

272 Todd M. Schmit, etc., "Economic Contribution of the Apple Industry Supply Chain in New York State" (Ithaca, NY: Charles H. Dyson School of Applied Economics and Management, Cornell University, March 2018).

273 shenandoahstories.org, Shenandoah County Library, "Bowman Apple Products Plant."

274 Peter Heerwagen, "Two Shenandoah County Plants Are Expanding" (Winchester, VA: QSBJ, May 2006).

275 James Heffernan, "Bowman to Expand Operations Through French Partnership" (Strasburg, VA: Northern Virginia Daily, November 13, 2018).

276 Michaela S. Pyle, "Knouse Foods is Monument to Enterprise, Courage and Vision of Fruit Growers" (Gettysburg Times, 6-29-1954).

277 whitehousefoods.com, "The Story of White House Foods."

278 Ibid.

279 fruitgrowersnews.com, Fruit Growers News (Sparta, MI: Great American Publishing, August 1998).

280 Ibid.

281 Sarah A. Reid, "National Fruit to Be Sold to Investors" (Winchester Star, 6-24-2006), 1.

282 Naomi Smoot, "Land Slated for Development" (Martinsburg, WV: The Journal, 7-25-2007).

283 Conor Gallagher, "Apples" (Winchester Star, 3-10-2012).

284 millcroftfarms.com, "About Millcroft Farms."

285 Ibid.

286 shawneesprings.com, "About Shawnee Springs Market."

287 "PET, Now Taken Over, Grew Up Via Takeovers" (St. Louis Post-Dispatch, 6-23-1978), 23.

288 lab2x.com, Through the Years, "Musselman's: A Family Favorite for Over 100 Years."

289 Matthew Umstead, "Applesauce Production to End in Inwood" (Hagerstown, MD: Herald-Mail, 8-8-2008).

290 Ibid.

291 "The Zeropack Company v. Commissioner" (United States Tax Court, Docket No. 20515-80, filed 10-27-1983).

292 Ibid.

293 David Foreman, "Zeropack Receiver Has Fast Timetable" (Winchester Star, 5-12-1998), 1.

294 winchesterva.gov, "Industrial History."

295 Brian Brehm, "Glaize Expanding to Support Cideries" (Winchester Star, 10-24-2018), AI.

296 Ibid.

297 rccolawinchester.com, Royal Crown Bottling Company, Company Info, "About Us."

298 Ibid.

299 Ibid., and bizfluent.com, David Bonner, "History of the Chero-Cola Company," 9-26-2017.

300 Ibid.

301 Ibid.

302 "The Purity of the Spring Water" (Museum of the Berkeley Springs pamphlet).

303 Peter Heerwagen, "Bottlers Sold" (Winchester, VA: QSBJ, April 2006), 22.

304 Ibid., 23.

305 John J. Scanlan, "$20 Million Poultry Co-op" (Washington, DC: News for Farmer Cooperatives, April 1952 - March 1953), 7.

306 ead.lib.virginia.edu, "A Guide to the Wampler Business Records, 1916-1972."

307 Rockinghamcountyva.com, "Resolution Honoring Elizabeth "Libby" Wampler Custer," 7-25-2008.

308 fundinguniverse.com, Funding Universe, "WLR Foods, Inc. History."

309 Ibid.

310 law.justia.com, "Blue Ridge Poultry v. Clark," Supreme Court of Virginia (Justia US Law, September 4, 1970).

311 Ibid.

312 "The History of Rocco, Inc." (company pamphlet, June 1989).

313 Ibid.

314 Ibid.

315 Tom Stanley, "Facing Change in Agriculture" (Virginia Cooperative Extension Service, Farm Business Management Update, June/July 2004).

316 Vic Bradshaw, "Rocco Sold, Broken Up" (Harrisonburg, VA: Daily News-Record, 8-3-2001), 1.

317 Jerry Knight, "WLR Buyout Isn't Chicken Feed" (Washington Post, 10-23-2000).

318 bloomberg.com/profiles, New Market Poultry Products, Inc., "Company Profile."

319 tiptoppoultry.com, Tip Top Poultry, "Our Company."

320 valleyproteins.com, About Us, History, "It Started with the Man with the Porkpie Hat."

321 Ibid.

322 Ibid.

323 Rona Kobell, "Rendering Plant Says It Is on Right Scent" (Baltimore Sun, 3-26-2004), and tmcapital.com, Mergermarket, "Valley Proteins Eyes Geographic Expansion Through Acquisitions - Co-Owner," 1-7-2020.

324 Winchester Star staff report, 12-30-21.

325 Alex Bridges, "Rendering Plant's Request to Step Up Processing Gets OK" (Strasburg, VA: Northern Virginia Daily, 9-5-2012).

326 Ibid.

327 poultry.com, Pierce Chicken, "About Us."

328 Anthony Faiola, "Feathers Fly Over a Marketing Coup D'état" (Washington Post, 1-27-1995).

329 Ibid.

330 foodonline.com, Food Online, "ConAgra Acquires Hester Industries," December 1997.

331 Rick Hemphill, "SVB Food & Beverage Company," Around the Panhandle (Martinsburg, WV: Hornby Publishing, LLC, March-April 2014), 12.

332 Ibid.

333 Thru the Valleys, "Swarming to Berkeley County" (Winchester, VA: QSBJ, June, 1998), 8.

334 gourmetretailer.com, Gourmet Retailer, "Vita Food Products, Inc. Purchases Virginia Honey Company," 7-1-2001.

335 columbiaunion.org, Columbia Union Conference, Elena Cornwell, "All in a Day's Work, Terry Hess: Spicing Up Life."

336 Ibid.

337 Ibid.

338 Sarah Grisriel, "Gunter's Honey Reigns Supreme During Va.'s Honey Month" (Hagerstown, MD: WDVM-TV, 9-6-2016).

339 Jack Markowitz, "Schrafft's Adds Restaurant in Pittsburgh" (Pittsburgh Post-Gazette, 11-29-1967), 35.

340 Clare M. Reckert, "PET Enters into a Pact for Sale of 22 Schrafft's Units to Riese" (New York Times, 6-21-1973), 63.

341 "Rich Products Purchases Schrafft's Plant in Winchester" (Statesville, NC: Statesville Daily Record, 5-5-1974), 32.

342 Peter Heerwagen, "Food and Plastic Plants in Winchester to Close Within Year" (Winchester, VA: QSBJ, July 2005), 15.

343 thefreelibrary.com, "Winchester Cold Storage Buys Former Rich Products Facility" (Fort Lee, NJ: E. W. Williams Publications, Inc., 2006).

344 Alex Bridges, "Cheese Factory Closes" (Strasburg, VA: Northern Virginia Daily, 12-16-2011).

345 Ibid.

346 Priscilla Lehman, "Out of the Past . . . from the Archives of the Winchester Star, 25 Years Ago," 10-26-2020, B5.

347 Barbara Greco, "Tabard Farm's Chips Taste Like Potatoes" (Winchester, VA: NVBJ, July 1991), 6.

348 Don Harrison, "Route 11 Potato Chips Finds Success as a Cult Favorite in a Fiercely Competitive Market" (Washington Post, 3-22-2014).

349 Ibid.

350 Peter Heerwagen, "General Foods' Road to the North Valley" (Winchester, VA: NVBJ, April 1991), 1.

351 David Conn, "Hershey Opts to Build Plant in Va., Not Md." (Baltimore Sun, 9-25-1991).

352 Thru the Valleys, "Leveraging Pasta" (Winchester, VA: QSBJ, January 1999), 8.

353 ebrofoods.es, "Ebro Puleva Will Acquire New World Pasta, Leader in Pasta in the USA and Canada" (Ebro press release, 6-7-2006), and rivianna.com, Rivianna, "About Us."

354 Peter Heerwagen, "Hood Spills into Frederick County" (Winchester, VA: QSBJ, April 1999), 1.

355 Ibid.

356 prnewswire.com, "HP Hood Celebrates Exponential Growth and the 15th Anniversary of Winchester, VA Processing Plant" (company press release, 9-10-2015).

357 Peter Heerwagen, "Interbake to Make Wafers in Warren County" (Winchester, VA: QSBJ, May 2005), 21.

358 Ibid.

359 wceda.com, "Nature's Touch Frozen Foods to Invest $1.8 million in Warren County and Create 25 New Jobs" (press release, Front Royal-Warren County Economic Development Authority, 12-3-2014).

360 santafetradingpost.com, "The CorningWare Story."

361 Ibid.

362 bizjournals.com, "Borden Buys Corning Consumer Products Company" (Columbus, OH: Columbus Business Journal, 5-2-1998), and Peter Heerwagen, "Westab Closes, World Kitchen Bankrupt" (Winchester, VA: QSBJ, July 2002), 15.

363 Peter Heerwagen, "Shockey Group Leases Part of Corning Complex" (Winchester, VA: QSBJ, August 2004), 15.

364 lamptech.co.uk, "Winchester Lamp" (Welcome to the Museum of Electric Lamp Technology, 5-4-2020).

365 Ibid.

366 Ibid.

367 Ibid.

368 Ibid.

369 Peter Heerwagen, "Pen-Tab Enrolls in Warren County Park" (Winchester, VA: QSBJ, April 1995), 1.

370 Ibid., 6.

371 Heerwagen, "Westab Closes, World Kitchen Bankrupt," 15, and sec.gov, U.S. Securities and Exchange Commission, Pen-Tab Industries, Inc., 8-K/A filing, 12-10-1998.

372 Ibid.

373 Ibid.

374 Peter Heerwagen, "Tissue Papers Tear into Region" (Winchester, VA: QSBJ, May 2008), 1.

375 Ibid.

376 Matthew Umstead, "Proctor & Gamble to Open Facility: Berkeley Co. Approves Proctor & Gamble PILOT Agreement" (Hagerstown, MD: Herald-Mail, 8-24-2017).

[377] Ibid, and Alexander Coolidge, "P&G Promises 'Mega Factory of the Future' As It Shuts Down Old Sites" (Cincinnati Enquirer, 7-24-2018).

[378] Matthew Umstead, "Employment at P&G Expected to Reach 1,400" (Hagerstown, MD: Herald-Mail, 11-13-2019), and Matt Welch, "Martinsburg Proctor & Gamble Facility Continues to Grow" (Winchester Star, 9-25-2020), A1.

[379] Matthew Umstead, "Berkeley Co. Approves Proctor & Gamble PILOT Agreement" (Hagerstown, MD: Herald-Mail, 8-24-2017).

[380] Josh Janney, "Hello Kitty? Cat Litter Maker Eyes Frederick" (Winchester Star, 3-7-2019), A1.

[381] Janney, "Supervisors' Vote Buries Cat Litter Plant" (Winchester Star, 5-24-2019).

[382] wvmetronews.com, Mike McCullough, "Clorox Announces Plans for Berkeley County Plant" (Charleston, WV: Metro News, 1-16-2020), and Josh Janney, "Clorox Official: W.Va. Plant Would Have Minimal Traffic Impact on Frederick County" (Winchester Star, 1-17-2020).

[383] Ibid.

[384] clarku.edu, Clark University, Robert J. S. Rodd. "NAFTA and the New Sweatshops: The Forces of Contradiction and Contention in the Emerging World Order."

[385] cnbc.com, CNBC-TV, Heesun Wee, "Made in USA Fuels New Manufacturing Hubs in Apparel," 9-23-2013.

[386] Wilbur S. Johnston, *Weaving a Common Thread* (Winchester, VA: Winchester-Frederick County Historical Society, 1980), 139.

[387] Ibid., 124.

[388] Ibid.

[389] Ibid., 135.

[390] Ibid., 139.

[391] Ibid.

[392] Ibid.

[393] Ibid.

[394] Ibid., 67.

[395] Ibid., 49.

[396] Kathy C. Kehoe, Strasburg Heritage Association Newsletter, Winter 2005.

[397] Blumer and Pomeroy, *Front Royal and Warren County, Images of America*, 56.

[398] law.justia.com, "The Schwarzenbach-Huber Company, Petitioner, v. National Labor Relations Board, Respondent, and Textile Workers Union of America," 3-5-1969.

[399] Lawrence Emerson, "On Labor Day, I Think About My Hometown's Old Factories" (Warrenton, VA: Fauquier Now, 9-1-2014).

[400] Christina Wulf, "The River and the Factory: Momentum and Shifting Dynamics Between the Shenandoah River and Avtex Fibers, 1939-1989" (master's thesis, Harrisonburg, VA: James Madison University, 2010), 83.

[401] Ibid.

[402] Ibid.

[403] Ibid.

[404] Ibid., 77.

[405] Heerwagen, "Apparel Industry May Be Out of Fashion," 1.

[406] Ibid., 6.

[407] Ibid.

[408] "Wanner Plant Taken Over by Aileen" (Winchester Star, 10-29-1962).

[409] Heerwagen, "Apparel Industry May Be Out of Fashion," 6.

[410] "Aileen Files for Bankruptcy" (New York Times, 1-25-1994).

[411] "Aileen to Sell 46 of its Stores" (New York Times, 7-18-1995).

[412] Heerwagen, "Apparel Industry May Be Out of Fashion," 6.

[413] just-style.com, Just-Style Apparel Sourcing Strategy, "USA: VF Corp. to Axe Seven US Plants, 3,000 Jobs," 10-18-2002.

[414] Priscilla Lehman, "Out of the Past . . . from the Archives of the Winchester Star, 100 Years Ago" (Winchester Star, 4-12-2021), B4.

[415] dhr.virginia.gov, Virginia Department of Historic Resources, National Register of Historic Places Nomination Form, Maral S. Kalbian, "Winchester Historic District (Boundary Increase)," 8-19-2002.

[416] Ibid.

[417] Hearings Before the Senate Interstate and Foreign Commerce Committee, "Problems in the Domestic Textile Industry, September 19

[418] Ibid., and Vaughn, *Luray and Page County Revisited, Images of America*, 38.

[419] Heerwagen, "Apparel Industry May Be Out of Fashion," 6, and Donald R. Serfass, "Death of an Industry Giant" (Lehighton, PA: Times News, 4-26-2013).

[420] sec.gov, "Letter to Shareholders," Shenandoah Telecommunications Company, 10-K Filing with U.S. Securities and Exchange Commission, Fiscal Year Ended December 31, 1999.

[421] Kristina Marie McIntyre, "Adaptive Reuse in Martinsburg: The Interwoven School of Crafts" (master's thesis, College Park, MD: University of Maryland, 2008), illustration.

[422] Ibid, and wvencyclopedia.org, e-WV, The West Virginia Encyclopedia, Jerra Jenrette, "Interwoven Mills," 2-3-2012.

[423] McIntyre, "Adaptive Reuse in Martinsburg," 38.

[424] Jenrette, "Interwoven Mills."

[425] Candice Bosely, "Help Available for Displaced Workers in Martinsburg" (Hagerstown, MD: Herald-Mail, 4-14-2004).

[426] Ibid.

[427] Ibid.

[428] okamotogroup.com, Okamoto Corporation, "History."

[429] wvculture.org, West Virginia Department of Arts, Culture and History, Jerra Jenrette, "Labor-Management Conflict in the Eastern Panhandle: Perfection Garment Company Battles the ILGWU" (Volume 52, 1993, West Virginia Archives and History), 109-126.

[430] Bob O'Connor, "The Centennial History of Ranson, W.V., 1910-2010" (Charles Town, WV: Spirit of Jefferson Farmer's Advocate, 6-23-2010), 3C.

[431] Ibid.

[432] Heerwagen, "Apparel Industry May Be Out of Fashion," 6.

[433] Craig Kaston and George Cox, *American Secret Projects 2: US Airlifters 1941 to 1961* (Manchester, UK: Crecy Publishing, Ltd., 2019).

[434] Ibid.

[435] Peter Heerwagen, "Texas Plane Maker Lands in Area After Long Flight" (Winchester, VA: NVBJ, October 1992), 13.

[436] Ibid.

[437] Heerwagen, "Swearingen Plant Ships Parts of First Plane" (Winchester, VA: QSBJ, June 2004), 25.

[438] Heerwagen, "Swearingen to Begin Producing Planes" (Winchester, VA: QSBJ, December 2005), 5.

[439] aopa.org, Alton A. Marsh, "Trials and Travails of the SJ30" (Frederick, MD: Aircraft Owners and Pilots Association, 1-1-2011).

[440] Heerwagen, "Dubai Investor Provides Fuel for SJ30-2" (Winchester, VA: QSBJ, July 2008), 9.

[441] Heerwagen, "Martinsburg Airport Home to Growing Taiwanese Airforce" (Winchester, VA: QSBJ, December 1997), 5.

[442] Heerwagen, "Tiger First on Runway" (Winchester, VA: QSBJ, August 2001), 6.

[443] aero-news.net, Aero News Network, "Tiger Files for Chapter 7 Bankruptcy: The Martinsburg, WV Airplane Builder Finally Folds," 1-24-2007.

[444] pagecounty.virginia.gov, Page County Comprehensive Plan, Volume II: Community Character, 4-21-2009.

[445] "Stanley Works," *Quad-State Industrial Directory, 2005/06 Edition* (Winchester, VA: QSBJ), 52, and cbc.ca, CBC Radio-Canada News, "Masonite to Buy Stanley Works Door Business for $160 Million," 12-9-2003.

[446] Peter Heerwagen, "Suppliers to Homebuilding Industry Increase Their Presence in Frederick County" (Winchester, VA: QSBJ, October 2003), 3.

[447] Ibid.

[448] Stan Hinden, "Dentist Fills Kitchen Cabinet Orders Instead of Teeth" (Washington Post, 9-8-1986).

[449] Ibid.

[450] Ibid.

[451] American Woodmark Annual Report, "Financial Highlights, Fiscal Years Ended April 30, 2008-2010," and Peter Heerwagen, "American Woodmark Finally Closes Plants" (Winchester, VA: QSBJ, May 2009), 20.

[452] James Heffernan, "A Year of Big Wins" (Richmond, VA: Virginia Business, 2-28-2017).

[453] referenceforbusiness.com, "Merillat Industries Inc. - Company Profile and History."

[454] Peter Heerwagen, "Two Shenandoah County Plants Are Expanding" (Winchester, VA: QSBJ, May 2006), 25.

[455] Ibid.

[456] Harry Culvyhouse, "After Nearly 53 Years, Blue Ridge Truss Closes" (Strasburg, VA: Northern Virginia Daily, 3-31-2015).

[457] dwmmag.com, "ProBuild to Open New Locations in Utah and Virginia" (Stafford, VA: Door & Window Market Magazine, 3-15-2010).

[458] amcasc.com, Annandale Millwork and Allied Systems, "History."

[459] Ibid.

[460] Ibid.

[461] Peter Heerwagen, "Northern Virginia Homebuilder to Make Building Components in Capon Bridge Park" (Winchester, VA: QSBJ, July 2005), 10.

[462] lbmjournal.com, "BMC Acquires Texas Plywood & Lumber and Code Plus Components" (Lakeville, MN: LBM Journal, 4-4-2017).

[463] Ibid.

[464] Yvonne Pfoutz, "Staying Foremost in Modular Homes" (Winchester, VA: QSBJ, June 2001), 25.

[465] fundinguniverse.com, Funding Universe, Browse Company Profiles, "Trex Company, Inc. History."

[466] Peter Heerwagen, "Fortune 500 Mobil Corp. Reworks Site" (Winchester, VA: NVBJ, April 1993), 1.

[467] Ibid.

[468] Trex Company, Inc. Prospectus, 4-8-1999.

[469] fundinguniverse.com, Trex Company, Inc., "History."

[470] Ibid.

[471] "Trex Closes Olive Branch Plant" (Memphis, TN: Memphis Business Journal, 5-25-2007).

[472] Adam Bryant, "Ron Kaplan of Trex, On Making Judgments Instead of Decisions" (New York Times, 5-3-2014).

[473] Michael O'Connor, "Trex to Deck Out Facilities in Virginia, Nevada" (Richmond, VA: Virginia Business, 6-17-2019), and Matt Welch, "Trex Begins Production at Expanded Site on Local Campus" (Winchester Star, 1-15-2021).

[474] sec.gov, "Champion Enterprises, Inc. Form 10-K for Fiscal Year Ended January 3, 2009," filed with U.S. Securities and Exchange Commission.

[475] whyy.org, John Blumgart and Steph Yin, "We Don't Build Them Like We Used To—Why New Houses Aren't Made of Brick" (WHYY Philadelphia, Public Broadcasting System, 8-9-2019).

[476] trademarkia.com, Trademarkia, "Shenado Chief of Construction Trademark Information."

[477] Matthew Umstead, "Former Brick-Making Plant Cleared for Use as Park Area" (Hagerstown, MD: Herald-Mail, 1-2-2011).

[478] Ibid.

[479] "Martinsburg Brick Plant Sold by Family" (Hagerstown, MD: The Morning Herald, 2-2-1974), 11.

[480] Matthew Umstead, "W.Va.'s Only Brick Manufacturer Marks 100 Years" (Hagerstown, MD: Herald-Mail, 6-12-2001).

[481] sec.gov, U.S. Securities and Exchange Commission, "ESSROC Press Release, 3-19-2002."

[482] Ibid.

[483] aggregateresearch.com, Rashmi Kalia, "Essroc's $500 Million Upgrade Nearly Complete," 4-27-2009.

[484] Ibid.

[485] Matthew Umstead, "Columbian Firm to Buy W.Va. Cement Plant for $660M" (Hagerstown, MD: Herald-Mail, 8-2-2016).

[486] Ibid.

[487] Peter Heerwagen, "Shockey Cements Sale of Ready-Mix Unit" (Winchester, VA: QSBJ, March 2008), 9.

[488] Rebecca A. Ebert and Teresa Lazazzera, *The Frederick County, Virginia: From the Frontier to the Future*, (Norfolk, VA:

The Donning Company, 1988), 166, and Heerwagen, "Shockey Cements Sale of Ready-Mix Unit."

[489] Ibid.

[490] Brian Brehm, "Shockey Precast Group Changing Hands" (Winchester Star, 1-4-2018).

[491] Susan Freinkel, "A Brief History of Plastic's Conquest of the World" (New York, NY: Scientific American, 5-29-2011).

[492] Stan Hinden, "O'Sullivan Rubber Well-Heeled Beginnings to Diversified 1980s" (Washington Post, 8-15-1988).

[493] Ibid.

[494] Ibid.

[495] Ibid., and sec.gov, "O'Sullivan Corporation, Form 10-Q for Quarter-Ended 9-30-1994," filed with U.S. Securities and Exchange Commission.

[496] Peter Heerwagen, "O'Sullivan's Calendar Hits Century Mark" (Winchester, VA: QSBJ, March 1996), 16.

[497] "Geon Offering $191 Million for O'Sullivan" (Santa Monica, CA: Plastics News, 6-7-1999).

[498] nytimes.com, Business Day, "Company Briefs: O'Sullivan Corp." (New York Times, 7-18-1997).

[499] "Geon Offering $191 Million for O'Sullivan."

[500] Onofrio Castiglia, "O'Sullivan Films Celebrates Employees, Announces Parent Company Change" (Winchester Star, 6-30-2017).

[501] acbs-bslol.com, Andreas Jordahl Rhude, "Larson Boats – Part 4, Larson Watercraft & Crestliner" (Land-O-Lakes Classic Boat Club, ACBS Chapter, 2002).

[502] Ibid.

[503] Ibid.

[504] rubbermaidcommercial.com, Rubbermaid Commercial Products, "Company Profile."

[505] Ibid.

[506] Thru the Valleys, "Rubber Hits the Road" (Winchester, VA: QSBJ, November 1998), 8.

[507] vedp.org, "Governor McDonnell Announces Rubbermaid Commercial Products' Expansion in the City of Winchester and Frederick County" (Richmond, VA: Virginia Economic Development Partnership press release, 12-14-2011).

[508] plasticnews.com, Rhoda Miel, "Rubbermaid Moving Commercial Products to North Carolina" (Detroit, MI: Plastic News, 12-12-2013).

[509] wtop.com, Neil Augenstein, "The Beatles' Abbey Road Came Through Virginia" (Washington's Top News, 4-13-2012).

[510] Ibid.

[511] "Capitol Records to Close Virginia Plant" (Washington Post, 12-7-1987).

[512] Peter Heerwagen, "He Liked the Machines, So He Bought the Company" (Winchester, VA: NVBJ, November 1994), 6.

[513] Ibid.

[514] Ibid.

[515] secontainer.com, "Southeastern Container History."

[516] Peter Heerwagen, "Great Britain-Based M&H Plastics Opens Plant in Fort Collier Industrial Park" (Winchester, VA: QSBJ, July 2004), 16.

[517] Matt Welch, "Berry Plastics Wants to Become an Employer of Choice" (Winchester Star, 10-20-2020).

[518] "Pactiv Corporation," *The Book of Lists, 2009 Edition* (Winchester, VA: QSBJ), 63.

[519] Catherine Kavanaugh, "Pactiv Selling Building Products Unit to Ireland's Kingspan" (Detroit, MI: Plastics News, 8-19-2014).

[520] Joan Tupponce, "Toray Plastics Expanding to Meet Growing Demand" (Richmond, VA: Virginia Business, 9-30-2016).

[521] Ibid.

[522] Ibid.

[523] Candice Bosely, "Siding Company to Move Distribution Center to W.Va." (Hagerstown, MD: Herald-Mail, 2-17-2005).

[524] Thru the Valleys, "Airing Out in Martinsburg" (Winchester, VA: QSBJ, November 1995), 9.

[525] Matt Welch, "Italian Manufacturing Plant Breaks Ground in Jefferson County" (Martinsburg, WV: The Journal, 4-10-2018).

[526] Ibid.

527 Peter Heerwagen, "Abex" (Winchester, VA: QSBJ, June 1992), 7.

528 Ibid.

529 Thru the Valleys, "Lifting Foot Off Brake" (Winchester, VA: QSBJ, April 2008), 8.

530 Sally Voth, "Federal Mogul Workers Say They Got a Raw Deal" (Strasburg, VA: Northern Virginia Daily, 10-9-2012).

531 Office of Remediation Programs, Virginia DEQ, "Statement of Basis, F-M Corp.," 10-31-2016.

532 Peter Heerwagen, "Total Quality Drives VDO Toward ISO 9000" (Winchester, VA: NVBJ, May 1993), 7.

533 Ibid.

534 Edmund Chew, "Sell-Offs Help Siemens" (Detroit, MI: Automotive News, 3-25-2002).

535 Peter Heerwagen, "Automotive Industries to Go Public" (Winchester, VA: NVBJ, April 1992), 6.

536 "Company News: "Lear Seating to Buy Automotive Industries" (New York, NY: Bloomberg News Archives, 1995).

537 Peter Heerwagen, "Food and Plastic Plants in Winchester to Close Within Year" (Winchester, VA: QSBJ, July 2005), 15, and Thru the Valleys, "New Venture for Supplier" (Winchester, VA: QSBJ, December 2006), 23.

538 Peter Heerwagen, "Auto Parts Supplier Downshifts at its Plants" (Winchester, VA: QSBJ, June 2009), 7.

539 John B. Willmann, "Front Royal: New Paint Plant May Brighten Economic Picture" (Washington Post, 3-1-1982).

540 Sally Voth, "Front Royal Plant Sold" (Strasburg, VA: Northern Virginia Daily, 8-30-2012).

541 Andrew Madigan, "Berryville, Va.: The Publishing World's Best-Kept Secret" (Washington Post, 4-2-2018).

542 Ibid.

543 Ibid.

544 fundinguniverse.com, Funding Universe, Browse Company Profiles, "Wallace Computer Services, Inc. History: Key Dates."

545 "Printing Company in Luray Closing in September, Jobs Moving to Fredericksburg" (AP, Fredericksburg, VA: Free-Lance Star, 7-9-2003).

546 Peter Heerwagen, "Judd's is Number One" (Winchester, VA: NVBJ, June 1990), 1.

547 Ibid., 6.

548 Thru the Valleys, "On Wisconsin" (Winchester, VA: QSBJ, December 1997), 14, and Peter Heerwagen, "Perry-Judd's Bought by an Acquisitive Printer" (Winchester, VA: QSBJ, March 2007), 15.

549 Peter Heerwagen, "Large Printers Invest in Technology" (Winchester, VA: NVBJ, April 1993), 12.

550 Ibid., 13 and referenceforbusiness.com, "History of Quebecor Inc."

551 Georgia Caldwell, "Quad/Graphics Inks Deal in Berkeley County" (Winchester, VA: NVBJ, April 1995), 1.

552 Ibid.

553 Thru the Valleys, "Printers Ink Deal" (Winchester, VA: QSBJ, August 1999), 10.

554 Euan Rocca, "Quad/Graphics to Pay $1.3 Billion for World Color Quebecor" (Toronto, ON: Thomson Reuters Corporation, 1-26-2010).

555 Ibid.

556 businesswire.com, LSC Communications Lunches as an Independent Company Following Spin-Off from R.R. Donnelley & Sons Company," 10-3-2016.

557 Rick Romell, "Quad/Graphics, LSC Communications Scrap Merger in Face of Antitrust Lawsuit" (Milwaukee Journal Sentinel, 7-23-2019).

558 Melissa Topey, "LSC Communications to Close" (Strasburg, VA: Northern Virginia Daily, 1-14-2020).

559 Matthew Umstead, "Quad/Graphics sells Berkeley County facility for $11.3M to Berryville Graphics" (Hagerstown, MD: Herald-Mail, 11-15-2020).

560 justjefferson.com, Jim Surkamp, "R. J. Funkhouser, 1885-1965, The Lord of the Manse."

561 Ibid.

562 cranems.com, Crane Merchandising Systems, "Our Heritage: Dixie-Narco," and amsvendors.com, AMS, "Our Story, The Heartbeat of Our Business."

563 Clay Chandler, "Court Backs Ex-Officer of Maytag in Rivalry Case" (Washington Post, 9-7-1987).

564 Daniel F. Cuff, "Maytag to Acquire Magic Chef for $740 Million" (New York Times, 3-25-1986), and AMS, "Our Story."

565 Chandler, "Battle Brews for Makers of Soda Machines."

566 Ibid.

567 Peter Heerwagen, "Jefferson County Cashes in on Vending Machine Industry" (Winchester, VA: QSBJ, October 1997), 1.

568 Ibid.

569 amsvendors.com, AMS, "Our Story, The Heartbeat of Our Business"

570 Ibid.

571 henkelharris.com, "About Us: Henkel Harris, Our Time-Honored Family Tradition."

572 Ibid.

573 Ibid.

574 Ibid.

575 Ibid.

576 Ibid.

577 gatcreek.com, "Gat Creek, Solid American-Made Furniture, Tom Seely."

578 Ibid.

579 Peter Heerwagen, "Tom Seely Furniture Defies Industry Trends" (Winchester, VA: QSBJ, December 2003), 3.

580 O'Connor, "The Centennial History of Ranson, WV, 1910-2010," and jacksoncatnapper.com, Jackson Furniture, "Born in America," and Thru the Valleys, "Logging on to Furniture" (Winchester, VA: QSBJ, January 2000), 23.

581 "FEMA Disaster Operations Center to be Housed at Facility in Winchester" (Washington, DC: Federal Emergency Management Administration press release, 4-8-2008), and thefreelibrary.com, "Binswanger/CBB Arranges Major Sale in Front Royal, VA" (company press release, 5-28-2003, and thefreelibrary.com, "Winchester Cold Storage Buys Former Rich Products Facility," 10-1-2006.

582 Candice Bosely, "Va. Company Buys General Motors Facility" (Hagerstown, MD: Herald-Mail, 11-19-2005).

583 Peter Heerwagen, "Trex Leases Former Lear Plant in Winchester" (Winchester, VA: QSBJ, May 2006), 3.

584 Thru the Valleys, "All in the Family" (Winchester, VA: QSBJ, October 2000), 26, and virginiahardwoodfloors.com, Virginia Hardwood Floors, "Winchester Distribution Center."

585 dhr.virginia.gov, Virginia Department of Historic Resources, National Register of Historic Places Nomination Form, Maral Kalbian, "Winchester Historic District (Boundary Increase)," 11-19-2002, and Brian Brehm, "Proposal to Raze Tax Credit Worries Preservationists" (Winchester Star, 11-7-2017).

586 Thru the Valleys, "Name Change for Park" (Winchester, VA: QSBJ, February 2004), 8, and Alex Bridges, "Three Area Sites Considered for New FBI Center" (Strasburg, VA: Northern Virginia Daily, 2-14-2015).

587 "Test Drives Will Raise Money for LFCC in Luray" (Lord Fairfax Community College press release, 5-17-2017.

588 Sally Voth, "Rubbermaid Buys Old Lamp Factory for $9 Million" (Strasburg, VA: Northern Virginia Daily, 8-29-2012).

589 Kathy Kuehner, "Local Habitat for Humanity Chapter Moving its Offices to ReStore Location" (Winchester Star, 1-6-2018).

590 Bosely, "Va. Company Buys General Motors Facility."

591 Peter Heerwagen, "Guardian Fills AT&T Facility with Jobs" (Winchester, VA: QSBJ, May 1997), 20.

592 "Verizon Distribution Center," *The Book of Lists*, 2009 Edition (Winchester, VA: QSBJ), 84.

593 Shenandoah Valley Industrial Report, "More Spec Development Planned for I-81 Corridor" (Toronto, ON: Colliers International, Third Quarter 2018), and John McVey, "Ecolab All About Cleaner, Safer World" (Martinsburg, WV: The Journal, 10-25-2013).

594 Peter Heerwagen, "Polo Ralph Lauren Takes Over Schwab Distribution Center at Martinsburg Airport" (Winchester, VA: QSBJ, July 2004), 3.

Endnotes: Chapter 7

595 Ibid.

596 Staff reports, "Ralph Lauren Move Will Leave S. Schwab Building Empty" (Cumberland, MD: Times-News, 8-7-2014).

597 Peter Heerwagen, "Ecolab and Orgill to Berkeley County" (Winchester, VA: QSBJ, May 1999), 1.

598 prnewswire.com, "W.P. Carey Announces Investments Totaling $188 Million" (company press release, 4-4-2019).

599 Peter Heerwagen, "GM to Build Anew in Berkeley County" (Winchester, VA: QSBJ, January 2000), 7.

600 Peter Heerwagen, "GM Plant is Big Money" (Winchester, VA: QSBJ, March 1999), 1.

601 marketwatch.com, "GM to Cut Jobs at W. Va. Plant – Roport" (9-29-2004)'

602 Ibid.

603 Ibid.

604 Voth, "Rubbermaid Buys Old Lamp Factory for $9 Million," and Samantha Cronk, "Company Will Move into Shockey Commerce Center" (Martinsburg, WV: The Journal, 2-19-2014).

605 Matthew Umstead, "Berkeley County Warehouse-Logistics Park Moves Ahead" (Hagerstown, MD: Herald-Mail, 1-7-2019).

606 Ibid.

607 equuspartners.com, Equus Capital Partners Ltd., "Mid-Atlantic 81 Logistics Park."

608 Onofrio Castiglia, "Former Winchester Cold Storage Celebrates Long Shelf Life" (Winchester Star, 9-20-2017).

609 wcslogistics.com, WCS Logistics, "About Us, Timeline."

610 Onofrio Castiglia, "New Facility Quadruples WCS Logistics' Freezer Space" (Winchester Star, 7-26-2019), A6.

611 Thru the Valleys, "Krafting a Warehouse" (Winchester, VA: QSBJ, December 2000), 8.

612 dbschenker.com, "The Story Behind DB Schenker."

613 Peter Heerwagen, "Home Depot Nails Down Another Warehouse" (Winchester, VA: QSBJ, April 2008), 13, and sec.gov, "Cole Real Estate Investments, Inc. 8-K/A Current Report," filed with U.S. Securities and Exchange Commission, 5-31-2013.

614 johnsondevelopment.net, Johnson Development Associates, Inc., "Fort Collier Industrial Park: Mercury Paper BTS."

615 Adrian Maties, "D.C. Area Industrial Properties Sold For $35M" (New York, NY: Commercial Property Executive, 1-6-2014), and James Heffernan, "A Year of Big Wins" (Richmond, VA: Virginia Business, 2-28-2017), and Josh Janney, "Rubbermaid to Lease New Warehouse" (Winchester Star, 4-17-2018).

616 Tom Crosby, "Winchester Plant State of the Art for Mopar" (Strasburg, VA: Northern Virginia Daily, 4-18-2017).

617 Peter Heerwagen, "Ford to Build Auto Parts Warehouse in Frederick County" (Winchester, VA: QSBJ, May 2003), 1.

618 Heffernan, "A Year of Big Wins."

619 shockeyproperties.com, "Graystone Industrial Park Welcomes Kirkland's."

620 Maggie Wolff Peterson, "Business Journal Profile – Kevin Adams" (Winchester, VA: QSBJ, May 1999), 18.

621 Peter Heerwagen, "It's Family Feud for Discount Chain's Distribution Center in Warren County" (Winchester, VA: QSBJ, September 1996), 3. and Thru the Valleys, "Ferguson to Warren County" (Winchester, VA: QSBJ, February 1998), and Heerwagen, "A Warehouse for Warehouses" (Winchester, VA: QSBJ, September 2002), 1.

622 Ibid.

623 Heerwagen, "Home Depot Nails Down Another Warehouse," 13, and Heerwagen, "More Warehouses Along I-81" (Winchester, VA: QSBJ, March 2007), 11, and taxes. cofrederick.va.us, Frederick County Property Records, "360 McGhee Rd."

624 Peter Heerwagen, "Economic Developers Talk Up the Start of the New Millennium" (Winchester, VA: QSBJ, January 2000), 6.

625 Ibid.

626 dailypay.com, Megan Wells, "Call Center Turnover Statistics in 2018" (New York, NY: DailyPay, 2-7-2019).

627 Peter Heerwagen, "ICT Group Hangs Up on Outbound Call Center in Jefferson County" (Winchester, VA: QSBJ, January 2006), 19, and Matthew Umstead, "Aerotek Settles Suit with Former Workers" (Hagerstown, MD:

Herald-Mail, 4-29-2009), and Heerwagen, "CFW to Move into Downtown Winchester" (Winchester, VA: QSBJ, December 1998), 9.

[628] Onofrio Castiglia, "Navy Federal Expansion Announced in State of Commonwealth Speech" (Winchester Star, 1-12-2017).

[629] Ibid.

[630] Onofrio Castiglia, "Navy Federal Credit Union Expansion on Schedule" (Winchester Star, 5-10-2019).

[631] Georgia Caldwell, "AB&C Spells Success in the Fulfillment Business" (Winchester, VA: QSBJ, February 1996), 1.

[632] Ibid.

[633] digitalcommerce360.com, Digital Commerce 360, Paul Demery, "AB&C Group to Provide Complete Catalog and Web Order Management, Call Center & Fulfillment Services to National Wildlife," 7-14-2006, and Ben Hammer, "NWF Shifts Catalog Work to McLean, Lays Off 105" (Washington Business Journal, 6-24-2006).

[634] Ibid.

[635] interchangeco.com, Tyler Yoder, "InterChange Purchases Winchester Warehouse" (company press release, 3-18-2015), and Paula Squires, "Threshold Enterprises Announces Opening of New East Coast Distribution Center in Winchester" (Richmond, VA: Virginia Business, 6-9-2015).

[636] thresholdenterprises.com, "About Us."

[637] jeffersoncountywvsitesearch.com, "Property Results, Burr Business Park."

[638] Peter Heerwagen, "Norm Thompson Finds Fulfillment Elsewhere" (Winchester, VA: QSBJ, August 2007), 10.

[639] Peter Heerwagen, "Skies Grow Dark at AB&C Group in Panhandle" (Winchester, VA: QSBJ, April 2008), 21.

[640] Ibid.

[641] Matthew Umstead, "Tomblin Visits Macy's Online Fulfillment Center Near Martinsburg" (Hagerstown, MD: Herald-Mail, 12-2-2013).

[642] Ibid.

[643] Ibid.

[644] Josh Janney, "Governor Tours Amazon Facility" (Winchester Star, 4-10-2019), A1.

[645] Ibid.

[646] Peter Heerwagen, "Realtors See Local Housing Market Staying on Solid Ground" (Winchester, VA: NVBJ, February 1990), 1.

[647] Journal staff, "Upscale Housing Market Finds Niche in North Valley" (Winchester, VA: NVBJ, November 1989), 1.

[648] growingformarket.com, "Live Poor, Die Rich? Not Exactly" (Skowhegan, ME: Growing for Market, 7-1-2005).

[649] Peter Heerwagen, "Land Rush Picks up in Potomac Highlands" (Winchester, VA: QSBJ, April 2004), 1.

[650] Peter Heerwagen, "Area Homebuilding Boom Fueled by National Firms" (Winchester, VA: QSBJ, April 2002), 1.

[651] Real Estate Price Chart (Winchester, VA: QSBJ, February 2009), 17.

[652] Peter Heerwagen, "The Region's Housing Market Slows as Inventories Build" (Winchester, VA: QSBJ, October 2005), 1.

[653] Real Estate Price Chart (Winchester, VA: QSBJ, February 2009), 17.

[654] Ibid.

[655] Building permit data from planning and zoning commissions in Berkeley and Frederick counties.

[656] realtor.com, Frederick County VA and Berkeley County WV Housing Markets, July 2020.

[657] retreatatcoolspring.com, The Retreat at Cool Spring, Suzanne Eblen, "About the Retreat."

[658] Ibid.

[659] Ibid.

[660] revolvy.com, Revolvy, "History of Shannondale, West Virginia."

[661] Ibid.

[662] Ibid.

[663] wapoava.org, Wilde Acres Property Owners Association - Mountain Falls Park, "About Us."

[664] shawneelandwinchester.com, "History of Shawneeland," and dcski.com, "Preserving the History of Snowsports in the Mid-Atlantic, Shawnee Land" (DCSKI, comments by former skiers).

[665] law.justia.com, "In Re Marjec, Inc., T/a Shawnee-land, Debtor," Marjec, Inc., etc.,

U.S. Court of Appeals for the Fourth Circuit (Law Justica, 11-12-1987).

666 Priscilla Lehman, "Out of the Past . . . from the Archives of the Winchester Star, 50 Years Ago," 9-15-2020.

667 lakeholidaypoa.com, Lake Holiday Property Owners Association, "Official Site of Lake Holiday Country Club, Inc."

668 Paula Ann Kirby, "Mountain Magic" (Richmond, VA: Virginia Living, 2-24-2016).

669 Ibid.

670 Ibid.

671 shenandoahfarms.org, Property Owners of Shenandoah Farms, "Oral History of Shenandoah Farms."

672 revolvy.com, Revolvy, "Coolfont Resort."

673 Ibid.

674 Peter Heerwagen, "New Coolfont Owner Makes Changes" (Winchester, VA: QSBJ, February 2006), 17.

675 coolfont.com, Coolfont Resort, "Now Open! Escape to WV."

676 thewoods.com, The Woods, "History," and obituaries of Ray Johnston and Robert Bernstein.

677 "Section of W.Va. 9 Named After Ray Johnston" (Hagerstown, MD: Herald-Mail, 2-6-2009).

678 Peter Heerwagen, "Minghini's Works the Panhandle" (Winchester, VA: QSBJ, September 1999), 18.

679 Ibid.

680 whmcontractors.com, W. Harley Miller Contractors, "Our History."

681 Ibid.

682 Peter Heerwagen, "Rickett's Name Returns to Region's Roster of Commercial Contractors" (Winchester, VA: QSBJ, March 2008), 26.

683 Ibid.

684 Robert Burke, "Held to High Standards: Shockey Maintains Culture Established by its Founder" (Richmond, VA: Virginia Business, 3-1-2016).

685 toanandassociates.com, Toan & Associates, "About Us."

686 Peter Heerwagen, "Lantz Handles Wide Range of Projects" (Winchester, VA: QSBJ, September 2007), 22.

687 Ibid.

688 Hilary Legge, "Local Alumni Part of Taylor Hotel Restoration" (Winchester, VA: Shenandoah University Alumni Link).

689 perryeng.com, "About Perry Engineering Company, Inc."

690 legacy.com, "Kathryn M. Perry Werner (1927-2016).

691 Joe Holley, "Banker, Developer Leo M. Bernstein" (Washington Post, 9-1-2008).

692 Ibid.

693 Shell Fisher, "Comeback of a Cave" (Winchester Star, 6-26-1998), B-3.

694 aikensgroup.com, "Aikens Group History."

695 Ibid.

696 Ibid.

697 Ibid.

698 Peter Heerwagen, "Business Journal Profile – Bruce Van Wyk" (Winchester, VA: QSBJ, January 1997), 16.

699 Ibid.

700 Jim Wright, "Ken Lowe Plays Down His Successes" (Winchester, VA: QSBJ, September 1998), 18.

701 Ibid.

702 "Foundation to Take Over Va. Battlefield" (Washington Post, 6-3-1989).

703 Allison Howard, "The Virginia Public Lake That Wasn't Really Public" (Washington Post, 1-27-1990).

704 Alison Howard, "Development to Begin Around Va. Lake" (Washington Post, 7-16-1990).

705 Brian Brehm, "George Washington Hotel to Mark 10th Anniversary After Reopening" (Winchester Star, 2-7-2018).

706 Ibid.

707 Brian Brehm, "City Denies Claims of Impropriety with Taylor Hotel Project" (Winchester Star, 2-2-2019), and oldtownwinchesterva.com, "You're Invited: Taylor Hotel Ribbon Cutting, 8-14-2014.

708 Matthew Umstead, "Shenandoah Hotel Sold to Virginia Firm for $550K" (Herald-Mail, 8-20-2019).

709 Ibid.

710 chicagofed.org, Christine Johnson and Tara Rice, "Assessing a Decade of Interstate Bank Branching" (Chicago Federal Reserve Bank, April 2007), 9.

711 Ibid.

712 Michelle Clark Neely, "Going Interstate: A New Dawn for U. S. Banking" (Central Banker, News and Notes from the Federal Reserve Bank of St. Louis, July 1994).

713 fred.stlouisfed.org, Federal Reserve Bank of St. Louis, Economic Research, "Commercial Banks in the U.S."

714 investopedia.com, Adam Hayes, "Dodd-Frank Wall Street Reform and Consumer Protection Act," 10-1-2020.

715 fdic.gov, Federal Deposit Insurance Corporation, Bank Data and Statistics, "Offices and Deposits."

716 ffiec.gov, Federal Financial Institutions Examination Council, National Information Center, "Institution History for First National Bank of Berryville."

717 Cathy Kuehner, "Feltner Dedicated Life to Community Banking, Philanthropy" (Winchester Star, 4-25-2018).

718 F&M National Corporation, 1992 and 2000 Annual Reports.

719 Peter Heerwagen, "Winchester's F&M Vaults to the South" (Winchester, VA: QSBJ, February, 2001), 1.

720 sec.gov, Form 8-K," Merger Agreement, BB&T and F&M National Corporation," filed with U.S. Securities and Exchange Commission, 2-27-2001, and su.edu, Shenandoah University, Stephanie Mangino, "In Memoriam: Wilbur M. Feltner."

721 Ibid.

722 Ibid.

723 ffiec.gov, National Information Center, "Institution History for Valley of Virginia Bankshares, Inc."

724 ffiec.gov, National Information Center, Institution History for each bank.

725 Peter Heerwagen, "Marathon Bank Runs a Different Race for the Gold" (Winchester, VA: NVBJ, July 1991), 1.

726 Peter Heerwagen, "Marathon Joins Up with Harrisonburg Bank" (Winchester, VA: QSBJ, May 2000), 15.

727 Ibid.

728 Peter Heerwagen, "Winchester Bank Will Unite with West Virginia Bank" (Winchester, VA: QSBJ, March 2007), 7.

729 ffiec.gov, National Information Center, "Institution History for Harpers Ferry Branch."

730 Ibid., and National Information Center, "Institution History for Potomac Bankshares, Inc."

731 Ibid.," Institution History for Mountaineer Bankshares of W. Va."

732 Ibid., "Institution History for Berkeley Springs Branch."

733 Ibid., and Peter Heerwagen, "Mountaineer Joins One Valley as Biggest W.Va. Bank" (Winchester, VA: NVBJ, September 1993), 1, and sec.gov, One Valley Bancorp of West Virginia, Inc. Form 10-K, Annual Report for Year Ending December 31, 1994, filed with U.S. Securities and Exchange Commission.

734 ffiec.gov, National Information Center, "Institution History for Charles Town Branch."

735 Ibid., "Institution History for Martinsburg Branch."

736 fdic.gov, Federal Deposit Insurance Corporation, *Changes Among Operating Banks and Branches: FDIC 1983.*

737 Peter Heerwagen, "Big Banks Merge, While Community Banks Add Branches" (Winchester, VA: QSBJ, January 2003), 11.

738 Jim Kudlinski, *The Tarnished Fed* (New York, NY: Page Publishing Inc., 2014).

739 fdic.gov, Federal Deposit Insurance Corporation, "The Savings and Loan Crisis and Its Relationship to Banking."

740 ffiec.gov, National Information Center, "Institution History for Old Dominion Savings Bank."

741 Ibid.

742 Ibid., and Comptroller of the Currency, Administrator of National Banks, "Decision on Application to Merge," 1-24-1984.

743 ffiec.gov, National Information Center, "Institution History for Front Royal Branch."

Endnotes: Chapter 7

[744] Ibid., and Thru the Valleys, "Taking it to the Bank" (Winchester, VA: QSBJ, February 2009), 8.

[745] Michael Schwartz, "Va. Bank Failure Marks First in State Since 1993" (Norfolk, VA: The Virginia-Pilot, 12-14-2009).

[746] Wendy Swallow, "Judge Orders Sale of Snowshoe Resort" (Washington Post, 6-15-1985).

[747] Peter Heerwagen, "New Bank Books Deposits in Former Jail" (Winchester, VA: NVBJ, November 1992), 14.

[748] ffiec.gov, National Information Center, "Institution History for Front Royal Branch."

[749] Joe Beck, "West Va. Firm Will Buy Virginia Savings Bank" (Strasburg, VA: Northern Virginia Daily, 11-15-2011), and "City Holding Buys Virginia Bank" (Charleston, WV: Charleston Gazette, 11-14-2011).

[750] "Credit Unions," *The Book of Lists, 2009 Edition* (Winchester, VA: QSBJ), 40.

[751] census.gov, U.S. Census Bureau, Statistical Abstracts of the United States, "Annual Retail Sales."

[752] statistica.com, Liam O'Connell, "Number of Shopping Centers in the U.S., from 1970 to 2017," 12-3-2019.

[753] Dave McMillion, "Plans for Bypass Go Through Berkeley Plaza" (Hagerstown, MD: Herald-Mail, 2-9-2000).

[754] Brian Brehm, "Once-Thriving Ward Plaza Still Struggling" (Winchester Star, 7-14-2017).

[755] Priscilla Lehman, "Out of the Past . . . from the Archives of the Winchester Star, 50 Years Ago," 2-26-2018, B5.

[756] winchesterva.gov, Winchester, Virginia, "Chronological History."

[757] malls.com, "Apple Blossom Mall."

[758] Peter Heerwagen, "Wal-Mart Comes to Town" (Winchester, VA: NVBJ, January 1990), 1.

[759] Priscilla Lehman, "Out of the Past . . . from the Archives of the Winchester Star, 25 Years Ago," 7-16-2018, B5, and Thru the Valleys, "Warehouse Clubs at War" (Winchester, VA: NVBJ, November 1994), 22.

[760] Peter Heerwagen, "Wal-Mart Supercenters to March Up I-81 Aisle" (Winchester, VA: QSBJ, July 1996), 1.

[761] Peter Heerwagen, "Two Area Malls Go Public with Operating Data" (Winchester, VA: NVBJ, August 1993), 1.

[762] Matthew Umstead, "Hobby Lobby to Replace J.C. Penney at Foxcroft Towne Center" (Hagerstown, MD: Herald-Mail, 6-5-2017), and paramountdevcorp.com, Paramount Development Corporation, "Foxcroft Towne Center – Martinsburg, WV."

[763] Peter Heerwagen, "Simon Says Make Over Apple Blossom Mall" (Winchester, VA: QSBJ, March 2007), 9.

[764] Sally Voth, "New Cinema, Facelift Coming to Apple Blossom Mall" (Strasburg, VA: Northern Virginia Daily, 5-29-2012).

[765] Josh Janney, "Winchester Sears Store to Close by February" (Winchester Star, 12-9-2019).

[766] Jennifer Hutchinson, "Creekside Lifestyle Center Continues to Expand" (Winchester, VA: QSBJ, November 2005), 17.

[767] Ibid.

[768] Peter Heerwagen, "More Shopping Centers to Open" (Winchester, VA: QSBJ, December 2005), 6.

[769] Maggie Wolff Peterson, "Finding New Outlets for Old Buildings" (Winchester, VA: NVBJ, December 1994), 15.

[770] Ibid.

[771] John McVey, "Recession Rebound" (Martinsburg, WV: The Journal, 4-10-2014).

[772] Ibid.

[773] Matthew Umstead, "Former Mountain State Campus in Martinsburg Sold for $2 Million" (Hagerstown, MD: Herald-Mail, 1-16-2015).

[774] Ibid.

[775] ache.org, "History of Health Insurance in the United States" (Chicago, IL: American College of Healthcare Executives).

[776] Ibid.

[777] hhs.gov, U.S. Department of Health and Human Services, "Medical Treatment in Hill-Burton Funded Healthcare Facilities."

[778] valleyhealthlink.com, Valley Health, Winchester Medical Center, "Our History."

[779] Ibid.

[780] Ibid.

[781] Ibid.

782 Daily staff report, "Valley Health Announces Sale of Cork Street Property" (Strasburg, VA: Northern Virginia Daily, 8-18-2014), and Brian Brehm, "Work to Start in October for Senior-Living Center at Old Hospital Location" (Winchester Star, 9-11-2020).

783 valleyhealthlink.com, Valley Health, Warren Memorial Hospital, "Our History."

784 Ibid., Valley Health, Shenandoah Memorial Hospital, "Our History."

785 Ibid., Valley Health, Page Memorial Hospital, "Our History."

786 cityofranson.net, Ranson, West Virginia, "Our City's History."

787 Ibid.

788 "Martinsburg Hospital Funded" (Hagerstown, MD: Daily Mail, 2-16-1967).

789 Ibid.

790 "City Hospital Rejects Purchase Proposal" (Hagerstown, MD: Morning Herald, 11-26-1976), 11.

791 Ibid.

792 Ibid.

793 Thru the Valleys, "City Hospital Ends Management Contract" (Winchester, VA: QSBJ, August 1999), 10.

794 Peter Heerwagen, "Business Coalition Continues Fight to Control Health Care Costs" (Winchester, VA: NVBJ, March 1994), 9.

795 Ibid., 10.

796 Peter Heerwagen, "Hospital to Businesses: No New Rate Hikes" (Winchester, VA: NVBJ, December 1992), 1.

797 Ibid.

798 Peter Heerwagen, "Local Health Care Providers Network in Face of Reform" (Winchester, VA: NVBJ, March 1994), 9.

799 Peter Heerwagen, "The Numbers Tell the Capacity Story" (Winchester, VA: QSBJ, January 1998), 15.

800 Valley Health System and Subsidiaries, Consolidated Financial Statements and other Financial Information, Year-Ended December 31, 2010.

801 valleyhealthlink.com, Valley Health, Shenandoah Memorial Hospital, "Our History."

802 Ibid., "Growing to Serve New Patients," Winter 2020, 13, and About Us, "Facts & Statistics."

803 Ibid.

804 Valley Health System and Subsidiaries Consolidated Financial Statements and Other Financial Information, Year-Ended December 31, 2014, 7.

805 Peter Heerwagen, "Eastern Panhandle Hospitals to Merge and Join WVU Hospitals" (Winchester, VA: QSBJ, October 2004), 1.

806 Ibid.

807 Ibid.

808 Peter Heerwagen, "Hospitals Become More Territorial as Local Competition Heats Up" (Winchester, VA: QSBJ, June 2006), 1.

809 Ibid.

810 Richard Belisle, "New Names Announced for Hospitals in Berkeley and Jefferson Counties" (Hagerstown, MD: Herald-Mail, 5-13-2013).

811 Adam Glasier, "Urgent Care Association of America Accredits Valley Health Urgent Care in Martinsburg With Highest Distinction" (Martinsburg, WV: The Journal, 2-15-2017).

812 valleyhealthlink.com, Valley Health, "Valley Health I Spring Mills Now Open."

813 Peter Heerwagen, "Assisted Living on the Rise in Area" (Winchester, VA: QSBJ, May 1998), 1.

814 Heerwagen, "Senior Living Sector Continues on Growth Path" (Winchester, VA: QSBJ, April 2009), 3.

815 Josh Janney, "Senior Community Celebrates 30th Anniversary" (Winchester Star, 5-12-2017).

816 Ibid.

817 Ibid.

818 Brian Brehm, "Westminster-Canterbury Proposes Major Expansion" (Winchester Star, 8-5-2020).

819 Peter Heerwagen, "Homewood Retirement Expands to Strasburg" (Winchester, VA: QSBJ, July 2008), 16.

820 Sally Voth, "Strasburg's Homewood Site for Sale" (Strasburg VA: Northern Virginia Daily, 3-31-2013).

821 Peter Heerwagen, "Some Continuing Care Communities Hit by Housing Slowdown" (Winchester, VA: QSBJ, December 2008), 15.

822 Josh Janney, "Village Expands Resident Options for Seniors" (Winchester Star, 6-2-2016), and thevillageatorchardridge.org, "Go Beyond the Typical CCRC."

823 Peter Heerwagen, "$20 Million Museum of the Shenandoah Valley on Display" (Winchester, VA: QSBJ, April 2005), 1.

824 Ibid.

825 themsv.org, Museum of the Shenandoah Valley, "Julian Wood Glass Jr."

826 nps.gov, National Park Service, Cedar Creek and Belle Grove National Historic Park, "Park Planning."

827 dcr.virginia.gov, Virginia Department of Conservation and Recreation, Shenandoah River State Park, "General Information."

828 vmi.edu, Virginia Military Institute, "The Virginia Museum of the Civil War and New Market Battlefield State Historical Park."

829 Ibid.

830 Maggie Wolff Peterson, "Civil War Battlefield Group Advances Its Plan" (Winchester, VA: QSBJ, July 2002), 1.

831 Ibid.

832 shrinemont.com, Shrine Mont, "Portlock Cottage."

833 Ibid.

834 Jenni Vincent, "Berkeley Springs Among Best Historical Towns" (Hagerstown, MD: Herald-Mail, 7-16-2020).

835 berkeleysprings.com, Berkeley Springs, "The Country's First Spa."

836 ngf.org, National Golf Foundation, "Statistics of Golf Industry."

837 Matthew Umstead, "Future of Stonebridge Golf Course Still Up in the Air" (Hagerstown, MD: Herald-Mail, 5-6-2015).

838 golflink.com, GolfLink, "Sleepy Hollow Golf Course Description," and Laura B. Withers, "Dick: Closing Carper's Valley Club Saddens Many" (Winchester Star, 12-29-2005), B1.

839 Georgia Caldwell, "Golf Housing Communities Gain Popularity in Region" (Winchester, VA: NVBJ, May 1995), 9.

840 Ibid.

841 Ibid.

842 cresscreek.com, Cress Creek, "Club History."

843 Caldwell, "Golf Housing Communities," 9, and Peter Heerwagen, "Mid-Length Course Opens at The Woods" (Winchester, VA: QSBJ, April 2002), 22.

844 Peter Heerwagen, "Changes Continue at Region's Golf Courses" (Winchester, VA: QSBJ, April 2006), 17.

845 Caldwell, "Golf Housing Communities," 9, and Peter Heerwagen, "Jackson's Chase Course Opens in Warren County" (Winchester, VA: QSBJ, April 1998), 9, and Heerwagen, "Several New Courses Are Planned for the Region" (Winchester, VA: QSBJ, April, 2000), 9.

846 Peter Heerwagen, "It's Show Us the Money for Several of the Area's Golf Courses" (Winchester, VA: QSBJ, April 2004), 21, and rockharborgolf.com, "Welcome to Rock Harbor Golf Course," and "The Course."

847 Barry Svriuga, "As U.S. Open Sets to Begin, Golf Looks for New Ways to Bolster Participation" (Washington Post, 6-7-2014), and National Golf Foundation report, 2019.

848 Ibid.

849 Peter Heerwagen, "More Closures May Be Par for Several Courses in Region" (Winchester, VA: QSBJ, April 2007), 17, and Roger Bianchini, "Blue Ridge Shadows Files for Re-Organizational Bankruptcy" (Front Royal VA: Warren County Report, December 2008).

850 su.edu, "Welcome to Cool Spring River Campus."

851 John McVey, "Stonebridge Auction a Whiff Among Bidders" (Martinsburg, WV: The Journal, 2-2-2013), and Matthew Umstead, "Future of Stonebridge Golf Club."

852 Bennett Liebman, "Reasons for the Decline of Horse Racing" (New York Times, 6-6-2010).

853 wvencyclopedia.org, e-WV, The West Virginia Encyclopedia, "Shenandoah Downs," 10-29-2010.

854 Ibid.

855 horseracing-racks.com, "No More Shenny," and e-WV, The West Virginia Encyclopedia, "Shenandoah Downs."

856 e-WV, The West Virginia Encyclopedia, William D. Theriault, "Charles Town Races," 1-28-2011.

857 Ibid.

858 drf.com, Daily Racing Form, Jay Privman, "Triple Crown Winners: The Second Act," 8-1-2015.

859 Theriault, "Charles Town Races."

860 Ibid.

861 Michael Trilling, "Two Charles Town Race Tracks Closed" (Washington Post, 1-4-1979).

862 Ibid.

863 Theriault, "Charles Town Races."

864 Josh Hafenbrack, "West Virginia Shows How to Cash in With Slots" (Deerfield Beach, FL: Sun-Sentinel, 3-13-2005).

865 Peter Heerwagen, "Charles Town Races Back on Track with Penn National" (Winchester, VA: QSBJ, December 1996), 1.

866 Ibid.

867 Peter Heerwagen, "Video Lottery to Open at Charles Town" (Winchester, VA: QSBJ, August 1997), 1.

868 Ibid.

869 Eric Bowen et al, "The Economic Impact of the Thoroughbred and Greyhound Racing Industries on West Virginia's Economy in 2012" (Morgantown, WV: West Virginia University, January 2014).

870 Ibid.

871 Richard Belisle, "Hollywood Casino at Charles Town Races to Lay Off 'Handful' of Poker Dealers" (Hagerstown, MD: Herald-Mail, 10-24-2013).

872 Matthew Umstead, "Hollywood Casino at Charles Town to Lay Off 541 Workers" (Hagerstown, MD: Herald-Mail, 7-24-2020).

873 shencofair.com, Shenandoah County Fair, "Visit Us."

874 virginiahorseracing.com, Virginia Equine Alliance, "About Us."

875 racingvirginia.com, Racing Virginia, "About Winchester Speedway."

876 Ibid.

877 "For the Record – Shenandoah Valley" (Richmond, VA: Virginia Business, 3-29-2010).

878 Ibid.

879 racingcircuits.info, "Summit Point, Circuit History."

880 Ibid.

881 pcapotomac.org, Porsche Club of America, Tom Neel, "New Horizons for Summit Point."

882 Tim Cool, "Allison's Goal: Keep Summit Point Humming" (Martinsburg, WV: The Journal, 12-11-2017).

883 Tom Crosby, "Summit Point Motorsports Park Undergoing Changes" (Winchester Star, 10-24-2018).

884 Karen Campbell, "Shenandoah Speedway Under Fire Again" (Harrisonburg, VA: WHSV, 6-17-2011).

885 shenandoah-speedway.com, Shenandoah Speedway, "Track Rental," 6-4-2018.

886 Drew Hartwell, "U.S. Radio's Top Player Blames AI for Layoffs: DJs Say That's Spin" (Washington Post, 2-9-1020).

887 E&P staff, "Virginia's Weekly Clarke Times-Courier Sold to Winchester Star" (Fountain Valley, CA: Editor & Publisher, 7-28-2008).

888 Philip Smith, "Shoestring Virginia Paper Still Alive" (Washington Post, 3-17-1996).

889 royalexaminer.com, Royal Examiner, "About Us."

890 wvencyclopedia.org, e-WV, West Virginia Encyclopedia, "Martinsburg Journal," 10-8-2010.

891 apnews.com, The Associated Press, "Ogden Newspapers to Buy Northern Virginia Daily," 2-6-2012, and Adrian O'Connor, "Byrd Family Selling Star to Ogden Newspapers" (Winchester Star, 3-7-2018), 1.

892 "WFTR Debuts as New Virginia MBS Outlet" (Washington, DC: Broadcasting, 9-27-1948).

893 Peter Heerwagen, "Radio Industry Enjoys Second Golden Era" (Winchester, VA: QSBJ, March 2001), 1.

894 Ibid.

895 Ibid., and enacademc.com, "WFQX (FM)."

896 *Decisions and Reports of the Federal Communications Commission, April 1-June 30, 1985*, "Application of Ruarck Associates," 345.

897 americanradiohistory.com, American Radio History, "Berkeley Springs, WCST(AM)."

898 wcstsports.wordpress.com, WCST 1010 AM Sports, "About – Brief History."

899 talkradiowrnr.com., WRNR, "About Us."

900 Kelsie LeRose, "WEPM Celebrates 75 Years of Serving the Community" (Martinsburg, WV: The Journal, 10-13-2021).

901 Peter Heerwagen, "Softer Music Emanates from Williamsport" (Winchester, VA: QSBJ, March 2001), 7.

902 Lance Venta, "West Virginia Radio Corporation Expands into Martinsburg and Hagerstown" (RadioInsight, 10-31-2014), and rbr.com, Radio + Television Business Report, "Price Revealed for West Virginia Radio Buy," 11-3-2014.

903 insideradio.com, Inside Radio, Deal Digest for the Week of September 17, 2015.

904 Mike Frank, "Area Radio Station Under New Ownership" (Martinsburg, WV: The Journal, 3-19-2017).

905 fccdata.org, FCC Data, Federal Communications Commission.

906 Broadcasting Magazine (Washington, DC, 8-4-1997).

907 Heerwagen, "Radio Industry Enjoys Second Golden Era."

908 worldradiohistory.com, "Clear Channel Buys West Virginia Combo" (Radio Business, 12-8-2000), 8.

909 Thru the Valleys, "Big Band Sold Out" (Winchester, VA: QSBJ, August 2000), 23.

910 Stephanie Mangino, "Sold! $26M for WINC's Corporate Parent" (Winchester Star, 5-17-2007).

911 Mickey Powell, "Owner of WINC-FM Selling 92.5 Frequency to Nonprofit Christian Radio Ministry" (Winchester Star, 12-1-2020).

912 Ibid.

913 Mike Lewis, "WHAG Unveils Programming Changes After Losing NBC" (Hagerstown, MD: Herald-Mail, 2-19-2016).

914 wikimill.com, WDCO-CD, "WAZT History."

915 Thru the Valleys, "TV Station Sold" (Winchester, VA: QSBJ, April 2006), 8.

916 Sally Voth, "Local Pastor $4.7M in Debt" (Strasburg, VA: Northern Virginia Daily, 11-4-2010).

917 Peter Heerwagen, "New Martinsburg TV Station Goes Airborne" (Winchester, VA: NVBJ, October 1991), 1.

918 Ibid.

919 Peter Heerwagen, "New TV Station to Hit the Airwaves in Winchester" (Winchester, VA: QSBJ, November 2006), 1.

920 Ibid.

921 Merrill Knox, "Gray Television Shutters TV3 Winchester" (New York, NY: Adweek, 12-5-2013).

922 calcable.org, California Cable & Telecommunications Association, "History of Cable."

923 Peter Krouse, "Lewis Family Sells Cable TV to Pa. Company" (Winchester Star, 1-5-1989), 7.

924 Peter Heerwagen, "More Clustering of Cable TV Systems" (Winchester, VA: QSBJ, February 1996), 16.

925 corporate.comcast.com, "Time Warner and Comcast Complete Adelphia Communications Transactions" (Comcast press release, 7-31-2006).

926 shentel.com, Shentel Management Company, "Shentel History," and Shentel 2009 Annual Report.

927 Ibid., "Shenandoah Telecommunications Company Reports First Quarter 2020 Results."

928 Brian Brehm, "Shentel Wants to Challenge Comcast's Cable Dominance in Winchester" (Winchester Star, 7-11-2019), 3.

929 Ibid.

930 hmdb.org, Historical Marker Database, "Veterans Administration Center."

931 "The Year in Brief, the VA in 1984," Veterans Administration."

932 nps.gov., National Park Service, Harpers Ferry Center, "Our History."

933 Ibid.

934 Patrick Farris, "U.S. Army Remount Depot Supported Two World Wars" (Byrd Newspapers, Shenandoah Summer, 2008), 42.

[935] Ibid., and nationalzoo.si.edu, Smithsonian's National Zoo & Conservation Biology Institute.

[936] cbp.gov, U.S. Customs and Border Protection, "Canine Center History."

[937] Ted Gup, "Civil Defense Doomsday Hideaway" (New York, NY: Time Magazine, 6-24-2001).

[938] Ibid.

[939] "FEMA Disaster Operations Center to be Housed at Facility in Winchester" (Washington, DC: Federal Emergency Management Administration press release, 4-8-2008).

[940] Ibid.

[941] Ibid.

[942] Robert P. Grathwol and Donita M. Moorhus, *Bricks, Sand, and Marble, U.S. Army Corps of Engineers Construction in the Mediterranean and Middle East 1947-1991* (Washington, DC: U.S. Government Printing Office, 2009).

[943] sad.usace.army.mil, "History of the Transatlantic Division of the U.S. Army Corps of Engineers, 1945-2011."

[944] lmi.workforcewv.org, Workforce West Virginia, "Employment and Wages 1995-2019."

[945] byrdcenter.org, Robert C. Byrd Center, Jody Brumage, "The Appalachian Fruit Research Station," 5-29-2018.

[946] Ibid.

[947] Wright, "Ken Lowe Plays Down His Successes."

[948] byrdcenter.org, Robert C. Byrd Center, Byrd's-Eye View, Senator Robert C. Byrd, "Two More Federal Agencies Plan Relocations to West Virginia," 7-3-1991.

[949] berkeleycounty.org, Berkeley County Development Authority, "Major Employers and Industries in Martinsburg–Berkeley County, WV," June 2016.

[950] Craig Collins, "The National Maritime Center" (Defense Media Center, 3-5-2011).

[951] nctc.fws.gov, National Conservation Training Center, U.S. Fish and Wildlife Service, "Byrd Legacy Remembered at NCTC," 6-28-2010.

[952] Wright, "Ken Lowe Plays Down His Successes."

[953] Beth Henry, "Harpers Ferry, WV Gets $122 Million Weapons Center" (Martinsburg, WV: Journal-News, 5-31-2008).

[954] Peter Heerwagen, "Byrd Secures Funds for V.A. Data Center" (Winchester, VA: QSBJ, December 2008), 5.

[955] fedweek.com, Federal Manager's Daily Report, "Management Development Center Moving," 11-4-2014.

[956] Nikki Wentling, "Two Years After Trump Promised a White House Veterans Hotline, It's Open–in West Virginia" (Washington, DC: Stars and Stripes, 7-27-2018).

[957] Ibid.

[958] David Foreman, "Changing the Daily Commute" (Winchester Star, 6-9-1998), A7.

[959] fedmanager.com, Fed Manager, "Seven DC-Area Telework Centers Close as GSA Ends Funding," 3-8-2011.

[960] "(FBI) Case Closed in Northern Valley," Thru the Valleys (Winchester, VA: QSBJ, March 2004), 8.

[961] federalregister.gov, Notice of Intent to Prepare a Supplemental Draft Environmental Impact Statement for the FBI Central Records Complex in Winchester, Virginia," 2-17-2015.

[962] Ibid.

[963] Josh Janney, "FBI Records Complex to Open This Spring" (Winchester Star, 2-13-2020).

BIBLIOGRAPHY

Aler, F. Vernon, *Aler's History of Martinsburg and Berkeley County, W. VA.*, Hagerstown, MD: The Mail Publishing Company, 1888.

Baldwin, Leland D., *Pittsburgh, The Story of a City*, Pittsburgh, PA: University of Pittsburgh Press, 1937.

Ball, Edward, "Slavery's Tail of Tears," Washington, DC: Smithsonian Magazine, November 2015.

Blumer, Thomas and Charles W. Pomeroy, *Front Royal and Warren County, Images of America*, Charleston, SC: Arcadia Publishing, 2004.

Brown, Stuart E. Jr., *Virginia Baron, The Story of Thomas 6th Lord Fairfax*, Berryville, VA: Chesapeake Book Company, 1965.

Bushong, Millard Kessler, *Historic Jefferson County*, Boyce, VA: Carr Publishing Company, Inc., 1972.

Byrne, John P., "The Civilian Conservation Corps in Virginia, 1933-1942," PhD dissertation, Missoula, MT: University of Montana, 1982.

Cadden, Virginia Hinkins, "The Story of Strasburg," Strasburg, VA: Northern Virginia Daily, 1961, reprinted by Strasburg Heritage Association in 2011.

Callahan, James Norton, *History of West Virginia, Old and New*, Chicago and New York: American Historical Society, Inc., 1923.

Cartmell, Thomas Kemp, *Shenandoah Valley Pioneers and Their Descendants*, Winchester, VA: The Eddy Press Corporation, 1909.

Comstock, H. E., "Redwell Ironworks," Winston-Salem, NC: The Museum of Early Southern Decorative Arts, Journal of Early Southern Decorative Arts, Volume VII, Number 1, May 1981.

Coulter, E. Merton, *The South During Reconstruction, 1865 – 1877,* Baton Rouge, LA: Louisiana State University Press, 1947.

Davis, Julia, *The Shenandoah,* New York, NY and Toronto: Rinehart & Company, Inc., 1945.

Dunaway, Wilma A., *The African American Family in Slavery and Reconstruction,* Cambridge, UK: Cambridge University Press, 2003.

Ebert, Rebecca A. and Teresa Lazazzera, *Frederick County, Virginia: From the Frontier to the Future,* Norfolk, VA: The Donning Company, 1988.

Evans, Willis F., *History of Berkeley County, West Virginia,* originally published 1927, reprinted by Westminster, MD: Heritage Books, Inc., 2001.

Fischer, David Hackett and James C. Kelly, *Bound Away: Virginia and the Westward Movement,* Charlottesville, VA and London: University of Virginia Press, 2000.

Foner, Eric, *Reconstruction, America's Unfinished Revolution, 1863-1877,* New York, NY: Harper & Row, 1998.

Foreman, Michael, Virginia L. Miller, Reed Nester and Charles Thorne, *Images of the Past: A Photographic Review of Winchester and Frederick County, Virginia,* Winchester, VA: Winchester-Frederick County Historical Society, 1980.

Fravel, Linden A. and Byron C. Smith, *Stephens City, Images of America,* Charleston, SC: Arcadia Publishing, 2008.

Gilbert, David T., *Waterpower: Mills, Factories, Machines & Floods at Harpers Ferry, West Virginia, 1762-1991,* Harpers Ferry, WV: Harpers Ferry Historical Association, 1999.

Grimsley, G. P., *West Virginia Geological Survey,* Vol. Four, Morgantown, WV: Acme Publishing Company, 1909.

Hammann, Conrad C., *History of Halltown Paperboard Company,* Shepherdstown, WV: self-published, 1984.

Hazen, Theodore R., *Flouring Milling in America, A General Overview*, Washington, DC: National Park Service, 2003.

Heinemann, Ronald L., *Depression and New Deal in Virginia, The Enduring Dominion*, Charlottesville, VA: The University Press of Virginia, 1983.

High, Mike, *The C&O Canal Companion: A Journal Through Potomac History*, Baltimore, MD: Johns Hopkins University Press, 2015.

Hildebrand, John R., *Iron Horses in the Valley: The Valley and Shenandoah Valley Railroads 1866–1882*, Shippensburg, PA: Burd Street Press, 2001.

Hofstra, Warren R., *A Separate Place: The Formation of Clarke County, Virginia*, Madison, WI: Madison House Publishers, Inc., 1986.

———. *The Planting of New Virginia*, Baltimore and London: Johns Hopkins University Press, 2004.

———. editor, *George Washington and the Virginia Backcountry*, Madison, WI: Madison House Publishers, Inc., 1998.

Hofstra, Warren R. and Karl Raitz, editors, *The Great Valley Road of Virginia*, Charlottesville, VA and London: University of Virginia Press, 2010.

Hotchkiss, Jed, "The Virginias, A mining, Industrial and Scientific Journal, Volume II, Staunton, VA, October 1881.

Hurst, Harold W., *Alexandria on the Potomac: The Portrait of an Antebellum Community*, Lanham, MD: University Press of America, 1991.

Johnston, Wilbur S., *Weaving a Common Thread*, Winchester, VA: Winchester-Frederick County Historical Society, 1980.

Joint Committee of Hopewell Friends and John Walter Wayland, *Hopewell Friends History, 1734 to 1934*, Strasburg, VA: Shenandoah Publishing House, 1936.

Jost, Scott, *Shenandoah Valley Apples*, Chicago, IL: Columbia College Chicago Press, 2013.

Kalbian, Maral S., *Frederick County, Virginia: History Through Architecture*, Winchester, VA: Winchester-Frederick County Historical Society, 1999.

"———. *Clarke County, Images of America*, Charleston, SC: Arcadia Publishing, 2011.

Kehoe, Kathy C., "Strasburg Heritage Association Newsletter," Winter 2005.

Kercheval, Samuel, *A History of the Valley of Virginia*, Fourth Edition, originally published in 1833, Strasburg, VA: Shenandoah Publishing House, 1925.

Kerns, Wilmer L., *Settlement and Some First Families of Back Creek Valley, 1730 to 1830*, Baltimore, MD: Gateway Press, Inc., 1995.

Koons, Kenneth E. and Warren R. Hofstra, editors, *After the Backcountry, Rural Life in the Great Valley of Virginia 1800-1900*, Knoxville, TN: University of Tennessee Press, 2000.

Lambert, Darwin, *The Undying Past of Shenandoah National Park*, Lanham, MD: Roberts Rinehart, Inc. Publishers, 1989.

Linhart, Mary Sullivan, "Up to Date and Progressive: Winchester and Frederick County, Virginia, 1870-1980," PhD dissertation, Fairfax, VA: George Mason University, 2014.

MacMaster, Richard, *The History of Hardy County, 1786-1986*, Salem, WV: Wadsworth Press, Inc., 1986.

Mahon, Michael G., *The Shenandoah Valley, 1861-1865*, Mechanicsburg, PA: Stackpole Books, 1999.

Martin, Jean M. and Shenandoah County Historical Society, *Shenandoah County, Images of America*, Charleston, SC: Arcadia Publishing, 2010.

McIntyre, Kristina Marie, "Adaptive Reuse in Martinsburg: The Interwoven School of Crafts," master's thesis, College Park, MD: University of Maryland, 2008.

Mitchell, Robert D., *Commercialism and Frontier: Perspectives on the Early Shenandoah Valley*, Charlottesville, VA: University of Virginia Press, 1977.

Morton, Frederic, *The Story of Winchester in Virginia*, Strasburg, VA: Shenandoah Publishing House, 1925.

Mozier, Jeanne and Betty Lou Harmison, *Berkeley Springs, Images of America*, Charleston, SC: Arcadia Publishing, 2011.

Munske, Roberta M. and Wilmer L. Kerns, editors, *Hampshire County, West Virginia, 1754- 2004,* Romney, WV: The Hampshire County 250th Anniversary Committee, 2004.

Nasby, Dolly, *Harpers Ferry, Images of America*, Charleston, SC: Arcadia Publishing, 2007.

——. *Shepherdstown, Images of America*, Charleston, SC: Arcadia Publishing, 2005.

——. *Charles Town, Images of America*, Charleston, SC: Arcadia Publishing, 2004.

Norris, J. E., *History of the Lower Shenandoah Valley: Counties of Frederick, Berkeley, Jefferson and Clarke*, Volume 1, Baltimore MD: Genealogical Publishing Company, 1923.

Noyalas, Jonathan A., *Two Peoples, One Community: The African American Experience in Newtown (Stephens City), Virginia, 1850-1870,"* Stephens City, VA: Stone House Foundation, 2007.

——. and Nancy T. Sorrells, editors, *Home Front to Front Line: The Civil War Era in the Shenandoah Valley*, New Market, VA: Shenandoah Valley Battlefields Foundation, 2009.

Parker, Kathryn, *Winchester, Images of America*, Charleston, SC: Arcadia Publishing, 2006.

Quarles, Garland R., *John Handley and the Handley Bequests*, Winchester, VA: Winchester-Frederick County Historical Society, 1969.

——. *Some Worthy Lives*, Winchester, VA: Winchester-Frederick County Historical Society, 1988.

Reynolds, Kirk and Dave Oroszi, *Baltimore & Ohio Railroad*, Minneapolis, MN: Voyageur Press, 2008.

Rice, A. H. and John Baer Stoudt, *The Shenandoah Pottery*, Strasburg, VA: Shenandoah Publishing House, 1929.

Ritenour, Jeanette Conner, James Harris Trott and Margaret Akers Trott, *Welcome to Fort Valley: The History and Culture of Virginia's Valley within a Valley*, Edgewater, MD: Fort Valley Book, LLC, 2011.

Rose, Kenneth W., "The Problematic Legacy of Judge John Handley," Winchester, VA: Winchester-Frederick County Historical Society Journal, Volume 25, 2003.

Sarles Jr., Frank B., *Harpers Ferry National Historical Park*, "Social and Economic History of Virginius Island," 6-20-1969.

Scharf, John Thomas, *History of Baltimore City and County, from the Earliest Period to the Present Day*, Philadelphia, PA: Lewis H. Everts, 1881.

Scott, Norman H., *Shenandoah Iron*, Verona, VA: self-published, 2017.

Strickler, Harry M., *A Short History of Page County*, Richmond, VA: The Dietz Press Incorporated, 1952.

Surkamp, Jim, "History of Jefferson County," Shepherdstown, WV: writings and Web sites, 2000-2010.

Theriault, William D., *History of Eastern Jefferson County of West Virginia*, Hagerstown, MD: self-published, 2009.

Todd, Richard Cecil, *Confederate Finance*, Athens, GA: The University of Georgia Press, 1954.

Vaughn, Dan, *Luray and Page County, Images of America*, Charleston, SC: Arcadia Publishing, 2005.

———. *Luray and Page County Revisited, Images of America*, Charleston, SC: Arcadia Publishing, 2008.

Wayland, John W., *A History of Shenandoah County, Virginia*, Strasburg, VA: Shenandoah Publishing House, Inc., 1969.

———. *Twenty-Five Chapters on the Shenandoah Valley*, Strasburg, VA: Shenandoah Publishing House, Inc., 1957.

———. *The Shenandoah Valley in History and Literature,* Harrisonburg, VA: State Normal School, 1915.

Westhaeffer, Paul J., *History of the Cumberland Valley Railroad, 1835-1919*, Washington DC: National Railway Society, 1979.

Williams, Edwin, "The Wheat Trade of the United States and Europe," an article in the National Magazine and Industrial Record, New York, NY, 1846.

Williamson, Mary Ann Lutz and Jean Allen Davis, *History of Edinburg, Virginia*, Edinburg, VA: Edinburg Heritage Foundation, 1994.

Winchester-Frederick County Historical Society, *More Images of the Past: A Photographic Review of Winchester and Frederick County, Virginia*, 2005.

———. *Men and Events of the Revolution in Winchester and Frederick County, Virginia,* 1975.

Winnemore, Lawrence P., *Winchester and Western Railroad,* Washington, DC: National Railway Historical Society, 1976.

Wolf, Christina, "The River and the Factory: Momentum and Shifting Dynamics Between the Shenandoah River and Avtex Fibers, 1939-1989," master's thesis, Harrisonburg, VA: James Madison University, 2010.

Wood, Don C., *Documented History of Martinsburg and Berkeley County, Volume I,* Martinsburg, WV: Berkeley County Historical Society, 2004.

———. *Documented History of Martinsburg and Berkeley County, Volume II,* Martinsburg, WV: Berkeley County Historical Society, 2007.

Young, Chester Raymond, "The Effects of the French and Indian War on Civilian Life in the Frontier Counties of Virginia, 1754-1763," PhD History Thesis, Nashville, TN: Vanderbilt University, 1969.

American Economic History

Carmichael, Richard E., *American Economic History,* Conover, NC: R. Carmichael Company, 2012.

Faulkner, Harold Underwood, *American Economic History,* New York, NY: Harper & Brothers Publishers, 1954.

Gordon, John Steele, *An Empire of Wealth; The Epic History of American Economic Power,* New York, NY: Harper Collins Publishers, 2004.

———. *The Business of America,* New York, NY: Walker Publishing Company, Inc., 2001.

Greenspan, Alan and Adrian Wooldridge, *Capitalism in America, A History,* New York, NY: Penguin Press, 2018.

Hindle, Brook and Steven Lubar, *Engines of Change: The American Industrial Revolution, 1790-1860,* Washington, DC and London: Smithsonian Institute Press, 1986.

Hughes, Jonathan and Louis Cain, *American Economic History, Fifth Edition,* Reading, MA: Addison Wesley Longman, Inc., 1998.

Licht, Walter, *Industrializing America, The Nineteenth Century*, Baltimore, MD: Johns Hopkins University Press, 1995.

Lind, Michael, *Land of Promise, An Economic History of the United States*, New York, NY: Harper Collins Publishers, 2012.

North, Douglass C., *The Economic Growth of the United States, 1790 to 1860*, New York, NY: W.W. Norton & Company, Inc., 1966.

INDEX

AB&C Group, 299, 304–5
Abex Friction Products Corp., 294
Adamantine Clay Products Co., 212, 291
Adelphia Communications
    Corporation, 336
Admiral Byrd Field, 192
Aerotek Staffing Services, 304
Agri-Tech, Inc., 206, 267
Agriculture Adjustment Act of 1933, 224
Aikens Group, 311
Aikens Sizzling Steaks, 311
Aikens, Harry, 311
Aileen, Inc., 283-4
Airport Business Center, 303
Airport Speedway, 237, 330
Alba Marl Lime Co., 217
Albertazzie, Albert, 335
Aldi, 319
Aldie and Ashby's Gap Turnpike, 37, 59
Alexandria and Harpers
    Ferry Railroad, 65
Alexandria, Loudoun and
    Hampshire Railroad, 66
Allegheny Power System, 193, 258
Allensville Planing Mill, 290
Amazon, Inc., 305, 318
American Alloy Corp., 216
American Bell Telephone Company, 122
American Brake Shoe and
    Foundry Co., 294
American Public University System, 264

American Strawboard Company, 163
American System, 25
American Telephone & Telegraph
    Company, 260
American Viscose Corporation,
    221, 226, 237–38, 247, 283
American Woodmark Company,
    288–89, 304
AmeriCold Logistics, 303
Amos, Walter, 234
Andersen Corporation, 288
Anderson, D. H. & Son, 146
Andros et Cie., 273
Annandale Millwork and Allied
    Systems Corporation, 289
Antietam Manufacturing and Land
    Improvement Company, 126
Apollo Civic Theater, 195
Appalachian Apple Service, 224
Appalachian Fruit Station Center, 338
Appalachian Regional Commission, 321
Apple Blossom Corners, 317
Apple Blossom Festival, 132
Apple Blossom Mall, 317-18
Apple Grading Law, 205
Apple Mountain Lake, 308
Apple Pie Ridge, 133
Apple Products Company, 207
Apple Show and Carnival, 132
Arcata Graphics Co., 297
Arctic Ice Company, 151

Argo Instruments, 295
Armstrong family, 273
Armstrong, Frank, Sr., 203
Army Corps of Engineers, 241, 337-38
Army Quartermaster's K-9 Corps, 337
Arthur, John & Co., 44
Arundel Newspapers, 332
Ashby's Ferry, 11
Ashby's Gap Turnpike, 37, 59
Ashby's Gap, 10, 29, 186
Ashelman, Sam, 309
Assumption Bill of 1790, 24
AT&T, 304
Auburn Wagon Company, 125, 156–57
Automated Merchandising
    Systems, Inc., 297
Automotive Industries, 292, 295
Avtex Fibers, 249, 283

B&O's Berkeley Springs and Potomac
    Railroad, 145, 171, 177, 187, 233
B&O's Frog Hollow Branch, 167, 213
B&O's Metropolitan Branch, 166, 256
B&O's Roundhouse, 66
B&O's Timber Preserving Plant, 188
B&O's Valley Branch, 115, 117, 134,
    137, 152, 166–70, 187-88, 216–17
B2B Magazine, 332
Baetjer, Henry, 104
Baker, Daniel, Sr., 167
Baker, J. E. Lime Company, 168, 216
Baker, Jacob, 65
Baker, W. B. & Sons, 109, 140
Baker, William, 65, 109, 126, 149
Baltimore & Ohio Railroad, 58,
    63-64, 69, 78–79, 92, 96, 98-100,
    102, 115, 117-18, 124, 138,
    159, 163, 167, 177, 187–88,
    194, 200, 212, 218, 246, 250
Baltimore Agricultural Aid Society, 97
Bank Holding Company
    Act of 1956, 312
Bank of Alexandria, 36
Bank of Berkeley Springs, 223
Bank of Berryville, 103, 173

Bank of Charles Town, 103, 173, 314
Bank of Clarke County, 173, 223, 314
Bank of Frederick County, 314
Bank of Harpers Ferry, 223, 314
Bank of Morgan County, 223
Bank of the Valley of Virginia,
    52, 90, 103
Bank of Warren, 103
Banks, Jos. A., 319
Barber & Ross Company, 288
Bardane Industrial Park, 247, 297, 304
Bardon, Plc, 270
Bare, Nasson, 86
Bartlett, Fred, 138, 177
Bartonsville Mill, 211, 272
Batt, Kermit, 237, 330
Battaile, William, 246
BB&T Corp., 304, 313-14
Beachley, Elmer E. Saw and
    Planing Mill, 126, 156
Beahm Memorial Hospital, 231, 321
Beahm, James Ambrose, 231
Bean-Zane Furnace, 19
Bean, Mordecai, 19, 42
Bean's Smelter, 18-19, 42
Beck's Steam Bakery, 152
Beckham, Townsend, 42, 45, 78
Beef Cattle Research Station, 240
Beeson Flour Mill, 79
Bell Atlantic Corporation, 260, 300
Bell Clothes Shop, 228
Bell, Peter, Jr., 51, 82
Bell, Samuel Pottery, 82, 161
Bell, Solomon, 82, 161
Belle Grove, 48
Belt Railroad, 125
Benchmark Communications, 333
Berkeley Aviation Club, 191
Berkeley Canning Company, 154
Berkeley Club Beverages, Inc., 275
Berkeley Cooperage Co., 158
Berkeley County Development
    Authority (BCDA), 251
Berkeley County Fair, 197

Berkeley County Horticulture
  Society, 131
Berkeley County Industrial Park,
  278, 280, 286, 294
Berkeley County Roundhouse
  Authority, 256
Berkeley Glass Sand Company, 172, 218
Berkeley Manufacturing Co., 148
Berkeley Medical Center, 323
Berkeley Plaza, 317
Berkeley Sand Works, 170
Berkeley Savings Bank, 90
Berkeley Springs and Potomac
  Railroad, 171, 177, 187
Berkeley Springs Bottling Works, 153
Berkeley Springs Hotel, 85, 112, 233
Berkeley Springs Sanitarium, 222
Berkeley Springs State Park, 326
Berkeley Woolen Company, 140,
  194, 201, 225, 239, 282
Bernstein, Bob, 309
Bernstein, Leo M., 311
Berry Plastics, 293
Berry's Ferry, 11, 29, 33, 59
Berryville and Charles Town
  Turnpike, 61
Berryville and Winchester Turnpike, 186
Berryville Basket Co., Inc., 210
Berryville Graphics, 295, 297
Berryville Horse Show, 236
Berryville Ice and Refrigerating
  Company, 200
Berryville Land and Improvement
  Company, 126
Bert, Charles and William, 148
Bertelsmann AG, 295
Bertschinger, Fred, 150
Bessemer Limestone Company, 168
Big Gem Cast Iron Furnace, 115, 141-43
Billmyer, David, 103
Bing, M. E. Company, 226
Binns, John Alexander, 38
Binswanger, H. P. Company, 215
Biser, George, 138, 177
Bishop Flour Mills, 110, 139

Bishop, John W., 110
Bixler's Landing on Shenandoah
  River, 43, 77
Black Tariff of 1842, 75
Blackburn Commerce Center, 303
Blackford, Arthur & Co., 44, 76
Blackford, Benjamin, 44
Blackford, Thomas, 76
Blair Limestone Company, 168, 218
Blakeley Bank and Trust Company, 227
Blandy Experimental Farm, 45
Blue Bell Overall Company,
  203, 239, 284
Blue Mountain, 308
Blue Ridge Acres, 308
Blue Ridge Bank, 314, 316
Blue Ridge Community and
  Technical College, 253, 263
Blue Ridge Factory Outlet
  Center, 263, 319
Blue Ridge Habitat for Humanity, 299
Blue Ridge Hospice, 320
Blue Ridge Hunt, 235
Blue Ridge Inn, 180
Blue Ridge Lime and Stone
  Company, 167
Blue Ridge Poultry & Egg Co., 276
Blue Ridge Shadows Golf Course, 328
Blue Ridge Technical Center, 262
Blue Ridge Truss and Supply, 289
Blue Ridge Woolen Company, 239
BlueSky Brands, Inc., 301, 305
Bluestone Flat Top-Pocahontas
  Coalfield, 142
Blunt, H. H., 107
BMC Stock Holdings, Inc., 290
Boise Cascade Corp., 287-88
Borden, F. H. Barrel and
  Stave Company, 158
Borst Tannery, 79, 91, 144
Borst, Peter Bock, 79, 91
Boteler, Henry, 81
Bowles Field, 191
Bowling Green Country Club, 328
Bowman Andros Foods, 273

Bowman Apple Products Co., 227, 266-67, 273
Bowman-Glaize partnership, 312
Bowman, Charles, 227
Bowman, Gordon, Sr., 273
Bowman, James, 270, 312
Boyce State Bank, 173, 223
Boyce, Upton, 115
Boyer, William, 108, 141, 165
Boyle, Albert, 236
BPG Development, 302
Bradford, J. M., & Co., 112
Braithwaite Bros., 209, 274
Brentwood Industries, Inc., 294
Bridgeforth, William E., Sr. and Ed, Jr., 275
Bridges, Henry P., 172, 218
Bridges, Robert, 171–72
British Parliament, 4, 17, 26
Brookfield Renewable Partners, 259
Brooklyn Brass Manufacturing Co., 125
Brucetown Woolen Co., 239
Bruin, Mackall, 182
Bryarly, Robert, 153
Bryce Hillside Cottages and Mineral Baths, 308
Bryce Resort, 308
Bryce, William and Peter, 308
Buena Vista Brewery, 79
Bunker Hill Mill, 211, 272
Bureau of Alcohol, Tobacco, Firearms & Explosives, 338
Burke, Glen and Kimberly, 312
Burner's White Sulphur Springs, 87
Burns, Ken, 326
Burnshire Hydroelectric LLC, 259
Burr Business Park, 294, 297, 305
Burwell-Morgan Mill, 33, 41, 82, 92, 211, 273, 311
Burwell, Nathaniel, 6, 33-34, 149
Buser, W. T., 153-54
Bush & Lobdell Company, 77, 108-09
Butler, H. W. & Brothers Packing Company, 207
Buxton Brick Works, 159, 212

Buxton, George, 159
Buzzerd, Jim and Lewis, 230
Buzzerd, Simon Strother, 175, 230
Byrd family, 6, 331-32
Byrd, Beverly, 267
Byrd, H. F., Inc., 199, 207, 224, 265, 288, 302, 311
Byrd, Harry, III, 267
Byrd, Harry, Sr., 135, 158, 170, 175, 186, 200, 224, 229, 266, 331
Byrd, Richard E., 174-5
Byrd, Robert C. Industrial Park, 252
Byrd, Robert C., 255, 311, 338-39
Byrne's Island, 177

Cacapon Camp, 222
Cacapon Lumber Company, 189
Cacapon State Park, 223, 251, 326
Cahill, Howard, 228
Camp Roosevelt, 222
Camp Wolf Gap, 222
Capen, Al, 309
Caperton, Gaston and Gat, 298
Capitol Cement Corp., 214, 218, 269–70, 291
Capitol Records, 290, 293
Capitol Rock Wool, 217
Capitol Theater, 195-96
Capon Bridge Tannery, 144
Capon Bridge Technology and Industrial Park, 289
Capon Iron Works, 77
Capper Broadcasting, 333
Capper, Emmitt, 333–34
Capper, John, 86
CapStar Broadcasting, Inc., 334
Cardinal IG, 250, 279
Carey, W. P., Inc., 301
Cargill Inc., 276
Carlyle Group, 295
Carmeuse Lime & Stone, Inc., 270, 281
Carnegie Steel Company, 168-69
Carnegie, Andrew, 131
Caroline Furnace, 77, 91, 108
Carpenter, Nathan, 214

Carpers Valley Golf Club, 327-28
Carr, Whitt, 276
Carraba's Italian Grill, 319
Carson Lime Company, 106, 170
Carson, Samuel, 106
Carson, William, 170, 235
Carter Hall, 33-34
Carter, Robert, 6, 33–34, 149
Carter, Shirley, 140, 149
Carter's Paper Mill, 50
Casey Jones Work-Clothes Company, 203, 239
Caskey Bakery & Ice Cream Company, 152
Caskey, W. Rufus, 152
Castleman's Ferry, 11, 59
Catherine Furnace, 76, 105, 141
Cedar Creek Battlefield Foundation, 312
Cementos Argos, 291
Central Chemical Corp., 270
Century Graphics Corporation, 296
CFW Communications Services, Inc., 260, 304
Chadbourne Hosiery Mils, Inc., 226, 284-85
Chalybeate Springs Hotel, 179
Champion Enterprises, Inc., 290
Chapin-Sachs Manufacturing Company, 152
Charles Town Farmers' Repository, 53
Charles Town General Hospital, 182, 230-31
Charles Town Horse and Colt Association, 236
Charles Town Jockey Club, 235, 329
Charles Town Race Track, 236, 327, 329-30
Chatfield-Taylor, Moncure, 319
Chesapeake and Ohio Canal National Historic Park, 326
Chesapeake and Ohio Canal, 31, 58, 61, 63, 79, 92, 102, 106, 118
Chesapeake and Ohio Railway, 129
Chesapeake and Potomac Telephone Company, 123, 260

Chew, Roger Preston, 125
Chewning, E. Taylor, 212-14, 291
Chicago Wool Company, 201
Chico's. 319
Child, Jonathan, 106
Child, McCreight & Co., 106
Christendom College, 264
Citicorp Venture Capital, 280
Citizens Concerned About Rockwool-Ranson, 251
Citizens Electric Light Company of Charles Town, 121
Citizens National Bank of Berkeley Springs, 223, 315
Citizens National Bank, 220
City Holding Company, 316
City Hospital, 321-23
Civil War Trails, 326
Civil Works Administration (CWA), 222
Civilian Conservation Corps (CCC), 222–23, 235, 309
Clark, E. W. Company, 101
Clarke County Industrial Park, 250
Clarke County Office of Economic Development, 250
Clarke Courier, 175
Clarke-Times Courier, 332
Clay, Henry, 25
Clear Channel Communications, Inc., 334
Clearbrook Woolen Company, 239, 282
Clohan, Alexander, 133, 154
Clorox Company, 281
CNB Bank, 315
Coblentz, Emory, 192
Coca-Cola Company, 293
Code Plus Components, 289
Cohen, Herman and Ben, 329
Cohen, Sarah, 279
Coin Acceptors, Inc., 297
Coleman Microwave Company, 285
Collins, George, 326
Collis, Craig and Berniece, 309
Colonial Brick Company, 140, 201, 213, 290

Columbia Furnace, 43–44, 77, 91, 109, 143, 222, 268, 276–77
Columbia-Liberty Iron Company, 143
Comcast Corporation, 336
Competitive Power Ventures, 258
Compromise of 1877, 94
Compton Mine, 165
ConAgra, Inc., 278
Cone, Dorastus, 105
Conrad, Holmes, 128–30
Conradt, Christian G., 49
Consolidated Orchard Company, 139, 208, 210, 252
Consolidated Rail Corporation (Conrail), 256
Construction Management, Inc., 310
Continental AG, 292
Continental Brick Company, 291
Continental Clay Products, 213, 291
Cooke, Jay, 96
Coolfont Resort, 309
Cooper Merchandise and Oil Company, 140
Cooper, Lewis, 140
Cora Miller Memorial Hospital, 231, 321
Corn Laws of 1815, 26, 33, 39, 41, 70
Corning Glass Works, 247, 263, 280, 299
Cornwell Lime Marl Co., 217
Cornwell, John and William, 188–90, 217
Costco, 318
Country Inn, The, 233, 309
Courtlauds plc, 226
Cover Brothers Tannery, 104, 144
Cover, Drayton & Leonard, 144
Cover, Franklin, 144
Cover, Loring, 144, 168, 213
Cover, Thomas, 104, 144
Covia Holdings Corporation, 272
Coxe, Tench, 25
Crawford Woolen Company, 125, 148-50
Crawford, William Henry, 147–49

Creekside Village, 319
Crestliner, Inc., 292
Crestmanor Homes, Inc., 294
Crider & Shockey, 291
Crider, James, 291
Crimean War, 70, 72
Crown American Realty Trust, 318
Crown Bottling Works, 154
Crown Door Company, 288
Crystal Caverns, 234, 311
CSX Corporation, 256
Cuba Rica Tobacco Co., 160
Cullen, Orin C., 179
Cumberland Road, 59
Cumberland Valley Fruit Products Company, 155, 205
Cumberland Valley Railroad, 101–2, 115, 117-18, 124, 129, 155, 168, 187, 204, 206–7, 256
Cumbo Yard Industrial Park, 251, 296, 301, 305
Currency Acts, 9
Cushwa, Jonathan, 48
CyberStreet Winchester, 252

Dawson International, Plc., 285
Dearing Beverage Company, 228
Dearing, Eugene, 228
Declaration of Independence, 8
Dee's Family Fun Center, 278
Deer Meadow Vineyard, 268
Defense Plant Corporation, 237
Deford Leather Company, 115, 144-45, 211
Deford, Benjamin, 144
Depot House Hotel, 65, 97
Depression of 1882-85, 98, 106, 114-15, 117, 129, 142
Digges, J. C. & Sons, Inc., 218
Dixie-Narco, Inc., 227, 297, 299, 304
Dodd-Frank Wall Street Reform and Consumer Protection Act, 313
Dominion Bankshares, 314
Dominion Energy, 258-59
Dominion Savings Bank, F.S.B., 316

Donnelley, RR, 296
Doubleday & Company, 295
Dovel, I. N., 154, 208
Dowell J. Howard Vocational-
　　Technical Center, 262
Downing, H. H., 127
Dr. Oates Hospital, 230
Drennen family, 328
Dulles Corridor, 244, 252
Dunn Woolen Company, 148, 194,
　　201, 225, 239, 282, 319
Dunn, Thomas, 148, 150
DuPont Potomac Works, 259
DuPont, E. I. Co., 247, 295
Duvall, Rezin, 55

Eagle Financial Services, Inc., 314
East Valley Road, 9, 34, 61
Eastern Board and Paper Company, 214
Eastern College, 176
Eastern Fruit Growers Association, 133
Eastern Management Development
　　Center, 339
Eastern Panhandle Health and
　　Human Service Council, 321
Eastern Silicate & Chemical Corp., 218
Eastern West Virginia Regional
　　Airport, 240, 255, 286–87, 300
Eastgate Commerce Center, 303
Eastman, George, 174
Eberly, J. J. & Co., 161
Eberly, Jacob Jeremiah, 161
Ebro Puleva S.A., 279
Echo-Star International, 247
Ecolab, Inc., 300
Eddy Paper, 215
EDF Renewables, 259
Edinburg Board of Trade, 194
Edinburg Mill, 74, 92, 211, 272
Edinburg Silk Mill, 226
Edison, Thomas, 119
Education Media Foundation, 335
Eisenhower, Dwight D., 254
Elizabeth Furnace, 141, 183s
Elsea Springs Hotel, 180

Elsea, Thomas, 180
Emancipation Proclamation, 93
Embargo Act of 1807, 26, 32
EMCO Enterprises, Inc., 288
Emivest Aerospace Corp., 287
Emmert Oil Company, 228
Emmert, Howard H., 201
Emmert, W. H., 228
Endless Caverns, 181, 234
Engle, William, 167
Episcopal Diocese of Virginia, 326
Equality Mill, 74
Equity Improvement Company
　　of Winchester, 128–31
Equus Capital Partners, 301-02
Erie Canal, 27, 61, 70
Ervin, Allen, 310
ESSROC Corporation, 291
Eureka Mine, 165, 215
Evans, Oliver, 41
Evening Journal, The, 332
Eyster & Son, 104, 163

F&M National Corporation, 304, 313-14
Fairfax Inn, 55
Fairfax, Thomas Lord, 6, 7, 12, 34
Family Dollar Stores, Inc., 303
Fansler, Willard, 289
Farmer's Advocate, 175
Farmers and Merchants National
　　Bank, 146, 173-74, 223
Farmers Bank of Winchester, 52, 90
Farmers Mutual Telephone System of
　　Shenandoah County, 123, 260
Federal Bureau of Investigation
　　(FBI), 299, 305, 339-40
Federal Emergency Management
　　Agency (FEMA), 299, 337
Federal Highway Act of 1916, 115
Federal Mogul Corporation, 294
Federal Reserve System, 114
Federated Fruit and Vegetable
　　Growers, 206-07
Feltner, Wilbur, 313
Ferguson Enterprises, Inc., 303

First Bank of the United States, 51
First Bank, 174, 314
First Energy Corp, 258
First Federal Savings and Loan
    Association, 316
First Federal Savings Bank of the
    Shenandoah Valley, 316
First National Bank of Berryville, 313
First National Bank of Luray,
    173–74, 220
First National Bank of Shenandoah, 220
First National Bank of Strasburg, 220
First National Corporation, 314
First National Tannery, 145
First Virginia Bank, 314
Fitz Steel Water Wheel, 75
Fitz, Samuel, 74
Flintkote Corp., 270
Follow the Apple Trail, 326
Foltz Milling Co., 140, 211
Food and Drug Act of 1906, 154
Ford Motor Company, 292, 302
Ford, Henry, 115, 157
Forecast Furniture, Inc., 298
Foreign Affairs Security
    Training Center, 331
Forrer, Daniel and Henry, 76
Fort Collier Industrial Park, 246,
    279, 288, 293, 302, 337
Fort Loudoun, 13
Fort Steam Furnace, 77, 91
Fortessa, Inc., 303
Foxcroft Towne Center, 318
Franklin & Armfield, 68
Fravel, Roy, 231, 321
Frederick County Economic
    Development Authority, 399–400
Frederick County Farmers' Bureau, 197
Free Press, The, 332
Freeman, Carl L. Companies, 309
Freeman, E. M., 307
Freezland Orchard, 135
French and Indian War, 8, 13
French, Warren and Christopher, 260
Frey Company, Inc., 270

Friend, Israel, 19
Friend's Orebank, 47
Friendly Grove Woolen Factory, 49
Frogale, William, 289
Front Royal and Riverton
    Improvement Company, 126
Front Royal and Winchester
    Turnpike Company, 29
Front Royal Beef Cattle
    Research Center, 337
Front Royal Community
    Hospital, 231, 321
Front Royal Credit Union, 316
Front Royal Golf Course, 235
Front Royal Ice and Storage
    Company, 150
Front Royal Milling Co., 211
Front Royal Savings and Loan
    Association, 316
Front Royal-Riverton Milling Co., 211
Front Royal-Warren County Airport, 255
Front Royal-Warren County
    Chamber of Commerce, 333
Front Royal-Warren County
    Economic Development
    Authority, 248-49, 290
Frontier Communications, Inc., 260
Fruit Hill Orchards, 266
Frye-Martin shops, 51
Funk, Michael, 316
Funkhouser, H. N. & Co., 228
Funkhouser, Hugh, 228
Funkhouser, Raymond J.,
    227, 292, 297, 321

Galise, Hugh, 77
Gallatin, Albert, 26
Gant, Ulysses, 91
Garber's Ice Cream, 152
Gardena Holding A.G., 292
Gat Creek Furniture, 298
Gatrell, Jacob W., 200
General Agreement on Trade
    and Tariffs, 282
General Chemical Company, 238

General Electric Company, 280
General Foods Company, 279
General Motors, 285, 300-01, 305
General Services Administration (GSA), 339–40
Genie Company, 288
Genstar Stone Products Company, 270
Gentile Brothers Folder Factory, 285
Geon Company, 292
George Washington Hotel Corporation, 135, 195, 312
George Washington National Forest, 141, 143, 183, 220, 223
George Weston, Ltd., 279
George's Inc., 277
German Brewing Company, 153
Gibbons, Samuel, 76
Gibbs, Edward, 48
Giddings, James, 80
Gilded Age, 113-14, 178
Gilpin family, 246
Glaize & Bros., 210, 156
Glaize Apple Packing House, 200
Glaize Apples, 266, 274
Glaize Components, 289
Glaize Developments, Inc., 312
Glaize, David and Philip III, 274
Glaize, Fred L. & Co., 135
Glaize, Fred L., III, 312
Glaize, Fred L., Sr., 135, 156, 189, 233, 274
Glaize, Fred, Jr., 289
Glaize, George F., 156
Glass-Glen Burnie Foundation, 325
Glass, Julian Wood, Jr., 325
Glenwood Forest, 309
Glover, John D. & Son, 228
Godlove Mine, 216
Goetz, A. D. Company, 125
Golden Gate Capital, 271, 305
Goldsmith, Chandlee, 51
Golliday, Leslie, 230, 247
Gooch, William, 5
Goodlatte, Bob, 249
Gooney Manor Copper Company, 164

Graber, Richard, 319
Grabill Manufacturing Company, 206
Graichen, F. A. Glove Company, 109
Graichen, Fred, 109
Graichen, W. C. Glove Company, 109–10, 146, 212
Graichen, William, 110, 146, 212
Granada Sales Corp., 286
Grandstaff, George, 74, 92
Gray Television, 335
Graystone Commerce Center, 247, 303
Great Atlantic Financial Corp., 316
Great Cacapon Power Company, 120-21
Great Cacapon Silica Sand Company, 171
Great Recession, 243, 288-90, 305-06, 310, 313, 325, 327, 335, 339
Great Wagon Road, 5–6, 9–12, 29, 34, 39, 46, 59–60
Greenway Court Hotel, 126
Greenway Court, 7
Greenway Engineering and Survey Company, 310
Gregory's Gap, 10
Grove, M. J. Lime Company, 116, 158, 169, 217-18, 270
GS Communications, 336
Gulfstream Corporation, 292, 295
Gum, David and Paige, 273, 298
Gunter, Greg, 278, 330
Gunter's Honey Motorsports, 330
Gunter's Honey, 278

H&W Construction, 311
Hable, Joseph and Herman, 104
Hable, S. H., 104
Haldeman, J. S., 151
Hall, John Harris, 48
Hall's Rifle Works, 48
Hallauer, John W. & Sons, 155
Halltown Paper Board Company, 163, 214
Hamilton, Alexander, 24-25
Hampshire Memorial Hospital, 322

Hampshire Southern Railroad Company, 188
Hancock White Sand Company, 171, 218
Hancock White Sand Works, 170
Hancock, Edward Joseph, Jr., 12
Handley High School, 131, 222, 262
Handley Library, 131
Handley, John, 128–31, 190
Hannisville Distillery, 107, 153, 158, 203
Hansbrough & Carter, 149
Hanson Aggregates, 291
Hanson Building Materials, 271
Happy Creek Industrial Park, 248, 252
Happy Creek Mine, 165
Happy Creek Technology Park, 252
Harmison, Walter, 233
Harmony Forge, 77
Harnsberger, J. B., 154, 204
Harper, Robert, 12, 29
Harpers Ferry & Shenandoah Manufacturing Co., 80
Harpers Ferry Brewing Company, 153
Harpers Ferry Center, 337
Harpers Ferry Electric Light & Power Co., 119-20, 162, 193, 214
Harpers Ferry Mining, Manufacturing and Improvement Company, 126
Hart-Clohan Canning Company, 154
Hawksbill Cannery, 154
Hawksbill Retreat, 235
Hazel-Atlas Glass Sand Company, 171, 218
HealthCare Development Partners, 320
Hectate Energy, LLC, 259
Heidelberg Cement Co., 291
Heinz, H. J. Company, 226, 274
Heller, Henry, 157
Henkel Harris, 298
Henkel Press, 53
Henkel, Mary, 298
Henrietta Furnace, 78, 91, 112
Herr, Abraham, 81, 106
Herr's Mill, 74, 82

Hershey Pasta Company, 279
Hess, Terry, 278
Hester Industries, 277-78
Hester, Wendell and Jeff, 277
Hickman, Boynton J., 147
High Knob, 308
Hill-Burton Act of 1946, 320-21
Hill, Reynolds, 275
Hill, Roland, 235
Hillman's Tollgate, 60
Hite, John, 17
Hite, Jost, 5, 17
Hoenshel, George Washington, 176
Holler, Grover, Jr., 276
Holley, Guy, 308
Hollingsworth Woolen Mill, 123, 151
Hollingsworth, Jonah, 49
Hollywood Casino at Charles Town Races, 330
Holt Limited Partnership of Pennsylvania, 333
Home Depot, 302-03
Homewood at the Shenandoah Valley, 325
Honeywood Paper Mill, 119, 161
Hospital Corporation of America (HCA), 321-22
Hotchkiss, Jedediah, 93, 163-64
Hotel Machir, 179
Hotel Powhatan, 125-26
Hotel Strasburg, 311
Hoyt, Joseph, 107
HP Hood, LLC, 279
Hudson Cement & Supply Co., 213
Hunt, HH Corporation, 324
Hunter, Henry Harrison, 171
Hupp, Bruce, 234
Hupp, George, 77, 234
Hupp's Cave, 234
Hupp's Homestead, 48
Hy-Grade Manganese Company, 216

I-66 (Interstate 66), 250, 252, 257
I-81 Logistics Corridor, 300
IAC North America, 295

ICT Group, Inc., 304
Imperial Corporation, 291
Industrial Revolution, 38, 57,
    67, 94, 123, 147
Insull, Samuel, 193
Interbake Foods Company, 279
Interchange Company, 304
Internal Revenue Service, 338
Interstate 81 (I-81), 244, 246, 250,
    254-55, 257, 299, 300-01, 342
Interstate Banking and Branching
    Efficiency Act, 313
Interwoven Stocking Company,
    147, 201-02, 225, 252, 285
Inwood Park, 118
Iron Act of 1750, 17
Isabella Furnace, 44, 76
Island Mills, 74
Island Park, 177
IT Federal, 249
Italcementi Group, 291
ITT Corporation, 271

Jack Frost Ice Cream, 152
Jackson Furniture Company, 298
Jackson, Thomas "Stonewall," 92-93, 164
Jackson's Chase Golf Club, 328
James River and Kanawha Canal, 61
James Rumsey Vo-Tech Center, 262
JC Penney, 195, 317-18
Jeanne Dixon Museum, 311
Jefferson Bankshares, 314
Jefferson Cooperage Co., 158, 210
Jefferson County Building
    Association, 103
Jefferson County Chamber
    of Commerce, 247
Jefferson County Development
    Authority (JCDA), 247, 251
Jefferson Creamery, 151
Jefferson Medical Center, 323
Jefferson Memorial Hospital, 321, 323
Jefferson Orchards, 207, 266
Jefferson Security Bank, 173, 315
Jefferson Storage, 302

Jefferson, Thomas, 268
Jenkins, Kable, Johnson
    Woolen Factory, 80
JLA Media and Publishing, LLC, 335
Jobe Mill, 148
John D. Rockefeller, IV Science and
    Technology Center, 286, 300
Johnson Development
    Associates, Inc., 302
Johnson, Charles M., 308
Johnson, Sidney, 231
Johnston, Ray, 309, 328
Jones & Laughlin Steel Company, 168
Jones Creamery, 152
Jones, Arthur G., 202
Jones, Arthur Woolen Mill, 202
Jones, Bobby, 234
Jones, Josiah, 17
Jordan Springs, 86, 112, 179
Jordan, Edwin Clarenden, Jr., 179
Jordan, Edwin Clarenden, Sr., 86
Jouan, S.A., 299
Journal, The, 332
Judd's Inc., 296
Judd's OnLine, 252

Kagey, D. F. and Company, 128, 173
Kauffman's Mill, 110
Kaylor-Fleming Manganese
    Company, 216
Kayser-Roth Corporation, 285
Kearneysville Creamery, 151
Kee Construction Services, Inc., 310
Keep Tryst Furnace, 19, 24, 42–43, 47
Keffer, William, 86
Keister, A. & Co., 82, 161
Keister, Adam, Jr. and Henry, 161
Keister, Adam, Sr., 50, 82
Keister, E. E., 175, 229-30, 331
Keller, O. J. Lime Company, 167-68
Kelley Industrial Park, 249, 280
Kembler, A. F., 125, 156
Kenner, Thomas, 110
Kenton Corporation, 329
Kernstown Distillery, 110

Kerr, John, 108
Keyes Ferry Acres, 308
Keyes' Ferry, 11
Keyes' Gap, 10, 78, 80
Keynes, Maynard, 221
Kieckhefer Container Company, 215
Kilbourn Knitting Machine Co., 125
Kilbourn, Charles, 147
King, Frank, 106
King, Newton, 103
King's Daughter's Hospital, 230, 321-22
Kingspan Group Plc., 293
Kirkland's Home Furnishings, 303
Kistler, James, 155
KKR & Co., 280
Kline's Mill, 42
Knouse Foods Cooperative, 273-74
Kohl's Department Stores, 303
Kownslar, Conrad, 50
Kraft Heinz, Inc., 279, 302
Kunkle Field, 191
Kurtz, George W., 108
KVK Precision Specialties, 331

Lacy, Benjamin, 135
Lake Holiday, 308
Lang, Rosana Oberdorff, 79
Lantz Construction of
    Winchester, Inc., 310
Lantz Mills, 77, 92, 110, 211
Lantz Roller Mill Co., 139
Larrick, Herbert, 190
Larson Boat Works, 292
Laurel Ridge Community College, 262
Lawrence, William, Jr., 239, 282
LCS Services, Inc., 291
Lear Seating Corp., 295
Leather Trust, 144, 212
Lee Ranger District, 220
Lee, Robert E., 42, 100
Leesburg and Snicker's Gap
    Turnpike, 59
Leggett's (Belk's), 318
Lehew, William H. & Co., 161
Leicester Piano Company, 127

Leicester, George, 127
Lenoir City Corporation, 246
Letterkenny Ordinance Depot, 240
Lewis family, 334, 336
Lewis Jones Knitting Mill,
    149, 225, 284, 299
Lewis, Richard F., Jr., 230
Liberty Business Park, 311, 338
Liberty Forge, 44
Liberty Furnace, 44, 77, 141, 143, 183
Liberty Iron Company, 143
Lichliter, Lawrence, 330
Limeton Lime Company, 169
Lindbergh, Charles, 191
Linden Beverage Company, 278
Linden Vineyard, 268
Linden Virginia Copper Company, 108
Lippert Components, 252
Lloyd Steam Bakery, 152
Locke, T. H., 211
Locke's Mill, 218, 273
Locksley Corporation, 284
Locust Grove Furnace, 141
Locust Hills Golf Course, 328
Lord Fairfax Community
    College, 262, 299
Lord Fairfax, 6, 12, 33, 55, 132
Lost City Tannery, 144
Lost River Lumber Company, 188
Lost River Railroad, 190
Lovett, John, 138
Lowe, Ken, 311
LSC Communications, 296
Lucas & Stirewalt Cannery, 208
Lukens Iron & Steel Company, 143
Lupton, John, 133
Lupton, Lewis and Joel, 81
Lupton, S. Lucien, 133, 199, 207
Luray and Front Royal Turnpike, 61
Luray Canning Company, 154, 208
Luray Caverns, 128, 177,
    180–81, 209, 234
Luray Ice Company, 151, 200
Luray Textile Corporation, 238
Luter, Joseph, 308

M&H Plastics, Ltd., 293
Macadam, John, 28
Machir, Lewis, 179
Macy's, Inc., 305
Magic Chef, 297
Major, Julian Neville, 209
Manassas Gap Railroad, 58, 66–67, 69, 74, 86, 92, 96, 100, 112
Manganese & Iron Company, 165
Marathon Bank, 314
Marjec, Inc., 308
Marker, William, 86
Market House, 35, 69, 97
Marlboro Iron Works, 19–20, 24, 42, 44, 46
Marshall, Edward, 66
Marston, Joseph, 91
Martin Distributing Company, 228
Martin-Marietta Corporation, 270
Martin, Howard, 228
Martinsburg and Potomac Railroad, 98, 101-02, 117
Martinsburg and Winchester Turnpike, 60
Martinsburg Board of Trade, 123, 147
Martinsburg Cold Storage and Canning Company, 125
Martinsburg Golf and Country Club, Inc., 327
Martinsburg Improvement, Building and Loan Association, 124, 156
Martinsburg Journal, The, 229
Martinsburg Mall, 263, 311, 318–19
Martinsburg Mining, Manufacturing and Improvement Company, 124-25
Martinsburg Power Company, 119–20, 161, 192
Martinsburg Statesman, 111
Martinsburg Street Railway Company, 125
Martinsburg Water Board, 123
Martinsburg West Va. Evening Journal, 175, 229
Martinsburg Worsted and Cashmere Co., 148

Martinsburg-Berkeley County Chamber of Commerce, 247
Marval Poultry Company, Inc., 276
Maryland and Virginia Milk Producers Cooperative Association, 197
Maryland Area Regional Commuter (MARC), 256
Masco Corporation, 289
Maslin, Thomas, 110
Masonite International, 288
Massanutten Canning Company, 208
Massey family, 274
Massey, Carl, 205
Mauck's Mill, 92
Mayberry, George, 43
Mayberry, Thomas, 18, 42
Maytag Corporation, 297
McCool, Mike, 332
McCormac, H. B. Sr., 150, 201
McCormick Harvesting Machine Company, 71, 132
McCormick Reaper and Twine Binder, 71
McCormick, Cyrus, 71
McCreight, John, 106
McCrory's, 195, 317
McDole Library Furniture, 298
McDonald's Corporation, Inc., 293, 319
McGraw, James and J. C., 153
McInturff, A. P., 179
McKesson Corp., 302
Mead Corporation, 280
Mechlenburg Tobacco Warehouse, 62, 104
Medical College of the Valley, 181
Meem's Bottom Covered Bridge, 135
Melnor Industries, 292
Mendenhall, James, 48
Mercury Paper Inc., 281, 302
Merillat Industries, 247, 289
Metro Radio, Inc., 334
Metromont Corp., 291
Mettler, John W., Jr., 285
Mettler, John W., Sr., 147
Mid Atlantic Network, 334–36

Mid-Atlantic 81 Logistics Park, 301
Mid-Atlantic Industrial and
    Tech Park, 246
Mid-Atlantic Industrial Park,
    251, 290, 300
Middlesex Knitting Co., 125, 147
Middletown Land and Improvement
    Company, 127
Middletown Railway, 63
Middletown Weekly, 175
Midwesco Filter Resources, Inc., 299
Millar, Samuel Rolfe, 176
Millcroft Farms Company, 274
Miller, Charles H., 154
Miller, Harley W., Inc., 310
Miller, Harold, 231
Miller, Henry W., Sr., 134, 208
Miller, Susan B. Nursing Home, 231
Miller, William Smith and John, 133
Millwood Country Club, 235
Milnes, William, Jr., 105, 141-42
Mine Run Furnace, 109, 141, 165
Mineral Ridge Manganese Corp., 216
Mineral Ridge Mine, 83, 165
Miners Lode Copper Company, 107, 180
Minghini, S. L. & Son, Inc., 309
Mobil Chemical Corporation, 290
Mobil Oil Corporation, 287
Monoflo International, Inc., 293
Montgomery Ward, 195
Moore and Dorsey, Inc., 267, 302
Moore Corporation, 296
Morgan Arts Council, 138
Morgan County Cold Storage
    Company, 138
Morgan County Economic
    Development Corporation, 251
Morgan County State Bank, 315
Morgan Messenger, 175, 230
Morgan, Daniel, 33
Morgan, E. Knitting Mills, Inc., 285
Morrison, Lynwood, 327
Mount Jackson Industrial
    Park, 247, 279, 289
Mount Jackson Mill, 211

Mount Jackson National Bank, 122
Mount Vernon Compact, 30
Mount Weather, 183, 219, 222, 240, 337
Mountain Falls Park, 308
Mountain State University, 263
Mountain View Golf Course, 328
Mountain View Rendering, 277
Mountaineer Bankshares of
    West Virginia, 315
Moyer Brothers Cannery, 209
Mt. Vernon Tannery, 79
Municipal Shale Brick &
    Block Company, 212
Museum of the Shenandoah Valley, 325
Musselman, C. H. Company,
    204-05, 274
Myers, Abraham and Fyanna, 112, 178
Myers, John and Samuel, 91, 112

Nadenbousch Distillery, 107
Nadenbousch, John Quincy Adams, 79
Napoleonic Wars, 26, 41
Narrow Passage Press, 332
National Bank of Martinsburg, 173
National Banking Acts, 102
National Carbon Company, 215
National Citizens Bank of
    Charles Town, 223
National Forest Service, 141, 183, 220
National Fruit Product Company,
    Inc., 149, 194, 203-05,
    227, 265-67, 273, 298
National Gypsum Company, 217
National Labor Relations Board, 225
National Lutheran Home, 325
National Media Services, Inc., 332
National Park Service, 232, 325, 337
National Turnpike, 27
National Wildlife Federation, 304
Nature's Touch Frozen Foods, 279
Navy Federal Credit Union, 304
Nebel, Oscar Company, 226
Nelson, Charles, 165, 216
Nerangis family, 319
NetTech Center, 253

Index 447

New Dominion Paper Mill, 104, 163
New England Development
   Company, 317
New Market Battlefield State
   Historical Park, 326
New Market Poultry Products, Inc., 276
New Shenandoah Company,
   31, 62-63, 102
New South, 94
New World Pasta Company, 279
Newberry, J. J., 195
Newell Company, 293
Newman, Benjamin Pennybacker,
   109, 135, 174
Newman, Edgar Douglas, 174
Newman, Walter, 44, 77, 109
Newton D. Baker Army General
   Hospital, 240, 337
Newtown Freight Wagon, 46
Nichols, S. E. Company, 318
Nicodemus, A. W. & Sons, 152
Norfolk & Western Railroad,
   115-16, 125, 127, 142, 150,
   152, 187, 207, 215, 238, 250
Norfolk & Western Shenandoah
   Yard, 115
Norfolk Southern Railway,
   254, 256-57, 302
Norm Thompson Outfitters, 305
North American Free Trade
   Agreement, 282
North American Housing Corp., 290
North American Rockwell
   Corporation, 292
North Mountain Brick Plant, 159
North Mountain Vineyard
   and Winery, 268
North Shenandoah Industrial
   Park, 249, 280, 303
North Valley Business Journal, 332
Northcott, Theodore, 181
Northern Neck Proprietary, 6
Northern Shenandoah Valley Health
   Care Task Force, 322
Northern Virginia Daily, 230, 331

Northern Virginia Power Company,
   120–21, 149, 190, 192
Northwestern Turnpike, 58-60, 86, 186
Norwalk Motor Car Company, 157–58
nTelos Holdings Corporation, 260-61

O'Sullivan Films, 292, 295, 299
O'Sullivan Rubber Company,
   224, 227, 282, 292-93
OakCrest Companies, 299
Oates, T. K., 182, 321
Office of Economic Redevelopment, 250
Office of Management and Budget, 244
Ogden Newspapers, 229, 332
Ogden, H. C., 229
Oglebay Norton, 270
Ohio River Valley, 13, 28, 30, 59, 62, 92
Okamoto Corporation, 285
Old Dominion Paper Company, 163, 214
Old Dominion Savings and
   Loan Association, 316
Old Dominion Savings Bank, 316
Old Mill Cold Storage, 207
Old National Bank, 103, 201, 315
Old Virginia Orchard Company,
   154, 204, 209
Old Virginia Packing
   Company, 209, 247
Omni Direct Mail Services Ltd., 247
Omni TRAX, 257
Omps, Larry, 309
One Valley Bancorp of West
   Virginia, 315
Ontario Power Generation, 258
Opequon Country Club, 235, 327
Orange and Alexandria Railroad, 66, 100
Orange, Alexandria and Manassas
   Railroad, 100, 105, 109,
   112, 127, 160, 165
Orchard Products Co., 204
Orgill, Inc., 301
Orkney Springs, 55, 78, 86, 96,
   112, 178, 233, 308, 326
Orndorff, M. M., 170, 217, 270
Orr, George Jr., 266

Orr's Farm Market, 266
Orrick, Robert, 108
Orrick's Livery Stables, 108
Ottowa Silica Co., 271
Outback Steakhouse, 319
Overhead Door Company, 288
Owen and Trenary Glove Company, 212
Owen, C. T., 212
Oxford Ochre Company, 164

Pack Horse Ford, 5, 10, 12
Pactiv Corporation, 293
Paddy Run Mine, 165, 216
Page Cooperative Farm Bureau, 197
Page County Industrial and
 Technology Park, 250
Page County Technical Center, 262
Page Memorial Hospital, 321
Page News & Currier, 331
Page Power Company, 193
Page Valley Courier, 111
Page Woolen & Cotton
 Manufacturing Co, 110
Page Woolen Mill, 110, 140, 148
Palace Theater, 195
Palmer Lime and Cement Company, 217
Palmer, W. H., 137
Panic of 1819, 26
Panic of 1837, 36, 58, 67, 70, 72, 76
Panic of 1857, 58, 67, 72, 75
Panic of 1873, 96, 101, 109, 132
Panic of 1893, 114, 117, 119, 121,
 124-28, 130, 132, 143, 178, 181
Panic of 1907, 114, 163
Panorama Resort, 232
Paoli Forge, 43
Paramount Development
 Corporation, 318-19
Park View Inn, 233
Patowmack Company, 30–31
Pembroke Springs Hotel, 86
Pen-Tab Industries, Inc., 280, 299
Penn Central, 256
Penn National Gaming, Inc., 329-30

Pennsylvania Glass Sand Company,
 171–72, 218, 247, 271-72
Pennsylvania Portage and
 Canal System, 27
Pennsylvania Railroad, 70, 100-01,
 117–18, 187, 190, 256
Pennsylvania Steel Company, 168
Pennybacker, Benjamin, 43-44, 77
Pennybacker, Dirck, 43
People's Bank, 173
People's National Bank 103
Peoples Bank of Charles Town, 315
Peoples Bank of Front Royal, 314
Peoples Bank of Stephens City, 223
Peoples National Bank of
 Martinsburg, 315
Peoples National Bank of
 Strasburg, 173-74, 220
Peoples Trust Company, 223
Perdue, Nichols & Co., 78
Perfection Garment Company,
 148, 202-03, 239, 286
Perin, Nelson E., 172, 218
Perry Engineering Company, 310
Perry Graphics, 296
Perry Kathryn, 31
Perry, Denny, 328
Perry, Ferman, 310
Perry, Stuart M., 229, 328
PET, Inc., 274, 278
Phoenix Mill, 50
Pierce Pre-Cooked Foods, 277
Pilgrim's Pride Corporation, 276
PILOT (Payment in Lieu of Property
 Taxes) program, 248, 259, 281,
 291, 294, 296, 301, 305
Pimlico Race Course, 329
Pine Grove Woolen Factory, 21
Pines Crippled Children's Clinic, 231
Pines Opportunity Center, 253, 263
Pioneer Bank, 314
Pittsburgh Limestone
 Company, 168, 218
Platt, Charles, 226

Plumly, P. W. Lumber
    Company, 228, 299
Plumly, Paul, 228
Plummer, Art, 278
Poland, John, Sr., 148, 202
Pollock, George Freeman, 180, 232
Polo Ralph Lauren Corporation, 301
Portlock, Miles, 326
Potomac Bankshares, Inc., 314
Potomac Limestone Company, 167
Potomac Mills 81, 106
Potomac Mills, Mining and
    Manufacturing Company, 106
Potomac Public Service
    Company, 192-93
Potomac Pulp Mill, 119, 162, 193, 214
Potomac Sportswear, Inc., 286
Potomac Tannery, 144
Potomak Guardian, 53
Powell's Fort Mining
    Company, 109, 141
Powhatan Brass, 126
Powhatan Lime Co., 158
Pratt, A. S., 112
Premier Community
    Bankshares, Inc., 314
Prettyman Broadcasting Company, 334
Price, Charles D., Jr., 208
Prime Retail Outlet Center, 319
Pritchard, Cornelius, 77, 91
ProBuilt Holding, 289
Proctor & Gamble Company,
    251, 281, 301
Proctor-Biggs Feed Mill, 211
ProLogis, Inc., 302
Pure Food and Drug Act, 209

Quad-State Business Journal, 332-33
Quad/Graphics, Inc., 296
Quartermaster K-9 Corps, 240
Quebecor World, 296
Quesos La Ricura, Ltd., 279

Rader, Helmut, 293
Randolph Macon Academy, 127

Rapid American Corporation, 329
Rappahannock Electric Cooperative, 258
Redbull GmbH, 303
Redwell Furnace, 43–44
Reliant Equity Investors LLC, 305
Residence Act of 1790, 24
Reynolds, George, 81
Rice, Lacy I., Jr., 315
Rich Products Corporation, 278, 299
Richmond Vinegar Works, Inc., 204
Ricketts Construction Company, 310
Ricketts, Charles, 310
Ridge State Fish Hatchery, 222
Ridgewood Fruit Growers, Inc., 205
Riklis, Meshulum, 329
Rinaca, U. S., 152
Rivenite Corporation, 290
Riverdale Canning Company, 208
Riverton Hydro Plant, 121-22
Riverton Investment
    Corporation, 270, 291
Riverton Lime and Stone
    Company, 170, 235
Riverton Mills Co., 105, 211
Riviana Foods, 279
Roaring Twenties, 224, 235
Robinson, C. L. Ice and Cold
    Storage Company, 137, 155,
    159, 199, 200, 226, 274
Robinson, Charles Lee, 137-38, 199
Rocco Farm Foods, 276–77
Rock Enon Springs Resort,
    86, 112, 190–91, 233
Rock Harbor Golf Course, 328
Rockefeller, John D., IV, 286
Rockingham Poultry Marketing
    Cooperative, 275–77
Rockwool-Ranson, 251
Roosevelt, Franklin, 221, 223, 231
Rosenberger, John, 189
Ross, Alexander, 5
Rosser's, Frank Page County Fair, 197
Rossi American Hardwoods, Inc., 299
Roth, Chester H. Company, 285
Rothwell & Co., 138, 200

Rothwell-Gatrell Fruit Company, 207
Rouss City Hall, 97
Rouss Springs, 123
Rouss, Charles Baltzell, 69, 123, 160
Route 11 Potato Chips, 279
Roxul, Inc., 251
Royal Crown Bottling Company, 275
Royal Examiner, 332
Royal Light, Heat and Power Co., 121
Royal Silk Mill, 150, 283
Royal Vendors, Inc., 297
Royce Hosiery Mills, Inc., 285
Royce Too LLC, 285
Ruarch Associates, 333, 335
Rubbermaid Commercial Products, 293, 299, 301-02,
Rumsey, James, 30, 55
Rust-Oleum Corporation, 301
Ryland Homes, 306

Sager, B. J. Inc., 228
Sandusky Cooperage and Lumber Company, 158
Sanwa Shutter Company, 288
Savage, Lycurgus, 110
Savage's L. E. & Sons (Kernstown) Distillery, 110
Savery, Thomas, 119, 162, 193, 214
Schaffer, W. B., 216
Schenck Foods Company, 228
Schenck, Bob, 228
Schenker, DB Logistics, 302
Schlegell, Max von, 175
Schoeneman, J., Inc., 246, 337
Schrafft's Frozen Foods, Inc., 278
Schwab Company, 300-01
Schwarzenbach-Huber Company, 150, 238, 283
Scott, Barbara, 331
Scott, Bill, 330
SCR-Sibelco NV, 256, 272
Sears Roebuck & Co., 195, 318
Secessionist Women of Baltimore, 97
Security Cement & Lime, 213
Seely, Tom Furniture, 298

Seely, Tom, 298
Seibel, H. J., Jr., 165
Semple, John, 19, 42
Sencindiver, David, 191
Seven Years War, 8
Seymour, A. R., 86
Shady Elm Woolen Factory, 149
Shaffer, C. V., 208
Shannondale Furnace, 78, 91
Shannondale Springs Hotel, 55, 85, 178-79
Shannondale, Inc., 308
Shawnee Springs Foods Canning, 209, 274
Shawneeland, 308
Shearer, John, 51
Sheetz, Philip, 23
Shen-Valley Lime Corporation, 271
Shenandoah Alum Springs Hotel, 112, 178
Shenandoah Apple Products Co., Inc., 204
Shenandoah Bakery, 152
Shenandoah Bee Company, 278
Shenandoah Brick and Tile Corporation, 290
Shenandoah Candy Company, Inc., 205, 274
Shenandoah Caverns, 234
Shenandoah Company, 31
Shenandoah Corporation, 329
Shenandoah Country Q102, 333-34
Shenandoah County Bank and Trust, 174
Shenandoah County Economic Development Agency, 260
Shenandoah County Fair Association, 197
Shenandoah County Industrial Development Authority, 247, 249, 283
Shenandoah County Office of Economic Development, 249
Shenandoah Downs, 329-30
Shenandoah Driving Park, 236
Shenandoah Farmers Milling Company, 122

Shenandoah Farms, 308
Shenandoah Federal Savings and
    Loan Association, 316
Shenandoah Herald, 111
Shenandoah Hotel, 196, 312
Shenandoah Industrial Park, 250
Shenandoah Iron & Coal Company, 143
Shenandoah Iron Works,
    91, 96, 102, 105
Shenandoah Iron, Lumber,
    Mining and Manufacturing
    (SILMM), 105, 141–42
Shenandoah Knitting Mills, 226, 284
Shenandoah Manganese Company, 165
Shenandoah Memorial Hospital,
    231, 260, 321, 323
Shenandoah Milling Company, 140
Shenandoah National Forest, 183, 220
Shenandoah National Park, 170,
    208, 221-22, 232, 234
Shenandoah Normal College, 176
Shenandoah Pants Company, 125, 148
Shenandoah Publishing House, 230
Shenandoah Pulp Mill, 119, 162, 214
Shenandoah Retreat Country
    Club, 307, 328
Shenandoah River Navigation
    Company, 102
Shenandoah River State Park, 326
Shenandoah Silica Co., Inc., 219, 272
Shenandoah Speedway, 331
Shenandoah Spirits Trail, 326
Shenandoah Telecommunications
    Company (Shentel), 123,
    260-61, 285, 336
Shenandoah University, 262,
    264, 310, 313, 320, 335
Shenandoah Valley Apple Cider &
    Vinegar Company, 116, 134,
    155, 158, 199, 203, 205, 273
Shenandoah Valley Bank and
    Trust, 220, 223
Shenandoah Valley Barrel
    Company, 158, 210
Shenandoah Valley Barrel Group, 209
Shenandoah Valley Business
    Journal, 332
Shenandoah Valley Electric
    Cooperative, 258
Shenandoah Valley Golf Club, 327
Shenandoah Valley Jockey Club, Inc., 236
Shenandoah Valley Manganese
    Corporation, 215
Shenandoah Valley Music Festival, 326
Shenandoah Valley National Bank, 97,
    103, 109, 135, 140, 149, 173, 190
Shenandoah Valley National
    Historic Battlefields District
    Commission, 326
Shenandoah Valley Partnership, 249
Shenandoah Valley Press, 296
Shenandoah Valley Railroad,
    96, 99, 101–2, 105, 115–16,
    124–25, 128, 141–42, 144,
    150, 164–65, 177, 180–81
Shenandoah Valley Telecommuting
    Center, 253, 339
Shenandoah Valley Travel
    Association, 232
Shenandoah Valley Westminster-
    Canterbury, 324
Shenandoah Valley Wine Growers
    Association, 269
Shenandoah Valley Wine Trail, 326
Shenandoah Valley-Herald, 332
Shendow, Sam, 228
ShenVal Communications, 333
Shenvalee Golf Resort, 235
Shepherd Community and
    Technical College, 253, 263
Shepherd Field, 191-92
Shepherd Normal School, 111, 176, 264
Shepherd University, 262, 264
Shepherd, Thomas, Sr., 17
Shepherdstown Building
    Association, 103
Shepherdstown Chronicle, 332
Shepherdstown Fruit Growers Club, 207
Shepherdstown Mining, Manufacturing
    and Improvement Company, 126

Sheridan, Philip, 91, 93
Shihadeh, Emil and Grace
    Innovation Center, 262
Shipman Brothers Mattress
    and Box Springs, 298
Shockey Commerce Center, 285, 301
Shockey Companies, 246, 291, 299
Shockey Precast Group, 291
Shockey Properties, 259, 301–03, 310
Shockey, Donald, 310
Shockey, Howard & Sons
    Inc., 246, 302, 310
Shockey, Howard, 157, 310
Shockey, James R. and Ralph, 310
Shockey, James, Sr., 291
Shumpeter, Joseph, 113
Shutt, Philip, 79
Shutt's Cream Beer, 79
Sibert, Lorenzo and George, 75
Siemens Automotive Systems Group, 295
Signal Knob Radio Partners, 334
Silver, Gray, 204, 206
Simon Property Group, 318
Sino Swearingen, 286-87
Sirota, Benjamin, 285
Skadden, Arthur E, 157
Sky Bryce Airport, 255
Sky-Park Broadcasting Company, 333
Skyland Resort, 83, 180, 222, 232
Skyline Caverns, 234
Skyline Drive, 140, 222, 224, 232, 259
Sleepy Hollow Golf and Country
    Club, Inc., 327
Smalley, Herbert, 210
Smith, Clyde, Gerald, Sr. and J.J., 277
Smith, German Bark & Sumac Mill, 109
Smithsonian's Conservation
    Biology Institute, 337
Smoot-Hawley Tariff Act, 225
Snapp Foundry, 138
Snapp, Alfred, 267
Snicker's Gap, 10, 29, 66, 179, 186
Solenberger, Robert, 266
Sonabank, 316
Sonner, J. H. & Co., 161

Sonner, John Henry, 161
Sonner, Samuel H., 82
South Berkeley National Bank, 315
Southeastern Container, Inc., 293
Southern Merchant Tailoring
    Co., 148, 150
Southern Railway, 115, 117, 121,
    126, 135, 143, 165, 169,
    179, 181, 234, 256, 292
Speedwell Forges, 44, 76
Speer White Sand Company, 171
Speer, Noah Q., 170-71
Spirit of Jefferson and Farmer's
    Advocate, 220
Spirit of Jefferson, 84
Spring Arbor, 324
Spring Mills Business Park, 338
Springdale Flour Mills, 272
Sprint, 260
Standard Lime & Stone Company, 158,
    167–68, 213–14, 217, 251, 269
Stanley Furnace and Land
    Improvement Company, 128
Stanley Mine, 216
Stanley Works, 288
Star Tannery, 104, 144, 213
Staub, Henry L., 79
Stauffer Chemical Company, 238
Steeley, Roy, 297
Stein, Samuel, 286
Stephen, Adam, 23
Stephens City Station, 116, 155
Stephens Industrial Park, 249, 279
Stephens, Lewis, 19
Stephens, Peter, 12
Stewart Vehicle Co., 156–57
Stickley, Keith, 332
Stonebridge Golf Club, 328
Stoner-Keller Mill, 211, 272
Stonewall Broadcasting Company, 334
Stonewall Industrial Park,
    246, 296, 302-304
Stonewall Jackson Bank & Trust, 314
Stonewall Jackson Museum, 311
Stony Creek Golf Course, 328

Index   453

Stony Man Mining Company, 83, 107
Storer College, 176, 367
Storer Normal School, 111, 176
Storer, John, 111
Stover, Peter, 20
Strasburg Antique Emporium, 311
Strasburg Fruit Products
    Co., Inc., 204, 227
Strasburg Hospital, 182
Strasburg Land and Improvement
    Company, 126, 161
Strasburg Manufacturing Co., 284
Strasburg Museum, 126
Strasburg News, 175
Strasburg Silk Mills, 226, 238, 283, 311
Strasburg Steam Flouring Mills, 126
Strasburg Stone and Earthenware
    Manufacturing Co., 126, 161
Strasburg Textile Manufacturing, 150
Strawboard Trust, 163, 214
Strickler, Charles and Robert, 276
Strother, John and David, 85
Stubblefield, James, 41
Summit Point Motorsports Park, 330
Summit, The, 308
Superior Ochre Company, 164
SVB Food & Beverage, 278
Swearingen Aircraft Company, 286
Swift Bros. & Co., 136
Swift, Gustavus, 136
SyberJet Aircraft Company, 287
Sysco Corporation, 303

T-Mobile, 261, 336
Tabard Farm, 279
Tabler Station Business Park, 251, 281
Talbot, Judge Walter R., 218
Talbot's, 319
Talk Radio WRNR, 334
Tanger Factory Outlet Center, 319
Tariff of 1816, 26, 49
Taylor Hotel, 68, 195, 250, 304, 312
Taylor, A. P., 42
Taylor, Bushrod, 60
Taylor, Samuel, 10

Taylor's Furnace, 42, 29
Technology Zone Winchester, 250, 252
Telegate AG, 304
TeMa North America, 294
Thieblot Aircraft, 286
Thieblot, Armond, 286
Thirteenth Amendment, 95
Thornton Gap, 10, 232
Threshold Enterprise Ltd., 305
Thwaite, John F., 134, 210, 266
Timberlake, Ambrose, 110
Tip Top Poultry, Inc., 277
TischlerBise, 261
TLM Aerospace Inc., 287
Toan, Charles and Doug, 310
Toray Plastics (America), Inc., 294
Torch Clean Energy, 259
Total Structural Solutions, 289
Trammel Crow, 306
Travel Berkeley Springs, 327
Tredegar Iron Works, 90-91, 105
Trenary, Charles W., 212
Trex Company, 288, 290, 293, 299, 303
Triplett Business and Technical
    Institute, 262
Triplett, Joseph I., 122
Trump Broadcasting, Inc., 333
Trump, Charles S., 333
Trump, Donald, 339
Tuley, Joseph, Jr., 79
Tuley, Joseph, Sr., 45, 79
Tuleyries, 45
TV3 Winchester, 335
Tyler, Paul, 215
Tyson Foods, 278

U. S. Borax, Inc., 271
U. S. Manganese & Mineral
    Company, 216
U. S. Silica, 172, 271
U.S. 522 South Business Park, 252
U.S. Armory and Arsenal,
    47, 73, 90, 111, 162
U.S. Army Remount Station,
    183, 219, 240, 337

U.S. Bureau of Mines, 337
U.S. Cavalry, 125, 219, 337
U.S. Coast Guard, 338
U.S. Customs Service, 337
U.S. Department of Agriculture, 197, 205-06, 219, 240
U.S. Department of Commerce, 222
U.S. Department of Homeland Security, 337
U.S. Department of Labor, 265
U.S. Fish and Wildlife Service, 339
U.S. Food and Drug Administration, 182
U.S. Office of Personnel Management, 311, 339
U.S. Patent Office, 55, 113
U.S. State Department, 330
U.S. War Department, 201
U.S. Weather Bureau, 183
UAW-Abex Employees Credit Union, 316
Unger, Donald, 314
Unimin Corporation, 256, 271
Union Bank of Winchester, 103, 129, 173, 201, 223
Union Forge, 44, 77
Union Relief Association of Baltimore, 97
United Bankshares, Inc., 314
United Church of Christ, 325
United Clay Products Co., 159, 212, 291
United Merchants and Manufacturers, Inc., 282
United States Army, 201
United States Leather Company, 144, 213
United States Steel Company, 168
Urban Grid Solar Projects, 259

Valley College, 263
Valley Evaporating Company, 155
Valley Foods Company, 228
Valley Health, 250, 320, 322–24
Valley Land and Improvement Company, 128
Valley Mills Cotton Factory, 80

Valley of Virginia Milk Producers Cooperative Association, 197
Valley Proteins, Inc., 277
Valley Railroad, 97, 100–101, 116
Valley Regional Enterprises, 323
Valley Star, 111
Valley Turnpike, 29, 59–60, 69, 99–100, 116, 133, 174, 186
Valley Woolen Mills, 110
Van Buren Furnace, 76, 106
Van Meter, Soloman, 45
Van Metre Company, 289
Van Swearingen, Thomas, 11
Van Wyk, Bruce, 311
Vanguard Industries, 251
Varel Mills, Inc., 282
Variform, Inc., 294
Vaughan, Jeff, 331
VDO-Argo Instruments, 295, 299, 337
Venning, Richard E., 182, 321
Verdier, James, 45
Verizon Communications, Inc., 260, 304
Vestal Bloomery, 18, 21, 42-43
Vestal, William, Jr., 18
Vestal's Ferry, 11
Vesuvius Crucible Company, 252
Vesuvius Tannery, 107, 145, 212
Veterans Affairs Administration, 337, 339
VF Corporation, 283
Victor Products Company, 227, 297
Viking Way Center, 319
Village, The at Orchard Ridge, 325
Virginia and Maryland Bridge Company, 29
Virginia and Tennessee Railroad, 99
Virginia Apple Storage, 135, 200
Virginia Barrel Co., 158-59, 210
Virginia Beverage Corp., 153
Virginia Board of Public Works, 27, 59, 63, 64, 66, 99, 118
Virginia Cave and Karst Trail, 326
Virginia Consolidated Copper Company, 164
Virginia Department of Environmental Quality, 294

Virginia Department of Health, 321
Virginia Equine Alliance, 330
Virginia Glass Sand Corp., 191, 218, 272
Virginia Inland Port (VIP), 254, 257, 279–81, 299, 301, 303
Virginia Inland Port Industrial Park, 294
Virginia International Terminals, 257
Virginia Locust Pin, 156
Virginia Manufactory of Arms, 90
Virginia Military Institute (VMI), 326
Virginia National Golf Course, 328
Virginia Oak Tannery, 144-45, 212, 239
Virginia Port Authority, 257
Virginia Power Company, 193
Virginia Pride Fruit Packers, 207
Virginia Rock Wool Company, 169
Virginia Savings Bank, 316
Virginia Sky-Line Company, Inc., 232
Virginia Woolen Company, 135, 146, 148–50, 190, 194, 201, 225, 239, 282
Virginius Island, 31, 41–42, 45, 73–74, 79–82, 91, 96, 106, 138, 162
Vita Food Products, Inc., 278
Vitro Corporation of America, 286
Vocational Education Act of 1963, 262
Vulcan Road Machine Company, 126

Wachtel, Rick and Gregg, 334
Wager, Gerard, 29
Wallace Computer Services, 296
Walmart, Inc., 317
Wampler Feed and Seed Company, 268, 276
Wampler-Longacre, Inc., 276
Wampler, Charles, Sr., 268
Wanner Textile Company, 284
Wanner, John, 284
War Memorial Hospital, 231, 253, 323
War Production Board, 237–39
Ward's Plaza Shopping Center, 318
Warner, Rupert, 311
Warren County Technology Consortium, 252-53
Warren County Vocational-Technical Center, 262
Warren Memorial Hospital, 231, 321, 323
Warren Sentinel, 111, 321
Warren Sulphur Springs Hotel, 179
Washington and Old Dominion Railway, 121
Washington Building Lime Company, 167
Washington Heritage Trail, 326
Washington Homes, 306
Washington Hotel, 178
Washington, George, 7, 13, 19, 20, 24, 30, 47, 55, 132, 312
Washington, Ohio & Western Railway, 179
Waste Management, Inc., 291
Waterlick Station, 86, 109, 112, 165, 179
Waterlick White Sulphur Springs, 86, 112, 179
Watkins, Evan Ferry, 12
Wayside Foundation of American History and Arts, Inc., 311
WAZR-FM, 333-34
WAZT-TV, 335
WCS Logistics, 302
WCST-AM, 333
WCT Channel 20, 335
WDVM, 335
Webb and Markell Factory, 80
Wegenast, Christian, 79
Weis, John George, 50
Weller, Charles, 234
WEPM-AM, 230, 333
WEPM-FM, 334
West Penn Electric Company, 193, 258
West Virginia Air National Guard, 255
West Virginia Community Packing House, 206
West Virginia Economic Development Authority, 247, 251, 291, 294
West Virginia Health Care Authority, 321
West Virginia Racing Commission, 329

West Virginia Radio Corporation, 334
West Virginia Spring Water
    Company, 275
West Virginia University
    Health System, 323
West Virginia University
    Medicine East, 323
West Virginia University, 262
West, William H., 284
Western Frederick Bank, 220
Western Maryland Railroad, 168
Westminster Canterbury of
    Winchester, Inc., 324
WFQX-FM, 333
WFTR-AM, 333
WHAG-TV, 335
Whelan, Ashton & Co., 104
Whisneff, Brian & Associates, 312
Whitacre, George, 134
Whitacre, William, 274
White Henkle Cotton and
    Woolen Factory, 80
White House Bridge, 29, 93
Whitlock Herb Medicine Company, 182
Whitlock, Joseph and William, 182
WHSV-TV, 335
Wigginton, James Bean, 78, 104
Wilde Acres, 308
Wilderness Road, 34
Wilkins, James R. Sr., 263
Williams, C. A., Thomas and James, 149
Williams, J. Allen, 232
Williams, R. Gray, 189-90
Williamsport, Nessle &
    Martinsburg Railroad, 168
Willow Grove Mill, 41, 92, 110, 140
WINC-AM and FM, 230, 332-33, 335
Winchester & Washington City
    Railway Co., 121
Winchester and Berkeley
    Springs Turnpike, 84
Winchester and Berry's
    Ferry Turnpike, 59
Winchester and Front Royal
    Turnpike, 81

Winchester and Martinsburg
    Turnpike, 65
Winchester and Moorefield Turnpike, 59
Winchester and Potomac Railroad,
    58-59, 64-65, 67, 69, 81, 83, 92,
    99, 100, 104, 117, 125, 129, 156
Winchester and Strasburg
    Railroad, 100, 116, 160
Winchester and Wardensville
    Railroad, 190-91, 233
Winchester and Western Railroad,
    188-90, 217-18, 256-57, 272, 281
Winchester Apple Growers
    Association, 200
Winchester Asphalt Company, 310
Winchester Building and Loan
    Association, 316
Winchester Building Supply
    Company, 310
Winchester Chamber of Commerce, 194
Winchester Cold Storage Company,
    200, 278, 299, 301
Winchester Creamery, 151
Winchester Economic Development
    Authority, 312
Winchester Evening Star, 175, 229–30
Winchester Gas & Electric
    Light Co., 119-21, 140
Winchester Gas Company, 109
Winchester Gazette, 53-54, 84
Winchester Incubation Regional
    Enterprise (WIRE), 253
Winchester Industrial Credit Union, 316
Winchester Industrial Development
    Authority, 250
Winchester Industrial Park, 246, 249,
    275, 288–89, 292–93, 299, 338
Winchester Inn (Hotel Winchester), 130
Winchester Knitting Mill, 225-26, 284
Winchester Little Theater, 256
Winchester Lumber Company,
    135, 189-90
Winchester Medical Center,
    320, 322, 324–25
Winchester Medical College, 181

Winchester Memorial Hospital,
 69, 149, 182, 201, 230, 320
Winchester Milling Corp., 201
Winchester Municipal Airport, 192, 237
Winchester Paper Company, 135, 163
Winchester Regional Airport, 255
Winchester Rendering Company, 277
Winchester Research Laboratory, 199
Winchester Society for Human
 Resource Management, 322
Winchester Star, 332
Winchester Steam Laundry, 138
Winchester Times, 95, 111
Winchester Weekly, 111
Winchester Woolen Mill,
 149, 202, 239, 282
Winchester-Frederick County Chamber
 of Commerce, 246, 263
Winchester-Frederick County
 Economic Development
 Commission (EDC), 240, 250-52
Windsor Knitting Mills, Inc., 285
Wissler, Franklin, 78, 109,
 135, 143, 163, 199
Wissler, John, 77, 109
WLR Foods, Inc., 276
Wolf, Frank, 326, 339

Wood, James, 325
Wood, William J., Jr., 271
Woodbrier Golf Club, 327
Woods Resort, 309, 328
Woods, Tiger, 328
Woodstock Electric Light
 Power Co., 122
World Color Press, 216
World Kitchen, 280
Wyndham Worldwide Corp., 312
Wyoming Manufacturing
 Company, 128-29
WYVN-TV, 335

Xator Corporation, 331

Yager, N. W., 110
Yager, Nicholas, 77
Yard, H. H., 143

Zacharia family, 286
Zane, Isaac 19-20, 24, 43-45
Zepp Tannery, 45
ZeroPack Company, 226, 274
Zirkle Cave, 181
Zirkle, Ruben, 181

www.ingramcontent.com/pod-product-compliance
Lightning Source LLC
Chambersburg PA
CBHW071851290426
44110CB00013B/1098